Why Do You Need This New Edition?

If you're wondering why you should buy this new edition of *Human Evolution and Culture*, here are some good reasons!

1. **NEW!** MyAnthroLab is an online resource that contains book-specific practice tests, chapter summaries, learning objectives, flashcards, weblinks, MySearchLab, a complete E-book and media-rich activities that enhance topics covered in *Human Evolution and Culture 7/e*.

2. **NEW!** Chapter on The Arts.

3. **Expanded Methods Chapter:** Re-titled "Research Methods in Anthropology" that goes beyond archaeology and physical anthropology to include cultural anthropology as well.

4. **Thirteen Box Features:** Nine boxes that demonstrate how the four-field disciplines make important contributions to the lives of people, and four box features that deal with gender issues and roles.

5. **Chapter 9 has been extensively revised** to emphasize the importance of culture change and globalization, material has been moved further forward and integrated with this chapter, now re-titled "Culture and Culture Change."

6. **Chapter 11 has been thoroughly revised** to emphasize recent economic changes, now discussing commercialization by way of migratory labor and remittances, nonagricultural commercial production, supplementary cash crops, and commercial and industrial agriculture.

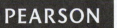

Why Do You Need This New Edition?

If you're wondering why you should buy this new edition of *[title]*, here are some good reasons!

Human Evolution and Culture

HIGHLIGHTS OF ANTHROPOLOGY

Seventh Edition

Carol R. Ember

Human Relations Area Files

Melvin Ember

Peter N. Peregrine

Lawrence University

PEARSON

Boston   Columbus   Indianapolis   New York   San Francisco   Upper Saddle River
Amsterdam   Cape Town   Dubai   London   Madrid   Milan   Munich   Paris   Montréal   Toronto
Delhi   Mexico City   São Paulo   Sydney   Hong Kong   Seoul   Singapore   Taipei   Tokyo

Editorial Director: Craig Campanella
Editor in Chief: Dickson Musslewhite
Publisher: Nancy Roberts
Editorial Project Manager: Nicole Conforti
Editorial Assistant: Nart Varoqua
Director of Marketing: Brandy Dawson
Senior Marketing Manager: Laura Lee Manley
Marketing Assistant: Paige Patunas
Senior Managing Editor: Ann Marie McCarthy
Project Manager: Debra A. Wechsler
Operations Specialist: Alan Fischer

Cover Designer: Bruce Kenselaar
Cover Art: Boat traffic on the narrow river of a
southern Chinese town. iamanewbee/shutterstock
Media Director: Brian Hyland
Digital Media Editor: Rachel Comerford
Lead Media Project Manager: Barbara Taylor-Laino
Full-Service Project Management: Patty Donovan
Composition: Laserwords
Printer/Binder: Edward Brothers Malloy
Cover Printer: Lehigh-Phoenix Color/Hagerstown
Text Font: Palatino Light 10/12

Credits and acknowledgments borrowed from other sources and reproduced, with permission, in this textbook appear on page 497.

Many of the designations by manufacturers and seller to distinguish their products are claimed as trademarks. Where those designations appear in this book, and the publisher was aware of a trademark claim, the designations have been printed in initial caps or all caps.

Library of Congress Cataloging-in-Publication Data
Ember, Carol R.
  Human evolution and culture : highlights of anthropology / Carol R. Ember, Melvin Ember, Peter
    N. Peregrine—7th ed.
    p. cm.
  ISBN-13: 978-0-205-23239-0
  ISBN-10: 0-205-23239-6
  1. Anthropology. I. Ember, Melvin. II. Peregrine, Peter N. (Peter Neal),
1963- III. Title.
  GN25.E46 2012
  301—dc23   2011044999

10 9 8 7 6 5 4 3 2

ISBN 10: 0-205-23239-6
ISBN 13: 978-0-205-23239-0

Brief Contents

Contents

PART III Cultural Variation

Preface

This book presents highlights from the thirteenth edition of *Anthropology.* The size of the book makes it useful for quarter courses, as well as for courses that encourage a lot of supplemental reading. We have made a number of major changes in this, the seventh edition. The most significant is greater emphasis on how the four-field disciplines make important contributions to the lives of people.

What's New to This Edition

- Nine new boxes emphasizing contributions anthropology makes to the lives of people;
- Three new boxes emphasizing gender issues and roles;
- A significantly revised chapter on culture, which now emphasizes culture change;
- A chapter titled "The Arts" is now included;
- A significantly revised methods chapter, which now includes cultural anthropology methods.

Although we made significant changes to this edition, we still tried to go beyond descriptions to explain not only *what* humans are and were like, but also *why* they got to be that way, in all their variety. An important part of updating the text is finding new explanations, and we try to communicate the necessity to evaluate these new explanations logically as well as on the basis of the available evidence. Throughout the book, we try to communicate that no idea, including ideas put forward in textbooks, should be accepted even tentatively without supporting tests that could have gone the other way.

Organization of the Text

Part I: Introduction

Chapter 1: The Importance of Anthropology Chapter 1 introduces the student to anthropology. We discuss what we think is distinctive about anthropology in general, and about each of its subfields in particular. We outline how each of the subfields is related to other disciplines such as biology, psychology, and sociology. We direct attention to the increasing importance of applied anthropology and the importance of understanding others in today's more globalized world. As a bridge to the revised methods chapter that follows, we discuss what it means to understand phenomena scientifically. The new box discusses the work of an applied anthropologist.

Chapter 2: Research Methods in Anthropology In this newly organized chapter we begin by describing the major types of study in anthropology distinguished by spatial scope and temporal scope. While our focus in that section is on ethnology or cultural anthropology, we point out the parallels in the other subfields. We follow this with an introduction to the unique methods employed by archaeologists and biological anthropologists, and end with an expanded discussion of ethics in anthropological research. The box explores changes in gender roles during the Shell Mound Archaic period in the southeastern United States.

Part II: Human Evolution: Biological and Cultural

Chapter 3: Genetics and Evolution This chapter discusses evolutionary theory as it applies to all forms of life, including humans. Following an extensive review of genetics and the processes of evolution, including natural selection and what it means, we discuss how natural selection may operate on behavioral traits and how cultural evolution differs from biological evolution. We discuss creationism and intelligent design. The box examines evidence suggesting that evolution proceeds abruptly rather than slowly and steadily.

Chapter 4: Human Variation and Adaptation Here we bring the discussion of human genetics and evolution into the present, dealing with physical variation in living human populations and how physical anthropologists study and explain such variation. We examine how both the physical environment and the cultural environment play important roles in human physical variation. In a section on "race" and racism we discuss why many anthropologists think the concept of "race" as applied to humans is not scientifically useful. We discuss the myths of racism and how "race" is largely a social category in humans. In a new box we discuss why forensic anthropologists are using the concept of "race" to identify remains when the concept is scientifically problematic.

Chapter 5: Primates: Present and Past After discussing common primate traits and how primates differ from other mammals, we provide an overview of the various living primates. We then discuss the distinctive features of humans in comparison with the other primates. The remainder of the chapter focuses on an overview of primate evolution: When, where, and why did the early primates emerge, and how and why did they diverge? Our overview covers the period from about 65 million years ago to the end of the Miocene, a little over 5 million years ago. To highlight how theory is generated and revised, the box deals with how a paleoanthropologist has reexamined his own theory of primate origins.

Chapter 6: The First Hominids and the Emergence of *Homo* This chapter begins with a discussion of the evolution of bipedal locomotion. Then we discuss what we know or suspect about the transition from hominoids to hominids, the various types of australopithecines and early *Homo* species, early hominid tools and lifestyles, and general trends in hominid evolution. We then turn to *Homo erectus* and Lower Paleolithic cultures. The new box discusses the evidence for when, how, and which hominid left Africa to migrate to other parts of the Old World.

Chapter 7: The Emergence of *Homo sapiens* This chapter examines the transition between *Homo erectus* and *Homo sapiens,* Middle Paleolithic cultures, the emergence of modern-looking humans, what happened to the Neandertals, and the Upper Paleolithic in Europe, Africa, Asia, and the New World. The box describes how forensic anthropologists reconstruct the faces of early humans.

Chapter 8: Food Production and the Rise of States This chapter deals with the emergence of broad-spectrum collecting and settled life, the domestication of plants and animals, the rise and fall of cities and states, and what may explain those developments. The new box describes the work of archaeologists who are re-creating ancient agricultural systems in the Andes and elsewhere to help local populations produce more food.

Part III: Cultural Variation

Chapter 9: Culture and Culture Change This extensively revised chapter (previously called "The Study of Culture") emphasizes that culture is always changing. Our previous edition discussed culture change, ethnogenesis, and globalization near the end of the book in a chapter called "Culture Change and Globalization." We have brought this material forward and integrated it into the present chapter. Particular aspects of culture change—economic, political, religious, and so on—are now included in their respective chapters. This chapter introduces the concept of culture. Rather than simply defining culture we try to convey a feeling for what culture is. We also discuss attitudes that hinder the study of culture, cultural relativism and the issue of human rights, patterning of culture, culture and adaptation, and mechanisms of culture change before getting to the emergence of new cultures and the impact of globalization. The box discusses the increasing cultural diversity within countries of the world as a result of immigration and migration.

Chapter 10: Language and Communication We begin by discussing communication in humans and other animals and the debate about the degree of difference between human and nonhuman primate language abilities. We discuss the origins of language and how creoles' and children's language acquisition may help us understand the origins. We then describe the fundamentals of descriptive linguistics, the historical processes of linguistic divergence, the interrelationships between language and other aspects of culture, the ethnography of speaking and the differences in speech by status and gender, multilingualism, code-switching, and at the end of the chapter we briefly discuss the history of writing and literacy. The new box tries to stimulate thinking about the possible impact of language on thought by asking whether the English language promotes sexist thinking.

Chapter 11: Economics Chapter 11 begins with a discussion of how societies vary in the ways they allocate resources (what "property" is and what ownership may mean), convert or transform resources through labor into usable goods, and distribute and perhaps exchange goods and services. We have added new research on the effects of money on sharing and a discussion of informal banking systems (*hawala* brokers). In this extensively revised chapter we emphasize recent change by incorporating material that used to be in a separate chapter on culture change. We now discuss commercialization by way of migratory labor and remittances, nonagricultural commercial production, supplementary cash crops, and commercial and industrial agriculture. The new box discusses some of the effects of food-getting on the environment.

Chapter 12: Social Stratification: Class, Ethnicity, and Racism This chapter explores the variation in degree of social stratification and how the various forms of social inequality may develop. We discuss how egalitarian societies work hard to prevent dominance. We then show how people in the United States generally deny the existence of class. We have expanded our section on caste, adding a discussion of occupational caste in Africa. The discussion of Rwanda is extensively revised to convey the sometimes complex relationship between class, caste, and ethnicity. We follow with an extensive discussion of "race," racism, and ethnicity and how they often relate to the inequitable distribution of resources. We have added a new discussion of the very different concepts of "race" in Latin America. We end with a discussion of theories about the origin of stratification. The new box discusses possible reasons for disparities in death by disease between African Americans and European Americans.

Chapter 13: Sex and Gender In the first part of Chapter 13 we open with a section on culturally varying gender concepts. We follow with sections on gender roles and personality, focusing on common patterns as well as cross-cultural differences. In addition to discussing the gender division of labor in primary and secondary subsistence and explanations of the observed patterns, we have added additional material on women hunters and discuss what impact it has on theories about the gender division of labor. In the second part of the chapter we discuss variation in sexual attitudes and practices. Following revised sections on marital sex and extramarital sex, there is a discussion of homosexuality, including female-female relationships. The new box examines the impact of economic development on women's status.

Chapter 14: Marriage, Family, and Kinship After discussing various theories about why marriage might be nearly universal, we move on to discuss variation in how one marries, whom one should or should not marry, and how many one should marry. We describe and explain variation in family form and household. We introduce recent research on the Hadza that supports one of the theories about marriage. We have updated our discussion of polygyny. To better prepare students for understanding kinship charts in the last part of the chapter, we have introduced a new diagram explaining different types of family structures. The section on marital residence and kinship has been rearranged so that explanations of all types of residence can be found together. We hope the discussion of kinship now flows more smoothly. The new box discusses how variation in residence and kinship affects the lives of women.

Chapter 15: Political Life We look at how societies have varied in their levels of political organization, the various ways people become leaders, the degree to which they participate in the political process, and the peaceful and violent methods of resolving conflict. We have added new material on different types of states, ranging from the more autocratic to the less autocratic that rely more on collective action and where leaders avoid personal aggrandizement. We discuss how colonialization has transformed legal systems and ways of making decisions and we include an expanded discussion of states as empires. The new box deals with the cross-national and cross-cultural relationship between economic development and democracy.

Chapter 16: Religion and Magic In this chapter we focus on variation in religious beliefs and practices, including the character and hierarchy of supernatural beings and the intervention of gods in human affairs. Consistent with increasing the visibility of culture change, we have expanded our discussion of the possible causes of religious conversion. We also discuss revitalization and fundamentalist movements. The new box raises the question of whether, and to what degree, religion promotes moral behavior, cooperation, and harmony.

Chapter 17: The Arts In this chapter, which is new to this edition, we focus on variation in body adornment, the visual arts, music, and folklore, and review how some of those variations might be explained. In regard to how the arts change over time, we discuss the myth that the art of "simpler" peoples is timeless, and how arts have changed as a result of European contact. We address the role of ethnocentrism in studies of art with a section on how Western museums and art critics look at the visual art of less complex cultures. The box, dealing with universal symbolism in art, reviews recent research on the emotions displayed in masks.

Part IV: Using Anthropology

Chapter 18: Global Problems In this chapter we discuss the relationship between basic and applied research, and how research may suggest possible solutions to various global social problems, including natural disasters and famines, homelessness, crime, family violence, war, and terrorism. The new box describes how the problem of refugees has become a global problem.

Chapter 19: Applied and Practicing Anthropology The field of applied or practicing anthropology is very diverse. In this chapter, after focusing on general issues we turn to some frequent types of applied work: *cultural resource management*—the "social impact" studies required in connection with many government or private programs and *forensic anthropology*—the use of physical anthropology to help identify human remains and assist in solving crimes. The chapter concludes with an extensive discussion of the application of anthropological knowledge to the study of health and illness. The new box explores eating disorders, biology, and the cultural construction of beauty.

Features of This Book

Feature Boxes The boxes in each chapter, New Perspectives on Gender, Current Research and Issues, Migrants and Immigrants, or Applied Anthropology, are designed to pique student interest in a research topic. Thirteen of the nineteen boxes are new to this edition and most focus on applied and practicing anthropology.

Readability We derive a lot of pleasure from trying to describe research findings, especially complicated ones, in ways that introductory students can understand. Thus, we try to minimize technical jargon, using only those terms students must know to appreciate the achievements of anthropology and to take advanced courses. We think readability is important, not only because it may enhance the reader's understanding of what we write, but also because it should make learning about anthropology more enjoyable! When new terms are introduced, which of course must happen sometimes, they are set off in boldface type and defined in the text (and in the Glossary at the end of the book).

Glossary Terms At the end of each chapter we list the new terms that have been introduced; these terms were identified by boldface type and defined in the text. We deliberately do not repeat the definitions at the end of the chapter to allow students to ask themselves if they know the terms. However, we do provide page numbers to find the definitions and we also provide all the definitions again in the Glossary at the end of the book.

Summaries In addition to the outline provided at the beginning of each chapter, there is a detailed summary at the end that will help the student review the major concepts and findings discussed.

Critical Questions We provide three or four questions at the end of each chapter that will stimulate thinking about the implications of the chapter. The questions do not ask for repetition of what is in the text. We want students to imagine, to go beyond what we know or think we know.

Read the Original Source Every chapter concludes with a suggested reading that can be found in MyAnthroLibrary, which is housed within MyAnthroLab. The reading illustrates a concept found in that chapter, and discussion questions provide helpful guidance.

Teacher and Student Resources

This textbook is part of a complete teaching and learning package that has been carefully created to enhance the topics discussed in the text.

MyAnthroLab MyAnthroLab is an interactive and instructive multimedia site designed to help students and instructors improve learning outcomes. It offers access to a wealth of resources geared to meet the individual teaching and learning needs of every instructor and student. Combining an e-book, video, audio, multimedia simulations, research support, and assessment, MyAnthroLab gives students tools they need to enhance their performance in the course.

MyAnthroLab can be used by itself or linked to any learning management system. Please see your Pearson sales representative or visit www.myanthrolab.com for more information.

Instructor's Manual with Tests (0205232418) For each chapter in the text, this valuable resource provides a chapter outline, preview questions, lecture topics, research topics, and questions for classroom discussion. In addition, test questions in multiple-choice and essay formats are available for each chapter; the answers are page-referenced to the text. For easy access, this manual is available within the instructor section of MyAnthroLab for *Human Evolution and Culture 7/e*, or at www.pearsonhighered.com

MyTest (020523349X) This computerized software allows instructors to create their own personalized exams, to edit any or all of the existing test questions, and to add new questions. Other special features of this program include random generation of test questions, creation of alternate versions of the same test, scrambling question sequence, and test preview before printing. For easy access, this software is available within the instructor section of MyAnthroLab for *Human Evolution and Culture 7/e*, or at www.pearsonhighered.com

PowerPoint Presentation Slides (0205232426) These PowerPoint slides combine text and graphics for each chapter to help instructors convey anthropological principles in a clear and engaging way. In addition, Classroom Response System (CRS) In-Class Questions allow for instant, class-wide student responses to chapter-specific questions during lectures for teachers to gauge student comprehension. For easy access, they are available within the instructor section of MyAnthroLab for *Human Evolution and Culture 7/e*, or at www.pearsonhighered.com

EthnoQuest® (013185013X) This interactive multimedia simulation includes a series of ten ethnographic encounters with the culture of a fictional Mexican village set in a computer-based learning environment. It provides students with a realistic problem-solving experience and is designed to help students experience the fieldwork of a cultural anthropologist. Please see your Pearson sales representative for more information about **EthnoQuest®**.

Acknowledgments

We thank the people at Prentice Hall for all their help, particularly Nancy Roberts, Publisher for Anthropology; Nicole Conforti, Editorial Project Manager; Carolyn Arcabascio, Permissions Project Manager; and Patty Donovan, Full Service Project Manager.

We want to thank the following for reviewing our chapters and making suggestions about them: Michael Polich, McHenry County College; Roberta Martine, Fort Hays State University; Jennifer Fillion, Mott Community College; Paula Marshall-Gray, Midland College; K. Jill Fleuriet, University of Texas, San Antonio; and Jennifer Basquiat, College of Southern Nevada.

Thank you all, named and unnamed, who gave us advice.

Carol R. Ember
and Peter N. Peregrine

About the Authors

Carol R. Ember started at Antioch College as a chemistry major. She began taking social science courses because some were required, but she soon found herself intrigued. There were lots of questions without answers, and she became excited about the possibility of a research career in social science. She spent a year in graduate school at Cornell studying sociology before continuing on to Harvard, where she studied anthropology, primarily with John and Beatrice Whiting.

For her Ph.D. dissertation she worked among the Luo of Kenya. While there she noticed that many boys were assigned "girls' work," such as babysitting and household chores, because their mothers (who did most of the agriculture) did not have enough girls to help out. She decided to study the possible effects of task assignment on the social behavior of boys. Using systematic behavior observations, she compared girls, boys who did a great deal of girls' work, and boys who did little such work. She found that boys assigned girls' work were intermediate in many social behaviors, compared with the other boys and girls. Later, she did cross-cultural research on variation in marriage, family, descent groups, and war and peace, mainly in collaboration with Melvin Ember, whom she married in 1970. All of these cross-cultural studies tested theories on data for worldwide samples of societies.

From 1970 to 1996, she taught at Hunter College of the City University of New York. She has served as president of the Society of Cross-Cultural Research and was one of the directors of the Summer Institutes in Comparative Anthropological Research, which were funded by the National Science Foundation. From 1996 until 2009 she served as executive director of the Human Relations Area Files, Inc. (HRAF), a nonprofit research agency at Yale University. She was appointed president of HRAF in 2010. She is also currently president-elect of the Society for Anthropological Sciences.

After graduating from Columbia College, **Melvin Ember** went to Yale University for his Ph.D. His mentor at Yale was George Peter Murdock, an anthropologist who was instrumental in promoting cross-cultural research and building a full-text database on the cultures of the world to facilitate cross-cultural hypothesis testing. This database came to be known as the Human Relations Area Files (HRAF) because it was originally sponsored by the Institute of Human Relations at Yale. Growing in annual installments and now distributed in electronic format, the HRAF database currently covers more than 410 cultures, past and present, all over the world.

Melvin Ember did fieldwork for his dissertation in American Samoa, where he conducted a comparison of three villages to study the effects of commercialization on political life. In addition, he did research on descent groups and how they changed with the increase of buying and selling. His cross-cultural studies focused originally on variation in marital residence and descent groups. He also did cross-cultural research on the relationship between economic and political development, the origin and extension of the incest taboo, the causes of polygyny, and how archaeological correlates of social customs can help us draw inferences about the past.

After four years of research at the National Institute of Mental Health, he taught at Antioch College and then Hunter College of the City University of New York. He has served as president of the Society for Cross-Cultural Research. From 1987 until his death in 2009, he was president of HRAF.

Peter N. Peregrine came to anthropology after completing an undergraduate degree in English. He found anthropology's social scientific approach to understanding humans more appealing than the humanistic approach he had learned as an English major. He undertook an ethnohistorical study of the relationship between Jesuit missionaries and Native American peoples for his master's degree and realized that he needed to study archaeology to understand the cultural interactions experienced by Native Americans prior to contact with the Jesuits.

While working on his Ph.D. at Purdue University, Peregrine did research on the prehistoric Mississippian cultures of the eastern United States. He found that interactions between groups were common and had been shaping Native American cultures for centuries. Native Americans approached contact with the Jesuits simply as another in a long string of intercultural exchanges. He also found that relatively little research had been done on Native American interactions and decided that comparative research was a good place to begin examining the topic. In 1990 he participated in the Summer Institute in Comparative Anthropological Research, where he met Carol R. Ember and Melvin Ember.

Peter Peregrine is currently Professor of Anthropology at Lawrence University in Appleton, Wisconsin. He serves as research associate for the eHRAF Archaeology collection and is president of the Society for Anthropological Sciences. He continues to do archaeological and cross-cultural research, and to teach anthropology and archaeology to undergraduate students.

The Importance of Anthropology

((•—[Listen to the **Chapter Audio** on **myanthrolab.com**   [□□]—[Read on **myanthrolab.com**

What is anthropology and what can it do? The term **anthropology** comes from the Greek *anthropos* for "man, human" and *logos* for "study." Anthropologists seek answers to an enormous variety of questions about humans. They are interested in both universals and differences in human populations. They want to discover when, where, and why humans appeared on the earth, how and why they have changed since then, and how and why modern human populations vary in their biological and cultural features. Anthropology has a practical side too. Applied and practicing anthropologists put anthropological methods, information, and results to use, in efforts to solve practical problems.

Defining anthropology as the study of human beings is not complete, however, for such a definition would appear to incorporate a whole catalog of disciplines: sociology, psychology, political science, economics, history, human biology, and perhaps even the humanistic disciplines of philosophy and literature. There must, then, be something unique about anthropology—a reason for its having developed as a separate discipline and for its having retained a separate identity over the last 100 years.

The Scope of Anthropology

Anthropologists are often thought of as individuals who travel to little-known corners of the world to study exotic peoples or who dig deep into the earth to uncover the fossil remains or the tools and pots of people who lived long ago. These views, though clearly stereotyped, do indicate how anthropology differs from other disciplines concerned with humans. Anthropology is broader in scope, both geographically and historically. Anthropology is concerned explicitly and directly with all varieties of people throughout the world, not just those close at hand. Anthropologists are also interested in people of all periods. Beginning with the immediate ancestors of humans, who lived a few million years ago, anthropology traces the development of humans until the present.

Anthropologists have not always been as global and comprehensive in their concerns as they are today. Traditionally, they concentrated on non-Western cultures and left the study of Western civilization to other disciplines. In recent years, however, this division of labor among the disciplines has begun to disappear. Now anthropologists work in their own and other complex societies.

What induces anthropologists to study humans so broadly? In part, they are motivated by the belief that any suggested generalization about human beings should be shown to apply to many times and places of human existence. If a generalization does not prove to apply widely, anthropologists are entitled or even obliged to be skeptical about it. The skeptical attitude, in the absence of persuasive evidence, is our best protection against accepting invalid ideas about humans.

For example, when American educators discovered in the 1960s that African American schoolchildren rarely drank milk, they assumed that lack of money or education was the cause. But evidence from anthropology suggested a different explanation. Anthropologists had known for years that people do not drink fresh milk in many parts of the world where milking animals are kept; rather, they sour it before they drink it, or they make it into cheese. Why they do so is now clear. Many people lack the enzyme lactase that is necessary for breaking down lactose, the sugar in milk. When such people drink regular milk, it actually interferes with digestion. Not only is the lactose in milk not digested, but other nutrients are less likely to be digested as well; in many cases, drinking milk will cause cramps, stomach gas, diarrhea, and nausea.[1]

Milk intolerance is common in adulthood among Asians, southern Europeans, Arabs and Jews, West Africans, North and South American native peoples, and African Americans. Because anthropologists are acquainted with human life in an enormous variety of geographic and historical settings, they are often able to correct mistaken beliefs about different groups of people.

The Holistic Approach

Another distinguishing feature of the discipline is its **holistic**, or multifaceted, approach to the study of human beings. Anthropologists study not only all varieties of people but many aspects of human experience. For example, when describing a group of people, an anthropologist might discuss the history of the area in which the people live, the physical environment, the organization of family life, the general features of their language, the group's settlement patterns, political and economic systems, religion, and styles of art and dress.

In the past, individual anthropologists tried to cover as many subjects as possible. Today, as in many other disciplines, so much information has been accumulated that anthropologists tend to specialize. Thus, one anthropologist may investigate the physical characteristics of some of our prehistoric ancestors. Another may study the biological effect of the environment on a human population over time. Still another will concentrate on many customs of a particular group of people. Despite this specialization, however, the discipline of anthropology retains its holistic orientation in that its many different specialties, taken together, describe many aspects of human existence, both past and present.

The Anthropological Curiosity

Thus far, we have described anthropology as being broader in scope, both historically and geographically, and more holistic in approach than other disciplines concerned with human beings. But this statement again implies that anthropology is the all-inclusive human science. How, then, is anthropology really different from the other disciplines? We suggest that anthropology's distinctiveness lies principally in the kind of curiosity it arouses.

Individuals may provide information to anthropologists, but the anthropological curiosity mostly focuses on the typical characteristics (traits, customs) of human groups and how to understand and explain them. For example, whereas economists take a monetary system for granted and study how it operates, anthropologists would ask how frequently monetary systems are found, why they vary, and why only some societies during the last few thousand years used money. This is not to imply that anthropologists are not interested in variation within human groups, but their focus is usually on typical characteristics of human groups—how and why populations and their characteristics have varied around the globe and throughout the ages.

Fields of Anthropology

Different anthropologists concentrate on different characteristics of societies. Some are concerned primarily with *biological* or *physical characteristics* of human populations; others are interested principally in what we call *cultural characteristics.* Hence, there are two broad classifications of subject matter in anthropology: *biological (physical) anthropology* and *cultural anthropology.* Biological anthropology is one major field of anthropology. Cultural anthropology is divided into three major subfields: *archaeology, linguistics,* and *ethnology.* Ethnology, the study of recent cultures, is now usually referred to by the parent name, cultural anthropology (see Figure 1.1). Crosscutting these four fields is a fifth, *applied* or *practicing anthropology.*

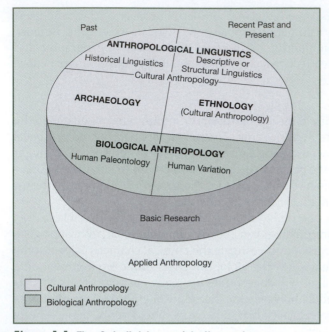

Past   Recent Past and Present

ANTHROPOLOGICAL LINGUISTICS
Historical Linguistics   Descriptive or Structural Linguistics
Cultural Anthropology

ARCHAEOLOGY   **ETHNOLOGY**
(Cultural Anthropology)

BIOLOGICAL ANTHROPOLOGY
Human Paleontology   Human Variation

Basic Research

Applied Anthropology

☐ Cultural Anthropology
☐ Biological Anthropology

Figure 1.1 The Subdivisions of Anthropology
The four major subdisciplines of anthropology (in bold type) may be classified according to subject matter (biological or cultural) and according to the period with which each is concerned (distant past versus recent past and present). There are applications of anthropology in all four subdisciplines.

Biological Anthropology

Biological (physical) anthropology, which deals with the biological or physical characteristics of humans, seeks to answer two distinct sets of questions. The first set is about the emergence of humans and their later evolution (this focus is called **human paleontology** or **paleoanthropology**). The second set is about how and why contemporary human populations vary biologically (this focus is called **human variation**).

To reconstruct human evolution, human paleontologists search for and study the buried, hardened remains or impressions—known as **fossils**—of humans, prehumans, and related animals. Paleontologists working in East Africa, for instance, have excavated the fossil remains of humanlike beings that lived more than 4 million years ago. These findings have suggested the approximate dates when our ancestors began to develop two-legged walking, very flexible hands, and a larger brain.

In attempting to clarify evolutionary relationships, human paleontologists may use not only the fossil record but also geological information on the succession of climates, environments, and plant and animal populations. Moreover, when reconstructing the past of humans, paleontologists are also interested in the behavior and evolution of our closest relatives among the mammals—the prosimians, monkeys, and apes, which, like ourselves, are members of the order of **Primates**. Anthropologists, psychologists, and biologists who specialize in the study of primates are called **primatologists**. The various species of primates are observed in the wild and in the laboratory. One especially popular subject of study is the chimpanzee, which bears a close resemblance to humans in behavior and physical appearance, has very similar genes, and is susceptible to many of the same diseases.[2]

The second major focus of biological anthropology, the study of human variation, investigates how and why contemporary human populations differ in biological or physical characteristics. All living people belong to one species, *Homo sapiens*, for all can successfully interbreed. Yet, much varies among human populations. Investigators of human variation ask such questions as: Why are some people taller than others? How have human populations adapted physically to their environmental conditions? Are some peoples, such as Inuit, better equipped than other peoples to endure cold? Does darker skin color offer special protection against the tropical sun?

To understand better the biological variations observable among contemporary human populations, biological anthropologists use the principles, concepts, and techniques of at least three other disciplines: human genetics (the study of human traits that are inherited), population

Birute Galdikas works with two orangutans in Borneo.

biology (the study of environmental effects on, and interaction with, population characteristics), and epidemiology (the study of how and why diseases affect different populations in different ways). Research on human variation, therefore, overlaps research in other fields.

Cultural Anthropology

Cultural anthropology is concerned with how and why cultures vary or are similar in the past and present. But what is culture? We discuss the concept of culture more fully in the chapter on culture and culture change. Briefly, the term *culture* refers to the customary ways that a particular population or society thinks and behaves. The culture of a social group includes many things—from the language that people speak, the way children are brought up, the roles assigned to males and females, religious beliefs and practices, and preferences in music. Anthropologists are interested in all of these and other learned behaviors and ideas that have come to be widely shared or customary in the group. The three main branches of cultural anthropology are **archaeology** (the study of past cultures, primarily through their material remains); **anthropological linguistics** (the anthropological study of languages); and **ethnology** (the study of existing and recent cultures), now usually referred to by the parent name, *cultural anthropology.*

Archaeology Archaeologists seek not only to reconstruct the daily life and customs of peoples who lived in the past but also to trace cultural changes and to offer possible explanations for those changes. This concern is similar to that of historians, but archaeologists reach much farther back in time. Historians deal only with societies that left written records and are therefore limited to the last 5,000 years of human history. Human societies, however, have existed for more than a million years, and only a small proportion in the last 5,000 years had writing. Lacking written records for study, archaeologists must try to reconstruct history from the remains of human cultures. Some of these remains are as grand as the Mayan temples discovered at Chichén Itzá in Yucatán, Mexico. More often, they are as ordinary as bits of broken pottery, stone tools, and garbage heaps.

In urban areas before new construction begins, archaeologists may be called upon to excavate and record information on historical sites, as shown here in New York City.

To collect the data they need to understand how and why ways of life have changed through time in different parts of the world, archaeologists use techniques and findings borrowed from other disciplines, as well as what they can infer from anthropological studies of recent and contemporary cultures. For example, to guess where to dig for evidence of early toolmaking, archaeologists rely on geology to tell them where sites of early human occupation are likely to be found, because of erosion and uplifting, near the surface of the earth. To infer when agriculture first developed, archaeologists date the relevant excavated materials by a process originally developed by chemical scientists. To try to understand why cities first emerged, archaeologists may use information from historians, geographers, and others about how recent and contemporary cities are related economically and politically to their hinterlands. If we can discover what recent and contemporary cities have in common, we can speculate on why cities developed originally. Thus, archaeologists use information from the present and recent past in trying to understand the distant past.

Anthropological Linguistics   Anthropological linguistics is another branch of cultural anthropology. Linguistics, or the study of languages, is a somewhat older discipline than anthropology, but the early linguists concentrated on the study of languages that had been written for a long time—languages such as English that had been written for nearly a thousand years. Anthropological linguists began to do fieldwork in places where the language was not yet written. This meant that anthropologists could not consult a dictionary or grammar to help them learn the language. Instead, they first had to construct a dictionary and grammar. Then they could study the structure and history of the language.

Like biological anthropologists, linguists study changes that have taken place over time, as well as contemporary variation. Some anthropological linguists are concerned with the emergence of language and also with the divergence of languages over thousands of years. The study of how languages change over time and how they may be related is known as **historical linguistics**. Anthropological linguists are also interested in how contemporary languages differ, especially in their construction. This focus of linguistics is generally called **descriptive (structural) linguistics**. The study of how language is used in social contexts is called **sociolinguistics**.

In contrast with human paleontologists and archaeologists, who have physical remains to help them reconstruct change over time, historical linguists deal only with languages—and usually unwritten ones at that. (Remember that writing is only about 5,000 years old, and most languages since then have not been written.) Because unwritten languages must be heard to be studied, they do not leave any trace once speakers have died. Linguists interested in reconstructing the history of unwritten languages must begin in the present, with comparisons of contemporary languages. On the basis of these comparisons, they draw inferences about the kinds of change in language that may have occurred in the past and that may account for similarities and differences observed in the present. Historical linguists typically ask such questions as these: Did two or more contemporary languages diverge from a common ancestral language? If they are related, how far back in time did they begin to differ?

Unlike historical linguists, the descriptive (or structural) linguists are typically concerned with discovering and recording the principles that determine how sounds and words are put together in speech. For example, a structural description of a particular language might tell us that the sounds *t* and *k* are interchangeable in a word without causing a difference in meaning. In American Samoa, one could say *Tutuila* or *Kukuila* as the name of the largest island, and everyone, except perhaps newly arrived anthropologists who know little yet about the Samoan language, would understand that the same island was being mentioned.

Sociolinguists are interested in the social aspects of language, including what people speak about and how they interact conversationally, their attitudes toward speakers of other dialects or languages, and how people speak differently in different social contexts. In English, for example, we do not address everyone we meet in the same way. "Hi, Sandy" may be the customary way a person greets a friend. But we would probably feel uncomfortable addressing a doctor by a first name; instead, we would probably say, "Good morning, Dr. Brown." Such variations in language use, which are determined by the social status of the people being addressed, are significant for sociolinguists.

Ethnology   Ethnologists, usually called "cultural anthropologists" nowadays, try to understand how and why peoples today and in the recent past differ or are similar in their customary ways of thinking and acting. How and why do cultures develop and change? How does one aspect of culture affect others? The aim of ethnologists is largely the same as that of archaeologists. However, ethnologists generally use data collected through observation and interviews of living peoples. Archaeologists, on the other hand, must work with fragmentary remains of past cultures, on the basis of which they can only make inferences about the customs of prehistoric peoples.

One type of ethnologist, **ethnographers**, usually spend a year or so living with, talking to, and observing the people whose customs they are studying. This fieldwork provides the data for a detailed description (an **ethnography**) of customary behavior and thought. Ethnographers vary in the degree to which they strive for completeness in their coverage of cultural and social life. Earlier ethnographers tended to strive for holistic coverage; more recent ethnographers have tended to specialize or focus on narrower realms such as ritual healing or curing, interaction with the environment, effects of modernization or globalization, or gender issues. Ethnographies often go beyond description; they may address current anthropological issues or try to explain some aspect of culture.

Many cultures have undergone extensive change in the recent past, so trying to understand what life was like in earlier times is important. Ethnographers can ask older people what life was like when they were young, and information about the past may be contained in historical documents usually not written by anthropologists. An **ethnohistorian** studies how the ways of life of a particular group of people have changed over time. Ethnohistorians investigate written documents, such as missionary accounts, reports by traders and explorers, and government records, to try to establish the cultural changes that have occurred. Unlike ethnographers, who rely mostly on their own observations and interviewing, ethnohistorians rely on the reports of others. Often, they must attempt to piece together and make sense of widely scattered, and even apparently contradictory, information. Thus, the ethnohistorian's research is very much like that of a historian, except that ethnohistorians are usually concerned with the history of a people who did not themselves leave written records.

Ethnographic and ethnohistorical research is very time-consuming, and it is rare for one person to study more than a few cultures. The **cross-cultural researcher** (who may be a cultural anthropologist or some other kind of social scientist) is interested in discovering general patterns about cultural traits—what is universal, what is variable, why traits vary, and what the consequences of the variability might be. Why, for example, is there more gender inequality in some societies than in others? Is family violence related to aggression in other areas of life? What are the effects of living in a very unpredictable environment? In testing possible answers to such questions, cross-cultural researchers use data from samples of cultures (usually described initially by ethnographers) to try to arrive at explanations or relationships that hold across cultures. Archaeologists may find the results of cross-cultural research useful for making inferences about the past, particularly if they can discover material indicators of cultural variation.

Because ethnologists may be interested in many aspects of customary behavior and thought—from economic behavior to political behavior to styles of art, music, and religion—ethnology overlaps with disciplines that concentrate on some particular aspect of human existence, such as sociology, psychology, economics, political science, art, music, and comparative religion. But the distinctive feature of cultural anthropology is its interest in how all these aspects of human existence vary from society to society, in all historical periods, and in all parts of the world.

Applied Anthropology

In the physical and biological sciences, it is well understood that technological breakthroughs like DNA splicing, spacecraft docking in outer space, and the development of miniscule computer chips could not have taken place without an enormous amount of basic research to uncover the laws of nature in the physical and biological worlds. If we did not understand fundamental principles, the technological achievements we are so proud of would not be possible. Researchers are often simply driven by curiosity, with no thought to where the research might lead, which is why such research is sometimes called *basic research.* The same is true of the social sciences. If a researcher finds out that societies with combative sports tend to have more wars, it may lead to other inquiries about the relationships between one kind of aggression and another. The knowledge acquired may ultimately lead to discovering ways to correct social problems, such as family violence and war.

Whereas basic research may ultimately help to solve practical problems, applied research is more explicit in its practical goals. Today, more than half of all professional anthropologists are applied, or practicing, anthropologists.[3] **Applied (practicing) anthropology** is explicit in its concern with making anthropological knowledge useful.[4] Applied anthropologists may be trained in any or all of the subfields of anthropology. In contrast to basic researchers, who are almost always employed in colleges, universities, and museums, applied anthropologists are commonly

Getting Development Programs to Notice Women's Contributions to Agriculture

When Anita Spring first did fieldwork in Zambia in the 1970s, she was not particularly interested in agriculture. Rather, medical anthropology was her interest. Her work focused on customary healing practices, particularly involving women and children. She was surprised at the end of the year when a delegation of women came to tell her that she didn't understand what it meant to be a woman. "To be a woman is to be a farmer," they said. She admits that it took her a while to pay attention to women as farmers, but then she began to participate in efforts to provide technical assistance to them. Like many others interested in women in development, Spring realized that all too often development agents downplay women's contributions to agriculture.

How does one bring about change in male-centered attitudes and practices? One way is to document how much women actually contribute to agriculture. Beginning with the influential writing of Ester Boserup in *Woman's Role in Economic Development* (1970), scholars began to report that in Africa south of the Sahara, in the Caribbean, and in parts of Southeast Asia, women were the principal farmers or agricultural laborers. Moreover, as agriculture became more complex, it required more work time in the fields, so women's contribution to agriculture increased. In

addition, men increasingly went away to work, so women had to do much of what used to be men's work on the farms.

In the 1980s, Spring designed and directed the Women in Agricultural Development Project in Malawi, funded by the Office of Women in the U.S. Agency for International Development. Rather than focusing just on women, the project aimed to collect data on both female and male agriculturalists and how development agents treated them. The project did more than collect information; mini-projects were set up and evaluated so that successful training techniques could be passed on to development agents in other regions. Spring points out that the success of the program was due not just to the design of the project. Much of the success depended on the interest and willingness of Malawi itself to change. It didn't hurt that the United Nations and other donor organizations increasingly focused attention on women. It takes the efforts of many to bring about change. Increasingly, applied anthropologists like Anita Spring are involved in these efforts from beginning to end, from the design stage to implementation and evaluation.

Source: Spring 1995; 2000b.

employed in settings outside traditional academia, including government agencies, international development agencies, private consulting firms, businesses, public health organizations, medical schools, law offices, community development agencies, and charitable foundations.

Biological anthropologists may be called upon to give forensic evidence in court, or they may work in public health, or design clothes and equipment to fit human anatomy. Archaeologists may be involved in preserving and exhibiting artifacts for museums and in doing contract work to find and preserve cultural sites that might be damaged by construction or excavation. Linguists may work in bilingual educational training programs or may work on ways to improve communication. Ethnologists may work in a wide variety of applied projects ranging from community development, urban planning, health care, and agricultural improvement to personnel and organizational management and assessment of the impact of change programs on people's lives.[5] We discuss applied anthropology in many of the boxes and more fully in the last part of this book, "Using Anthropology."

Forensic anthropology is one kind of applied anthropology. Kathy Reichs is a forensic anthropologist working in a medical examiner's office.

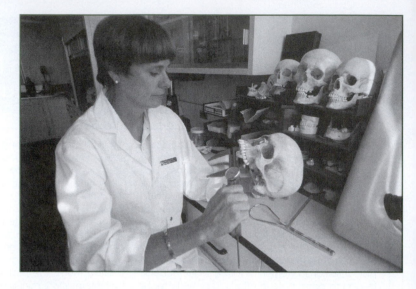

The Relevance of Anthropology

The idea that it is impossible to account for human behavior scientifically, either because our actions and beliefs are too individualistic and complex or because human beings are understandable only in otherworldly terms, is a self-fulfilling notion. We cannot discover general principles explaining human behavior if we neither believe such principles exist nor bother to look for them. People who do not believe that there can be general principles of human behavior will be reinforced by their finding none. If we are to increase our understanding of human beings, we first have to believe it is possible to do so.

If we aim to understand humans, it is essential that we study humans in all times and places. We must study ancient humans and modern humans. We must study their cultures and their biology. How else can we understand what is true of humans generally or how they are capable of varying? If we study just our own society, we may come up only with explanations that are culture-bound, not general or applicable to most or all humans. Anthropology is useful, then, to the degree that it contributes to our understanding of human beings everywhere.

In addition, anthropology is relevant because it helps us avoid misunderstandings between peoples. If we can understand why other groups are different from ourselves, we might have less reason to condemn them for behavior that appears strange to us. We may then come to realize that many differences between peoples are products of physical and cultural adaptations to different environments. For example, someone who first finds out about the San as they lived in the Kalahari Desert of southern Africa in the 1950s might assume that the San were "backward." The San wore little clothing, had few possessions, lived in meager shelters, and enjoyed none of our technological niceties like radio and computers. But let us reflect on how a typical North American community might react if it awoke to find itself in an environment similar to that in which the San lived. The people would find that the arid land makes both agriculture and animal husbandry impossible, and they might have to think about adopting a nomadic existence. They might then discard many of their material possessions so that they could travel easily, to take advantage of changing water and food supplies. Because of the extreme heat and the lack of extra water for laundry, they might find it more practical to be almost naked than to wear clothes. They would undoubtedly find it impossible to build elaborate homes. For social security, they might start to share the food brought into the group. Thus, if they survived at all, they might end up looking and acting far more like the San looked than like typical North Americans.

As the world becomes increasingly interconnected or globalized, the importance of understanding and trying to respect cultural and physical differences becomes more and more important. Minor misunderstandings

A large number of emigrants from the former Soviet Union, particularly from Black Sea cities and towns such as Odessa, live in the Brighton Beach neighborhood of Brooklyn. Migrant and immigrant communities, such as "Little Odessa," are an increasing focus of anthropological study.

can escalate quickly into more serious problems. Even when powerful countries think they are being helpful, they may convey that other countries are inferior. They may also unknowingly promote behaviors that are not in the best interest of the people they are trying to help. At the extreme, misunderstandings can lead to violent confrontations. In today's world, going to war with modern weapons of mass destruction can kill more people than ever before.

Knowledge of our past may bring both a feeling of humility and a sense of accomplishment. If we are to attempt to deal with the problems of our world, we must be aware of our vulnerability so that we do not think that problems will solve themselves. But we also have to think enough of our accomplishments to believe that we can find solutions to problems. Much of the trouble we get into may be a result of feelings of self-importance and invulnerability—in short, our lack of humility. Knowing something about our evolutionary past may help us to understand and accept our place in the biological world. Just as for any other form of life, there is no guarantee that any particular human population, or even the entire human species, will perpetuate itself indefinitely. The earth changes, the environment changes, and humanity itself changes. What survives and flourishes in the present might not do so in the future.

Yet, our vulnerability should not make us feel powerless. We have many reasons to feel confident about the future. Consider what we have accomplished so far. By means of tools and weapons fashioned from sticks and stones, we were able to hunt animals larger and more powerful than ourselves. We discovered how to make fire, and we learned to use it to keep ourselves warm and to cook our food. As we domesticated plants and animals, we gained greater control over our food supply and were able to establish more permanent settlements. We mined and smelted ores to fashion more durable tools. We built cities and irrigation systems, monuments and ships. We made it possible to travel from one continent to another in a single day. We conquered some illnesses and prolonged human life.

In short, human beings and their cultures have changed considerably over the course of history. Human populations have often been able to adapt to changing circumstances. Let us hope that humans continue to adapt to the challenges of the present and future.

Explanation and Evidence

Anthropologists in the field try to arrive at accurate answers to descriptive questions. How do the people make a living? How do they marry? What gods do they believe in? But as important as accurate description is, it is not the ultimate goal of anthropology. Anthropologists want to *understand*—to know *why* people have certain customs or beliefs, not just to see that they *do* have them. As difficult as the *how* and *what* questions are to answer, the *why* questions are even harder. *Why* questions deal with explanations, which are harder to generate and harder to evaluate. In science, to understand is to explain, and so the major goal of science is to arrive at trustworthy explanations.[6]

For many anthropologists, the plausibility or persuasiveness of an explanation cannot be considered a sufficient reason to accept it. The explanation must also be tested and supported by objective evidence that could have falsified it. And even when it is supported, there still may be grounds for skepticism. According to the scientific orientation, all knowledge is uncertain and therefore subject to increasing or decreasing confirmation as new tests are made. This means that we will never arrive at absolute truth. On the other hand, and this is encouraging, we should be able to achieve more and more reliable understanding if we keep testing our theories.

Explanations

An **explanation** is an answer to a *why* question. There are many types of explanations, some more satisfying than others. For example, suppose we ask why a society thinks that a couple should abstain from sex for a year or so after the birth of a baby. If we say their tradition is to practice a long postpartum sex taboo, is this a satisfactory explanation? We would have to say no, because the thing to be explained (the taboo) is being explained by itself, by its prior existence. To explain something in terms of tradition is to say that people do it because they already do it, which is not informative. What kinds of explanations are more satisfactory, then? In science, there are two kinds of explanations that are sought: associations and theories.

Associations or Relationships One way of explaining something (an observation, an action, or a custom) is to say how it conforms to a general principle or relationship. So to explain why the water left outside in the basin froze, we say that it was cold last night and that water freezes at 32°F (0°C). The statement that water solidifies (becomes ice) at 32°F is a statement of a relationship or association between two **variables**—things or quantities that vary. In this case, variation in the state of water (liquid vs. solid) is related to variation in the temperature of the air (above vs. below 32°F). The truth of the relationship is suggested by repeated observations. In the physical sciences, such relationships are called **laws** when almost all scientists accept them. We find such explanations satisfactory because they allow us to predict what will happen in the future or to understand something that has happened regularly in the past.

In the social sciences, associations are usually stated *probabilistically*; that is, we say that two or more variables tend to be related in a predictable way, which means that there are usually some exceptions. For example, to explain why a society has a long postpartum sex taboo, we can point to the association (or correlation) that John Whiting found in a worldwide sample of societies: Societies with apparently low-protein diets tend to have long postpartum sex taboos.[7] We call the relationship between low-protein diets and the sex taboo a **statistical association**, which means that the observed relationship is unlikely to be due to chance.

Theories Even though laws and statistical associations explain by relating what is to be explained to other things, we want to know more: why those laws or associations exist. Why does water freeze at 32°F? Why do societies with low-protein diets tend to have long postpartum sex taboos? Therefore, scientists try to formulate theories that will explain the observed relationships (laws and statistical associations). **Theories** are explanations of laws and statistical associations. By way of example, let us return to the question of why some societies have long postpartum sex taboos. We have already seen that a known statistical association can be used to help explain it. In general (but not always), if a society has a low-protein diet, it will have a long postpartum sex taboo. But most people would ask additional questions: Why does a low-protein diet explain the taboo? What is the mechanism by which a society with such a diet develops the custom of a long postpartum sex taboo? A theory is intended to answer such questions.

A thermometer provides a way of comparing or measuring the "heat" of different locations or over different time periods. While the physical sciences often use physical instruments and the social sciences often use humans to observe, all measurements compare things on some scale of variation.

John Whiting theorized that a long postpartum sex taboo may be an adaptation to certain conditions. Particularly in tropical areas, where the major food staples are low in protein, babies are vulnerable to the protein-deficiency disease called *kwashiorkor.* But if a baby could continue to nurse for a long time, it might have more of a chance to survive. The postpartum sex taboo might be adaptive, Whiting's theory suggests, because it increases the likelihood of a baby's survival. That is, if a mother puts off having another baby for a while, the first baby might have a better chance to survive because it can be fed mother's milk for a longer time. Whiting suggests that parents may be aware, whether unconsciously or consciously, that having another baby too soon might jeopardize the survival of the first baby, and so they might decide that abstaining from intercourse for more than a year after the birth of the first baby would be a good idea.

As this example of a theory illustrates, there are differences between a theory and an association. A theory is more complicated, containing a series of statements. An association usually states quite simply that there is a relationship between two or more measured variables. Another difference is that, although a theory may mention some things that are observable, such as the presence of a long postpartum sex taboo, parts of it are difficult or impossible to observe directly. For example, with regard to Whiting's theory, it would be difficult to find out if people had deliberately or unconsciously decided to practice a long postpartum sex taboo because they recognized that babies would thereby have a better chance to survive. Then, too, the concept of adaptation—that some characteristic promotes greater reproductive success—is difficult to verify because it is difficult to find out whether different individuals or groups have different rates of reproduction because they do or do not practice the supposedly adaptive custom. Thus, some concepts or implications in a theory are unobservable (at least at the present time), and only some aspects may be observable. In contrast, statistical associations or laws are based entirely on observations.[8]

Why Theories Cannot be Proved

Many people think that the theories they learned in physics or chemistry courses have been proved. Unfortunately, many students get that impression because their teachers present "lessons" in an authoritative manner. Scientists and philosophers of science now generally agree that no theory can be said to be proved or unquestionably true, although some theories may have considerable evidence supporting them. This is because many of the concepts and ideas in theories are not directly observable and therefore are not directly verifiable. For example, scientists may try to explain how light behaves by postulating that it consists of particles called photons, but photons cannot be observed, even with the most powerful microscope. So, exactly what a photon looks like and exactly how it works remain in the realm of the unprovable. The photon is a **theoretical construct**, something that cannot be observed or verified directly. Because all theories contain such constructs, theories cannot be proved entirely or with absolute certainty.[9]

Why should we bother with theories, then, if we cannot prove that they are true? Perhaps the main advantage of a theory as a kind of explanation is that it may lead to new understanding or knowledge. A theory can suggest new relationships or imply new predictions that might be supported or confirmed by new research. For example, Whiting's theory about long postpartum sex taboos has implications that researchers could investigate. Because the theory discusses how a long postpartum sex taboo might be adaptive, we would expect that certain changes would result in the taboo's disappearance. For example, suppose people adopted either mechanical birth control devices or began to give supplementary high-protein foods to babies. With birth control, a family could space births without abstaining from sex, so we would expect the custom of postpartum abstinence to disappear. As well, we would expect it to disappear with protein supplements for babies, because kwashiorkor would then be less likely to afflict the babies. Whiting's ideas might also prompt investigators to try to find out whether parents are consciously or unconsciously aware of the problem of close birth spacing in areas with low supplies of protein.

The Yanomamö Indians of Brazil (*left*) depend on root crops. The Inuit of arctic North America depend almost entirely on fish and marine mammals.

Although theories cannot be proved, they are rejectable. The method of **falsification**, which shows that a theory seems to be wrong, is the main way that theories are judged.[10] Scientists derive implications or predictions that should be true if the theory is correct. So, for example, Whiting predicted that societies with long postpartum sex taboos would be found more often in the tropics than in temperate regions and that they would be likely to have low-protein food supplies. Such predictions of what might be found are called **hypotheses**. If the predictions turn out not to be correct, the researcher is obliged to conclude that something may be wrong with the theory or with the test of the theory. Theories that are not falsified are accepted for the time being because the available evidence seems to be consistent with them. But remember that no matter how much the available evidence seems to support a theory, we can never be certain it is true. There is always the possibility that some implication of it, some hypothesis derivable from it, will not be confirmed in the future.

Evidence: Testing Explanations

In any field of investigation, theories are generally the most plentiful commodity. It is necessary, then, for us to have procedures that enable us to select from among the many available theories those that are more likely to be correct. "Just as mutations arise naturally but are not all beneficial, so hypotheses [theories] emerge naturally but are not all correct. If progress is to occur, therefore, we require a superfluity of hypotheses and also a mechanism of selection."[11] In other words, generating a theory or interpretation is not enough. We need some reliable method of testing whether or not that theory is likely to be correct. If a theory is not correct, it may detract from our efforts to achieve understanding by misleading us into thinking the problem is already solved.

The strategy in all kinds of testing in science is to predict what one would expect to find if a particular theory were correct, and then to conduct an investigation to see if the prediction is generally consistent with the data. If the prediction is not supported, the investigator is obliged to accept the possibility that the theory is wrong. If, however, the prediction holds true, then the investigator is entitled to say that evidence supports the theory. Thus, conducting research designed to test expectations derived from theory allows researchers to eliminate some theories and to accept others, at least tentatively.

Operationalization and Measurement To transform theoretical predictions into statements that might be verified, a researcher provides an **operational definition** of each of the concepts or variables mentioned in the prediction. An operational definition is a description of the procedure that is followed to measure the variable.[12]

Whiting predicted that societies with a low-protein diet would have a long postpartum sex taboo. Amount of protein in the diet is a variable; some societies have more, others have less. Length of the postpartum sex taboo is a variable; a society may have a short taboo or a long taboo. Whiting operationally defined the first variable, *amount of protein*, in terms of staple foods.[13] If a society depended mostly on root and tree crops (such as cassava and bananas), Whiting rated the society as having low protein. If the society depended mostly on cereal crops (such as wheat, barley, corn, and oats), he rated it as having moderate protein, because cereal crops have more protein by weight than root and tree crops. If the society depended mostly on hunting, fishing, or herding for food, he rated it as having high protein. The other variable in Whiting's prediction, *length of postpartum sex taboo*, was operationalized as follows: A society was rated as having a long taboo if couples customarily abstained from sex for more than a year after the birth of a baby; abstention for a year or less was considered a short taboo.

Specifying an operational definition for each variable is extremely important because it allows other investigators to check a researcher's results.[14] Science depends on *replication*, the repetition of results. Only when many researchers observe a particular association can we call that association or relationship a law. Providing operational definitions is also extremely important because it allows others to evaluate whether a measure is appropriate. Only when we are told exactly how something was measured can we judge whether the measure reflects what it is supposed to reflect. Specifying measures publicly is so important in science that we are obliged to be skeptical of any conclusions offered by a researcher who fails to say how variables were measured.

To **measure** something is to say how it compares with other things on some scale of variation.[15] People often assume that a measuring device is always a physical instrument, such as a scale or a ruler, but *classification* is also a form of measurement. When we classify people as male or female or employed versus unemployed, we are dividing them into *sets*. Deciding which set they belong to is a kind of measurement because doing so allows us to compare them. We can also measure things by deciding which cases or examples have more or less of something (e.g., more or less protein in the diet). The measures employed in physical science are usually based on scales that allow us to assign numbers to each case; we measure height in meters and weight in grams, for example. However we measure our variables, the fact that we can measure them means that we can test our hypotheses to see if the predicted relationships actually exist, at least most of the time.

Sampling   After deciding how to measure the variables in some predicted relationship, investigators must decide how to select which cases to study to see if the predicted relationship holds. If the prediction is about the behavior of people, the sampling decision involves which people to observe. If the prediction is about an association between societal customs, the sampling decision involves which societies to study. No researcher can investigate all the possible cases, so choices must be made. Some choices are better than others. The best sample is almost always some kind of random sample in which all cases selected have an equal chance of being included in the sample or subset. Almost all statistical tests used to evaluate the results of research require random sampling because only results based on a random sample can be assumed to be probably true for some larger set or universe of cases.

Statistical Evaluation   When researchers have measured the variables of interest for all the sample cases, they are ready to see if the predicted relationship actually exists in the data. Remember, the results may not turn out to be what the theory predicts. Sometimes researchers construct a *contingency table*, like that shown in Table 1.1, to see if the variables are associated as predicted. In Whiting's sample of 172 societies, each case is assigned to a box, or cell, in the table, depending on how the society is measured on the two variables of interest. For example, a society that has a long postpartum sex taboo and a low-protein diet is placed in the third row of the Long Duration column. (In Whiting's sample [see Table 1.1], there are 27 such societies.) A society that has a short postpartum sex taboo and a low-protein diet is placed in the third row in the Short Duration column. (There are 20 such societies in the sample.) The statistical question is, Does the way the cases are distributed in the six central cells of the table generally support Whiting's prediction? If we looked just at the table, we might not know what to answer. Many cases appear to be in the expected places. For example, most of the high-protein cases (47 of 62) have short taboos, and most of the low-protein cases (27 of 47) have long taboos. But there

TABLE 1.1 Association Between Availability of Protein and Duration of Postpartum Sex Taboo

Availability of Protein	Duration of Postpartum Sex Taboo		
	Short (0–1 Year)	Long (More Than 1 Year)	Total
High	47	15	62
Medium	38	25	63
Low	20	27	47
Total	105	67	172

Source: Based on Whiting 1964, 520.

are also many exceptions (e.g., 20 cases have low protein and a short taboo). So, although many cases appear to be in the expected places, there are also many exceptions. Do the exceptions invalidate the prediction? How many exceptions would compel us to reject the hypothesis? Here is where we resort to *statistical tests of significance.*

Statisticians have devised various tests that tell us how "perfect" a result has to be for us to believe that there is probably an association between the variables of interest, that one variable generally predicts the other. Essentially, every statistical result is evaluated in the same objective way. We ask: What is the chance that this result is purely accidental, that there is no association at all between the two variables? Although some of the mathematical ways of answering this question are complicated, the answer always involves a probability value (or *p*-value)—the likelihood that the observed result or a stronger one could have occurred by chance. The statistical test used by Whiting gives a *p*-value of less than .01 ($p < .01$) for the observed result. In other words, there is less than 1 chance out of 100 that the relationship observed is purely accidental. A *p*-value of less than .01 is a fairly low probability; most social scientists conventionally agree to call any result with a *p*-value of .05 or less (5 or fewer chances out of 100) a statistically significant, or probably true, result. When we describe relationships or associations in the rest of this book, we are almost always referring to results that have been found to be statistically significant.

But why should a probably true relationship have any exceptions? If a theory is really correct, shouldn't *all* the cases fit? There are many reasons why we can never expect a perfect result. First, even if a theory is correct (e.g., if a low-protein diet really does favor the adoption of a long postpartum sex taboo), there may still be other causes that we have not investigated. For example, societies that depend mostly on hunting for their food, and would therefore be classified as having a high-protein diet, may have a problem carrying infants from one campsite to another and may practice a long postpartum sex taboo so that two infants will not have to be carried at the same time.

Exceptions to the predicted relationship might also occur because of *cultural lag.*[16] Cultural lag occurs when change in one aspect of culture takes time to produce change in another aspect. Suppose that a society recently changed crops and is now no longer a low-protein society but still practices the taboo. This society would be an exception to the predicted relationship, but it might fit the theory if it stopped practicing the taboo in a few years. Measurement inaccuracy is another source of exception. Whiting's measure of protein, which is based on the major sources of food, is not a very precise measure of protein in the diet. It does not take into account the possibility that a "tree crop" society might get a lot of protein from fishing or raising pigs. So it might turn out that some supposedly low-protein societies have been misclassified, which may be one reason why there are 20 cases in the lowest cell in the left-hand column of Table 1.1. Measurement error usually produces exceptions.

Significant statistical associations that are predictable from a theory offer tentative support for the theory. But much more is needed before we can be fairly confident about the theory. Replication is needed to confirm whether other researchers can reproduce the predictions using other samples. Other predictions should be derived from the theory to see if they too are supported. The theory should be pitted against alternative explanations to see which theory works better. We may have to combine theories if alternative explanations also predict the relationship in question. The research process in science thus requires time and patience. Perhaps most important, it requires that researchers be humble. No matter how wonderful one's own theory seems, it is important to acknowledge that it may be wrong. If we don't test our theories, we can never tell the difference between a better or worse theory, and we will be saddled forever with our present ignorance. In the next chapter, we explore more specific ways that anthropologists do research to understand the past and the present.

✓ ─ Study and **Review** on **myanthrolab.com**

Summary

1. Anthropology is literally the study of human beings. It differs from other disciplines concerned with people in that anthropology is: (a) concerned with humans in all places of the world and traces human evolution and cultural development from millions of years ago to the present day; (b) holistic, that is, studies all aspects of peoples' experiences; (c) concerned with identifying and explaining typical characteristics (traits, customs) of particular human populations.

2. Biological (physical) anthropology, one of the major fields of anthropology, studies the emergence of humans and their later physical evolution (human paleontology) and how and why contemporary human populations vary biologically (human variation).

3. Cultural anthropology has three subfields—archaeology, anthropological linguistics, and ethnology (now usually referred to by the parent name, cultural anthropology). All the subfields deal with aspects of human culture, that is, with the customary ways of thinking and behaving of particular societies.

4. Archaeologists seek to reconstruct and explain the daily life and customs of prehistoric peoples from the remains of human cultures.

5. Anthropological linguists are concerned with the emergence of language and with the divergence of languages over time (historical linguistics) as well as how contemporary languages differ, both in construction (descriptive or structural linguistics) and in actual speech (sociolinguistics).

6. The ethnologist (now often called a cultural anthropologist) seeks to understand how and why peoples of today and the recent past differ in their customary ways of thinking and acting. There are three major types of cultural anthropologists: ethnographers, ethnohistorians, and cross-cultural researchers.

7. In all four major subdisciplines of anthropology, there are applied anthropologists, people who apply anthropological knowledge to achieve more practical goals.

8. By showing us why other people are the way they are, both culturally and physically, anthropology may make us more tolerant. Knowledge of our past may bring us both a feeling of humility and a sense of accomplishment.

9. Scientists try to achieve two kinds of explanations—associations and theories. Theories are falsified by deriving hypotheses or predictions that should be true if the theory is correct.

10. To select among many possible theories researchers predict what one would expect to find if a given theory is correct, then gather evidence to see if the prediction holds true.

11. It is unusual for a researcher to be able to investigate most or all possible cases, so sampling is used to select cases for testing.

12. Statistical evaluation is often used to determine how well a particular test fits the expectations derived from a theoretical prediction.

Glossary Terms

anthropological linguistics (p. 5)
anthropology (p. 2)
applied (practicing) anthropology (p. 8)
archaeology (p. 5)
biological (physical) anthropology (p. 4)
cross-cultural researcher (p. 8)
cultural anthropology (p. 5)
descriptive (structural) linguistics (p. 6)

ethnographer (p. 7)
ethnography (p. 7)
ethnohistorian (p. 8)
ethnology (p. 5)
explanation (p. 12)
falsification (p. 15)
fossils (p. 4)
historical linguistics (p. 6)
holistic (p. 3)
Homo sapiens (p. 4)
human paleontology (p. 4)
human variation (p. 4)
hypotheses (p. 15)

laws (p. 12)
measure (p. 16)
operational definition (p. 15)
paleoanthropology (p. 4)
Primates (p. 4)
primatologists (p. 4)
sociolinguistics (p. 6)
statistical association (p. 12)
theoretical construct (p. 14)
theories (p. 13)
variables (p. 12)

Critical Questions

1. Why study anthropology? What are its goals and how is it useful?

2. How does anthropology differ from other fields of study you've encountered that deal with humans? (Compare with psychology, sociology, political science, history, or biology, among others.)

3. Can a unique event be explained? Explain your answer.

4. Why is scientific understanding always uncertain?

Read the Original Source on myanthrolab.com

Read the chapter by Terence E. Hays, "From Ethnographer to Comparativist and Back Again," on MyAnthroLab, and answer the following questions.

1. Many researchers find that their interests change when they go to the field. What did Hays start out studying? What did he get more interested in?
2. Explain why Hays thinks that you need both ethnography and comparison.

Research Methods in Anthropology

2

((•─Listen to the **Chapter Audio** on **myanthrolab.com**   ▭─Read on **myanthrolab.com**

Anthropologists use several methods to conduct research. Each has certain advantages and disadvantages in generating and testing explanations. The types of research in anthropology can be classified according to two criteria. One is the spatial scope or breadth of the study (e.g., the analysis of a single society, analysis of societies in a region, or analysis of a worldwide sample of societies). The other criterion is the temporal scope of the study—historical versus nonhistorical. Combinations of these criteria are shown in Table 2.1.

Types of Research in Anthropology

In this section, we mostly discuss research strategies in cultural anthropology. However, most of these have parallels in archaeology and biological anthropology, as Table 2.1 makes clear. Archaeology and biological anthropology have special methods, and we devote the last section of the chapter to some of those methods.

Ethnography

Around the beginning of the twentieth century, anthropologists realized that, if they were to produce anything of scientific value, they would have to study their subject in depth. To describe cultures more accurately, they started to live among the people they were studying. They observed, and even took part in, the important events of those societies and carefully questioned the people about their native customs. This method is known as **participant-observation.** Participant-observation always involves **fieldwork,** which is firsthand experience with the people being studied, but fieldwork may also involve other methods, such as conducting a census or a survey.[1]

Fieldwork, the cornerstone of modern anthropology, is the means by which most anthropological information is obtained. Regardless of other methods that anthropologists may use, participant-observation conducted usually for a year or more is regarded as fundamental.

TABLE 2.1 Types of Research in Anthropology

Scope	Nonhistorical	Historical
Single case	Ethnography/fieldwork*	Ethnohistory*
	Archaeological site excavation*	Culture history*
	Single species study/fieldwork*	Evolutionary history of a species*
	Language study/fieldwork*	Language history
Region	Controlled comparison	Controlled comparison
	Regional comparison of archaeological or other sites	Regional comparison of archaeological or other sites
	Cross-species comparison	Cross-species comparison
	Language family comparison	Language family comparison
Worldwide sample	Cross-cultural research	Cross-historical research
	Cross-archaeological research	Cross-archaeological research
	Cross-species comparison	Cross-species comparison
	Cross-linguistic comparison	Comparative historical linguistics

*All of these can also involve comparisons within the research setting—of different individuals, social groups, or populations.

Anthropologist Margaret Kieffer conducts an ethnographic interview with a Mayan woman in Guatemala.

In contrast to the casual descriptions of travelers and adventurers, anthropologists' descriptions record, describe, analyze, and eventually formulate a picture of the culture, or at least part of it.[2] After doing fieldwork, an anthropologist may prepare an *ethnography,* a description and analysis of a single society.

How an anthropologist goes about doing long-term participant-observation in another culture—and, more important, doing it well—is not so straightforward. Much of it depends on the person, the culture, and the interaction between the two. Without a doubt, the experience is physically and psychologically demanding, comparable often to a rite of passage. Although it helps enormously to learn the local language before going, often it is not possible to do so, and so most anthropologists find themselves struggling to communicate in addition to trying to figure out how to behave properly. Participant-observation carries its own dilemma. Participation implies living like the people who are being studied, trying to understand subjectively what they think and feel by doing what they do, whereas observation implies a certain amount of objectivity and detachment.[3] Because participant-observation is such a personal experience, it is not surprising that anthropologists have begun to realize that *reflecting* on their experiences and their personal interaction with the people they live with is an important part of understanding the enterprise.

An essential part of the participant-observation process is finding some knowledgeable people who are willing to work with you (anthropologists call them *informants*), to help you interpret what you observe and tell you about aspects of the culture that you may not have a chance to see, or may not be entitled to see. For example, it is not likely that you will see many weddings in a village of 200 people in a year or two of fieldwork. So how can you know who will be a good informant? It is obviously important to find people who are easy to talk to and who understand what information you need. But how do you know who is knowledgeable? You can't just assume that the people you get along with have the most knowledge. (Besides, knowledge is often specialized; one person may know a whole lot more about some subjects than others.) At a minimum, you have to try out a few different people to compare what they tell you about a subject. What if they disagree? How do you know who is more trustworthy or accurate? Fortunately, formal methods have been developed to help anthropologists select the most knowledgeable informants. One method, called the "cultural consensus model," relies on the principle that those things that most informants agree on are probably cultural. After you establish which things appear to be cultural by asking a sample of informants the same questions about a particular cultural domain, it will be easy to discover which informants are very likely to give answers that closely match the cultural consensus. These individuals are your best bets to be the most knowledgeable in that domain.[4] It may seem paradoxical, but the most knowledgeable and helpful individuals are not necessarily "typical" individuals. Many anthropologists have pointed out that key informants are likely to feel somewhat marginal in their culture. After all, why would they want to spend so much time with the visiting anthropologist?[5]

Participant-observation is valuable for understanding some aspects of culture, particularly the things that are the most public, readily talked about, and most widely agreed upon. But more systematic methods are important too: mapping, house-to-house censuses, behavior observations (e.g., to determine how people spend their time), as well as focused interviews with a sample of informants. We discuss ethics in fieldwork in the last section of this chapter.

Within-Culture Comparisons

Ethnographers could test a theory within one society if they decide to compare individuals, families, households, communities, or districts. The natural variability that exists can be used to create a comparison. Suppose we want to verify Whiting's assumption that longer postpartum taboos enhance the survival of babies in a society with a low-protein diet. Although almost all couples might practice a long postpartum sex taboo because it is customary, some couples might not adhere to the taboo consistently and some couples might not conceive quickly after the taboo is lifted. So we would expect some variation in spacing between births. If we collected information on the births of each mother and the survival outcome of each birth, we would be able to compare the survival rates of children born a short time after the mother's last pregnancy with those of children born after longer intervals. A significantly higher survival rate for the births after longer intervals would support Whiting's theory. What if some communities within the society had access to more protein than others? If Whiting's theory were correct, those communities with more protein should also have a higher survival rate for babies. If there were variation in the length of the postpartum sex taboo, the communities with more protein should have shorter taboos.

Regional Controlled Comparisons

In a regional controlled comparison, anthropologists compare ethnographic information obtained from societies found in a particular region—societies that presumably have similar histories and occupy similar environments. Anthropologists who conduct a regional comparison are apt to be familiar with the complex of cultural features associated with that region. These features may provide a good understanding of the context of the phenomenon that is to be explained.

Because some of the societies being compared will have the characteristic that is to be explained and some will not, anthropologists can determine whether the conditions hypothesized to be related are in fact related, at least in that region. We must remember, however, that two or more conditions may be related in one region for reasons peculiar to that region. Therefore, an explanation supported in one region may not fit others.

Cross-Cultural Research

The most common use of worldwide comparisons has been to test explanations. An example is Whiting's test of his theory about the adaptive functions of a long postpartum sex taboo. Recall that Whiting hypothesized that, if his theory were correct, variation in protein supplies in the adult diet should predict variation in the duration of the postpartum sex taboo. Cross-cultural researchers first identify conditions that should generally be associated if a particular theory is correct. Then they look at a worldwide sample of societies to see if the expected association generally holds true. Most cross-culturalists choose a published sample of societies that was not constructed for any specific hypothesis test. Two of the most widely used samples are the Standard Cross-Cultural Sample (SCCS) of 186 societies and the HRAF Collection of Ethnography (much of which is available in eHRAF World Cultures online), an annually growing collection of original ethnographic books and articles on approximately 400 cultures past and present around the world.[6]

The advantage of cross-cultural research is that the conclusion drawn from it is probably applicable to most societies, if the sample used for testing has been more or less randomly selected and therefore is representative of the world. In other words, the results of a cross-cultural study are probably applicable to most societies and most regions, in contrast with the results of a regional comparison, which may or may not be applicable to other regions.

Historical Research

Ethnohistory consists of studies based on descriptive materials about a single society at more than one point in time. It provides the essential data for historical studies of all types, just as ethnography provides the essential data for all nonhistorical types of research. Ethnohistorical data may consist of sources other than the ethnographic reports prepared by anthropologists—accounts by explorers, missionaries, traders, and government officials. Ethnohistorians, like historians, cannot simply assume that all the documents they find are simply descriptions of fact; they were written by very different kinds of people with very different goals and purposes. So they need to separate carefully what may be fact from what may be speculative interpretation. To reconstruct how a culture changed over hundreds of years, where the natives left few or no written accounts, anthropologists have to seek out travelers' accounts and other historical documents that were written by non-natives.

An important goal of ethnohistory, and of cultural anthropology in general, is to explain variation in cultural patterns, that is, to specify what conditions will favor one cultural pattern rather than another. Such specification requires us to assume that the supposed

Ethnohistorians need to analyze pieces of information from a variety of sources such as the accounts of European explorers. Pictured here is a group of Roanoke Native Americans fishing in the late 1500s. It provides ethnohistorians with good information on how these people harvested fish.

Source: John White/Copyright The British Museum.

causal, or favoring, conditions antedated the pattern to be explained. Theories or explanations, then, imply a sequence of changes over time, which are the stuff of history. Therefore, if we want to come closer to an understanding of the reasons for the cultural variations we are investigating, we should examine historical sequences. They will help us determine whether the conditions we think caused various phenomena truly antedated those phenomena and thus might more reliably be said to have caused them.

Evidence of the Past

How can archaeologists and paleoanthropologists know about what may have happened thousands or even millions of years ago? There are no written records from those periods from which to draw inferences. But we do have other kinds of "records," other kinds of evidence from the past. And we have ways of "reading" this evidence, which tells us a lot about how our human ancestors evolved and how they lived long ago.

Archaeologists and paleoanthropologists rely on four kinds of evidence to learn about the past: *artifacts, ecofacts, fossils,* and *features.* As we will see, each provides unique information about the past. Together, artifacts, ecofacts, fossils, and features provide a story about human life long ago.

Artifacts

Anything made or modified by humans is an **artifact.** The book you are reading now, the chair you are sitting in, the pen you are taking notes with are all artifacts. Most artifacts we will lose or throw away. That is exactly how things enter what we call the "archaeological record." Think about it: How much garbage do you produce in a day? What kinds of things do you throw away? Mostly paper, probably, but also wood (from the ice cream bar you ate at lunch), plastic (like the pen that ran out of ink last night), and even metal (the dull blade on your razor). Into the garbage they go and out to the dump or landfill. Under the right conditions, many of those items will survive for future archaeologists to find. Most of the artifacts that make up the archaeological record are just this kind of mundane waste—the accumulated garbage of daily life that archaeologists may recover and examine to reconstruct what daily life was like long ago. By far, the most

Vietnamese archaeologists expose the remains of the ancient citadel of Hanoi, preserved below the modern city.

common artifacts from the past are stone tools, which archaeologists call **lithics.** Indeed, lithics are the only kind of artifact available for 99 percent of human history.

Ecofacts

Ecofacts are natural objects that humans have used or affected. A good example is the bone from animals that people have eaten. These bones are somewhat like artifacts, but they haven't been made or modified by humans, just used and discarded by them. Another example is pollen found at archaeological sites. Because humans bring plants back to their houses to use, pollens from many plants are commonly found. These pollens may not have come from the same location. The only reason they are together is that they have been brought together by human use. Other examples are the remains of insect and animal pests that associate with humans, such as cockroaches and mice. Their remains are found in sites because they associate with humans and survive by taking advantage of the conditions that humans create. Their presence is in part caused by human presence, and thus they are also considered ecofacts.

Fossils

Fossils, although rare, are particularly informative about human biological evolution. **Fossils** may be impressions of an insect or leaf on a muddy surface that now is stone. A fossil may also consist of the actual hardened remains of an animal's skeletal structure. When an animal dies, the organic matter that made up its body begins to deteriorate. The teeth and skeletal structure are composed largely of inorganic mineral salts, and soon they are all that remains. Under most conditions, these parts eventually deteriorate too. But once in a great while, conditions are favorable for preservation—for instance, when volcanic ash, limestone, or highly mineralized groundwater is present to form a high-mineral environment. If the remains are buried under such circumstances, the minerals in the ground may become bound into the structure of the teeth or bone, hardening the remains and thus making them less likely to deteriorate.

But we don't have fossil remains of everything that lived in the past, and sometimes we only have fragments from one or a few individuals. So the fossil record is very incomplete. For example, Robert Martin estimates that the earth has probably seen 6,000 primate species; remains of only 3 percent of those species have been found. It is hardly surprising that primate paleontologists cannot identify most of the evolutionary connections between early and later forms. The task is particularly difficult with small mammals, such as the early primates, which are less likely than large animals to be preserved in the fossil record.[7]

Features

Features are kinds of artifacts, but archaeologists distinguish them from other artifacts because they cannot be easily removed from an archaeological site. Hearths are good examples. When humans build a fire on bare ground, the soil becomes heated and is changed—all the water is driven out of it and its crystalline structure is broken down and reformed. When archaeologists find a hearth, what exactly is found? An area of hard, reddish, even slightly magnetic soil, often surrounded by charcoal and ash. Here, then, is an artifact—an object of human manufacture. But it would be very hard, if not impossible, for archaeologists to take the hearth back to the lab for study like a lithic or ceramic. A hearth is really an intrinsic feature of a site—hence the name *feature.*

Hearths are common features, but the most common features by far are called *pits.* Pits are simply holes dug by humans that are later filled with garbage or eroded soil. They are usually fairly easy to distinguish because the garbage or soil they are filled with is often different in color and texture from the soil the pit was dug into. *Living floors* are another common type of feature. These are the places where humans lived and worked. The soils in these locations are often compacted through human activity and are full of minute pieces of garbage—seeds, small stone flakes, beads, and the like—that became embedded in the floor. A large or very deep area of such debris is called a *midden.* Middens are often the remains of garbage dumps or areas repeatedly used over long periods of time, such as caves. Finally, *buildings* are common features on archaeological sites. These can range from the remains of stone rings that once held down the sides of tents to palaces built of stones that had been shaped and fitted together. Even the remains of wooden houses (or parts of them) have been preserved under some conditions.

Finding the Evidence of the Past

Evidence of the past is all around us, but finding it is not always easy or productive. Archaeologists and paleoanthropologists usually restrict their searches to what are called *sites.* **Sites** are known or suspected locations of human activity in the past that contain a record of that activity. Sites are created when the remnants of human activity are covered or buried by some natural process. The most dramatic process is volcanic activity, which can bury an entire city, such as Pompeii during the eruption of Mount Vesuvius in A.D. 79. Less dramatic processes are the natural processes that build up soil, such as the decay of falling leaves, or soil brought by floods or wind.

Because humans often reuse good locations to live and work in, many sites contain the remains of numerous human occupations. The most valuable sites to archaeologists and paleoanthropologists are those in which the burial processes worked quickly enough that each use of the site is clearly separated from the previous one. Such sites are called **stratified;** each layer, or *stratum,* of human occupation is separate, like a layer in a layer cake. Not only do stratified sites allow archaeologists or paleoanthropologists to distinguish the sequence of site occupations, but the strata themselves provide a way to know the relative ages of the occupations—earlier occupations will always be below later ones.

How Are Sites Found?

There is no single method of finding sites, and indeed many sites are found by happenstance. But when archaeologists and paleoanthropologists want to go out and find sites, they typically employ one of two basic methods: pedestrian survey and remote sensing. *Pedestrian*

Archaeologists examine the wall of an excavation at Nippur, Iraq. The thick white line in the wall is the plastered floor of a building, and defines the division between two different strata. Items found on the floor can all be assumed to date from the same time, whereas items found below it can be assumed to date from an earlier time.

NEW PERSPECTIVES ON GENDER

Women in the Shell Mound Archaic

One of the main issues that archaeologists interested in gender address is how we can learn about and understand gender roles in prehistoric cultures. Gender roles might seem impossible to study in archaeological contexts. How is gender preserved in the archaeological record? How can knowledge about gender roles be recovered? Information about gender roles can be recovered if one is aware of how particular kinds of material culture are associated ethnographically with particular gender roles, and changes in them over time. Archaeologists argue that such an awareness leads not only to a better understanding of gender in prehistory but can also lead to a fuller understanding of prehistoric cultures overall.

An example is Cheryl Claassen's work on the Shell Mound Archaic culture of the Tennessee River valley. The Shell Mound Archaic represents the remains of people who lived in Tennessee and Kentucky between about 5,500 and 3,000 years ago. They were hunters and gatherers who lived in small villages, and probably moved seasonally between summer and winter communities. The most distinctive feature of the Shell Mound Archaic is the large mounds of mollusk shells they constructed for burying their dead. Tens of thousands of shells were piled together to create these mounds. Yet, around 3,000 years ago, shellfishing and thus the creation of shell burial mounds stopped abruptly. Claassen wondered why.

Suggested explanations include climate change, overexploitation of shellfish, and the migration of shellfishing peoples from the area. None has proven wholly satisfactory. In contemporary cultures, women and children typically do the shellfishing, and Claassen wondered whether an approach that considered gender roles might be more productive. She decided to approach the problem through the perspective of women's workloads because women would have most likely been the ones shellfishing. The end of shellfishing would have meant that women would have had a lot of free time—free time that could have been put to use in some other way. What might have changed to lead women to stop shellfishing? Did some other activities become more important, so that women's labor was needed more for those other tasks?

Women's labor might have been redirected toward domesticated crops. There is archaeological evidence that about 3,000 years ago several productive crops that required intensive labor came into wide use. For example, *chenopodium,* one of the more plentiful and nutritious of these new crops, has tiny seeds that require considerable labor to harvest, clean, and process. Women were likely the ones burdened with such work. They not only would have harvested these crops but also would have been the ones to process and prepare meals from them. Thus, the emergence of agricultural economies would have required women to undertake new labor in food production and processing that may well have forced them to stop engaging in other tasks, like shellfishing, especially if the new tasks produced a larger food supply.

The development of agricultural activities might also have brought about changes in ritual and ceremonialism. The shell burial mounds were clearly central to Shell Mound Archaic death ceremonies. Considerable labor, mostly by women, would have been required to collect the shells and to build these mounds. Later societies in the region buried their dead in earthen mounds. Could this be a reflection of the new importance dirt had in an emerging agricultural economy? If so, what role did women play in ceremonies of death and burial? If they were no longer the providers of the raw materials needed for burial, does that mean their status in society as a whole changed?

We may never know exactly why the Shell Mound Archaic disappeared, or how women's work and women's roles in society changed. But as Claassen points out, taking a gender perspective provides new avenues along which to pursue answers to these questions, and interesting new questions to pursue.

Source: Claassen 1991; 2009.

survey is what the name suggests—walking around and looking for sites. But archaeologists and paleoanthropologists can use sampling and systematic surveying methods to reduce the area to be covered on foot. *Remote sensing* techniques allow archaeologists and paleoanthropologists to find archaeological deposits from a remote location, usually the current surface of the ground beneath which the archaeological deposits are buried. Most remote sensing techniques are borrowed from exploration geology, and are the same ones geologists use to find mineral or oil deposits. They typically involve the measurement of minute variations in phenomena like the earth's magnetic or gravitational field, or changes in an electric current or pulse of energy directed into the ground. When these subtle changes, called *anomalies,* are located, more detailed exploration can be done to map the extent and depth of the buried archaeological deposits.

How Are Artifacts, Ecofacts, and Features Recovered from Sites?

Once archaeological deposits are found there is only one way to recover them—by *excavation.* Excavation is a complex process with two goals: (1) to find every scrap of evidence (or a statistically representative sample) about the past that a given site holds, and (2) to record the horizontal and vertical location of that evidence with precision. Archaeologists and paleoanthropologists have developed many excavation strategies and techniques to accomplish these goals, but all of them involve the careful removal of the archaeological deposits; the recovery of artifacts, ecofacts, fossils, and features from the soil in which those deposits were buried; and the detailed recording of where each artifact, ecofact, fossil, and feature was located on the site.

To date, no one has figured out a way to recover artifacts, ecofacts, fossils, and features from a site without destroying the site in the process, and this is one of the ironies of archaeological research. As we discuss shortly, the relationships between and among artifacts, ecofacts, fossils, and features are of most interest to archaeologists, and precisely these relationships are destroyed when archaeologists remove them from a site. For this reason, most excavation by professional archaeologists today is done only when a site is threatened with destruction, and then only by highly trained personnel using rigorous techniques. Archaeologists and paleoanthropologists collect data in basically the same ways, with one important difference. Archaeologists are most concerned with recovering intact features, whereas paleoanthropologists are most concerned with recovering intact fossils.[8]

Putting It All in Context

You might have gained the impression from our discussion that archaeologists and paleoanthropologists analyze artifacts, ecofacts, fossils, and features as individual objects, separate from one another. Nothing could be farther from the truth. In fact, putting these materials in context with one another is really what archaeology and paleoanthropology are all about. **Context** is how and why the artifacts and other materials are related. Artifacts, ecofacts, fossils, and features in isolation may be beautiful or interesting by themselves, but only when they are placed in context with the other materials found on a site are we able to "read" and tell the story of the past.

To illustrate this point, let's consider a set of letters that were found separately: *A E G I M N N.* They are arranged here in alphabetical order, the way a set of beautiful artifacts might be arranged in a museum display in order of size. Do these arrangements tell us anything? No. What if we knew something about the relationships between and among these letters—their context? What if, for example, we knew that the *M* was the first letter found, and that the *A* and *E* were found next to the *M,* but in reverse order, that one *N* was found between the *E* and *I,* and that the other *N* was found between the *I* and the *G?* Knowing in what context the letters were found would tell us that the letters should be arranged like this: *M E A N I N G.* And meaning is exactly what context gives to artifacts, ecofacts, fossils, and features.

Dating the Evidence from the Past

An important, indeed vital, part of putting artifacts and other materials into context is putting them in chronological order. To reconstruct the evolutionary history of the primates, for example, one must know how old primate fossils are. For some time, relative dating methods were the only methods available. The last half-century has seen important advances in absolute dating, including techniques that allow the dating of the earliest phases of primate evolution. **Relative dating** is used to determine the age of a specimen or deposit relative to another specimen or deposit. **Absolute dating,** or **chronometric dating,** is used to measure how old a specimen or deposit is in years.

Relative Dating Methods

The earliest, and still the most commonly used, method of relative dating is based on **stratigraphy,** the study of how different rock or soil formations are laid down in successive layers or strata. Older layers are generally deeper or lower than more recent layers. Indicator artifacts are used to establish a stratigraphic sequence for the relative dating of new finds. These **indicator artifacts** are items of human manufacture that spread widely over short periods of time, or that disappeared or changed fairly rapidly. If a site has been disturbed, stratigraphy will not be a satisfactory way to determine relative age. As noted earlier, remains from different periods may be washed or blown together by water or wind. Or a landslide may superimpose an earlier layer on a later layer. Still, it may be possible using absolute, or chronometric, dating methods to estimate the relative age of the different fossils found together in a disturbed site.

Absolute, or Chronometric, Dating Methods

Many of the absolute dating methods are based on the decay of a radioactive isotope. Because the rate of decay is known, the age of the specimen can be estimated, within a range of possible error. **Radiocarbon,** or **carbon-14 (^{14}C), dating** is perhaps the most popularly known method of determining the absolute age of a specimen. It is based on the principle that all living matter possesses a certain amount of a radioactive form of carbon (carbon-14, or ^{14}C). Radioactive carbon, produced when nitrogen-14 is bombarded by cosmic rays, is absorbed from the air by plants and then ingested by animals that eat the plants (see Figure 2.1). After an organism dies, it no longer takes in any of the radioactive carbon. Carbon-14 decays at a slow but steady pace and reverts to nitrogen-14. (By *decays,* we mean that the ^{14}C gives off a certain number of beta radiations per minute.) The rate at which the carbon decays—its **half-life**—is known: ^{14}C has a half-life of 5,730 years. In other words, half of the original amount of ^{14}C in organic matter will have decayed 5,730 years after the organism's death; half of the remaining ^{14}C will have decayed after another 5,730 years; and so on. After about 50,000 years, the amount of ^{14}C remaining in the organic matter is too small to permit reliable dating.

To discover how long an organism has been dead—that is, to determine how much ^{14}C is left in the organism and therefore how old it is—we either count the number of beta radiations given off per minute per gram of material, or use a particle accelerator to measure

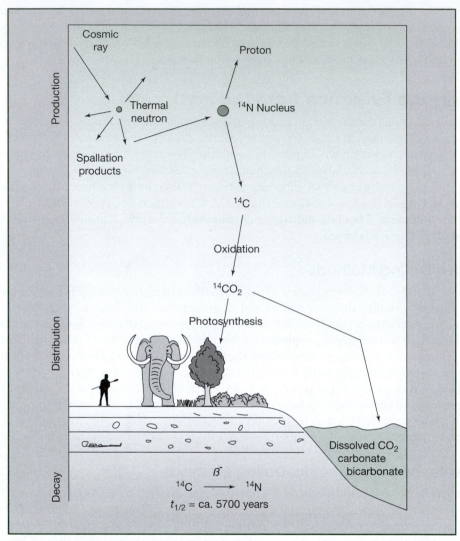

Figure 2.1 The Carbon-14 Cycle

Source: Taylor and Aitken 1997.

the actual amount of ^{14}C in a sample. Modern ^{14}C emits about 15 beta radiations per minute per gram of material, but ^{14}C that is 5,730 years old emits only half that amount (the half-life of ^{14}C) per minute per gram. So, if a sample of some organism gives off 7.5 radiations a minute per gram, which is only half the amount given off by modern ^{14}C, the organism must be 5,730 years old. Similarly, because the amount of ^{14}C in a sample slowly declines over time, the atoms in a sample can be sent through a particle accelerator to separate them by weight (the lighter ^{12}C accelerates faster than the heavier ^{14}C) and measure the actual amount of each. This method, called accelerator mass spectrometry (AMS), is more accurate than the beta radiation method, requires only a very small sample of material, and provides a way to date specimens that are up to 80,000 years old.[9]

Another very common absolute dating technique based on radioactive decay uses potassium-40 (^{40}K), a radioactive form of potassium that decays at an established rate and forms argon-40 (^{40}Ar). The half-life of ^{40}K is a known quantity, so the age of a material containing potassium can be measured by the amount of ^{40}K compared with the amount of ^{40}Ar it contains.[10] Radioactive potassium's (^{40}K's) half-life is very long—1,330 million years. This means that **potassium-argon (K-Ar) dating** may be used to date samples from 5,000 years up to 3 billion years old.

The K-Ar method is used to date potassium-rich minerals in rock, not the fossils that may be found in the rock. A very high temperature, such as occurs in a volcanic event, drives off any original argon in the material. The amount of argon that accumulates afterward from the decay of radioactive potassium is directly related to the amount of time since the volcanic event. This type of dating has been extremely useful in East Africa, where volcanic events have occurred frequently since the Miocene, which began 24 million years ago. If the material to be dated is not rich in potassium, or the area did not experience any high-temperature events, other methods of absolute dating are required.

There are many other methods of absolute dating; indeed, new methods are being developed all the time.

Ethics in Anthropological Research

Anthropologists have many ethical obligations—to the people they study, their anthropological colleagues, to the public and world community, and even to their employers and their own and host countries. But anthropologists agree that, should a conflict arise in ethical obligations, the most important obligation is to protect the interests of the people they study. According to the profession's code of ethics, anthropologists should tell people in the field site (or, if they are archaeologists, people who are direct descendants of the prehistoric people they are studying) about the research, and they should respect the right of people to remain anonymous if they so choose.[11] For this reason, informants are often given "pseudonyms" or fake names; many anthropologists have extended this principle to using a fake name for the community as well. But the decision to create a fake name for a community is questionable in many circumstances.[12] First, anthropologists "stick out," and it is not hard for anyone interested to figure out where they lived and worked. Governments may have to be asked for research clearance, which means that they know where the anthropologist is going to do the fieldwork. Second, people who are studied are often proud of their place and their customs and they may be insulted if their community is called something else. Third, important geographic information is often vital to understanding the community. You have to reveal if it is located at the confluence of two major rivers, or if it is the trading center of the region. And lastly, it may be difficult for future anthropologists to conduct follow-up studies if the community is disguised. Of course, if a community were truly in danger, there would be no question that an anthropologist has an obligation to try to protect it.

Honest, objective reporting is also an obligation to the anthropological profession, to the public at large, and to the observed community. But suppose a custom or trait that appears perfectly reasonable to the observed community is considered objectionable by outsiders? Such customs could range from acts that outsiders consider criminal, such as infanticide, to those that are considered repugnant, such as eating dogs. Archaeologists have caused outrage by presenting evidence of cannibalism in ancient populations.[13] An anthropologist may believe that publication of the information could bring harm to the population. Kim Hill and Magdalena Hurtado faced this situation when they realized that infanticide rates were high in the group they studied in South America. They did not want to play up their findings, nor did they want to dissimulate. After they met with community leaders to discuss the situation, they agreed not to publish their findings in Spanish to minimize the possibility that the local media or neighboring groups might learn of their findings.[14]

Everyday decisions like how to compensate people for their time are not easy either. Nowadays, many if not most informants expect to be paid or receive gifts. But in the early days of anthropology, in places where money was not an important part of the native economy, the decision to pay people was not a clear ethical choice. If money is rare, paying people increases the importance of money in that economy. Even nonmonetary gifts can increase inequalities or create jealousies. On the other hand, doing nothing by way of compensation doesn't seem right either. As an alternative, some anthropologists try to find some community project that they can help with—that way, everyone benefits. This is not to say that the anthropologists are necessarily a burden on the community. People often like to talk about their customs, and they may want others to appreciate their way of life. And anthropologists are often amusing. They may ask "funny" questions, and when they try to say or do customary things, they often do them all wrong. Probably every anthropologist has been laughed at sometimes in the field.

Archaeologists must be aware of the effects of their work on descendant communities. Many people, for example, find the excavation of ancestors' remains to be offensive.

Many people find the idea of archaeologists or physical anthropologists excavating, cleaning, and preserving the remains of ancestors to be offensive. Therefore, they must be sensitive to the desires and beliefs of the populations that descend from the ones they are researching. In addition, artifacts from some ancient cultures are in great demand by art and antiquities collectors, and archaeological finds can lead to uncontrolled looting if archaeologists are not careful about how and to whom they report their discoveries. Wholesale ransacking of ancient cemeteries in some parts of China, for example, started because new archaeological discoveries led Chinese antiquities to become increasingly popular among collectors, and hence, increasingly valuable to those able to discover them.[15]

It is also an ethical responsibility of anthropologists to present the results of their work to the profession and the general public. For example, when archaeologists excavate sites, they also destroy some of the context of the artifacts, ecofacts, fossils, and features found in the sites. But if they leave some of the sites unexcavated, they are preserving them (at least partially) for future investigation. To offset their partial destruction, archaeologists are ethically obligated to publish the results of their work.

✓•—Study and Review on myanthrolab.com

Summary

1. Anthropologists use several different methods to conduct research. The types of research in anthropology can be classified according to two criteria: the spatial scope of the study (analysis of a single case, analysis of several or more cases in a region, or analysis of a worldwide sample of cases), and the temporal scope of the study (historical vs. nonhistorical). The cases might be societies, archaeological traditions, languages, sites, or species. In cultural anthropology, the basic research methods, then, are ethnographic fieldwork and ethnohistory, historical and nonhistorical regional controlled comparisons, and historical and nonhistorical cross-cultural research.

2. Archaeologists and paleoanthropologists have four basic sources of evidence about the past: artifacts, ecofacts, fossils, and features. Artifacts are any objects made by humans. Ecofacts are natural objects that humans use or modify. Fossils are the preserved remains of ancient plants and animals. Features are artifacts that cannot be removed from archaeological sites.

3. Archaeological sites are locations where the evidence of the past has been buried and preserved. Sites are found through pedestrian survey or remote sensing, and artifacts, ecofacts, fossils, and features are recovered from sites through excavation.

4. Much information can be gained through the analysis of archaeological materials, but the materials themselves are not the primary focus of analysis. Rather, the context between and among artifacts, ecofacts, fossils, and features allows archaeologists or paleoanthropologists to gain insights about the past.

5. A key aspect of putting archaeological material into context is being able to date material accurately. Many kinds of dating techniques are used. Relative dating techniques determine the age of archaeological materials relative to other materials of known ages. Absolute dating techniques determine the age of the archaeological deposits or materials themselves.

6. Ethics are important to all anthropologists. Anthropologists must inform the people they are studying (or the descendants of those people if they are studying an archaeological culture) about their work and its purpose. Anthropologists must ensure that their work does no harm, and that the confidentiality of people with whom they work is protected.

Glossary Terms

absolute dating (p. 31)
artifact (p. 26)
chronometric dating (p. 31)
context (p. 30)
ecofacts (p. 27)
features (p. 27)
fieldwork (p. 22)

fossils (p. 27)
half-life (p. 31)
indicator artifacts (p. 31)
lithics (p. 27)
participant-observation (p. 22)
potassium-argon (K-Ar) dating (p. 33)

radiocarbon, or carbon-14 (^{14}C), dating (p. 31)
relative dating (p. 31)
sites (p. 28)
stratified (p. 28)
stratigraphy (p. 31)

Critical Questions

1. Anthropological methods vary from single-case studies to broad comparisons across space and time. Compare the different strategies with respect to their usefulness in generating and testing explanations.

2. Why is context so important in archaeological research?

3. Why do anthropologists find it so important to protect the interests of the people they study?

Read the Original Source on myanthrolab.com

Read the chapter by Carol R. Ember and Melvin Ember, "On Cross-Cultural Research," on MyAnthroLab and answer the following questions.

1. Give a few examples of questions that can be answered by cross-cultural research.

2. What are the basic assumptions and steps in a cross-cultural study?

Genetics and Evolution

3

((•──│Listen to the **Chapter Audio** on **myanthrolab.com**   📖─│Read on **myanthrolab.com**

Astronomers estimate that the universe has been in existence for some 15 billion years, plus or minus a few billion. To make this awesome history more understandable, Carl Sagan devised a calendar that condenses this span into a single year.[1] Using 24 days for every billion years and 1 second for every 475 years as a scale, Sagan moves from the "big bang" or beginning of the universe on January 1, to the origin of the Milky Way on May 1. In this system, September 9 marks the beginning of our solar system, and September 25 the origin of life on earth. At 10:30 in the evening of December 31, the first humanlike primates appear. Sagan's compression of history provides us with a manageable way to compare the short span of human existence with the total time span of the universe. Humanlike beings have been around for only about 90 minutes out of a 12-month period. In this book, we are concerned with what happened in the last few hours of that year.

Some 55 million to 65 million years ago, the first primates appeared. They were ancestral to all living primates, including monkeys, apes, and humans. The early primates may or may not have lived in trees, but they had flexible digits and could grasp things. Later, about 35 million years ago, the first monkeys and apes appeared. About 15 million years ago, some 20 million years after the appearance of monkeys and apes, the immediate apelike ancestors of humans probably emerged. About 4 million years ago, the first humanlike beings appeared. Modern-looking humans evolved only about 100,000 years ago.

How do we account for the biological and cultural evolution of humans? The details of the emergence of primates and the evolution of humans and their cultures are covered in subsequent chapters. In this chapter, we focus on how the modern theory of evolution developed and how it accounts for change over time.

The Evolution of Evolution

Older Western ideas about nature's creatures were very different from Charles Darwin's theory of evolution, which suggested that different species developed, one from another, over long periods of time. In the fourth and fifth centuries B.C., the Greek philosophers Plato and Aristotle believed that animals and plants form a single, graded continuum going from more perfection to less perfection. Humans, of course, were at the top of this scale. Later Greek philosophers added the idea that the creator gave life or "radiance" first to humans, but some of that essence was lost at each subsequent creation.[2] Macrobius, summarizing the thinking of Plotinus, used an image that was to persist for centuries, the image of what came to be called the "chain of being": "The attentive observer will discover a connection of parts, from the Supreme God down to the last dregs of things, mutually linked together and without a break. And this is Homer's golden chain, which God, he says, bade hand down from heaven to earth."[3]

Belief in the chain of being was accompanied by the conviction that an animal or plant species could not become extinct. In fact, all things were linked to one another in a chain, and all links were necessary. Moreover, the notion of extinction threatened people's trust in God; it was unthinkable that a whole group of God's creations could simply disappear.

The idea of the chain of being persisted through the years, but philosophers, scientists, poets, and theologians did not discuss it extensively until the eighteenth century. Those discussions prepared the way for evolutionary theory. Ironically, although the chain of being did not allow for evolution, its idea that nature had an order of things encouraged studies of natural history and comparative anatomical studies, which stimulated the development of the idea of evolution.

People were also now motivated to look for previously unknown creatures. Moreover, humans were not shocked when naturalists suggested that humans were close to apes. This notion was perfectly consistent with the idea of a chain of being; apes were simply thought to have been created with less perfection.

Early in the eighteenth century, an influential scientist, Carolus Linnaeus (1707–1778), classified plants and animals in a *systema naturae,* which placed humans in the same order (Primates) as apes and monkeys. Linnaeus did not suggest an evolutionary relationship between humans and apes; he mostly accepted the notion that all species were created by God and fixed in their form. Not surprisingly, then, Linnaeus is often viewed as an anti-evolutionist. But Linnaeus's hierarchical classification scheme—in descending order from kingdom to class, order, **genus** (a group of related species), and species—provided a framework for the idea that humans, apes, and monkeys had a common ancestor.

Others did not believe that species were fixed in their form. According to Jean-Baptiste Lamarck (1744–1829), acquired characteristics could be inherited and therefore species could evolve; individuals who in their lifetime developed characteristics helpful to survival would pass those characteristics on to future generations, thereby changing the physical makeup of the species. For example, Lamarck explained the long neck of the giraffe as the result of successive generations of giraffes stretching their necks to reach the high leaves of trees. The stretched muscles and bones of the necks were somehow transmitted to the offspring of the neck-stretching giraffes, and eventually all giraffes came to have long necks. But because Lamarck and later biologists failed to produce evidence to support the hypothesis that acquired characteristics can be inherited, this explanation of evolution is now generally dismissed.[4]

By the nineteenth century, some thinkers were beginning to accept evolution whereas others were trying to refute it. For example, Georges Cuvier (1769–1832) was a leading opponent of evolution. Cuvier's theory of catastrophism proposed that a quick series of catastrophes accounted for changes in the earth and the fossil record. Cataclysms and upheavals such as Noah's flood had killed off previous sets of living creatures, which each time were replaced by new creations.

Major changes in geological thinking occurred in the nineteenth century. Earlier, geologist James Hutton (1726–1797) had questioned catastrophism, but his work was largely ignored. In contrast, Sir Charles Lyell's (1797–1875) volumes of the *Principles of Geology* (1830–1833), which built on Hutton's earlier work, received immediate acclaim. Their concept of *uniformitarianism* suggested that the earth is constantly being shaped and reshaped by natural forces that have operated over a vast stretch of time. Lyell also discussed the formation of geological strata and paleontology. He used fossilized fauna to define different geological epochs. Lyell's works were read avidly by Charles Darwin before and during Darwin's now-famous voyage on the *Beagle.* The two corresponded and subsequently became friends.

After studying changes in plants, fossil animals, and varieties of domestic and wild pigeons, Charles Darwin (1809–1882)

Although Darwin's idea of evolution by natural selection was strongly challenged when first published (particularly, as illustrated here, the idea that humans and primates shared a common ancestor), it has withstood rigorous testing and is the foundation of many anthropological theories.

rejected the notion that each species was created at one time in a fixed form. The results of his investigations pointed clearly, he thought, to the evolution of species through the mechanism of natural selection. While Darwin was completing his book on the subject, naturalist Alfred Russel Wallace (1823–1913) sent him a manuscript that came to conclusions about the evolution of species that matched Darwin's own.[5] In 1858, the two men presented the astonishing theory of natural selection to their colleagues at a meeting of the Linnaean Society of London.[6]

In 1859, when Darwin published *The Origin of Species by Means of Natural Selection,*[7] he wrote, "I am fully convinced that species are not immutable; but that those belonging to what are called the same genera are lineal descendants of some other and generally extinct species, in the same manner as the acknowledged varieties of any one species."[8] His conclusions outraged those who believed in the biblical account of creation, and the result was bitter controversy that continues to this day.[9]

Until 1871, when his *The Descent of Man* was published, Darwin avoided stating categorically that humans were descended from nonhuman forms, but the implications of his theory were clear. People immediately began to take sides. In June 1860, at the annual meeting of the British Association for the Advancement of Science, Bishop Wilberforce saw an opportunity to attack the Darwinists. Concluding his speech, he faced Thomas Huxley, one of the Darwinists' chief advocates, and inquired, "Was it through his grandfather or his grandmother that he claimed descent from a monkey?" Huxley responded,

> If . . . the question is put to me would I rather have a miserable ape for a grandfather than a man highly endowed by nature and possessing great means and influence and yet who employs those faculties and that influence for the mere purpose of introducing ridicule into a grave scientific discussion—I unhesitatingly affirm my preference for the ape.[10]

Although Huxley's retort to Bishop Wilberforce displays both humor and quick wit, it does not answer the bishop's question very well. A better answer, and one we pursue later in this chapter, is that Darwinists would claim that we descended from monkeys neither through our grandmother or our grandfather, but that both we and monkeys are descended from a common ancestor who lived long ago. Darwinists would further argue that natural selection was the process through which the physical and genetic form of that common ancestor diverged to become both monkey and human.

The Principles of Natural Selection

Charles Darwin was not the first person to view the creation of new species in evolutionary terms, but he was the first to provide a comprehensive, well-documented explanation—natural selection—for the way evolution had occurred. **Natural selection** is the main process that increases the frequency of adaptive traits through time. The operation of natural selection involves three conditions or principles.[11] The first is *variation:* Every species is composed of a great variety of individuals, some of which are better adapted to their environment than others. The existence of variety is important. Without it, natural selection has nothing on which to operate; without variation, one kind of characteristic could not be favored over another. The second principle of natural selection is *heritability:* Offspring inherit traits from their parents, at least to some degree and in some way. The third principle of natural selection is *differential reproductive success:* Because better-adapted individuals generally produce more offspring over the generations than poorer-adapted individuals, the frequency of adaptive traits gradually increases in subsequent generations. A new species emerges when changes in traits or geographic barriers result in the reproductive isolation of the population.

When we say that certain traits are **adaptive** or advantageous, we mean that they result in greater reproductive success in a particular environment. The phrase "particular environment" is very important. Even though a species may become more adapted to a particular environment over time, we cannot say that one species adapted to its environment is "better" than another species adapted to a different environment. For example, we may like to think of ourselves as "better" than other animals, but humans are clearly less adapted than fish for living underwater, than bats for catching flying insects, or than raccoons for living on suburban garbage.

Although the theory of natural selection suggests that disadvantageous or **maladaptive** traits will generally decline in frequency or even disappear eventually, it does not necessarily follow that all such traits will do so. After all, species derive from prior forms that have certain structures. This means that not all changes are possible; it also means that some traits are linked to others that might have advantages that outweigh the disadvantages. Choking may be very maladaptive for any animal, yet all vertebrates are capable of choking because their digestive and respiratory systems cross in the throat. This trait is a genetic legacy, probably from the time when the respiratory system developed from tissue in the digestive system of some ancestral organism. Apparently, the propensity to choke has not been correctable evolutionarily.[12]

Changes in a species can be expected to occur as the environment changes or as some members of the species move into a new environment. With environmental change, different traits become adaptive. The forms of the species that possess the more adaptive traits will become more frequent, whereas those forms whose characteristics make continued existence more difficult or impossible in the modified environment will eventually become extinct.

Consider how the theory of natural selection would explain why giraffes became long-necked. Originally, the necks of giraffes varied in length, as happens with virtually any physical characteristic in a population. During a period when food was scarce, those giraffes with longer necks, who could reach higher tree leaves, might be better able to survive and suckle their offspring, and thus they would leave more offspring than shorter-necked giraffes. Because of heredity, the offspring of long-necked giraffes are more likely to have long necks. Eventually, the shorter-necked giraffes would diminish in number and the longer-necked giraffes would increase. The resultant population of giraffes would still have variation in neck length but on the average would be longer-necked than earlier forms.

Natural selection does not account for all variation in the frequencies of traits. In particular, it does not account for variation in the frequencies of neutral traits—that is, those traits that do not seem to confer any advantages or disadvantages on their carriers. Changes in the frequencies of

The giraffe's long neck is adaptive for eating tree leaves high off the ground. When food is scarce, longer-necked giraffes would get more food and reproduce more successfully than shorter-necked giraffes; in this environment, natural selection would favor giraffes with longer necks.

neutral traits may result rather from random processes that affect gene frequencies in isolated populations—*genetic drift*—or from matings between populations—*gene flow.* We discuss these other processes later in the chapter.

Observed Examples of Natural Selection

Natural selection is a process we can see at work in the world today. It is a process that has been studied in both the laboratory and in nature, and it is a process that most scientists would argue is very well understood. However, as in all scientific endeavors, understanding grows and changes as new information is obtained. The understanding of natural selection we have today is quite different from that originally put forward by Darwin. A century and a half of research has added tremendously to the information Darwin had to work with, and entirely new fields, like population genetics, have emerged. With this new information, we know that Darwin was unaware of some things. For example, it seems clear that natural selection is not always a uniform process, but can act in jumps and starts. The fact that the ideas put forward by Darwin have changed, and are changing as new research is done, does not mean they were wrong. Darwin's ideas were simply incomplete. As we add to our knowledge base each day, we move closer to an even more complete understanding of natural selection. Because the process of natural selection may involve nearly imperceptible gradations over generations, it is often difficult to observe directly. Nevertheless, because some life forms reproduce rapidly, some examples of natural selection have been observed over relatively short periods in changing environments.

For example, scientists think they have observed natural selection in action in British moths. In 1850, an almost black moth was spotted for the first time in Manchester. That was quite unusual, for most of the moths were speckled gray. A century later, 95 percent of the moths in industrial parts of Britain were black; only in the rural areas were the moths mostly gray. How is this to be explained? It seems that, in the rural areas, the gray-speckled moth is hard to spot by bird predators against the lichen growing on the bark of trees. But in industrial areas, lichen is killed by pollution. The gray-speckled moths, formerly well adapted to blend into their environment, became clearly visible against the darker background of the lichen-free trees and were easier prey for birds. In contrast, the black moths, which previously would have had a disadvantage against the lighter bark, were now better adapted for survival. Their dark color was an advantage, and subsequently the darker moths became the predominant variety in industrial regions.

How can we be sure that natural selection was the mechanism accounting for the change? Consistent evidence comes from a series of experiments performed by H. B. D. Kettlewell. He deliberately released specially marked moths, black and gray, into two areas of England—one urban industrial and one rural—and then set light traps to recapture them subsequently. The proportions of the two kinds of moths recovered tell us about differential survival. Kettlewell found that proportionately more black moths compared with gray moths were recovered in the urban industrial area. Just the reverse happened in the rural area; proportionately more gray-speckled moths were recovered.[13] Questions have been raised recently about whether the Kettlewell experiments were properly conducted.[14] However, the basic conclusion has been replicated by subsequent research.[15] The same transformation—the switch to darker color—has occurred in 70 other species of moth, as well as in a beetle and a millipede. And the transformation did not just occur in Britain; it also happened in other highly polluted areas, including the Ruhr area of Germany and the Pittsburgh area of the United States. Moreover, in the Pittsburgh area, antipollution measures in the last 50 years have apparently caused the black moth to dwindle in number once again.[16]

The type of natural selection in the moth example is called **directional selection** because a particular trait seems to be positively favored and the average value shifts over time toward the adaptive trait. But there can also be **normalizing selection.** In this type of selection, the average value does not change, but natural selection removes the extremes. An example is the birth weight of babies. Both very low birth weights and very high birth weights are disadvantageous and would be selected against. Directional and normalizing selection both assume that natural selection will either favor or disfavor genes, but there is a third possibility: balancing selection. **Balancing selection** occurs when a *heterozygous* (varied) combination of *alleles* (genes) is positively favored, even though a *homozygous* (genes in the pairs are the same) combination is disfavored. In the chapter on human variation, we discuss a trait that apparently involves balancing selection—sickle-cell anemia—which is found in people of West African ancestry, among other populations.

Another well-known example of observed natural selection is the acquired resistance of houseflies to the insecticide DDT. When DDT was first used to kill insects, beginning in the 1940s, several new, DDT-resistant strains of housefly evolved. In the early DDT environment, many houseflies were killed, but the few that survived were the ones that reproduced, and their resistant characteristics became common to the housefly populations. To the chagrin of medical practitioners, similar resistances develop in bacteria. A particular antibiotic may lose its effectiveness after it comes into wide use because new, resistant bacterial strains emerge. These new strains will become more frequent than the original ones because of natural selection. In the United States now, a few strains are resistant to all antibiotics on the market, a fact that worries medical practitioners. One possible way to deal with the problem is to stop using antibiotics for a few years, so resistance to those antibiotics might not develop or develop only slowly.

The theory of natural selection answered many questions, but it also raised at least one whose answer eluded Darwin and others. The appearance of a beneficial trait may assist the survival of an organism, but what happens when the organism reproduces by mating with members that do not possess this new variation? Will not the new adaptive trait eventually disappear if subsequent generations mate with individuals that lack this trait? Darwin knew variations were transmitted through heredity, but he did not have a clear model of the mode of inheritance. Gregor Mendel's pioneering studies in the science of genetics provided the foundation for such a model, but his discoveries did not become widely known until 1900.

Heredity
Gregor Mendel's Experiments

Mendel (1822–1884), a monk and amateur botanist who lived in what is now the Czech Republic, bred several varieties of pea plants and made detailed observations of their offspring. He chose as breeding partners plants that differed by only one observable trait. Tall plants were crossed with short ones, and yellow ones with green, for example.

When the pollen from a yellow pea plant was transferred to a green pea plant, Mendel observed a curious phenomenon: All of the first-generation offspring bore yellow peas. It seemed that the green trait had disappeared. But when seeds from this first generation were crossed, they produced both yellow and green pea plants in a ratio of three yellow to one green pea plant. Apparently, Mendel reasoned, the green trait had not been lost or altered; the yellow trait was simply **dominant** and the green trait was **recessive.** Mendel observed similar results with other traits. Tallness dominated shortness, and the factor for smooth-skinned peas dominated the factor for wrinkled ones. In each cross, the three-to-one ratio appeared in the second generation. Self-fertilization, however, produced different results. Green pea plants always yielded green pea plants, and short plants always produced short plants.

From his numerical results, Mendel concluded that some yellow pea plants were pure (*homozygous*) for that trait, whereas others also possessed a green factor (the plants were *heterozygous*). That is, although two plants might both have yellow peas, one of them might produce offspring with green peas. In such cases, the genetic makeup, the **genotype,** differed from the observable appearance, or **phenotype.**

Genes: The Conveyors of Inherited Traits

Mendel's units of heredity were what we now call **genes.** He concluded that these units occurred in pairs for each trait and that offspring inherited one unit of the pair from each parent. Each member of a gene pair or group is called an **allele.** If the two genes, or alleles, for a trait are the same, the organism is **homozygous** for that trait; if the two genes for a characteristic differ, the organism is **heterozygous** for that trait. A pea plant that contains a pair of genes for yellow is homozygous for the trait. A yellow pea plant with a dominant gene for yellow and a recessive gene for green, although phenotypically yellow, has a heterozygous genotype. As Mendel demonstrated, the recessive green gene can reappear in subsequent generations. But Mendel knew nothing of the composition of genes or the processes that transmit them from parent to offspring. Many years of scientific research have yielded much of the missing information.

The genes of higher organisms (not including bacteria and primitive plants such as blue-green algae) are located on ropelike bodies called **chromosomes** within the nucleus of every one of the organism's cells. Chromosomes, like genes, usually occur in pairs. Each allele for a given trait is carried in the identical position on corresponding chromosomes. The two genes that determined the color of Mendel's peas, for example, were opposite each other on a pair of chromosomes.

Mitosis and Meiosis The body cells of every plant or animal carry chromosome pairs in a number appropriate for its species. Humans have 23 pairs, or a total of 46 chromosomes, each carrying many times that number of genes. Each new body cell receives this number of chromosomes during cellular reproduction, or **mitosis,** as each pair of chromosomes duplicates itself.

But what happens when a sperm cell and an egg cell unite to form a new organism? What prevents the human baby from receiving twice the number of chromosomes characteristic of its species—23 pairs from the sperm and 23 pairs from the egg? The process by which the reproductive cells are formed, **meiosis,** ensures that this will not happen (see Figure 3.1). Each reproductive cell contains half the number of chromosomes appropriate for the species. Only one member of each chromosome pair is carried in every egg or sperm. At fertilization, the human embryo normally receives 23 separate chromosomes from its mother and the same number from its father, which add up to the 23 pairs.

DNA Each gene carries a set of instructions encoded in its chemical structure. It is from this coded information carried in genes that a cell makes all the rest of its structural parts and chemical machinery. It appears that, in most living organisms, heredity is controlled by the same chemical substance, **DNA**—deoxyribonucleic acid. An enormous amount of research has been directed

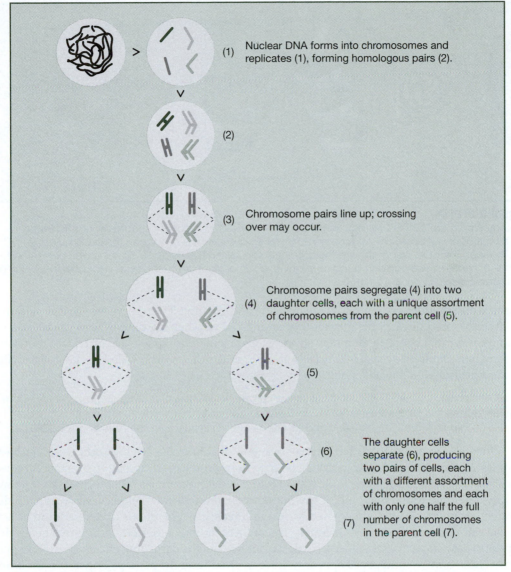

(1) Nuclear DNA forms into chromosomes and replicates (1), forming homologous pairs (2).

(2)

(3) Chromosome pairs line up; crossing over may occur.

(4) Chromosome pairs segregate (4) into two daughter cells, each with a unique assortment of chromosomes from the parent cell (5).

(5)

(6) The daughter cells separate (6), producing two pairs of cells, each with a different assortment of chromosomes and each with only one half the full number of chromosomes in the parent cell (7).

(7)

Figure 3.1 Meiosis (Sex Cells)

toward understanding DNA—what its structure is, how it duplicates itself in reproduction, and how it conveys or instructs the formation of a complete organism.

One of the most important keys to understanding human development and genetics is the structure and function of DNA. In 1953, American biologist James Watson, with British molecular biologist Francis Crick, proposed that DNA is a long, two-stranded molecule shaped like a double helix (see Figure 3.2). Genetic information is stored in the linear sequences of the bases; different species have different sequences, and every individual is slightly different from every other individual. Notice that each base in the DNA molecule always has the same opposite base;

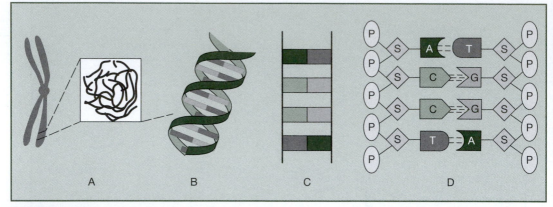

Figure 3.2 DNA
Chromosomes are built of DNA (A), which consists of two spiral sugar-phosphate strands (B) linked by the nitrogenous bases adenine, guanine, thymine, and cytosine (C). When the DNA molecule reproduces, the bases separate and the spiral strands unwind (D). Because adenine can only bond to thymine, and cytosine can only bond to guanine, each original strand serves as a mold along which a new complementary chain is formed.

adenine and thymine are paired, as are cytosine and guanine. The importance of this pattern is that the two strands carry the same information, so that, when the double helix unwinds, each strand can form a template for a new strand of complementary bases. Because DNA stores the information required to make up the cells of an organism, it has been called the language of life. As George and Muriel Beadle put it,

> the deciphering of the DNA code has revealed our possession of a language much older than hieroglyphics, a language as old as life itself, a language that is the most living language of all—even if its letters are invisible and its words are buried deep in the cells of our bodies.[17]

Once it was understood that genes are made of DNA, concerted efforts were begun to map DNA sequences and their locations on the chromosomes of different organisms. A project known as the Human Genome Project set out to assemble a complete genetic map for humans. In July 2000, the initial mapping of the human genome was completed.[18] This was a significant achievement and has already led to several breakthroughs in our understanding of how the genetic code functions.[19] For example, researchers recently reported finding two genes that appear to provide partial resistance to malaria, but without the damaging effects of the sickle-cell gene. These newly found genes appear to have evolved recently, perhaps only a few thousand years ago. If researchers can discover how these genes help to defend their carriers against malaria, that may help medical science discover how to prevent or treat this devastating disease.[20]

Messenger RNA DNA stores the information to make cells, but it does not directly affect the formation of cells. One type of ribonucleic acid (RNA), **messenger RNA (mRNA),** is copied from a portion of DNA and moves outside the cell nucleus to direct the formation of proteins. Proteins have so many functions that they are considered to be responsible for most of the characteristics of an organism. They act as catalysts for synthesizing DNA and RNA and for the activities of cells; they also contribute many structural elements that determine the shape and movement of cells. Messenger RNA is like DNA in that it has a linear sequence of bases attached to a sugar-phosphate backbone, but it is slightly different chemically. One difference is that messenger

RNA has the base uracil instead of the base thymine. Messenger RNA also has a different sugar-phosphate backbone and is single- rather than double-stranded. Messenger RNA is formed when a double-stranded DNA molecule unwinds and forms a template for the mRNA. After a section of DNA is copied, the mRNA releases from the DNA and leaves the nucleus, and the double helix of the DNA is reformed.

Protein Synthesis Once the mRNA is released from the DNA, it travels out of the cell nucleus and into the body of the cell. There it attaches to a structure in the cell called a **ribosome,** which uses the information on the mRNA to make proteins. The ribosome essentially "reads" the chemical bases on the mRNA in commands that tell the ribosome the specific amino acids to join together to form a protein (see Figure 3.3). For example, the mRNA sequence adenine, adenine, guanine (AAG) tells the ribosome to place the amino acid lysine in that location, whereas the sequence adenine, adenine, cytosine (AAC) calls for the amino acid histidine. There are also mRNA commands that tell the ribosome when to begin and when to stop constructing a protein. Thus, the DNA code copied onto mRNA provides all the information necessary for ribosomes to build the proteins that make up the structures of organisms and drive the processes of life.

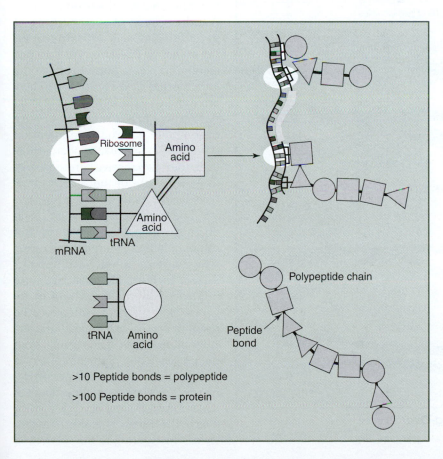

Figure 3.3 Translation and Protein Synthesis The mRNA copy of the cellular DNA is "read" by a ribosome that attaches the amino acid with the corresponding transfer RNA (tRNA) to a growing chain of amino acids (called a polypeptide chain because the amino acids are linked together by peptide bonds). A chain more than 100 amino acids long is called a protein.

Sources of Variability

Natural selection proceeds only when individuals within a population vary. There are two main genetic sources of new variation: genetic recombination and mutation. There are also two processes through which variations are shuffled through populations: *gene flow* and *genetic drift.* Scholars have recently begun to consider one other potential source of variability: *hybridization.*

Genetic Recombination

The distribution of traits from parents to children varies from one offspring to another. Brothers and sisters, after all, do not look exactly alike, nor does each child resemble 50 percent of the mother and 50 percent of the father. This variation occurs because, when a sperm cell or an egg is formed, the single member of each chromosome pair it receives is a matter of chance. Each reproductive cell, then, carries a random assortment of chromosomes and their respective genes. At fertilization, the egg and sperm that unite are different from every other egg carried by the mother and every other sperm carried by the father. A unique offspring is thus produced by a shuffling of the parents' genes. One cause of this shuffling is the random **segregation,** or sorting, of chromosomes in meiosis. Conceivably, an individual could get any of the possible assortments of the paternal and maternal chromosomes. Another cause of the shuffling of parental genes is **crossing-over,** the exchange of sections of chromosomes between one chromosome and another (see Figure 3.4). Thus, after meiosis, the egg and sperm do not receive just a random mixture of complete paternal and maternal chromosomes; because of crossing-over, they also receive chromosomes in which some of the sections may have been replaced.

The traits displayed by each organism are not simply the result of combinations of dominant and recessive genes, as Mendel had hypothesized. In humans, most traits are influenced by the activity of many genes. Skin color, for example, is the result of several inherited characteristics. A brownish shade results from the presence of a pigment known as *melanin;* the degree of darkness in the hue depends largely on the amount of melanin present and how it is distributed in the layers of the skin. Another factor contributing to the color of all

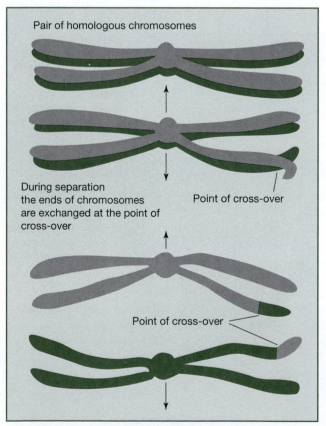

Pair of homologous chromosomes

During separation the ends of chromosomes are exchanged at the point of cross-over

Point of cross-over

Point of cross-over

Figure 3.4 Crossing-Over

Source: From Boaz and Almquist 1997.

human skin is the blood that flows in blood vessels located in the outer layers of the skin. Humans carry at least five different genes for the manufacture of melanin and many other genes for the other components of skin hue. In fact, almost all physical characteristics in humans are the result of the concerted action of many genes. Some traits are sex-linked. The X chromosome, which together with the presence or absence of a Y chromosome determines sex, may also carry the gene for hemophilia or the gene for color blindness. The expression of these two characteristics depends on the sex of the organism.

Genetic recombination produces variety, which is essential for the operation of natural selection. Ultimately, however, the major source of variability is mutation. This is because mutation replenishes the supply of variability, which is constantly being reduced by the selective elimination of less fit variants. Mutation also produces variety in organisms that reproduce asexually.

A mutation in a fruit fly causes legs to grow where antennae should be. Although most mutations are either neutral or harmful (like this one), some can be adaptive and spread rapidly through a population.

Mutation

A **mutation** is a change in the DNA sequence. Such a change produces an altered gene. The majority of mutations are thought to occur because of occasional mismating of the chemical bases that make up DNA. Just as a typist will make errors in copying a manuscript, so will DNA, in duplicating itself, occasionally change its code. A mutation will result from such an error. Some mutations have more drastic consequences than others. Suppose the error is in one base on a DNA strand. The effect depends on what that portion of the DNA controls. The effect may be minimal if the product hardly affects the organism. On the other hand, if the change occurs at a place where the DNA regulates the production of many proteins, the effect on the organism can be serious.

Although it is very difficult to estimate the proportions of mutations that are harmful, neutral, or beneficial, there is no doubt that some mutations have lethal consequences. We can discuss the relative merits or disadvantages of a mutant gene only in terms of the physical, cultural, and genetic environment of that gene. Galactosemia, for example, is caused by a recessive mutant gene and usually results in mental retardation and blindness. But it can be prevented by dietary restrictions begun at an early age. In this instance, the intervention of human culture counteracts the mutant gene and allows the afflicted individual to lead a normal life. Thus, some cultural factors can modify the effects of natural selection by helping to perpetuate a harmful mutant gene. People with the galactosemia trait who are enabled to function normally can reproduce and pass on one of the recessive genes to their children. Without cultural interference, natural selection would prevent such reproduction. Usually, natural selection acts to retain only those mutations that aid survival.

Even though most mutations may not be adaptive, those that are will multiply in a population relatively quickly by natural selection. As Theodosius Dobzhansky has suggested:

> Consistently useful mutants are like needles in a haystack of harmful ones. A needle in a haystack is hard to find, even though one may be sure it is there. But if the needle is valuable, the task of finding it is facilitated by setting the haystack on fire and looking for the needle among the ashes. The role of the fire in this parable is played in biological evolution by natural selection.[21]

The black moth that was spotted in Manchester in 1850 probably resulted from a mutation. If the tree trunks had been light-colored, that moth or its offspring probably would have died out. But as industrialization increased and the tree trunks became darker, a trait that was once maladaptive became adaptive.

Genetic recombination and mutation are the sources of new variations, but evolutionary biologists have identified two other processes that are important in distributing those variations through populations: genetic drift and gene flow.

Genetic Drift

The term **genetic drift** refers to various random processes that affect gene frequencies in small, relatively isolated populations. Genetic drift is also known as the *Wright effect,* after geneticist Sewall Wright, who first directed attention to this process. Over time in a small population, genetic drift may result in a neutral or nearly neutral gene becoming more or less frequent just by chance.

One variety of genetic drift, called the *founder effect,* occurs when a small group of organisms recently derived from a larger population migrates to a relatively isolated location. If a particular gene is absent just by chance in the migrant group, the descendants are also likely to lack that gene, assuming that the group remains isolated. Similarly, if all members of the original migrant group just by chance carried a particular gene, their descendants would also be likely to share that gene. Isolation can occur for physical reasons, such as when a group moves to a previously uninhabited place and does not return. The populations that traveled over land when the Bering land bridge connected Asia to North America could not readily return when the sea level rose. This may explain why Native Americans have a higher proportion of individuals with type O blood than other populations—the first migrants may have had, by chance, a predominance of individuals with type O blood.

Isolation can also occur for social reasons. A religious sect of Anabaptists called "Dunkers" emigrated from Germany to the United States in the early 1700s. The fact that the 50 original families kept to themselves probably explains why some of their gene frequencies differ from what is found in both the German and general U.S. populations.[22]

Gene Flow

Gene flow is the process whereby genes pass from one population to another through mating and reproduction. Unlike the other processes of natural selection and genetic drift, which generally increase the differences between populations in different environments, gene flow tends to work in the opposite direction—it *decreases* differences between populations. Two populations at opposite ends of a region may have different frequencies of a particular gene, but the populations located between them have an intermediate gene frequency because of gene flow between them. The variation in gene frequency from one end of the region to the other is called a **cline.** In Europe, for example, there is a cline in the distribution of type B blood, which gradually diminishes in frequency from east to west.[23]

Most genetically determined characteristics in humans have gradually or clinally varying frequencies as one moves from one area to another. Neighboring regions have more similar gene frequencies than regions widely separated. But these clines do not always coincide, which makes the concept of "race" as applied to humans not very useful for understanding human biological variation.[24] We discuss this in more detail in the chapter on human variation.

Gene flow may occur between distant as well as close populations. Long-range movements of people, to trade or raid or settle, may result in gene flow. But they do not always do so.

Hybridization

A **species** is a population that consists of organisms able to interbreed and produce fertile and viable offspring. In general, individuals from one species do not successfully mate with members of a different species because of genetic and behavioral differences. If members of different species do mate, fertilization usually does not occur and, if it does, the embryo does not survive. In the cases where offspring are born, they are usually infertile. However,

Hybridization is an important source of variation in some plant species, such as these hybrid grapes.

recent studies have suggested that **hybridization,** the creation of a viable offspring from two different species, may be more possible than once thought. Hybridization may be an important source of new variation in some populations.

The finches of the Galápagos Islands that Darwin used as evidence for natural selection and that we refer to in the box "Is Evolution Slow and Steady or Fast and Abrupt?" also provide an example of hybridization in action. Many female cactus finches (*Geospiza scandens*) died during a period of severe drought, leaving an abundance of males. High competition for mates led some female ground finches (*Geospiza fortis*) to mate with the abundant male cactus finches, something that would not normally occur. The result was hybrid offspring with unique characteristics. These hybrids, both male and female, went on to mate only with cactus finches because they imprinted on the male cactus finch song as infants. The end result was a one-time influx of ground finch genes into the cactus finch population, adding new variations upon which natural selection could work.[25]

The Origin of Species

One of the most controversial aspects of Darwin's theory was the suggestion that one species could, over time, evolve into another. What is the explanation for this differentiation? How does one group of organisms become so unlike another group with the same ancestry that it forms a totally new species? **Speciation,** or the development of a new species, may occur if one subgroup of a species finds itself in a radically different environment. In adapting to their separate environments, the two populations may undergo enough genetic changes to prevent them from interbreeding, should they renew contact. Numerous factors can prevent the exchange of genes.

CURRENT RESEARCH AND ISSUES   Is Evolution Slow and Steady or Fast and Abrupt?

Darwin's evolutionary theory suggested that new species emerge gradually over time. Through the process of natural selection, frequencies of traits would slowly change, and eventually a new species would appear. But Darwin did not explain why so much speciation has occurred. If trait frequencies change only gradually over time, wouldn't descendant populations retain their ability to interbreed and therefore continue to belong to the same species?

In the 1930s and 1940s, biologists and geneticists advanced what came to be called the "modern synthesis" in evolutionary theory, adding what was known from genetics about heredity. Mutation and the recombination of genes now provided for genetic variety. The driving force of change was still adaptation to environments through natural selection; gene frequencies of a population presumably changed slowly as adaptive traits in prevalence and maladaptive traits decreased. As for the development and divergence of different species, the modern synthesis postulated that it would occur when subpopulations became isolated by geographic barriers or when different subpopulations encountered different climatic conditions or moved into new ecological niches; those environmental isolating processes would eventually result in the development of reproductive isolation and therefore new species.

Niles Eldredge and Stephen Jay Gould challenged this gradualist view of evolution in 1972. Their alternative model of evolution, "punctuated equilibrium," still assumes that natural selection is the primary mechanism of evolutionary change, but in contrast to the modern synthesis, Eldredge and Gould do not think the world's species commonly change gradually into descendant species. Rather, species are born more or less abruptly, they have lifetimes during which they do not change much, and they become extinct. As examples, Eldredge and Gould cite the history of North American trilobites and Bermudan land snails. In both groups of animals, it looks as if the different species did not change for a long period of time—millions of years for some species—but then certain species seem to have been quickly replaced by related species from nearby areas.

Most evolutionists today agree that change could occur relatively quickly. Recent research suggests that some relatively quick climate changes in the earth's history helped bring about massive extinctions of species and families of species and exponential increases in the subsequent number of new families. For example, there is considerable evidence that a large meteorite collided with the earth at the end of the Cretaceous geological period, about 65 million years ago. Louis Alvarez and his colleagues proposed that so much dust

Two species living in the same area may breed at different times of the year, or their behavior during breeding—their courtship rituals—may be distinct. The difference in body structure of closely related forms may in itself bar interbreeding. Geographic barriers may be the most common barriers to interbreeding.

Speciation versus Creation

But some people, particularly those who call themselves "scientific creationists," argue that, although natural selection can produce variation within species (often referred to as *microevolution*), it cannot produce new species (often referred to as *macroevolution*). Creationists argue that God created all living things, and that evolution has only changed those living things in minor ways and has not created new kinds of living things. The major problem with the creationist view is that there is solid empirical evidence for speciation. For example, William Rice and George Salt demonstrated that, if they sorted fruit flies by their environmental preferences (such as light intensity and temperature) and then bred the sorted groups separately, they

was sent into the atmosphere by the collision that the earth was shrouded in darkness for months, if not longer. Some investigators now think that the meteorite impact may have also triggered a great deal of volcanic activity, even on the opposite side of the world, which would also have reduced solar radiation to the earth's surface. Not only the dinosaurs disappeared about 65 million years ago, so also did many sea animals and plants. Afterward, the earth saw the proliferation of many other kinds of animals, such as fish, lizards, birds, and mammals, as well as flowering trees. As we shall see in the chapter on the primates, our own biological order, the Primates, is believed to have emerged around that time.

Peter Grant recently studied the same finches on the Galápagos Islands that partially inspired Darwin's theory. But, unlike Darwin, Grant had the chance to see natural selection in action. It was surprisingly quick. Central to the project was the attachment of colored bands to each individual bird, which allowed each bird to be identified at a distance. In the midst of the project, in 1977, when half the birds had been banded, there was a serious drought. Of the two main species of finch on one island, the cactus finch and the medium ground finch, only the cactus finches were able to breed, but they had no surviving offspring. During the next 18 months, 85 percent of the adult medium ground finches disappeared. Those finches that survived tended to be larger and to have larger beaks than the ones that died. Why larger beaks? Both species of finch eat seeds, but small seeds produced by grasses and herbs are scarce in a drought; bigger seeds are more available. So it seems that natural selection under conditions of drought favored finches with bigger beaks, which are better at cracking the husks of large seeds.

If it were not for the fact that wet years, which favor smaller finches, occur between years of drought, we might see the quick evolution of new finch species. An estimated 20 drought episodes would be sufficient to produce a new species of finch. Galápagos finches do not really provide an example of punctuated equilibrium since no replacement from outside occurred, but they do suggest that evolutionary change could be a lot quicker than Darwin imagined.

Controversy continues over whether evolution is slow and steady or fast and abrupt. In any case, much more investigation of evolutionary sequences is needed to help us evaluate the two competing theoretical models.

Sources: Alvarez et al. 1980; Devilliers and Chaline 1993; Eldredge and Gould 1972; Grant and Grant 2008, 82–87; Tattersall 2009; Weiner 1994.

could produce flies incapable of interbreeding—separate species—in as little as 35 generations.[26] The fossil record contains numerous examples of speciation and even the development of entirely new kinds of creatures. For example, the evolution of birds from terrestrial creatures is clearly evidenced in the fossil record.[27] Although many creationists downplay the evidence for speciation, the evidence is plentiful, and can be seen by the public in museums all over the world.

With the abundant evidence for speciation found in both the fossil record and in experimental observations, creationists have recently developed a new argument to discount the role of natural selection in the process of speciation. The new argument is that life in general, and species in particular, are so complex that a random, undirected process like natural selection could never have created them. The complexity of life, these creationists argue, must stem from "intelligent design." This new appeal to intelligent design in the origin of species is actually an old, and widely discredited, one. In his 1802 book *Natural Theology,* William Paley wrote, "Suppose I had found a watch upon the ground, and it should be enquired how the watch happened to be in that place . . . the inference, we think, is inevitable; that the watch must have had a maker. . . ."[28] By this, Paley implied that if we find a complex mechanism at work in the world, like a watch, we must conclude that a maker exists. Paley extended the argument to the complexity of life, and concluded that life must stem from an intelligent designer—God.

Darwin wrote *On the Origin of Species* in part as a response to Paley, and Darwinists have been responding ever since. But in recent years, the "intelligent design" movement, or as proponents call it, the "wedge," has brought Paley's ideas back with force. Indeed, the force is an active political one, with the explicit purpose "to reverse the stifling dominance of the materialist world view, and to replace it with a science consonant with Christian and theistic convictions."[29] Intelligent design is, at the core, a political movement. The problem, however, is that intelligent design cannot explain speciation in a scientific way. The central argument made by proponents of intelligent design is simply that what we see in the world is too complex to be accounted for by natural selection, but they offer no alternative natural mechanism. They argue that, if natural selection may not account for all cases of speciation, then the only alternative is divine intervention. Clearly, this reasoning is flawed. Just because we do not understand something today does not mean we should toss out all we do know. Rather, the scientific approach is to continue to examine unexplained phenomena to learn more about them.

Intelligent design proponents also fail to answer critics who point out that natural selection can and has accounted for even the most complex of features—such as wings and eyes—and hence that intelligent design arguments lack a basis in fact. The key facts that intelligent design and other creationist scholars appeal to are biblical ones. But it is important to point out that most biblical scholars do not agree with creationist arguments. As theologian Ernan McMullin suggests, the Bible "ought to be understood as conveying fundamental theological truths about dependence of the natural and human worlds on their Creator, rather than explaining how exactly these worlds first took shape."[30] On the other hand, there is nothing in science that can absolutely rule out supernatural intervention in the natural world, because supernatural activities are beyond the realm of scientific explanation. For example, although we now know that people with a condition called hypertrichosis grow hair all over their faces because of a single mutation on the X chromosome, science cannot rule out the possibility that the mutation was caused by the "curse of the werewolf" or a divine punishment for sin.[31] Science cannot rule out such possibilities because they cannot be observed, measured, or experimentally tested. Science and religion should be regarded as different ways of understanding the world, the former relying on evidence, the latter relying on faith.

Natural Selection of Behavioral Traits

Until now, we have discussed how natural selection might operate to change a population's physical traits, such as the color of moths or the neck length of giraffes. But natural selection can also operate on the behavioral characteristics of populations. Although this idea is not new, it is now receiving more attention. The approaches called sociobiology,[32] behavioral ecology,[33] evolutionary psychology,[34] and dual-inheritance theory[35] involve the application of evolutionary principles to the behavior of animals and humans. *Behavioral ecology* looks at how all kinds of behavior related to the environment; *sociobiology* looks at social organization and social behavior; *evolutionary psychology* looks at how evolution may have produced lasting variation in the way humans behave, interact, and perceive the world; and *dual-inheritance theory* looks at how beneficial cultural traits might be selected for and transmitted. The typical behaviors of a species are assumed to be adaptive and to have evolved by natural selection. For example, why do related species exhibit different social behaviors even though they derive from a common ancestral species?

Consider the lion, as compared with other cats. Although members of the cat family are normally solitary creatures, lions live in social groups called *prides.* Why? George Schaller has suggested that lion social groups may have evolved primarily because group hunting is a more successful way to catch large mammals in open terrain. He has observed that not only are several lions more successful in catching prey than are solitary lions, but several lions are more likely to catch and kill large and dangerous prey such as giraffes. Then, too, cubs are generally safer from predators when in a social group than when alone with their mothers. Thus, the social behavior of lions may have evolved primarily because it provided selective advantages in the lions' open-country environment.[36]

It is important to remember that natural selection operates on expressed characteristics, or the phenotype, of an individual. In the moth example, the color of the moth is part of its *phenotype,* subject to natural selection. Behavior is also an expressed characteristic. If hunting in groups, a behavioral trait, gets you more food, then individuals who hunt in groups will do better. But we must also remember that natural selection requires traits to be heritable. Can the concept of heritability be applied to learned behavior, not just genetically transmitted behavior? And, even more controversially, if the concept of heritability can include learning, can it also include cultural learning? Recent research on domesticated dogs suggests it may. Domesticated dogs appear to inherently understand social cues used by humans, such as pointing, whereas wolves do not. These findings suggest that some aspects of cultural learning in animals may be heritable.[37]

Early theorizing in sociobiology and behavioral ecology appeared to emphasize the genetic component of behavior. For example, Edward O. Wilson, in his book *Sociobiology,* defined sociobiology as "the systematic study of the biological causes of behavior."[38] But Bobbi Low points out that, although the term *biological* may have been interpreted to mean "genetic," most biologists understand that expressed or observable characteristics are the results of genes, environment, and life history all interacting. Behavior is a product of all three. If we say that some behavior is heritable, we mean that the child's behavior is more likely to resemble the parents' behavior than the behavior of others.[39] Learning from a parent could be an important part of why the offspring is like the parent. If the

Domesticated dogs have evolved the ability to understand human social cues far better than wolves.

child is more like the parent than like others, then the likeness is heritable, even if it is entirely learned from the parent.

The sociobiological approach has aroused considerable controversy in anthropology, probably because of its apparent emphasis on genes, rather than experience and learning, as determinants of human behavior. Anthropologists have argued that the customs of a society may be more or less adaptive because cultural behaviors also have reproductive consequences. It is not just an individual's behavior that may have reproductive consequences. So, does natural selection also operate in the evolution of culture? Many biologists think not. They say there are substantial differences between biological and cultural evolution. How do cultural evolution and biological evolution compare? To answer this question, we must remember that the operation of natural selection requires three conditions, as we already noted: variation, heritability or mechanisms that duplicate traits in offspring, and differential reproduction because of heritable differences. Do these three requirements apply to cultural behavior?

In biological evolution, variability comes from genetic recombination and mutation. In cultural evolution, it comes from recombination of learned behaviors and from invention.[40] Cultures are not closed or reproductively isolated, as species are. A species cannot borrow genetic traits from another species, but a culture can borrow new things and behaviors from other cultures. The custom of growing corn, which has spread from the New World to many other areas, is an example of this phenomenon. As for the requirement of heritability, although learned traits obviously are not passed to offspring through purely genetic inheritance, parents who exhibit adaptive behavioral traits are more likely to "reproduce" those traits in their children, who may learn them by imitation or by parental instruction. Children and adults may also copy adaptive traits they see in people outside the family. Finally, as for the requirement of differential reproduction, it does not matter whether the trait in question is genetic or learned or both. As Henry Nissen emphasized, "behavioral incompetence leads to extinction as surely as does morphological disproportion or deficiency in any vital organ. Behavior is subject to selection as much as bodily size or resistance to disease."[41]

Many theorists are comfortable with the idea of applying the theory of natural selection to cultural evolution, but others prefer to use different terminology when dealing with traits that do not depend on purely genetic transmission from one generation to the next. For example, Robert Boyd and Peter Richerson discuss human behavior as involving "dual inheritance." They distinguish cultural transmission, by learning and imitation, from genetic transmission, but they emphasize the importance of understanding both and the interaction between them.[42] William Durham also deals separately with cultural transmission, using the term *meme* (analogous to the term *gene*) for the unit of cultural transmission. He directs our attention to the interaction between genes and culture, calling that interaction "coevolution," and provides examples of how genetic evolution and cultural evolution may lead to changes in each other, how they may enhance each other, and how they may even oppose each other.[43]

So biological and cultural evolution in humans may not be completely separate processes. As we will discuss, some of the most important biological features of humans—such as our relatively large brains—may have been favored by natural selection because our ancestors made tools, a cultural trait. Conversely, the cultural trait of informal and formal education may have been favored by natural selection because humans have a long period of immaturity, a biological trait.

As long as the human species continues to exist and the social and physical environment continues to change, there is reason to think that natural selection of biological and cultural traits will also continue. However, as humans learn more about genetic structure, they will become more capable of curing genetically caused disorders and even altering the way evolution proceeds. Genetic researchers are capable of diagnosing genetic defects in developing fetuses, and parents may decide to terminate a pregnancy. Soon, genetic engineering will probably allow humans to fix defects and even try to "improve" the genetic code of a growing fetus. Whether and to what extent humans should alter genes will undoubtedly be the subject of continuing debate. Whatever the decisions we eventually make about genetic engineering, they will affect the course of human biological and cultural evolution.

✓●─[Study and **Review** on **myanthrolab.com**

Summary

1. Ideas about evolution took a long time to take hold because they contradicted the biblical view of events; species were viewed as fixed in their form by the creator. But in the 18th and early 19th centuries, increasing evidence suggested that evolution was a viable theory. In geology, the concept of uniformitarianism suggested that the earth is constantly subject to shaping and reshaping by natural forces working over vast stretches of time. A number of thinkers during this period began to discuss evolution and how it might occur.

2. Charles Darwin and Alfred Wallace proposed the mechanism of natural selection to account for the evolution of species. Basic principles of the theory of natural selection are that (1) every species is composed of a great variety of individuals, some of which are better adapted to their environment than others; (2) offspring inherit traits from their parents at least to some degree and in some way; and (3) because better-adapted individuals generally produce more offspring over the generations than the poorer-adapted individuals, the frequency of adaptive traits increases in subsequent generations. In this way, natural selection results in increasing proportions of individuals with advantageous traits.

3. Mendel's and subsequent research in genetics and our understanding of the structure and function of DNA and mRNA help us to understand the biological mechanisms by which traits may be passed from one generation to the next.

4. Natural selection depends on variation within a population. The primary sources of new biological variation are genetic recombination and mutation. New biological variations move through a population by the processes of genetic drift, gene flow, and hybridization.

5. Speciation, the development of a new species, may occur if one subgroup becomes separated from other subgroups. In adapting to different environments, these subpopulations may undergo enough genetic changes to prevent interbreeding, even if they reestablish contact. Once species differentiation occurs, it is believed that the evolutionary process cannot be reversed.

6. So-called "creation scientists" and proponents of "intelligent design" theory argue that the origin of species cannot be accounted for through natural selection. This argument ignores the enormous body of evidence—experimental, fossil, and field data—that demonstrates how natural selection works to create new species.

7. Natural selection can also operate on the behavioral characteristics of populations. The approaches such as sociobiology and behavioral ecology involve the application of evolutionary principles to the behavior of animals. Much controversy surrounds the degree to which the theory of natural selection can be applied to human behavior, particularly cultural behavior. There is more agreement that biological and cultural evolution in humans may influence each other.

Glossary Terms

adaptive (p. 41)
allele (p. 44)
balancing selection (p. 43)
chromosome (p. 44)
cline (p. 50)
crossing-over (p. 48)
directional selection (p. 43)
DNA (p. 44)
dominant (p. 43)
gene flow (p. 50)
genes (p. 44)

genetic drift (p. 50)
genotype (p. 44)
genus (p. 39)
heterozygous (p. 44)
homozygous (p. 44)
hybridization (p. 51)
maladaptive (p. 41)
meiosis (p. 44)
messenger RNA
   (mRNA) (p. 46)
mitosis (p. 44)

mutation (p. 49)
natural selection (p. 40)
normalizing
   selection (p. 43)
phenotype (p. 44)
recessive (p. 43)
ribosome (p. 47)
segregation (p. 48)
speciation (p. 51)
species (p. 51)

Critical Questions

1. Do you think the theory of natural selection is compatible with religious beliefs? Explain your reasoning.

2. How might the discovery of genetic cures and the use of genetic engineering affect the future of evolution?

3. Why do you think humans have remained one species?

Read the Original Source on myanthrolab.com

Read the chapter by Jonathan Marks titled "Genes, Bodies, and Species" on MyAnthroLab. Answer the following questions.

1. Compare Marks's discussion of the "Hardy-Weinberg Law" and the discussion of Mendel's experiments with pea plants in this chapter. Explain how the Hardy-Weinberg Law relates to Mendel's discovery.

2. Marks argues that speciation requires a gene pool to be divided into isolated groups. Explain why this is the case. Given the enormous gene flow in human populations, is it likely (or even possible) that a new species of human will evolve under current conditions?

3. Marks concludes his essay by stating that genetic mutation is more complex than we had previously thought. In what ways does Marks's discussion of mutation and its effects differ from that we present in this text? Does Marks's discussion appear to make the process of mutation more complex than ours?

Human Variation and Adaptation

((•─[**Listen** to the **Chapter Audio** on **myanthrolab.com**   [📖]─[**Read** on **myanthrolab.com**

In any given human population, individuals vary in external features such as skin color or height and in internal features such as blood type or susceptibility to a disease. If you measure the frequencies of such features in different populations, you will typically find differences on average from one population to another. So, for example, some populations are typically darker in skin color than other populations.

Why do these physical differences exist? They may be largely the product of differences in genes. They may be largely due to growing up in a particular environment, physical and cultural. They are perhaps the result of an interaction between environmental factors and genes.

We turn first to the processes that may singly or jointly produce the varying frequencies of physical traits in different human populations. Then we discuss specific differences in external and internal characteristics and how they might be explained. Finally, we close with a critical examination of racial classification and whether it helps or hinders the study of human variation.

Processes in Human Variation and Adaptation

Mutations—changes in the structure of a gene—are the ultimate source of all genetic variation. Because different genes make for greater or lesser chances of survival and reproduction, natural selection results in more favorable genes becoming more frequent in a population over time. We call this process **adaptation.** Adaptations are genetic changes that give their carriers a better chance to survive and reproduce than individuals without the genetic change who live in the same environment. It is the environment, of course, that favors the reproductive success of some traits rather than others.

How adaptive a gene or trait is depends on the specific environment; what is adaptive in one environment may not be adaptive in another. For example, in the chapter on genetics and evolution, we discussed the advantage that dark moths had over light moths when certain areas of England became industrialized. Predators could not easily see the darker moths against the newly darkened trees, and these moths soon outnumbered the lighter variety. Similarly, human populations live in a great variety of environments, so we would expect natural selection to favor different genes and traits in those different environments. Variations in skin color and body build are among the many features that may be at least partly explainable by how natural selection works in different environments.

Acclimatization

Natural selection may favor certain genes because of certain physical environmental conditions, as in the case of the moths in England. But the physical environment can sometimes produce variation even in the absence of genetic change. As we shall see, climate may influence the way the human body grows and develops, and therefore some kinds of human variation may be explainable largely as a function of environmental variation. We call this process *acclimatization.* **Acclimatization** involves physiological adjustments to environmental conditions in individuals. Acclimatizations may have underlying genetic factors, but they are not themselves genetic. Individuals develop them during their lifetimes, rather than being born with them.

Many acclimatizations are simple physiological changes in the body that appear and disappear as the environment changes. For example, when we are chilled, our bodies attempt to create heat by making our muscles work, a physiological response to the environment that we experience as shivering. Longer exposure to cold weather leads our bodies to increase our metabolic rates so that we generate more internal heat. Both these physiological changes are acclimatizations, one short term (shivering), one long term (increased metabolic rate).

As we discuss later in this chapter, some long-term acclimatizations are difficult to distinguish from adaptations because they become established as normal operating processes, and they may persist even after the individual moves into an environment that is different from the one that originally fostered the acclimatization. It also appears that some acclimatizations are closely related to genetic adaptations. For example, tanning, an acclimatization among light-skinned people when exposed to high levels of solar radiation, is likely in people where light skin color is adapted to environments with typically low solar radiation.

Influence of the Cultural Environment

Humans are not only influenced by their environments through adaptations and acclimatizations, but humans can also dramatically affect their environments. Culture allows humans to modify their environments, and such modifications may lessen the likelihood of genetic adaptations and physiological acclimitizations. For example, the effects of cold may be modified by the culture traits of living in houses, harnessing energy to create heat, and clothing the body to insulate it. In these cultural ways, we alter our "microenvironments." Iron deficiency may be overcome by the culture trait of cooking in iron pots. If a physical environment lacks certain nutrients, people may get them by the culture trait of trading for them; trading for salt has been common in world history. Culture can also influence the direction of natural selection. As we shall see, the culture of dairying seems to have increased the frequency of genes that allow adults to digest milk.[1]

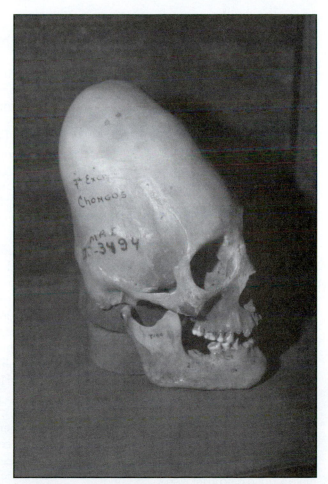

In addition, individual cultures sometimes practice behaviors that lead to physical variations between their members and between members of one culture and another. For example, elites in many highland Andean societies (the Inca, for example) practiced head binding. The heads of elite children were tightly bound with cloth. As the children grew, the binding forced the skull to take on an elongated, almost conical shape. This cultural practice, then, created physical variations among individuals that were

A cranium from the prehistoric Paracas culture of Peru, showing the effects of head binding.

intended to identify members of elite groups.[2] Many cultures have practices that are intended to create physical variations that distinguish members of their culture from members of other cultures. The Hebrew Bible, for example, tells the story of how Abraham was instructed by God to circumcise himself and all his male descendants as a sign of the covenant between them.[3] Thus, male descendants of Abraham traditionally share a culturally induced physical variation (lack of a foreskin) to identify themselves as a group.

Physical Variation in Human Populations

The most noticeable physical variations among populations are those that are external, on the surface—body build, facial features, skin color, and height. No less important are those variations that are internal, such as variation in susceptibility to different diseases and differences in the ability to produce certain enzymes.

We begin our survey with some physical features that appear to be strongly linked to variation in climate, particularly variation in temperature, sunlight, and altitude.

Body Build and Facial Construction

Scientists have suggested that the body build of many birds and mammals may vary according to the temperature of the environment in which they live. Bergmann and Allen, two nineteenth-century naturalists, suggested some general rules for animals, but researchers did not begin to examine whether these rules applied to human populations until the 1950s.[4] **Bergmann's rule** describes what seems to be a general relationship between body size and temperature: The slenderer populations of a species inhabit the warmer parts of its geographic range, and the more robust populations inhabit the cooler areas.

D. F. Roberts's studies of variation in mean body weight of human populations in regions with widely differing temperatures have provided support for Bergmann's rule.[5] Roberts discovered that the lowest body weights were found among residents of areas with the highest mean annual temperatures, and vice versa. Figure 4.1 shows the relationship between body weight of males and average annual temperature for four different geographic populations. Although the slope of the relationship is slightly different for each group, the trend is the same—with colder temperatures, weight is greater. Looking at the general trend across populations (see the "Total" line), we see that, where the mean annual temperatures are about freezing (32°F; 0°C), the average weight for males is about 143 pounds (65 kilograms); where the mean annual temperatures are about 77°F (25°C), men weigh, on the average, about 110 pounds (50 kilograms).

These Samburu people from Kenya illustrate Bergmann's rule. They have the long-limbed, lean body type that is often found in equatorial regions. Such a body type provides more surface area in relation to body mass and thus may facilitate the dissipation of body heat.

Allen's rule refers to another kind of variation in body build among birds and mammals: Protruding body parts (e.g., limbs) are relatively shorter in the cooler areas of a species' range than in the warmer areas. Research comparing human populations tends to support Allen's rule.[6]

The rationale behind these theories is that the long-limbed, lean body type often found in equatorial regions provides more surface area in relation to body mass and thus facilitates the dissipation of body heat. In contrast, the chunkier, shorter-limbed body type found among residents of cold regions promotes retention of body heat because the amount of surface area relative to body mass is lessened. The build of the Inuit (Eskimo) appears to exemplify Bergmann's and Allen's rules. The relatively large bodies and short legs of the Inuit may be adapted to the cold temperatures in which they live.

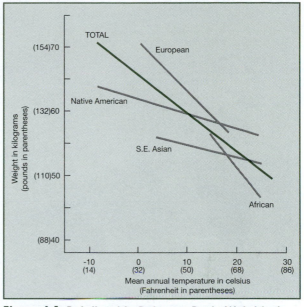

Figure 4.1 Relationship Between Body Weight of Males and Average Annual Temperature for Four Major Population Groups

Source: From Roberts 1953.

Skin Color

Human populations obviously differ in average skin color. Many people consider skin color the most important indicator of "race," and they sometimes treat others differently solely on this basis. But anthropologists, in addition to being critical of prejudice, also note that skin color is not a good indicator of ancestry. For example, dark skin is commonly found in sub-Saharan Africa. However, natives of southern India have skin as dark or darker than that of many Africans. Yet, these people are not closely related to Africans, either genetically or historically.

How can we explain the wide range of skin colors among the peoples of the world? The color of a person's skin depends on both the amount of dark pigment, or melanin, in the skin and the amount of blood in the small blood vessels of the skin.[7] Despite the fact that there is still much to understand about the genetics of skin color, we can explain much of the variation.

The amount of melanin in the skin seems to be related to the climate in which a person lives. **Gloger's rule** states that populations of birds and mammals living in warmer climates have more melanin and, therefore, darker skin, fur, or feathers, than do populations of the same species living in cooler areas. On the whole, this association with climate holds true for people as well as for other mammals and birds.

The populations of darker-skinned humans do live mostly in warm climates, particularly sunny climates (see Figure 4.2). Dark pigmentation seems to have at least one specific advantage in sunny climates. Melanin protects the sensitive inner layers of the skin from the sun's damaging ultraviolet rays; therefore, dark-skinned people living in sunny areas are safer from sunburn and skin cancers than are light-skinned people. Dark skin may also confer other important biological advantages in tropical environments, such as greater resistance to tropical diseases.[8]

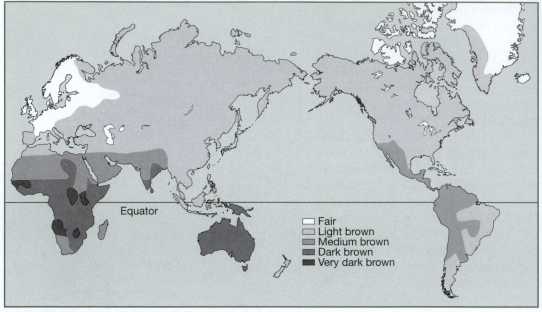

Figure 4.2 **Variation in Skin Color**

Source: From Robins 1991.

What, then, might be the advantages of light-colored skin? Presumably, there must be some benefits in some environments; otherwise, all human populations would tend to have relatively dark skin. Although light-skinned people are more susceptible to sunburn and skin cancers, the ultraviolet radiation that light skin absorbs also facilitates the body's production of vitamin D. Vitamin D helps the body incorporate calcium and thus is necessary for the proper growth and maintenance of bones. Too much vitamin D, however, can cause illness.[9] Light skin may also confer another advantage in colder environments: It is less likely to be damaged by frostbite.[10]

We now have direct evidence that confirms the connection between solar radiation and skin pigmentation. Anthropologists Nina Jablonski and George Chaplin used data from NASA satellites to determine the average amount of ultraviolet radiation people were exposed to in different parts of the world. They compared these average radiation amounts to data on skin reflectance (the lighter one's skin, the more light it reflects) and found that dark skin is more prevalent where ultraviolet radiation is more intense. Interestingly, there seems to be one notable exception—Native Americans tend to be lighter-skinned than expected. Jablonski and Chaplin suggest that this is because they are recent migrants to the New World, and their skin colors have not adapted to the varying levels of ultraviolet radiation they encountered in the Americas, just as the skin colors of European colonizers have not.[11]

Adaptation to High Altitude

Oxygen constitutes 21 percent of the air we breathe at sea level. At high altitudes, the percentage of oxygen in the air is the same, but because the barometric pressure is lower, we take in less oxygen with each breath.[12] We breathe more rapidly, our hearts beat faster, and all activity is more difficult. The net effects are discomfort and a condition known as **hypoxia,** or oxygen deficiency.

If high altitude presents such difficulties for many human beings, how is it that populations numbering in the millions can live out their lives, healthy and productive, at altitudes of 6,000, 12,000, or even 17,000 feet? Populations in the Himalayas and the Andes have adapted to their environments and do not display the symptoms that low-altitude dwellers suffer when they are exposed to high altitudes. Moreover, high-altitude dwellers have come to terms physiologically with extreme cold, deficient nutrition, strong winds, rough countryside, and intense solar radiation.[13]

Early studies of Andean high-altitude dwellers found that they differed in certain physical ways from low-altitude dwellers. Compared with low-altitude dwellers, high-altitude Andean Indians had larger chests and greater lung capacity, as well as more surface area in the capillaries of the lungs (which was believed to facilitate the transfer of oxygen to the blood).[14] Early researchers thought that genetic changes had allowed the Andeans to maximize their ability to take in oxygen at the lower barometric pressure of their high-altitude environment. Recent research, however, has cast some doubt on this conclusion. It appears now that other populations living at high altitudes do not show the Andean pattern of physical differences. In the Himalayas, for example, low-altitude dwellers and high-altitude dwellers do not differ in chest size or lung size, even though both groups show adequate lung functioning.[15]

Thus, current research does not suggest that high-altitude living requires biological adaptations that are purely genetic. In fact, some evidence suggests that humans who grow up in a high-altitude environment may adapt to hypoxia during their lifetimes as they mature. For example, Peruvians who were born at sea level but who grew up at high altitudes developed the same amount of lung capacity as people who spent their entire lives at high altitudes.[16] Consistent with a presumed environmental effect, the children of high-altitude Peruvians who grow up in the lowlands do not develop larger chests. What appeared to earlier researchers to be a genetic adaptation among highland Andean populations appears in fact to be an acclimatization that develops early in childhood and persists for the lifetime of an individual. As with other traits that have been studied, it appears that life experiences can have profound effects on how the body grows.

Height

Studies of identical twins and comparisons of the height of parents and children suggest that heredity plays a considerable role in determining height,[17] so genetic differences must at least partly explain differences between populations in average height. But if average height can increase dramatically in a few decades, as in Japan between 1950 and 1980, and in many other countries in recent times,[18] then environmental influences are also likely to be important.

In recent times, there has been a dramatic increase in average height, which may be due to one or more environmental factors. Here we see an Asian American woman who is much taller than her mother.

The considerable variation in average height among human populations may be partly explained by temperature differences. The Dutch, in Europe, are among the tallest populations in the world on average, and the Mbuti of Zaire, in central Africa, are among the shortest.[19] We already know that weight is related to mean annual temperature (Bergmann's rule). Weight is also related to height (taller people are likely to be heavier). So, because the taller (heavier) Dutch live in a cooler climate, some of the population variation in height would appear to involve adaptation to heat and cold.[20] Other factors besides heat and cold must also be operating, however, because tall and short peoples can be found in most areas of the world.

Many researchers think that poor nutrition and disease lead to reduced height and weight. In many parts of the world, children in higher social classes are taller on the average than children in lower social classes,[21] and this difference is more marked in economically poorer countries,[22] where the wealth and health differences between the classes are particularly large. During times of war and poor nutrition, children's stature often decreases. For example, in Germany during World War II, the stature of children 7–17 years of age declined as compared with previous time periods, despite the fact that stature had generally increased over time.[23]

More persuasive evidence for the effects of poor nutrition and disease comes out of longitudinal studies of the same individuals over time. For example, Reynaldo Martorell found that children in Guatemala who had frequent bouts of diarrhea were on the average over an inch shorter at age 7 than children without frequent diarrhea.[24] Although malnourished or diseased children can catch up in their growth, follow-up research on Guatemalan children suggests that, if stunting occurs before 3 years of age, stature at age 18 will still be reduced.[25]

A controversial set of studies links a very different environmental factor to variation in height in human populations. The factor at issue is stress, both physical and emotional, in infancy.[26] Contrary to the view that any kind of stress is harmful, a body of evidence suggests that short-term stresses in infancy (vaccinations, circumcision, piercing, separating infants from their mothers) are associated with greater height and weight. Experimental studies with rats provided the original stimulus for the studies investigating the possible effect of stress on height. Cross-cultural evidence suggests that after applying controls for nutrition, climate, and geography, *both* physical stress and mother–infant separation, *if practiced before 2 years of age,* predict greater adult height; males are on the average 2 inches taller in societies customarily practicing some form of infant stress. (It is important to note that the stresses being discussed are short in duration, often a one-time occurrence, and do not constitute prolonged stress or abuse, which can have opposite effects.) Because the cross-cultural evidence is associational, not experimental, it is possible that the results are due to some factor confounded with infant stress. More persuasive evidence for the stress hypothesis also comes from an experimental study conducted in Kenya.[27] Consistent with the cross-cultural evidence on the possible effect of stress on height, the children vaccinated before the age of 2 were significantly taller than the children vaccinated later. The children vaccinated before the age of 2 were selected randomly for early vaccination, so it is unlikely that nutritional or other differences between the two groups account for their difference in height.

As we noted earlier, people have been getting taller in several areas of the world. What accounts for this recent trend toward greater height? Several factors may be involved. Some researchers think that it may be the result of improved nutrition and lower incidence of infectious diseases.[28] But it might also be that infant stress has increased as a result of giving birth in hospitals, which usually separate babies from mothers and also subject the newborns to medical tests, including taking blood. Various kinds of vaccinations have also become more common in infancy.[29]

In short, differences in human size seem to be the result of both adaptations and acclimatizations, with both of these, in turn, affected by cultural factors such as nutrition and stress.

Susceptibility to Infectious Diseases

Certain populations seem to have developed inherited resistances to particular infectious diseases. That is, populations repeatedly decimated by certain diseases in the past now have a high frequency of genetic characteristics that ameliorate the effects of these diseases. As Arno Motulsky pointed out, if there are genes that protect people from dying when they are infected by one of the diseases prevalent in their area, these genes will tend to become more common in succeeding generations.[30]

A field study of the infectious disease myxomatosis in rabbits supports this theory. When the virus responsible for the disease was first introduced into the Australian rabbit population, more than 95 percent of the infected animals died. But among the offspring of animals exposed to successive epidemics of myxomatosis, the percentage of animals that died from the disease decreased from year to year. The more epidemics the animals' ancestors had lived through, the smaller the percentage of current animals that died of the disease. Thus, the data suggested that the rabbits had developed a genetic resistance to myxomatosis.[31]

Infectious diseases seem to follow a similar pattern among human populations. When tuberculosis first strikes a population that has had no previous contact with it, the disease is usually fatal. But some populations seem to have inherited a resistance to death from tuberculosis. For example, the Ashkenazi Jews in America (those whose ancestors came from central and eastern Europe) are one of several populations whose ancestors survived many years of exposure to tuberculosis in the crowded European ghettos where they had previously lived. Although the

Permanent settlements and high population densities allow diseases to spread rapidly and produce epidemics. Shown here is Banda Aceh's Peunayong Market in Indonesia. Close contact between chickens and humans in markets like this one provided the opportunity for the deadly H5N1 strain of bird flu to evolve.

rate of tuberculosis infection is identical among American Jews and non-Jews, the rate of tuber-culosis mortality is significantly lower among Jews than among non-Jews in the United States.[32] After reviewing other data on this subject, Motulsky thought it likely "that the present relatively high resistance of Western populations to tuberculosis is genetically conditioned through natural selection during long contact with the disease."[33]

We tend to think of measles as a childhood disease that kills virtually no one, and we now have a vaccine against it. But when first introduced into populations, the measles virus can kill large numbers of people. In 1949, the Tupari Indians of Brazil numbered about 200 people. By 1955, two-thirds of the Tupari had died of measles introduced into the tribe by rubber gatherers in the area.[34] Large numbers of people died of measles in epidemics in the Faeroe Islands in 1846, in Hawaii in 1848, in the Fiji Islands in 1874, and among the Canadian Inuit very recently. It is possible that, where mortality rates from measles are low, populations have acquired a genetic resistance to death from this disease.[35]

Why is a population susceptible to a disease in the first place? Epidemiologist Francis Black suggests that lack of genes for resistance is not the whole answer. A high degree of genetic homogeneity in the population may also increase susceptibility.[36] A virus grown in one host is preadapted to a genetically similar new host and is therefore likely to be more virulent in the new host. For example, the measles virus adapts to a host individual; when it replicates, the viral forms that the host cannot kill are those most likely to survive and con-tinue replicating. When the virus passes to a new host with similar genes, the preadapted virus is likely to kill the new host. On the other hand, if the next host is very different geneti-cally, the adaptation process starts over again; the virus is not so virulent at first because the host can kill it.

Populations that recently came to an area, and that had a small group of founders (as was probably true for the first Native Americans and the Polynesian seafarers who first settled many islands in the Pacific), tended to have a high degree of genetic homogeneity. Therefore, epidemic diseases introduced by Europeans (such as measles) would be likely to kill many of the natives within the first few years after contact. An estimated 56 million people died in the New World after contact with Europeans, mostly because of introduced diseases such as smallpox and measles. Similarly caused depopulation occurred widely in the Pacific.[37]

Some researchers suggest that nongenetic factors may also partly explain differential resis-tance to infectious disease. For example, cultural practices may partly explain the epidemics of measles among the Yanomamö Indians of Venezuela and Brazil. The Yanomamö frequently visit other villages, and that, together with the nonisolation of sick individuals, promoted a very rapid spread of the disease. Because many individuals were sick at the same time, there were not enough healthy people to feed and care for the sick; mothers down with measles could not even nurse their babies. Thus, cultural factors may increase exposure to a disease and worsen its effect on a population.[38]

Epidemics of infectious disease may occur only if many people live near each other. Hunter-gatherers, who usually live in small dispersed bands, do not have enough people in and near the community to keep an epidemic going. Without enough people to infect, short-lived microor-ganisms that cause or carry diseases die out. In contrast, among agriculturalists, there are larger numbers of people in and around the community to whom a disease can spread. Permanent settlements, particularly urban settlements, also are likely to have poor sanitation and contami-nated water.[39] Tuberculosis is an example of an infectious disease that, although very old, began to kill large numbers of people only after the emergence of sedentary, larger communities.[40]

Sickle-Cell Anemia

Another biological variation is an abnormality of the red blood cells known as **sickle-cell anemia,** or **sicklemia.** This is a condition in which normal, disk-shaped red blood cells assume a crescent (sickle) shape when deprived of oxygen. The sickle-shaped red blood cells do not move through the body as readily as normal cells, and thus cause more oxygen deficiency and damage to the heart, lungs, brain, and other vital organs. In addition, the red blood cells tend to "die" more rapidly, and the anemia worsens still more.[41]

Sickle-cell anemia is caused by a variant form of the genetic instructions for hemoglobin, the protein that carries oxygen in the red blood cells.[42] Individuals who have sickle-cell anemia have inherited the same allele (Hb^S) from both parents and are therefore homozygous for that gene. Individuals who receive this allele from only one parent are heterozygous; they have one Hb^S allele and one allele for normal hemoglobin (Hb^A). Heterozygotes generally will not show the full-blown symptoms of sickle-cell disease, although a heterozygous individual may have a mild case of anemia in some cases. A heterozygous person has a 50 percent chance of passing on the sickle-cell allele to a child. And if the child later mates with another person who is also a carrier of the sickle-cell allele, the statistical probability is that 25 percent of their children will develop sickle-cell anemia. Without advanced medical care, most individuals with two Hb^S alleles are unlikely to live more than a few years.[43]

Why has the allele for sickle-cell persisted in various populations? If people with sickle-cell anemia do not usually live to reproduce, we would expect a reduction in the frequency of Hb^S to near zero through the process of *normalizing selection.* But the sickle-cell allele occurs fairly often in some parts of the world, particularly in the wet tropical belt of Africa, where frequencies may be between 20 and 30 percent, and in Greece, Sicily, and southern India.[44]

Because the sickle-cell gene occurs in these places much more often than expected, researchers in the 1940s and the 1950s began to suspect that heterozygous individuals (who carry one HbS allele) might have a reproductive advantage in a malarial environment.[45] If the heterozygotes were more resistant to attacks of malaria than the homozygotes for normal hemoglobin (who get the HbA allele from both parents), the heterozygotes would be more likely to survive and reproduce, and therefore the recessive HbS allele would persist at a higher-than-expected frequency in the population. This kind of outcome is an example of balancing selection.[46]

A number of pieces of evidence support the "malaria theory." First, geographic comparisons show that the sickle-cell allele tends to be found where the incidence of malaria is high (see Figure 4.3). Second, as land in the tropics is opened to yam and rice agriculture, the incidence of the sickle-cell allele also increases. Indeed, recent studies suggest malaria may have evolved alongside agriculture in these regions.[47] The reason seems to be that malaria, carried principally by the *Anopheles gambiae* mosquito, becomes more prevalent as tropical forest gives way to more open land where mosquitoes can thrive in warm, sunlit ponds. Indeed, even among peoples of similar cultural backgrounds, the incidence of the sickle-cell allele increases with greater rainfall and surpluses of water. Third, children who are heterozygous for the sickle-cell trait tend to have fewer malarial parasites in their bodies than do homozygous normal individuals, and they are more likely to survive.[48] The sickling trait does not necessarily keep people from contracting malaria, but it greatly decreases the rate of mortality from malaria—and in evolutionary terms, the overall effect is the same.[49] Fourth, if there is no balancing selection because malaria is no longer present, we should find a rapid decline in the incidence of the sickle-cell allele. Indeed, we find such a decline in populations with African ancestry. Those who live in malaria-free zones

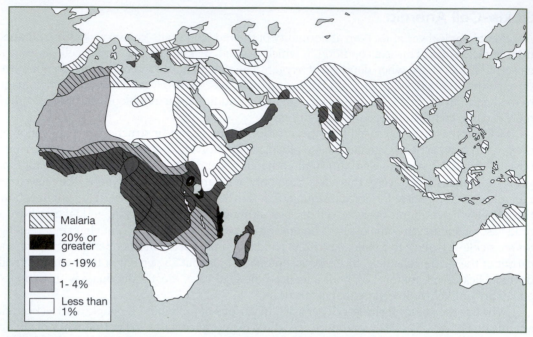

Figure 4.3 Geographic Distribution of Sicklemia and Its Relationship to the Distribution of Malaria

Source: John Buettner-Janusch, *Physical Anthropology: A Perspective* (New York: Wiley, 1973).

of the New World have a much lower incidence of sicklemia than do those who live in malarial regions of the New World.[50]

Hb[S] is not the only abnormal hemoglobin to have a distribution related to malaria. It seems that a number of abnormal hemoglobins may be widespread because of the advantage that heterozygotes have against the disease. For example, another abnormal hemoglobin, Hb[E], occurs in populations from India through Southeast Asia and New Guinea where malaria occurs, but Hb[S] is not that common. Why should Hb[E] heterozygotes have resistance to malaria? One possibility is that malarial parasites are less able to survive in an individual's blood with some normal and some abnormal hemoglobin. Abnormal hemoglobin cells are more delicate and live less long, so they may not readily support malarial parasites.[51]

Lactase Deficiency

When American educators discovered that African American schoolchildren very often did not drink milk, they assumed that lack of money or education was the reason. These assumptions provided the impetus for establishing the school milk programs prevalent around the country. However, it now appears that, after infancy, many people lack the enzyme lactase, which is necessary for breaking down the sugar in milk—lactose—into simpler sugars that can be absorbed into the bloodstream.[52] Thus, a person without lactase cannot digest milk properly, and drinking it may cause bloating, cramps, stomach gas, and diarrhea. A study conducted in Baltimore among 312 African American and 221 European American children in grades 1–6 in two elementary schools indicated that 85 percent of the African American children and 17 percent of the European American children were milk-intolerant.[53]

More recent studies indicate that lactose intolerance occurs frequently in adults in many parts of the world.[54] The condition is common in Southeast and East Asia, India, the Mediterranean and the Near East, sub-Saharan Africa, and among Native North and South Americans. The widespread incidence of lactose intolerance should not be surprising. After infancy, mammals normally stop producing lactase.[55]

If lactose intolerance in adulthood in mammals is normal, we need to understand why only some human populations have the ability to make lactase in adulthood and digest lactose. Why would selection favor this genetic ability in some populations but not in others? In the late 1960s, F. J. Simoons and Robert McCracken noted a relationship between lactose absorption and dairying (raising cows for milk). They suggested that, with the advent of dairying, individuals with the genetic ability to produce lactase in adulthood would have greater reproductive success; hence, dairying populations would come to have a high proportion of individuals with the ability to break down lactose.[56]

But people in some dairying societies do not produce lactase in adulthood. Rather, they seem to have developed a cultural solution to the problem of lactase deficiency; they transform their milk into cheese, yogurt, sour cream, and other milk products that are low in lactose. To make these low-lactose products, people separate the lactose-rich whey from the curds or treat the milk with a bacterium (*Lactobacillus*) that breaks down the lactose, thus making the milk product digestible by a lactase-deficient person.[57]

So, why did natural selection favor a biological solution (the production of the enzyme lactase in adulthood) in some dairying societies rather than the cultural solution? William Durham has collected evidence that natural selection may favor the biological solution in dairying societies farther from the equator. The theory is that lactose behaves biochemically like vitamin D, facilitating the absorption of calcium—but only in people who produce lactase so that they can absorb the lactose. Because people in more temperate latitudes are not exposed to that much sunlight, particularly in the winter, and therefore make less vitamin D in their skin, natural selection may have favored the lactase way of absorbing dietary calcium.[58] In other words, natural selection may favor lactase production in adulthood, as well as lighter skin, at higher latitudes (where there is less sunlight).

(Left) Milking a cow in Barnstable, Massachusetts. Natural selection may favor production of the enzyme lactase, a genetic way of making milk digestible in dairying populations far from the equator. (Right) A Masai woman milking a cow in Kenya. Natural selection may favor the souring of milk, a cultural way of making it digestible in dairying populations close to the equator.

This is an example of how culture may influence the way natural selection favors some genes over others. Without dairying, natural selection may not have favored the genetic propensity to produce lactase. This propensity is yet another example of the complex ways in which genes, environment, and culture interact to create human variation.

Race and Racism

Fortunately, internal variations such as lactase deficiency have never been associated with inter-group tensions—perhaps because such differences are not immediately obvious. Unfortunately, the same cannot be said for some of the more obvious external human differences such as skin color.

For as long as any of us can remember, countless aggressive actions—from fistfights to large-scale riots and civil wars—have stemmed from tensions and misunderstandings between various groups commonly referred to by many as "races." *Race* has become such a common term that most of us take the concept for granted, not bothering to consider what it does and does not mean. We may talk about the "human race," which means that all humans belong to the same breeding population. Yet we are often asked to check a box to identify our particular "race." We discuss first how biologists sometimes use the term *race;* then we turn to why most biological anthropologists now conclude that the concept of race does not apply usefully to humans. We discuss how racial classifications are largely social constructions that have been used to justify discrimination, exploitation, and even the extermination of certain categories of people.

Race as a Construct in Biology

Biological variation is not uniformly distributed in any species. Although all members of a species can potentially interbreed with others, most matings take place within smaller groups or breeding populations. Through the processes of natural selection and genetic drift, populations inhabiting different geographic regions will come to exhibit some differences in biological traits. When differences within a species become sufficiently noticeable, biologists may classify different populations into different *varieties,* or *races.* If the term *race* is understood to be just a shorthand or classificatory way that biologists describe slight population variants within a species, the concept of race would probably not be controversial. Unfortunately, as applied to humans, racial classifications have often been confounded with *racism,* the belief that some "races" are innately inferior to others. The misuse and misunderstanding of the term *race* and its association with racist thinking is one reason why many biological anthropologists and others have suggested that the term should not be applied to human biological differences.

A second reason for not applying racial classification to humans is that humans have exhibited so much interbreeding that different populations are not clearly classifiable into discrete groups that can be defined in terms of the presence or absence of particular biological traits.[59] Therefore, many argue that "race" is not scientifically useful for describing human biological variation. The difficulty in employing racial classification is evident by comparing the number of "races" that classifiers come up with. The number of "racial" categories in humans has varied from as few as 3 to more than 37.[60]

How can human groups be clearly divided into "races" if most adaptive biological traits show clines or gradual differences from one region to another?[61] Skin color is a good example of clinal variation. In the area around Egypt, there is a gradient of skin color as one moves from north to south in the Nile Valley. Skin generally becomes darker closer to the equator (south) and lighter closer to the Mediterranean. But other adaptive traits may not have north–south clines because the environmental predictors may be distributed differently. Nose shape varies with humidity, but clines in humidity do not particularly correspond to variation in latitude. So the gradient for skin color would not be the same as the gradient for nose shape. Because adaptive traits tend to be clinally distributed, there is no line you could draw on a world map that would separate "white" from "black" people or "whites" from "Asians."[62] Only traits that are neutral in terms of natural selection will tend (because of genetic drift) to cluster in regions.[63]

Racial classification is problematic also because there is sometimes more physical, physiological, and genetic diversity *within* a single geographic group that might be called a "race" (e.g., Africans) than there is *between* supposed "racial" groups. Africans vary more among themselves than they do in comparison with people elsewhere.[64] Analyses of all human populations have demonstrated that between 93 and 95 percent of genetic variation is due to individual differences within populations, whereas only 3–5 percent of genetic variation is due to differences between major human population groups.[65] "Race," when applied to humans, is a social category, not a scientific one.

Race and Civilization

Many people hold the racist viewpoint that the biological inferiority of certain groups, which they call "races," is reflected in the supposedly "primitive" quality of their cultures. They will argue that the "developed" nations are "white" and the "underdeveloped" nations are not. (We put terms like "white," which are used as racial categories, in quotes to indicate the problematic nature of the categories.) But to make such an argument ignores much of history. Many of today's so-called underdeveloped nations—primarily in Asia, Africa, and South America—had developed complex and sophisticated civilizations long before European nations expanded and acquired considerable power. The advanced societies of the Shang dynasty in China, the Mayans in Mesoamerica, and the African empire of Ghana were all founded and developed by "nonwhites."

Between 1523 and 1028 B.C., China had a complex form of government, armies, metal tools and weapons, and production and storage facilities for large quantities of grain. The early Chinese civilization also had writing and elaborate religious rituals.[66] From A.D. 300 to 900, the Mayans were a large population with a thriving economy. They built many large and beautiful cities in which were centered great pyramids and luxurious palaces.[67] According to legend, the West African civilization of Ghana was founded during the second century A.D. By A.D. 770, the time of the Sonniki rulers, Ghana had developed two capital cities—one Muslim and the other non-Muslim—each with its own ruler and both supported largely by Ghana's lucrative gold market.[68]

Considering how recently northern Europeans developed cities and central governments, it seems odd that some "whites" should label Africans, Native Americans, and others backward in terms of historical achievement, or biologically inferior in terms of

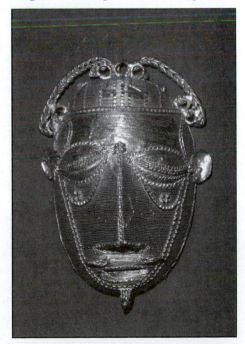

African metal workers created magnificent works of art like this golden head from Ghana long before Europeans arrived.

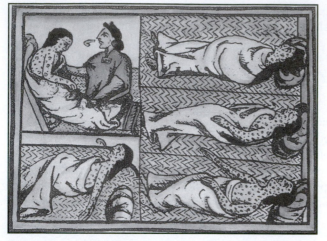

The conquest of the Aztecs was aided by smallpox contracted from the Spanish, which killed at least half the population.

capacity for civilization. But racists, both "white" and "nonwhite," choose to ignore the fact that many populations have achieved remarkable advances in civilization. Most significant, racists refuse to believe that they can acknowledge the achievements of another group without in any way downgrading the achievements of their own.

Race, Conquest, and the Role of Infectious Disease

There are those who would argue that Europeans' superiority accounted for their ability to colonize much of the world during the last few hundred years. But it now appears that Europeans were able to dominate at least partly because many native peoples were susceptible to diseases they introduced.[69] Earlier, we discussed how continued exposure to epidemics of infectious diseases, such as tuberculosis and measles, can cause succeeding generations to acquire a genetic resistance to death from such diseases. Smallpox had a long history in Europe and Africa; genetic resistance eventually made it mostly a survivable childhood disease. But in the New World, it was quite another story. Cortez and the conquistadores were inadvertently aided by smallpox in their attempt to defeat the Aztecs of Mexico. In 1520, a member of Cortez's army unwittingly transmitted smallpox to the natives. The disease spread rapidly, killing at least 50 percent of the population, and so the Aztecs were at a considerable disadvantage in their battling with the Spanish.[70]

Outbreaks of smallpox repeatedly decimated many Native American populations in North America a century or two later. In the early nineteenth century, the Massachusett and Narragansett Indians, with populations of 30,000 and 9,000, respectively, were reduced by smallpox to a few hundred members. Extremely high mortality rates were also noted among the Crow, the Blackfoot, and other Native American groups during the nineteenth century. The germ theory alone may not completely explain these epidemics; Europeans may have deliberately encouraged the spread of one new disease, smallpox, by purposely distributing infected blankets to the natives. Motulsky calls the spread of smallpox "one of the first examples of biological warfare."[71]

Race and Behavior

As an outgrowth of earlier attempts to show that inferior "races" have "primitive" cultures, some scholars have attempted to demonstrate behavioral differences between "races." One of the most active has been psychologist J. Philippe Rushton, whose 1995 book *Race, Evolution, and Behavior* purports to demonstrate behavioral differences between the "Negroid," "Caucasoid," and "Mongoloid" "races" in terms of sexual practices, parenting, social deviance, and family structure, among others.

Rushton argues that these behaviors have a genetic basis rooted in adaptations to particular environments. He suggests that "Negroids" are adapted to the warm environments of East Africa, where humans first evolved, through a reproductive strategy in which individuals have many offspring but put little energy into their children's upbringing and care. This strategy is known in evolutionary theory as *r-selected,* and is well documented among creatures such as fish, reptiles, and even some mammals (rabbits, for example).[72] Rushton further suggests that, as humans left Africa they adapted to the "colder" climates of Asia by adopting a more *K-selected* reproductive strategy, which involves having few offspring but putting lots of energy into their upbringing and care. K-selected strategies are also well documented in the animal world, and it is interesting to note that apes (and humans) are often presented as examples of highly K-selected species.[73]

The data Rushton uses to support his argument come almost entirely from modern nations, many with a history of racial discrimination (such as South Africa, Japan, and the United States). But if genetic differences in behavior do exist among these three "races," differences that have their origins in the exodus of modern humans from Africa more than 100,000 years ago, then those differences should be apparent both between and among all the cultures of the world. That is, "Negroid" cultures should all share behaviors that are clearly different from those of "Caucasoid" cultures; "Caucasoid" cultures should all share behaviors that are different from those of "Mongoloid" cultures; and so on. Do such differences exist?

The authors of this text used information about the 186 cultures composing the Standard Cross-Cultural Sample to test whether Rushton's ideas hold up.[74] We examined 26 separate behaviors that Rushton predicted would differ among the "races." Contrary to Rushton's predictions, most of the behaviors showed no differences between the supposed "racial" groups. Only one of them showed the differences that Rushton predicted, and five of them demonstrated a pattern that was the *opposite* of what Rushton predicted. So Rushton's gross division of humans into three "races" does not generally predict variation in human behavior. The data do not support the belief that it is scientifically useful to distinguish human "races."[75]

Race and Intelligence

The first large-scale intelligence testing in the United States began with the nation's entry into World War I, in 1917. Thousands of draftees were given the so-called alpha and beta IQ tests to determine military assignments. Later, psychologists arranged the test results according to the "racial" categories of "white" and "black" and found what they had expected—"blacks" scored consistently lower than "whites." This result was viewed as scientific proof of the innate intellectual inferiority of "blacks" and was used to justify further discrimination against them, both in and out of the army.[76]

Otto Klineberg's subsequent statistical analyses of IQ test results demonstrated that "blacks" from northern states scored higher than "blacks" from the South. Although dedicated racists explained that this difference was due to the northward migration of innately intelligent "blacks," most academics attributed the result to the influence of superior education and more stimulating environments in the North. When further studies showed that northern "blacks" scored higher than southern "whites," the better-education-in-the-North theory gained support, but again racists insisted such results were due to northward migration by more intelligent "whites."[77]

As a further test of his conclusions, Klineberg gave IQ tests to "black" schoolgirls born and partly raised in the South who had spent varying lengths of time in New York City. He found that the longer the girls had been in the North, the higher their average IQ. In addition to providing support for the belief that "blacks" are not inherently inferior to "whites," these findings suggested that cultural factors can and do influence IQ scores, and that IQ is not a fixed quantity.

The controversy about race and intelligence was fueled again in 1969 by Arthur Jensen.[78] He suggested that, although the IQ scores of American "blacks" overlapped considerably with the IQ scores of "whites," the average score for "blacks" was 15 points lower than the average for

APPLIED ANTHROPOLOGY

The Use of Race in Forensic Anthropology

In this chapter, we have made the point that human "races" are not valid biological entities. There is more genetic variation within alleged "races" than between them, and the characteristics used to define "races" are primarily visual—skin color, hair form, eye form, and the like. Most anthropologists (over 70 percent according to a recent survey) disagree with the statement "There are biological races in the species *Homo sapiens*." Given this fact, it seems odd that many forensic anthropologists still employ "race" as one of the categories for identifying skeletal remains.

Diana Smay and George Armelagos argue that forensic anthropologists still employ the concept of "race" for three primary reasons. First, they suggest that some forensic anthropologists genuinely believe that "race" is a useful analytical tool. For these anthropologists, the fact that it is easy for anyone to categorize others into "races" must mean something is genuine about the concept. Indeed, some forensic anthropologists suggest that they can determine "race" with 80 percent accuracy from skeletal remains (although others argue that, without clear information about the specific geographical location where the remains were found, accuracy drops to less than 20 percent). This leads to a second reason (according to Smay and Armelagos) that may lead forensic anthropologists to employ the "race" concept—it works for them. Within local areas, at least, a well-trained forensic anthropologist can determine whether a skeleton comes from one of the major "race" groups. But as forensic anthropologist Madeleine Hinkes explains: "sometimes it is only the anthropologist's experience that tells

him there is an undefinable 'something' about the skeleton that suggests one race over another"—not a very convincing argument for the analytical utility of "race."

A third reason Smay and Armelagos give for why many forensic anthropologists continue to employ the concept of "race" is that they are asked to do so. As Stanley Rhine points out, "The forensic anthropologist who can tell officials that an unknown skull is, for instance, Hispanic, provides a datum useful in narrowing search parameters. By contrast, the forensic anthropologist who delivers a philosophical lecture to the sheriff on the non-existence of human races is unlikely to be consulted again." But is this a good reason to employ the concept of "race"? Might there be a better way to provide information to police and other officials to help them identify a set of human remains? Alice Brues thinks so. She argues that forensic anthropologists should focus on local, geographic variations among populations that we know do exist and avoid the large "race" categories that we know do not. In Alaska, for example, forensic anthropologists might be able to distinguish between Inuit and Aleut remains, or between Chinese, Japanese, and Polynesian in California. Brues argues that, by lumping the real variation that is present in these local populations into predefined "racial" categories, forensic anthropologists limit their ability to use the full range of variation to identify unique, local variations that might be useful in identifying human remains.

Sources: Brues 1992; Hinkes 1993, 51; Lieberman et al. 2003; Rhine 1993, 55; Smay and Armelagos 2000.

"whites." IQ scores presumably have a large genetic component, so the lower average score for "blacks" implied to Jensen that "blacks" were genetically inferior to "whites." Jensen's arguments were further developed by Richard Herrnstein and Charles Murray in their 1994 book, *The Bell Curve.* Herrnstein and Murray purported to show that the intelligence of an individual was largely inherited and unchangeable throughout the life span, that an individual's success was largely based on intelligence, and that African Americans were likely to remain at the bottom of society because they had less intelligence than European Americans.[79] Herrnstein and Murray appealed to a lot of studies to buttress their argument. But their argument was still faulty. Herrnstein and Murray, like Jensen and others before them, fail to distinguish between a measure, such as a particular IQ test, and what is supposedly being measured, intelligence. If a test only imperfectly measures what it purports to measure, lower average IQ scores merely mean lower scores on that particular IQ test; they do not necessarily reflect lower intelligence.[80]

First, there is widespread recognition now that IQ tests are probably not accurate measures of "intelligence" because they are probably biased in favor of the subculture of those who construct the tests. That is, many of the questions on the test refer to things that "white," middle-class children are familiar with, thus giving such children an advantage.[81] So far, no one has come up with a "culture-fair," or bias-free, test. There is more agreement that, although the IQ test may not measure "intelligence" well, it may predict scholastic success or how well a child will do in the primarily "white"-oriented school system.[82] The tests also do not measure some kinds of intelligence such as social "smarts" and creativity.

A second major problem with a purely genetic interpretation of the IQ difference is that many studies show that IQ scores can be influenced by the social environment. Economically deprived children, whether "black" or "white," will generally score lower than affluent "white" or "black" children. And training of children with low IQ scores clearly improves their test scores.[83] More dramatic evidence is provided by Sandra Scarr and her colleagues. "Black" children adopted by well-off "white" families have IQ scores above the average for "whites." And those "blacks" with more European ancestry do not have higher IQ scores.[84] So the average difference between "blacks" and "whites" in IQ cannot be attributed to a presumed genetic difference. For all we know, the 15-point average difference may be due completely to differences in environment or to test bias. New studies show very subtle effects of the social environment on test and school performance. Simply reminding "blacks" of their "race" before a test causes them to do worse. The difference on the Graduate Record Exam between "blacks" and "whites" disappeared after President Barack Obama's election. These and other results strongly suggest that the pervasive stereotype of "blacks" not performing as well as "whites" (particularly potent prior to Obama's election) caused worse performance among "blacks."[85]

Geneticist Theodosius Dobzhansky reminded us that conclusions about the causes of different levels of achievement on IQ tests cannot be drawn until all people have equal opportunities to develop their potentials. He stressed the need for an open society operating under the democratic ideal, where all people are given an equal opportunity to develop whatever gifts or aptitudes they possess and choose to develop.[86]

The Future of Human Variation

Laboratory fertilization, subsequent transplantation of the embryo, and successful birth have been accomplished with humans and nonhumans. *Cloning*—the exact reproduction of an individual from cellular tissue—has been achieved with frogs, sheep, and other animals. *Genetic engineering*—the substitution of some genes for others—is increasingly practiced in nonhuman organisms. And *stem cells,* which can be induced to grow into any tissue type, are in clinical trials for human use. What are the implications of such practices for the genetic future of humans? Will it really be possible someday to control the genetic makeup of our species? If so, will the effects be positive or negative?

It is interesting to speculate on the development of a "perfect human." Aside from the serious ethical question of who would decide what the perfect human should be like, there is the serious biological question of whether such a development might in the long run be detrimental to the human species, for what is perfectly suited to one physical or social environment may be totally unsuited to another. The collection of physical, emotional, and intellectual attributes that might be "perfect" in the early twenty-first century might be inappropriate in the twenty-second century.[87] Even defects such as the sickle-cell trait may confer advantages under certain conditions, as we have seen.

In the long run, the perpetuation of genetic variability is probably more advantageous than the creation of a "perfect" and invariable human being. In the event of dramatic changes in the world environment, absolute uniformity in the human species might be an evolutionary dead end. Such uniformity might lead to the extinction of the human species if new conditions favored genetic or cultural variations that were no longer present in the species. Perhaps our best hope for maximizing our chances of survival is to tolerate, and even encourage, the persistence of many aspects of human variation, both biological and cultural.[88]

✓●─ **Study** and **Review** on **myanthrolab.com**

Summary

1. Physical variation—variation in the frequencies of physical traits—from one human population to another is the result of one or more of the following factors: adaptation, acclimatization, and the influence of the social or cultural environment.

2. Some physical variations in human populations involve genetic variations that do not appear to be adaptive; other variations, including body build, facial construction, and skin color, may be adapted to variation in climate. Some adaptations to climate do not involve genetic changes, but rather physiological changes that develop during an individual's lifetime. Still other variations, such as the ability to make lactase, may be adapted partially to variation in cultural environment.

3. Most biological anthropologists today agree that "race" is not a useful way of referring to human biological variation because human populations do not unambiguously fall into discrete groups defined by a particular set of biological traits. Physical traits that are adaptive vary clinally, which makes it meaningless to divide humans into discrete "racial" entities. Rather, it is suggested that "racial" classifications are mostly social categories that are presumed to have a biological basis.

4. Perhaps the most controversial aspect of racial discrimination is the relationship supposed between "racial" categories and intelligence. Attempts have been made to show, by IQ tests and other means, the innate intellectual superiority of one "racial" category over another. But there is doubt that IQ tests measure intelligence fairly. Because evidence indicates that IQ scores are influenced by both genes and environment, conclusions about the causes of differences in IQ scores cannot be drawn until all the people being compared have equal opportunities to develop their potentials.

Glossary Terms

acclimatization (p. 60)
adaptation (p. 60)
Allen's rule (p. 63)

Bergmann's rule (p. 62)
Gloger's rule (p. 63)
hypoxia (p. 65)

sickle-cell anemia
  (sicklemia) (p. 69)

Critical Questions

1. Why is skin color used more often than hair or eye color or body proportions in "racial" classifications?
2. If Europeans had been more susceptible to New World and Pacific diseases, would the world be different today?
3. How might studies of natural selection help increase tolerance of other populations?

Read the Original Source on myanthrolab.com

Read the chapter by C. Loring Brace titled "The Concept of Race in Physical Anthropology" on MyAnthroLab. Answer the following questions.

1. What does Brace mean when he states that "'race' is whatever people think it should be"?
2. How do geographic populations (or clines) differ from biological races?
3. How might the concept of "race" limit our ability to understand human variation?

5 Primates: Past and Present

((•─Listen to the **Chapter Audio** on **myanthrolab.com**   [□]─Read on **myanthrolab.com**

H umans belong to the order of Primates. All living primates, including humans, evolved from earlier primates that are now extinct. How do primates differ from other mammals? And what distinguishes humans from the other primates? After discussing these questions, we turn to the evolution of the primates: When, where, and why did the early primates emerge, and how and why did they diverge? Our overview covers the period from about 65 million years ago to the end of the Miocene, a little over 5 million years ago.

Common Primate Traits

All primates belong to the class Mammalia, and they share all the common features of mammals. Except for humans, the bodies of primates are covered with dense hair or fur, which provides insulation. Even humans have hair in various places, though perhaps not always for insulation. Mammals are *warm-blooded;* that is, their body temperature is more or less constantly warm and usually higher than that of the air around them. Almost all mammals give birth to live young that develop to a considerable size within the mother and are nourished by suckling from the mother's mammary glands. The young have a relatively long period of dependence on adults after birth. This period is also a time of learning, for a great deal of adult mammal behavior is learned rather than instinctive. Play is a learning technique common to mammal young and is especially important to primates.

The primates have a number of physical and social traits that set them apart from other mammals. No one of the primates' physical features is unique to primates; animals from other orders share one or more of the following described characteristics. But the complex of all these physical traits is unique to primates.[1]

Many skeletal features of the primates reflect an **arboreal** (tree-living) existence. All primate hind limbs are structured principally to provide support, but the "feet" in most primates can also grasp things (see Figure 5.1). Some primates—orangutans, for instance—can suspend themselves from their hind limbs. The forelimbs are especially flexible, built to withstand both pushing and pulling forces. Each of the hind limbs and forelimbs has one bone in the upper portion and two bones in the lower portion (with the exception of the tarsier). This feature has changed little since the time of the earliest primate ancestors. It has remained in modern primates (although many other mammals have lost it) because the double bones give great mobility for rotating arms and legs.

Another characteristic structure of primates is the clavicle, or collarbone. The clavicle also gives primates great freedom of movement, allowing them to move the shoulders both up and down and back and forth. Although humans obviously do not use this flexibility for arboreal activity, we do use it for other activities. Without a clavicle, we could not throw a spear or a ball; we could not make any fine tools or turn doorknobs if we did not have rotatable forearms.

Primates generally are **omnivorous;** that is, they eat all kinds of food, including insects and small animals, as well as fruits, seeds, leaves, and roots. The teeth of primates reflect this omnivorous diet. The chewing teeth—the *molars* and *premolars*—are unspecialized, particularly in comparison with those of other groups of animals, such as the grazers. The front teeth—the *incisors* and *canines*—are often very specialized, principally in the lower primates. For example, the slender, tightly packed lower incisors and canines in many prosimians form a "dental comb" that the animals use in grooming or for scraping hardened tree gum (which is a food for them) from tree trunks.[2]

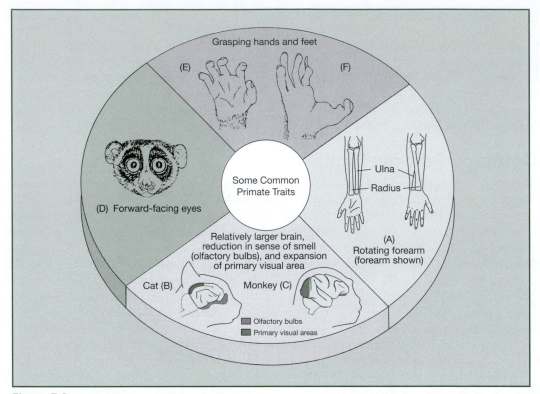

Figure 5.1 Some Common Primate Traits

Sources: (A) From Wolff 1991, 255. Reprinted with permission of D.C. Heath; (B, C) from Deacon 1992, 110; (D) from Cartmill 1992b, 25; and (E, F) from Cartmill 1992b, 24.

Primate hands are extremely flexible. All primates have prehensile—grasping—hands, which can be wrapped around an object. Primates have five digits on both hands and feet (in some cases, one digit may be reduced to a stub), and their nails, with few exceptions, are broad and flat, not clawlike. This structure allows them to grip objects; the hairless, sensitive pads on their fingers, toes, heels, and palms also help them to grip. Most primates have **opposable thumbs,** a feature that allows an even more precise and powerful grip.

Vision is very important to primate life. Compared with other mammals, primates have a relatively larger portion of the brain devoted to vision rather than smell. Primates are characterized by stereoscopic, or depth, vision. Their eyes are directed forward rather than sideways, as in other animals—a trait that allows them to focus on an object (insects or other food or a distant branch) with both eyes at once. Most primates also have color vision, perhaps to recognize when plant foods are ready to eat.

Another important primate feature is a large brain relative to body size. That is, primates generally have larger brains than animals of similar size, perhaps because their survival depends on an enormous amount of learning, as we discuss later. In general, animals with large brains seem to mature more slowly and to live longer than animals with small brains.[3] The more slowly an animal matures and the longer it lives, the more it can learn.

For the most part, primates are social animals. For most primates, particularly those that are **diurnal**—that is, active during the day—group life may be crucial to survival. Social relationships begin with the mother and other adults during the fairly long dependency period of primates. The prolonged dependency of infant monkeys and apes probably offers an evolutionary advantage in that it allows infants more time to observe and learn the complex behaviors essential to survival while enjoying the care and protection of mature adults.

The Various Living Primates

The order Primates is often divided into two suborders: the *prosimians*—literally, premonkeys—and the *anthropoids*. The prosimians include lemurs, lorises, and tarsiers. The anthropoid suborder includes New World monkeys, Old World monkeys, the lesser apes (gibbons, siamangs), the great apes (orangutans, gorillas, and chimpanzees), and humans.

Prosimians

The **prosimians** resemble other mammals more than the anthropoid primates do. For example, the prosimians depend much more on smell for information than do anthropoids. Also in contrast with the anthropoids, they typically have more mobile ears, whiskers, longer snouts, and relatively fixed facial expressions. The prosimians also exhibit many traits shared by all primates, including grasping hands, stereoscopic vision, and enlarged visual centers in the brain.

Lemurlike Forms Lemurs and their relatives, the indris and the aye-ayes, are found only on two island areas off the southeastern coast of Africa: Madagascar and the Comoro Islands. These primates range in size from the mouse lemur to the 4-foot-long indri. Members of the lemur group usually produce single offspring, although twins and even triplets are common in some species. Many of the species in this group are **quadrupeds**—animals that move on all fours; they walk on all fours in the trees as well as on the ground. Some species, such as the indris, use their hind limbs alone to push off from one vertical position to another in a mode of locomotion called **vertical clinging and leaping.** Lemurs are mostly vegetarians, eating fruit, leaves, bark, and flowers. Lemur species vary greatly in their group size. Many lemur species, particularly those that are **nocturnal** (active during the night), are solitary during their active hours. Others are much more social, living in groups ranging in size from a small family to as many as 60 members.[4] An unusual feature of the lemurlike primates is that females often dominate males, particularly over access to food. In most primates, and in most other mammals, female dominance is rarely observed.[5]

A ring-tailed lemur mother and its baby holding on. Prosimians such as ring-tailed lemurs depend much more on smell than do anthropoids. Prosimians also have more mobile ears, whiskers, longer snouts, and relatively fixed facial expressions.

Lorislike Forms Members of the loris group, found in both Southeast Asia and sub-Saharan Africa, are all nocturnal and arboreal. They eat fruit, tree gum, and insects, and usually give birth to single infants.[6] There are two major subfamilies, the lorises and the bush babies (galagos), and they show wide behavioral differences. Bush babies are quick, active animals that hop between branches and tree trunks in the vertical-clinging-and-leaping pattern. On the ground, they often resort to a kangaroo-like hop. Lorises are much slower, walking sedately along branches hand over hand in the quadrupedal fashion.

Tarsiers The nocturnal, tree-living tarsiers, found now only on the islands of the Philippines and Indonesia, are the only primates that depend completely on animal foods. They are usually insect eaters, but they sometimes capture and eat other small animals. They are well equipped for night vision, possessing enormous eyes, extraordinary eyesight, and enlarged visual centers in the brain. The tarsiers get their name from their elongated tarsal bones (the bones of the ankle), which give them tremendous leverage for their long jumps. Tarsiers are very skilled at vertical clinging and leaping. They live in family groups composed of a mated pair and their offspring. Like some higher primates, male and female tarsiers sing together each evening to advertise their territories.[7] The classification of tarsiers is somewhat controversial. Some classifiers group tarsiers with anthropoids rather than with prosimians. Tarsiers have chromosomes similar to those of other prosimians; they also have claws for grooming on some of their toes, more than two nipples, and a uterus shaped like that of other prosimians (two-horned). Tarsiers are more like anthropoids in having a reduced dependence on smell. And, in common with the anthropoids, their eyes are closer together and are protected by bony orbits.[8]

Nocturnal tree-living tarsiers, like this one in the Philippines, are the only primates that depend completely on animal foods. Their enormous eyes equip them to find insects and other prey in the night. Their elongated anklebones (tarsals) make them very good at vertical clinging and leaping.

Anthropoids

The anthropoid suborder includes humans, apes, and monkeys. Most **anthropoids** share several traits in varying degrees. They have rounded braincases; reduced, nonmobile outer ears; and relatively small, flat faces instead of muzzles. They have highly efficient reproductive systems. They also have highly dextrous hands.[9] The anthropoid order is divided into two main groups: **platyrrhines** and **catarrhines** (see Figure 5.2). Platyrrhines have broad, flat-bridged noses, with nostrils facing outward; these monkeys are found only in the New World, in Central and South America. Catarrhines have narrow noses with nostrils facing downward. Catarrhines include monkeys of the Old World (Africa, Asia, and Europe), as well as apes and humans.

New World Monkeys Besides the shape of the nose and the position of the nostrils, other anatomical features distinguish the New World monkeys (platyrrhines) from the catarrhine anthropoids. The New World species have three premolars, whereas the Old World species have two. Some New World monkeys have a **prehensile** (grasping) tail; no Old World monkeys do. All the New World monkeys are completely arboreal; they vary a lot in the size of their groups; and their food ranges from insects to nectar and sap to fruits and leaves.[10]

Two main families of New World monkeys have traditionally been defined. One family, the *callitrichids,* contains marmosets and tamarins; the other family, the *cebids,* contains all

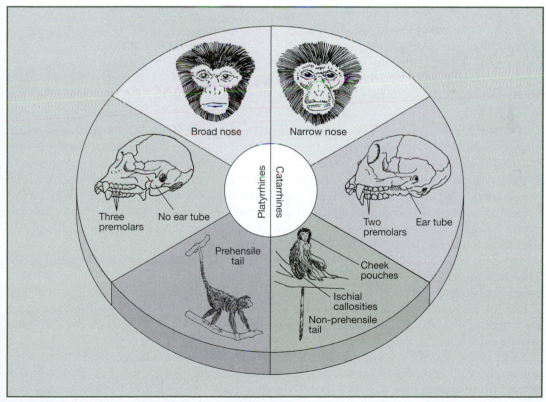

Figure 5.2 **Features of Platyrrhines and Catarrhines**

Source: Boaz and Almquist 1999.

the other New World monkeys. The callitrichids are very small, have claws instead of fin-
gernails, and give birth to twins who mature
in about 2 years. Perhaps because twinning
is so common and the infants have to be carried, callitrichid mothers cannot take care of
them alone. Fathers and older siblings have
often been observed carrying infants. Indeed,
males may do more carrying than females.
Callitrichid groups may contain a mated pair
(monogamy) or a female mated to more than
one male (polyandry). The callitrichids eat a
lot of fruit and tree sap, but like other very
small primates, they obtain a large portion of
their protein requirements from insects.[11]

Cebids are generally larger than callitrichids, take about twice as long to mature, and
tend to bear only one offspring at a time.[12] The
cebids vary widely in size, group composition,
and diet. For example, squirrel monkeys weigh
about 2 pounds, whereas woolly spider monkeys weigh more than 16 pounds. Some cebids
have small groups with one male–female pair;
others have groups of up to 50 individuals.

The squirrel monkey, like all platyrrhines, almost
never leaves the trees. It is well suited to an
arboreal lifestyle; note how it uses both hands
and feet to grasp branches.

Some of the smallest cebids have a diet of leaves, insects, flowers, and fruits, whereas others
are mostly fruit eaters with lesser dependence on seeds, leaves, or insects.[13]

Old World Monkeys The Old World monkeys, or **cercopithecoids,** are related more closely to
humans than to New World monkeys. They have the same number of teeth as apes and humans.
The Old World monkey species are not as diverse as their New World cousins, but they live in
a greater variety of habitats. Some live both in trees and on the ground; others, such as the
gelada baboon, are completely **terrestrial,** or ground-living. Macaques are found both in tropical
jungles and on snow-covered mountains, and they range from the Rock of Gibraltar to Africa to
northern India, Pakistan, and Japan. There are two major subfamilies of Old World monkeys:
the *colobines* and the *cercopithecines.*

The colobines live mostly in trees, and their diet consists principally of leaves and seeds.
Their digestive tracts are equipped to obtain maximum nutrition from a high-cellulose diet; they
have pouched stomachs, which provide a large surface area for breaking down plant food, and
very large intestinal tracts. One of the most noticeable features of colobines is the flamboyant
color typical of newborns. For example, in one species, dusky gray mothers give birth to brilliant
orange babies.[14]

The cercopithecine subfamily of monkeys includes more terrestrial species than any other
subfamily of Old World monkeys. Many of these species are characterized by a great deal of
sexual dimorphism (the sexes look very different); the males are larger, have longer canines,
and are more aggressive than the females. Cercopithecines depend more on fruit than do colobines. They are also more capable of surviving in arid and seasonal environments.[15] Pouches
inside the cheeks allow cercopithecines to store food for later eating and digestion. An unusual

physical feature of these monkeys is the ischial callosities, or callouses, on their bottoms—an adaptation that enables them to sit comfortably in trees or on the ground for long periods of time.[16]

The Hominoids: Apes and Humans

The **hominoid** group includes three separate families: the lesser apes, or **hylobates** (gibbons and siamangs); the great apes, or **pongids** (orangutans, gorillas, and chimpanzees); and humans, or **hominids.** Their brains are relatively large, especially the areas of the cerebral cortex associated with the ability to integrate data. All hominoids have fairly long arms; short, broad trunks; and no tails. The wrist, elbow, and shoulder joints of hominoids allow a greater range of movement than in other primates. Hominoid hands are longer and stronger than those of other primates. These skeletal features probably evolved along with the hominoids' unique abilities in suspensory locomotion. Unlike other anthropoids, who move quadrupedally along the ground or along the tops of tree branches, hominoids often suspend themselves from below the branches and swing or climb hand over hand from branch to branch.[17] This suspensory posture also

This langur, like all catarrhines, has a relatively narrow nose with nostrils that point downward. Langurs are Asian members of the colobine family and are primarily leaf eaters.

translates to locomotion on the ground; all hominoids, at least occasionally, move bipedally, as we discuss in more detail later in this chapter.

The dentition of hominoids demonstrates some unique features as well (see Figure 5.3). Hominoid molars are flat and rounded compared to those of other anthropoids, and have what is called a "Y-5" pattern on the lower molars—that is, the lower molars have five cusps with a Y-shaped groove opening toward the cheek running between them. Other anthropoids have what is called a **bilophodont** pattern—their molars have two ridges or "loafs" running perpendicular to the cheeks. All hominoids except for humans also have long canine teeth that project beyond the tops of the other teeth, and a corresponding space on the opposite jaw, called a **diastema,** where the canine sits when the jaws are closed. The contact of the upper canine and the lower third premolar creates a sharp cutting edge, in part due to the premolar being elongated to accommodate the canine.[18] These dental features are related to the hominoids' diets, which often include both fibrous plant materials, which can be efficiently cut with sharp canines against elongated premolars, and soft fruits, which can be efficiently chewed with wide, flat molars.

A troop of baboons in Ethiopia spends most of its time on the ground.

The skeletal and dental features that the hominoids share point toward their common ancestry. Their proteins and DNA show many similarities, too. This genetic likeness is particularly strong among chimpanzees, gorillas, and humans.[19] For this reason, primatologists think chimpanzees and gorillas are evolutionarily closer to humans than are the lesser apes and orangutans, which probably branched off at some earlier point. We discuss the fossil evidence that supports an early split for the orangutans later in the chapter.

Gibbons and Siamangs　The agile gibbons and their close relatives the siamangs are found in the jungles of Southeast Asia. The gibbons are small, weighing only between 11 and 15 pounds. The siamangs are somewhat larger, but no more than 25 pounds. Both are mostly fruit eaters,

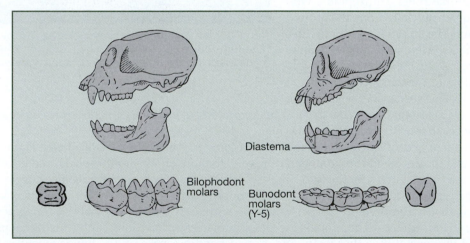

Bilophodont molars

Diastema

Bunodont molars (Y-5)

Figure 5.3 Difference in dentition between an Old World monkey (left) and an ape (right).
In Old World monkeys, the cusps of the lower molars form two parallel ridges; in apes, the five cusps form a Y-shaped pattern. Apes also have a space between the lower canine and first premolar, called a diastema.

Source: Adapted from Boaz and Almquist 1999, 164.

although they also eat leaves and insects. They are spectacular **brachiators;** their long arms and fingers let them swing hand over hand through the trees.[20] A gibbon can move more than 30 feet in a single forward swing.

Gibbons and siamangs live in small family groups consisting of an adult pair, who appear to mate for life, and one or two immature offspring. When the young reach adulthood, they are driven from home by the adults. There is little sexual dimorphism—males and females do not differ in size or appearance—nor is there any clear pattern of dominance by either sex. These lesser apes are also highly territorial; an adult pair advertises their territory by singing and defends it by chasing others away.[21]

Orangutans Orangutans survive only on the islands of Borneo and Sumatra. Unlike gibbons and siamangs, they are clearly recognizable as males or females. Males not only weigh almost twice as much as females (up to 200 pounds), but they also have large cheek pads, throat pouches, beards, and long hair.[22] Like gibbons and siamangs, orangutans are primarily fruit eaters and arboreal. They are the heaviest of the arboreal primates, and perhaps they move slowly and laboriously through the trees for this reason. Orangutans are unusual among the higher primates in that, except for mothers and their young, adults spend much of their time alone.

Gorillas Gorillas are found in the lowland areas of western equatorial Africa and in the mountain areas of Congo, Uganda, and Rwanda.[23] Unlike the other apes, who are mostly fruit eaters, gorillas mostly eat other parts of plants—stems, shoots (e.g., bamboo), pith, leaves, roots, and flowers. In many populations, fruit eating is rare; in some, however, fruit is a common part of the diet.[24]

Gorillas are by far the largest of the surviving apes. In their natural habitats, adult males weigh up to 450 pounds and females up to 250 pounds. To support the weight of massive chests, gorillas travel mostly on the ground on all fours in a form of locomotion known as **knuckle walking:** They

A white-handed gibbon demonstrates its ability as a brachiator.

A young gorilla shows how it knuckle-walks. The back feet are flat on the ground, and only the knuckles of the "hands" touch the ground.

walk on the thickly padded middle joints of their fingers. Gorillas' arms and legs, especially those of the young, are well suited for climbing. As adults, their heavier bodies make climbing more precarious.[25] They sleep on the ground or in tub-shaped nests they make from nonfood plants each time they bed down.[26]

Gorillas tend to live in groups consisting of a dominant male, called a silverback, other adult males, adult females, and immature offspring. Both males and females, when mature, seem to leave the groups into which they were born to join other groups. The dominant male is very much the center of attention; he acts as the main protector of the group and the leader in deciding where the group will go next.[27]

Chimpanzees Chimpanzees live in the forested areas of Africa, from Sierra Leone in the west to Tanzania in the east. There are two distinct species of chimpanzee—the common chimpanzee (*Pan troglodytes*) and the bonobo, or pygmy, chimpanzee (*Pan paniscus*). Bonobos tend to be more slender than common chimpanzees, with longer limbs and digits, smaller heads, darker faces, and a distinct part in their hair. Unlike common chimpanzees, bonobos show almost no sexual dimorphism in dentition or skeletal structure. More significant seem to be differences in social behavior. Bonobos are more gregarious than common chimpanzees, and groups tend to be more stable. Groups also tend to be centered around females rather than males.[28]

Although they are primarily fruit eaters, chimpanzees show many similarities to their close relatives, the gorillas. Both are arboreal and terrestrial. Like gorillas, chimpanzees move best on the ground, and when they want to cover long distances they come down from the trees and move by knuckle walking. Occasionally, they stand and walk upright, usually when they are traveling through tall grass or are trying to see long distances. Chimpanzees sleep in tree nests that they carefully prepare anew, complete with a bunch of leaves as a pillow, each time they bed down.[29]

Chimpanzees (including bonobos) are less sexually dimorphic than the other great apes. Males weigh a little more than 100 pounds on the average, females somewhat less. Males also have longer canines.

After three decades of studies at Gombe National Park in Tanzania and elsewhere, researchers have found that common chimpanzees not only eat insects, small lizards, and birds, but they also actively hunt and kill larger animals.[30] At Gombe, the red colobus monkey is by far the most often hunted animal. Hunting appears to be undertaken more often during the dry season when food is scarce.[31] Prey is caught mostly by the males, which hunt either alone or in small groups. It is then shared with—or, perhaps more accurately, begged by—as many as 15 other chimpanzees in friendly social gatherings that may last up to 9 hours.[32]

A bonobo's slender limbs, dark face, and parted hair are some of the traits that distinguish them from common chimpanzees.

Chimpanzees, though they spend much time in the trees, can also move very quickly on the ground.

Hominids According to the classification we use here, the hominoids we call hominids include only one living species—modern humans. Humans have many distinctive characteristics that set them apart from other anthropoids and other hominoids, which lead many to place humans in a category separate from the pongids. (These traits are discussed throughout much of the rest of the book.) However, others believe that the differences are not so great as to justify a separate hominid category for humans.

Distinctive Hominid Traits

We turn now to some of the features that distinguish us—the hominids—from the other primates. Although we like to think of ourselves as unique, many of the traits we discuss here are at the extreme of a continuum that can be traced from the prosimians through the apes.

Physical Traits

Of all the primates, only hominids consistently walk erect on two feet. All other primates require thick, heavy musculature to hold their heads erect; this structure is missing in hominids, for our heads are more or less balanced on top of our spinal columns. A dish-shaped pelvis (peculiar to hominids), a lumbar curve in the spine, straight lower limbs, and arched, nonprehensile feet are all related to **bipedalism.** Because hominids are fully bipedal, we can carry objects without impairing our locomotor efficiency.

Although many primates have an opposable thumb, which enables them to grasp and examine objects, the greater length and flexibility of the hominid thumb allow us to handle objects with greater dexterity. We are capable of both a power grip, to hold large or heavy objects firmly, and a precision grip, to hold small or delicate objects without dropping or breaking them. We also have remarkable hand–eye coordination, as well as a remarkably sophisticated brain.

The hominid brain is large and complex, particularly the **cerebral cortex,** the center of speech and other higher mental activities. The brain of the average adult modern human measures more than 79 cubic inches (1,300 cubic centimeters), compared with 32 cubic inches (525 cubic centimeters) for the gorilla, the primate with the next largest brain. The frontal areas of the hominid brain are also larger than those of other primates, so that hominids have more prominent foreheads than monkeys or gorillas. Hominids have special areas of the brain that are dedicated to speech and language. The large hominid brain requires an enormous amount of blood, and the way blood is carried to and from the brain is also unique.[33] We'll say more about the hominid brain and its evolution in the next chapter.

Hominid teeth reflect our completely omnivorous diet, and they are not very specialized, which may reflect the fact that we use tools and cooking to prepare our food. As discussed earlier, other hominoids have long canines and a diastema, whereas hominid canines do not usually project beyond the tops of the other teeth. This allows hominids to move their jaws both vertically and horizontally when chewing; horizontal movement would be prevented by the long upper canines of the other hominoids. Hominid molars have thicker enamel than the molars of other hominoids, and both horizontal movement and thickened molars may be related to a dietary emphasis on coarse grains and seeds. The hominid jaw is shaped like a parabolic arch, rather than a U-shape, as in the apes, and is composed of relatively thin bones and light muscles. Modern humans have chins; other primates do not.

One other distinctive hominid trait is the sexuality of hominid females, who may engage in intercourse at any time throughout the year; most other primate females engage in sex only periodically, just around the time they can conceive.[34] Hominids are also unusual among the primates in having female–male bonding.[35]

Why, then, does hominid female sexuality differ from that of most other primates? One suggestion is that more or less continuous female sexuality became selectively advantageous in hominids after female–male bonding developed in conjunction with local groups consisting of at least several adult males and adult females.[36] More specifically, the combination of group living and male–female bonding—a combination unique to hominids among the primates—may have favored a switch from the common higher-primate pattern of periodic female sexuality to the pattern of more or less continuous female sexuality. Such a switch may have been favored in hominids because periodic rather than continuous female sexuality would undermine female–male bonding in multi-male–multi-female groups.

Field research on nonhuman primates strongly suggests that males usually attempt to mate with any females ready to mate. If the female (or females) a male was bonded to was not interested in sex at certain times, but other females in the group were, it seems likely that the male would try to mate with those other females. Frequent "extramarital affairs" might jeopardize the male–female bond and thereby presumably reduce the reproductive success of both males and females. Hence, natural selection may have favored more or less continuous sexuality in hominid females if hominids already had the combination of group living (and the possibility of "extramarital affairs") and marriage. If bonded adults lived alone, as do gibbons, noncontinuous female sexuality would not threaten bonding, because "extramarital" sex would not be likely to occur. Similarly, seasonal breeding would also pose little threat to male–female bonds, because all females would be sexually active at more or less the same time.[37] So the fact that the combination of group living and male–female bonding occurs only in hominids may explain why continuous female sexuality developed in hominids. The bonobo, or pygmy chimpanzee, female does engage in intercourse throughout the year, but bonobos do not have male–female bonding and the females are not interested in sex quite as often as hominid females.[38]

Behavioral Abilities

In comparison with other primates, a much greater proportion of hominid behavior is learned and culturally patterned. As with many physical traits, we can trace a continuum in the learning abilities of all primates. The great apes, including orangutans, gorillas, and chimpanzees, are probably about equal in learning ability.[39] Old and New World monkeys do much less well in learning tests, and, surprisingly, gibbons perform more poorly than most monkeys.

Toolmaking The same kind of continuum is evident in inventiveness and toolmaking. There is no evidence that any nonhuman primates except great apes use tools, although several species of monkeys use "weapons"—branches, stones, or fruit dropped onto predators below them on the ground. Chimpanzees both fashion and use tools in the wild. They strip leaves from sticks and then use the sticks to "fish" termites from their mound-shaped nests. They use leaves to mop up termites, to sponge up water, or to wipe themselves clean. Indeed, tool use varies enough in chimpanzees that primatologist Christophe Boesch has suggested that local chimpanzee groups have cultural differences in terms of the tools they employ.[40]

One example of chimpanzee tool use suggests planning. In Guinea, West Africa, observers watched a number of chimpanzees crack oil palm nuts with two stones. The "platform" stone had a hollow depression; the other stone was used for pounding. The observers assumed that the stones had been brought by the chimpanzees to the palm trees because no stones like them were nearby and the chimps were observed to leave the pounding stone on top of or near the platform stone when they were finished.[41] Observers in other areas of West Africa have also reported that chimpanzees use stones to crack nuts. In one location in Liberia, an innovative female appeared to have started the practice; it seems to have been imitated within a few months by 13 others who previously showed no interest in the practice.[42]

Hominids have usually been considered the only toolmaking animal, but observations such as these call for modification of the definition of toolmaking. If we define toolmaking as adapting a natural object for a specific purpose, then at least some of the great apes are toolmakers too. Perhaps it would be more accurate to say hominids are the only habitual toolmaking animal, just as we say hominids are the only habitual bipedal hominoid, even though the other hominoids all can and do walk bipedally sometimes. As far as we know, though, hominids are unique in their ability to use one tool to make another.

Language Only modern humans have spoken, symbolic language. But, as with toolmaking abilities, the line between modern human language and the communications of other primates is not as sharp as we once thought. In the wild, vervet monkeys make different alarm calls to warn of different predators. Observers playing

Chimps in the wild use tools—in this case, a stone to crack palm nuts. As far as we know, though, they don't use tools to make other tools, as humans do.

tape recordings of these calls found that monkeys responded to them differently, depending on the call. If the monkeys heard an "eagle" call, they looked up; if they heard a "leopard" call, they ran high into the trees.[43]

Common chimpanzees are also communicative, using gestures and many vocalizations in the wild. Researchers have used this "natural talent" to teach chimpanzees symbolic language in experimental settings. In their pioneering work, Beatrice T. Gardner and R. Allen Gardner raised a female chimpanzee named Washoe and trained her to communicate with startling effectiveness by means of American Sign Language hand gestures.[44] After a year of training, she was able to associate gestures with specific activities. For example, if thirsty, Washoe would make the signal for "give me" followed by the one for "drink." As she learned, the instructions grew more detailed. If all she wanted was water, she would merely signal for "drink." But if she craved soda pop, as she did more and more, she prefaced the drink signal with the sweet signal— a quick touching of the tongue with her fingers. Later, the Gardners had even more success in training four other common chimpanzees, who were taught by fluent deaf users of American Sign Language.[45]

Bonobos have provided strong evidence that they understand simple grammatical "rules," very much like 2-year-old humans. Pointing to graphic symbols for different particular meanings, a bonobo named Kanzi regularly communicated sequences of types of symbols; for example, he would point to a symbol for a verb ("bite") and then point to a symbol for an object ("ball," "cherry," or "food").[46]

Other Hominid Traits   Although many primates are omnivores, eating insects and small reptiles in addition to plants—some even hunt small mammals—only hominids hunt very large animals. Also, hominids are one of the few primates that are completely terrestrial. We do not even sleep in trees, as many other ground-living primates do. Perhaps our ancestors lost their perches when the forests receded, or cultural advances such as weapons or fire may have eliminated the need to seek nightly shelter in the trees. In addition, as we have noted, we have the longest dependency period of any of the primates, requiring extensive parental care and support for up to 20 years or so.

Finally, hominids are unlike almost all other primates in having a division of labor by gender in food-getting and food-sharing in adulthood. Among nonhuman primates, both females and males forage for themselves after infancy. Hominids have more gender-role specialization, perhaps because men, unencumbered by infants and small children, were freer to hunt and chase large animals.

Having examined our distinctive traits, those traits we share with other primates, now we turn to the fossil evidence about primate evolution, from the earliest forms to apes.

Reconstruction of *Carpolestes simpsoni,* an arboreal creature from the late Paleocene that may be the common ancestor of the primates.

The Emergence of Primates

When did the primates first emerge? This question turns out to be hard to answer with the current fossil record. Some paleoanthropologists have suggested that fossil finds from the **Paleocene** epoch, which began about 65 million years ago, are from archaic primates. These are the *plesiadapiforms.* They have been found in both Europe and North America, which were one connected landmass in the Paleocene. The best known plesiadapiform is ***Plesiadapis***. This squirrel-like animal had a large snout and large incisors. It also had a large nasal cavity and eye orbits located on the sides of the skull, suggesting a well-developed sense of smell and little or no stereoscopic vision (depth perception). The fingers of *Plesiadapis* had claws, and its hands and feet did not appear to allow for grasping. These features suggest that *Plesiadapis* was not a primate. However, the elbow and ankle joints suggest great mobility, and the teeth suggest a primatelike omnivorous diet despite the large incisors. The structure of their inner ears also resembled that of modern primates. Because it had these primatelike features, some scholars believe that the plesiadipiforms were archaic primates.[47]

Other paleoanthropologists find so few similarities between the plesiadapiforms and later obvious primates that they do not include the plesiadapiforms in the order Primates.[48] There is no dispute, however, about fossils dating from the early **Eocene,** about 55 million years ago. These oldest definite primates appear in two major groups of prosimians—*adapids* and *omomyids.* Because these two kinds of primate are different from each other in major ways, and because they both appeared rather abruptly at the border of the Paleocene and Eocene, there presumably was an earlier common primate ancestor. One strong candidate for the common primate ancestor is *Carpolestes simpsoni,* a mouse-sized arboreal creature from Wyoming dating to about 56 million years ago. ***Carpolestes*** has an interesting mix of primate and nonprimate characteristics. Although it lacks stereoscopic vision, *Carpolestes* has nails instead of claws on its big toes, and it has grasping hands and feet.[49] Not all scholars are convinced that *Carpolestes* is the common ancestor of all primates, and in Figure 5.4, the circled P represents where paleontologist Robert D. Martin placed the common ancestor of primates, in the late Cretaceous.

The Environment

It is generally agreed that the earliest primate may have emerged by the Paleocene, 65 million to 55 million years ago, and perhaps earlier, in the late **Cretaceous.** The beginning of the Paleocene marked a major geological transition, what geologists call the transition from the Mesozoic to the Cenozoic era. About 75 percent of all animal and plant life that lived in the last part of the Cenozoic (the late Cretaceous) vanished by the early Paleocene. The extinction of the dinosaurs is the most famous of these disappearances.[50]

The climate of the Cretaceous period was almost uniformly damp and mild, but temperatures began falling at the end of the Cretaceous. Around the beginning of the Paleocene epoch, both seasonal and geographic fluctuations in temperature began to develop. The climate became much drier in many areas, and vast swamplands disappeared. The climate of the Paleocene was generally somewhat cooler than in the late Cretaceous, but by no means cold. Forests and savannas thrived in fairly high latitudes. Subtropical climates existed as far north as latitude 62 in Alaska.[51]

One important reason for the very different climates of the past is **continental drift** (Figure 5.5). In the early Cretaceous (circa 135 million years ago), the continents were actually clumped into two large landmasses or "supercontinents"—*Laurasia,* which included North America and Eurasia, and *Gondwanaland,* which included Africa, South America, India, Australia,

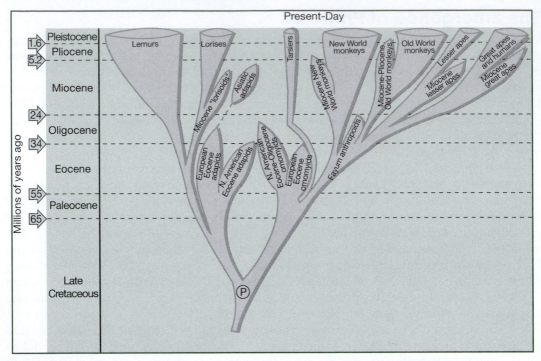

Figure 5.4   A view of the evolutionary relationships between early primates and living primates, adapted from one suggested by R. D. Martin. The primate lineages that do not extend to the present day indicate presumed extinctions. Branching from a common "stalk" suggests divergence from a common ancestor. P represents the unknown common ancestor of all primates.

Source: From Martin 1990. The dates for the Paleocene, Eocene, Oligocene, and the beginning of the Miocene are from Berggren et al. 1992, 29–45. The dates for the end of the Miocene, Pliocene, and Pleistocene are from Jones et al. 1992.

and Antarctica. By the beginning of the Paleocene (circa 65 million years ago), Gondwanaland had broken apart, with South America drifting west away from Africa, India drifting east, and Australia and Antarctica drifting south. As the continents changed position, they moved into locations with different climatic conditions. More importantly, however, the very movement of the continents affected the climate, sometimes on a global scale.[52]

With changes in climate come changes in vegetation. Although the first deciduous trees (that lose their leaves in winter) and flowering plants (called *angiosperms*) arose during the Cretaceous, large trees with large fruits and seeds also became common during the late Paleocene and early Eocene.[53] Although some mammals date from the Cretaceous, the Paleocene saw the evolution and diversification of many different types of mammals, and the expansion and diversification of deciduous trees and flowering plants probably played a large role in mammalian expansion and diversification. Indeed, primate paleontologists think primates evolved from one of these mammalian *radiations*, or extensive diversifications, probably from the **insectivore** order of mammals, including modern shrews and moles, that is adapted to eating insects—insects that would have lived off the new deciduous trees and flowering plants. The insectivores were very adaptable and were able to take advantage of many different habitats—under the ground, in water, on the ground, and above the ground, including the woody habitat of bushes, shrubs, vines, and trees. It was the last kind of adaptation, above

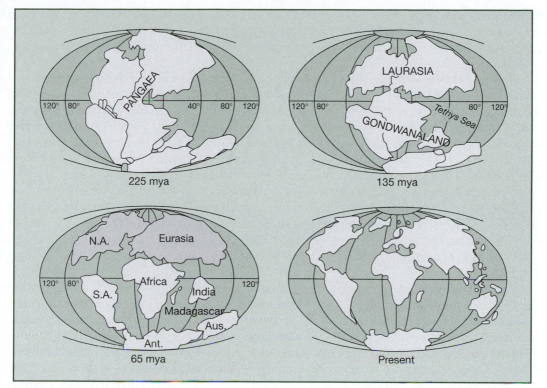

Figure 5.5 **Continental Drift**
The supercontinent Pangea split into Laurasia and Gondwanaland 135 million years ago (mya).
These further divided into the continents as we know them today.

Source: Boaz and Almquist 1999.

the ground, that may have been the most important for primate evolution. The woody habitat had been exploited only partially in earlier periods. But then several different kinds, or taxa, of small animals, one of which may have been the archaic primate, began to take advantage of the woody habitat.

What in Particular May Have Favored the Emergence of Primates?

The traditional explanation of primate origins (the *arboreal theory*) suggests that the primates evolved from insectivores that took to the trees. Different paleoanthropologists emphasized different possible adaptations to life in the trees. In 1912, G. Elliot Smith suggested that taking to the trees favored vision over smell. Vision would be more useful in an animal that searched for food in the maze of tree branches. With smaller snouts and the declining importance of the sense of smell, the eyes of the early primates would have come to face forward. In 1916, Frederic Wood Jones emphasized changes in the hand and foot. He thought that tree climbing would favor grasping hands and feet, with the hind limbs becoming more specialized for support and propulsion. In 1921, Treacher Collins suggested that the eyes of the early primates came to face forward not just because the snout got smaller. Rather, he thought that three-dimensional binocular vision would be favored because an animal jumping from branch to branch would be more likely to survive if it could accurately judge distances across open space.[54] In 1968, Frederick Szalay suggested that a shift in diet—from insects to seeds, fruits, and leaves—might have been important in the differentiation of primates from insectivores.[55]

Arboreal theory still has some proponents, but Matt Cartmill highlighted some crucial weaknesses in the theory.[56] He argued that tree living is not a good explanation for many of the primate features because there are living mammals that dwell in trees but seem to do very well without primatelike characteristics. One of the best examples, Cartmill says, is the tree squirrel. Its eyes are not front-facing, its sense of smell is not reduced in comparison with other rodents, it has claws rather than nails, and it lacks an opposable thumb. Yet these squirrels are very successful in trees. They can leap accurately from tree to tree, they can walk over or under small branches, they can go up and down vertical surfaces, and they can even hang from their hind legs to get food below them. Furthermore, other animals have some primate traits but do not live in trees or do not move around in trees as primates do. For example, carnivores, such as cats, hawks, and owls, have forward-facing eyes, and the chameleon, a reptile, and some Australian marsupial mammals that prey on insects in bushes and shrubs have grasping hands and feet.

Cartmill thinks, then, that some factor other than moving about in trees may account for the emergence of the primates. He proposes that the early primates may have been basically insect eaters, and that three-dimensional vision, grasping hands and feet, and reduced claws may have been selectively advantageous for hunting insects on the slender vines and branches that filled the undergrowth of tropical forests. Three-dimensional vision would allow insect hunters to gauge the prey's distance accurately. Grasping feet would allow predators to move quietly up narrow supports to reach the prey, which could then be grabbed with the hands. Claws, Cartmill argues, would make it difficult to grasp very slender branches. And the sense of smell would have become reduced, not so much because it was no longer useful, but because the location of the eyes at the front of the face would leave less room for a snout. (See the box "Matt Cartmill Reexamines His Own Theory of Primate Origins" for a discussion of Cartmill's recent revision in response to criticisms.)

We still have very little fossil evidence of the earliest primates. *Carpolestes* suggests that grasping hands and feet evolved first, sometime in the late Paleocene, and stereoscopic vision evolved somewhat later. When more fossils become available, we may be better able to evaluate the various explanations that have been suggested for the emergence of primates.

Early Eocene Primates: Omomyids and Adapids

Two groups of prosimians appear in the early Eocene. One group, called **omomyids,** had many tarsierlike features; the other group, **adapids,** had many lemurlike features. The omomyids were very small, no bigger than squirrels; the adapids were kitten- and cat-sized.

Omomyids are considered tarsierlike because of their large eyes, long tarsal bones, and very small size. The large eyes suggest that they were active at night; the smaller-sized omomyids may have been insect eaters and the larger ones may have relied more on fruit.[57] Most of the omomyids had dental formulas characteristic of modern prosimians: two incisors and three premolars on each side of the lower jaw rather than the three incisors and four premolars of early mammals.[58] The importance of vision is apparent in a fossilized skull of the Eocene omomyid *Tetonius.* Imprints in the skull show that the brain had large occipital and temporal lobes, the regions associated with perception and the integration of visual memory.[59]

Matt Cartmill Reexamines His Own Theory of Primate Origins

Matt Cartmill originally conceived his visual predation theory to explain primate origins because he thought that the arboreal theory did not explain enough. Why do other animals, such as tree squirrels, manage very well in the trees, even though they don't have primate traits? Cartmill's theory attracted some criticism. How did he respond?

One criticism, by J. Allman, is that, if visual predation is such an important predictor of forward-facing eyes, then why don't some visual predators have such eyes? Cats and owls have forward-facing eyes, but mongooses and robins do not. A second criticism, by Paul Garber, is that, if claws were disadvantageous for moving on slender branches, why does at least one small primate—the Panamanian tamarin—feed on insects among small twigs and vines but have claws on four of its five digits? And Robert Sussman pointed out that most small nocturnal prosimians eat more fruit than insects. Sussman suggests that the need for precise finger manipulation to grasp small fruits and flowers at the ends of small branches, while hanging on by the hind feet, might favor both clawless digits and grasping extremities.

Cartmill acknowledged these problems and responded to them by revising his theory. He also suggests how new research could test some of the implications of his revised theory.

In regard to the problem of forward-facing eyes, Cartmill says that Allman's own research suggests a solution: namely, that forward-facing eyes are advantageous for seeing something in front more clearly in dim light. Daytime predators have eye pupils that constrict to see ahead more clearly, so fully forward-facing eyes are not necessary for daytime predation. Nocturnal predators relying on sight are more likely to have forward-facing eyes because constricting pupils would be disadvantageous at night. So Cartmill now believes that the earliest primates were probably nocturnal. And he now thinks that they also probably ate fruit (in addition to insects), as Sussman suggests, just as many contemporary nocturnal prosimians do. If they ate fruit and insects at the ends of small branches and twigs, claws may have been disadvantageous. The Panamanian tamarin is not a case to the contrary; it has claws, to be sure, but it also eats tree gum on the tree trunks to which it clings, using its claws as a tree squirrel does.

Cartmill thinks that his modified theory explains the changes in primate vision better than Sussman's theory. For example, how can we explain stereoscopic, forward-facing eyes in the early primates? Sussman says that the early primates were fruit eaters, but Cartmill points out that, although stereoscopic, forward-facing eyes are not necessary for getting nonmoving fruit. Rather, forward-facing eyes might be essential for catching insects.

Cartmill suggests how future research on other arboreal mammals may help us answer some of the remaining questions about the origins of primates. Arboreal marsupials, for instance, tend to have grasping hind feet with clawless divergent first toes, and many have reduced claws on some other toes and fingers. The eyes of arboreal marsupials are also somewhat convergent (not as much, of course, as the eyes of primates). One genus of marsupial, an opossum in South America (*Caluromys*), has many additional primatelike features, including a relatively large brain, more forward-facing eyes, a short snout, and a small number of offspring at one time. Studies by Tab Rasmussen suggest that *Caluromys* fits both Cartmill's and Sussman's theories because it eats fruit on terminal branches and catches insect prey with its hands. More field research on marsupials and other animals with some primatelike habits or features could tell us a lot more. So would new fossil finds.

Sources: Cartmill 1992a; 2009; Rasmussen 1990; Sussman 1991.

The lemurlike adapids were more active during the day and relied more on leaf and fruit vegetation. In contrast to the omomyids, adapid remains show considerable sexual dimorphism in the canines. They also retain the four premolars characteristic of earlier mammals (although with fewer incisors).[60] One adapid known from its abundant fossil finds is *Notharctus*. It had a small, broad face with full stereoscopic vision and a reduced muzzle. It appears to have lived in

An artist's reconstruction of *Notharctus,* a lemurlike primate from the Eocene.

the forest and had long, powerful hind legs for leaping from tree to tree.[61]

There was a great deal of diversity among all mammals during the Eocene epoch, and the primates were no exception. Evolution seems to have proceeded rapidly during those years. Both the omomyids and adapids had a few features that suggest links between them and the anthropoids that appear later, in the Oligocene, but there is no agreement that either group gave rise to the anthropoids.[62] Although the omomyids had some resemblances to modern tarsiers and the adapids had some resemblances to lemurs and lorises, paleoanthropologists are not sure that either group was ancestral to modern prosimians. But it is generally thought that the populations ancestral to lemurs and lorises as well as tarsiers did emerge in the Eocene or even earlier, in the late Paleocene.[63]

The Emergence of Anthropoids

The anthropoids of today—monkeys, apes, and humans—are the most successful living primates and include well over 150 species. Unfortunately, the fossil record documenting the emergence of the anthropoids is extremely spotty, and there is no clear fossil record of the Old World forms (the catarrhines) in the two areas where they are most abundant today—the rain forests of sub-Saharan Africa and Southeast Asia.[64] Some paleoanthropologists think that recent Eocene primate finds from China, Southeast Asia, and Algeria have anthropoid affinities, but there is no clear agreement on their evolutionary status.[65]

Undisputed remains of early anthropoids date from a somewhat later period, the late Eocene and early Oligocene, about 34 million years ago, in the Fayum area, southwest of Cairo, Egypt. One of the earliest fossil primates at Fayum is *Catopithecus,* dating to around 35 million years ago. *Catopithecus* was about the size of a modern marmoset or squirrel monkey. Its dentition suggests a mixed diet of fruit and insects. Its eyes were small, suggesting it was active during the day (diurnal). The few skeletal remains of *Catopithecus* suggest it was an agile arboreal quadruped.[66]

Oligocene Anthropoids

The Fayum is an uninviting area of desert badlands, but it has yielded a remarkable array of early anthropoid fossils. During the **Oligocene** epoch, 34 million to 24 million years ago, the Fayum was a tropical rain forest very close to the shores of the Mediterranean Sea. The area had a warm climate, and it contained many rivers and lakes. The Fayum, in fact, was far more inviting than the northern continents then, for the climates of both North America and Eurasia were beginning to cool during the Oligocene. The general cooling seems to have resulted in the virtual disappearance of primates from the northern areas, at least for a time.

Oligocene anthropoids from the Fayum are grouped into two main types: the monkeylike **parapithecids** and the apelike **propliopithecids.** Dating from 35 million to 31 million years ago, the parapithecids and the propliopithecids had enough features to be unquestionably classified as anthropoids.

Parapithecids The monkeylike parapithecids had three premolars (in each quarter), as do most prosimians and the New World monkeys. They were similar to modern anthropoids, with a bony partition behind the eye sockets, broad incisors, projecting canines, and low, rounded cusps on their molars. But they had prosimianlike premolars and relatively small brains. The parapithecids were small, generally weighing less than 3 pounds, and resembled the squirrel monkeys living now in South and Central America.[67] Their relatively small eye sockets suggest that they were not nocturnal. Their teeth suggest that they ate mostly fruits and seeds. Locomotion is best known from one of the parapithecids, *Apidium,* an arboreal quadruped that also did a considerable amount of leaping.[68] The parapithecids are the earliest definite anthropoid group, and although there is still disagreement among paleoanthropologists, most believe that the emergence of the anthropoids preceded the split between the New World monkeys (platyrrhines) and the Old World monkeys (catarrhines).[69]

That parapithecids may be ancestral to New World monkeys (platyrrhines) raises an interesting puzzle in primate evolution: the origin of the New World monkeys. Anthropoidal primates such as *Dolichocebus,* a small fruit-eating monkey similar to the modern squirrel monkey,[70] appear suddenly and without any apparent ancestors in South America around 25 million years ago. Because the parapithecids predate the appearance of anthropoids in South America, and resemble them in many ways, it seems reasonable to view them as part of the population ancestral to the New World monkeys.[71]

But how did anthropoidal primates get from Africa to South America? Although the continents were closer together in the late Oligocene, when primates first appear in South America, at least 1,864 miles (3,000 kilometers) separated South America and Africa. An extended continental shelf and islands created by lower sea levels in the late Oligocene may have made it possible to "island-hop" from Africa to South America over ocean stretches as short as 125 miles (200 kilometers), but that is still a long distance for an arboreal primate.

Going from Africa to Europe and North America, which were still joined in the late Oligocene, is not a likely route either. North America and South America were not joined until some 5 million years ago, so even if the ancestors of the New World monkeys made it to North America, they would still have needed to make a long ocean crossing to reach South America. One suggestion is that the ancestors of the New World monkeys "rafted" across the Atlantic on large mats of vegetation. Such "rafts" of matted plants, roots, and soil break away from the mouths of major rivers today, and they can be quite large. It seems an unlikely scenario, but many scholars believe such drifting vegetation must have been the means of bringing anthropoids to South America.[72]

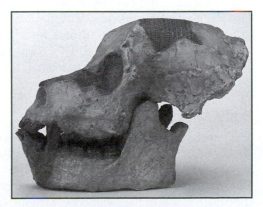

The fossil skull of an *Aegyptopithecus* from the Fayum. Its dentition, small bony eye sockets, and relatively large brain make it an unambiguous ancestor of Old World monkeys and apes.

Propliopithecids The other type of anthropoid found in the Fayum, the propliopithecids, had the dental formula of modern catarrhines. This trait clearly places the propliopithecids with the catarrhines.[73] In contrast with the parapithecids, which had three premolars (in each quarter of the jaw), the propliopithecids had only two premolars, as do modern apes, humans, and Old World monkeys. Propliopithecids shared with the parapithecids the anthropoid dental characteristics of broad lower incisors, projecting canines, and lower molars with low, rounded cusps. And, like parapithecids, propliopithecids had a bony partition behind the eye socket.

Aegyptopithecus, the best-known propliopithecid, probably moved around quadrupedally in the trees, and weighed about 13 pounds. Its molars were low with large cusps, and it had relatively large incisors, suggesting that *Aegyptopithecus* ate mostly fruit. Its eyes were relatively small, and thus it was probably active during the day. It had a long muzzle and a relatively small brain. Endocasts of the brain cavity suggest *Aegyptopithecus* had a relatively large area of the brain dedicated to vision and a relatively small area dedicated to smell. The skulls of *Aegyptopithecus* show considerable sexual dimorphism, and individuals also changed dramatically as they aged, developing bony ridges along the top and across the back of the skull, much like modern great apes. Although its teeth, jaws, and some aspects of the skull were apelike, the rest of *Aegyptopithecus*'s skeleton was monkeylike,[74] and most scholars classify them as primitive catarrhines. Because the propliopithecids lack the specialized characteristics of living Old World monkeys and apes (catarrhines), but share the dental formula of the catarrhines, some paleoanthropologists think that the propliopithecids included the ancestor of both the Old World monkeys and the hominoids (apes and humans).[75]

The Emergence of Hominoids

During the **Miocene** epoch, 24 million to 5.2 million years ago, monkeys and apes clearly diverged in appearance, and numerous kinds of apes appeared in Europe, Asia, and Africa. In the early Miocene, the temperatures were considerably warmer than in the Oligocene. From early to late Miocene, conditions became drier, particularly in East Africa. The reasons for this relate again to continental drift. By about 18 million years ago, Africa came into contact with Eurasia, ending the moderating effect that the Tethys Sea, which separated Africa from Eurasia, had on the climates of both continents. The contact of Africa and, more significantly, India with the Eurasian continent also initiated mountain building, changing established weather patterns. The overall effect was that southern Eurasia and eastern Africa became considerably drier than they had been. Once again, these changes appear to have significantly influenced primate evolution.

Early Miocene Proto-Apes

Most of the fossils from the early Miocene are described as proto-apes. They have been found mostly in Africa. The best-known genus is **Proconsul,** found in sites in Kenya and Uganda that are about 20 million years old.[76]

All of the various *Proconsul* species that have been found were much bigger than any of the anthropoids of the Oligocene, ranging from about the size of a gibbon to that of a female gorilla.[77] They lacked a tail. That lack is one of the most definitive features of hominoids, and most paleoanthropologists now agree that *Proconsul* was definitely hominoid, but quite unlike any ape living today. Modern hominoids have many anatomical features of the shoulder, elbow, wrists, and fingers that are adapted for locomotion by suspension (brachiation). Suspension was apparently not *Proconsul's* method of getting around. Its elbows, wrists, and fingers may have permitted brachiation,[78] but, like the Oligocene anthropoids, *Proconsul* was primarily an arboreal quadruped. Some of the larger forms may have sometimes moved on the ground. Judging by teeth, most *Proconsul* species appear to have been fruit eaters, but larger species may have also consumed leaves.[79]

Middle Miocene Apes

The first definitely apelike finds come from the middle Miocene, 16 million to 10 million years ago.

An artist's reconstruction of *Proconsul,* a Miocene proto-ape.

The oldest, dating to about 13 million years ago, is **Pierolapithecus,** and was recently found near Barcelona, Spain.[80] Another hominoid, **Kenyapithecus,** was found on Maboko Island and nearby locations in Kenya.[81]

Both *Pierolapithecus* and *Kenyapithecus* have many of *Proconsul's* features, but have teeth and faces that resemble those of more modern hominoids. And, in contrast to *Proconsul, Kenyapithecus* was probably more terrestrial. It also had very thickly enameled teeth and robust jaws, suggesting a diet of hard, tough foods, or possibly a great deal of grit in the food because *Kenyapithecus* lived mostly on the ground. Whether *Kenyapithecus* is ancestral to the later apes and humans is something of a puzzle because its limbs do not show the capacity for brachiation that is characteristic of all the later apes.[82] *Pierolapithecus,* however, has wrists and vertebrae that would have made it capable of brachiation, but also has relatively short fingers like modern monkeys. *Pierolapithecus* probably spent most of its time in trees, walking along larger branches as monkeys do, and also brachiating among smaller branches, as apes do.[83] Thus, *Pierolapithecus* is a good candidate for the ancestor of later forest-dwelling apes.

Late Miocene Apes

From the end of the middle Miocene into the late Miocene, the apes diversified and moved into many areas. Fossils are abundant in Europe and Asia, less so in Africa. This does not mean that apes were more numerous than monkeys. In fact, the fossil record suggests that monkeys in the Old World became more and more numerous than apes toward the end of the Miocene, and this trend continues to the present day.

One well-known late Miocene ape from Europe is *Oreopithecus*, which dates from about 8 million years ago. It is particularly interesting because, despite being well represented by fossils, including nearly complete ones preserved in beds of hard coal, its classification is enigmatic. *Oreopithecus* was clearly adapted to life in thickly forested marshlands. It had extremely long arms and hands and mobile joints, and was likely an agile brachiator. Its dentition suggests it had a diet that consisted mostly of leaves. However, the dentition and skull of *Oreopithecus* also had a number of unique features that suggest affinity to some Old World monkeys. In short, *Oreopithecus* had an apelike body and a monkeylike head. Because of its suspensory locomotion and other apelike features, most scholars today consider it an early, albeit specialized, ape.[84]

Most paleoanthropologists divide the later Miocene apes into at least two main groups: the sivapithecids, represented primarily by the genus *Sivapithecus* and found primarily in western and southern Asia, and the dryopithecids, represented primarily by the genus *Dryopithecus* and found primarily in Europe.

Sivapithecids At one time, ***Sivapithecus,*** which dates from roughly 13 million to 8 million years ago, was thought to be ancestral to hominids. It had flat and thickly enameled molars, smaller canines, and less sexual dimorphism than other Miocene apes, and had a parabolic dental arcade in some reconstructions (now considered faulty)—all hominid features. It also lived in a mixed woodland–grassland environment. However, as more fossil material was uncovered, scholars recognized that *Sivapithecus* was remarkably similar to the modern orangutan in the face, and it is now thought to be ancestral to the orangutan.[85]

Dryopithecids ***Dryopithecus,*** which appears about 15 million years ago, was a chimpanzee-sized ape that lived in the forests of Eurasia. It was mainly arboreal and apparently omnivorous. *Dryopithecus* had thinner tooth enamel than *Sivapithecus*, lighter jaws, and pointed molar cusps. In the palate, jaw, and mid face, *Dryopithecus* looked like the African apes and humans. In contrast to later hominoids, however, *Dryopithecus* had a very short face and a relatively small brow ridge.[86]

The fingers and elbows of *Dryopithecus* and *Sivapithecus* suggest that they were much more capable of suspending themselves than were earlier hominoids. *Sivapithecus* may have moved about more on the ground than *Dryopithecus,* but both were probably mostly arboreal.[87] Indeed, recent finds of *Dryopithecus* hand, arm, shoulder, and leg bones strongly suggest that *Dryopithecus* was highly efficient at suspensory locomotion and probably moved through the trees like modern orangutans do.

It is still very difficult to identify the particular evolutionary lines leading from the Miocene apes to modern apes and humans. Only the orangutans have been linked to a late Miocene ape genus, *Sivapithecus*, so presumably that lineage continued into modern times.[88] *Dryopithecus* disappears from the fossil record after about 10 million years ago, leaving no descendants, perhaps because less rainfall and more seasonality reduced the forests where they lived.[89]

The Divergence of Hominids from the Other Hominoids

The later Miocene apes are best known from Europe and Asia. Until recently, there has been an almost complete lack of African fossil hominoids dating between 13.5 million and 5 million years ago.[90] Recently, two species, *Orrorin tugenensis,* from Kenya and dated to about 6 million years ago, and *Sahelanthropus tchadensis,* from Chad and dated to perhaps 7 million years ago, have provided a glimpse of hominoid evolution during this time period. Still, this scarcity of fossils from 13.5 to 5 million years ago is unfortunate for our understanding of human evolution because the earliest unambiguous bipedal primates (hominids) appear in Africa near the beginning of the Pliocene, after 5 million years ago. To understand the evolutionary links between the apes of the Miocene and the hominids of Africa, we need more fossil evidence from late Miocene times in Africa.

✔●─Study and Review on myanthrolab.com

Summary

1. Although no living primate can be a direct ancestor of humans, we do share a common evolutionary history with the other surviving primates. Studying the behavioral and anatomical features of our closest living relatives may help us make inferences about primate evolution. Studying distinctive human traits may help us understand why the line of primates that led to humans branched away from the line leading to chimpanzees and gorillas.

2. No one trait is unique to primates. However, primates do share the following features: two bones in the lower part of the leg and in the forearm, a collarbone, flexible prehensile (grasping) hands, stereoscopic vision, a relatively large brain, only one (or sometimes two) offspring at a time, long maturation of the young, and a high degree of dependence on social life and learning.

3. The order Primates is divided into two suborders: the prosimians and the anthropoids. Compared with the anthropoids, prosimians depend more on smell for information. They have mobile ears, whiskers, longer snouts typically, and relatively fixed facial expressions. Anthropoids have rounded braincases; reduced, nonmobile outer ears; and relatively small, flat faces instead of muzzles. They have highly dextrous hands.

4. The Anthropoid order is divided into two main groups: platyrrhines (monkeys of the New World) and catarrhines. The catarrhines are subdivided into cercopithecoids (Old World monkeys) and hominoids (apes and humans). The anthropoid apes consist of the hylobates, or lesser apes (gibbons and siamangs), and the pongids, or great apes (orangutans, gorillas, and chimpanzees).

5. Along with the gorilla, the chimpanzee has proteins and DNA remarkably similar to those of humans, as well as anatomical and behavioral similarities to humans. Wild chimpanzees have been seen to create and use tools, modifying a natural object to fulfill a specific purpose. High conceptual ability is also demonstrated by both the chimpanzee's and the gorilla's facility in learning sign language.

6. The differences between hominids and the other anthropoids show us what makes humans distinctive as a species. Hominids are totally bipedal; they walk on two legs and do not need the arms for locomotion. The hominid brain, particularly the cerebral cortex, is the largest and most complex. Hominid offspring have a proportionately longer dependency stage. And in comparison with other primates, more hominid behavior is learned and culturally patterned. Spoken, symbolic language and the use of tools to make other tools are uniquely modern human behavioral traits. Hominids also generally have a division of labor in food-getting and food-sharing in adulthood.

7. The surviving primates—prosimians, New World monkeys, Old World monkeys, apes, and humans—are thought to be descendants of small, originally terrestrial insectivores (the order, or major grouping, of mammals, including modern shrews and moles, that is adapted to feeding on insects). However, exactly who the common ancestor was and when it emerged are not yet known.

8. The earliest definite primates, dating from the early Eocene, about 55 million years ago, are definitely primates. They are classified into two major groups of prosimians—adapids and omomyids. These two kinds of primates have major differences so their common ancestor would have had to emerge earlier, probably in the Paleocene.

9. The traditional view of primate evolution was that arboreal (tree) life would have favored many of the common primate features, including distinctive dentition, greater reliance on vision over smell, three-dimensional binocular vision, and grasping hands and feet. Another theory proposes that some of the distinctive primate characteristics were selectively advantageous for hunting insects on the slender vines and branches that filled the undergrowth of forests.

10. Undisputed remains of early anthropoids unearthed in Egypt date from the early Oligocene (after 34 million years ago). They include the monkeylike parapithecids and the propliopithecids with apelike teeth.

11. During the Miocene epoch (24 million to 5.2 million years ago), monkeys and apes clearly diverged in appearance, and numerous kinds of apes appeared in Europe, Asia, and Africa. Most of the fossils from the early Miocene are described as proto-apes. From the end of the middle Miocene into the late Miocene, the apes diversified and spread geographically. Most paleoanthropologists divide the later Miocene apes into at least two main groups: dryopithecids, found primarily in Europe, and sivapithecids, found primarily in western and southern Asia.

Glossary Terms

adapid (p. 98)
Aegyptopithecus (p. 102)
anthropoids (p. 85)
arboreal (p. 81)
bilophodont (p. 87)
bipedalism (p. 91)
brachiators (p. 89)
Carpolestes (p. 95)
catarrhines (p. 85)
cercopithecoids (p. 86)
cerebral cortex (p. 92)
continental drift (p. 95)
Cretaceous (p. 95)
diastema (p. 87)
diurnal (p. 83)

Dryopithecus (p. 104)
Eocene (p. 95)
hominids (p. 87)
hominoid (p. 87)
hylobates (p. 87)
insectivore (p. 96)
Kenyapithecus (p. 103)
knuckle walking (p. 89)
Miocene (p. 102)
nocturnal (p. 83)
Oligocene (p. 100)
omnivorous (p. 81)
opposable thumbs (p. 82)
omomyid (p. 98)
Paleocene (p. 95)

parapithecids (p. 101)
Pierolapithecus (p. 103)
platyrrhines (p. 85)
Plesiadapis (p. 95)
pongids (p. 87)
prehensile (p. 85)
Proconsul (p. 102)
propliopithecids (p. 101)
prosimians (p. 83)
quadrupeds (p. 83)
sexual dimorphism (p. 86)
Sivapithecus (p. 104)
terrestrial (p. 86)
vertical clinging
   and leaping (p. 83)

Critical Questions

1. How could you infer that a fossil primate lived in the trees?

2. We like to think of the human lineage as biologically unique, which of course it is (like all evolutionary lineages). But some paleoanthropologists say that humans, chimpanzees, and gorillas are so similar that all three should be grouped as hominids. What do you think, and why do you think so?

3. Why might humans have the longest period of childhood among the primates?

▌●▐ **Read** the **Original Source** on **myanthrolab.com**

Read the chapter by Craig B. Stanford titled "Chimpanzee Hunting Behavior and Human Evolution" on MyAnthroLab. Answer the following questions.

1. How might the study of chimpanzee behavior, and particularly hunting behavior, benefit our understanding of early hominid behavior and of human evolution in general?

2. For many years chimpanzees were thought to be vegetarians. Why did it take so long for chimpanzee hunting to be identified and studied?

3. What do you think is the best answer to the question "Why do chimpanzees hunt"?

6 The First Hominids and the Emergence of *Homo*

B ipedal locomotion is a defining feature of the hominids. Undisputed bipedal hominids lived in East Africa about 4 million years ago. These hominids, and some others who may have lived later in eastern and southern Africa, are generally classified in the genus *Australopithecus*. In this chapter, we discuss what we know or suspect about the transition from hominoids to hominids, the emergence of australopithecines, and their relationship to later hominids, including ourselves. Then we turn to early hominid tools and lifestyles.

The Evolution of Bipedal Locomotion

Perhaps the most crucial change in early hominid evolution was the development of *bipedal locomotion,* or walking on two legs. We know from the fossil record that other important physical changes—including the expansion of the brain, modification of the female pelvis to allow bigger-brained babies to be born, and reduction of the face, teeth, and jaws—did not occur until about 2 million years after the emergence of bipedalism. Other human characteristics, such as an extended period of infant and child dependency and increased meat-eating, may also have developed after that time.

We do not know whether bipedalism developed quickly or gradually, because the fossil record for the period between 8 million and 4 million years ago is very skimpy. We do know, on the basis of their skeletal anatomy, that many of the Miocene anthropoids were capable of assuming an upright posture. For example, *brachiation,* swinging by the arms through the trees, puts an animal in an upright position; so does climbing up and down trees with the use of grasping hands and feet.[1] It is also likely that the protohominids were capable of occasional bipedalism, just as many modern monkeys and apes are.[2]

Definitely bipedal hominids emerged in Africa, judging by the available fossil record. The emergence of bipedal hominids coincides with a change about 16 million to 11 million years ago from extensive tropical forest cover to more discontinuous patches of forest and open country.[3] Gradually, the African rain forests, deprived of intense humidity and rainfall, dwindled in extent; areas of **savanna** (grasslands) and scattered deciduous woodlands became more common. The tree-dwelling primates did not completely lose their customary habitats because some tropical forests remained in wetter regions, and natural selection continued to favor the better-adapted tree dwellers in those forested areas. But the new, more open country probably favored characteristics adapted to ground living in some primates as well as other animals. In the evolutionary line leading to humans, these adaptations included bipedalism.

Theories for the Evolution of Bipedalism

What may have favored the emergence of bipedal hominids? One early idea is that bipedalism was adaptive for life amid the tall grasses of the savannas because an erect posture may have made it easier to spot ground predators as well as potential prey.[4] But baboons and some other Old World monkeys also live in savanna environments, yet, although they occasionally stand erect, they have not evolved fully bipedal locomotion. And recent evidence suggests that the area where early hominids lived in East Africa was not predominantly savanna; rather, it seems to have been a mix of woodland and open country.[5]

Other theories stress the importance of freeing the hands to perform other activities at the same time. Gordon Hewes emphasized the importance of carrying hunted or scavenged meat,[6] but many paleoanthropologists now question whether early hominids hunted or even scavenged.[7]

However, the ability to carry any food to a place safe from predators may have been one of the more important advantages of bipedalism. C. Owen Lovejoy has suggested that food carrying might have been important for another reason. If males provisioned females and their babies by carrying food back to a home base, the females would have been able to conserve energy by not traveling and therefore might have been able to produce and care for more babies.[8]

But carrying food or provisioning families might not have been the only benefit of freeing the hands; feeding itself may have been more efficient. Clifford Jolly has argued that bipedalism would have allowed early hominids to efficiently harvest small seeds and nuts because both hands could be used to pick up food and move it directly to the mouth.[9] In the changing environments of East Africa, where forests were giving way to more open woodlands and savannas, an advantage in foraging for small seeds and nuts might well have proven important for survival, and thus have been favored by natural selection.

Bipedalism might also have been favored by natural selection because the freeing of the hands would allow protohominids to use, and perhaps even make, tools that they could carry with them. Sherwood Washburn noted that some contemporary ground-living primates dig for roots to eat, "and if they could use a stone or a stick they might easily double their food supply."[10] David Pilbeam suggested that tool use by the more open-country primates may have appreciably increased the number and amount of plant foods they could eat: In order to be eaten, many of the plant foods in the grassy areas probably had to be chopped, crushed, or otherwise prepared with the aid of tools.[11] Tools may also have been used to kill and butcher animals for food. Without tools, primates in general are not well equipped physically for regular hunting or even scavenging.

Mary Leakey's expedition discovered a trail about 70 yards long of 3.8-million-year-old fossilized footprints at Laetoli, Tanzania. Shown here is one part of the trail left by two adults who were clearly upright walkers. The footprints shows a well-developed arch and forward-facing big toe.

Their teeth and jaws are not sharp and strong enough, and their speed afoot is not fast enough. Finally, tools may have been used as weapons against predators, which would have been a great threat to the relatively defenseless ground-dwelling protohominids. In Milford Wolpoff's opinion, it was the advantage of carrying weapons *continuously* that was responsible for transforming occasional bipedalism to completely bipedal locomotion.[12] In particular, Sue Savage-Rumbaugh has suggested that the ability to abduct or snap the wrist would have permitted early humans "to perfect both throwing and rock-striking skills [for toolmaking] and consequently to develop throwing as a much more effective predator defense system than apes could ever manage."[13]

But some anthropologists question the idea that tool use and toolmaking favored bipedalism. They point out that the first clear evidence of stone tools appears more than 2 million years *after* the emergence of bipedalism. So how could toolmaking be responsible for bipedalism? Wolpoff suggests an answer. Even though bipedalism appears to be at least 2 million years older than stone tools, it is not unlikely that protohominids used tools made of wood and bone, neither of which would be as likely as stone to survive in the archaeological record. Moreover, unmodified stone tools present in the archaeological record might not be recognizable as tools.[14]

Some researchers have taken a closer look at the mechanics of bipedal locomotion to see if it might be a more efficient form of locomotion in the savanna-woodland environment, where resources are likely to be scattered. Compared with the quadrupedal locomotion of primates such as chimpanzees, bipedalism appears to be more efficient for long distances.[15] But why travel long distances? If the ancestors of humans had the manipulative ability and tool-using capability of modern chimpanzees (e.g., using stones to crack nuts), and those ancestors had to move around in a more open environment, then those individuals who could efficiently travel longer distances to exploit those resources might do better.[16]

Finally, bipedalism might have been favored by natural selection as a way of regulating body temperature, particularly in the increasingly hot and dry environments of East Africa at the end of the Miocene and the beginning of the Pliocene. Peter Wheeler has argued that a bipedal posture limits the area of the body directly exposed to the sun, especially when the sun is at its hottest, at midday.[17] Bipedal posture would also facilitate convective heat loss by allowing heat to rise up and away from the body rather than being trapped underneath it. Cooling through the evaporation of sweat would also be facilitated by a bipedal posture, as more skin area would be exposed to cooling winds. Thus, natural selection may have favored bipedalism because it reduced heat stress in the warming environments of East Africa.

All theories about the origin of bipedalism are speculative. We do not yet have direct evidence that any of the factors we have discussed were actually responsible for bipedalism. Any or all of the factors may explain the transformation of an occasionally bipedal protohominid to a completely bipedal hominid.

The "Costs" of Bipedalism

We must remember that there are also "costs" to bipedal walking. Bipedalism makes it harder to overcome gravity to supply the brain with sufficient blood,[18] and the weight of the body above the pelvis and lower limbs puts greater stress on the hips, lower back, knees, and feet. As Adrienne Zihlman points out, the stresses on the lower body are even greater for pregnant and nursing females who carry their infants.[19]

We must also remember that the evolution of bipedalism required some dramatic changes in the ancestral ape skeleton. Although apes today can and do walk bipedally, they cannot do so efficiently or for long periods of time. To be habitually bipedal, the ancestral ape skeleton had to be modified, and the major changes that allowed the early hominids to become fully bipedal occurred primarily in the skull, pelvis, knees, and feet.[20] Let's take a look at each of these changes.

In both ancient and modern apes, the spinal column enters the skull toward the back, which makes sense because apes generally walk on all fours, with the spine roughly parallel to the ground. In bipedal hominids, the spinal column enters the skull at the bottom, through a hole called the **foramen magnum**. Thus, when hominids became bipedal, the skull ended up on top of the spinal column.

The shape of ancient and modern ape pelvises is considerably different from that of a bipedal hominid. Ape pelvises are long and flat, forming a bony plate in the lower back to which the leg muscles attach. In bipedal hominids, the pelvis is bowl-shaped, which supports the internal organs and also lowers the body's center of gravity, allowing better balance on the legs. The hominid pelvis also provides a different set of muscle attachments and shifts the orientation of the femurs (the upper leg bones) from the side of the pelvis to the front. These changes allow hominids to move their legs forward in a bipedal stride (and do things like kick a soccer ball). Apes, in comparison, move their legs forward (when they walk bipedally) by shifting their pelvis from side to side, not by kicking each leg forward alternately as we do.[21]

Another change associated with the hominid ability to kick the leg forward is our "knock-kneed" posture. Ape legs hang straight down from the pelvis. Bipedal hominid legs, on the other hand, angle inward toward one another. This configuration not only helps us move our legs forward but also helps us maintain a center of gravity in the midline of our bodies, so that our center of gravity does not shift from side to side when we walk or run.

Finally, the feet of bipedal hominids have two major changes compared to those of apes. First, hominid feet have an enlarged group of ankle bones forming a robust heel that can withstand the substantial forces placed on them as a result of habitual bipedalism. Second, hominid feet have an arch, which also aids in absorbing the forces endured by the feet during bipedal locomotion. ("Flat-footed" people who lack it have chronic problems in their feet, ankles, knees, and back).[22]

We don't know for sure when these changes took place, but fossils from East Africa—Ethiopia, Tanzania, and Kenya—clearly show that bipedal hominids lived there between 4 million and 5 million years ago.

The Transition from Hominoids to Hominids

Western Chad, in north-central Africa, and its windswept deserts do not seem a likely place to find fossil apes or hominids, but paleoanthropologist Michel Brunet thinks it might be.[23] Western Chad was covered by an ancient lake, and for several million years was a location where forest-dwelling mammals, including primates, congregated. Around 7 million years ago, a primate called *Sahelanthropus tchadensis* lived on the shores of the lake, where Brunet and his colleagues recovered its fossilized bones in 2001. *Sahelanthropus,* represented by an almost complete skull, has a unique mix of hominid and hominoid traits. Although the skull itself is hominoid, with a small brain, large brow ridges, and wide face, the teeth seem more hominidlike, especially the canines, which do not project below the tooth row.[24] Unfortunately, there is no evidence that *Sahelanthropus* was bipedal. For now, we have to wait for additional evidence to know whether *Sahelanthropus* was the first bipedal ape.

There is, however, tantalizing evidence that another possible early hominid, **Orrorin tugenensis,** was bipedal. Discovered in western Kenya by Brigitte Senut and colleagues in 1998, *Orrorin tugenensis* consists of 19 specimens of jaw, teeth, finger, arm, and leg bones, including the top of a femur.[25] The femur in *Orrorin,* according to Brian Richmond and William Jungers, shows adaptations to bipedalism, including a long, angled "head" (or top).[26] *Orrorin* dates between 5.8 and 6 million years, so it may turn out to be the earliest hominid if further research supports *Orrorin* bipedalism.

In 1992, a team of researchers led by anthropologist Tim White began surveying a

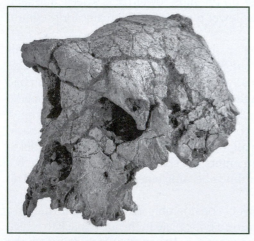

Reconstructed skull of *Sahelanthropus tchadensis,* possibly the earliest hominid, dating to almost 7 million years ago.

4.4-million-year-old fossil deposit at Aramis, in the Middle Awash region of Ethiopia. There, they discovered 17 fossils of what may be the earliest hominid (more have been found since, including some fragments dating perhaps as early as 5.8 million years ago): *Ardipithecus ramidus.*[27]

What makes **Ardipithecus ramidus** unique is the combination of apelike dentition along with evidence of bipedal locomotion and an overall hominidlike skeleton. Like apes, *Ardipithecus* has relatively small cheek teeth with thin enamel and relatively large canines. However, its arm bones seem hominidlike, and the base of its skull shows the foramen magnum positioned underneath the skull, just as in definitely bipedal hominids.[28] The feet of *Ardipithecus* also seem adapted to bipedalism.[29] Although more evidence is needed to be sure, *Ardipithecus* may be the earliest hominid yet found.

Australopithecus: The First Definite Hominid

Although some doubt remains about the status of *Ardipithecus* as a hominid genus, there is no doubt that the australopithecines (members of the genus **Australopithecus**) dating from about 4 million years ago in eastern Africa were hominids. Their teeth share the basic hominid characteristics of small canines, flat and thickly enameled molars, and a parabolic dental arch, and there is unambiguous evidence that even the earliest australopithecines were fully bipedal. Not only do their skeletons reflect bipedal locomotion, but at Laetoli, Tanzania, more than 50 hardened humanlike footprints about 3.6 million years old give striking confirmation that the hominids there were fully bipedal. However, all of the australopithecines, including the later ones, seem also to have been capable of climbing and moving in trees, judging by arm versus leg length and other skeletal features.[30]

Most scholars divide the various australopithecine species into two groups, the "gracile" australopithecines and the "robust" australopithecines.[31]

Gracile Australopithecines

The **gracile australopithecines** include *A. anamensis, A. afarensis,* and *A. africanus.* All of them have smaller dentition and lighter facial and dental musculature than the robust australopithecines.

Australopithecus anamensis The earliest australopithecine species, dating between 3.9 million and 4.2 million years ago, is **Australopithecus anamensis,** found in several locations in northern Kenya.[32] It was a small bipedal hominid with teeth similar to those of the later *A. afarensis.*[33] The more controversial specimens have long bones, suggesting well-developed bipedalism, but their elbow and knee joints look more like those of the later *Homo* genus than like those of any other species of *Australopithecus.* It has been said that *A. anamensis* is "*afarensis*-like from the neck up and *Homo*-like from the neck down."[34]

Australopithecus afarensis **Australopithecus afarensis** dates from about 4 to 3 million years ago. Remains from at least two dozen individuals were unearthed at Laetoli, Tanzania.[35] There is no question that the Laetoli hominids were bipedal, because the now-famous trail of footprints was found at the Laetoli site. Two hominids walking erect and side by side left their tracks in the ground 3.6 million years ago. The remains of at least 35 individuals have been found at another site, Hadar, in Ethiopia. The Hadar finds are remarkable for their completeness. Whereas paleoanthropologists often find just parts of the cranium and jaws, many parts of the skeleton were also found at Hadar. For example, paleoanthropologist Donald Johanson found 40 percent of the skeleton of a female hominid he named Lucy, after the Beatles' song "Lucy in the Sky with Diamonds."[36]

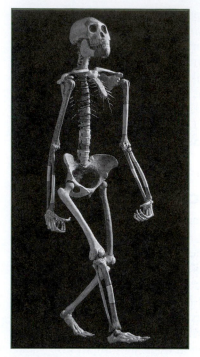

A reconstruction of a female *Australopithecus afarensis* skeleton. Note how long the arms are relative to the legs, and the long fingers. Both suggest *A. afarensis* was at least partially arboreal.

Dating of the hominid remains at Laetoli suggests that the hominids there lived between 3.8 million and 3.6 million years ago.[37] Recent dating of the Hadar remains suggests that they are somewhat younger—less than 3.2 million years old. Lucy probably lived 2.9 million years ago.[38] The environment Lucy lived in was semiarid, upland savanna with rainy and dry seasons.[39]

A. afarensis was a small hominid, but, like most of the living great apes, was sexually dimorphic. Females weighed perhaps 65 pounds and stood a little more than 3 feet tall; males weighed more than 90 pounds and stood about 5 feet tall.[40] *A. afarensis* teeth were large compared to their body size, and they had thick molar enamel. They also had large, apelike canines, which, on some specimens, projected beyond the adjacent teeth. However, even the longer canines did not rub against the lower teeth or fit into a diastema (a space between the teeth), and thus did not prevent side-to-side movement of the lower jaw.[41] This is important, because side-to-side movement of the lower jaw allowed *A. afarensis* to efficiently chew small seeds and nuts. The thick enamel on the molars and wear patterns on the molar crowns suggest that such small, hard materials made up a significant part of the diet of *A. afarensis*.[42] The cranium of *A. afarensis* reflects its dentition. The face juts forward because of the large teeth and jaws, and the base of the skull flares out to provide attachment areas for large neck muscles to support the heavy face. The brain is small, about 400 cubic centimeters (cc), but relatively large for an animal this size.[43]

The arms and legs of *A. afarensis* were about the same length, and the fingers and toe bones are curved, suggesting they were heavily muscled. Most scholars believe these limb proportions and strong hands and feet point to spending a lot of time in the trees, probably feeding, sleeping, and avoiding terrestrial predators.[44] The pelvis and leg bones of *A. afarensis*, however, demonstrate that it moved bipedally when on the ground. The pelvis is wide and flaring, but has the bowl-like shape of all later hominids. The legs angle inward, and the feet have an arch and an ankle much like later hominids.[45] Detailed analyses of the Laetoli footprints suggest that *A. afarensis* may have had a shorter and less efficient stride than modern humans.[46]

Although *A. afarensis* is the most well-represented australopithecine species, it was not the first one discovered. That distinction rests with *Australopithecus africanus*.

Australopithecus africanus In 1925, Raymond Dart, professor of anatomy at the University of Witwatersrand in Johannesburg, South Africa, presented the first evidence that an erect bipedal hominid existed in the Pliocene epoch—the skull of an infant bipedal hominid, which has come to be known as the Taung Child. Since the Taung child's discovery 80 years ago, the remains of hundreds of other similar australopithecines have been unearthed from caves at Sterkfontein and Makapansgat in South Africa. Dating of the australopithecine finds from the South African limestone caves is difficult because absolute dating techniques cannot be applied. Relative dating suggests that the South African **Australopithecus africanus** lived between 3 million and 2 million years ago. The climate was prob- ably semiarid, not too different from the climate of today.[47] *A. africanus* had a rounded braincase, a fairly well-developed forehead, moderate brow ridges, and a projecting face.[48] The estimated cra- nial capacity for the various finds from Taung and Sterkfontein is between 428 and 485 cc.[49]

Like *A. afarensis*, *A. africanus* was very small; the adults were 3½–4½ feet tall, weighed 60–90 pounds, and were sexually dimorphic.[50] The large, chinless jaw of *A. africanus* resembles that of *A. afarensis*, but some of the dental features of *A. afri- canus* are similar to those of modern humans— broad incisors and small, short canines. And, although the premolars and molars were larger than in modern humans, their form was very simi- lar. Presumably, function and use were also similar.

Fossil skull of an *Australopithecus africanus* (STS 5) nicknamed "Mrs. Ples" found by Robert Broom at Sterkfontein cave in 1947.

Other Gracile Australopithecines New fossils from eastern Africa found in the last two decades suggest some other species of gracile australopithecine. Two groups of fossils are con- sidered by most scholars to represent new australopithecine species, named ***Australopithecus bahrelghazali*** and ***Australopithecus garhi***. *A. bahrelghazali* is currently represented by a single, fragmentary jaw, and only a handful of skull and limb fragments represent *A. garhi*.

Australopithecus garhi, found in rock dating to approximately 2.5 million years ago, is par- ticularly interesting. *A. garhi* has larger molars than *A. afarensis*, yet does not have the huge face and jaws of the robust australopithecines. It also lacks the enlarged brain of early *Homo*. Several limb bones were found in the same rock layers, and these do resemble *A. afarensis*. *A. garhi*, then, looks like *afarensis* but with greatly enlarged molars.[51] It may represent one end of the range of variation in *afarensis*, or it may represent an adaptation to eating tough foods, similar to that made by the robust australopithecines, discussed shortly.

It is interesting that the remains of butchered animals were found in the same rock layer as the *A. garhi* remains. Several bones found near the *A. garhi* fossils show unambiguous cut marks and signs of having been broken with a stone tool. Unfortunately, no stone tools have been found, but the evidence for butchery suggests they must have been used. And since no other species of hominid have been found in the area, it is reasonable to think that *A. garhi* was the toolmaker and butcher. The fossil's discoverer, Berhane Asfaw, suggests that *A. garhi* is in the right place, at the right time, and has the right physical and behavioral traits to be the direct ancestor of early *Homo*.[52]

Equally intriguing is *Australopithecus bahrelghazali*, not so much because of its physical fea- tures, but because it was found further west, in what is now central Chad. Most scholars assume the early hominids represent a specific adaptation to the Rift Valley (a long valley in East Africa where the earth is pulling apart, exposing fossils from millions of years ago). The discovery of an early australopithecine some 2,500 kilometers (1,550 or so miles) west of the Rift Valley calls this assumption into question.[53] *A. bahrelghazali* dates to about 3 million years ago, and is very similar to contemporary *A. afarensis* fossils from the Rift Valley. It differs from *A. afarensis* in some distinct ways (its premolars, for example, have thinner enamel and more well-defined roots).

A related hominid genus, ***Kenyanthropus platyops,*** is thought by some scholars to be yet another australopithecine (and hence should not be regarded as a separate genus). The nearly

Fossil skull of *Australopithecus boisei* found by Louis and Mary Leakey in 1959. Note its huge face and teeth and its sagittal crest.

complete 3.5-million-year-old skull of *Kenyanthropus platyops* from western Kenya shows traits that Meave Leakey and her colleagues suggest separate it from the australopithecines that lived at the same time. Its face is smaller and flatter, and its molars are smaller than those of the australopithecines. Leakey believes *Kenyanthropus* may be a direct link to *Homo,* but others are not so sure. The skull is distorted, and scholars are not convinced that its features lie outside the range of the australopithecines.[54]

Robust Australopithecines

The **robust australopithecines** lived in eastern Africa and in southern Africa from about 2.7 million to 1 million years ago, and are quite distinct from the gracile australopithecines. Indeed, some paleoanthropologists think these fossils are so different that they deserve to be classified in a different genus, which they call *Paranthropus,* literally, "beside humans." The three main robust australopithecines, from oldest to youngest, are: *Australopithecus aethiopicus, Australopithecus robustus,* and *Australopithecus boisei.*

In contrast to the gracile australopithecines, the robust australopithecines had thicker jaws, with larger molars and premolars but smaller incisors, more massive muscle attachments for chewing, and well-developed sagittal crests and ridges to support heavy chewing.[55] In addition, *A. robustus* and *A. boisei* have somewhat larger cranial capacities (about 490–530 cc) than the gracile species.

It used to be thought that the robust australopithecines were substantially bigger than the other australopithecines, but recent calculations suggest that these australopithecines were not substantially different in body weight or height. The robustness is primarily in the skull and jaw, most strikingly in the teeth. The body of the robust forms is similar to that of *A. africanus,* so the brain of the robust australopithecines was relatively larger than the brain of *A. africanus.*[56]

Australopithecus aethiopicus *Australopithecus aethiopicus* is the earliest and least known of the robust australopithecines. *A. aethiopicus* fossils were found in northern Kenya and southern Ethiopia and date between 2.3 million and 2.7 million years ago. *A. aethiopicus* differed from *A. afarensis* specimens from roughly the same region and perhaps even the same time period by having much larger dentition, particularly molars; huge cheekbones; projecting and dish-shaped (round and flat) faces; and large sagittal crests. But they are similar to *A. afarensis* in most other ways. Overall, *A. aethiopicus* resembles *A. afarensis,* but with a massively "scaled-up" dental apparatus.[57]

Australopithecus robustus In 1936, Robert Broom, then curator of vertebrate paleontology at the Transvaal Museum in South Africa, began seeking fossils for the museum, particularly hominids that might support Raymond Dart's earlier discovery of the Taung Child. In 1938, a quarry manager gave Broom a hominid jaw that had been found in a nearby cave called Kromdraai. Broom immediately began excavating in the cave, and within days was able to piece together the skull of what would prove to be a new australopithecine species—*Australopithecus robustus.*[58]

Although Broom had expected another example of *A. africanus,* this one was different. It had larger teeth, a massive jaw, and a flatter face than *A. africanus.*[59] Because of these differences,

Broom and many scholars today believe the robust australopithecines are unique enough to warrant classification in a separate *Paranthropus* genus.

How did two strikingly different hominid species evolve in the same environment? In 1954, John T. Robinson proposed that *A. africanus* and *A. robustus* had different dietary adaptations— *A. africanus* being an omnivore (dependent on meat and plants) and *A. robustus* a vegetarian, with a need for heavy chewing. Robinson's view was hotly debated for many years. Evidence from electron microscopy supports Robinson's view that *A. robustus* ate mostly small, hard objects such as seeds, nuts, and tubers. But how different was *A. africanus* in this respect? Recent analyses suggest that *A. africanus* also practiced fairly heavy chewing.[60]

The idea that *A. robustus* was just a vegetarian is also questioned by a relatively new chemical technique that analyzes strontium–calcium ratios in teeth and bones to estimate the proportion of plant versus animal food in the diet. This new kind of analysis suggests that *A. robustus* was an omnivore.[61] Thus *A. robustus* may have needed large teeth and jaws to chew seeds, nuts, and tubers, but that doesn't mean that it didn't eat other things too. Most paleoanthropologists think that *A. robustus* died out shortly after 1 million years ago[62] and is not ancestral to our own genus, *Homo*.[63]

Australopithecus boisei Legendary paleoanthropologist Louis Leakey began his search for a human ancestor in 1931, at Olduvai Gorge in western Tanzania. It was not until 1959 that his efforts paid off with the discovery of *A. boisei* (named after a benefactor, Charles Boise). ***Australopithecus boisei*** lived between about 2.3 million and 1.3 million years ago.[64] Like *A. robustus,* it seems to have lived in a dry, open environment and ate a lot of coarse seeds, nuts, and roots. And, like *A. robustus,* most paleoanthropologists think *A. boisei* is not ancestral to our genus, *Homo*.[65] What did *A. boisei* look like? Compared with *A. robustus, A. boisei* had even more extreme features that reflected a huge chewing apparatus—enormous molar teeth and expanded premolars that look like molars; a massive, thick and deep jaw; thick cheekbones; and a more pronounced sagittal crest.[66] Indeed, *A. boisei* has been called a "hyper-robust" australopithecine—a name that definitely captures the species.

The picture that emerges from this brief overview of the australopithecines is one of diversity. There seem to have been many different species of australopithecine, and even within species there seems to be a relatively high level of variation.[67] All shared similar environments in eastern and southern Africa, but those environments were diverse and changing. Forests were giving way to open woodlands and grasslands. Large lakes were formed and then broken apart through uplifting and volcanic activity in the Rift Valley of eastern Africa. And the climate continued to warm until the end of the **Pliocene,** some 1.6 million years ago.

At this point, you may well be wondering how all these species fit together. Figure 6.1 shows one model about how the known fossils may be related. The main disagreement among paleontologists concerns which species of *Australopithecus* were ancestral to the line leading to modern humans. For example, the model shown in Figure 6.1 suggests that *A. africanus* is not ancestral to *Homo,* only to one line of robust australopithecines. *Australopithecus afarensis* is viewed as ancestral to both lines of robust australopithecines and to the line leading to modern humans. Those who think that *A. afarensis* was the last common ancestor of all the hominid lines shown in Figure 6.1 think the split to *Homo* occurred over 3 million years ago.[68]

Despite the uncertainty and disagreements about what species was ancestral to the *Homo* line, paleoanthropologists widely agree about other aspects of early hominid evolution: (1) There were at least two separate hominid lines between 3 million and 1 million years ago; (2) the robust australopithecines were not ancestral to modern humans but became extinct about 1 million

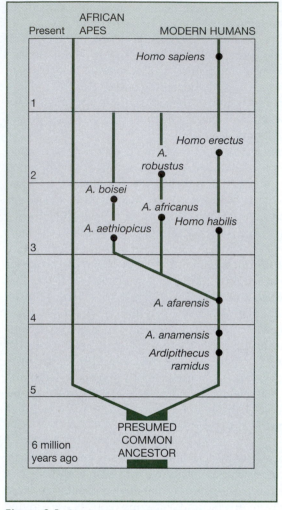

Figure 6.1 Phylogenetic Time Lines

Source: Adapted from *The New York Times,* September 5, 1995, p. C9. Dates changed slightly to reflect recent redating.

years ago; and (3) *Homo habilis* (and successive *Homo* species) were in the direct ancestral line to modern humans. Now we turn to our direct ancestors, the first members of the *Homo* genus.

Early *Homo* Species

Early hominids classified in our own genus, *Homo,* are generally divided into two species: **Homo habilis** and **Homo rudolfensis.** Both are known primarily from the western parts of Kenya and Tanzania, but remains have been found elsewhere in eastern and southern Africa, including the Omo Basin of Ethiopia and Sterkfontein cave in South Africa. Both lived in the same place and time as the robust australopithecine, *Australopithecus boisei,* and may later have lived at the same time as *Homo erectus.*

Homo habilis appears to be the earlier of these two species, appearing around 2.3 million years ago. Compared with the australopithecines, *H. habilis* had a significantly larger brain, averaging 630–640 cc,[69] and reduced molars and premolars.[70] The rest of the skeleton is reminiscent of the australopithecines, including the presence of powerful hands and relatively long arms, suggesting that *H. habilis* was at least partially arboreal. *H. habilis* may also have been sexually dimorphic like the australopithecines, as individuals seem to have greatly differed in size.

Homo rudolfensis is roughly contemporary with *Homo habilis,* and shares many of its features. Indeed, many paleoanthropologists make no distinction between the two species, putting *H. rudolfensis* into *H. habilis.* Those who do see them as distinct species point to the larger and more thickly enameled cheek teeth of *H. rudolfensis,* its flatter and broader face, and its more modernlike limb proportions. Even with its larger teeth and broader face, the dentition of *H. rudolfensis* is considerably reduced over the australopithecines and, as in *H. habilis,* its brain is at least a third larger. We have little postcranial skeletal material for either early *Homo* species, so it is impossible to tell whether the female pelvis had changed. However, with brains averaging a third larger than that of the australopithecines, it seems likely that some modifications must have developed to allow bigger-brained babies to be born.

The expansion of the brain is only one of a number of trends in hominid evolution. Another is the routine use of patterned or nearly standardized stone tools, which is considered one sign of the emergence of culture. It is assumed, but not known for sure, that patterned stone tools were made by the first members of our own genus, *Homo,* for we first see a number of trends in the genus *Homo* that probably started because of habitual stone toolmaking and use—expansion of the brain, modification of the female pelvis to accommodate bigger-brained babies, and reduction in the teeth, face, and jaws.

Even though stone tools are found at various sites in East Africa before the time early *Homo* appeared, most anthropologists surmise that members of early *Homo* species, rather than the australopithecines, made those tools. But the fact is that none of the earliest stone tools is clearly associated with early *Homo,* so it is impossible as yet to know who made them.[71]

The earliest identifiable stone tools found so far come from various sites in East Africa and date from about 2.5 million years ago,[72] and maybe earlier. They range from very small flakes (thumb-size) to cobble or core tools that are fist-size.[73] These early tools were apparently made by striking a stone with another stone, a technique called **percussion flaking.** Both the sharp-edged flakes and the sharp-edged cores (the pieces of stone left after flakes are removed) were probably used as tools. Unfortunately, little can be inferred about lifestyles from the earliest tool sites because little else was found with the tools. In contrast, finds of later tool assemblages at Olduvai Gorge in Tanzania have yielded a rich harvest of cultural information. Of the Olduvai site, Louis Leakey wrote,

> [It] is a fossil hunter's dream, for it shears 300 feet through stratum after stratum of earth's history as through a gigantic layer cake. Here, within reach, lie countless fossils and artifacts which but for the faulting and erosion would have remained sealed under thick layers of consolidated rock.[74]

The oldest cultural materials from Olduvai (Bed I) date from Lower Pleistocene times (about 1.6 million years ago). The stone artifacts include core tools and sharp-edged flakes. Flake tools predominate. Among the core tools, so-called choppers are common. Choppers are cores that have been partially flaked and have a side that might have been used for chopping. Other core tools, with flaking along one side and a flat edge, are called scrapers. Whenever a stone has facets removed from only one side of the cutting edge, we call it a **unifacial tool.** If the stone has facets removed from both sides, we call it a **bifacial tool.** Although there are some bifacial tools in the early stone tool assemblages, they are not as plentiful or as elaborated as in later tool traditions. The kind of tool assemblage found in Bed I and to some extent in later (higher) layers is referred to as **Oldowan** (see Figure 6.2).[75]

Archaeologists have experimented with what can be done with Oldowan tools. The flakes appear to be very versatile; they can be used for slitting the hides of animals, dismembering animals, and whittling wood into sharp-pointed sticks (wooden spears or digging sticks). The larger stone tools (choppers and scrapers) can be used to hack off branches or cut and chop tough animal joints.[76] Those who have made and tried to use stone tools for various purposes are so impressed by the sharpness and versatility of flakes that they wonder whether most of the core tools were really used as tools. The cores could mainly be what remained after wanted flakes were struck off.[77] Archaeologists surmise that many early tools were also made of wood and bone, but these do not survive in the archaeological record. Present-day populations use sharp-pointed digging sticks for extracting roots and tubers from the ground; stone flakes are very effective for sharpening wood to a very fine point.[78] None of the early flaked stone tools can plausibly be thought of as weapons. So, if the toolmaking hominids were hunting or defending themselves with weapons, they had to have used wooden spears, clubs, or unmodified stones as missiles. Later, Oldowan tool assemblages also include stones that were flaked and battered into

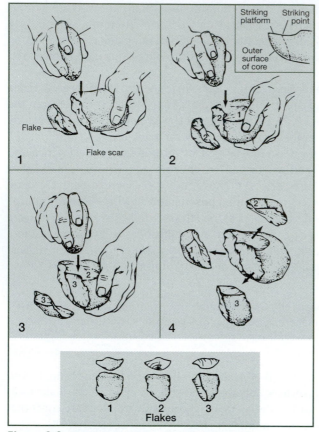

Striking platform   Striking point

Outer surface of core

Flake

Flake scar

1   2   3   4

Flakes

Figure 6.2 The Production of a Simple Oldowan Chopper Core and the Resultant Flakes

Source: Freyman 1987. Reprinted by permission of the artist, Ed Hanson.

a rounded shape. The unmodified stones and the shaped stones might have been lethal projectiles.[79]

Experiments may indicate what can be done with tools, but they cannot tell us what was *actually* done with them. Other techniques, such as microscopic analysis of the wear on tools, are more informative. Lawrence Keeley used high-powered microscopes in his experimental investigations of tools and found that different kinds of "polish" develop on tools when they are used on different materials. The polish on tools used for cutting meat is different from the polish on tools used for woodworking. On the basis of microscopic investigation of the 1.5-million-year-old tools from the eastern side of Lake Turkana, Keeley and his colleagues concluded that at least some of the early tools were probably used for cutting meat, others for cutting or whittling wood, and still others for cutting plant stems.[80]

For many years, it seemed plausible to assume that hominids were the hunters and the animals their prey. However, archaeologists had to reexamine this assumption with the emergence of the field of *taphonomy,* which studies the processes that can alter and distort an assemblage of bones. So, for example, flowing water can bring bones and artifacts together, which may have happened at Olduvai Gorge about 1.8 million years ago. (The area of what is now the gorge bordered the shores of a shallow lake at that time.) Other animals such as hyenas could have also brought carcasses to some of the same places that hominids spent time.[81]

But there is little doubt that hominids were cutting up animal carcasses for meat shortly after 2 million years ago. Pat Shipman suggested that scavenging, not hunting, was the major meat-getting activity of the hominids living there between 2 million and 1.7 million years ago. For example, the cut marks made by the stone tools usually (but not always) overlie teeth marks made by carnivores. This suggests that the hominids were often scavenging the meat of animals killed and partially eaten by nonhominid predators. The fact that the cut marks were sometimes made first, however, suggested to Shipman that the hominids were also sometimes the hunters.[82] There is also no consensus about how to characterize the Olduvai sites that contain concentrations of stone tools and animal bones. In the 1970s, there was a tendency to think of them as home bases to which hominids (presumably male) brought meat to share with others (presumably nursing mothers and young children). Indeed, Mary Leakey identified two locations where she thought early hominids had built simple structures. One was a stone circle that she suggested formed the base of a small brush windbreak. The other was a circular area of dense debris surrounded by an area virtually without debris. Leakey suggested that the area lacking debris may represent the location of a ring of thorny brush with which early hominids surrounded their campsite in order to keep out predators—much like pastoralists living in the region do today.[83] But archaeologists today are not so sure that these sites were home bases. For one thing,

A replica of an Oldowan stone tool is used to chop into a large bone to extract the nutrient-rich marrow. Few animals have jaws powerful enough to break open the bones of large mammals, but stone tools would have allowed early humans to do so.

carnivores also frequented the sites. Places with meaty bones lying around may not have been so safe for hominids to use as home bases. Second, the animal remains at the sites had not been completely dismembered and butchered. If the sites had been hominid home bases, we would expect more complete processing of carcasses.[84] Third, natural processes as simple as trees growing through a site can create circular areas of debris such as the ones Leakey identified as structures, and without better evidence that early hominids made them, one cannot be sure that the circles of debris were indeed structures.[85]

Alternatively, some archaeologists are beginning to think that these early sites with many animal bones and tools may just have been places where hominids processed food but did not live. Why would the hominids return repeatedly to a particular site? Richard Potts suggests one possible reason—that hominids left caches of stone tools and stones for toolmaking at various locations to facilitate recurrent food-collecting and -processing activities.[86]

Stone Tools and Culture

The presence of patterned stone tools means that these early hominids had probably developed *culture*. Archaeologists consider a pattern of behavior, such as a particular way to make a tool that is shared and learned by a group of individuals, to be a sign of cultural behavior. To be sure, toolmaking does not imply that early humans had anything like the complex cultures of humans today. Chimpanzees have patterns of tool use and toolmaking that appear to be shared and learned, but they do not have that much in the way of cultural behavior.

It seems clear from the archaeological record that early hominids were making and using stone tools on a regular basis. Tools are frequently found in discrete concentrations, and often in association with animal bones and other debris from human activity suggesting, as we have already noted, campsites or even small shelters used by groups of individuals over periods of time. In such a situation, sharing of food at least amongst closely related individuals is very likely. Even when food-sharing takes place among chimpanzees, it is usually among closely related individuals.[87] Thus, the ancient locations of early hominid social activity may be evidence of family groups. How would such a system of social behavior—the creation of a common meeting, resting, and living place for a group of related individuals to share food—have evolved? Let's consider one model.

One Model for the Evolution of Culture

Early *Homo* had a brain almost one-third larger than that of the australopithecines. As we discuss later in the section on trends in hominid evolution, one of the possible consequences of brain expansion was the lessening of maturity at birth. Compared with other animals, we spend not only a longer proportion of our life span, but also the longest absolute period in a dependent state. Prolonged infant dependency has probably been of great significance in human cultural evolution. According to Theodosius Dobzhansky,

> it is this helplessness and prolonged dependence on the ministrations of the parents and other persons that favors . . . the socialization and learning process on which the transmission of culture wholly depends. This may have been an overwhelming advantage of the human growth pattern in the process of evolution.[88]

It used to be thought that the australopithecines had a long period of infant dependency, just as modern humans do, but the way their teeth apparently developed suggests that the early australopithecines followed an apelike pattern of development. Thus, prolonged maturation may be relatively recent, but just how recent is not yet known.[89]

Although some use of tools for digging, defense, or scavenging may have influenced the development of bipedalism, full bipedalism may have made possible more efficient toolmaking and consequently more efficient foraging and scavenging. Indeed, we have fairly good evidence that early hominids were butchering and presumably eating big game some 2 million years ago.

Whenever it was that hominids began to scavenge for game and perhaps hunt regularly, the development of scavenging would have required individuals to travel long distances frequently in search of suitable carcasses. Among groups of early *Homo,* longer infant and child dependency may have fostered the creation of home bases or at least established meeting places. The demands of childbirth and caring for a newborn might have made it difficult for early *Homo* mothers to travel for some time after the birth. Certainly, it would have been awkward for a mother carrying a nursing child to travel long distances to hunt. Although carrying an infant might be possible with a sling, successful hunting might not be so likely with a needy and potentially noisy child along. Because early *Homo* males (and perhaps females without young children) would have been freer to roam farther from home, they probably became the scavengers or hunters. Women with young children may have gathered wild plants within a small area that could be covered without traveling far from the home base or meeting place.

The creation of home bases or meeting places among early *Homo* groups may itself have increased the likelihood of wider food-sharing. If mothers with young children were limited to gathering plant foods in a relatively small area, the only way to ensure that they and their children could obtain a complete diet would have been to share the other foods obtained elsewhere. Sharing would have made it more likely that their offspring would survive to have offspring. Thus, if early *Homo* had home bases and families, those characteristics could have encouraged the development of the learned and shared behaviors we call culture.[90] Obviously this is a "just-so" story—a tale that we may never be able to prove really happened. However, it is a tale that is consistent with the archaeological record.[91] Patterned stone tools do not appear until early *Homo* comes on the scene. With early *Homo,* we see the start of several trends in hominid evolution that appear to reflect the manufacture and use of patterned stone tools—the expansion of the brain, the modification of the female pelvis to accommodate bigger-brained babies, and a general reduction in the size of teeth, face, and jaws.

Trends in Hominid Evolution

Expansion of the Brain

The australopithecines had relatively small cranial capacities, about 380–530 cubic centimeters (cc)—not much larger than that of chimpanzees. But around 2.3 million years ago, close to the time that patterned stone tools first appeared, some hominids show evidence of enlarged brain capacity. These hominids, early *Homo,* had cranial capacities averaging about 630–640 cc, which is about 50 percent of the brain capacity of modern humans (which averages slightly more than 1,300 cc). (See Figure 6.3.) The australopithecines were small, and the earliest *Homo* finds were hardly bigger, so much of the increase in brain size over time might have been a result of later hominids' bigger bodies. When we correct for body size, however, it turns out that brain size increased not only absolutely but also relatively after 2 million years ago. Between about 4 million and 2 million years ago, relative brain size remained just about the same. Only in the last 2 million years has the hominid brain doubled in relative size and tripled in absolute size.[92] Many anthropologists think that the increase is linked to the emergence of stone toolmaking about 2.5 million years ago. The reasoning is that stone toolmaking was important for the survival of our ancestors, and therefore natural selection would have favored bigger-brained individuals because they had motor and conceptual skills that enabled them to be better tool-makers. According to this view, the expansion of the brain and more sophisticated toolmaking would have developed together. Other anthropologists think that the expansion of the brain may have been favored by other factors, such as warfare, hunting, longer life, and language.[93] One intriguing theory is that life in complex social groups requires increased intelligence and memory, and that the creation of home bases and family groups may have fostered the expansion of the hominid brain.[94] Whatever the factors favoring bigger brains, they also provided

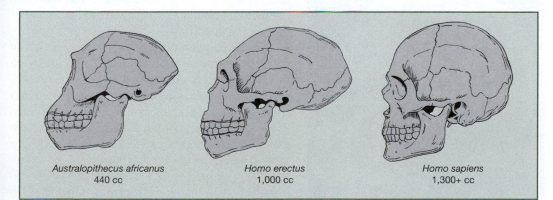

| *Australopithecus africanus* | *Homo erectus* | *Homo sapiens* |
| 440 cc | 1,000 cc | 1,300+ cc |

Figure 6.3 Comparison of the estimated cranial capacities of *Australopithecus africanus*, *Homo erectus*, and *Homo sapiens*, demonstrating the expansion of the brain in hominid evolution

Source: Estimated cranial capacities from Tattersall, Delson, and Van Couvering 2000. Reproduced by permission of Routledge, Inc., part of The Taylor & Francis Group.

humans with an expanded capacity for culture. Thus, along with bipedalism, the expansion of the brain marks a watershed in human evolution.

As the hominid brain expanded, natural selection also favored the widening of the female pelvis to allow larger-brained babies to be born.[95] But there was probably a limit to how far the pelvis could widen and still be adapted to bipedalism. Something had to give, and that something was the degree of physical development of the human infant at birth—for instance, the human infant is born with cranial bones so plastic that they can overlap. Because birth takes place before the cranial bones have hardened, the human infant with its relatively large brain can pass through the opening in the mother's pelvis. Human infants are born at a relatively early stage of development, and are wholly dependent on their parents for many years. As we have noted, this lengthy period of infant dependency may have been an important factor in the evolution of culture.

Reduction of the Face, Teeth, and Jaws

As in the case of the brain, substantial changes in the face, teeth, and jaws do not appear in hominid evolution until after about 2 million years ago. The australopithecines all have cheek teeth that are very large relative to their estimated body weight, perhaps because the diet of the australopithecines was especially high in plant foods,[96] including small, tough objects such as seeds, nuts, and tubers. The australopithecines have thick jawbones, probably also related to their chewing needs. The australopithecines have relatively large faces that project forward below the eyes. But when we get to the *Homo* forms, we see reduction in the size of the face, cheek teeth, and jaws (see Figure 6.4). It would seem that natural selection in favor of a bigger and stronger chewing apparatus was relaxed. One reason might be that members of the *Homo* genus started to eat foods that were easier to chew. Such foods might have included roots, fruits, and meat. As we discuss later, it may have been the development of habitual tool use and the control of fire that allowed members of the *Homo* genus to change their diet to include foods that are easier to chew, including meat. If food is cooked and easy to chew, individual humans with smaller jaws and teeth would not be disadvantaged, and therefore the face, cheek teeth, and jaw would get smaller on average over time.[97]

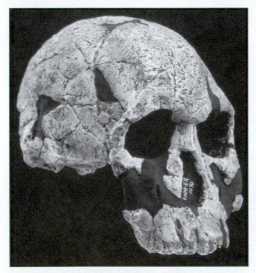

The skull of a *Homo habilis/rudolfensis* (ER-1470) found by Richard Leakey in 1972. Note its high forehead and large braincase.

The expansion of the brain and reduction of the face occurred at about the same time, and were probably related. A recent discovery in human genetics appears to provide direct evidence of a connection. Researchers studying muscle diseases in modern humans discovered that humans have a unique myosin gene called MYH16 (myosin is a protein in muscle tissue) that is only present in jaw muscles. Comparing MYH16 to related genes in primates, the researchers determined that MYH16 evolved about 2.4 million years ago—around the time the brain began to enlarge and the face and jaw began to shrink. So, the expansion of the brain appears to have been aided by a mutation in myosin that caused jaw muscles to shrink.[98]

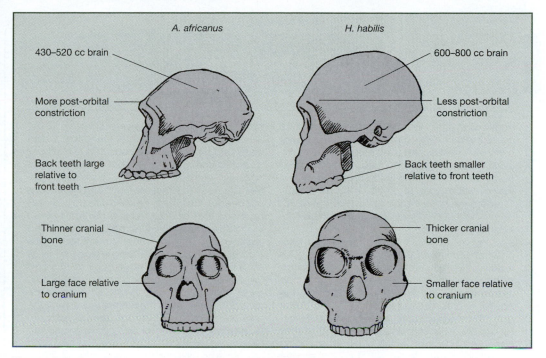

Figure 6.4 Comparison of **A. africanus** and **H. habilis**

Homo erectus

Homo erectus was the first hominid species to be widely distributed in the Old World (see the box "The First Migrants"). Until recently, it was assumed that it was *H. erectus* who moved out of Africa because *H. erectus* lived in East Africa about 1.6 million years ago but not until after about 1 million years ago in Asia.[99] However, recent redating suggests that *H. erectus* in Java is somewhat older, dating to perhaps 1.8 million years ago.[100] And newer *H. erectus* fossils from Dmanisi, in the southeastern European nation of Georgia, have recently been dated to at least 1.7 million years ago.[101] If these dates are accurate, earlier hominids, possibly *H. habilis*, probably moved out of Africa earlier. Indeed, one well-preserved skull found at Dmanisi in 2001 has some features that are reminiscent of *H. habilis*—a brain only about 600 cc, relatively large canines, and a relatively thin browridge.[102]

Some scholars see enough differences between Asian and African populations of *H. erectus* to argue that they should be separated into two distinct species, *Homo erectus* for the Asian populations and **Homo ergaster** for the African ones. Furthermore, *Homo erectus* (or *Homo ergaster*) fossils are also found in Europe. But some paleoanthropologists think that the finds in Europe typically classified as *H. erectus* are actually early examples of *H. sapiens*.[103] Others think that the European fossils and similar ones found in southern Africa and the Near East should be grouped into a distinct species, *Homo heidelbergensis*. There is also *Homo floresiensis*, a diminutive hominid that appears to be a miniature form of *Homo erectus* that evolved only on the isolated island of Flores, Indonesia. It is all a bit confusing; later we will try to sort it all out.

MIGRANTS AND IMMIGRANTS

The First Migrants

Hominids evolved in Africa, yet today hominids are found on every continent. Who were the first hominids to leave Africa, and when did they first leave? For many years, the clear answer was that *Homo erectus* were the first to leave Africa, and they did so perhaps 700,000 to 1 million years ago. In recent years, new findings and sources of evidence have led scholars to question this established answer.

The first new information came from geochemist Carl Swisher, who in the mid-1990s redated the Java sites where *Homo erectus* fossils had been found and determined they dated to perhaps 1.8 million years ago. Because the earliest *H. erectus* fossils in Africa share a similar date, this created a problem—how did *H. erectus* appear in Java at about the same time they appeared in Africa? As this question was being pondered, a remarkable set of new *H. erectus* fossils were being uncovered in Dmanisi, Georgia. Dated at 1.7 million years ago, these fossils made it clear that *H. erectus* left Africa almost as soon as they had evolved. The discovery of a *Homo habilis*–like fossil at Dmanisi, and of Oldowan-like tools at Riwat, Pakistan, and Longgupo, China, suggested that *H. habilis* may have been the first to leave Africa, and *H. erectus* followed a path their predecessors blazed. If they were following an earlier migration, it could explain how *H. erectus* were able to move so quickly across Asia.

A more unusual source of information on when hominids first left Africa comes from the parasites that accompanied them. All hominoids are plagued by lice, but humans host a distinct species, *Pediculus humanus*. Geneticist David Reed and his colleagues found that *P. humanus* diverged from other lice about 5.6 million years ago—about the time the first hominids appeared. More interesting, however, Reed and colleagues discovered that there are two subspecies of *P. humanus* that appear to have diverged about 1.2 million years ago. One subspecies is found worldwide today; the other is restricted to the New World. Reed and colleagues suggest this is evidence that at least some hominid migrants (probably *H. erectus*) became isolated in Asia by at least 1.2 million years ago, where their lice diverged from that of other hominid populations, only to be picked up much later by modern human migrants who ended up colonizing the New World.

So, who were the first hominid migrants? They may have been *H. habilis,* or they may have been very early *H. erectus.* When did the first hominid migrations out of Africa take place? Probably slightly less than 2 million years ago, but once these hominids left, they moved quickly, and they moved long distances. By 1.6 million years ago, *H. erectus* was in both western and southern Asia, and by 1.2 million years ago, their populations had moved far enough to have become isolated from one another. Whether or not they were the first migrants out of Africa, *H. erectus* migrated fast and far.

Sources: Reed et al. 2004; Tattersall 1997.

Physical Characteristics of *Homo erectus*

The *Homo erectus* skull generally was long, low, and thickly walled, with a flat frontal area and prominent browridges. It had a unique pentagonal shape when looked at from the back, formed in part by a rounded ridge, called a **sagittal keel,** running along the crest of the skull. There was also a ridge of bone running horizontally along the back of the skull, called an **occipital torus,** which added to the skull's overall long shape (see Figure 6.5).[104]

Compared with early *Homo, H. erectus* had relatively small teeth. *H. erectus* was the first hominid to have third molars that were smaller than the second or first molars, as in modern humans. The molars also had an enlarged pulp cavity, called **taurodontism,** which may have allowed the teeth to withstand harder use and wear than the teeth of modern humans. But the *H. erectus* jaw was lighter and thinner than in either early *Homo* or the australopithecines, and the face was less **prognathic,** or forward thrusting, in the upper and lower jaw. The brain, averaging 895–1,040 cc, was larger than that found in any of the australopithecines or early *Homo* species, but smaller than the average brain of a modern human.[105] Endocasts, which provide a picture of the surface of the brain, suggest that it was organized more like the brain of modern humans than like that of australopithecines.

    Homo erectus had a prominent, projecting nose, in contrast to the australopithecines' flat, nonprojecting nose.[106] From the neck down, *H. erectus* was practically indistinguishable from *H. sapiens.* In contrast to the smaller australopithecines and early *Homo* species living in East Africa

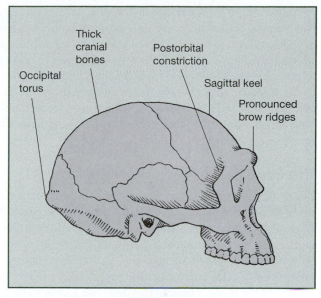

Figure 6.5 *Homo erectus* **Features**

around the same time, *H. erectus* was comparable to modern humans in size. The almost complete skeleton of the boy at Nariokotome, Kenya, suggests that he was about 5½ feet tall and about 8 years of age when he died; researchers estimate that he would have been over 6 feet tall had he lived to maturity. About 1.6 million years ago, the Nariokotome region was probably open grassland, with trees mostly along rivers.[107] *Homo erectus* in East Africa was similar in size to Africans today who live in a similarly open, dry environment.[108] *H. erectus* was also less sexually dimorphic than either the australopithecines or early *Homo,* comparable to modern humans.

Homo floresiensis

Whether or not there are distinct African and Asian species of *Homo erectus,* most scholars agree that **Homo floresiensis** is a distinct species that is closely related to *Homo erectus. H. floresiensis* has only been found on the Indonesian island of Flores, and only a handful of individuals have been located to date. All are tiny (they stood perhaps 3 feet tall), and have very small brains, on the order of 380 cc.[109] The structure of the brain, however, seems closely related to that of *H. erectus,* as do the structures of the skull.[110] In other words, *H. floresiensis* appears to be a tiny version of *H. erectus. H. floresiensis* even made tools that look similar to those made by *H. erectus,* and in some cases the tools look even more sophisticated.

The skull of the dwarf species *Homo floresiensis* next to that of a modern human. Note how small it is in comparison.

How might a miniature version of *H. erectus* have evolved? The answer is that both dwarfism and gigantism are common phenomena in isolated populations. Dwarfism appears to be an adaptation that occurs when there are few predators—a species in isolation can become smaller, and have a large population, if there are no predators threatening them. This may be what happened on Flores.[111] It is interesting that the island also hosted a number of dwarf species in addition to *H. floresiensis,* including a dwarf elephant that appears to have been one of the favorite foods of *H. floresiensis.* Perhaps even more interesting is the fact that *H. floresiensis* may have survived until as recently as 12,000 years ago—well into the time period when modern humans were living in Indonesia.

The Evolution of *Homo erectus*

The evolution of *Homo erectus* reflects a continuation of the general evolutionary trends we discussed previously. The brain continued to expand, increasing more than a third over early *Homo* (just as early *Homo* had increased more than a third over the australopithecines). The face, teeth, and jaws continued to shrink, taking on an almost modern form. An increasing use and variety of tools may have led to a further development of the brain. *Homo erectus* was eating and probably cooking meat, and this may have led to further reduction in the teeth and jaws.

As noted above, *Homo erectus* does not appear to be as sexually dimorphic as earlier hominids. What might have caused this change? In other primates, sexual dimorphism appears to be linked to social systems in which males are at the top of dominance hierarchies due to physical size and prowess and such males control sexual access to multiple females in the group. In contrast, lack of sexual dimorphism seems most pronounced in the animals where *pair bonding* exists—that is, where a male and a female form a breeding pair that lasts for a long period of time (as we will learn in later chapters, there are several distinct variations of male–female bonding in modern human cultures).[112] Could male–female bonding have developed in *Homo erectus?* It seems possible.

In animal species where females can feed themselves and their babies after birth, pair bonding is rare. But in species where females cannot feed both themselves and their babies, pair bonding is common. Why? We think it is because a strong male–female bond provides a good solution to the problem of incompatibility between a mother's feeding requirements and tending a newborn baby. A male partner can bring food and/or watch the newborn while the mother gets food.[113] But most primates lack pair bonding. This may be because primate infants are able to cling to their mother's fur soon after birth, so that the mother's hands are free to forage. Human infants demonstrate a residual form of this innate ability to cling during their first few weeks of life. This is called the *Moro reflex.*[114]

We have no way of knowing if *Homo erectus* had fur like other primates, but we think probably not, because we think they may have worn clothing, as we discuss later. The brain in *Homo erectus* may also have already expanded enough that *Homo erectus* infants, like modern human infants, could not adequately support their heads even if they could hold onto their mother's fur. In any case, when early hominids began to depend on scavenging and hunting for food (and for skins to be used in clothing), it would have been difficult and hazardous for a parent with a newborn baby to engage in these activities with a baby along. Marriage would have been an effective solution to this problem because each parent could help protect the baby while the other was away getting food. (For further discussion of this theory, see the chapter on marriage, family, and kinship.)

Another important aspect of the evolution of *Homo erectus* was the movement of populations out of eastern and southern Africa. It seems likely that cultural innovations were the key to allowing *Homo erectus* to move into new environments. Why? Because upon entering new environments, *Homo erectus* would have been faced with new (and generally colder) climatic conditions, new and different sources of raw material for tools, and new plants and animals to rely on for food. All animals adapt to such changes through natural selection, but natural selection typically takes a relatively long time and requires physical changes in the adapting organisms. *Homo erectus* was able to adapt to new environments very quickly and without apparent physical changes. This suggests that the primary mechanisms of adaptation for *Homo erectus* were cultural rather than biological.

What cultural adaptations might *Homo erectus* have made? Fire usage might have been the crucial cultural adaptation to colder climates. As we discuss below, there is tantalizing evidence that *Homo erectus* used fire. But fire can only warm people when they are stationary; it doesn't help when people are out collecting food. To be mobile in colder climates, *Homo erectus* may have begun to wear animal furs for warmth. Some *Homo erectus* tools look like the hide-processing tools used by more recent human groups,[115] and it seems unlikely that *Homo erectus* could have survived in the colder locations where they have been found, in eastern Europe and Asia, without some form of clothing. And if *Homo erectus* was wearing furs for warmth, they must have been hunting. *Homo erectus* could not have depended on scavenging to acquire skins—the skin is the first thing predators destroy when they dismember a carcass.

Lower Paleolithic Cultures

The stone tool traditions of *Homo erectus* are traditionally called **Lower Paleolithic.** These stone tool traditions involve "core" tool techniques, in which a core of stone, rather than a flake, is used as the basic raw material for finished tools (we will talk more about Lower Paleolithic stone tool technology shortly). Because stone tools are the most common cultural material in the archaeological record of these ancient peoples, the entire culture of *Homo erectus* is often termed *Lower Paleolithic,* a practice we follow here.

The archaeological finds of tools and other cultural artifacts dating from 1.5 million years to about 200,000 years ago are assumed to have been produced by *Homo erectus.* But hominid fossils are not usually associated with these materials. Therefore some of the tools during this period were possibly produced by hominids other than *H. erectus,* such as australopithecines earlier and *H. sapiens* later. But the so-called *Acheulian* tool assemblages dating from 1.5 million years ago to more than a million years later are very similar to each other, and *H. erectus* is the only hominid that spans the entire period. Thus, it is conventionally assumed that *H. erectus* was responsible for most if not all of the Acheulian tool assemblages.[116]

The Acheulian Tool Tradition

The stone toolmaking tradition known as the **Acheulian** was named after the site at St. Acheul, France, where the first examples were found. But the oldest Acheulian tools recovered are from East Africa, on the Peninj River in Tanzania, dating back about 1.5 million years.[117] In contrast to Oldowan, Acheulian assemblages have more large tools created according to standardized designs or shapes. Oldowan tools have sharp edges made by a few blows. Acheulian toolmakers shaped the stone by knocking more flakes off most of the edges. Many of these tools were made from very large flakes that had first been struck from very large cores or boulders.

One of the most characteristic and common tools in the Acheulian tool kit is the so-called **hand axe,** which is a teardrop-shaped, bifacially flaked tool with a thinned sharp tip. Other large tools resemble cleavers and picks. There were also many kinds of flake tools, such as scrapers with a wide edge.

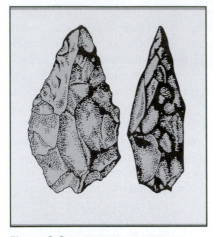

Figure 6.6 In later Acheulian technology, the characteristic hand axes were made by the soft-hammer method

Early Acheulian tools appeared to have been made by blows with a hard stone, but later tools are wider and flatter and may have been made with a **soft hammer** of bone or antler.[118] Tools made by a **hard hammer** technique, rock against rock, have limits in terms of their sharpness and form because only large and thick flakes can be made with a hard hammer technique. Flakes created by soft hammer flaking are much thinner and longer than hard hammer flakes, and the flintknapper generally has better control over their size and shape. This means that thinner and sharper tools can be made, as well as tools with complex shapes.

Were hand axes made for chopping trees, as their name suggests? Experiments suggest that they are not good for cutting trees; they seem more suited for butchering large animals.[119] Lawrence Keeley microscopically examined some Acheulian hand axes, and the wear on them is more consistent with animal butchery. They may also have been used for woodworking, particularly hollowing and shaping wood, and they are also good for digging.[120] William Calvin has even suggested that a hand axe could be used as a projectile thrown like a discus into a herd of animals in the hope of injuring or killing an animal.[121]

Acheulian tools are found widely in Africa, Europe, and western Asia, but bifacial hand axes, cleavers, and picks are not found as commonly in eastern and southeastern Asia.[122] Because *H. erectus* has been found in all areas of the Old World, it is puzzling that the tool traditions seem to differ from west to east. Some archaeologists have suggested that large bifacial tools may be lacking in eastern and southeastern Asia because *H. erectus* in Asia had a better material to make tools out of—bamboo. Bamboo has been used recently in Southeast Asia for many purposes, including incredibly sharp arrows and sticks for digging and cutting. Geoffrey Pope has shown that bamboo is found precisely in those areas of Asia where hand axes and other large bifacial tools are largely missing.[123]

Big Game Eating

Some of the Acheulian sites have produced evidence of big game eating. F. Clark Howell, who excavated sites at Torralba and Ambrona, Spain, found a substantial number of elephant remains and unmistakable evidence of human presence in the form of tools. Howell suggests that the humans at those sites used fire to frighten elephants into muddy bogs from which they would be unable to escape.[124] To hunt elephants in this way, the humans would have had to plan and work cooperatively in fairly large groups.

But do these finds of bones of large- and medium-sized animals, in association with tools, tell us that the humans definitely were big game hunters? Some archaeologists who have reanalyzed the evidence from Torralba think that the big game may have been scavenged. Because the Torralba and Ambrona sites are near ancient streams, many of the elephants could have died naturally, their bones accumulating in certain spots because of the flow of water.[125] What seems fairly clear is that the humans did deliberately butcher different kinds of game—different types of tools are found with different types of animals.[126] Thus, whether the humans hunted

Homo erectus ate—and probably hunted—large game animals, and they probably also learned to control fire.

big game at Torralba and Ambrona is debatable; all we can be sure of, as of now, is that they consumed big game and probably hunted smaller game.

Control of Fire

One way in which *H. erectus* is thought to have hunted is by using *fire drives*—a technique still used by hunting and gathering peoples in recent times. It is highly effective: Animals are driven out of their hiding places and homes by fire and dispatched by hunters positioned downwind of the oncoming flames. Most peoples who use this technique today set fires deliberately, but fires caused by lightning strikes may have also been utilized. Did *H. erectus* set these fires? Because *H. erectus* was the first hominid to be found throughout the Old World and in areas with freezing winters, most anthropologists presume that *H. erectus* had learned to control fire, at least for warmth. There is archaeological evidence of fire in some early sites, but fires can be natural events.[127]

   Suggestive but not conclusive evidence of the deliberate use of fire comes from Kenya in East Africa and is over 1.4 million years old.[128] More persuasive evidence of human control of fire, dating from nearly 800,000 years ago, comes from the site of Gesher Benot Ya'aqov in Israel. Here, researchers found evidence of burned seeds, wood, and stone, as well as concentrations of burned items suggestive of hearths.[129] Evidence of the deliberate use of fire comes from Europe somewhat later. Unfortunately, the evidence of control of fire at Gesher Benot Ya'aqov and European sites is not associated with *H. erectus* fossils, so the link between deliberate use of fire and *H. erectus* cannot definitely be established yet.[130] The control of fire was a major step in increasing the energy under human control. Cooking would have made all kinds of food (not just meat) more safely digestible and therefore more usable.[131] Fires would also have kept predators away, a not inconsiderable advantage given that there were many.

Campsites

Acheulian sites were usually located close to water sources, lush vegetation, and large stocks of herbivorous animals. Some camps have been found in caves, but most were in open areas surrounded by rudimentary fortifications or windbreaks. Several African sites are marked by stony rubble brought there by *H. erectus,* possibly for the dual purpose of securing the windbreaks and providing ammunition in case of a sudden attack.[132]

The presumed base campsites display a wide variety of tools, indicating that the camp was the center of many group functions. More specialized sites away from camp have also been found. These are marked by the predominance of a particular type of tool. For example, a butchering site in Tanzania contained dismembered hippopotamus carcasses and rare heavy-duty smashing and cutting tools. Workshops are another kind of specialized site encountered with some regularity. They are characterized by tool debris and are located close to a source of natural stone suitable for toolmaking.[133]

A camp has been excavated at the Terra Amata site near Nice, on the French Riviera. The camp appears to have been occupied in the late spring or early summer, judging by the pollen found in fossilized human feces. The excavator describes stake holes driven into the sand, paralleled by lines of stones, presumably marking the spots where the people constructed huts of roughly 30 × 15 feet (see Figure 6.7). A basic feature of each hut was a central hearth that seems to have been protected from drafts by a small wall built just outside the northeast corner of the hearth. The evidence suggests that the Terra Amata occupants gathered seafood such as oysters and mussels, did some fishing, and hunted in the surrounding area. The animal remains suggest that they obtained both small and large animals but mostly got the young of larger animals such as stags, elephants, boars, rhinoceroses, and wild oxen. Some of the huts contain recognizable toolmakers' areas, scattered with tool debris; occasionally, the impression of an animal skin shows where the toolmaker actually sat.[134]

Figure 6.7 A Reconstruction of the Oval Huts Built at Terra Amata. These huts were approximately 30 × 15 feet.

Source: Copyright © 1969 by Eric Mose.

✔●[Study and Review on myanthrolab.com

Summary

1. The drying trend in climate that began about 16 million to 11 million years ago diminished the extent of African rain forests and gave rise to areas of savanna and scattered deciduous woodlands. The new, more open country probably favored characteristics adapted to ground living in some primates. In the evolutionary line leading to humans, these adaptations included bipedalism, a crucial change in early hominid evolution.

2. There are several theories for the development of bipedalism: It may have increased the emerging hominid's ability to see predators and potential prey while moving through the tall grasses of the savanna; by freeing the hands for carrying, it may have facilitated transferring food from one place to another, for tool use for subsistence activities or weapons, for more efficient traveling over long distances, or for cooling the body.

3. *Sahelanthropus, Orrorin,* and *Ardipithecus* are likely candidates for the first hominid. They date as early as 6 million years ago, and may have walked bipedally. Undisputed hominids dating before 4 million years ago have been found in East Africa. These definitely bipedal hominids are now generally classified in the genus *Australopithecus.*

4. At least six species of australopithecine have been identified, and these are generally divided into two types: gracile and robust. The gracile australopithecines have relatively smaller teeth and jaws, and include *A. anamensis, A. afarensis,* and *A. africanus.* The robust australopithecines have relatively larger teeth and jaws, and are more muscular than the gracile australopithecines. They include *A. aethiopicus, A. robustus,* and *A. boisei.*

5. The earliest identifiable stone tools found so far come from various sites in East Africa and date from about 2.5 million years ago. Flake tools predominate, but choppers are also common. These early stone tools are referred to as Oldowan.

6. The presence of stone tools and perhaps home bases suggests that early hominids had culture.

7. Important physical changes in early hominids that led to the evolution of our genus, *Homo,* include the expansion of the brain, the modification of the female pelvis to allow bigger-brained babies to be born, and the reduction of the face, teeth, and jaws. These physical changes are seen in the species *Homo habilis* and *Homo rudolfensis,* both of which date to around 2.3 million years ago. Early *Homo* appears to have used tools and scavenged or possibly hunted meat, so culture, or the evolution of cultural behavior, seems to have played a role in these physical changes as well.

8. *Homo erectus* emerged about 1.8 million to 1.6 million years ago and was the first hominid species to be widely distributed in the Old World. It had a larger brain capacity than *Homo habilis* and an essentially modern postcranial skeleton. What differentiates *Homo erectus* most from modern humans is the shape of the skull, which is long, low, and has prominent browridges.

9. Some of the locations where *Homo erectus* lived in eastern Europe and Asia were quite cold, and *Homo erectus* was probably able to adapt to these new and often colder environments through cultural adaptations, such as use of fire for warmth and cooking, furs for clothing, and hunting.

10. Lower Paleolithic tools and other cultural artifacts from about 1.6 million to about 200,000 years ago were probably produced by *H. erectus.* Acheulian is the name given to the most well-known tool tradition of this period. Acheulian tools include both small flake tools and large tools, but hand axes and other large bifacial tools are characteristic.

Glossary Terms

Acheulian (p. 129)
Ardipithecus ramidus (p. 113)
Australopithecus (p. 113)
Australopithecus aethiopicus (p. 116)
Australopithecus afarensis (p. 113)
Australopithecus africanus (p. 114)
Australopithecus anamensis (p. 113)
Australopithecus bahrelghazali (p. 115)
Australopithecus boisei (p. 117)
Australopithecus garhi (p. 115)

Australopithecus robustus (p. 116)
bifacial tool (p. 119)
foramen magnum (p. 111)
gracile australopithecines (p. 113)
hand axe (p. 129)
hard hammer (p. 130)
Homo erectus (p. 125)
Homo ergaster (p. 125)
Homo floresiensis (p. 127)
Homo habilis (p. 118)
Homo rudolfensis (p. 118)
Kenyanthropus platyops (p. 115)
Lower Paleolithic (p. 129)

occipital torus (p. 126)
Oldowan (p. 119)
Orrorin tugenensis (p. 112)
percussion flaking (p. 119)
Pliocene (p. 117)
prognathic (p. 127)
robust australopithecines (p. 116)
sagittal keel (p. 126)
Sahelanthropus tchadensis (p. 112)
savanna (p. 109)
soft hammer (p. 130)
taurodontism (p. 126)
unifacial tool (p. 119)

Critical Questions

1. How could there have been more than one species of hominid living in East Africa at the same time?

2. Why might early hominids have begun to make stone tools? How would stone tools have been more useful than wood or bone tools?

3. When compared to earlier hominids, *Homo erectus* is larger and has a larger brain and smaller teeth. How might these physical changes correlate with apparent behavioral changes in *Homo erectus?*

4. *Homo erectus* lived in many places in the Old World. What may have enabled them to spread so widely?

📖 Read the Original Source on myanthrolab.com

Read the chapter by Scott Simpson titled *"Australopithecus afarensis* and Human Evolution" on MyAnthroLab. Answer the following questions.

1. Why is the Afar region of Ethiopia such a rich and important area for finding early hominid fossils?
2. How does Simpson come to the conclusion that only one species, *A. afarensis,* is represented in the collections from Hadar and Laetoli?

The Emergence of
Homo sapiens

7

Recent finds in Africa indicate the presence of *Homo sapiens* perhaps 160,000 years ago. Completely modern-looking humans, *Homo sapiens sapiens*, appeared by 50,000 years ago. One paleoanthropologist, Christopher Stringer, characterizes the modern human, *Homo sapiens sapiens,* as having "a domed skull, a chin, small eyebrows, browridges, and a rather puny skeleton."[1] Some of us might not like to be called puny, but except for our larger brain, most modern humans definitely are puny compared with *Homo erectus* and even with earlier forms of our own species, *H. sapiens*. We are relatively puny in several respects, including our thinner and lighter bones, as well as our smaller teeth and jaws.

In this chapter, we discuss the fossil evidence, as well as the controversies, about the transition from *H. erectus* to modern humans, which may have begun 500,000 years ago. We also overview what we know archaeologically about the Middle Paleolithic (about 300,000 to 40,000 year ago) and Upper Paleolithic (40,000 to 10,000) years ago.

The Transition from *Homo erectus* to *Homo sapiens*

Most paleoanthropologists agree that *H. erectus* evolved into *H. sapiens,* but they disagree about how and where the transition occurred. There is also disagreement about how to classify some fossils from about 500,000 years to 200,000 years ago that have a mix of *H. erectus* and *H. sapiens* traits.[2] A particular fossil might be called *H. erectus* by some anthropologists and "archaic" *Homo sapiens* by others. And, as we shall see, still other anthropologists see so much continuity between *H. erectus* and *H. sapiens* that they think it is completely arbitrary to call them different species. According to these anthropologists, *H. erectus* and *H. sapiens* may just be earlier and later varieties of the same species and therefore all should be called *H. sapiens*. (*H. erectus* would then be *H. sapiens erectus*.)

Homo heidelbergensis

Some scholars have suggested that the "transitional" fossils share common traits and may actually represent a separate species—***Homo heidelbergensis***, named after a jaw found in 1907, near Heidelberg, Germany.[3] Other specimens that have been suggested as members of this species have been found in many parts of the Old World.[4] Although the classification of these "transitional" specimens is somewhat controversial, to simplify things, we will call all these "transitional" specimens *H. heidelbergensis*.

Homo heidelbergensis differs from *Homo erectus* in having smaller teeth and jaws, a much larger brain (on the order of 1,300 cc), a skull that lacks a sagittal keel and occipital torus, a browridge that divides into separate arches above each eye, and a more robust skeleton (see Figure 7.1). *Homo heidelbergensis* differs from *Homo sapiens* in retaining a large and prognathic face with relatively large teeth and jaws, a browridge, a long, low cranial vault with a sloping forehead, and in its more robust skeleton.[5]

Neandertals: *Homo sapiens* or *Homo neandertalensis*?

There may be disagreement about how to classify the mixed-trait fossils from 500,000 to 200,000 years ago, but recently an outright battle has emerged about many of the fossils that are less than 200,000 years old. Some anthropologists argue that they were definitely *Homo sapiens* and classify them as *Homo sapiens neandertalensis.* Other anthropologists argue that they were part of a distinct species, ***Homo neandertalensis,*** more commonly referred to as the **Neandertals.**

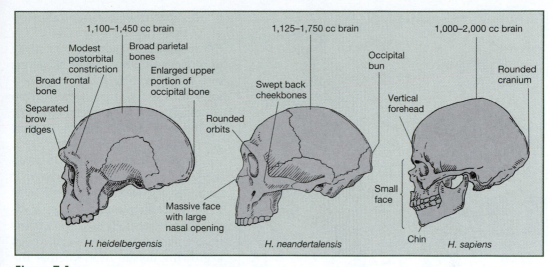

Figure 7.1 Comparison of the crania of *Homo heidelbergensis*, *Homo neandertalensis*, and *Homo sapiens*, showing important differences.

The Neandertals have been a confusing hominid fossil group since the first specimen was found in 1856. Somehow through the years, the Neandertals have become the victims of their cartoon image, which usually misrepresents them as burly and more ape than human. Actually, they might go unnoticed in a cross-section of the world's population today. Were they part of our species? For a while, the answer seemed to be yes. But recent archaeological and genetic evidence has led most to question the relationship between Neandertals and modern humans, and today the tide seems to have turned against those who would group them together. Let's take a look at some of the history of research on the Neandertals.

In 1856, three years before Darwin's publication of *Origin of Species,* a skullcap and other fossilized bones were discovered in a cave in the Neander Valley (*tal* is the German word for "valley"), near Düsseldorf, Germany. The fossils in the Neander Valley were the first that scholars could tentatively consider as an early hominid. (The fossils classified as *Homo erectus* were not found until later in the nineteenth century, and the fossils belonging to the genus *Australopithecus* were not found until the twentieth century.) After Darwin's revolutionary work was published, the Neandertal find aroused considerable controversy. A few evolutionist scholars, such as Thomas Huxley, thought that the Neandertal was not that different from modern humans. Others dismissed the Neandertal as irrelevant to human evolution; they saw it as a pathological freak, a peculiar, disease-ridden individual. However, similar fossils turned up later in Belgium, Yugoslavia, France, and elsewhere in Europe, which meant that the original Neandertal find could not be dismissed as an oddity.[6]

The view that the Neandertals were too "brutish" and "primitive" to have been ancestral to modern humans prevailed in the scholarly community until well into the 1950s. Now scholars agree that the skeletal traits of the Neandertals are completely consistent with bipedalism. Perhaps more important, when the australopithecine and *H. erectus* fossils were accepted as hominids in the 1940s and 1950s, anthropologists realized that the Neandertals did not look that different from modern humans—despite their sloping foreheads, large browridges, flattened braincases, large jaws, and nearly absent chins (see Figure 7.1).[7] And they had larger brains on the average than modern humans (about 150 cc larger).[8] Some scholars believe that the large

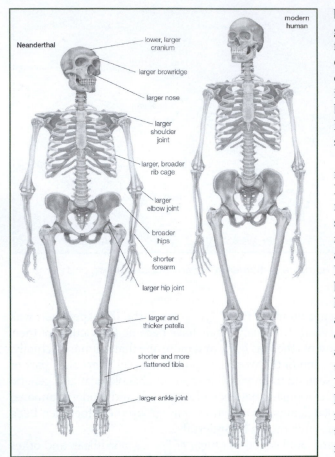

A comparison of a Neandertal (left) and a modern human skeleton. Note how similar they are, yet the Neandertal appears more stocky and robust.

brain capacity of Neandertals suggests that they were capable of the full range of behaviors characteristic of modern humans. Their skeletons did, however, attest to one behavioral trait markedly different from behaviors of most modern humans: Neandertals apparently made very strenuous use of their bodies.[9]

While it took almost 100 years for scholars to accept the idea that Neandertals were not that different from modern humans and perhaps should be classified as *Homo sapiens neandertalensis,* recently there has been a growing debate over whether the Neandertals in western Europe interbred with modern-looking people who lived later in western Europe, after about 40,000 years ago. In 1997, a group of researchers from the United States and Germany published findings that forced a reconsideration of the Neandertals' relationship to modern humans. These scholars extracted mitochondrial DNA (mtDNA) from the original Neandertal specimen found in 1856.[10] Among individual modern humans, there are usually five to ten differences in the sequence of mtDNA examined by the U.S. and German researchers. Between modern humans and the Neandertal specimen, there tend to be about 25 differences—more than three times that among modern humans (see Figure 7.2). This suggested to the researchers that the ancestors of modern humans and the Neandertal must have diverged about 600,000 years ago.[11] If the last common ancestor of ours and the Neandertal lived that long ago, the Neandertal would be a much more distant relative than previously thought. This research has since been replicated with mtDNA from other Neandertal fossils.[12]

But mtDNA is only part of the story. Subsequently, nuclear DNA has been recovered and sequenced from Neandertals. Researchers have found that Neandertals and modern humans have identical versions of the FOXP2 gene, suggesting to some that they may have had language abilities similar to modern humans.[13] Neandertals also had fair skin, and at least some had red hair.[14] While these nuclear DNA findings suggest more similarity, some significant differences between Neandertal and modern human nuclear DNA have also been identified. For example, Neandertals apparently lack the modern human version of *microcephalin,* a gene that is associated with brain development.[15] And initial analyses of the nuclear DNA suggest that the ancestral modern human and Neandertal populations split more than a half million years ago, with only modest admixture after that time.[16]

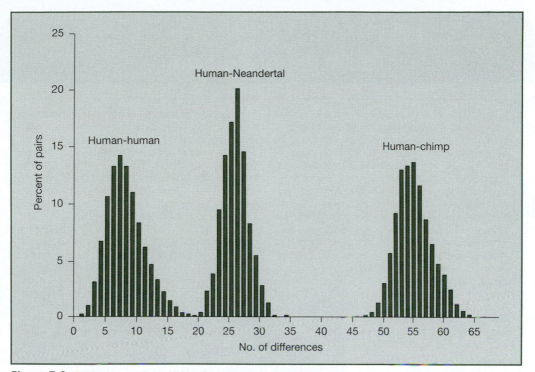

Figure 7.2 **Differences in mtDNA Sequences among Humans, Humans and Neandertals, and Humans and Chimpanzees**
The *x*-axis shows the number of sequence differences; the *y*-axis shows the percent of individuals that share that number of sequence differences.

Source: Krings 1997, 25.

Archaeological findings from Europe and the Near East also seem to indicate that Neandertals and modern humans were different species. It has been known for decades that both modern human and Neandertal fossils are found in the same locations in parts of the Levant, but recent improvements in dating technology and newly discovered fossils have even more clearly demonstrated that the two kinds of hominid coexisted. In fact, several caves in the Mount Carmel region of Israel contain both modern human and Neandertal occupations. The fact that these two groups of hominids coinhabited the Near East for perhaps as much as 30,000 years and did not interbreed much or share much in the way of tool technology strongly suggests that the two are different species.[17] Finds in Europe seem to corroborate that assessment. As early modern humans began moving into Europe, they appear to have displaced populations of Neandertals already living there. Sites with tools thought to be associated with Neandertals disappear throughout Europe as sites with tools thought to be associated with modern humans expand their range.[18] Significantly, the area of Europe last colonized by modern humans (Iberia) contains the very latest Neandertal fossils yet found, dating to some 30,000 years ago.[19]

With all this evidence pointing to Neandertals not being part of the modern human species, why is there an ongoing debate? In part, this is because none of the evidence is conclusive, and much of it can be interpreted in alternate ways. Perhaps more important, however, Neandertal culture, typically referred to as Middle Paleolithic after the predominant tool technology, has some features that make it seem similar to the culture of early modern humans.

Facial Reconstruction

Have you ever wondered how we know what early humans looked like? We have pictures of them throughout this book, but how did the artists determine what to sculpt or draw? The answer lies in the field of forensic anthropology and more particularly in the field of facial reconstruction.

Facial reconstruction is based on knowledge of skull musculature and the thickness of soft tissue, determined over many years (the first such analysis was done in 1895) from cadavers and, more recently, magnetic resonance images of living people. From these measurements, forensic anthropologists have established a standard set of 21–34 locations on the skull where the average soft tissue thicknesses are known. The first step in facial reconstruction is to mark these locations on a cast of the skull to be reconstructed, using pegs that are the same length as the thickness of muscle and soft tissue at that location. Clay is then used to cover the skull cast to the depth of these pegs (the musculature of the face is first modeled in more sophisticated reconstructions, then clay is used to represent the soft tissues, up to the depth of the pegs).

The size and shape of the nose are reconstructed based on the size and shape of the nasal opening. The size and shape of lips and ears are more difficult to determine, and the skull itself can tell the forensic anthropologist almost nothing about hair or eye color, whether the person had facial hair, or how the person's hair was cut. Those aspects of facial reconstruction require some artistic intuition, and it is helpful to know something about the person, such as sex, age, and ethnicity.

But what about ancient humans? The standard measurements used to reconstruct faces

Boule's reconstruction of a Neandertal, as displayed at Chicago's Field Museum in 1929, illustrates how subjective fossil reconstructions can be. It falsely implies that Neandertals could not stand upright or straighten their knees, and that they were more primitive than we know today that they actually were.

from modern human skulls cannot be assumed to work for ancient skulls. For those, the forensic anthropologists have to go back to the basis of facial reconstruction—muscle and soft tissue. When reconstructing the faces of ancient humans, forensic anthropologists begin with a careful reconstruction of skull musculature, often aided by the comparative anatomy of modern great apes. Once the muscles are in place, glands, fatty tissue, and skin are added, and the face begins to take shape. The size and shape of the nose are determined much like that for modern humans, from the size and shape of the nasal opening. Lips, ears, eyes, and hair are, however, subject to almost pure guesswork—we really have no way of knowing how hairy our ancestors were, whether they had full lips like ours or thin lips like other great apes, or whether their ears were large or small.

Though based on study of the likely muscular anatomy in fossils and the comparative anatomy of modern humans and great apes, it is important to realize that the reconstruction of ancient faces is in part an artistic exercise. We can never know for sure what, for example, *Homo erectus* really looked like. We do not know how hairy they were or how they "styled" their hair. We do not know if their ears were like ours. We do not know the color of their eyes or skin. This is why reconstructions vary in the ways they depict ancient humans. We need to keep in mind when we look at reconstructions that they are educated, perhaps biased, guesses, and not necessarily true depictions of ancient people.

Sources: Moser 1998; Prag and Neave 1997.

Middle Paleolithic Cultures

The period of cultural history associated with the Neandertals is traditionally called the **Middle Paleolithic** in Europe and the Near East and dates from about 300,000 years to about 40,000 years ago.[20] For Africa, the term *Middle Stone Age* is used instead of Middle Paleolithic. The tool assemblages from this period are generally referred to as Mousterian in Europe and the Near East and as *post-Acheulian* in Africa.

Tool Assemblages

The Mousterian The Mousterian type of tool complex is named after the tool assemblage found in a rock shelter at Le Moustier in the Dordogne region of southwestern France. Compared with an Acheulian assemblage, a **Mousterian tool assemblage** has a smaller proportion of large core tools such as hand axes and cleavers and a bigger proportion of small flake tools such as scrapers.[21] Although many flakes struck off from a core were used "as is," the Mousterian is also characterized by flakes that were often altered or "retouched" by striking small flakes or chips from one or more edges (see Figure 7.3).[22] Studies of the wear on scrapers suggest that many were used for scraping hides or working wood. The fact that some of the tools, particularly points, were thinned or shaped on one side suggests that they were hafted or attached to a shaft or handle.[23]

Toward the end of the Acheulian period, a technique developed that enabled toolmakers to produce flake tools of a predetermined size instead of simply chipping flakes away from the core at random. In this **Levalloisian method,** toolmakers first shaped the core and prepared a

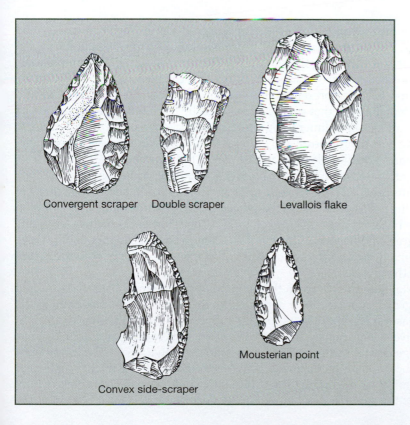

Convergent scraper   Double scraper   Levallois flake

Convex side-scraper   Mousterian point

Figure 7.3 Stone Tools of the Typical Mousterian Industry
Flakes were carefully retouched, usually on two sides. Mousterian tools, associated with Neandertals, are part of what archaeologists call the Middle Paleolithic, about 200,000 to 35,000 years before the present.
Source: Klein 1974.

"striking platform" at one end. Flakes of predetermined and standard sizes could then be knocked off. Although some Levallois flakes date as far back as 400,000 years ago, they are found more frequently in Mousterian tool kits.[24]

The tool assemblages in particular sites may be characterized as Mousterian, but one site may have more or fewer scrapers, points, and so forth, than another site. A number of archaeologists have suggested possible reasons for this variation. For example, Sally Binford and Lewis Binford suggested that different activities may have occurred in different sites. Some sites may have been used for butchering and other sites may have been base camps; hence, the kinds of tools found in different sites should vary.[25] And Paul Fish has suggested that some sites may have more tools produced by the Levalloisian technique because larger pieces of flint were available.[26]

The Post-Acheulian in Africa   Like Mousterian tools, many of the post-Acheulian tools in Africa during the Middle Stone Age were struck off prepared cores in the Levalloisian way. The assemblages consist mostly of various types of flake tools. A well-described sequence of such tools comes from the area around the mouth of the Klasies River on the southern coast of South Africa. This area contains rock shelters and small caves in which early and later *Homo sapiens* lived. The oldest cultural remains in one of the caves may date back 120,000 years.[27] These earliest tools include parallel-sided flake blades (probably used as knives), pointed flakes (possibly spearpoints), burins or gravers (chisel-like tools), and scrapers. Similar tools discovered at Border cave, South Africa, may have been used almost 200,000 years ago.[28]

Homesites

Most of the excavated Middle Paleolithic homesites in Europe and the Near East are located in caves and rock shelters. The same is true for the excavated Middle Stone Age homesites in sub-Saharan Africa. We might conclude, therefore, that Neandertals (as well as many early modern humans) lived mostly in caves or rock shelters. But that conclusion could be incorrect. Caves and rock shelters may be overrepresented in the archaeological record because they are more likely to be found than are sites that originally were in the open but now are hidden by thousands of years, and many feet, of sediment. Sediment is the dust, debris, and decay that accumulate over time; when we dust the furniture and vacuum the floor, we are removing sediment.

Still, we know that many Neandertals lived at least part of the year in caves. This was true, for example, along the Dordogne River in France. The river gouged deep valleys in the limestone of that area. Below the cliffs are rock shelters with overhanging roofs and deep caves, many of which were occupied during the Middle Paleolithic. Even if the inhabitants did not stay all year, the sites do seem to have been occupied year after year.[29] Although there is evidence of some use of fire in earlier cultures, Middle Paleolithic humans seem to have relied more on it. There are thick layers of ash in many rock shelters and caves and evidence that hearths were used to increase the efficiency of the fires.[30]

Quite a few Neandertal homesites were in the open. In Africa, open-air sites were located on floodplains, at the edges of lakes, and near springs.[31] Many open-air sites have been found in Europe, particularly eastern Europe. The occupants of the well-known site at Moldova in western Russia lived in river-valley houses framed with wood and covered with animal skins. Bones of mammoths, huge elephants now extinct, surround the remains of hearths and were apparently used to help hold the animal skins in place. Even though the winter climate near the edge of the glacier nearby was cold at that time, there still would have been animals to hunt because the plant food for the game was not buried under deep snow.

The hunters probably moved away in the summer to higher land between the river valleys. In all likelihood, the higher ground was grazing land for the large herds of animals the Moldova hunters depended on for meat. In the winter river valley sites, archaeologists have found skeletons of wolf, arctic fox, and hare with their paws missing. These animals probably were skinned for pelts that were made into clothing.[32]

Getting Food

How Neandertals and early modern humans got their food probably varied with their environment. In Africa, they lived in savanna and semiarid desert. In western and eastern Europe, they had to adapt to cold; during periods of increased glaciation, much of the environment was steppe grassland and tundra.

The European environment during this time was much richer in animal resources than the tundra of northern countries today. Indeed, the European environment inhabited by Neandertals abounded in big and small game, such as reindeer, bison, wild oxen, horses, mammoths, rhinoceroses, and deer, as well as bears, wolves, and foxes.[33] Some European sites have also yielded bird and fish remains. For example, people in a summer camp in northern Germany apparently hunted swans and ducks and fished for perch and pike.[34] Little, however, is known about the particular plant foods the European Neandertals may have consumed; the remains of plants are unlikely to survive thousands of years in a nonarid environment.

In Africa, too, early *Homo sapiens* varied in how they got food. For example, we know that the people living at the mouth of the Klasies River in South Africa ate shellfish as well as meat from small grazers such as antelopes and large grazers such as eland and buffalo.[35] But archaeologists disagree about how the Klasies River people got their meat when they began to occupy the caves in the area. Richard Klein thinks they hunted both large and small game. Klein speculates that, because the remains of eland of all ages have been found in Cave 1 at the Klasies River site, the people there probably hunted the eland by driving them into corrals or other traps, where animals of all ages could be killed. Klein thinks that buffalo were hunted differently. Buffalo tend to charge attackers, which would make it difficult to drive them into

Neandertals appear to have hunted a wide variety of game. In this reconstruction, two Neandertals are shown attacking a mastodon they have trapped in a pit.

traps. Klein believes that, because bones from mostly very young and very old buffalo are found in the cave, the hunters were able to stalk and kill only the most vulnerable animals.[36]

Lewis Binford thinks the Klasies River people hunted only small grazers and scavenged the eland and buffalo meat from the kills of large carnivores. He argues that sites should contain all or almost all of the bones from animals that were hunted. According to Binford, because more or less complete skeletons are found only from small animals, the Klasies River people were not, at first, hunting all the animals they used for food.[37]

However, evidence suggests that people were hunting big game as much as 400,000 years ago. Wooden spears that old were found in Germany in association with stone tools and the butchered remains of more than 10 wild horses. The heavy spears resemble modern aerodynamic javelins, which suggests they would have been thrown at large animals such as horses, not at small animals. This new evidence strongly suggests that hunting, not just scavenging, may be older than archaeologists once thought.[38]

Rituals

At Drachenloch cave in the Swiss Alps, a stone-lined pit holding the stacked skulls of seven cave bears was found in association with a Neandertal habitation. Why preserve these skulls? One reason might be for rituals intended to placate or control bears. Cave bears were enormous—some nearly 9 feet tall—and competed with Neandertals for prime cave living sites. Perhaps the Neandertals preserved the skulls of bears they killed in the cave as a way of honoring or appeasing either the bears or their spirits. But the evidence is not completely persuasive. In our own society, some may hang a deer or moose head on the wall without any associated ritual. At this point, we cannot say for certain whether or not Neandertals engaged in ritual behavior.[39]

The Emergence of Modern Humans

Cro-Magnon humans, who appear in western Europe about 35,000 years ago, were once thought to be the earliest specimens of modern humans, or *Homo sapiens sapiens.* (The Cro-Magnons are named after the rock shelter in France where they were first found in 1868.[40]) But we now

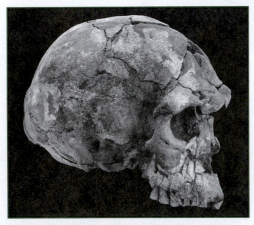

This *Homo sapiens* skull from Ethiopia is the oldest member of our species yet found, dating to 160,000 years ago.

know that modern-looking humans appeared earlier outside of Europe. As of now, the oldest unambiguous fossils classified as *H. sapiens* come from Ethiopia and date to perhaps 160,000 years ago.[41] Additional fossils, discovered in one of the Klasies River mouth caves in South Africa, are possibly as old as 100,000 years.[42] Other *Homo sapiens* fossils of about the same age have been found in Border cave in South Africa.[43] Remains of anatomically modern humans (*Homo sapiens sapiens*) found at two sites in Israel, at Skhul and Qafzeh, which used to be thought to date back 40,000 years to 50,000 years, may be 90,000 years old.[44] There are also anatomically modern human finds in Borneo, at Niah, from about 40,000 years ago and in Australia, at Lake Mungo, from about 30,000 years ago.[45]

These modern-looking humans differed from the Neandertals and other early *H. sapiens* in that they had higher, more bulging foreheads, thinner and lighter bones, smaller faces and jaws, chins (the bony protuberances that remain after projecting faces recede), and only slight browridges (or no ridges at all; see Figure 7.1).

Theories about the Origins of Modern Humans

Two theories about the origins of modern humans continue to be debated among anthropologists. One, which can be called the *single-origin theory,* suggests that modern humans emerged in Africa and then spread to other parts, replacing Neandertals. The second theory, which has been called the multiregional theory, suggests that modern humans evolved in various parts of the Old World after *Homo erectus* spread out of Africa.[46]

Single-Origin Theory According to the single-origin theory, the Neandertals did not evolve into modern humans. Rather, Neandertals were replaced by modern humans around 30,000 years ago. Single-origin theorists think that the originally small population of *H. sapiens sapiens* had some biological or cultural advantage, or both, that allowed them to spread and replace Neandertals.

The main evidence for the single-origin theory comes from the genes of living peoples. In 1987, Rebecca Cann and colleagues used genetic differences between living peoples to determine how long ago modern humans separated from our closest ancestors. Cann relied on the genes within a tiny structure found in all of our eukaryotic cells called *mitochondria.* Mitochondria produce enzymes needed for energy production, and they have their own DNA, which replicates when a cell replicates but is not thought to be under any pressure from natural selection.[47]

The only source of change in mitochondrial DNA (usually referred to as *mt*DNA) is random mutation. Mitochondrial DNA is inherited only from mothers in animals; it is not carried into an egg cell by sperm, but is left with the sperm's tail on the outside of the egg. These unique characteristics make it possible to use mtDNA to measure the degree of relatedness between two species, and even to say how long ago those species diverged.[48] The longer two species have been separated, the more differences there will be in their mtDNA, which is thought to mutate at a fairly constant rate of about 2 percent per million years. Thus, the number of differences between the mtDNA of two organisms can be converted into an estimated date in the past when those organisms stopped being part of the same breeding population. Although controversy remains over many of the details of how and why mtDNA mutates and about its accuracy for determining absolute dates of divergence, most scholars agree that it is a powerful tool for examining relative degrees of relatedness between species.[49]

Rebecca Cann and her colleagues presented evidence that the mtDNA from people in the United States, New Guinea, Africa, and East Asia showed differences suggesting that their common ancestor lived only 200,000 years ago. Cann and colleagues further claimed that, because the amount of variation among individuals was greatest in African populations, the common ancestor of all lived in Africa.[50] (It is generally the case that people living in a homeland exhibit more variation than any emigrant descendant population.)

There were many problems with early mtDNA studies, but those problems have been addressed over the years and new and better mtDNA analyses have been performed. Most scholars now agree that the mtDNA of modern humans shows a remarkably small degree of variation (in fact, less than half the variation found in most chimpanzee populations), which strongly suggests that we all share a very recent, common ancestry.[51] More detailed analyses of mtDNA diversity in modern humans have allowed scholars to identify the ancestral roots of contemporary populations around the world, and these analyses also point to modern human origins in East Africa and a subsequent spread out of that region.[52]

Evidence for an East African origin of modern humans and the subsequent expansion also comes from research on variation in the Y chromosome. The Y chromosome is the chromosome that determines whether a person is male. A male inherits an X chromosome from his mother and a Y chromosome from his father. Only men have a Y chromosome, and because there is only one copy in any given man, the Y chromosome is the only nuclear chromosome that, like mtDNA, does not undergo recombination. Although the Y chromosome can be affected by selection, it is thought that most variation in the Y chromosome, like variation in mtDNA, is caused by random mutations. Variation in the Y chromosome can therefore be analyzed in much the same way as variation in mtDNA.[53]

The results of research on variation in the Y chromosome mirror those on variation in mtDNA to a remarkable extent. Analysis of Y chromosome variation points to Africa as the source of modern humans, and suggests an exodus from Africa of modern humans. One of the major differences between mtDNA studies and those employing the Y chromosome is in the dating of the most recent common ancestor. As noted previously, studies of mtDNA suggest the most recent common ancestor lived about 200,000 years ago, whereas studies of the Y chromosome suggest the most recent ancestor lived only about 100,000 years ago.[54] Additional research, including new research on variation in nuclear DNA, may help to resolve these differences. For now, however, it seems clear that the modern human gene pool has a single, and fairly recent, origin in Africa.[55]

The mtDNA analyses of Neandertals, and the archaeological evidence suggesting that Neandertals and modern humans lived without much interaction or interbreeding in Europe and the Near East, also tend to support the single-origin theory. The *Homo sapiens* skeletal material from Ethiopia, Africa, in the 150,000–200,000-year-ago time range, further supports the single-origin theory.[56] However, such evidence does not necessarily contradict the validity of the multiregional theory of human origins.

Multiregional Theory   According to the multiregional theory, *Homo erectus* populations in various parts of the Old World gradually evolved into anatomically modern-looking humans. The few scholars who continue to support this view believe that the "transitional" or "archaic" *H. sapiens* and the Neandertals represent phases in the gradual development of more "modern" anatomical features. Indeed, as we have noted, some of these scholars see so much continuity between *Homo erectus* and modern humans that they classify *Homo erectus* as *Homo sapiens erectus*.

Continuity is the main evidence multiregional theorists use to support their position. In several parts of the world, there seem to be clear continuities in distinct skeletal features between *Homo erectus* and *Homo sapiens*. For example, *Homo erectus* fossils from China tend to have broader faces with more horizontal cheekbones than specimens from elsewhere in the world, traits that also appear in modern Chinese populations.[57] Southeast Asia provides more compelling evidence, according to multiregional theorists. There, a number of traits—relatively thick cranial bones, a receding forehead, an unbroken browridge, facial prognathism, relatively large cheekbones, and relatively large molars—appear to persist from *Homo erectus* through modern populations (see Figure 7.4).[58] But others suggest that these traits cannot be used to establish a unique continuation from *Homo erectus* in Southeast Asia because these traits are found in modern humans all over the world. And still others argue that the traits are not as similar as the multiregional theorists claim.[59]

In support of their position, multiregional theorists argue that the mtDNA and Y chromosome evidence supports multiregional evolution rather than a single-origin theory of modern humans, that genetic variation in modern humans may reflect the emigration of *Homo erectus* out of Africa rather than the emigration of *Homo sapiens sapiens.* This interpretation would mean that the accepted rates of mutation in both mtDNA and the Y chromosome are wrong, that both actually mutate much more slowly than currently thought.[60] However, this interpretation is contradicted by established correlations between differences in mtDNA among human groups known to have colonized New Guinea and Australia at particular points in time, which seem to fit the accepted rate of mutation, and with the divergence between humans and apes, the date of which also seems to accord with the accepted faster rate of mtDNA mutation.

To explain why human evolution would proceed gradually and in the same direction in various parts of the Old World, multiregional theorists point to cultural improvements in cutting-tool and cooking technology that occurred all over the Old World. These cultural improvements may have relaxed the prior natural selection for heavy bones and musculature in the skull. The argument is that, unless many plant and animal foods were cut into small pieces and

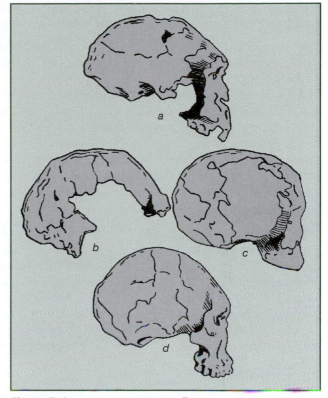

Figure 7.4 Fossil Evidence for Regional Continuity
Continuity in Southeast Asian and Australian populations: Skulls of (a) *Homo erectus*, (b) early *Homo sapiens*, and (d) modern *Homo sapiens*, all from Southeast Asia and Australia, have similar foreheads, browridges, and occipital and facial shapes, whereas skulls from Africa, represented here by (c), an early *Homo sapiens*, have different forms. The similarity in Southeast Asian and Australian populations over more than 500,000 years argues for regional continuity rather than replacement.

thoroughly cooked in hearths or pits that were efficient thermally, they would be hard to chew and digest. Thus, people would have needed robust jaws and thick skull bones to support the large muscles that enabled them to cut and chew their food. But robust bone and muscle would no longer be needed after people began to cut and cook more effectively.[61]

Intermediate Theories There is also the intermediate interpretation that there may have been some replacement of one population by another, some local continuous evolution, and some interbreeding between early modern humans who spread out of Africa, and populations encountered in North Africa, Europe, and Asia.[62] As biologist Alan Templeton has noted, the debates over a single-origin versus multiregional evolution

are based on the myth that replacement of one physical feature in a fossil series with another feature can only be created by one population replacing another (by exterminating them, for example), but such fossil patterns could be a reflection of one genotype replacing another through gene flow and natural selection. Morphological replacement should not be equated with population replacement when one is dealing with populations that can interbreed.[63]

Interestingly, data on the genetic diversity of human body lice seems to support an intermediate theory of human origins. Humans are plagued by a single species of hair lice, *Pediculus humanus,* which happens to have two distinct genetic lineages. One is found worldwide, the other only in the Americas. These two genetic lineages of lice appear to have diverged over 1 million years ago. If modern humans evolved less than 200,000 years ago (and the worldwide louse lineage suggests it experienced some dramatic changes about 100,000 years ago, which may relate to modern humans leaving Africa), then how did the other lineage continue? One answer is that they were transferred to modern humans from a previously isolated population of *Homo erectus* in Asia.[64] But if that were the case, then very close contact—either body to body or sharing clothing—would had to have taken place between modern and archaic humans.

What Happened to the Neandertals?

Regardless of which theory (single-origin, multiregional, or intermediate) is correct, it seems clear that Neandertals and modern humans (*H. sapiens sapiens*) coexisted in Europe and the Near East for at least 20,000 years, and maybe as long as 60,000 years. What happened to the Neandertals? Three answers have generally been considered. First, they interbred with modern humans and the unique Neandertal characteristics slowly disappeared from the interbreeding population. Second, they were killed off by modern humans. Third, they were driven to extinction due to competition with modern humans. Let's take a look at each of these scenarios.

Interbreeding

The interbreeding scenario seems the most probable, yet evidence supporting it is weak. If modern humans and Neandertals interbred, we should be able to find "hybrid" individuals in the fossil record. In fact, a group of scholars has argued that an Upper Paleolithic skeleton from Portugal demonstrates a combination of modern human and Neandertal features.[65] The finding remains controversial, however, because it is a child's skeleton (approximately 4 years old) and its Neandertal-like features have not been corroborated by other scholars. More significantly, if the interbreeding hypothesis is correct, then the mtDNA analysis we have discussed several times in this chapter must be wrong. On the other hand, recent research on Neandertal tools suggests that some Neandertal groups adopted new techniques of tool manufacture that are thought to be uniquely associated with modern humans.[66] If Neandertals were learning from modern humans, then the idea that they could have interbred and perhaps been absorbed within the modern human population gains credibility.

Genocide

The genocide scenario, that modern humans killed off Neandertals, has appeal as a sensational story, but little evidence. Not a single "murdered" Neandertal has ever been found, and one might wonder, in a fight between the powerful Neandertals and the more gracile modern humans, who might get the better of whom.

Extinction

Finally, the extinction scenario, that Neandertals simply could not compete with modern humans, seems to have the best archaeological support. As we discussed earlier, there appear to be "refugee" populations of Neandertals in Iberia as recently as perhaps 30,000 years ago.

The "retreat" of Neandertals from the Near East, eastern Europe, and finally western Europe following the movement of modern humans into the region seems to support the "refugee" interpretation.[67] More importantly, physical anthropologist Erik Trinkaus has argued, based on both physical characteristics of the Neandertal skeleton and their apparent patterns of behavior, that Neandertals were less efficient hunters and gatherers than modern humans.[68] And they may have needed more food. Steve Churchill has suggested that Neandertals' stocky bodies and great muscle mass might have required 25 percent more calories than modern humans.[69] If this is true, a modern human group would have been able to live and reproduce more easily than a Neandertal group in the same territory, and this would likely drive the Neandertals away. When there were no new territories to run to, the Neandertals would go extinct—precisely what the archaeological record seems to suggest.[70]

But were modern humans and their cultures really that much more efficient than Middle Paleolithic cultures? As we will see, the Upper Paleolithic does seem to mark a watershed in the evolution of human culture, allowing humans to expand their physical horizons throughout the world and their intellectual horizons into the realms of art and ritual.

The Upper Paleolithic World

The period of cultural history in Europe, the Near East, and Asia known as the **Upper Paleolithic** dates from about 40,000 years ago to the period known as the *Neolithic* (beginning about 10,000 years ago, depending on the area). In Africa, the cultural period comparable to the Upper Paleolithic is known as the *Later Stone Age* and may have begun much earlier. In North and South

America, the period begins when humans first entered the New World, some time before 12,000 years ago (these colonizers are typically called *Paleo-Indians*) and continues until what are called *Archaic traditions* emerged some 10,000 years ago. To simplify terminology, we use the term *Upper Paleolithic* to refer to cultural developments in all areas of the Old World during this period.

In many respects, lifestyles during the Upper Paleolithic were similar to lifestyles before. People were still mainly hunters, gatherers, and fishers who probably lived in small mobile bands. They made their camps out in the open in skin-covered huts and in caves and rock shelters. And they continued to produce smaller and smaller stone tools.

But the Upper Paleolithic is also characterized by a variety of new developments. One of the most striking is the emergence of art—painting on cave walls and stone slabs, and carving tools, decorative objects, and personal ornaments out of bone, antler, shell, and stone. Because more archaeological sites date from the Upper Paleolithic than from any previous period and some Upper Paleolithic sites seem larger than any before, many archaeologists think that the human population increased considerably during the

Upper Paleolithic bone needle and spear or harpoon points. Upper Paleolithic peoples made a much wider variety of tools than their predecessors.

Upper Paleolithic.[71] In addition, new inventions, such as the bow and arrow, the spear thrower, and tiny replaceable blades that could be fitted into handles, appear for the first time.[72]

The Last Ice Age

The Upper Paleolithic world had an environment very different from today's. The earth was gripped by the last ice age, with glaciers covering Europe as far south as Berlin and Warsaw, and North America as far south as Chicago. To the south of these glacial fronts was a tundra zone extending in Europe to the Alps and in North America to the Ozarks, Appalachians, and well out onto the Great Plains. Environmentally, both Europe and North America probably resembled contemporary Siberia and northern Canada. Elsewhere in the world conditions were not as extreme, but were still different from conditions today.[73] Annual temperatures were as much as 50 degrees Fahrenheit (10 degrees Celsius) below today's, and changes in ocean currents would have made temperature contrasts (i.e., the differences between summer and winter months) more extreme as well. Europe experienced heavy annual snowfall. The presence of huge ice sheets in the north changed the climate throughout the world. North Africa, for example, appears to have been much wetter than today, and South Asia was apparently drier. And everywhere the climate seems to have been highly variable.[74]

The plants and animals of the Upper Paleolithic world were adapted to these extreme conditions. Among the most important, and dramatic, were the large game animals collectively known as *Pleistocene megafauna*.[75] These animals, as their name suggests, were huge compared to their contemporary descendants. For example, in North America, giant ground sloths stood some 8–10 feet tall and weighed several thousand pounds. Siberian mammoths were the largest elephants ever to live—some standing more than 14 feet tall.

Upper Paleolithic Europe

With the vast supplies of meat available from megafauna, it is not surprising that many Upper Paleolithic cultures relied on hunting, and this was particularly true of the Upper Paleolithic peoples of Europe, on whom we focus here. Their way of life represents a common pattern throughout the Old World. But as people began to use more diverse resources in their environments, the use of local resources allowed Upper Paleolithic groups in much of the Old World to become more sedentary than their predecessors. They also began to trade with neighboring groups to obtain resources not available in their local territories.[76]

As was the case in the known Middle Paleolithic sites, most of the Upper Paleolithic remains that have been excavated were situated in caves and rock shelters. In southwestern France, some groups seem to have paved parts of the shelter floors with stones. Tentlike structures were built in some caves, apparently to keep out the cold.[77] Some open-air sites have also been excavated.

The site at Dolni Vestonice in what is now the Czech Republic, dated to around 25,000 years ago, is one of the first for which there is an entire settlement plan.[78] The settlement seems to have consisted of four tentlike huts, probably made from animal skins, with a great open hearth in the center. Around the outside were mammoth bones, some rammed into the ground, which suggests that the huts were surrounded by a wall. All in all, there were bone heaps from about 100 mammoths. Each hut probably housed a group of related families—about 20–25 people. (One hut was approximately 27 by 45 feet and had five hearths distributed inside it, presumably one for each family.) With 20–25 people per hut, and assuming that all four huts were occupied at the same time, the population of the settlement would have been 100–125 people.

Up a hill from the settlement was a fifth and different kind of hut. It was dug into the ground and contained a bake oven and more than 2,300 small, fired fragments of animal figurines. There were also some hollow bones that may have been musical instruments. Another interesting feature of the settlement was a burial find of a woman with a disfigured face. She may have been a particularly important personage; her face was found engraved on an ivory plaque near the central hearth of the settlement.

Upper Paleolithic Tools

Upper Paleolithic toolmaking appears to have had its roots in the Mousterian and post-Acheulian traditions because flake tools are found in many Upper Paleolithic sites. But the Upper Paleolithic is characterized by a preponderance of blades; there were also burins, bone and antler tools, and microliths. In addition, two new techniques of toolmaking appeared: *indirect percussion* and *pressure flaking.* Blades were found in Middle Paleolithic assemblages, but they were not widely used until the Upper Paleolithic. Although blades can be made in a variety of ways, **indirect percussion** using a hammer-struck punch was common in the Upper Paleolithic. After shaping a core into a pyramidal or cylindrical form, toolmakers put a punch of antler, wood, or other hard material into position and struck it with a hammer. Because the force is readily directed, toolmakers were able to strike off consistently shaped **blades,** which are more than twice as long as they are wide.[79]

The Upper Paleolithic is also noted for the production of large numbers of bone, antler, and ivory tools; needles, awls, and harpoons made of bone appear for the first time.[80] The manufacture of these implements may have been made easier by the development of many varieties of burins. **Burins** are chisel-like stone tools used for carving; bone and antler needles, awls, and projectile points could be produced with them.[81] Burins have been found in Middle and Lower Paleolithic sites but are present in great number and variety only in the Upper Paleolithic.

Pressure flaking also appeared during the Upper Paleolithic. Rather than using percussion to strike off flakes as in previous technologies, pressure flaking works by employing pressure with a bone, wood, or antler tool at the edge of the tool to remove small flakes. Pressure flaking would usually be used in the final stages of retouching a tool.[82]

As time went on, all over the Old World, smaller and smaller blade tools were produced. The very tiny ones, called **microliths,** were often hafted or fitted into handles, one blade at a time or several blades together, to serve as spears, adzes, knives, and sickles. The hafting required inventing a way to trim the blade's back edge so that it would be blunt rather than sharp. In this way, the blades would not split the handles into which they might be inserted; the blunting would also prevent the users of an unhafted blade from cutting themselves.[83]

Some archaeologists think that the blade technique was adopted because it made for more economical use of flint. André Leroi-Gourhan calculated that, with the old Acheulian technique, a 2-pound lump of flint yielded 16 inches of working edge and produced only two hand axes. If the more advanced Mousterian technique were used, a lump of equal size would yield 2 yards of working edge. The indirect percussion method of the Upper Paleolithic would yield as much as 25 yards of working edge.[84] Getting the most out of a valuable resource may have been particularly important in areas lacking large flint deposits.

Jacques Bordaz suggested that the evolution of toolmaking techniques, which continually increased the amount of usable edge that could be gotten out of a lump of flint, was significant because people could then spend more time in regions where flint was unavailable.[85] Another reason for adopting the blade toolmaking technique may have been that it made for easy repair of tools. For example, the cutting edge of a tool might consist of a line of razorlike microliths set into a piece of wood. The tool would not be usable if just one of the cutting edge's microliths broke off or was chipped. But if the user carried a small prepared core of flint from which an identical-sized microlith could be struck off, the tool could be repaired easily by replacing the lost or broken microlith. A spear whose point was lost could be repaired similarly. Thus, the main purpose of the blade toolmaking technique may not have been to make more economical use of flint but rather to allow easy replacement of damaged blades.[86]

How Were the Tools Used? One way of suggesting what a particular tool was used for in the past is to observe the manner in which similar tools are used by members of recent or contemporary societies, preferably societies with subsistence activities and environments similar to those of the ancient toolmakers. This method of study is called reasoning from **ethnographic analogy.** The problem with such reasoning, however, is obvious: We cannot be sure that the original use of a tool was the same as the present use. When selecting recent or contemporary cultures that may provide the most informative and accurate comparisons, we should try to choose those that derive from the ancient culture in which we are interested. If the cultures being compared are historically related, there is a greater likelihood that the two groups used a particular kind of tool in similar ways and for similar purposes.[87]

Another way of suggesting what a particular kind of tool was used for is to compare the visible and microscopic wear marks on the prehistoric tools with the wear marks on similar tools made and experimentally used by researchers. The idea behind this approach is that different uses leave different wear marks. A pioneer in this research was S. A. Semenov. For example, by cutting into meat with his re-created stone knives, he produced a polish on the edges that was like the polish found on blades from a prehistoric site in Siberia. This finding led Semenov to infer that the Siberian blades were probably also used to cut meat.[88]

The tools made by Upper Paleolithic peoples suggest that they were much more effective hunters and fishers than their predecessors.[89] During the Upper Paleolithic, and probably for the first time, spears were shot from a spear thrower rather than thrown with the arm. We know this because bone and antler **atlatls** (the Aztec word for "spear thrower") have been found in some sites. A spear propelled off a grooved board could be sent through the air with increased force, causing it to travel farther and hit harder, and with less effort by the thrower. The bow and arrow was also used in various places during the Upper Paleolithic; and harpoons, used for fishing and perhaps for hunting reindeer, were invented at this time.

These new tools and weapons for more effective hunting and fishing do not rule out the possibility that Upper Paleolithic peoples were still scavenging animal remains. Olga Soffer suggests that Upper Paleolithic peoples may have located their settlements near places where many mammoths died naturally in order to make use of the bones for building (see Figure 7.5). For example, in Moravia, the mammoths may have come to lick deposits of calcite and other sources of magnesium and calcium, particularly during the late spring and early summer when resources were short and mortality was high. Consistent with this idea is that there are few human-made cut marks on mammoth bones in some places. For example, at Dolni Vestonice, where bones of 100 mammoths were found, few bones show cut marks from butchering and few bones were found inside the huts. In contrast, the site is littered with bison, horse, and reindeer bones, suggesting that these other animals were deliberately killed and eaten by humans. If the people had been able to kill all the mammoths we find the remains of, why would they have hunted so many other animals?[90]

Upper Paleolithic Art The earliest discovered traces of art are beads and carvings, and then paintings, from Upper Paleolithic sites. We might expect that early artistic efforts were crude,

Figure 7.5 Here we see the type of mammoth-bone shelters constructed about 15,000 years ago on the East European Plain. Often mammoth skulls formed part of the foundation for the tusk, long bone, and wooden frame, covered with hide. As many as 95 mammoth mandibles were arranged around the outside in a herringbone pattern.

but the cave paintings of Spain and southern France show a marked degree of skill. So do the naturalistic paintings on slabs of stone excavated in southern Africa. Some of those slabs appear to have been painted as much as 28,000 years ago, which suggests that painting in Africa is as old as painting in Europe.[91] But painting may be even older than that. The early Australians may have painted on the walls of rock shelters and cliff faces at least 30,000 years ago and maybe as much as 60,000 years ago.[92] And at Blombos Cave in South Africa, engraved pieces of red ochre date back to more than 77,000 years ago.[93]

Peter Ucko and Andrée Rosenfeld identified three principal locations of paintings in the caves of western Europe: (1) in obviously inhabited rock shelters and cave entrances—art as decoration or "art for art's sake"; (2) in "galleries" immediately off the inhabited areas of caves; and (3) in the inner reaches of caves, whose difficulty of access has been interpreted by some as a sign that magical-religious activities were performed there.[94]

The subjects of the paintings are mostly animals. The paintings are on bare walls, with no backdrops or environmental trappings. Perhaps, like many contemporary peoples, Upper Paleolithic men and women believed that the drawing of a human image could cause death or injury. That might explain why human figures are rarely depicted in cave art. Another explanation for the focus on animals is that these people sought to improve their luck at hunting. This theory is suggested by evidence of chips in the painted figures, perhaps made by spears thrown at the drawings. Or perhaps the paintings were inspired by the need to increase the supply of animals. Cave art seems to have reached a peak toward the end of the Upper Paleolithic period, when the herds of game were decreasing.

The particular symbolic significance of the cave paintings in southwestern France is more explicitly revealed by the results of Patricia Rice and Ann Paterson's statistical study.[95] The data suggest that the animals portrayed in the cave paintings were mostly the ones that the painters preferred for meat and for materials such as hides. For example, wild cattle (bovines) and horses are portrayed more often than we would expect by chance, probably because they were larger and heavier (meatier) than the other animals in the environment. In addition, the paintings

Paintings of wild horses from Chauvet cave in France. Cave paintings like this demonstrate the remarkable skill of Upper Paleolithic artists.

mostly portray animals that the painters may have feared the most because of their size, speed, natural weapons such as tusks and horns, and unpredictability of behavior (mammoths, bovines, and horses). Thus, the paintings are consistent with the idea that "the art is related to the importance of hunting in the economy of Upper Paleolithic people."[96] Consistent with this idea is the fact that the art of the cultural period that followed the Upper Paleolithic, when getting food no longer depended on hunting large game because they were becoming extinct, the art ceased to focus on portrayals of animals.

Upper Paleolithic Cultures in Africa and Asia

Europe was not the only region where Upper Paleolithic peoples thrived. In North Africa, for example, Upper Paleolithic peoples hunted large animals on the grasslands that covered the region during that period. They lived in small communities located within easy access to water and other resources, and moved regularly, probably to follow the animal herds. Trade took place between local groups, particularly for high-quality stone used in making tools.[97] In eastern and southern Africa, a way of life known as the Later Stone Age developed that persisted in some areas until very recently. People lived in small, mobile groups, hunting large animals and collecting a wide variety of plant foods.

In South Asia, the Upper Paleolithic saw an increasingly sedentary lifestyle developing along the banks of freshwater streams. The Upper Paleolithic peoples in South Asia combined hunting, fishing, and gathering with seasonal movements to exploit seasonally abundant resources.[98] In East and Southeast Asia, ocean resources became vital to coastal-dwelling peoples, whereas those inland lived primarily in caves, hunting and collecting broadly in the local environment. Many of these sites appear to have been occupied for long periods of time, suggesting some degree of sedentism. During the Upper Paleolithic, peoples from Asia also populated Australia, New Guinea, and some of the islands of western Melanesia, clearly demonstrating the ability of these peoples to navigate on the sea and to use its resources.[99]

The Earliest Humans and Their Cultures in the New World

So far in this chapter, we have dealt only with the Old World—Africa, Europe, and Asia. What about the New World—North and South America? How long have humans lived there, and what were their earliest cultures like?

Because only *Homo sapiens sapiens* fossils have been found in North and South America, migrations of humans to the New World had to have taken place some time after the emergence of *H. sapiens sapiens*. But exactly when these migrations occurred is subject to debate, particularly about when people got to areas south of Alaska. On the basis of similarities in biological traits such as tooth

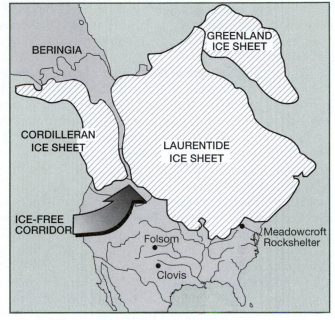

Figure 7.6 Beringia and the Ice Sheets

Source: Meltzer 1993.

forms and blood types, and on possible linguistic relationships, anthropologists agree that Native Americans originally came from Asia. The traditional assumption is that they came to North America from Siberia, walking across a land bridge (Beringia) that is now under water (the Bering Strait) between Siberia and Alaska. The ice sheets or glaciers that periodically covered most of the high latitudes of the world contained so much of the world's water (the ice sheets were thousands of feet thick in some places) that Beringia was dry land in various periods (see Figure 7.6).

Until recently, the prevailing view was that humans were not present south of Alaska until after 11,500 years ago. Now it appears from an archaeological site called Monte Verde in Chile that modern humans got to southern South America by at least 12,500 years ago, and maybe as much as 33,000 years ago. The Monte Verde site contains more than 700 stone tools, the remains of hide-covered huts, and a child's footprint next to a hearth.[100] The site suggests that there was at least one wave of human migration into the New World before 11,500 years ago, by walking and/or perhaps in boats. Even when the last glaciers were at their fullest extent, there was a small ice-free corridor through which people could have walked. And there were ice-free corridors earlier.

It was geologically possible then for humans to have walked into the New World at various times, or they could have traveled by boat. Parts of the Beringia land bridge were exposed from about 60,000 years to 25,000 years ago. Not until between 20,000 years and 18,000 years ago was the land bridge at its maximum. When did the last land bridge disappear? It used to be widely believed that the land bridge was flooded around 14,000 years ago, but recent evidence suggests that walking across Beringia was still possible until about 10,000 years ago. An ice-free corridor between the Laurentide and Cordilleran ice sheets may have been present after 25,000 years ago, but that corridor is not likely to have supported big game, and permitted humans to hunt enough for sustenance, until after about 14,000 years ago. So some investigators suggest that moving through the ice-free corridor to what is now south of Canada was not likely until after that time.[101]

The people moving into North America through the ice-free corridor may or may not have hunted big game, but just a little while later people were living in the Amazon jungle of what is now Brazil, and they were definitely not hunters of mammoths and other big game, as the contemporaneous Clovis people of North America were. In other words, it looks like the earliest inhabitants of the New World—in Chile, Brazil, and North America—varied in culture. The people in the Amazon lived by collecting fruits and nuts, fishing, and hunting small game. They lived in caves with painted art on the walls and left 30,000 stone chips from making tips of spears, darts, or harpoons.[102]

There is no disagreement that humans were living south of Canada after 11,000 years ago. The Clovis people, as they are called (after an archaeological site near Clovis, New Mexico), left finely shaped spear points in many locations in North America. And we have human skeletal remains from after 11,000 years ago. Now that the Monte Verde site has been reliably dated to before 12,000 years ago, we know that there were people south of Canada before the Clovis people were in New Mexico. And there are other possible sites of pre-Clovis occupation.[103] For example, the Cactus Hill site in Virginia, the Gault site in Texas, and the Shriver site in Missouri all contain a stratum of blades and other stone tools below a Paleo-Indian stratum containing Clovis tools. Meadowcroft Rockshelter in western Pennsylvania contains the most carefully reported pre-Clovis occupation in North America.[104] In the bottom third of a stratum that seems to date from 19,600 years to 8,000 years ago, the Meadowcroft site shows clear signs of human occupation—a small fragment of human bone, a spearpoint, and chipped knives and scrapers. Surprising physical evidence for pre-Clovis people in the Americas comes from the Paisley Caves in southern Oregon. Here, human coprolites (dried feces) have been found and dated to 14,400 years ago. Because the coprolites contain human DNA, and radiocarbon samples were taken directly from the coprolites, it seems conclusive that at least a small group of humans were in North America more than a thousand years before Clovis people.[105]

According to comparative linguists Joseph Greenberg and Merritt Ruhlen, there were three waves of migration into the New World.[106] They compared hundreds of languages in North and South America, grouping them into three different language families. Because each of these language families has a closer relationship to an Asian language family than to the other New World language families, it would appear that three different migrations came out of Asia. The first arrivals spoke a language that diverged over time into most of the languages found in the New World, the Amerind family of languages; the speakers of these related languages came to occupy all of South and Central America as well as most of North America. Next came the ancestors of the people who speak languages belonging to the Na-Dené family, which today includes Navajo and Apache in the southwestern United States and the various Athapaskan languages of northern California, coastal Oregon, northwestern Canada, and Alaska. Finally, perhaps 4,000 years ago, came the ancestors of the Inuit (Eskimo) and Aleut (the latter came to occupy the islands southwest of Alaska and the adjacent mainland), who speak languages belonging to the Inuit–Aleut family.

Christy Turner's study of New World teeth supports the Greenberg and Ruhlen proposal of three separate migrations. Turner looked at the proportions of shovel-shaped incisors, a common Asian trait, in New World populations. The varying proportions fall into three distinct

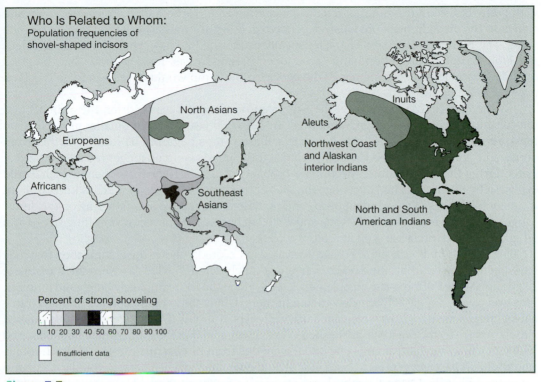

Who Is Related to Whom:
Population frequencies of
shovel-shaped incisors

North Asians

Europeans

Africans

Southeast
Asians

Inuits

Aleuts

Northwest Coast
and Alaskan
interior Indians

North and South
American Indians

Percent of strong shoveling

0 10 20 30 40 50 60 70 80 90 100

Insufficient data

Figure 7.7 Inuit (Eskimos) and Aleuts, speakers of Na-Dené languages, and other Native American language groups differ in the frequency of shovel-shaped incisors and other genetically based traits. These genetic differences seem to reflect three waves of migration into the New World.

Source: Turner 1987; 2005.

groupings, the same three suggested by the linguists[107] (see Figure 7.7). But genetic analyses suggest that the peopling of the New World may have been even more complicated. There could have been four separate migrations from the Old World, from different regions of Asia, or there could have been only one, with languages and genes diverging after humans arrived.[108]

The Paleo-Indians Archaeological remains of early New World hunters, called *Paleo-Indians*, have been found in the United States, Mexico, and Canada. Just south of the farthest reaches of the last glaciations, the area east of the Rockies known as the High Plains abounded with mammoths, bison, wild camels, and wild horses. The tools found with mammoth kills are known as the *Clovis complex*, which includes the Clovis projectile point as well as stone scrapers and knives and bone tools. The Clovis projectile point is large and leaf-shaped, flaked on both sides. It has a broad groove in the middle, presumably so that the point could be attached to a wooden spear shaft.[109] Because one mammoth was found with eight Clovis points in it, there is little dispute that Clovis people hunted large game.[110] Recent dating places most Clovis sites between 11,200 years and 10,900 years ago.[111]

The mammoth disappeared about 10,000 years ago, and the largest game animal became the now-extinct large, straight-horned bison. The hunters of that bison used a projectile point called the *Folsom point,* which was much smaller than the Clovis point. Tools are also found with many other kinds of animal remains, including wolf, turtle, rabbit, horse, fox, deer, and camel, so the bison hunters obviously depended on other animals as well.[112] In the Rio Grande valley, the Folsom toolmakers characteristically established a base camp on low dune ridges overlooking both a large pond and broad, open grazing areas. If we assume that the pond provided water for the grazing herds, the people in the camp would have been in an excellent position to watch the herds.[113]

As the climate of what is now the American Southwest became drier, the animals and the cultural adaptations changed somewhat. About 9,000 years ago, the smaller modern bison replaced the earlier straight-horned variety.[114] Base camps began to be located farther from ponds and grazing areas and closer to streams. If the ponds were no longer reliable sources of water during these drier times, the animals probably no longer frequented them, which would explain why the hunters had to change the sites of their base camps. Not much is known about the plant foods these Paleo-Indian people may have exploited, but plant-gathering on the desert fringes may have been vital. In Nevada and Utah, archaeologists have found milling stones and other artifacts for processing plant food.[115]

The Olsen-Chubbuck site, a kill site excavated in Colorado, shows the organization that may have been involved in hunting bison.[116] In a dry gulch dated to 6500 B.C. were the remains of 200 bison. At the bottom were complete skeletons and at the top, completely butchered animals. This find clearly suggests that Paleo-Indian hunters deliberately stampeded the animals into a natural trap—an arroyo, or steep-sided dry gully. The animals in front were probably pushed into the arroyo by the ones behind. Joe Ben Wheat estimated that the hunters may have obtained 55,000 pounds of meat from this one kill. If we judge from nineteenth-century Plains Indians, who could prepare bison meat to last a month, and estimate that each person would eat a pound a day, the kill at the Olsen-Chubbuck site could have fed more than 1,800 people for a month (they probably did not all live together throughout the year). The hunters must have been highly organized not only for the stampede itself but also for butchering. It seems that the enormous carcasses had to be carried to flat ground for that job. In addition, the 55,000 pounds of meat and hides had to be carried back to camp.[117]

Although big game may have been most important on the High Plains, other areas show different adaptations. For example, Paleo-Indian people in woodland regions of what is now the United States seem to have depended more heavily on plant food and smaller game. In some woodland areas, fish and shellfish may have been a vital part of the diet.[118] On the Pacific coast, some Paleo-Indian people developed food-getting strategies more dependent on fish.[119] And in other areas, the lower Illinois River valley being one example, Paleo-Indian people who depended on game and wild vegetable foods managed to get enough food to live in permanent villages of perhaps between 100 and 150 people.[120]

The End of the Upper Paleolithic

After about 10,000 years ago, the glaciers began to disappear, and with their disappearance came other environmental changes. The melting of the glacial ice caused the oceans to rise, and, as the seas moved inland, the waters inundated some of the richest fodder-producing coastal plains, creating islands, inlets, and bays. Other areas were opened up for human occupation as the glaciers retreated and the temperatures rose.[121] The cold, treeless plains, tundras, and grasslands eventually gave way to dense mixed forests, mostly birch, oak, and pine, and the Pleistocene megafauna became extinct. The warming waterways began to be filled with fish and other aquatic resources.[122]

Archaeologists believe that these environmental changes induced some populations to alter their food-getting strategies. When the tundras and grasslands disappeared, hunters could no longer obtain large quantities of meat simply by remaining close to large migratory herds of animals, as they probably did during Upper Paleolithic times. Even though deer and other game were available, the number of animals per square mile (density) had decreased, and it became difficult to stalk and kill animals sheltered in the thick woods. Thus, in many areas, people seemed to have turned from a reliance on big game hunting to the intensive collecting of wild plants, mollusks, fish, and small game to make up for the extinction of the large game animals they had once relied upon.

The Maglemosian Culture of Northern Europe Some adaptations to the changing environment can be seen in the cultural remains of the settlers in northern Europe who archaeologists call *Maglemosians*. Their name derives from the peat bogs (*magle mose* in Danish means "great bog") where their remains have been found.

To deal with the new, more forested environment, the Maglemosians made stone axes and adzes to chop down trees and form them into various objects. Large timbers appear to have been split for houses; trees were hollowed out for canoes; and smaller pieces of wood were made into paddles. The canoes presumably were built for travel and perhaps for fishing on the lakes and rivers that abounded in the postglacial environment.

We do not know to what extent the Maglemosians relied on wild plant foods, but there were a lot of different kinds available, such as hazelnuts. However, we do know many other things about the Maglemosians' way of life. Although fishing was fairly important, as suggested by the frequent occurrence of bones from pike and other fish, as well as fishhooks, these people apparently depended mainly on hunting for food. Game included elk, wild ox, deer, and wild pig. In addition to many fishing implements and the adzes and axes, the Maglemosians' tool kit included the bow and arrow. Some of their tools were ornamented with finely engraved designs. Ornamentation independent of tools also appears in amber and stone pendants and small figurines representing, for example, the head of an elk.[123]

Like the Maglemosian finds, many of the European post–Upper Paleolithic sites are found near water—lakes, rivers, and ocean. But these sites probably were not inhabited year-round; there is evidence that at least some groups moved seasonally from one place of settlement to another, perhaps between the coast and inland areas.[124] Finds such as kitchen middens (piles of shells) that centuries of post–Upper Paleolithic seafood eaters had discarded, and the remains of fishing equipment, canoes, and boats indicate that these people depended much more heavily on fishing than had their ancestors in Upper Paleolithic times.

The Archaic Cultures of Eastern North America A related set of adaptations to the changing environment can be seen among the peoples who inhabited eastern North America at the end of the ice age. As the climate became warmer and drier, the flora and fauna of North America changed. Megafauna, as elsewhere in the world, went extinct, and were replaced by smaller mammals, particularly deer. The availability of meat was greatly reduced—hunters could count on coming home with pounds, not tons, of meat. Warmer-adapted plants replaced cold-adapted plants, and were used for food to replace the meat that was no longer available. Warmer-adapted plants had advantages as food resources for humans over cold-adapted ones because edible seeds, fruits, and nuts were more common, and often more plentiful and accessible, on the warmer-adapted plants. Thus, the Archaic peoples came to use a much greater diversity of plants and animals.[125]

The **Archaic** peoples of North America, like the Maglemosian peoples in Europe, began to follow a more sedentary lifestyle. Two forms of Archaic settlement appear to have been typical. One was a residential base camp, which would have been inhabited seasonally by several, probably related, families. The other was a special-purpose camp, which would have been a short-term habitation near a particular resource or perhaps used by a group of hunters for a short period of time.[126] On the Atlantic coast, for example, individual groups apparently moved seasonally along major river valleys, establishing summer base camps in the piedmont and winter camps near the coast. Special-purpose camps were created year-round as groups went out from the base camp to hunt and collect particular resources, such as stone for making tools.[127]

One of the innovations of the Archaic peoples was the development of ground stone woodworking tools. Axes, adzes, and tools for grinding seeds and nuts become more and more common in the tool kit.[128] This probably reflects the emergence of greater areas of forest following the retreat of the glaciers from North America, but it also demon-

Some examples of Archaic ground stone woodworking tools from eastern North America (wooden handles are reproductions) Archaic peoples apparently used wood more extensively than the Paleo-Indians.

strates a greater reliance on forest products and, most likely, a greater use of wood and wood products. Fish and shellfish also came to be relied upon in some areas, and this too reflects the adjustment made by the Archaic peoples to the changing conditions they faced at the end of the last ice age.

The innovation of most lasting importance in both the New and Old Worlds, however, was the development of domesticated plants and animals. In both parts of the world, peoples at the end of the ice age began to experiment with plants. By around 14,000 years ago in the Old World, and 10,000 years ago in the New World, some species had been domesticated. We turn to this fundamental change in food-getting—the invention of agriculture—in the next chapter.

✓●⃞**Study** and **Review** on **myanthrolab.com**

Summary

1. Most anthropologists agree that *Homo erectus* began to evolve into *Homo sapiens* after about 500,000 years ago. But there is disagreement about how and where the transition occurred. The mixed traits of the transitional fossils include large cranial capacities (well within the range of modern humans), together with low foreheads and large browridges, which are characteristic of *H. erectus* specimens.

2. *Homo sapiens* have been found in many parts of the Old World—in Africa and Asia as well as in Europe. Some of these *H. sapiens* may have lived earlier than the Neandertals

of Europe. There is still debate over whether the Neandertals in western Europe became extinct or survived and were ancestral to the modern-looking people who lived in western Europe after about 40,000 years ago.

3. The period of cultural history associated with the Neandertals is traditionally called the Middle Paleolithic in Europe and the Near East and dates from about 300,000 years to about 40,000 years ago. For Africa, the term *Middle Stone Age* is used. The assemblages of flake tools from this period are generally referred to as Mousterian in Europe and the Near East and as post-Acheulian in Africa. Compared with an Acheulian assemblage, a Mousterian tool assemblage has a smaller proportion of large hand axes and cleavers and a larger proportion of small flake tools such as scrapers. Some Mousterian sites show signs of intentional burial.

4. Fossil remains of fully modern-looking humans, *Homo sapiens sapiens,* have been found in Africa, the Near East, Asia, and Australia, as well as in Europe. The oldest of these fossils have been found in East Africa and may be 160,000 years old.

5. Two theories about the origins of modern humans continue to be debated among anthropologists. One, the *single-origin theory,* suggests that modern humans emerged in just one part of the Old World—the Near East and, more recently, Africa have been the postulated places of origin—and spread to other parts of the Old World, superseding Neandertals. The second theory, the *multiregional theory,* suggests that modern humans emerged in various parts of the Old World, becoming the varieties of humans we see today.

6. The period of cultural history known as the Upper Paleolithic in Europe, the Near East, and Asia or the Later Stone Age in Africa dates from about 40,000 years ago to about 14,000 to 10,000 years ago. During this ice age, glaciers covered much of northern Europe and North America, and annual temperatures were much lower than today's temperatures.

7. The Upper Paleolithic tool kit is characterized by the preponderance of blades; there were also burins, bone and antler tools, and (later) microliths. In many respects, lifestyles were similar to lifestyles before. People were still mainly hunters, gatherers, and fishers who probably lived in highly mobile bands. They made their camps out in the open and in caves and rock shelters.

8. The Upper Paleolithic is also characterized by a variety of new developments: new techniques of toolmaking, the emergence of art, population growth, and new inventions such as the bow and arrow, the spear thrower (atlatl), and the harpoon.

9. Only *Homo sapiens sapiens* remains have been found in the New World. The prevailing opinion is that humans migrated to the New World over a land bridge between Siberia and Alaska in the area of what is now the Bering Strait. Until recently, it was thought that humans were not present south of Alaska until after 11,500 years ago. Now it appears that modern humans arrived in southern South America by at least 12,500 years ago and perhaps as much as 33,000 years ago.

10. At the end of the ice age, around 14,000 years ago, the climate began to become more temperate. Many large animals that Upper Paleolithic peoples relied upon for food went extinct, and at the same time new, warmer-adapted plants provided a rich, new food source. Around the world, people began to use more plant foods and a broader range of resources overall. In many parts of the world, people began experimenting with domesticating plants and animals.

Glossary Terms

Archaic (p. 160)
atlatl (p. 152)
blade (p. 151)
burin (p. 151)
Cro-Magnon (p. 144)
ethnographic analogy (p. 152)

Homo heidelbergensis (p. 136)
Homo neandertalensis (p. 136)
Homo sapiens sapiens (p. 136)
indirect percussion (p. 151)
Levalloisian method (p. 141)
microlith (p. 151)

Middle Paleolithic (p. 141)
Mousterian tool assemblage
 (p. 141)
Neandertal (p. 136)
pressure flaking (p. 151)
Upper Paleolithic (p. 149)

Critical Questions

1. If the single-origin or "out-of-Africa" theory were correct, by what mechanisms could *Homo sapiens* have been able to replace *Homo erectus* and *Homo neandertalensis* populations?

2. How do Middle Paleolithic cultures differ from Lower Paleolithic cultures?

3. Upper Paleolithic cave paintings arouse our imaginations. We have described some research that tested ideas about what these paintings might mean. Can you think of other ways to understand the significance of cave art?

Read the Original Source on myanthrolab.com

Read the chapter by David Frayer titled "Testing Theories and Hypotheses about Modern Human Origins" on MyAnthroLab. Answer the following questions.

1. What does Frayer identify as the key elements of debate between the "Out of Africa" (or, as he calls it, "Noah's Ark") and "Multiregional" models of modern human origins?

2. What problems does Frayer identify with mitochondrial DNA evidence of modern human origins?

3. Frayer is in the minority among physical anthropologists today in supporting the multiregional model of human evolution. What reasons does he give for rejecting the more broadly accepted "Out of Africa" model?

Food Production and the Rise of States

8

CHAPTER OUTLINE

((•─┤**Listen** to the **Chapter Audio** on **myanthrolab.com**   ┤📖├─┤**Read** on **myanthrolab.com**

B
eginning about 14,000 years ago, people in some regions began to depend less on big game hunting and more on relatively stationary food resources, such as fish, shellfish, small game, and wild plants (see Figure 8.1). In some areas, particularly Europe and the Middle East, the exploitation of local, relatively permanent resources may account for an increasingly settled way of life. The cultural period in which these developments took place is usually now called the **Epipaleolithic** in the Middle East and the **Mesolithic** in Europe. Other areas of the world show a similar switch to what is called *broad-spectrum* food-collecting, but they do not always show an increasingly settled lifestyle, as, for example, in Mesoamerica where this period is called the *Archaic*.

We see the first clear evidence of a changeover to **food production**—the cultivation and domestication of plants and animals—in the Middle East, about 8000 B.C.[1] This shift, called the *Neolithic revolution* by archaeologist V. Gordon Childe, occurred, probably independently, in other areas of the Old and New Worlds within the next few thousand years. In the Old World, there were independent centers of domestication in China, Southeast Asia (what is now Malaysia, Thailand, Cambodia, Vietnam, and New Guinea), and Africa around 6000 B.C.[2] In the New World, there were centers of cultivation and domestication in the highlands of Mesoamerica

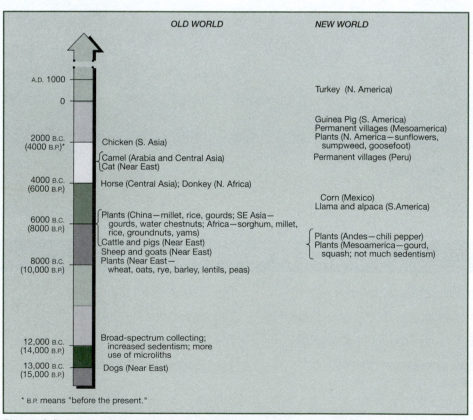

Figure 8.1 The Evolution of Domestication

Source: Dates for animal domestication are from Clutton-Brock 1992.

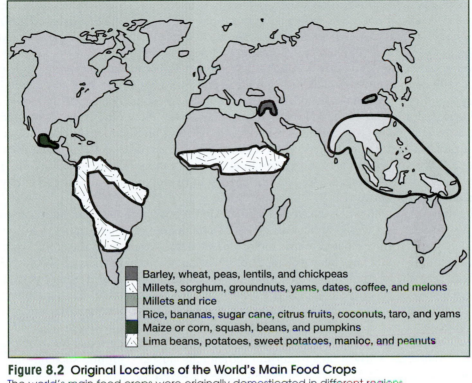

Figure 8.2 Original Locations of the World's Main Food Crops
The world's main food crops were originally domesticated in different regions.

Source: Hole 1992.

✳ Explore on **myanthrolab.com**

(about 7000 B.C.), the central Andes around Peru (about 7000 B.C.), and the Eastern Woodlands of North America (about 2000 B.C., but perhaps earlier).[3] Most of the world's major food plants and animals were domesticated well before 2000 B.C. Also developed by that time were techniques of plowing, fertilizing, fallowing, and irrigation.[4] Figure 8.2 shows the regions of the world that domesticated today's main food crops.

In this chapter, we discuss what is believed about the origins of food production and settled life, called **sedentarism**—how and why people in different places may have come to cultivate and domesticate plants and animals (referred to as **agriculture**) and to live in permanent villages. We then discuss the origin of cities and states. Much of our discussion focuses on the Middle East and Mesoamerica, the areas we know best archaeologically for the developments leading to food production and the rise of states.

Preagricultural Developments

The Middle East

In the Middle East, there seems to have been a shift from mobile big game hunting to the utilization of a broad spectrum of natural resources at the end of the Upper Paleolithic, similar to those changes that happened in Europe, which we discussed at the end of the last chapter.[5] There is evidence that people subsisted on a variety of resources, including fish, mollusks, and other water life; wild deer, sheep, and goats; and wild grains, nuts, and legumes.[6] The increased utilization of stationary food sources such as wild grain may partly explain why some people in the Middle East began to lead more sedentary lives during the Epipaleolithic.

Even today, a traveler passing through the Anatolian highlands of Turkey and other mountainous regions in the Middle East may see thick stands of wild wheat and barley growing as densely as if they had been cultivated.[7] Wielding flint sickles, Epipaleolithic people could easily have harvested a bountiful crop from such wild stands. Just how productive these resources can be was demonstrated in a field experiment duplicating prehistoric conditions. Using the kind of flint-blade sickle an Epipaleolithic worker would have used, researchers were able to harvest a little over 2 pounds of wild grain in an hour. A family of four, working only during the few weeks of the harvest season, probably could have reaped more wheat and barley than they needed for the entire year.[8]

The amount of wild wheat harvested in the experiment prompted Kent Flannery to conclude, "Such a harvest would almost necessitate some degree of sedentism—after all, where could they go with an estimated metric ton of clean wheat?"[9] Moreover, the stone equipment used for grinding would have been a clumsy burden to carry. Part of the harvest would probably have been set aside for immediate consumption, ground, and then cooked either by roasting or boiling. The rest of the harvest would have been stored to supply food for the remainder of the year. A grain diet, then, could have been the impetus for the construction of roasters, grinders, and storage pits by some preagricultural people, as well as for the construction of solid, fairly permanent housing. Once a village was built, people may have been reluctant to abandon it. We can visualize the earliest preagricultural settlements clustered around such naturally rich regions, as archaeological evidence indeed suggests they were.

The Natufians of the Middle East   Eleven thousand years ago, the Natufians, a people living in the area that is now Israel and Jordan, inhabited caves and rock shelters and built villages on the slopes of Mount Carmel in Israel. For example, the site of Eynan contains the remains of three villages in sequence, one atop another. Each village consisted of about 50 circular *pit houses.* The floor of each house was sunk a few feet into the ground, so that the walls of the house consisted partly of earth, below ground level, and partly of stone, above ground level. The villages appear to have had stone-paved walks; circular stone pavements ringed with what seem to be permanent hearths; and the dead were interred in village cemeteries.

The tools suggest that the Natufians harvested wild grain intensively. Sickles recovered from their villages have a specific sheen, which experiments have shown to be the effect of flint striking grass stems, as the sickles would have been used in the cutting of grain. The Natufians are the earliest Epipaleolithic people known to have stored surplus crops. Beneath the floors of their stone-walled houses, they constructed plastered storage pits.[10] The remains of many wild animals are found in Natufian sites; Natufians appear to have concentrated on hunting gazelle, which they would take by surrounding whole herds.[11]

Natufian food-collecting was different from foragers in earlier periods.[12] Not only was Natufian foraging based on a more intensive use of stationary resources such as wild grain, but the archaeological evidence suggests increasing social complexity. Natufian sites on the average were five times larger than those of their predecessors. Communities were occupied for most of the year, if not year-round. Burial patterns suggest more social differences between people. Although the available wild cereal resources appear to have enabled the Natufians to live in relatively permanent villages, their diet seems to have suffered. Their tooth enamel shows signs of nutritional deficiency, and their stature declined over time.[13]

Mesoamerica

A similar shift toward more broad-spectrum hunting and gathering occurred in the New World at the end of the Paleo-Indian period, about 10,000 years ago. The retreat of glacial ice from North America and overall warmer and wetter climate brought dramatic changes to plant and animal communities throughout North America and Mesoamerica. Pleistocene megafauna, such as mammoths, mastodon, rhinoceros, giant ground sloth, and others, as well as a variety of smaller game animals, such as the horse, all went extinct in a relatively short period of time.[14] Hunting strategies shifted toward a broader range of game species, particularly deer, antelope, bison, and small mammals. At the same time, deciduous woodlands and grasslands expanded, providing a range of new plants to exploit. Ground stone woodworking tools such as axes and adzes first appeared, as did nut-processing tools such as mortars and pestles. Shellfish began to be exploited in some areas. Throughout North America and Mesoamerica, people began to expand the range of plants and animals they relied upon.[15]

The Archaic Peoples of Highland Mesoamerica In Highland Mesoamerica, the mountainous regions of central and southern Mexico, we also see a shift from big game hunting to a broader use of resources, in part due to a change in climate more like today's. Altitude became an important factor in the hunting and collecting regime, as different altitudes have different plant and animal resources. Valleys tend to have scrubby, grassland vegetation, whereas foothills and mountains have "thorn forests" of cactuses and succulents, giving way to oak and pine forests at higher altitudes, where there is more moisture. This vertical zonation means that a wide range of plants and animals were available in relatively close proximity—different environments were close by—and the Archaic peoples took advantage of these varied conditions to hunt and collect a broad range of resources.[16]

About 8,000 years ago, the Archaic peoples in Mesoamerica appear to have moved seasonally between communities of two different sizes: camps with 15–30 residents (*macrobands*) and camps with only 2–5 residents (*microbands*). Macroband camps were located near seasonally abundant resources, such as acorns or mesquite pods. Several families would have come together when these resources were in season, both to take advantage of them and to work together to harvest them while they were plentiful, perhaps to perform rituals, and simply to socialize. Microband camps were also inhabited seasonally, probably by a single family, when groups were not assembled into macroband camps. Remains of these microband camps are often found

These young Fulbe-Waila girls in Chad are collecting seeds much like preagricultural peoples did.

in caves or rock shelters from which a variety of environments could be exploited by moving either upslope or downslope from the campsite.[17] Unlike the Natufians of the Middle East, there is no evidence of social differences among the Archaic peoples of Highland Mesoamerica.

Other Areas

The still-sparse archaeological record suggests that a change to broad-spectrum collecting occurred in Southeast Asia, which may have been one of the important centers of original plant and animal domestication.[18] For example, at inland base camps, we find the remains of animals from high mountain ridges as well as lowland river valleys, birds and primates from nearby forests, bats from caves, and fish from streams. The few coastal sites indicate that many kinds of fish and shellfish were collected and that animals such as deer, wild cattle, and rhinoceros were hunted.[19] The preagricultural developments in Southeast Asia probably were responses to changes in the climate and environment, including a warming trend, more moisture, and a higher sea level.[20]

In Africa, too, the preagricultural period was marked by a warmer, wetter environment. The now-numerous lakes, rivers, and other bodies of water provided fish, shellfish, and other resources that apparently allowed people to settle more permanently than they had before. For example, there were lakes in what is now the southern and central Sahara Desert, where people fished and hunted hippopotamuses and crocodiles. This pattern of broad-spectrum food-collecting seems also to have been characteristic of the areas both south and north of the Sahara.[21] One area showing increased sedentarism is the Dakhleh Oasis in the Western Desert of Egypt. Between 9,000 years and 8,500 years ago, the inhabitants lived in circular stone huts on the shores of rivers and lakes. Bone harpoons and pottery are found there and in other areas from the Nile Valley through the central and southern Sahara westward to what is now Mali. Fishing seems to have allowed people to remain along the rivers and lakes for much of the year.[22]

Why Did Broad-Spectrum Collecting Develop?

It is apparent that the preagricultural switch to broad-spectrum collecting was fairly common throughout the world. Climate change was probably at least partly responsible for the exploitation of new sources of food. For example, the worldwide rise in sea level because of glacial melting may have increased the availability of fish and shellfish. Changes in climate may have also been partly responsible for the decline in the availability of big game, particularly the large herd animals. Another possible cause of that decline was human activity, specifically overkilling of some of these animals.[23] The extinction in the New World of many of the large Pleistocene animals, such as the mammoth, coincided with the movement of humans from the Bering Strait region into the Americas.[24] However, an enormous number of bird species also became extinct during the last few thousand years of the North American Pleistocene, and it is difficult to argue that human hunters caused all of those extinctions. Because the bird and mammal extinctions occurred simultaneously, it is likely that most or nearly all the extinctions were due to climatic and other environmental changes.[25] Then again, the example of the New Zealand moas, which went extinct soon after humans colonized the islands, may be instructive. Moas had low reproductive rates; computer simulations suggest their population would have been very sensitive to increases in adult mortality. Because many large animals have low reproductive rates like moas, human overhunting may have been responsible for their extinction.[26]

Population growth may have also led to the shift to broad-spectrum collecting. As Mark Cohen has noted, hunter-gatherers were "filling up" the world, and they may have had to seek new, possibly less desirable sources of food.[27] We might think of shellfish as more desirable than mammoths, but only because we don't have to do the work to get such food. A lot of shellfish have to be collected, shelled, and cooked to produce the amount of animal protein obtainable from one large animal.

Broad-spectrum collecting does not necessarily mean that people were eating better. A decline in stature often indicates a poorer diet. During the preagricultural period, height apparently declined by as much as 2 inches in many parts of the Old World (Greece, Israel, India, and northern and western Europe).[28] In other areas of the world, such as Australia and what is now the midwestern United States, skeletal evidence also suggests a decline in the general level of health with the rise of broad-spectrum collecting.[29]

Broad-Spectrum Collecting and Sedentarism

Does the switch to broad-spectrum collecting explain the increasingly sedentary way of life we see in various parts of the world in preagricultural times? The answer seems to be both yes and no. In some areas of the world—some sites in Europe, the Middle East, Africa, and Peru—settlements became more permanent. In other areas, such as the semiarid highlands of Mesoamerica, the switch to broad-spectrum collecting was not associated with increasing sedentarism. Even after the Highland Mesoamericans began to cultivate plants, they still did not live in permanent villages.[30] Why?

It would seem that it is not simply the switch to broad-spectrum collecting that accounts for increasing sedentarism in many areas. Rather, a comparison of settlements on the Peruvian coast suggests that the more permanent settlements were located nearer, within 3½ miles, to most, if not all, of the diverse food resources exploited during the year. The community that did not have a year-round settlement seems to have depended on more widely distributed resources. What accounts for sedentarism may thus be the nearness[31] or the high reliability and yield[32] of the broad-spectrum resources, rather than the broad spectrum itself.

Population Growth and Sedentarism

Although some population growth undoubtedly occurred throughout the hunting and gathering phase of world history, some anthropologists have suggested that populations would have increased dramatically when people began to settle down.

The settling-down of a nomadic group may reduce the typical spacing between births.[33] Nomadic San have children spaced 4 years apart on the average; in contrast, recently sedentarized San have children about 3 years apart. Why might birth spacing change with settling down? If effective contraceptives are not available, prolonged sexual abstinence after the birth of a child (the postpartum sex taboo), common in many recent societies, may be one way of reducing births. Another way is abortion or infanticide.[34] Nomadic groups may be motivated to have children farther apart because of the problem of carrying small children.

Although some nomadic groups may have deliberately spaced births by abstinence or infanticide, there is no evidence that such practices explain why 4 years separate births among nomadic San. There may be another explanation, involving an unintended effect of how babies are fed. Nancy Howell and Richard Lee have suggested that the presence of baby foods other than mother's milk may be responsible for the decreased birth spacing in sedentary agricultural San groups.[35] It is now well established that the longer a mother nurses her baby without supplementary foods, the longer it is likely to be before she starts ovulating again. Nomadic San women have little to give their babies in the way of soft, digestible food, and the babies depend largely on mother's milk for 2–3 years. But sedentary San mothers can give their babies soft foods such as cereal (made from cultivated grain) and milk from domesticated animals. Such changes in feeding

A San group moving camp. When hunters and gatherers move, they have to carry their children and all their possessions with them. Spacing births an average of 4 years apart helps to ensure that a woman will not have to carry more than 2 children at a time.

practices may shorten birth spacing by shortening the interval between birth and the resumption of ovulation. In preagricultural sedentary communities, it is possible that baby foods made from wild grains might have had the same effect. For this reason alone, therefore, populations may have grown even before people started to farm or herd.

Some investigators suspect that a critical minimum of fat in the body may be necessary for ovulation. A sedentary San woman may have more fatty tissue than a nomadic San woman, who walks many miles daily to gather wild plant foods, often carrying a child with her. Thus, sedentary San women might resume ovulating sooner after the birth of a baby, and so for that reason alone may be likely to have more closely spaced children. If some critical amount of fat is necessary for ovulation, that would explain why many women who have little body fat in our own society—long-distance runners, gymnasts, and ballet dancers are examples—do not ovulate regularly.[36]

The Domestication of Plants and Animals

Neolithic means "of the new stone age"; the term originally signified the cultural stage in which humans invented pottery and ground-stone tools. We now know, however, that both were present in earlier times, so we cannot define a Neolithic state of culture purely on the basis of the presence of pottery and ground-stone tools. At present, archaeologists generally define the **Neolithic** in terms of the presence of domesticated plants and animals. In this type of culture, people began to produce food rather than merely collect it. The line between food-collecting and food-producing occurs when people begin to plant crops and to keep and breed animals. How do we know when this transition occurred? In fact, archaeologically we do not see the beginning of food production; we can see signs of it only after plants and animals show differences from their wild varieties. When people plant crops, we refer to the process as cultivation. It is only when the crops cultivated and the animals raised are *modified*—different from wild varieties—that we speak of plant and animal **domestication.**

We know, in a particular site, that domestication occurred if plant remains have characteristics different from those of wild plants of the same types. For example, wild grains of barley and wheat have a fragile **rachis**—the seed-bearing part of the stem—which shatters easily, releasing the seeds. Domesticated grains have a tough rachis, which does not shatter easily. In addition, the grain of wild barley and wheat has a tough shell protecting the seed from premature exposure, whereas domesticated grain has a brittle shell that can be easily separated, which facilitates preparing the seed for grinding into flour.

Consider how the rachis of wheat and barley may have changed. When humans arrived with sickles and flails to collect the wild stands of grain, the seeds harvested probably contained a high proportion of tough-rachis mutants because these could best withstand the rough treatment of harvest processing. If planted, the harvested seeds would be likely to produce tough-rachis plants. If, in each successive harvest, seeds from tough-rachis plants were the least likely to be lost, tough-rachis plants would come to predominate.[37]

Domesticated species of animals also differ from the wild varieties. For example, the horns of wild goats in the Middle East are shaped differently from those of domesticated goats.[38]

Domestication in the Middle East

For some time, most archaeologists have thought that the Fertile Crescent (see Figure 8.3), the arc of land stretching up from Israel and the Jordan Valley through southern Turkey and then downward to the western slopes of the Zagros Mountains in Iran, was one of the earliest centers of plant and animal domestication. We know that several varieties of domesticated wheat were being grown there after about 8000 B.C., as were oats, rye, barley, lentils, peas, and various fruits and nuts (apricots, pears, pomegranates, dates, figs, olives, almonds, and pistachios).[39] It appears that animals were first domesticated in the Middle East. Dogs were first domesticated before the rise of agriculture, around 13,000 B.C., goats and sheep around 7000 B.C., and cattle and pigs around 6000 B.C.[40]

Ali Kosh At the stratified site of Ali Kosh in what is now southwestern Iran (see Figure 8.3), we see the remains of a community that started out about 7500 B.C., living mostly on wild plants and animals. Over the next 2,000 years, until about 5500 B.C., agriculture and herding became increasingly important. After 5500 B.C., we see the appearance of two innovations—irrigation and the use of domesticated cattle—that seem to have stimulated a minor population explosion during the following millennium.[41]

From 7500 to 6750 B.C., the people at Ali Kosh cut little slabs of raw clay out of the ground to build small, multiroom structures. There is evidence that the people at Ali Kosh may have moved for the summer (with their goats) to the grassier mountain valleys nearby, which were just a few days' walk away.

We have a lot of evidence about what the people at Ali Kosh ate. They got some of their food from cultivated emmer wheat and a kind of barley and a considerable amount from domesticated goats. We know the goats were domesticated because wild goats do not seem to have lived in the area. Also, the fact that virtually no bones from elderly goats were found in the site suggests that the goats were domesticated and herded rather than hunted.[42] Moreover, it would seem from the horn cores found in the site that mostly young male goats were eaten, so the females probably were kept for breeding and milking. But with all these signs of deliberate food production, there is an enormous amount of evidence—literally tens of thousands of seeds and bone fragments—that the people at the beginning of Ali Kosh depended mostly on wild plants (legumes and grasses) and wild animals (including gazelles, wild oxen, and wild pigs). They also collected fish, such as

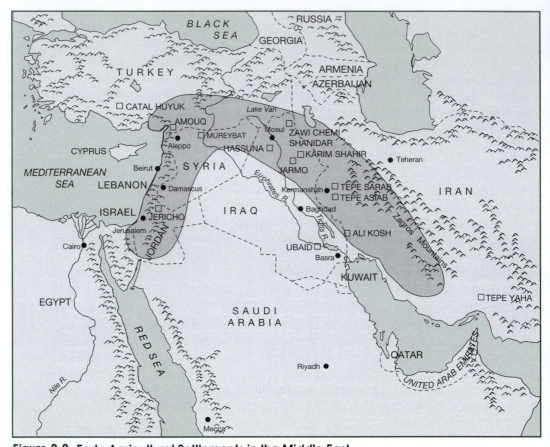

Figure 8.3 Early Agricultural Settlements in the Middle East
Modern cities are represented by a dot, early settlements by a square. The shaded arc indicates the
area known as the Fertile Crescent.

✳ Explore on **myanthrolab.com**

carp and catfish, and shellfish, such as mussels, as well as waterfowl that visited the area during
part of the year.

The flint tools used during this earliest phase at Ali Kosh were varied and abundant.
Finds from this period include tens of thousands of tiny flint blades, some only a few milli-
meters wide. About 1 percent of the chipped stone that archaeologists found was **obsidian,**
or volcanic glass, which came from what is now eastern Turkey, several hundred miles away.
Thus, the people at Ali Kosh during its earliest phase definitely had some kind of contact with
people elsewhere.

From 6750 to 6000 B.C., the people increased their consumption of cultivated food plants;
40 percent of the seed remains in the hearths and refuse areas were now from emmer wheat
and barley. The proportion of the diet coming from wild plants was much reduced, probably
because the cultivated plants have the same growing season and grow in the same kind of soil
as the wild plants. Grazing by the goats and sheep that were kept may also have contributed to
the reduction of wild plant foods in the area and in the diet. The village may or may not have
grown larger, but the multiroom houses definitely had. The rooms were now larger than 10 by

10 feet; the walls were much thicker; and a mud mortar now held the clay-slab bricks together. Also, the walls now often had a coat of smooth mud plaster on both sides. There were courtyards with domed brick ovens and brick-lined roasting pits.[43]

Even though the village probably contained no more than 100 individuals, it participated in an extensive trading network. Seashells were probably obtained from the Persian Gulf, which is some distance to the south; copper may have come from what is now central Iran; obsidian was still coming from eastern Turkey; and turquoise somehow made its way from what is now the border between Iran and Afghanistan. Some of these materials were used as ornaments worn by both sexes—or so it seems from the remains of bodies found buried under the floors of houses.

After about 5500 B.C., the area around Ali Kosh began to show signs of a much larger population, apparently made possible by a more complex agriculture employing irrigation and plows drawn by domesticated cattle. In the next thousand years, by 4500 B.C., the population of the area probably tripled. This population growth was apparently part of the cultural developments that culminated in the rise of urban civilizations in the Middle East.[44]

Domestication in Mesoamerica

A very different pattern of domestication is seen in Mesoamerica. Here the seminomadic Archaic hunting and gathering lifestyle persisted long after people first domesticated plants.[45] People sowed a variety of plants, but after doing so, they went on with their seasonal rounds of hunting and gathering, and came back later to harvest what they had sown. Domestication may have been a way for Archaic peoples to make desirable plants more common in their environment. For example, one of the first domesticates was the bottle gourd. These were not eaten but were used to carry water. Joyce Marcus and Kent Flannery hypothesize that people deliberately domesticated the bottle gourd by planting them in areas where they did not grow naturally, so that as groups moved through those areas, they always had access to gourds for carrying water.[46]

Other domesticates include tomatoes, cotton, a variety of beans and squashes, and, perhaps most importantly, maize. The earliest domesticated form of maize (corn), dating from about 5000 B.C., has been found in Tehuacán, Mexico. Genetic studies of maize show that it was domesticated from teosinte, a tall wild grass that still grows widely in Mexico.[47] Indeed, these genetic studies suggest that changes occurred in only two genes, one related to the kernel glumes (outer casing) and one related to the stalk shape.[48] The genes of modern corn were already established 4,000–6,000 years ago.

Early maize was considerably different from modern maize. The oldest maize cobs—dating to about 7,000 years ago—are tiny, only about an inch long. They have only a half-dozen rows of seeds, and each seed is tiny. Maize is almost completely dependent on humans to reproduce—the shift from seeds with brittle coats to cobs with a tough husk meant that someone had to open the husk without damaging the seeds for them to be dispersed and reproduce.[49]

People who lived in Mesoamerica, Mexico, and Central America are often credited with the invention of planting maize, beans, and squash together in the same field. This planting strategy provides some important advantages. Maize takes nitrogen from the soil; beans, like all legumes, put nitrogen back into the soil. The maize stalk provides a natural pole for the bean plant to twine around, and the low-growing squash can grow around the base of the tall maize plant. Beans supply people with the amino acid lysine, which is missing in maize. Thus, maize and beans together provide all the essential amino acids that humans need to obtain from their food. Teosinte may have provided the model for this unique combination, as wild runner beans and wild squash occur naturally where teosinte grows.[50]

APPLIED ANTHROPOLOGY

Raised Field Agriculture

Most agricultural systems in the Americas today rely upon either animal power or large machines to cultivate the soil and harvest food. But in the past, people had no traction animals or machines to help with agricultural production. How did the ancient farmers in the Americas till the soil and harvest crops? The answer is that they used human labor. In most cases, animal or mechanical power is much more efficient than human power, and allows more food to be grown on the same piece of land. Archaeologists, however, have found that some ancient, human-powered agricultural systems are actually better suited to specific local environments, and produce more food than modern, mechanized systems. These archaeologists have started to use their knowledge of ancient food production to help modern communities improve their lives.

Archaeologist Clark Erickson calls this work "applied archaeology," and he has been conducting applied archaeological work in South America since the early 1980s. One of his most significant projects involved the reconstruction of raised fields in the community of Huatta near Lake Titicaca in highland Peru. The environment there is relatively harsh. Agricultural development projects in the 1960s tried and failed to make the land surrounding Huatta productive. But Erickson recognized that most of the area surrounding the community had once been highly productive raised fields, and he wondered if rebuilding these ancient agricultural structures might help the community.

Raised fields are created by piling soil into a long mound, which becomes surrounded by a ditch as soil is taken from it and piled on the mound. Over time, the ditch fills with water and aquatic plants. The aquatic plants are harvested annually and placed on top of the mound as fertilizer. The water in the ditch both keeps the mound soil moist and helps control the soil temperature. As a system, raised fields form a self-sustaining agricultural microenvironment. The major drawback is that mechanized equipment cannot be used easily on these mounds and ditches, so significant amounts of human labor are often required.

In 1981, Erickson began working with members of the Huatta community to rebuild several of the ancient raised fields. By 1986, it was clear that raised field agriculture was well suited to the area. Raised fields were not as labor-intensive as initially thought, and were as or more productive than nearby agricultural fields built upon better soils. More significantly, the "green manure" from aquatic plants maintained the soils in the raised fields and actually improved them over time. So, although more labor-intensive, raised fields were able to bring otherwise marginal land into full agricultural production. Throughout the late 1980s, a number of indigenous communities in the Lake Titicaca basin turned to raised field agriculture with the help of a number of organizations. Due to many complex factors beginning in the 1990s such as guerrilla activities, urban migration, and pullout of development organizations, raised field agriculture is only practiced by a few communities today despite its potential (see photo).

Sources: Erickson 1988; 1989; 1998, 2003.

Domestication Elsewhere in the World

South America and the Eastern United States Evidence of independent domestication of plants comes from at least two areas in the New World: South America and the eastern United States. In addition to plants domesticated in Mesoamerica, we can trace more than 200 domesticated plants to the Andes in South America, including potatoes, lima beans, amaranth, and quinoa. The first clear domesticates were squashes and gourds, which may date back to 8000 B.C., which makes domestication in the Andes as old as in Mesoamerica, and perhaps even older.[51] The origins of the root crops manioc and sweet potato are less certain, but those crops probably originated in lowland tropical forest regions of South America.[52]

Many of the plants grown in North America, such as corn, beans, and squash, were apparently introduced from Mesoamerica. However, at least three seed plants were probably domesticated independently in North America at an earlier time—sunflowers, sumpweed, and

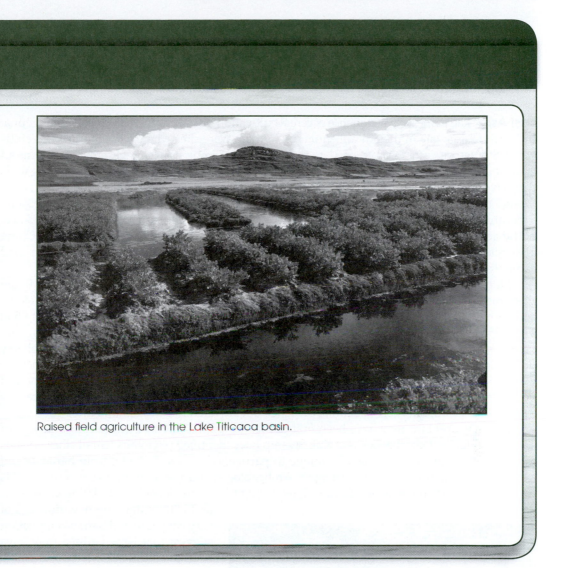

Raised field agriculture in the Lake Titicaca basin.

goosefoot. Sunflowers and sumpweed contain seeds that are highly nutritious in terms of protein and fat; goosefoot is high in starch and similar to corn in food value.[53] Sumpweed is an unusually good source of calcium, rivaled only by greens, mussels, and bones. It is also a very good source of iron (better than beef liver) and thiamine.[54] These plants may have been cultivated in the area of Kentucky, Tennessee, and southern Illinois beginning around 2000 B.C. (Corn was introduced about A.D. 200.)

On the whole, domestic animals were less important economically in the New World than they were in many parts of the Old World. The central Andes was the only part of the New World where animals were a significant part of the economy. Used for meat, transportation, and wool, llamas and alpacas (members of the camel family) were domesticated in the Andes as early as 5000 B.C.[55] Guinea pigs, misnamed because they are neither pigs nor from Guinea, are rodents that were domesticated in the Andes sometime later. They were an important source of food even before domestication.[56] Since they were domesticated, they have been raised in people's dwellings.

Animal domestication in the New World differed from that in the Old World because different wild species were found in the two hemispheres. The Old World plains and forests were the homes for the wild ancestors of the cattle, sheep, goats, pigs, and horses we know today. In the New World, the Pleistocene herds of horses, mastodons, mammoths, and other large animals were long extinct, allowing few opportunities for domestication of large animals.[57]

East Asia The earliest clear evidence of cereal cultivation outside the Middle East is from China. In North China, late in the 6th millennium B.C., there were sites where foxtail millet was cultivated. Storage pits, storage pots, and large numbers of grinding stones suggest that millet was an enormously important item in the diet. The wild animal bones and the hunting and fishing tools that have been found suggest that people still depended on hunting and fishing somewhat, even though domesticated pigs (as well as dogs) were present. In South China, from about the same time, archaeologists have found a village by the edge of a small lake where people cultivated rice, bottle gourds, water chestnuts, and the datelike fruit called jujube. The people in South China also raised water buffalo, pigs, and dogs. And, as in the North China sites, some of their food came from hunting and fishing.[58]

Mainland Southeast Asia may have been a place of domestication as early as the Middle East was. The dating of domestication in Southeast Asia is not yet clear; the dates of the oldest site with probable domesticates—Spirit cave in northwest Thailand—range from about 9500 B.C. to 5500 B.C. Some of the plants found at Spirit cave are not clearly distinguishable from wild varieties, but others, such as gourds, betel nut, betel leaf, and water chestnut, were probably domesticates.[59] Some early cultivated crops may not have been used for food at all. In particular, bamboo may have been used to make cutting tools and for a variety of building purposes, and gourds were probably used as containers or bowls. We do not know yet exactly when rice was first domesticated, but there is definite evidence of cultivated rice in Thailand after 4000 B.C.

Bananas and taro may have been first domesticated in New Guinea. Recent analyses of soils from archaeological deposits at Kuk Swamp have identified phytoliths (small silica crystals formed between plant cells that are unique to particular species of plants) from bananas and taro dating from almost 7,000 years ago.[60] Archaeologists have known that agricultural fields with soil mounds and irrigation features have a long history in New Guinea, dating back as far as 10,000 years. The new findings of very early taro and banana cultivation suggest that New Guinea may have been the location where these plants were first domesticated. Other major food plants domesticated in Southeast Asia include yams, breadfruit, and coconuts.[61]

Bananas and taro were domesticated in New Guinea nearly 7,000 years ago. Bananas are now grown in many tropical regions, including Ghana pictured here.

Africa Some plants and animals were domesticated first in Africa. Most of the early domestications probably occurred in the wide, broad belt of woodland-savanna country south of the Sahara and north of the equator. Among the cereal grains, sorghum was probably first domesticated in the central or eastern part of this belt, bulrush millet and a kind of rice (different from Asian rice) in the western part, and finger millet in the east. Bambara groundnuts (similar to peanuts) and yams were first domesticated in West Africa.[62] We do know that farming became widespread in the northern half of Africa after 6000 B.C.; investigators continue to debate whether the earliest crops grown there were indigenous or borrowed from the Middle East. There is little doubt, however, that some of the plant foods were first domesticated in sub-Saharan Africa because the wild varieties occur there.[63] Many of the important domestic animals in Africa today, especially sheep and goats, were first domesticated elsewhere in the Old World, but one form of cattle, as well as donkey and guinea fowl, were probably first domesticated in Africa.[64]

Why Did Food Production Develop?

Why did domestication occur? And why did it occur independently in many different places within a period of a few thousand years? Considering that people depended only on wild plants and animals for millions of years, the differences in exactly when domestication first occurred in different parts of the world seem small.

There are many theories of why food production developed; most have tried to explain the origin of domestication in the area of the Fertile Crescent. Gordon Childe's theory, popular in the 1950s, was that a drastic change in climate caused domestication in the Middle East.[65] According to Childe, the postglacial period was marked by a decline in summer rainfall in the Middle East and northern Africa. As the rains decreased, people were forced to retreat into shrinking pockets, or oases, of food resources surrounded by desert. The lessened availability of wild resources provided an incentive for people to cultivate grains and to domesticate animals, according to Childe. However, the climatic changes that occurred in the Middle East after the retreat of the last glaciers had probably occurred at earlier interglacial periods too, but there had never been a similar food-producing revolution before. Hence, according to Robert Braidwood, there must be more to the explanation of why people began to produce food than simply changes in climate.[66]

Lewis Binford and Kent Flannery thought that the incentive to domesticate animals and plants may have been a desire to reproduce what was wildly abundant in the most bountiful or optimum hunting and gathering areas. Because of population growth in the optimum areas, people might have moved to surrounding areas containing fewer wild resources. In those marginal areas, people might have first turned to food production to reproduce what they used to have. The Binford-Flannery model seems to fit the archaeological record in the Levant, the southwestern part of the Fertile Crescent, where population increase did precede the first signs of domestication.[67] But, as Flannery admitted, in some regions, such as southwestern Iran, the optimum hunting and gathering areas do not show population increase before the emergence of domestication.[68]

The Binford-Flannery model focuses on population pressure in a small area as the incentive to turn to food production. Mark Cohen theorizes that population pressure on a global scale explains why so many of the world's peoples adopted agriculture within the span of a few thousand years.[69] He argues that hunter-gatherers all over the world gradually increased in population so that the world was more or less filled with foragers by about 10,000 years ago. Thus, people could no longer relieve population pressure by moving to uninhabited areas. To support their increasing populations, they would have had to exploit a broader range of less desirable wild foods; that is, they would have had to switch to broad-spectrum collecting, or they would have had to increase the yields of the most desirable wild plants by weeding, protecting them from animal pests, and perhaps deliberately planting the most productive among them. Cohen thinks that people might have tried a variety of these strategies but would generally have ended up depending on cultivation because that would have been the most efficient way to allow more people to live in one place.

Recently, some archaeologists have returned to the idea that climatic change might have played a role in the emergence of agriculture. It seems clear from the evidence now available that the climate of the Middle East about 13,000 years to 12,000 years ago became more seasonal: The summers got hotter and drier than before and the winters became colder. These climatic changes may have favored the emergence of annual species of wild grain, which archaeologically we see proliferating in many areas of the Middle East.[70] People such as the Natufians intensively exploited the seasonal grains, developing an elaborate technology for storing and processing the grains and giving up their previous nomadic existence to do so. The transition to agriculture may have occurred when sedentary foraging no longer provided sufficient resources for the population. This could have happened because sedentarization led to population increase and therefore resource scarcity,[71] or because local wild resources became depleted after people settled down in permanent villages.[72] In the area of Israel and Jordan where the Natufians lived, some of the people apparently turned to agriculture, probably to increase the supply of grain, whereas other people returned to nomadic foraging because of the decreasing availability of wild grain.[73]

Change to a more seasonal climate might also have led to a shortage of certain nutrients for foragers. In the dry seasons, certain nutrients would have been less available. For example, grazing animals get lean when grasses are not plentiful, so meat from hunting would have been in short supply in the dry seasons. Although it may seem surprising, some recent hunter-gatherers have starved when they had to rely on lean meat. If they could have increased their carbohydrate or fat intake somehow, they might have been more likely to get through the periods of lean game.[74] So it is possible that some foragers in the past thought of planting crops to get them through the dry seasons when hunting, fishing, and gathering did not provide enough carbohydrates and fat for them to avoid starvation.

Mesoamerica presents a very different picture because the early domesticates were not important to subsistence. Theories about population pressure and nutrient shortage don't seem to fit Mesoamerica well. However, there were apparently shortages of desired plants, such as bottle gourds, and domestication may well have occurred as humans actively sowed these desired plants. The difference between this model and the ones described previously is that humans in Mesoamerica were apparently not forced into domestication by climate change or population pressure, but actively turned to domestication to obtain more of the most desired or useful plant species. The most interesting case is maize, which only became a staple food some 2,500 or more years after it was first domesticated. Why did it become a staple? Probably because it was both a suitable staple crop (especially when intercropped with beans and squash, as discussed earlier) and because people liked it, so they grew it in large quantities. Over time, and perhaps because of conflict, population pressure, and other forces similar to those that apparently led to domestication in the Middle East, people in Mesoamerica and later North and South America came to rely on maize as their dietary mainstay.

Consequences of the Rise of Food Production

We know that intensive agriculture (permanent rather than shifting cultivation) probably developed in response to population pressure, but we do not know for sure that population pressure was even partly responsible for plant and animal domestication in the first place. Still, population growth certainly accelerated after the rise of food production, possibly because the spacing between births was reduced further and therefore fertility (the number of births per mother)

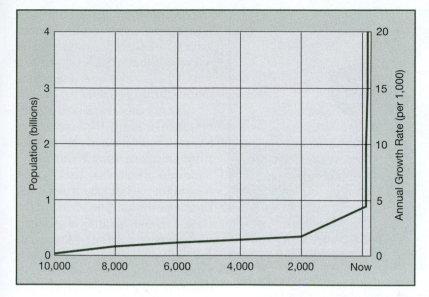

Figure 8.4 Population Growth since 10,000 Years Ago
The rate of population growth accelerated after the emergence of farming and herding 10,000 years ago. The rate of growth accelerated even more dramatically in recent times.

Source: Coale 1974.

increased (see Figure 8.4). Increased fertility may have been advantageous because of the greater value of children in farming and herding economies; there is evidence from recent population studies that fertility rates are higher where children contribute more to the economy.[75] The increased workload of mothers may also (but inadvertently) decrease birth spacing. The busier a mother is, the less frequently she may nurse and the more likely her baby will be given supplementary food by other caretakers such as older siblings.[76] Less frequent nursing[77] and greater reliance on food other than mother's milk may result in an earlier resumption of ovulation after the birth of a baby.

Although the rise of food production may have led to increased fertility, it appears that health declined at least sometimes with the transition to food production. The two trends may seem paradoxical, but rapid population growth can occur if each mother gives birth to a large number of babies, even if many of them die early because of disease or poor nutrition. Nutritional and disease problems are indicated by such features as incomplete formation of tooth enamel, nonaccidental bone lesions (incompletely filled-in bone), reduction in stature, and decreased life expectancy. Many of the studied prehistoric populations that relied heavily on agriculture seem to show less adequate nutrition and higher infection rates than populations living in the same areas before agriculture.[78] Some of the agricultural populations are shorter and had lower life expectancies.

The reasons for a decline in health in those populations are not yet clear. Greater malnutrition can result from an overdependence on a few dietary staples that lack some necessary nutrients. Overdependence on a few sources of food may also increase the risk of famine because the fewer the staple crops, the greater the danger to the food supply posed by a weather-caused crop failure. But some or most nutritional problems may be the result of social and political factors, particularly the rise of different socioeconomic classes of people and unequal access, between and within communities, to food and other resources.[79]

For the first time, apparel made of woven textiles appeared. This development was not simply the result of the domestication of flax (for linen), cotton, and wool-growing sheep. These sources of fiber alone could not produce cloth. It was the development by Neolithic society of the

As this reconstruction shows, transforming grain into flour was a "daily grind," putting a great deal of stress on the lower back and knees. Studies of Neolithic skeletons of women show marks of stress on bone and arthritis, probably reflecting their long hours of work at the grinding stone.

Source: Osti 1994. Courtesy of *Scientific American*, August 1994, p. 73, top.

spindle and loom for spinning and weaving that made textiles possible. True, textiles can be woven by hand without a loom, but to do so is a slow, laborious process, impractical for producing garments.

There is also evidence of long-distance trade in the Neolithic, as we have noted. Obsidian from southern Turkey was being exported to sites in the Zagros Mountains of Iran and to what are now Israel, Jordan, and Syria in the Levant. Great amounts of obsidian were exported to sites about 190 miles from the source of supply; more than 80 percent of the tools that residents of those areas used were made of this material.[80] Marble was being sent from western to eastern Turkey, and seashells from the coast were traded to distant inland regions.

The Rise of Cities and States

From the time agriculture first developed until about 6000 B.C., people in the Middle East lived in fairly small villages. There were few differences in wealth and status from household to household, and apparently there was no governmental authority beyond the village. There is also no evidence that these villages had any public buildings or craft specialists or that one community was very different in size from its neighbors. In short, these settlements had none of the characteristics we commonly associate with "civilization."

But sometime around 6000 B.C., in parts of the Middle East—and at later times in other places—a great transformation in the quality and scale of human life seems to have begun. For the first time, we can see evidence of differences in status among households. For example, some are much bigger than others. Communities begin to differ in size and to specialize in certain crafts. And there are signs that some political officials had acquired authority over several communities, that what anthropologists call "chiefdoms" had emerged.

Somewhat later, by about 3500 B.C., we can see many, if not all, of the conventional characteristics of **civilization**: the first inscriptions, or writing; cities; many kinds of full-time craft specialists; monumental architecture; great differences in wealth and status; and the kind of strong, hierarchical, centralized political system we call the **state** (see Figure 8.5).

This type of transformation has occurred many times and in many places in human history (see Figure 8.5). The most ancient civilizations arose in the Middle East around 3500 B.C., in northwestern India and in Peru about 2500 B.C., in northern China around 1750 B.C., in Mexico a few hundred years before the time of Christ, and in tropical Africa somewhat later.[81] At least some of these civilizations evolved independently of the others—for example, those in the New

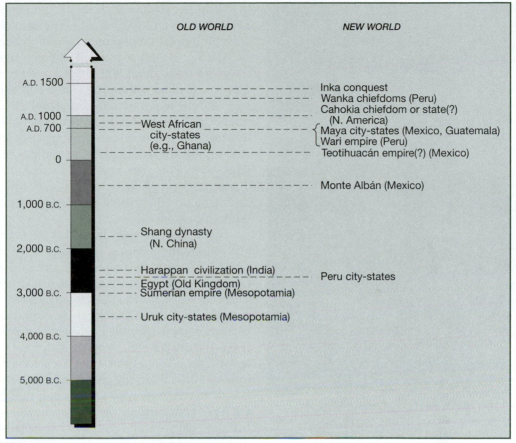

Figure 8.5 The Emergence of Civilization

World and those in the Old World. Why did they do so? What conditions favored the emergence of centralized, statelike political systems? What conditions favored the establishment of cities? In discussing some of the things archaeologists have learned or suspect about the growth of ancient civilizations, we focus primarily on the Middle East and Mexico because archaeologists know the most about the sequences of cultural development in those two areas.

Archaeological Inferences about Civilization

Archaeologists rather than historians have studied the most ancient civilizations because those civilizations evolved before the advent of writing. How do archaeologists infer that a particular people in the preliterate past had social classes, cities, or a centralized government? It appears that the earliest Neolithic societies were *egalitarian;* that is, people did not differ much in wealth, prestige, or power. Some later societies show signs of social inequality, indicated by burial finds. Archaeologists generally assume that inequality in death reflects inequality in life, at least in status and perhaps also in wealth and power. Thus, we can be fairly sure that a society had differences in status if only some people were buried with special objects, such as jewelry or pots filled with food. And we can be fairly sure that high status was assigned at birth rather

Reconstruction of the burial of a prehistoric Peruvian king, known as the "Lord of Sipan." Note the carefully laid-out wood tomb and the ornate cloth and gold items buried with the individual. Archaeologists assume that such special treatment indicates elite status.

than achieved in later life if we find noticeable differences in children's tombs. For example, some (but not all) child burials from as early as 5500 B.C. to 5000 B.C. at Tell es-Sawwan in Iraq, and from about 800 B.C. at La Venta in Mexico, are filled with statues and ornaments, suggesting that some children had high status from birth.[82] But burials indicating differences in status do not necessarily mean a society had significant differences in wealth. Only when archaeologists find other substantial differences, as in house size and furnishings, can we be sure the society had different socio-economic classes of people.

Some archaeologists think that states first evolved around 3500 B.C. in greater Mesopotamia, the area now shared by southern Iraq and southwestern Iran. Archaeologists do not always agree on how a state should be defined, but most think that hierarchical and centralized decision making affecting a substantial population is the key criterion. States usually have cities with a substantial part of the population not involved directly in the collection or production of food (which means that people in cities are heavily dependent on people elsewhere); full-time religious and craft specialists; public buildings; and often an official art style. There is a hierarchical social structure topped by an elite class from which the leaders are drawn. The government tries to claim a monopoly on the use of force. (Our own state society says that citizens do not have the right "to take the law into their own hands.") The state uses its force or threat of force to tax its population and to draft people for work or war.[83]

How can archaeologists tell, from the information provided by material remains, whether a society was a state or not? This depends in part on what is used as the criterion for a state. For example, Henry Wright and Gregory Johnson defined a state as a centralized political hierarchy with at least three levels of administration.[84] But how might archaeologists infer that such a hierarchy existed in some area? Wright and Johnson suggested that the way settlement sites differ in size is one indication of how many levels of administration there were in an area.

During the early Uruk period (just before 3500 B.C.), in what is now southwestern Iran, there were some 50 settlements that seem to fall into three groups in terms of size.[85] There were about 45 small villages, three or four "towns," and one large center, Susa. These three types of settlements seem to have been part of a three-level administration hierarchy, because many small villages could not trade with Susa without passing through a settlement intermediate in size. Because a three-level hierarchy is Wright and Johnson's criterion of a state, they think a state had emerged in the area by early Uruk times.

Evidence from the next period, middle Uruk, suggests more definitely that a state had emerged. This evidence takes the form of clay seals that were apparently used in trading.[86] *Commodity sealings* were used to keep a shipment of goods tightly closed until it reached its destination, and *message sealings* were used to keep track of goods sent and received. The clay seals found in Susa include many message seals and *bullae,* clay containers that served as bills of lading for goods received. The villages, in contrast, had few message seals and bullae. Again, this finding suggests that Susa administered the regional movement of goods and that Susa was the "capital" of the state.

Let us turn now to the major features of the cultural sequences leading to the first states in southern Iraq.

Cities and States in Southern Iraq

Farming communities older than the first states have not been found in the arid lowland plains of southern Iraq—the area known as Sumer, where some of the earliest cities and states developed. Perhaps silt from the Tigris and Euphrates rivers has covered them. Or, as has been suggested, Sumer may not have been settled by agriculturalists until people learned how to drain and irrigate river-valley soils otherwise too wet or too dry for cultivation. At any rate, small communities depending partly on agriculture had emerged in the hilly areas north and east of Sumer early in the Neolithic. Later, by about 6000 B.C., a mixed herding and farming economy developed in those areas.

The Formative Era Elman Service called the period from about 5000 B.C. to 3500 B.C. the *formative era,* for it saw the coming-together of many changes that seem to have played a part in the development of cities and states. Service suggested that, with the development of small-scale irrigation, lowland river areas began to attract settlers. The rivers provided not only water for irrigation but also mollusks, fish, and waterbirds for food. And they provided routes by which to import needed raw materials, such as hardwood and stone, which were lacking in Sumer.[87]

Changes during this period suggest an increasingly complex social and political life. Differences in status are reflected in the burial of statues and ornaments with children. Different villages specialized in the production of different goods—pottery in some, copper and stone tools in others.[88] Temples were built in certain places that may have been centers of political as well as religious authority for several communities.[89] Furthermore, some anthropologists think that chiefdoms, each having authority over several villages, had developed by this time.[90]

Sumerian Civilization By about 3500 B.C., there were quite a few cities in the area of Sumer. Most were enclosed in a fortress wall and surrounded by an agricultural area. About 3000 B.C., all of Sumer was unified under a single government. After that time, Sumer became an empire. It had great urban centers. Imposing temples, commonly set on artificial mounds, dominated the cities. In the city of Warka, the temple mound was about 150 feet high. The empire was very complex and included an elaborate system for the administration of justice, codified laws, specialized government officials, a professional standing army, and even sewer systems in the cities. Among the many specialized crafts were brickmaking, pottery, carpentry, jewelry making, leatherworking, metallurgy, basketmaking, stonecutting, and sculpture. Sumerians learned to construct and use wheeled wagons, sailboats, horse-drawn chariots, and spears, swords, and armor of bronze.[91]

As economic specialization developed, social stratification became more elaborate. Sumerian documents describe a system of social classes: nobles, priests, merchants, craftworkers,

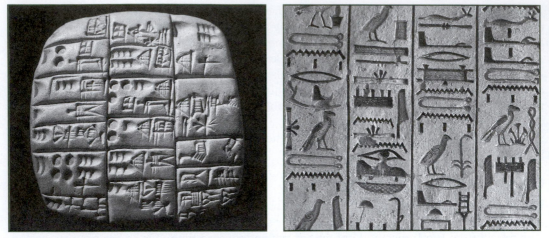

Examples of two of the earliest writing systems on earth. On the left is a cuneiform tablet and on the right is a section of a hieroglyphic panel.

metallurgists, bureaucrats, soldiers, farmers, free citizens, and slaves. Slaves were common in Sumer; they often were captives, brought back as the spoils of war.

We see the first evidence of writing around 3000 B.C. The earliest Sumerian writings were in the form of ledgers containing inventories of items stored in the temples and records of livestock or other items owned or managed by the temples. Sumerian writing was wedge-shaped, or **cuneiform,** formed by pressing a stylus against a damp clay tablet. For contracts and other important documents, the tablet was fired to create a virtually permanent record. Egyptian writing, or hieroglyphics, appeared about the same time. **Hieroglyphics** were written on rolls woven from papyrus reeds, from which our word *paper* derives.

Cities and States in Mesoamerica

Cities and states emerged in Mesoamerica—Mexico and Central America—later than they did in the Middle East. The later appearance of civilization in Mesoamerica may be linked to the later emergence of agriculture in the New World, and possibly to the near-absence of large animals such as cattle and horses that could be domesticated.[92] We focus primarily on the developments that led to the rise of the city-state of Teotihuacán, which reached its height shortly after the time of Christ. Teotihuacán is located in a valley of the same name, which is the northeastern part of the larger Valley of Mexico.

The Formative Period The formative period in the area around Teotihuacán (1000 B.C. to 300 B.C.) was characterized initially by small, scattered farming villages on the hilly slopes just south of the Teotihuacán Valley. There were probably a few hundred people in each hamlet, and each of these scattered groups was probably politically autonomous. After about 500 B.C., there seems to have been a population shift to settlements on the valley floor, probably in association with the use of irrigation. Between about 300 B.C. and 200 B.C., small "elite" centers emerged in the valley; each had an earthen or stone raised platform. Residences or small temples of poles and thatch originally stood on these platforms. That some individuals, particularly those in the elite centers, were buried in special tombs supplied with ornaments, headdresses, carved bowls, and a good deal of food indicates some social inequality.[93] The various elite centers may indicate the presence of chiefdoms.

The City and State of Teoti-huacán About 150 years before the time of Christ, no more than a few thousand people lived in scattered villages in the Teotihuacán Valley. In A.D. 100, there was a city of 80,000. By A.D. 500, well over 100,000 people, or approximately 90 percent of the entire valley population, seem to have been drawn or coerced into Teotihuacán.[94]

The layout of the city of Teotihuacán, which shows a tremendous amount of planning, suggests that the valley was politically unified under a centralized state from its beginning. Mapping has revealed that the streets and most of the

The city of Teotihuacán, which had its peak in A.D. 500, was a planned city built on a grid pattern. At the center was the Pyramid of the Sun, seen in the background on the left here.

buildings are laid out in a grid pattern following a basic modular unit of 57 square meters. Residential structures are often squares of this size, and many streets are spaced according to multiples of the basic unit. Even the river that ran through the center of the city was channeled to conform to the grid pattern. Perhaps the most outstanding feature of the city is the colossal scale of its architecture. Two pyramids dominate the metropolis, the so-called Pyramid of the Moon and the Pyramid of the Sun. At its base, the latter is as big as the great Pyramid of Cheops in Egypt.

The thousands of residential structures built after A.D. 300 follow a standard pattern. Narrow streets separate the one-story buildings, each of which has high, windowless walls. Patios and shafts provide interior light. The layout of rooms suggests that each building consisted of several apartments; more than 100 people may have lived in one of these apartment compounds. There is variation from compound to compound in the size of rooms and the elaborateness of interior decoration, suggesting considerable variation in wealth.[95]

At the height of its power (A.D. 200 to A.D. 500), the metropolis of Teotihuacán encompassed an area larger than imperial Rome.[96] Much of Mesoamerica seems to have been influenced by Teotihuacán. Archaeologically, its influence is suggested by the extensive spread of Teotihuacán-style pottery and architectural elements. Undoubtedly, large numbers of people in Teotihuacán were engaged in production for, and the conduct of, long-distance trade. Perhaps 25 percent of the city's population worked at various specialized crafts, including the manufacture of projectile points and cutting and scraping tools from volcanic obsidian. Teotihuacán was close to major deposits of obsidian, which was apparently in some demand over much of Mesoamerica. Materials found in graves indicate that there was an enormous flow of foreign goods into the city, including precious stones, feathers from colorful birds in the tropical lowlands, and cotton.[97]

Cities and States in Other Areas

So far, we have discussed the emergence of cities and states in southern Iraq and Mesoamerica whose development is best, if only imperfectly, known archaeologically. But other state societies probably arose more or less independently in many other areas of the world as well. We say "independently" because such states seem to have emerged without colonization or conquest by other states.

Almost at the same time as the Sumerian empire, the great dynastic age was beginning in the Nile Valley in Egypt. The Old Kingdom, or early dynastic period, began about 3100 B.C., with a capital at Memphis. The archaeological evidence from the early centuries is limited, but most of the population appears to have lived in largely self-sufficient villages. Many of the great pyramids and palaces were built around 2500 B.C.[98]

Elsewhere in Africa, states also arose. In what is present-day Ethiopia, the Axum (or Aksum) state evolved beginning sometime early in the 1st millennium A.D., and ultimately became a center of trade and commerce between Africa and the Arabian Peninsula. Among the unique accomplishments of the Axum state were multistory stone residences built in a singular architectural style. Axum is also notable as being perhaps the first officially Christian state in the world.[99]

In sub-Saharan Africa, by A.D. 800, the savanna and forest zones of western Africa had a succession of city-states. One of them was called Ghana, and it became a major source of gold for the Mediterranean world (as did other states in what came to be known as the "Gold Coast").[100] In the Congo River basin, a powerful kingdom had evolved by A.D. 1200, with cities described as having tens of thousands of residences and a king that was recognized as an equal by the Portuguese king in the early 1500s.[101] Farther south, states apparently arose in several areas early in the 2nd millennium A.D. One of these was responsible for the large, circular stone structures known today as the Great Zimbabwe.[102]

In the Indus Valley of northwestern India, a large state society had developed by 2300 B.C. This Harappan civilization did not have much in the way of monumental architecture, such as pyramids and palaces, and it was also unusual in other respects. The state apparently controlled an enormous territory—over a million square kilometers. There was not just one major city but many, each built according to a similar pattern and with a municipal water and sewage system.[103]

The Shang dynasty in northern China (1750 B.C.) has long been cited as the earliest state society in the Far East. But recent research suggests that an even earlier one, the Xia dynasty, may have emerged in the same general area by 2200 B.C.[104] In any case, the Shang dynasty had all the earmarks of statehood: a stratified, specialized society; religious, economic, and administrative unification; and a distinctive art style.[105]

Artist's reconstruction of the ancient city of Harappa. Despite large public works like this water control system, there was little display of grandeur at Harappa. Unlike many other ancient civilizations, all Harappan cities were laid out according to the same basic plan.

In South America, a group of distinct state societies may have emerged as early as 2500 B.C. in the Supe and Pativilca valleys north of Lima, Peru. The valley contains a group of large cities that seem to have been interdependent—cities on the coast supplied inland cities with fish, whereas inland cities served as political and economic centers. The cities contain plaza areas and large pyramids, which are thought to be temple structures.[106] After 200 B.C. the major river valleys leading from the Andes to the sea witnessed the development of a complex agricultural system dependent on irrigation. The separate, but similar, states participated in a widespread system

Artist's reconstruction of what Cahokia may have looked like during its fluorescence.

of religious symbols and beliefs called Chavín. The various states included the well-known Moche state, creators of some of the most remarkable effigy ceramics ever known, and the Nazca state, the people of which constructed a huge landscape of intaglios (inscribed images and lines) on the hard ground of highland deserts. By A.D. 700, these regional states were integrated into a large, militaristic empire called Wari (or Huari).[107]

And in North America, a huge settlement, with over 100 earthen mounds (one of them, Monk's Mound, is the largest pre-Columbian structure north of Mexico), and covering an area of more than 5 square miles (13 square kilometers), developed near present-day St. Louis late in the 1st millennium A.D. The site is called Cahokia, and it was certainly the center of a large and powerful chiefdom. Whether it had achieved a state level of organization is controversial. There is evidence for religious and craft specialists and there is clear social stratification, but whether or not the leaders of Cahokian society were able to govern by force is still unclear.[108]

Theories About the Origin of States

We have seen that states developed in many parts of the world. Why did they evolve when and where they did? We consider those that archaeologists have discussed frequently.[109]

Irrigation

Irrigation seems to have been important in many of the areas in which early state societies developed. Irrigation made the land habitable or productive in parts of Mesoamerica, southern Iraq, the Nile Valley, China, and South America. It has been suggested that the labor and management needed for the upkeep of an irrigation system led to the formation of a political elite, the overseers of the system, who eventually became the governors of the society.[110] Proponents of this view believe that both the city and civilization were outgrowths of the administrative requirements of an irrigation system.

Critics note that this theory does not seem to apply to all areas where cities and states may have emerged independently. For example, in southern Iraq, the irrigation systems serving the early cities were generally small and probably did not require extensive labor and management. Large-scale irrigation works were not constructed until after cities had been fully established.[111] Thus, irrigation could not have been the main stimulus for the development of cities and states in

Sumer. Even in China, for which the irrigation theory was first formulated, there is no evidence of large-scale irrigation as early as Shang times.[112]

Although large-scale irrigation may not always have preceded the emergence of the first cities and states, even small-scale irrigation systems could have resulted in unequal access to productive land and so may have contributed to the development of a stratified society.[113] In addition, irrigation systems may have given rise to border and other disputes between adjacent groups, thereby prompting people to concentrate in cities for defense and stimulating the development of military and political controls.[114] Finally, as Robert Adams and Elman Service both suggested, the main significance of irrigation, either large or small scale, may have been its intensification of production, a development that in turn may have indirectly stimulated craft specialization, trade, and administrative bureaucracy.[115]

Population Growth, Circumscription, and War

Robert Carneiro has suggested that states may emerge because of population growth in an area that is physically or socially limited. Competition and warfare in such a situation may lead to the subordination of defeated groups, who are obliged to pay tribute and to submit to the control of a more powerful group.[116] Carneiro illustrated his theory by describing how states may have emerged on the northern coast of Peru.

After the people of that area first settled into an agricultural village life, population grew at a slow, steady rate. Initially, new villages were formed as population grew. But in the narrow coastal valleys—blocked by high mountains, fronted by the sea, and surrounded by desert—this splintering-off process could not continue indefinitely. The result, according to Carneiro, was increasing land shortage and warfare between villages as they competed for land. Because the high mountains, the sea, and the desert blocked any escape for losers, the defeated villagers had no choice but to submit to political domination. In this way, chiefdoms may have become kingdoms as the most powerful villages grew to control entire valleys. As chiefs' power expanded over several valleys, states and empires may have been born.

Marvin Harris suggested a somewhat different form of circumscription. He argued that the first states with their coercive authority could emerge only in areas that supported intensive grain agriculture (and the possibility of high food production) and were surrounded by areas that could not support intensive grain agriculture. So people in such areas might put up with the coercive authority of a state because they would suffer a sharp drop in living standards if they moved away.[117]

Carneiro suggested that his theory applies to many areas besides the northern coast of Peru, including southern Iraq and the Indus and Nile valleys. Although there were no geographic barriers in areas such as northern China or the Mayan lowlands on the Yucatán Peninsula, the development of states in those areas may have been the result of social circumscription. Carneiro's theory seems to be supported for southern Iraq, where there is archaeological evidence of population growth, circumscription, and warfare.[118] And there is evidence of population growth before the emergence of the state in the Teotihuacán Valley.[119]

But population growth does not necessarily mean population pressure. For example, the populations in the Teotihuacán and Oaxaca valleys apparently did increase prior to state development, but there is no evidence that they had even begun to approach the limits of their resources. More people could have lived in both places.[120] Nor is population growth definitely associated with state formation in all areas where early states arose. For example, according to Wright and Johnson, there was population growth long before states emerged in southwestern Iran, but the population apparently declined just before the states emerged.[121]

In addition, Carneiro's circumscription theory leaves an important logical question unanswered: Why would the victors in war let the defeated populations remain and pay tribute? If the victors wanted the land so much in the first place, why wouldn't they try to exterminate the defeated and occupy the land themselves, which has happened many times in history?

Local and Long-Distance Trade

It has been suggested that trade was a factor in the emergence of the earliest states.[122] Wright and Johnson theorized that the organizational requirements of producing items for export, redistributing the items imported, and defending trading parties would foster state formation.[123] Does the archaeological evidence support such a theory?

In southern Iraq and the Mayan lowlands, long-distance trade routes may indeed have stimulated bureaucratic growth. In the lowlands of southern Iraq, as we have seen, people needed wood and stone for building, and they traded with highland people for those items. In the Mayan lowlands, the development of civilization seems to have been preceded by long-distance trade. Farmers in the lowland regions traded with faraway places to obtain salt, obsidian for cutting blades, and hard stone for grinding tools.[124] In southwestern Iran, long-distance trade did not become very important until after Susa became the center of a state society, but short-distance trade may have played the same kind of role in the formation of states.

Kwang-chih Chang put forward a similar theory for the origin of states in China. He suggested that Neolithic societies in the Yellow River valley developed a long-distance trade network, which he called an *interaction sphere,* by about 4000 B.C. Trade spread cultural elements among the societies in the interaction sphere, so that they came to share some common elements. Over time, these societies came to depend on each other both as trade partners and as cultural partners, and around 2000 B.C., they unified into a single political unit under the Shang dynasty.[125] Thus, Chang sees political unification in China as an outgrowth of a preexisting system of trade and cultural interaction.

The Various Theories: An Evaluation

Why do states form? As of now, no one theory seems to fit all the known situations. The reason may be that different conditions in different places may have favored the emergence of centralized government. After all, the state, by definition, implies an ability to organize large populations for a collective purpose. In some areas, this purpose may have been the need to organize trade with local or far-off regions. In other cases, the state may have emerged as a way to control defeated populations in circumscribed areas. In still other instances, a combination of factors may have fostered the development of the state type of political system.[126]

The Consequences of State Formation

We have considered several areas where states arose, as well as a number of theories to explain the origin of states. But what were the consequences for the people living in those societies? The consequences seem to have been dramatic.

One of the ways states change the lifestyles of people is by allowing for larger and denser populations.[127] As we have already seen, agriculture itself gives populations the potential to grow, and the development of a state only furthers that potential. Why? Because a state is able to build infrastructure—irrigation systems, roadways, markets—that allows both the production and distribution of agricultural products to become more efficient. States are able

Shown is a street in the old city of Jaipur, India. The rise of states allows cities with dense populations to develop and, along with them, the many potentials and problems that cities and their populations create.

to coordinate information to manage agricultural production cycles and to anticipate or manage droughts, blights, or other natural disasters. States are also able to control access to land (through laws and a military) and thus can both maintain farmers on the land and prevent others (from either within or outside of the state) from removing the farmers or interfering with their ability to produce food.

With increased efficiency of agricultural production and distribution, states also allow many (if not most) people in the society to be relieved of food production. These people are freed to become craftspeople, merchants, and artists, as well as bureaucrats, soldiers, and political leaders. People may also live apart from agricultural fields, and thus cities with dense populations can arise. Cities can also arise in locations that are not suited to agriculture but that perhaps are suited to trade (such as the cities on rivers in southern Mesopotamia) or defense (such as on top of a mountain, as in the case of Monte Albán). Art, music, and literature often flourish in such contexts, and these too are often consequences of the rise of states. Organized religion also often develops after states appear. Thus, all the hallmarks we associate with civilization can be seen as resulting from the evolution of states.[128]

The development of states can have many negative impacts as well. When states develop, people become governed by force and are no longer able to say "no" to their leaders. Police and military forces can become instruments of oppression and terror.[129] On a less obvious level, the class stratification of states creates differences in access to resources and an underclass of poor, uneducated, and frequently unhealthy people. Health issues are exacerbated by the concentration of people in cities, an environment in which epidemic diseases can flourish.[130] Without direct access to food supplies, people in cities also face the threat of malnutrition or outright starvation if food production and distribution systems fail.[131]

All states appear to be expansionistic, and the emergence of state warfare and conquest seems one of the most striking negative impacts of the evolution of states. In fact, more human suffering can probably be linked to state expansion than to any other single factor. Why do states expand? One basic reason may be that they are able to. States have standing armies ready to fight or be sent to conquer enemies. Another reason for state expansion might be related to the threat of famine and disease, which is more likely with intensive agriculture.[132] A third answer to the question of why states tend to expand might be that belligerence is simply part of the nature of states. States often arise through military means, and it may be vital to the continuation of some states that military power be continually demonstrated.[133]

Regardless of the causes, war and conquest are the consequences of state formation. Often, too, defeat in war is the fate of states.

The Decline and Collapse of States

When you look over the list of ancient states we have discussed in this chapter—such as Teotihuacán, Sumer, and pharonic Egypt—you will notice one element common to them all: Each eventually collapsed; none maintained its power and influence into historic times. Why? It is an important question because, if collapse is the ultimate fate of many if not all states, then we can anticipate that our own state is likely to collapse eventually. Perhaps knowing something about how and why other states have fallen can prevent (or at least hold off) the fall of our own.

One suggested explanation for the decline and collapse of states is environmental degradation. If states originally arose where the environment was conducive to intensive agriculture and harvests big enough to support social stratification, political officials, and a state type of political system, then perhaps environmental degradation—declining soil productivity, persistent drought, and the like—contributed to the collapse of ancient states. Archaeologist Harvey Weiss has suggested that persistent drought helped to bring about the fall of the ancient Akkadian empire in the Middle East. By 2300 B.C., the Akkadians had established an

The history of Ephesus, a former city lying in ruins in what is now western Turkey, illustrates the waxing and waning of states and empires. From about 1000 B.C. to 100 B.C., it was controlled by the Greeks, Lydians, Persians, Macedonians, and Romans, among others.

empire stretching over 800 miles (1,300 kilometers) from the Persian Gulf in what is now Iraq to the headwaters of the Euphrates River in what is now Turkey. But a century later, the empire collapsed. Weiss thinks that a long-term drought brought the empire down, as well as other civilizations around at that time too. Many archaeologists doubted there was such a widespread drought, but new evidence indicates that the worst dry spell of the past 10,000 years began just as the Akkadians' northern stronghold was being abandoned.[134] The evidence of the drought, windblown dust in sediment retrieved from the bottom of the Persian Gulf, indicates that the dry spell lasted 300 years. Other geophysical evidence suggests that the drought was worldwide.[135]

Environmental degradation may also have contributed to the collapse of Mayan civilization.[136] Lake sediments show that the region the Maya inhabited experienced an extended period of drought lasting between roughly A.D. 800 and A.D. 1000. The Maya, who depended on rainfall agriculture for subsistence, may not have been able to produce enough food in areas around temple complexes during this long period of drought to feed the resident populations. People would have been forced to move into less populated areas to survive, and the temple complexes would have slowly been abandoned.[137]

The behavior of humans may sometimes be responsible for environmental degradation. Consider the collapse of Cahokia, a city of at least 15,000 people that thrived for a while in the area where the Missouri and Mississippi rivers converge. In the twelfth century A.D., Cahokia had large public plazas, a city wall constructed from some 20,000 logs, and massive mounds. But within 300 years, only the mounds were left. Silt from flooding covered former croplands and settled areas. Geographer Bill Woods thinks that overuse of woodlands for fuel, construction, and defense led to deforestation, flooding, and persistent crop failure. The result was the abandonment of Cahokia.[138]

Many other ideas have been put forward to explain collapse, ranging from catastrophes, overextension, internal conflict, and almost mystical factors such as "social decadence," but, as with theories for the origin of states, no single explanation seems to fit all or even most of the situations. Although it is still not clear what specific conditions led to the emergence, or collapse, of the state in each of the early centers of civilization, the question of why states form and decline is a lively focus of research today. More satisfactory answers may come out of ongoing and future investigations.

✓─[Study and **Review** on **myanthrolab.com**

Summary

1. In the period immediately before plants and animals were domesticated, there seems to have been a shift in many areas of the world to less dependence on big game hunting and greater dependence on broad-spectrum collecting.

2. In some sites in Europe, the Middle East, Africa, and Peru, the switch to broad-spectrum collecting seems to be associated with the development of more permanent communities. In other areas, such as the semiarid highlands of Mesoamerica, permanent settlements may have emerged only after the domestication of plants and animals.

3. The shift to the cultivation and domestication of plants and animals has been referred to as the Neolithic revolution, and it occurred, probably independently, in a number of areas. To date,

the earliest evidence of domestication comes from the Middle East at about 8000 B.C. Dating for the earliest domestication in other areas of the Old World is not so clear, but the presence of different domesticated crops in different regions suggests that there were independent centers of domestication in China, Southeast Asia (what is now Malaysia, Thailand, Cambodia, and Vietnam), New Guinea, and Africa some time around or after 6000 B.C. In the New World, there appear to have been several early areas of cultivation and domestication: the highlands of Mesoamerica (about 7000 B.C.), the central Andes around Peru (about the same time, but perhaps even earlier), and the Eastern Woodlands of North America (about 2000 B.C.).

4. Theories about why food production originated remain controversial, but most archaeologists think that certain conditions must have pushed people to switch from collecting to producing food. Some possible causal factors include (1) population growth in regions of bountiful wild resources (which may have pushed people to move to marginal areas where they tried to reproduce their former abundance); (2) global population growth (which filled most of the world's habitable regions and may have forced people to utilize a broader spectrum of wild resources and to domesticate plants and animals); and (3) the emergence of hotter and drier summers and colder winters (which may have favored sedentarism near seasonal stands of wild grain; population growth in such areas may have forced people to plant crops and raise animals to support themselves).

5. Regardless of why food production originated, it seems to have had important consequences for human life: increases in population, sedentarism, and some decline in health.

6. Archaeologists do not always agree on how a state should be defined, but most seem to agree that hierarchical and centralized decision making affecting a substantial population is the key criterion. Most states have cities with public buildings, full-time craft and religious specialists, an official art style, and a hierarchical social structure topped by an elite class from which the leaders are drawn. Most states maintain power with a monopoly on the use of force. The state uses force or the threat of force to tax its population and to draft people for work or war.

7. The earliest states arose in the Middle East around 3500 B.C., Other early states in the Old World emerged in Egypt around 3100 B.C., the Indus Valley by 2300 B.C., and the Yellow River Valley of China by 1750 B.C. (and perhaps earlier). States first arose in the New World around 150 B.C.

8. Theories about the rise of states suggest the importance of irrigation, circumscription and war, and trade. At this point, no one theory is able to explain the formation of every state. Perhaps different organizational requirements in different areas all favored centralized government.

9. When states arise, they have a dramatic impact. Populations grow and become concentrated in cities. Agriculture becomes more efficient, allowing many people to be removed from food production. States provide a context in which what we commonly call civilization—art, music, literature, and organized religion—can develop and flourish. But states also provide a context in which warfare and political terror can flourish. The social differentiation found in states produces an underclass of poor and often unhealthy people. States are prone to epidemic disease and periodic famine.

10. History suggests that all ancient states collapsed eventually.

Glossary Terms

agriculture (p. 165)
civilization (p. 180)
cuneiform (p. 184)
domestication (p. 170)
Epipaleolithic (p. 164)

food production (p. 164)
hieroglyphics (p. 184)
Mesolithic (p. 164)
Neolithic (p. 170)

obsidian (p. 172)
rachis (p. 171)
sedentarism (p. 165)
state (p. 180)

Critical Questions

1. Do the various theories of the rise of food production explain why domestication occurred in many areas of the world within a few thousand years?

2. Cities and states did not appear until after the emergence of food production. Why might food production be necessary, but not sufficient, for cities and states to develop?

3. Like the emergence of food production, the earliest cities and states developed within a few thousand years of each other. What might be the reasons?

4. Can you imagine a future world without states? What conditions might lead to that "state" of the world?

📖⊙ Read the Original Source on myanthrolab.com

Read the chapter by Mark Nathan Cohen titled "Were Early Agriculturalists Less Healthy than Food Collectors?" on MyAnthroLab. Answer the following questions.

1. Describe the basic arguments behind Cohen's question. What benefits did agriculture provide to human groups? What problems may have resulted from agriculture?

2. What does Cohen suggest his comparative data from modern foragers and modern agriculturalists demonstrate about the relative health of the two groups? Do data from ancient skeletons demonstrate a similar or a different pattern?

Culture and Culture Change

W e all consider ourselves to be unique individuals with our own set of personal opinions, preferences, habits, and quirks. Indeed, all of us are unique; and yet most of us also share many feelings, beliefs, and habits with most of the people who live in our society. If we live in North America, we are likely to have the feeling that eating dogs is wrong, have the belief that bacteria or viruses cause illness, and have the habit of sleeping on a bed. These ideas and behaviors are part of what we mean by *culture*.

We only begin to become aware that our culture is different when we become aware that other peoples have different feelings, different beliefs, and different habits from ours. So most North Americans would never even think of the possibility of eating dog meat if they did not know that people in some other societies commonly do so. They would not realize that their belief in germs was cultural if they were not aware that people in some societies think that witchcraft or evil spirits causes illness. They might not become aware that it is their custom to sleep on beds if they were not aware that people in many societies sleep on the floor or on the ground. Only when we compare ourselves with people in other societies may we become aware of cultural differences and similarities. This is, in fact, the way that anthropology as a profession began. When Europeans began to explore and move to faraway places, they were forced to confront the sometimes striking facts of cultural variation.

Most of us are aware that "times have changed," especially when we compare our lives with those of our parents. Some of the most dramatic changes have occurred in attitudes about sex and marriage, changes in women's roles, and changes in technology. But such culture change is not unusual. Throughout history, humans have replaced or altered customary behaviors and attitudes as their needs have changed. Just as no individual is immortal, no particular cultural pattern is impervious to change. Anthropologists want to understand how and why such change occurs. Culture change may be gradual or rapid. Although there has always been contact between different societies, contact between faraway cultures through exploration, colonization, trade, and more recently multinational business has accelerated the pace of change within the last 600 years or so. Globalization has made the world more and more interconnected. We conclude this chapter with a discussion of the future of cultural diversity.

Defining Culture

In everyday usage, the word *culture* refers to a desirable quality we can acquire by attending a sufficient number of plays and concerts and visiting art museums and galleries. Anthropologists, however, have a different definition, as Ralph Linton explained:

> *Culture* refers to the total way of life of any society, not simply to those parts of this way which the society regards as higher or more desirable. Thus culture, when applied to our own way of life, has nothing to do with playing the piano or reading Browning. For the social scientist such activities are simply elements within the totality of our culture. This totality also includes such mundane activities as washing dishes or driving an automobile, and for the purposes of cultural studies these stand quite on a par with "the finer things of life." It follows that for the social scientist there are no uncultured societies or even individuals. Every society has a culture, no matter how simple this culture may be, and every human being is cultured, in the sense of participating in some culture or other.[1]

Culture, then, refers to innumerable aspects of life, including many things we consider ordinary. Linton emphasized common habits and behaviors in what he considered culture, but the totality of life also includes not just what people do, but also how they commonly think and feel. As we define it here, **culture** is the set of learned behaviors and ideas (including beliefs, attitudes, values, and ideals) that are characteristic of a particular society or other social group. Behaviors can also produce products or *material culture*—things like houses, musical instruments, and tools that are the products of customary behavior.

Different kinds of groups can have cultures. People come to share behaviors and ideas because they communicate with and observe each other. Although groups from families to societies share cultural traits, anthropologists have traditionally been concerned with the cultural characteristics of *societies.* Many anthropologists define **society** as a group of people who occupy a particular territory and speak a common language not generally understood by neighboring peoples. By this definition, societies may or may not correspond to countries. There are many countries, particularly newer ones, that have within their boundaries different peoples speaking mutually unintelligible languages. By our definition of society, such countries are composed of many different societies and therefore many cultures. Also, by our definition of society, some societies may even include more than one country. For example, we would have to say that Canada and the United States form a single society because the two groups generally speak English, live next to each other, and share many common ideas and behaviors. That is why we refer to "North American culture" in this chapter. The terms *society* and *culture* are not synonymous. Society refers to a group of people; culture refers to the learned and shared behaviors, ideas, and characteristics of those people. As we will discuss shortly, we also have to be careful to describe culture as of a particular time period; what is characteristic of one time may not be characteristic of another.

Culture Is Commonly Shared

If only one person thinks or does a certain thing, that thought or action represents a personal habit, not a pattern of culture. For a thought or action to be considered cultural, some social group must commonly share it. We usually share many behaviors and ideas with our families and friends. We commonly share cultural characteristics with those whose ethnic or regional origins, religious affiliations, and occupations are the same as or similar to our own. We share certain practices and ideas with most people in our society. We also share some cultural traits with people beyond our society who have similar interests (such as rules for international sporting events) or similar roots (as do the various English-speaking nations).

When we talk about the commonly shared customs of *a* society, which constitute the traditional and central concern of cultural anthropology, we are referring to *a* culture. When we talk about the commonly shared customs of a group within a society, which are a central concern of sociologists and increasingly of concern to anthropologists, we are referring to a **subculture**. (A subculture is not necessarily the same as an ethnic group; we discuss the concept of ethnicity further in the chapter on social stratification, ethnicity, and racism.) When we study the commonly shared customs of some group that includes different societies, we are talking about a phenomenon for which we do not have a single word—for example, as when we refer to *Western culture* (the cultural characteristics of societies in or derived from Europe) or the *culture of poverty* (the presumed cultural characteristics of poor people the world over).

We must remember that, even when anthropologists refer to something as cultural, there is always individual variation, which means that not everyone in a society shares a particular cultural characteristic of that society. For example, it is cultural in North American society for adults to live apart from their parents. But not all adults in our society do so, nor do all adults wish to do so. The custom of living apart from parents is considered cultural because most adults practice that custom. In every society studied by anthropologists—in the simplest as well as the most complex—individuals do not all think and act the same.[2] Indeed, individual variation is a major source of new culture.[3]

Culture Is Learned

Not all things shared generally by a group are cultural. Typical hair color is not cultural, nor is eating. For something to be considered cultural, it must be learned as well as shared. A typical hair color (unless dyed) is not cultural because it is genetically determined. Humans eat because they must; but what and when and how they eat are learned and vary from culture to culture. Most North Americans do not consider dog meat edible, and indeed the idea of eating dogs horrifies them. But in China, as in some other societies, dog meat is considered delicious. In North American culture, many people consider a baked ham to be a holiday dish. In several societies of the Middle East, however, including those of Egypt and Israel, eating the meat of a pig is forbidden by sacred writings.

To some extent, all animals exhibit learned behaviors, some of which most individuals in a population may share and may therefore consider cultural. But different animal species vary in the degree to which their shared behaviors are learned or are instinctive. The sociable ants, for instance, despite all their patterned social behavior, do not appear to have much, if any, culture. They divide their labor, construct their nests, form their raiding columns, and carry off their dead—all without having been taught to do so and without imitating the behavior of other ants. Our closest biological relatives, the monkeys and the apes, not only learn a wide variety of behaviors on their own, they also learn from each other. Some of their learned responses are as basic as those involved in maternal care; others are as frivolous as the taste for candy. Frans de Waal reviewed seven long-term studies of chimpanzees and identified at least 39 behaviors that were clearly learned from others.[4] If shared and socially learned, these behaviors could be described as cultural.

A daughter braids her doll's hair, imitating what her mother is doing.

Although humans may acquire much learned behavior by trial and error and imitation, as do monkeys and apes, most human ideas and behaviors are learned from others. Much of it is probably acquired with the aid of spoken, symbolic language. Using language, a human parent can describe a snake and tell a child that a snake is dangerous and should be avoided. If symbolic language did not exist, the parent would have to wait until the child actually saw a snake and then, through example, show the child that such a creature is to be avoided. To sum up, we may say that something is cultural if it is a learned behavior or idea (belief, attitude, value, ideal) that the members of a society or other social group generally share.

Attitudes That Hinder the Study of Cultures

Many of the Europeans who first traveled to faraway places were revolted or shocked by customs they observed. Such reactions are not surprising. People commonly feel that their own behaviors and attitudes

Because we are ethnocentric about many things, it is often difficult to criticize our own customs, some of which might seem shocking to a member of another society. The elderly in America often spend their days alone. In contrast, the elderly in Japan often live in a three-generational family.

are the correct ones and that people who do not share those patterns are immoral or inferior.[5] People who judge other cultures solely in terms of their own culture are **ethnocentric**—that is, they hold an attitude called **ethnocentrism**. Most North Americans would think that eating dogs or insects is disgusting, but most do not feel the same way about eating beef. Similarly, they would react negatively to child betrothal or digging up the bones of the dead.

Our own customs and ideas may appear bizarre or barbaric to an observer from another society. Hindus in India, for example, would consider our custom of eating beef disgusting. In their culture, the cow is a sacred animal and may not be slaughtered for food. In many societies, a baby is almost constantly carried by someone, in someone's lap, or asleep next to others.[6] People in such societies may think it is cruel of us to leave babies alone for long periods of time, often in devices that resemble cages (cribs and playpens). Even our most ordinary customs—the daily rituals we take for granted—might seem thoroughly absurd when viewed from an outside perspective. An observer of our society might justifiably take notes on certain strange behaviors that seem quite ordinary to us, as the following description shows:

> The daily body ritual performed by everyone includes a mouth-rite. Despite the fact that these people are so punctilious about the care of the mouth, this rite involves a practice which strikes the uninitiated stranger as revolting. It was reported to me that the ritual consists of inserting a small bundle of hog hairs into the mouth, along with certain magical powders, and then moving the bundle in a highly formalized series of gestures. In addition to the private mouth-rite, the people seek out a holy-mouth man once or twice a year. These practitioners have an impressive set of paraphernalia, consisting of a variety of augers, awls, probes, and prods. The use of these objects in the exorcism of the evils of the mouth involves almost unbelievable ritual torture of the client. The holy-mouth man opens the client's mouth and, using the above-mentioned tools, enlarges any holes which decay may have created in teeth. Magical materials are put into these holes. If there are no naturally occurring holes in the teeth, large sections of one or more

teeth are gouged out so that the supernatural substance can be applied. In the client's view, the purpose of these ministrations is to arrest decay and to draw friends. The extremely sacred and traditional character of the rite is evident in the fact that the natives return to the holy-mouth man year after year, despite the fact that their teeth continue to decay.[7]

We are likely to protest that to understand the behaviors of a particular society—in this case, our own—the observer must try to find out what the people in that society say about why they do things. For example, the observer might find out that periodic visits to the "holy-mouth man" are for medical, not magical, purposes. Indeed, the observer, after some questioning, might discover that the "mouth-rite" has no sacred or religious connotations whatsoever. Actually, Horace Miner, the author of the passage on the "daily rite ritual," was not a foreigner. An American, he described the "ritual" the way he did to show how the behaviors involved might be interpreted by an outside observer.

Ethnocentrism hinders our understanding of the customs of other people and, at the same time, keeps us from understanding our own customs. If we think that everything we do is best, we are not likely to ask why we do what we do or why "they" do what "they" do.

We may not always glorify our own culture. Other ways of life may sometimes seem more appealing. Whenever we are weary of the complexities of civilization, we may long for a way of life that is "closer to nature" or "simpler" than our own. For instance, a young North American whose parent is holding two or three jobs just to provide the family with bare necessities might briefly be attracted to the lifestyle of the San of the Kalahari Desert in the 1950s. The San shared their food and therefore were often free to engage in leisure activities during the greater part of the day. They obtained all their food by men hunting animals and women gathering wild plants. They had no facilities for refrigeration, so sharing a large freshly killed animal was clearly more sensible than hoarding meat that would soon rot. Moreover, the sharing provided a kind of social security system for the San. If a hunter was unable to catch an animal on a certain day, he could obtain food for himself and his family from someone else in his band. Then, at some later date, the game he caught would provide food for the family of another, unsuccessful hunter. This system of sharing also ensured that people too young or too old to help with collecting food would still be fed.

Could we learn from the San? Perhaps we could in some respects, but we must not glorify their way of life either or think that their way of life might be easily imported into our own society. Other aspects of San life would not appeal to many North Americans. For example, when the nomadic San decided to move their camps, they had to carry all the family possessions, substantial amounts of food and water, and all young children below age 4 or 5. This is a sizable burden to carry for any distance. The nomadic San traveled about 1,500 miles in a single year and families had few possessions.[8] It is unlikely that most North Americans would find the San way of life enviable in all respects.

Both ethnocentrism and its opposite, the glorification of other cultures, hinder effective anthropological study.

Cultural Relativism

As we discussed in the chapter on the history of theory in anthropology, the early evolutionists tended to think of Western cultures as being at the highest or most progressive stage of evolution. Not only were these early ideas based on very poor evidence of the details of world ethnography, they could also be ethnocentric glorifications of Western culture.

But Franz Boas and many of his students—like Ruth Benedict, Melville Herskovits, and Margaret Mead—challenged the attitude that Western cultures were obviously superior. The anthropological attitude that a society's customs and ideas should be described objectively and understood in the context of that society's problems and opportunities became known as **cultural relativism**. Does cultural relativism mean that the actions of another society, or of our own, should not be judged? Does our insistence on objectivity mean that anthropologists should not make moral judgments about the cultural phenomena they observe and try to explain? Does it mean that anthropologists should not try to bring about change? Not necessarily. Although the concept of cultural relativism remains an important anthropological tenet, anthropologists differ in their interpretation of the principle of cultural relativism.

Many anthropologists are uncomfortable with the strong form of cultural relativism that suggests that all patterns of culture are equally valid. What if the people practice slavery, violence against women, torture, or genocide? If the strong doctrine of relativism is adhered to, then these cultural practices are not to be judged, and we should not try to eliminate them. A weaker form of cultural relativism asserts that anthropologists should strive for objectivity in describing a people and should be wary of superficial or quick judgment in their attempts to understand the reasons for cultural behavior. Tolerance should be the basic mode unless there is strong reason to behave otherwise.[9] The weak version of cultural relativity does not preclude anthropologists from making judgments or from trying to change behavior they think is harmful. But judgments need not, and should not, preclude accurate description and explanation.

Now that we have defined what is cultural, we must ask a further question: How does an anthropologist go about deciding which particular behaviors, values, and beliefs of individuals are cultural?

Describing a Culture

Earlier we discussed *participant-observation* and some other methods of research that cultural anthropologists use in doing fieldwork.

But here we focus on another question: If all individuals are unique and all cultures have some internal variation, how do anthropologists discover what may be cultural? Understanding what is cultural involves two parts: separating what is shared from what is very individually variable, and understanding whether common behaviors and ideas are learned.

Individual Variation

To understand better how an anthropologist might make sense of diverse behaviors, let us examine the diversity at a professional football game in the United States. When people attend a football game, various members of the crowd behave differently while "The Star-Spangled Banner" is being played. As they stand and listen, some people remove their hats; a child munches popcorn; a veteran of the armed forces stands at attention; a teenager searches the crowd for a friend; and the coaches take a final opportunity to intone secret chants and spells designed to sap the strength of the opposing team. Yet, despite these individual variations, most of the people at the game respond in a basically similar manner: Nearly everyone stands silently, facing the flag. Moreover, if you go to several football games, you will observe that many aspects of the event are notably similar. Although the plays will vary from game to game, the rules of the game are never different, and although the colors of the uniforms of the teams are different, the players never appear on the field dressed in swimsuits.

Although the variations in individual reactions to a given stimulus are theoretically limitless, in fact they tend to fall within easily recognizable limits. A child listening to the anthem may continue to eat popcorn but will probably not do a rain dance. Similarly, the coaches will unlikely react to that same stimulus by running onto the field and embracing the singer.

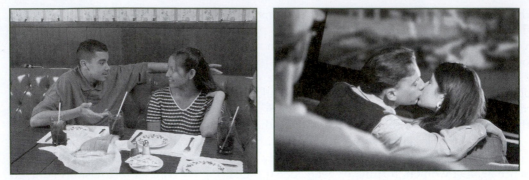

In deciding what is cultural behavior, anthropologists look for commonalities, understanding that there is always considerable variation. In North American culture, unmarried couples are allowed and even encouraged to spend time with each other, but how they spend their time varies.

Variations in behavior, then, are confined within socially acceptable limits, and part of the anthropologists' goals is to find out what those limits are. They may note, for example, that some limitations on behavior have a practical purpose: A spectator who disrupts the game by wandering onto the field would be required to leave. Other limitations are purely traditional. In our society, it is considered proper for a man to remove his overcoat if he becomes overheated, but others would undoubtedly frown upon his removing his trousers even if the weather were quite warm. Using observation and interviewing, anthropologists discover the customs and the ranges of acceptable behavior that characterize the society under study.

Similarly, anthropologists interested in describing courtship and marriage in our society would encounter a variety of behaviors. Dating couples vary in where they go (coffee shops, movies, restaurants, bowling alleys), what behaviors they engage in on dates, how long they date before they split up or move on to more serious relationships. If they decide to marry, ceremonies may be simple or elaborate and involve either religious or secular rituals. Despite this variability, anthropologists would begin to detect certain regularities in courting practices. Although couples may do many different things on their first and subsequent dates, they nearly always arrange the dates by themselves; they try to avoid their parents when on dates; they often manage to find themselves alone at the end of a date; they put their lips together frequently; and so forth. After a series of more and more closely spaced encounters, a man and woman may decide to declare themselves publicly as a couple, either by announcing that they are engaged or by revealing that they are living together or intend to do so. Finally, if the two of them decide to marry, they must in some way have their union recorded by the civil authorities.

In our society, a person who wishes to marry cannot completely disregard the customary patterns of courtship. If a man saw a woman on the street and decided he wanted to marry her, he could conceivably choose a quicker and more direct form of action than the usual dating procedure. He could get on a horse, ride to the woman's home, snatch her up in his arms, and gallop away with her. In Sicily, until the 1960s, such a couple would have been considered legally married, even if the woman had never met the man before or had no intention of marrying. But in North American society, any man who acted in such a fashion would be arrested and jailed for kidnapping and would probably have his sanity challenged. Although individual behaviors may vary, most social behavior falls within culturally acceptable limits.

In the course of observing and interviewing, anthropologists also try to distinguish actual behavior from the ideas about how people in particular situations ought to feel and behave. In everyday terms, we speak of these ideas as *ideals*; in anthropology, we refer to them as *ideal cultural traits.* Ideal cultural traits may differ from actual behavior because the ideal is based on the way society used to be. (Consider the ideal of "free enterprise," that industry should be totally free of governmental regulation.) Other ideals may never have been actual patterns and may represent merely what people would like to see as correct behavior. Consider the idealized belief, long cherished in North America, that everybody is "equal before the law," that everybody should be treated in the same way by the police and courts. Of course, we know that this is not always true. The rich, for example, may receive less jail time and be sent to nicer prisons. Nevertheless, the ideal is still part of our culture; most of us continue to believe that the law should be applied equally to all.

Cultural Constraints

Noted French sociologist Émile Durkheim stressed that culture is something *outside* us, exerting a strong coercive power on us. We do not always feel the constraints of our culture because we generally conform to the types of conduct and thought it requires. Social scientists refer to standards or rules about what is acceptable behavior as **norms**. The importance of a norm usually can be judged by how members of a society respond when the norm is violated.

Cultural constraints are of two basic types, *direct* and *indirect.* Naturally, the direct constraints are the more obvious. For example, if you choose to wear a casual shorts outfit to a wedding, you will probably be subject to some ridicule and a certain amount of social isolation. But if you choose to wear nothing, you may be exposed to a stronger, more direct cultural constraint—arrest for indecent exposure.

Although indirect forms of cultural constraint are less obvious than direct ones, they are no less effective. Durkheim illustrated this point when he wrote, "I am not obliged to speak French with my fellow-countrymen, nor to use the legal currency, but I cannot possibly do otherwise. If I tried to escape this necessity, my attempt would fail miserably."[10] In other words, if Durkheim had decided he would rather speak Icelandic than French, nobody would have tried to stop him. But hardly anyone would have understood him either. And although he would not have been put into prison for trying to buy groceries with Icelandic money, he would have had difficulty convincing the local merchants to sell him food.

In a series of classic experiments on conformity, Solomon Asch revealed how strong social pressure can be. Asch coached the majority of a group of college students to give deliberately incorrect answers to questions involving visual stimuli. A "critical subject," the one student in the room who was not so coached, had no idea that the other participants would purposely misinterpret the evidence presented to them. Asch found that, in one-third of the experiments, the critical subjects consistently gave incorrect answers, seemingly allowing their own correct perceptions to be distorted by the obviously incorrect statements of the others. And in another 40 percent of the experiments, the critical subject yielded to the opinion of the group some of the time.[11] These studies have been replicated in the United States and elsewhere. Although the degree of conformity appears to vary in different societies, most studies still show conformity effects.[12] Many individuals still do not give in to the wishes of the majority, but a recent study using magnetic resonance imaging has shown that perceptions can actually be altered if participants consciously alter their answers to conform to others.[13]

How to Discover Cultural Patterns

There are two basic ways in which an anthropologist can discover cultural patterns. When dealing with customs that are overt or highly visible within a society—for example, the custom of sending children to school—an investigator can determine the existence of such practices by direct observation and by interviewing a few knowledgeable people. But when dealing with a domain of behavior that may include many individual variations, or when the people studied are unaware of their pattern of behavior and cannot answer questions about it, the anthropologist may need to collect information from a larger sample of individuals to establish what the cultural trait is.

One example of a cultural trait that most people in a society are not aware of is how far apart people stand when they are having a conversation. Yet there is considerable reason to believe that unconscious cultural rules govern such behavior. These rules become obvious when we interact with people who have different rules. We may experience considerable discomfort when another person stands too close (indicating too much intimacy) or too far (indicating unfriendliness). Edward Hall reported that Arabs customarily stand quite close to others, close enough, as we have noted, to be able to smell the other person. In interactions between Arabs and North Americans, then, the Arabs will move closer at the same time that the North Americans back away.[14]

If we wanted to arrive at the cultural rule for conversational distance between casual acquaintances, we could study a sample of individuals from a society and determine the *modal response,* or *mode.* The mode is a statistical term that refers to the most frequently encountered response in a given series of responses. So, for the North American pattern of casual conversational distance, we would plot the actual distance for many observed pairs of people. Some pairs may be 2 feet apart, some 2.5, and some 4 feet apart. If we count the number of times every particular distance is observed, these counts provide what we call a *frequency distribution.* The distance with the highest frequency is the *modal pattern.* Very often the frequency distribution takes the form of a *bell-shaped curve,* as shown in Figure 9.1.

There, the characteristic being measured is plotted on the horizontal axis (in this case, the distance between conversational pairs), and the number of times each distance is observed (its frequency) is plotted on the vertical axis. If we were to plot how a sample of North American casual conversational pairs is distributed, we would probably get a bell-shaped curve that peaks at around 3 feet.[15] Is it any wonder, then, that we sometimes speak of keeping others "at arm's length"?

Distance between people conversing varies cross-culturally. The faces of the Rajput Indian men on the left are much closer than the faces of the American women on the right.

Although we may be able to discover by interviews and observation that a behavior, thought, or feeling is widely shared within a society, how do we establish that something commonly shared is learned, so that we can call it cultural? Establishing that something is or is not learned may be difficult. Because children are not reared apart from adult caretakers, the behaviors they exhibit as part of their genetic inheritance are not clearly separated from those they learn from others around them. We suspect that particular behaviors and ideas are largely learned if they vary from society to society. We also suspect genetic influences when particular behaviors or ideas are found in all societies. For example, as we will see in the chapter on language, children the world over seem to acquire language at about the same age, and the structure of their early utterances seems to be similar. These facts suggest that human children are born with an innate grammar. However, although early childhood language seems similar the world over, the particular languages spoken by adults in different societies show considerable variability. This variability suggests that particular languages have to be learned. Similarly, if the courtship patterns of one society differ markedly from those of another, we can be fairly certain that those courtship patterns are learned and therefore cultural.

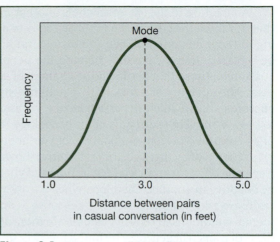

Figure 9.1 Frequency Distribution Curve

Culture Is Patterned

Anthropologists have always known that culture is not a hodgepodge of unrelated behaviors and ideas—that a culture is mostly integrated. In saying that a culture is mostly *integrated*, we mean that the elements or traits that make up that culture are not just a random assortment of customs but are mostly adjusted to or consistent with one another.

A culture may also tend to be integrated for psychological reasons. The ideas of a culture are stored in the brains of individuals. Research in social psychology has suggested that people tend to modify beliefs or behaviors that are not cognitively or conceptually consistent with other information.[16] We do not expect cultures to be completely integrated, just as we do not expect individuals to be completely consistent. But if a tendency toward cognitive consistency is found in humans, we might expect that at least some aspects of a culture would tend to be integrated for that reason alone.

Humans are also capable of rational decision making; they can usually figure out that certain things are not easy to do because of other things they do. For example, if a society has a long postpartum sex taboo (a custom in which couples abstain from sex for a year or more after the birth of a baby), we might expect that most people in the society could figure out that it would be easier to observe the taboo if husband and wife did not sleep in the same bed. Or if people drive on the left side of the road, as in England, it is easier and less dangerous to drive a car with a steering wheel on the right because that placement allows you to judge more accurately how close you are to cars coming at you from the opposite direction. Consistency or integration of culture traits may also be produced by less conscious psychological processes. As we discuss in the chapters on religion and magic and the arts, people may generalize (transfer) their experiences from one area of life to another.

Adaptation to the environment is another major reason for traits to be patterned. Customs that diminish the survival chances of a society are not likely to persist. Either the people clinging to those customs will become extinct, taking the customs with them, or the customs will be replaced, thereby possibly helping the people to survive. By either process, **maladaptive customs**—those that diminish the chances of survival and reproduction—are likely to disappear. The customs of a society that enhance survival and reproductive success are **adaptive customs** and are likely to persist. Hence, we assume that if a society has survived long enough to be described in the annals of anthropology (the "ethnographic record"), much, if not most, of its cultural repertoire is adaptive, or was at one time.

When we say that a custom is adaptive, however, we mean it is adaptive only with respect to a specific physical and social environment. What may be adaptive in one environment may not be adaptive in another. Therefore, when we ask why a society may have a particular custom, we really are asking if that custom makes sense as an adaptation to that society's particular environmental conditions. If certain customs are more adaptive in particular settings, then those "bundles" of traits will generally be found together under similar conditions. For example, the San, as we have mentioned, subsisted by hunting wild animals and gathering wild plants. Because wild game is mobile and different plants mature at different times, a nomadic way of life may be an adaptive strategy. That food-getting strategy cannot support that many people in one area, so small social groups make more sense than large communities. Because people move frequently, it is probably more adaptive to have few material possessions. As we will see, these cultural traits usually occur together when people depend on hunting and gathering for their food.

We must remember that not all aspects of culture are consistent, nor is a society forced to adapt its culture to changing environmental circumstances.

How and Why Cultures Change

When you examine the history of a society, it is obvious that its culture has changed over time. Some of the shared behaviors and ideas that were common at one time are modified or replaced at another time. That is why, in describing a culture, it is important to understand that a description pertains to a particular time period. For example, the San of the 1950s were mostly dependent on the collection of wild plants and animals and moved their campsites frequently, but later they became more sedentary to engage in wage labor.

When we compare our lives with those of our parents, it is obvious that many culture changes have occurred. Witness the recent changes in attitudes about sex and marriage, as well as the changes in women's roles. But such culture change is not unusual. Throughout history humans have replaced or altered customary behaviors and attitudes as their needs have changed. Anthropologists want to understand how and why cultures change.

Three general questions can be asked about culture change: What is the source of a new trait? Why are people motivated unconsciously, as well as consciously, to adopt it? And is the new trait adaptive? In general, the impetus for change may come from within the society or from without. From within, the unconscious or conscious pressure for consistency will produce culture change if enough people adjust old behavior and thinking to new. And change can also occur if people try to invent better ways of doing things. Michael Chibnik suggests that people who confront a new problem conduct mental or small "experiments" to decide how to behave. These experiments may give rise to new cultural traits.[17] A good deal of culture change may be stimulated by changes in the external environment. Many North Americans, for example, started to think seriously about conserving energy and about using sources of energy other than oil only after oil supplies from the Middle East were curtailed in 1973 and 1974. As we noted earlier, a significant amount of the radical and rapid culture change that has occurred in the last few hundred years has been due to the imperial expansion of Western societies into other areas of the world. Native Americans, for instance, were forced to alter their lifestyles drastically when they were driven off their lands and confined to reservations.

Discovery and Invention

The new thing discovered or invented, the innovation, may be an object—the wheel, the plow, the computer—or it may involve behavior and ideas—buying and selling, democracy, monogamy. According to Ralph Linton, a discovery is any addition to knowledge, and an invention is a new application of knowledge.[18] Thus, a person might discover that children can be persuaded to eat nourishing food if the food is associated with an imaginary character that appeals to them. And then someone might exploit that discovery by inventing a character named Popeye who appears in a series of animated cartoons, acquiring miraculous strength by devouring cans of spinach.

Unconscious Invention In discussing the process of invention, we should differentiate between various types of inventions. One type is the consequence of a society's setting itself a specific goal, such as eliminating tuberculosis or placing a person on the moon. Another type emerges less intentionally. This second process of invention is often referred to as *accidental juxtaposition* or *unconscious invention.* Linton suggested that some inventions, especially those of prehistoric days, were probably the consequences of literally dozens of tiny initiatives by "unconscious" inventors. These inventors made their small contributions, perhaps over many hundreds of years, without being aware of the part they were playing in bringing one invention, such as the wheel or a better form of hand ax, to completion.[19] In reconstructing the process of invention in prehistoric times, however, we should be careful not to look back on our ancestors with a smugness generated by our more highly developed technology. We have become accustomed to reading science news in magazines, newspapers and online, finding, almost daily, reports of miraculous new discoveries and inventions. From our point of view, it is difficult to imagine such a simple invention as the wheel taking so many centuries to come into being. We are tempted to surmise that early humans were less intelligent than we are. But the capacity of the human brain has been the same for perhaps 100,000 years; there is no evidence that the inventors of the wheel were any less intelligent than we are.

Intentional Innovation Some discoveries and inventions arise out of deliberate attempts to produce a new idea or object. It may seem that such innovations are obvious responses to perceived needs. For example, during the Industrial Revolution, there was a great demand for inventions that would increase productivity. James Hargreaves, in eighteenth-century England, is an example of an inventor who responded to an existing demand. Textile manufacturers were clamoring for such large quantities of spun yarn that cottage laborers, working with foot-operated spinning wheels, could not meet the demand. Hargreaves, realizing that prestige and financial rewards would come to the person who invented a method of spinning large quantities of yarn in a short time, set about the task and developed the spinning jenny.

A study of innovation among Ashanti artist carvers in Ghana suggests that creativity is more likely in some socioeconomic groups than in others.[20] Some carvers produced only traditional designs; others departed from tradition and produced "new" styles of carving. Two groups were found to innovate the most—the wealthiest and the poorest carvers. These two groups of carvers may tolerate risk more than the middle socioeconomic group. Innovative carving entails some risk because it may take more time and it may not sell. Wealthy carvers can afford the risk, and they may gain some prestige as well as income if their innovation is appreciated. The poor are not doing well anyway, and they have little to lose by trying something new.

Mayan woman from San Martin Jilotepeque working on a hip-strap loom. Designs became more individual and complex by the 1990s.

Some societies encourage innovativeness more than others, and this can vary substantially over time. Patricia Greenfield and her colleagues describe the changes in weaving in a Mayan community in the Zinacantán region of Chiapas, Mexico.[21] In 1969 and 1970, innovation was not valued. Rather, tradition was; there was the old "true way" to do everything, including how one dressed. There were only four simple weaving patterns, and virtually all males wore ponchos with the same pattern. By 1991, virtually no poncho was the same and the villagers had developed elaborate brocaded and embroidered designs. In a period of 20 years, innovation had increased dramatically.

Who Adopts Innovations? Once someone discovers or invents something, there is still the question of whether others will adopt the innovation. Many researchers have studied the characteristics of "early adopters." Such individuals tend to be educated, high in social status, upwardly mobile, and, if they are property owners, have large farms and businesses. The individuals who most need technological improvements—those who are less well off—are generally the last to adopt innovations. The theory is that only the wealthy can afford to take the substantial risks associated with new ways of doing things. In periods of rapid technological change, therefore, the gap between rich and poor is likely to widen because the rich adopt innovations sooner, and benefit more from them, than the poor.[22]

Costs and Benefits An innovation that is technologically superior is not necessarily going to be adopted. There are costs as well as benefits for both individuals and large-scale industries. Take the computer keyboard. The keyboard used most often on computers today is called the QWERTY keyboard (named after the letters on the left side of the line of keys below the row of number keys). This keyboard was actually invented to slow typing speed down! Early typewriters had mechanical keys that jammed if the typist went too fast.[23] Computer keyboards don't have that problem, so an arrangement of keys that allowed faster typing would probably be better. Different keyboard configurations have been invented, but they haven't caught on. Most people probably would find it too hard or too time-consuming to learn a new style of typing, so the original style of keyboard persists.

Diffusion

The source of new cultural elements in a society may also be another society. The process by which cultural elements are borrowed from another society and incorporated into the culture of the recipient group is called **diffusion**. Borrowing sometimes enables a group to bypass stages or mistakes in the development of a process or institution. For example, Germany was able to accelerate its program of industrialization in the nineteenth century because it was able to avoid some of the errors its English and Belgian competitors made by taking advantage of technological borrowing. Japan did the same somewhat later. Indeed, in recent years, some of the earliest industrialized countries have fallen behind their imitators in certain areas of production, such as automobiles, televisions, cameras, and computers.

In a well-known passage, Linton conveyed the far-reaching effects of diffusion by considering the first few hours in the day of an American man in the 1930s. This man

> . . . awakens in a bed built on a pattern which originated in the Near East but which was modified in northern Europe before it was transmitted to America. He throws back covers made from cotton, domesticated in India, or linen, domesticated in the Near East, or silk, the use of which was discovered in China. All of these materials have been spun and woven by processes invented in the Near East. . . . He takes off his pajamas, a garment invented in India, and washes with soap invented by the ancient Gauls. He then shaves, a masochistic rite which seems to have derived from either Sumer or ancient Egypt.
>
> Before going out for breakfast he glances through the window, made of glass invented in Egypt, and if it is raining puts on overshoes made of rubber discovered by the Central American Indians and takes an umbrella, invented in southeastern Asia. . . .
>
> On his way to breakfast he stops to buy a paper paying for it with coins, an ancient Lydian invention. . . . His plate is made of a form of pottery invented in China. His knife is of steel, an alloy first made in southern India, his fork a medieval Italian invention, and his spoon a derivative of a Roman original. . . . After his fruit (African watermelon) and first coffee (an Abyssinian plant), . . . he may have the egg of a species of bird domesticated in Indo-China, or thin strips of the flesh of an animal domesticated in eastern Asia which have been salted and smoked by a process developed in northern Europe. . . .

A Masai man in Kenya can call home or around the world from the plains of Kenya.

While smoking (an American Indian habit), he reads the news of the day, imprinted in characters invented by the ancient Semites upon a material invented in China by a process invented in Germany. As he absorbs the accounts of foreign troubles he will, if he is a good conservative citizen, thank a Hebrew deity in an Indo-European language that he is 100 percent American.[24]

The Selective Nature of Diffusion   Although there is a temptation to view the dynamics of diffusion as similar to a stone sending concentric ripples over still water, this would be an oversimplification of the way diffusion actually occurs. Not all cultural traits are borrowed as readily as the ones we have mentioned, nor do they usually expand in neat, ever-widening circles. Rather, diffusion is a selective process. The Japanese, for instance, accepted much from Chinese culture, but they also rejected many traits. Rhymed tonal poetry, civil service examinations, and foot binding, which the Chinese favored, were never adopted in Japan. The poetry form was unsuited to the structure of the Japanese language; the examinations were unnecessary in view of the entrenched power of the Japanese aristocracy; and foot binding was repugnant to a people who abhorred body mutilation of any sort.

Not only would we expect societies to reject items from other societies that are repugnant, we would also expect them to reject ideas and technology that do not satisfy some psychological, social, or cultural need. After all, people are not sponges; they don't automatically soak up the things around them. If they did, the amount of cultural variation in the world would be extremely small, which is clearly not the case. Finally, diffusion is selective because the overt form of a particular trait, rather than its function or meaning, frequently seems to determine how the trait will be received. For example, the enthusiasm in women for bobbed hair (short haircuts) that swept through much of North America in the 1920s never caught on among the Native Americans of northwestern California. To many women of European ancestry, short hair was a symbolic statement of their freedom. To Native American women, who traditionally cut their hair short when in mourning, it was a reminder of death.[25]

Acculturation

On the surface, the process of change called **acculturation** seems to include much of what we have discussed under the label of diffusion because acculturation refers to the changes that occur when different cultural groups come into intensive contact. As in diffusion, the source of new cultural items is the other society. But more often than not, anthropologists use the term *acculturation* to describe a situation in which one of the societies in contact is much more powerful than the other. Thus, acculturation can be seen as a process of extensive cultural borrowing in the context of superordinate–subordinate relations between societies.[26] There is probably always some borrowing both ways, but generally the subordinate or less powerful society borrows the most.

External pressure for culture change can take various forms. In its most direct form—conquest or colonialization—the dominant group uses force or the threat of force to try to bring about culture change in the other group. For example, in the Spanish conquest of Mexico, the conquerors forced many of the native groups to accept Catholicism. Although such direct force is not always exerted in conquest situations, dominated peoples often have little choice but to change. Examples of such indirectly forced change abound in the history of Native Americans in the United States. Although the federal government made few direct attempts to force people to adopt American culture, it did drive many native groups from their lands, thereby obliging them to give up many aspects of their traditional ways of life. To survive, they had no choice but to adopt many of the dominant society's traits. When Native American children were required to go to school, which taught the dominant society's values, the process was accelerated.

A subordinate society may acculturate to a dominant society even in the absence of direct or indirect force. Perceiving that members of the dominant society enjoy more secure living conditions, the dominated people may identify with the dominant culture in the hope that they will be able to share some of its benefits by doing so. Or, they may elect to adopt cultural elements from the dominant society because they perceive that the new element has advantages. For example, in Arctic areas, many Inuit and Saami (or Lapp) groups seemed eager to replace dog sleds with snowmobiles without any coercion.[27] There is evidence that the Inuit weighed the advantages and disadvantages of the snowmobile versus the dog sled and that its adoption was gradual. Similarly, rifles were seen as a major technological improvement, increasing the success rate in hunting, but the Inuit did not completely abandon their former ways of hunting. More recently the Inuit are trying out GPS devices for navigating.[28]

Acculturation processes vary considerably depending on the wishes of the more powerful society, the attitudes of the less powerful, and whether there is any choice. More powerful societies do not always want individuals from another culture to assimilate or "melt into" the dominant culture completely; instead, they may prefer and even actively promote a *multicultural* society. Multiculturalism can be voluntary or it may arise out of deliberate segregation.

Many millions of people, however, never had a chance to acculturate after contact with Europeans. They simply died, sometimes directly at the hands of the conquerors, but probably more often as a result of the new diseases the Europeans inadvertently brought with them. Depopulation because of measles, smallpox, and tuberculosis was particularly common in North and South America and on the islands of the Pacific. Those areas had previously been isolated from contact with Europeans and from the diseases of that continuous landmass we call the Old World—Europe, Asia, and Africa.[29]

Nowadays, many powerful nations—and not just Western ones—may seem to be acting in more humanitarian ways to improve the life of previously subjugated as well as other "developing" peoples. For better or worse, these programs, however, are still forms of external pressure. The tactic used may be persuasion rather than force, but most of the programs are nonetheless designed to bring about acculturation in the direction of the dominant societies' cultures. For example, the introduction of formal schooling cannot help but instill new values that may contradict traditional cultural patterns. Even health care programs may alter traditional ways of life by undermining the authority of shamans and other leaders and by increasing population beyond the number that can be supported in traditional ways. Confinement to "reservations" or other kinds of direct force are not the only ways a dominant society can bring about acculturation.

The process of acculturation also applies to immigrants, most of whom, at least nowadays, choose to leave one country for another. Immigrants are almost always a minority in the new country and therefore are in a subordinate position. If the immigrant's culture changes, it is almost always in the direction of the dominant culture. Immigrant groups vary considerably in the degree and speed with which they adopt the new culture and the social roles of the new society in which they live. An important area of research is explaining the variation in acculturation and assimilation. (*Assimilation* is a concept very similar to acculturation, but *assimilation* is a term more often used by sociologists to describe the process by which individuals acquire the social roles and culture of the dominant group.) Why do some immigrant groups acculturate or assimilate faster than others? A comparative study by Robert Schrauf assessed the degree to which immigrant groups coming to North America retained their native language over time. He looked at whether they lived in tightly knit communities, retained religious rituals, had separate schools and special festivals, visited their homeland, did not intermarry, or worked with others of their ethnic group. All of these factors might be expected to lead to retention of the native language (and presumably other cultural patterns), but only living in tightly knit communities and retaining religious rituals strongly predicted retaining the native language over a long period of time.[30]

Culture Change and Adaptation

Earlier in this chapter when we discussed the fact that culture is patterned, we indicated that adaptation to the environment is one reason why certain culture traits will cluster because more than one trait is likely to be *adaptive* in a particular environment. We make the assumption that most of the customary behaviors of a culture are probably *adaptive*, or at least not maladaptive, in that environment. Even though customs are learned and not genetically inherited, cultural adaptation may resemble biological adaptation in one major respect. The frequency of certain genetic alternatives is likely to increase over time if those genetic traits increase their carriers' chances of survival and reproduction. Similarly, the frequency of a new learned behavior will increase over time and become customary in a population if the people with that behavior are most likely to survive and reproduce.

One of the most important differences between cultural evolution and genetic evolution is that individuals often can decide whether or not to accept and follow the way their parents behave or think, whereas they cannot decide whether or not to inherit certain genes. When enough individuals change their behavior and beliefs, we say that the culture has changed. Therefore, it is possible for culture change to occur much more rapidly than genetic change.

A dramatic example of intentional cultural change was the adoption and later elimination of the custom of *sepaade* among the Rendille, a pastoral population that herds camels, goats, and sheep in the desert in northern Kenya. According to the *sepaade* tradition, some women had to wait to marry until all their brothers were married. These women could well have been over 40 by the time they married. The Rendille say that this tradition was a result of intense warfare between the Rendille and the Borana during the mid-nineteenth century. Attacked by Borana on horseback, the male warriors had to leave their camels unattended and the frightened camels fled. The daughters of one male age-set were appointed to look after the camels, and the *sepaade* tradition developed. In 1998, long after warfare with the Borana ceased, the elders decided to free the *sepaade* from their obligation to postpone their own marriages. Interviews with the Rendille in the 1990s revealed that many individuals were fully aware of the reason for the tradition in the first place. Now, they said, there was peace, so there was no longer any reason for the *sepaade* tradition to continue.[31]

The adoption of the *sepaade* is an example of culture change in a changing environment. But what if the environment is stable? Is culture change more or less likely? Robert Boyd and Peter Richerson have shown mathematically that, when the environment is relatively stable and individual mistakes are costly, staying with customary modes of behavior (usually transmitted by parents) is probably more adaptive than changing.[32] But what happens when the environment, particularly the social environment, is changing? It is particularly when circumstances change that individuals are likely to try ideas or behaviors that are different from those of their parents. We can expect that the choices individuals make may often be adaptive ones. But it is important to note that adopting an innovation from someone in one's own society or borrowing an innovation from another society is not always or necessarily beneficial, either in the short or the long run. Why, for example, have smoking and drug use diffused so widely even though they are likely to reduce a person's chances of survival? Second, even if people are correct in their short-term judgment of benefit, they may be wrong in their judgment about long-run benefit. A new crop may yield more than the old crop for five consecutive years, but the new crop may fail miserably in the sixth year because of lower-than-normal rainfall or because the new crop depleted soil nutrients. Third, people may be forced by the more powerful to change, with few if any benefits for themselves.

Whatever the motives for humans to change their behavior, the theory of natural selection suggests that new behavior is not likely to become cultural or remain cultural over generations if it has harmful reproductive consequences, just as a genetic mutation with harmful consequences is not likely to become frequent in a population.[33] Still, we know of many examples of culture change that seem maladaptive—the switch to bottle-feeding rather than nursing infants, which may spread infection because contaminated water is used, or the adoption of alcoholic beverages, which may lead to alcoholism and early death.

Revolution

Certainly the most drastic and rapid way a culture can change is as a result of **revolution**—replacement, usually violent, of a country's rulers. Historical records, as well as our daily newspapers, indicate that people frequently rebel against established authority. Rebellions, if they occur, almost always occur in state societies, where there is a distinct ruling elite. They take the form of struggles between rulers and ruled, between conquerors and conquered, or between representatives of an external colonial power and segments of the native society. Rebels do not always succeed in overthrowing their rulers, so rebellions do not always result in revolutions. And even successful rebellions do not always result in culture change; the individual rulers may change, but customs or institutions may not. The sources of revolution may be mostly internal, as in the French Revolution, or partly external, as in the Russian-supported 1948 revolution in Czechoslovakia and the United States–supported 1973 revolution against President Allende in Chile.

The American War of Independence toward the end of the eighteenth century is a good example of a colonial rebellion, the success of which was at least partly a result of foreign intervention. The American rebellion was a war of neighboring colonies against the greatest imperial power of the time, Great Britain. In the nineteenth century and continuing into the middle and later years of

Revolutionary leaders are often from high-status backgrounds. Here we see a depiction of Patrick Henry giving his famous speech to the aristocratic landowners in the Virginia General Assembly on March 23, 1775. Urging the Virginians to fight the British, Henry said that the choice was "liberty or death."

Source: Currier & Ives, "Give Me Liberty or Give Me Death!", 1775. Lithograph, 1876. c. The Granger Collection, New York.

the twentieth century, there would be many other wars of independence, in Latin America, Europe, Asia, and Africa. We don't always remember that the American rebellion was the first of these anti-imperialist wars in modern times, and the model for many that followed. And just like many of the most recent liberation movements, the American rebellion was also part of a larger worldwide war, involving people from many rival nations. Thirty thousand German-speaking soldiers fought, for pay, on the British side; an army and navy from France fought on the American side. There were volunteers from other European countries, including Denmark, Holland, Poland, and Russia.

One of these volunteers was a man named Kosciusko from Poland, which at the time was being divided between Prussia and Russia. Kosciusko helped win a major victory for the Americans, and subsequently directed the fortification of what later became the American training school for army officers, West Point. After the war, he returned to Poland and led a rebellion against the Russians, which was only briefly successful. In 1808, he published the *Manual on the Maneuvers of Horse Artillery*, which was used for many years by the American army. When he died, he left money to buy freedom and education for American slaves. The executor of Kosciusko's will was Thomas Jefferson.

As in many revolutions, those who were urging revolution were considered "radicals." At a now-famous debate in Virginia in 1775, delegates from each colony met at a Continental Congress. Patrick Henry put forward a resolution to prepare for defense against the British armed forces. The motion barely passed, by a vote of 65 to 60. Henry's speech is now a part of American folklore. He rose to declare that it was insane not to oppose the British and that he was not afraid to test the strength of the colonies against Great Britain. Others might hesitate, he said, but he would have "liberty or death." The "radicals" who supported Henry's resolution included many aristocratic landowners, two of whom, George Washington and Thomas Jefferson, became the first and third occupants of the highest political office in what became the United States of America.[34]

Not all peoples who are suppressed, conquered, or colonialized eventually rebel against established authority. Why this is so, and why rebellions and revolts are not always successful in bringing about culture change, are still open questions. The classic revolutions of the past occurred in countries that were industrialized only incipiently at best. For the most part, the same is true of the rebellions and revolutions in recent years; they have occurred mostly in countries we call "developing." The evidence from a worldwide survey of developing countries suggests that rebellions have tended to occur where the ruling classes depended mostly on the produce or income from land, and therefore were resistant to demands for reform from the rural classes that worked the land. In such agricultural economies, the rulers are not likely to yield political power or give greater economic returns to the workers because to do so would eliminate the basis (landownership) of the rulers' wealth and power.[35]

Globalization: Problems and Opportunities

Investment capital, people, and ideas are moving around the world at an ever faster rate.[36] Transportation now allows people and goods to circle the globe in days; telecommunications and the Internet make it possible to send a message around the world in seconds and minutes. Economic exchange is enormously more global and transnational. The word **globalization** is often used nowadays to refer to "the massive flow of goods, people, information, and capital across huge areas of the earth's surface."[37] The process of globalization has resulted in the worldwide spread of cultural features, particularly in the domain of economics and international trade. We buy from the same companies (that have factories all over the world), we sell our products and services for prices that are set by world market forces. We can eat pizza, hamburgers, curry, or sushi in most urban centers. In some ways, cultures are changing in similar directions. They have become

Television has dramatically enhanced world communication. Using other new inventions, a family in the village of Tiele in Mali watch TV powered by a car battery which was recharged with a solar home system.

more commercial, more urban, and more international. The job has become more important, and kinship less important, as people travel to and work in other countries, and return just periodically to their original homes. Ideas about democracy, the rights of the individual, and alternative medical practices and religions have become more widespread; people in many countries of the world watch the same TV shows, wear similar fashions, and listen to the same or similar music. In short, people are increasingly sharing behaviors and beliefs with people in other cultures, and the cultures of the world are less and less things "with edges," as Paul Durrenberger says.[38]

But diffusion of a culture trait does not mean that it is incorporated in exactly the same way, and the spread of certain products and activities through globalization does not mean that change happens in the same way everywhere. For example, the spread of multinational fast-food restaurants like McDonald's or Kentucky Fried Chicken has come to symbolize globalization. But the behavior of the Japanese in such restaurants is quite different from behavior in the United States. Perhaps the most surprising difference is that the Japanese in McDonald's actually have more familial intimacy and sharing than in more traditional restaurants. We imagine that establishments like McDonald's promote fast eating. But Japan has long had fast food—noodle shops at train stations, street vendors, and boxed lunches. Sushi, which is usually ordered in the United States at a sit-down restaurant, is usually served in Japan at a bar with a conveyor belt—individuals only need to pluck off the wanted dish as it goes by. Observations at McDonald's in Japan suggest that mothers typically order food for the family while the father spends time with the children at a table, a rare event since fathers often work long hours and cannot get home for dinner often. Food, such as French fries, is typically shared by the family. Even burgers and drinks are passed around, with many people taking a bite or a sip. Such patterns typify long-standing family practices. Japan has historically borrowed food, such as the Chinese noodle soup, now called ramen. Indeed, in a survey, ramen was listed as the most representative Japanese food. The burger was the second most-often listed. McDonald's has become Japanese—the younger generation does not even know that McDonald's is a foreign company—they think it is Japanese.[39]

Globalization is not new. The world has been global and interdependent since the sixteenth century.[40] What we currently call "globalization" is a more widespread version of what we used to call by various other names—diffusion, acculturation, colonialism, imperialism, or

MIGRANTS AND IMMIGRANTS

Increasing Cultural Diversity within the Countries of the World

The modern world is culturally diverse in two ways. There are native cultures in every part of the world, and today most countries have people from different cultures who have arrived relatively recently. Recent arrivals may be migrants coming for temporary work, or they may be refugees, forced by persecution or genocide to migrate, or they may be immigrants who voluntarily come into a new country. Parts of populations have moved away from their native places since the dawn of humanity. The first modern-looking humans moved out of Africa only in the last 100,000 years. People have been moving ever since. The people we call Native Americans were actually the first to come to the New World; most anthropologists think they came from northeast Asia. In the last 200 years, the United States and Canada have experienced extensive influxes of people. As is commonly said, they have become nations of migrants and immigrants, and Native Americans are now vastly outnumbered by the people and their descendants who came from Europe, Africa, Asia, Latin America, and elsewhere. North America not only has native and regional subcultures, but also ethnic, religious, and occupational subcultures, each with its own distinctive set of culture traits. Thus, North American culture is partly a "melting pot" and partly a mosaic of cultural diversity. Many of us, not just anthropologists, like this diversity. We like to go to ethnic restaurants regularly. We like salsa, sushi, and spaghetti. We compare and enjoy the different geographic varieties of coffee. We like music and artists from other countries. We often choose to wear clothing that may have been manufactured halfway around the world. We like all of these things not only because they may be affordable. We like them mostly, perhaps, because they are different.

Many of the population movements in the world today, as in the past, are responses to persecution and war. The word *diaspora* is often used nowadays to refer to these major dispersions. Most were and are involuntary; people are fleeing danger and death. But not always. Scholars distinguish different types of diaspora, including "victim," "labor," "trade," and "imperial" diasporas. The Africans who were sold into slavery, the Armenians who fled genocide in the early twentieth century, the Jews who fled persecution and genocide in various places over the centuries, the Palestinians who fled to the West Bank, Gaza, Jordan, and Lebanon in the mid-twentieth century, and the Rwandans who fled genocide toward the end of the twentieth century may have mostly been victims. The Chinese, Italians, and the Poles may have mostly moved to take advantage of job opportunities, the Lebanese to trade, and the British to extend and service their empire. Often these categories overlap; population movements can and have occurred for more than one reason. Some of the recent diasporas are less one-way than in the past. People are more "transnational," just as economics and politics are more "globalized." The new global communications have facilitated the retention of homeland connections—socially, economically, and politically. Some diasporic communities play an active role in the politics of their homelands, and some nation-states have begun to recognize their far-flung emigrants as important constituencies.

As cultural anthropologists increasingly study migrant, refugee, and immigrant groups, they focus on how the groups have adapted their cultures to new surroundings, what they have retained, how they relate to the homeland, how they have developed an ethnic consciousness, and how they relate to other minority groups and the majority culture.

Sources: M. Ember et al. 2005; Levinson and M. Ember 1997.

commercialization. But globalization is now on a much grander scale; enormous amounts of international investment fuel world trade. Shifts in the world marketplace may drastically affect a country's well-being more than ever before. For example, 60 percent of Pakistan's industrial employment is in textile and apparel manufacturing, but serious unemployment resulted when that manufacturing was crippled by restrictive American import policies and fears about war between India and Afghanistan.[41]

As we have seen in this chapter, there are many negative effects of colonialism, imperialism, and globalization. Many native peoples in many places lost their land and have been forced to work for inadequate wages in mines and plantations and factories that foreign capitalists own. Frequently, there is undernutrition if not starvation. Global travel has resulted in the quick spread of diseases such as HIV and severe acute respiratory syndrome (SARS), and increasing deforestation has led to a spread of malaria.[42] But are there any positive consequences? The "human development indicators" collected by the United Nations suggest an improvement in many respects, including increases in life expectancy and literacy in most countries. Much of the improvement in life expectancy is undoubtedly due to the spread of medicines developed in the advanced economies of the West. There is generally less warfare as colonial powers enforced pacification within the colonies that later became independent states. Most important, perhaps, has been the growth of middle classes all over the world, whose livelihoods depend on globalizing commerce. The middle classes in many countries have become strong and numerous enough to pressure governments for democratic reforms and the reduction of injustice.

World trade is the primary engine of economic development. Per capita income is increasing. Forty years ago, the countries of Asia were among the poorest countries in the world in terms of per capita income. Since then, because of their involvement in world trade, their incomes have risen enormously. In 1960, South Korea was as poor as India. Now its per capita income is 20 times higher than India's. Singapore is an even more dramatic example. In the late 1960s, its economy was a disaster. Today, its per capita income is higher than Britain's.[43] Mexico used to be a place where North Americans built factories to produce garments for the North American market. Now its labor is no longer so cheap. But because it has easy access to the North American market and because its plentiful labor is acquiring the necessary skills, Mexico is now seeing the development of high-tech manufacturing with decent salaries.[44]

There is world trade also in people. Many countries of the world now export people to other countries. Mexico has done so for a long time. Virtually every family in a Bangladesh village depends on someone who works overseas and sends money home. Without those remittances, many would face starvation. The government encourages people to go abroad to work. Millions of people from Bangladesh are now overseas on government-sponsored work contracts.[45]

But does a higher per capita income mean that life has improved generally in a country? Not necessarily. As we will see in the chapter on social stratification, inequality within countries can increase with technological improvements because the rich often benefit the most. In addition, economic wealth is increasingly concentrated in a relatively small number of countries. Obviously, then, not everyone is better off even if most countries are doing better on average. Poverty has become more common as countries have become more unequal.

Although many of the changes associated with globalization seem to be driven by the economic and political power of the richer countries, the movement of ideas, art, music, and food is more of a two-way process. A large part of that process involves the migration of people who bring their culture with them. Movements of people have played a large role in the entry of food such as tortilla chips and salsa, sushi, and curries into the United States; music like reggae and many types of dance music from Latin America; and African carvings and jewelry such as beaded necklaces. Recently there has even been increased interest in acquiring indigenous knowledge of plants, the knowledge of indigenous healers, and learning about shamanistic trances.

It is probably not possible to go back to a time when societies were not so dependent on each other, not so interconnected through world trade, not so dependent on commercial exchange. Even those who are most upset with globalization find it difficult to imagine that it is possible to return to a less connected world. For better or worse, the world is interconnected and will remain so. The question now is whether the average economic improvements in countries will eventually translate into economic improvements for most individuals.

Many of the processes that we have discussed—the expansion and domination by the West and other powerful nations, the deprivation of the ability of peoples to earn their livelihoods by traditional means, the imposition of schools or other methods to force acculturation, the attempts to convert people to other religions, and globalization—have led to profound changes in culture. But if culture change in the modern world has made cultures more alike in some ways, it has not eliminated cultural differences. Often, in the aftermath of violent events such as depopulation, relocation, enslavement, and genocide by dominant powers, deprived peoples have created new cultures in a process called **ethnogenesis**.[46]

Some of the most dramatic examples of ethnogenesis come from areas where escaped slaves (called Maroons) created new cultures. Maroon societies emerged in the past few hundred years in a variety of New World locations, from the United States to the West Indies and northern parts of South America. One of the new cultures, now known as Aluku, emerged when slaves fled from coastal plantations in Suriname to the swampy interior country along the Cottica River. After a war with the Dutch colonists, this particular group moved to French Guiana. The escaped slaves, originating from widely varying cultures in Africa or born on Suriname plantations, organized themselves into autonomous communities with military headmen.[47] They practiced slash-and-burn cultivation, with women doing most of the work. Although settlements shifted location as a way of evading enemies, coresidence in a community and collective ownership of land became important parts of the emerging identities. Communities took on the names of the specific plantations from which their leaders had escaped. Principles of inheritance through the female line began to develop, and full-fledged matriclans became the core of each village. Each village had its own shrine, the *faaka tiki*, where residents invoked the clan ancestors, as well as a special house where the deceased were brought to be honored and feted before being taken to the forest for burial. Clans also inherited avenging spirits with whom they could communicate through mediums.The Aluku case is a clear example of ethnogenesis because the culture did not exist 350 years ago. It emerged and was created by people trying to adapt to circumstances not of their own making. In common with other cases of emerging ethnic identity, the Aluku came not only to share new patterns of behavior but also to see themselves as having a common origin (a common ancestor), a shared history, and a common religion.[48]

Cultural Diversity in the Future

Measured in terms of travel time, the world today is much smaller than it has ever been. It is possible now to fly halfway around the globe in the time it took people to travel to the next state less than a century ago. In the realm of communication, the world is even smaller. We can talk to someone on the other side of the globe in a matter of minutes, we can send that person a message (by fax or e-mail) in seconds, and through television we can see live coverage of events in that person's country. More and more people are drawn into the world market economy, buying and selling similar things and, as a consequence, altering the patterns of their lives in sometimes similar ways. Still, although modern transportation and communication facilitate the rapid spread of some cultural characteristics to all parts of the globe, it is highly unlikely that all parts of the world will end up the same culturally. Cultures are bound to retain some of their original characteristics or develop distinctive new adaptations. Even though television has diffused around the world, local people continue to prefer local programs when they are available. And even when people all over the world watch the same program, they may interpret it in very different ways. People are not just absorbing the messages they get; they often resist or revise them.[49]

Until recently, researchers studying culture change generally assumed that the differences between people of different cultures would become minimal. But in the last 30 years or so, it has become increasingly apparent that, although many differences disappear, many people are affirming ethnic identities in a process that often involves deliberately introducing cultural difference.[50] Eugeen Roosens describes the situation of the Huron of Quebec, who in the late 1960s seemed to have disappeared as a distinct culture. The Huron language had disappeared and the lives of the Huron were not obviously distinguishable from those of the French Canadians around them. The Huron then developed a new identity as they actively worked to promote the rights of indigenous peoples like themselves. That their new defining cultural symbols bore no resemblance to the past Huron culture is beside the point.

One fascinating possibility is that ethnic diversity and ethnogenesis may be a result of broader processes. Elizabeth Cashdan found that the degree of ethnic diversity appears to be related to environmental unpredictability, which is associated with greater distance from the equator.[51] There appear to be many more cultural groups nearer to the equator than in very northern and southern latitudes. Perhaps, Cashdan suggests, environmental unpredictability in the north and south necessitates wider ties between social groups to allow cooperation in case local resources fail. This may minimize the likelihood of cultural divergence, that is, ethnogenesis. Hence, there will be fewer cultures further from the equator.

Future research on culture change should increase our understanding of how and why various types of change are occurring. If we can increase our understanding of culture change in the present, we should be better able to understand similar processes in the past. We may be guided in our efforts to understand culture change by the large number of cross-cultural correlations that have been discovered between a particular cultural variation and its presumed causes.[52] All cultures have changed over time; variation is the product of differential change. Thus, the variations we see are the products of change processes, and the discovered predictors of those variations may suggest how and why the changes occurred. In the chapters that follow, we hope to convey the main points of what anthropologists think they know about aspects of cultural variation and culture change, and what they do not know.

✓•─ **Study** and **Review** on **myanthrolab.com**

Summary

1. Culture may be defined as the set of learned behaviors and ideas (including beliefs, attitudes, values, and ideals) that are characteristic of a particular society or other social group.

2. When anthropologists refer to *a* culture, they usually are referring to the cultural patterns of a particular society—that is, a particular territorial population speaking a language not generally understood by neighboring territorial populations.

3. Ethnocentrism, judging other cultures in terms of your own, and its opposite—the glorification of other cultures—impede anthropological inquiry. An important tenet in anthropology is the principle of cultural relativism: the attitude that a society's customs and ideas should be studied objectively and understood in the context of that society's culture. But when it comes to some cultural practices such as violence against women, torture, slavery, or genocide, most anthropologists can no longer adhere to the strong form of cultural relativism that asserts that all cultural practices are equally valid.

4. Anthropologists seek to discover the customs and ranges of acceptable behavior that constitute the culture of a society under study. In doing so, they focus on general or shared patterns of behavior rather than on individual variations.

5. Cultures have patterns or clusters of traits. They tend to be integrated for psychological and adaptive reasons.

6. Culture is always changing. Because culture consists of learned behaviors and ideas, cultural traits can be unlearned and learned anew as human needs change.

7. Discoveries and inventions, though ultimately the sources of all culture change, do not necessarily lead to change. Only when society accepts an invention or discovery and uses it regularly can culture change be said to have occurred.

8. The process by which cultural elements are borrowed from another society and incorporated into the culture of the recipient group is called diffusion. Cultural traits do not necessarily diffuse; that is, diffusion is a selective, not automatic, process. A society accepting a foreign cultural trait is likely to adapt it in a way that effectively harmonizes it with the society's own traditions.

9. When a group or society is in contact with a more powerful society, the weaker group is often obliged to acquire cultural elements from the dominant group. This process of extensive borrowing in the context of superordinate–subordinate relations between societies is called acculturation. Acculturation processes vary considerably depending on the wishes of the more powerful society, the attitudes of the less powerful, and whether there is any choice.

10. Even though customs are not genetically inherited, cultural adaptation may be similar to biological adaptation in one major respect. Traits (cultural or genetic) that are more likely to be reproduced (learned or inherited) are likely to become more frequent in a population over time. Particularly when the environment changes, individuals may try out ideas and behaviors that are different than their parents.

11. Perhaps the most drastic and rapid way a culture can change is by revolution—a usually violent replacement of the society's rulers. Rebellions occur primarily in state societies, where there is a distinct ruling elite. However, not all peoples who are suppressed, conquered, or colonized eventually rebel or successfully revolt against established authority.

12. Globalization—the widespread flow of people, information, technology, and capital over the earth's surface—has minimized cultural diversity in some respects, but it has not eliminated it.

Glossary Terms

acculturation (p. 210)
adaptive customs (p. 206)
cultural relativism (p. 201)
culture (p. 197)
diffusion (p. 209)

ethnocentric (p. 199)
ethnocentrism (p. 199)
ethnogenesis (p. 218)
globalization (p. 214)
maladaptive customs (p. 206)

norms (p. 203)
revolution (p. 213)
society (p. 197)
subculture (p. 197)

Critical Questions

1. Would it be adaptive for a society to have everyone adhere to the cultural norms? Explain your answer.

2. Not all people faced with external pressure to change do so or do so at the same rate. What factors might explain why some societies rapidly change their culture?

3. Does the concept of cultural relativism promote international understanding, or does it hinder attempts to have international agreement on acceptable behavior, such as human rights?

Read the Original Source on myanthrolab.com

Read the case study by Regina Smith Oboler, "Nandi: From Cattle-Keepers to Cash-Crop Farmers," on MyAnthroLab, and answer the following questions.

1. Who are the Nandi? Give a brief description of them, and include the time period and community being described by Oboler.

2. As you read about the Nandi, you may be surprised by some of their customs. Indicate which specific customs surprise you. Describe whether you think you are reacting simply because their customs are different from your customs, whether you are being ethnocentric, or if you prefer their customs.

3. Anthropologists have to learn not to judge behavior in another culture in terms of their own culture. Give an example from Regina Smith Oboler's fieldwork among the Nandi.

10 Language and Communication

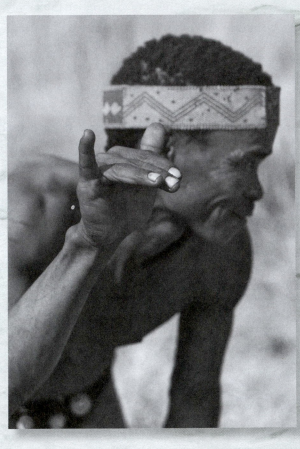

Few of us can remember when we first became aware that words signified something. Yet that moment was a milestone for us, not just in the acquisition of language but in becoming acquainted with all the complex, elaborate behavior that constitutes our culture. Without language, the transmission of complex traditions would be virtually impossible, and each person would be trapped within his or her own world of private sensations.

Helen Keller, left deaf and blind by illness at the age of 19 months, gives a moving account of the afternoon she first established contact with another human being through words:

> [My teacher] brought me my hat, and I knew I was going out into the warm sunshine. This thought, if a wordless sensation may be called a thought, made me hop and skip with pleasure.
>
> We walked down the path to the well house, attracted by the fragrance of the honeysuckle with which it was covered. Someone was drawing water and my teacher placed my hand under the spout. As the cool stream gushed over one hand she spelled into the other the word water, first slowly, then rapidly. Suddenly I felt a misty consciousness as of something forgotten—a thrill of returning thought; and somehow the mystery of language was revealed to me. I knew then that w-a-t-e-r meant the wonderful cool something that was flowing over my hand. That living word awakened my soul, gave it light, hope, joy, set it free! There were barriers still, it is true, barriers that could in time be swept away.
>
> I left the well house eager to learn. Everything had a name, and each name gave birth to a new thought. As we returned to the house every object which I touched seemed to quiver with life. That was because I saw everything with the strange, new sight that had come to me.[1]

Communication

Against all odds, Helen Keller had come to understand the essential function that language plays in all societies—namely, that of communication. The word *communicate* comes from the Latin verb *communicare*, "to impart," "to share," "to make *common*." We communicate by agreeing, consciously or unconsciously, to call an object, a movement, or an abstract concept by a common name. For example, speakers of English have agreed to call the color of grass *green*, even though we have no way of comparing precisely how two people actually experience this color. What we share is the agreement to call similar sensations *green*. Any system of language consists of publicly accepted symbols by which individuals try to share private experiences. Spoken or vocal language is probably the major transmitter of culture, allowing us to share and pass on our complex configuration of attitudes, beliefs, and patterns of behavior.

Nonverbal Human Communication

As we all know from experience, the spoken word does not communicate all that we know about a social situation. We can usually tell when someone says, "It was good to meet you," whether he or she really means it. We can tell if people are sad from their demeanor, even if they just say, "I'm fine," in response to the question "How are you?"

Obviously, our communication is not limited to spoken language. We communicate directly through facial expression, body stance, gesture, and tone of voice and indirectly through systems of signs and symbols, such as writing, algebraic equations, musical scores, dancing, painting, code flags, and road signs. As Anthony Wilden put it, "every act, every pause, every movement in living and social systems is also a message; silence is communication; short of death it is impossible for an organism or person not to communicate."[2] How can silence be a communication? Silence may reflect companionship, as when two people work side by side on a project, but silence can also communicate unfriendliness. An anthropologist can learn a great deal from what people in a society do not talk about. For example, in India, sex is not supposed to be talked about. HIV infection is spreading very fast in India, so the unwillingness of people to talk about sex makes it extraordinarily difficult for medical anthropologists and health professionals to do much to reduce the rate of spread.[3]

Some nonverbal communication appears to be universal in humans. For example, humans the world over appear to understand facial expression in the same way; that is, they are able to recognize a happy, sad, surprised, angry, disgusted, or afraid face. How the face is represented in art appears to evoke similar feelings in many different cultures. As we explore later in the arts chapter, masks intended to be frightening have sharp, angular features and inward- and downward-facing eyes and eyebrows.

Nonverbal communication is also culturally variable. In the chapter on culture and culture change, we discussed how the distance between people standing together is culturally variable. In the realm of facial expression, different cultures have different rules about the emotions that are acceptable to express. One study compared how Japanese and Americans express emotion. Individuals from both groups were videotaped while they were shown films intended to evoke feelings of fear and disgust. When the subjects saw the films by themselves, without other people present, they showed the same kinds of facial expressions of fear and disgust. But there was a cultural effect too. When an authority figure was present during the videotaping, the Japanese subjects tried to mask their negative feelings with a half-smile more often than did the Americans.[4] Many gestures are culturally variable. In some cultures, an up-and-down nod of the head means "yes," in others it means "no."

Nonverbal communication can even involve the voice. Consider how we might know that a person is not fine even though she just said "I'm fine." We can tell a lot by tone of voice. A depressed person might speak very quietly and use a flat tone of voice. If a person thought about explaining what was really wrong but thought better of it, a significant pause or silence might come before the words, "I'm fine." Even a person's **accent** (differences in pronunciation) can tell a lot about the person's background, such as place of origin and education. There are also nonverbal (nonword) sounds that people make—grunts, laughs, giggles, moans, and sighs.

Nonhuman Communication

Systems of communication are not unique to human beings, nor is communication by sound. Other animal species communicate in a variety of ways. One way is by sound. A bird may communicate by a call that "this is my territory"; a squirrel may utter a cry that leads other squirrels to flee from danger. Another means of animal communication is odor. An ant releases a chemical when it dies, and its fellows then carry it away to the compost heap. Apparently the communication is highly effective; a healthy ant painted with the death chemical will be dragged to the funeral heap again and again. Bees use another means of communication, body movement, to convey the location of food sources. Karl von Frisch discovered that the black Austrian honey-bee—by choosing a round dance, a wagging dance, or a short, straight run—can communicate not only the precise direction of the source of food but also its distance from the hive.[5]

One of the biggest scholarly debates is the degree to which nonhuman animals, particularly nonhuman primates, differ from humans in their capacity for language. Some scholars see so much discontinuity that they postulate that humans must have acquired (presumably through mutation) a specific genetic capability for language. Others see much more continuity between humans and nonhuman primates and point to research that shows much more cognitive capacity in nonhuman primates than previously thought possible. They point out that the discontinuity theorists are constantly raising the standards for the capacities thought necessary for language.[6] For example, in the past, only human communication was thought to be symbolic. But recent research suggests that some monkey and ape calls in the wild are also symbolic.

When we say that a call, word, or sentence is **symbolic communication,** we mean at least two things. First, the communication has meaning even when its *referent* (whatever is referred to) is not present. Second, the meaning is arbitrary; the receiver of the message could not guess its meaning just from the sound(s) and does not know the meaning instinctively. In other words, symbols have to be learned. There is no compelling or "natural" reason that the word *dog* in English should refer to a smallish four-legged omnivore.

Vervet monkeys in Africa are not as closely related to humans as are African apes. Nevertheless, scientists who have observed vervet monkeys in their natural environment consider at least three of their alarm calls to be symbolic because each of them *means* (refers to) a different kind of predator—eagles, pythons, or leopards—and monkeys react differently to each call. For example, they look up when they hear the "eagle" call. Experimentally, in the absence of the referent, investigators have been able to evoke the normal reaction to a call by playing it back electronically. Another indication that the vervet alarm calls are symbolic is that infant vervets appear to need some time to learn the referent for each. When they are very young, infants apply a particular call to more animals than adult vervets apply the call to. So, for example, infant vervets will often make the eagle warning call when they see any flying bird. The infants learn the appropriate referent apparently through adult vervets' repetition of infants' "correct" calls; in any case, the infants gradually learn to restrict the call to eagles.

How is human vocalization different? All of the nonhuman vocalizations we have described so far enable individual animals to convey messages. The sender gives a signal that is received and "decoded" by the receiver, who usually responds with a specific action or reply. How is human vocalization different? Because monkeys and apes appear to use symbols at least some of the time, it is not appropriate to emphasize symbolism as the distinctive feature of human language. However, there is a significant quantitative difference between human language and other primates' systems of vocal communication. All human languages employ a much larger set of symbols.

Another often-cited difference between human and nonhuman vocalizations is that the other primates' vocal systems are *closed*—that is, different calls are not combined to produce new, meaningful utterances. In contrast, human languages are *open* systems, governed by

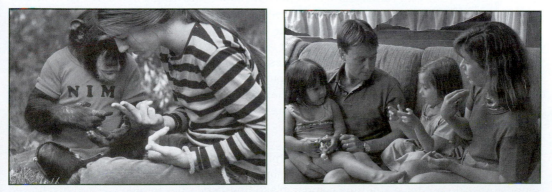

Apes lack the human capacity for speech, so researchers have explored the capacity of chimpanzees and other apes to communicate with hand gestures. Researcher Joyce Butler teaches Nim, a chimpanzee, a sign for "drink." A family employs sign language to communicate with a deaf child.

complex rules about how sounds and sequences of sounds can be combined to produce an infinite variety of meanings.[7] For example, an English speaker can combine *care* and *full* (*careful*) to mean one thing, then use each of the two elements in other combinations to mean different things. *Care* can be used to make *carefree, careless,* or *caretaker; full* can be used to make *powerful* or *wonderful.* And because language is a system of shared symbols, it can be reformed into an infinite variety of expressions and be understood by all who share these symbols. In this way, for example, T. S. Eliot could form a sentence never before formed—"In the room the women come and go/talking of Michelangelo"[8]—and all speakers of English could understand the sense of his sentence, though not necessarily his private meaning.

Although no primatologist disputes the complexity and infinite variety with which human languages can combine sounds, other primates (cotton-top tamarins, pygmy marmosets, capuchin monkeys, and rhesus macaques) also combine calls in orderly sequences,[9] but not nearly as much as humans do.

Another trait thought to be unique to humans is the ability to communicate about past or future events. But Sue Savage-Rumbaugh has observed wild bonobos leaving what appear to be messages to other bonobos to follow a trail. They break off vegetation where trails fork and point the broken plants in the direction to follow.

Perhaps most persuasive are the successful attempts to teach apes to communicate with humans and with each other using human-created signs. These successes have led many scholars to question the traditional assumption that the gap between human and other animal communication is enormous. Even a parrot, which has a small brain, has been taught to communicate with a human trainer in ways once thought impossible. Alex (a parrot) could correctly answer questions in English about what objects were made of, how many objects of a particular type there were, and even what made two objects the same or different.[10] When he was not willing to continue a training session, Alex said, "I'm sorry . . . Wanna go back."[11] Chimpanzees Washoe and Nim and the gorilla Koko were taught hand signs based on American Sign Language (ASL; used by the hearing impaired in the United States).

Some of the best examples of linguistic ability come from a chimpanzee named Kanzi. In contrast to other apes, Kanzi initially learned symbols just by watching his mother being taught, and he spontaneously began using the computer symbols to communicate with humans, even indicating his intended actions. Kanzi did not need rewards or to have his hands put in the right position. And he understood a great deal of what was spoken to him in English. For example, when he was 5 years old, Kanzi heard someone talk about throwing a ball in the river, and he turned around and did so. Kanzi has come close to having a primitive English grammar when he strings symbols together.[12] If chimpanzees and other primates have the capacity to use nonspoken language and even to understand spoken language, then the difference between humans and nonhumans may not be as great as people used to think.

Are these apes really using language in some minimal way? Many investigators do agree about one thing—nonhuman primates have the ability to "symbol," to refer to something (or a class of things) with an arbitrary "label" (gesture or sequence of sounds).[13] For example, Washoe originally learned the sign *dirty* to refer to feces and other soil and then began to use it insultingly, as in "dirty Roger," when her trainer Roger Fouts refused to give her things she wanted.

When we discuss the structure of sounds (phonology) later in this chapter, we will see that every human language has certain ways of combining sounds and ways of not combining those sounds. Apes do not have anything comparable to linguistic rules for allowed and disallowed combinations of sounds. In addition, humans have many kinds of discourse. We make lists and speeches, tell stories, argue, and recite poetry. Apes do none of these things.[14] But apes do have at least some of the capacities for language. Therefore, understanding their capacities may help us better understand the evolution of human language.

The Origins of Language

How long humans have had spoken language is not known. Some think that the earliest *Homo sapiens,* perhaps 100,000 years ago, may have had the beginnings of language. Others believe that language developed only after 100,000 years ago, with the emergence of modern humans. Because the only unambiguous remains of language are found on written tablets, and the earliest stone tablets date back only about 5,000 years,[15] pinpointing the emergence of the earliest languages remains speculative. Theories about when language developed are based on nonlinguistic information such as when cranial capacity expanded dramatically, when complex technology and symbolic artifacts (such as art) started to be made, and when the anatomy of the throat, as inferred from fossil remains, began to resemble what we see in modern humans.

Noam Chomsky and other theoreticians of grammar suggest that there is an innate *language-acquisition device* in the human brain, as innate to humans as call systems are to other animals.[16] If humans are unique in having an innate capacity for language, then some mutation or series of mutations had to be favored in human evolution, not before the human line separated from apes. Whether such a mechanism in fact exists is not clear. But we do know that the actual development of individual language is not completely biologically determined; if it were, all human beings would speak the same brain-generated language. Instead, about 4,000–5,000 mutually unintelligible languages have been identified. More than 2,000 of them were still spoken as of recently, most by peoples who did not traditionally have a system of writing.

Can we learn anything about the origins of language by studying the languages of nonliterate (without writing) and technologically simpler societies? The answer is no, because such languages are not simpler or less developed than ours. The sound systems, vocabularies, and grammars of technologically simpler peoples are in no way inferior to those of peoples with more complex technology.[17] Of course, people in other societies, and even some people in our own society, will not be able to name the sophisticated machines used in our society. All languages, however, have the potential for doing so. As we will see later in this chapter, all languages possess the amount of vocabulary their speakers need, and all languages expand in response to cultural changes. A language that lacks terminology for some of our conveniences may have a rich vocabulary for events or natural phenomena that are of particular importance to the people in that society.

If there are no primitive languages, and if the earliest languages have left no traces that would allow us to reconstruct them, does that mean we cannot investigate the origins of language? Some linguists think that understanding the way children acquire language, which we discuss shortly, can help us understand the origins of language. Other linguists have suggested that an understanding of how creole languages develop will also tell us something about the origins of language.

Pidgin and Creole Languages

In many contact situations where one group is much more powerful than the other, people shift to the dominant language, and their native language gradually becomes lost. However, some contact situations led to a different result—the development of a new language, different from the dominant language or the previous native languages.

Some languages developed where European colonial powers established commercial enterprises that relied on imported labor, generally slaves. The laborers in one place often came from many different societies and, in the beginning, would speak with their masters and with each other in some kind of simplified way, using linguistic features of one or more of the languages. Often, most of the vocabulary is drawn from the masters' language.[18] These *pidgin languages* become a new way of communicating. Pidgins are simplified languages and lack many of the building blocks found in the languages of whole societies, building blocks such as prepositions (*to, on,* and so forth) and auxiliary verbs (designating future and other tenses). Many pidgin languages developed into and were replaced by so-called *creole languages,* which incorporate much of the vocabulary of another language (often the masters' language) but also have a grammar that differs from it and from the grammars of the laborers' native languages.[19]

Derek Bickerton argues that there are striking grammatical similarities in creole languages throughout the world. This similarity, he thinks, is consistent with the idea that some grammar is inherited by all humans. Creole languages, therefore, may resemble early human languages. All creoles use intonation instead of a change in word order to ask a question. The creole equivalent of the question "Can you fix this?" would be "You can fix this?" The creole version puts a rising inflection at the end; in contrast, the English version reverses the subject and verb without much inflection at the end. All creoles express the future and the past in the same grammatical way, by the use of particles (such as the English *shall*) between subject and verb, and they all employ double negatives, as in the Guyana English Creole "Nobody no like me."[20]

It is possible that many other things about language are universal, that all languages are similar in many respects, because of the way humans are "wired" or because people in all societies have similar experiences. For example, names for frogs may usually contain *r* sounds because frogs make them.[21]

Children's Acquisition of Language

Apparently a child is equipped from birth with the capacity to reproduce all the sounds used by the world's languages and to learn any system of grammar. Research on 6-month-old infants finds that they can distinguish sounds of approximately 600 consonants and 200 vowels—all the sounds of all the languages of the world. But, by about the time of their first birthdays, babies become better at recognizing the salient sounds and sound clusters of their parents or caretakers and become less adept at distinguishing those of other languages.[22]

Children's acquisition of the structure and meaning of language has been called the most difficult intellectual achievement in life. If that is so, it is pleasing to note that they accomplish it with relative ease and vast enjoyment. As we have noted, many believe that this "difficult intellectual achievement" may in reality be a natural response to the capacity for language that is one of humans' genetic characteristics. All over the world, children begin to learn language at about the same age, and in no culture do children wait until they are 7 or 10 years old. By 12 or 13 months of age, children are able to name a few objects and actions, and by 18–20 months, they can make one key word stand for a whole sentence: "Out!" for "Take me out for a walk right now"; "Juice!" for "I want some juice now." Evidence suggests that children acquire the concept of a word as a whole,

A lot of language instruction occurs by pointing to something and saying what it is called.

learning sequences of sounds that are stressed or at the ends of words (e.g., "raffe" for giraffe). Even children with hearing impairments who are learning signs in ASL tend to acquire and use signs in a similar fashion.[23]

Children the world over tend to progress to two-word sentences at about 18–24 months of age. In their sentences, they express themselves in "telegraph" form—using nounlike words and verblike words but leaving out the seemingly less important words. So a two-word sentence such as "Shoes off" may stand for "Take my shoes off," or "More milk" may stand for "Give me more milk, please."[24] They do not utter their two words in random order, sometimes saying "off" first, other times saying "shoes" first. If children say, "Shoes off," then they will also say, "Clothes off" and "Hat off." They seem to select an order that fits the conventions of adult language, so they are likely to say, "Daddy eat," not "Eat Daddy." In other words, they tend to put the subject first, as adults do. And they tend to say "Mommy coat" rather than "Coat Mommy" to indicate "Mommy's coat."[25] Adults do not utter sentences such as "Daddy eat," so children seem to know a lot about how to put words together with little or no direct teaching from their caretakers.

If there is a basic grammar imprinted in the human mind, we should not be surprised that children's early and later speech patterns seem to be similar in different languages. We might also expect children's later speech to be similar to the structure of creole languages. And it is, according to Derek Bickerton.[26] The "errors" children make in speaking are consistent with the grammar of creoles. For example, English-speaking children 3–4 years old tend to ask questions by intonation alone, and they tend to use double negatives, such as "I don't see no dog," even though the adults around them do not speak that way and consider the children's speech "wrong."

But some linguists argue that the evidence for an innate grammar is weak because children the world over do not develop the same grammatical features at similar ages. For example, word order is a more important determinant of meaning in English than in Turkish; the endings of words are more important in Turkish. The word at the beginning of the sentence in English is likely to be the subject. The word with a certain ending in Turkish is the likely subject. Consistent with this difference, English-speaking children learn word order earlier than Turkish children do.[27]

Future research on children's acquisition of language and on the structure of creole languages may bring us closer to an understanding of the origins of human language. But, even if much of grammar is universal, we still need to understand how and why the thousands of languages in the world vary, which brings us to the conceptual tools linguists have had to invent to study languages.

Descriptive Linguistics

In every society, children do not need to be taught "grammar" to learn how to speak. They begin to grasp the essential structure of their language at a very early age, without direct instruction. If you show English-speaking children a picture of one "gork" and then a picture of two of these creatures, they will say there are two "gorks." Somehow they know that adding an s to a noun means more than one. But they do not know this consciously, and adults may not either. One of the most surprising features of human language is that meaningful sounds and sound sequences are combined according to rules that the speakers often do not consciously know.

These rules should not be equated with the "rules of grammar" you were taught in school so that you would speak "correctly." Rather, when linguists talk about rules, they are referring to the patterns of speaking that are discoverable in actual speech. Needless to say, there is some overlap between the actual rules of speaking and the rules taught in school. But there are rules that children never hear about in school, because their teachers are not linguists and are not aware of them. When linguists use the term *grammar,* they are *not* referring to the prescriptive rules that people are supposed to follow in speaking. Rather, *grammar* to the linguist consists of the actual, often unconscious principles that predict how most people talk. As we have noted, young children may speak two-word sentences that conform to a linguistic rule, but their speech is hardly considered "correct."

Discovering the mostly unconscious rules operating in a language is a very difficult task. Linguists have had to invent special concepts and methods of transcription (writing) to permit them to describe: (1) the rules or principles that predict how sounds are made and how they are used (slightly varying sounds are often used interchangeably in words without creating a difference in meaning—this aspect of language is called **phonology**); (2) how sound sequences (and sometimes even individual sounds) convey meaning and how meaningful sound sequences are strung together to form words (this aspect is called **morphology**); and (3) how words are strung together to form phrases and sentences (this aspect is called **syntax**).

Phonology

Most of us have had the experience of trying to learn another language and finding that some sounds are exceedingly difficult to make. Although the human vocal tract theoretically can make a very large number of different sounds—**phones,** to linguists—each language uses only some of them. It is not that we cannot make the sounds that are strange to us; we just have not acquired the habit of making those sounds. And until the sounds become habitual for us, they continue to be difficult to make.

Finding it difficult to make certain sounds is only one of the reasons we have trouble learning a "foreign" language. Another problem is that we may not be used to combining certain sounds or making a certain sound in a particular position in a word. Thus, English speakers find it difficult to combine *z* and *d,* as Russian speakers often do (because we never do so in English), or to pronounce words in Samoan, a South Pacific language, that begin with the sound English speakers write as *ng,* even though we have no trouble putting that sound at the end of words, as in the English *sing* and *hitting.*

To study the patterning of sounds, linguists who are interested in *phonology* have to write down speech utterances as sequences of sound. This task would be almost impossible if linguists were restricted to using their own alphabet (say, the one we use to write English), because other languages use sounds that are difficult to represent with the English alphabet or because the alphabet we use in English can represent a particular sound in different ways. (English writing represents the sound *f* by *f* as in *food,* but also as *gh* in *tough* and *ph* in *phone.*) In addition, in English, different sounds may be represented by the same letter. English has 26 letters but more than 40 significant sounds (sounds that can change the meaning of a word).[28] To overcome these difficulties in writing sounds with the letters of existing writing systems, linguists have developed systems of transcription with special alphabets in which each symbol represents only one particular sound.

Once linguists have identified the sounds or phones used in a language, they try to identify which sounds affect meaning and which sounds do not. One way is to start with a simple word like *lake* and change the first sound to *r* to make the word *rake.* A linguist will ask if this new combination of sounds means the same thing. An English speaker would say *lake* means something completely different from *rake.* These minimal contrasts enable linguists to identify a **phoneme** in a language—a sound or set of sounds that makes a difference in meaning in that language.[29] So the sound *l* in *lake* is different phonemically from the sound *r* in *rake.* The ways in which sounds are grouped together into phonemes vary from language to language. We are so used to phonemes in our own language that it may be hard to believe that the contrast between *r* and *l* may not make a difference in meaning in some languages. For example, in Samoan, *l* and *r* can be used interchangeably in a word without changing the meaning (therefore, these two sounds belong to the same phoneme in Samoan). So Samoan speakers may say "Leupena" sometimes and "Reupena" at other times when they are referring to someone who in English would be called "Reuben."

English speakers may joke about languages that "confuse" *l* and *r*, but they are not usually aware that we do the same thing with other sets of sounds. For example, in English, the word we spell *and* may be pronounced quite differently by two different English speakers without changing the meaning, and no one would think that a different word was spoken. We can pronounce the *a* in *and* as in the beginning of the word *air*, or we can pronounce it as the *a* in *bat*. If you say those varying *a* sounds and try to think about how you are forming them in your mouth, you will realize that they are two different sounds. English speakers might recognize a slight difference in pronunciation but pay little or no attention to it because the two ways to pronounce the *a* in *and* do not change the meaning. Now think about *l* and *r*. If you form them in your mouth, you will notice that they are only slightly different with respect to how far the tongue is from the ridge behind the upper front teeth. As early as 6 months of age, infants "ignore" sound shifts within the same phoneme of their own language, but they "hear" a sound shift within the phoneme of another language.[30] Languages do tend to consider sounds that are close as belonging to the same phoneme, but why they choose some sounds and not others to group together is not yet fully understood.

Why, for example, are two or more consonants strung together in some languages, whereas in other languages, vowels are *almost* always put between consonants? The Samoan language now has a word for "Christmas" borrowed from English, but the borrowed word has been changed to fit the rules of Samoan. In the English word, two consonants come first, *k* and *r*, which we spell as *ch* and *r*. The Samoan word is *Kerisimasi* (pronounced as if it were spelled Keh-ree-see-mah-see). It has a vowel after each consonant, or five consonant–vowel syllables.

Why do some languages like Samoan alternate consonants and vowels more or less regularly? Recent cross-cultural research suggests three predictors of this variation. One predictor is a warmer climate. Where people live in warmer climates, the typical syllable is more likely to be a consonant–vowel syllable. Linguists have found that consonant–vowel syllables provide the most contrast in speech. Perhaps when people converse outdoors at a distance, which they are likely to do in a warmer climate, they need more contrast between sounds to be understood. A second predictor of consonant–vowel alternation is literacy. Languages that are written have fewer consonant–vowel syllables. If communication is often in written form, meaning does not have to depend so much on contrast between adjacent sounds. A third (indeed the strongest) predictor of consonant–vowel alternation is the degree to which babies are held by others. Societies with a great deal of baby-holding have a lot of consonant–vowel syllables. Later, in the chapter on the arts, you will read about research that relates baby-holding to a societal preference for regular rhythm in music. The theory is that, when babies are held on a person much of the day, they begin to associate regular rhythm with pleasurable experiences. The baby senses the regular rhythm of the caretaker's heartbeats or the caretaker's rhythmic work, and the reward value of that experience generalizes to a preference for all regular rhythms in adult life, including apparently a regular consonant–vowel alternation in adult speech. Compare the rhythm of the Samoan word *Kerisimasi* with the English word *Christmas*.[31]

Morphology

A phoneme in a language usually does not mean something by itself. Usually phonemes are combined with other phonemes to form a meaningful sequence of sounds. *Morphology* is the study of sequences of sounds that have meaning. Often these meaningful sequences of sounds make up what we call *words,* but a word may be composed of a number of smaller meaningful units. We take our words so much for granted that we do not realize how complicated it is to say what words are. People do not usually pause very much between words when they speak; if we did not know our language, a sentence would seem like a continuous stream of sounds. This is how we first hear a foreign language. Only when we understand the language and write down what we say do we separate (by spaces) what we call words. But a word is really only an arbitrary sequence of sounds that has a meaning; we would not "hear" words as separate units if we did not understand the language spoken.

Because anthropological linguists traditionally investigated unwritten languages, sometimes without the aid of interpreters, they had to figure out which sequences of sounds conveyed meaning. And because words in many languages can often be broken down into smaller meaningful units, linguists had to invent special words to refer to those units. Linguists call the smallest unit of language that has a meaning a **morph.** Just as a phoneme may have one or more phones, one or more morphs with the same meaning may make up a **morpheme.** For example, the prefix *in-,* as in *indefinite,* and the prefix *un-,* as in *unclear,* are morphs that belong to the morpheme meaning *not.* Although some words are single morphs or morphemes (e.g., *for* and *giraffe* in English), many words are a combination of morphs, generally prefixes, roots, and suffixes. Thus *cow* is one word, but the word *cows* contains two meaningful units—a root (*cow*) and a suffix (pronounced like *z*) meaning more than one. The **lexicon** of a language, which a dictionary approximates, consists of words and morphs and their meanings.

In English, the meaning of an utterance (containing a subject, verb, object, and so forth) usually depends on the order of the words. "The dog bit the child" is different in meaning from "The child bit the dog." But in many other languages, the grammatical meaning of an utterance does not depend much, if at all, on the order of the words. Rather, meaning may be determined by how the morphs in a word are ordered. For example, in Luo, a language of East Africa, the same bound morpheme may mean the subject or object of an action. If the morpheme is the prefix to a verb, it means the subject; if it is the suffix to a verb, it means the object. Another way that grammatical meaning may be conveyed is by altering or adding a bound morpheme to a word to indicate what part of speech it is. For example, in Russian, when the subject of a sentence, the word for *mail* is pronounced something like *pawchtah.* When *mail* is used as the object of a verb, as in "I gave her the mail," the ending of the word changes to *pawchtoo.* And if I say, "What was in the mail?" the word becomes *pawchtyeh.*

Some languages have so many bound morphemes that they might express as a complex but single word what is considered a sentence in English. For example, the English sentence, "He will give it to you" can be expressed in Wishram, a Chinookan dialect that was spoken along the Columbia River in the Pacific Northwest, as *acimluda* (a-c-i-m-l-ud-a, literally "will-he-him-thee-to-give-will"). Note that the pronoun *it* in English is gender-neutral; Wishram requires that *it* be given a gender, in this case, "him."[32]

Syntax

Because language is an open system, we can make up meaningful utterances that we have never heard before. We are constantly creating new phrases and sentences. Just as they do for morphology, speakers of a language seem to have an intuitive grasp of *syntax*—the rules that predict how phrases and sentences are generally formed. These "rules" may be partly learned in school, but children know many of them even before they get to school. In adulthood, our understanding of morphology and syntax is so intuitive that we can even understand a nonsense sentence, such as this famous one from Lewis Carroll's *Through the Looking-Glass:*

> 'Twas brillig, and the slithy toves
> Did gyre and gimble in the wabe

Simply from the ordering of the words in the sentence, we can surmise which part of speech a word is, as well as its function in the sentence. *Brillig* is an adjective; *slithy,* an adjective; *toves,* a noun and the subject of the sentence; *gyre* and *gimble,* verbs; and *wabe,* a noun and the object of a prepositional phrase. Of course, an understanding of morphology helps too. The *-y* ending in *slithy* is an indication that the latter is an adjective, and the *-s* ending in *toves* tells us that we most probably have more than one of these creatures. In addition to producing and understanding an infinite variety of sentences, speakers of a language can tell when a sentence is not "correct" without consulting grammar books. For example, an English speaker can tell that "Child the dog the hit" is not an acceptable sentence but "The child hit the dog" is fine. There must, then, be a set of rules underlying how phrases and sentences are constructed in a language.[33] Speakers of a language know these implicit rules of syntax but are not usually consciously aware of them. The linguist's description of the syntax of a language tries to make these rules explicit.

Historical Linguistics

The field of **historical linguistics** focuses on how languages change over time. Written works provide the best data for establishing such changes. For example, the following brief passage from Chaucer's *Canterbury Tales,* written in the English of the fourteenth century, has recognizable elements but is different enough from modern English to require a translation.

> *A Frere ther was, a wantowne and a merye,*
> *A lymytour, a ful solempne man.*
> *In alle the ordres foure is noon that kan*
> *So muche of daliaunce and fair language.*
> *He hadde maad ful many a mariage*
> *Of yonge wommen at his owene cost.*

> *A Friar there was, wanton and merry,*
> *A limiter [a friar limited to certain districts], a very important man.*
> *In all the orders four there is none that knows*
> *So much of dalliance [flirting] and fair [engaging] language.*
> *He had made [arranged] many a marriage*
> *Of young women at his own cost.*[34]

In this passage, we can recognize several changes. Many words are spelled differently today, and in some cases, meaning has changed: *Full,* for example, would be translated today as *very.* What is less evident is that changes in pronunciation have occurred. For example, the *g* in *mariage* (marriage) was pronounced *zh,* as in the French from which it was borrowed, whereas now it is usually pronounced like either *g* in *George.*

An illustration accompanies the ornate script text on a page from Chaucer's famed *The Canterbury Tales.*

Because languages spoken in the past leave no traces unless they were written, and most of the languages known to anthropology were not written by their speakers, you might think that historical linguists can study linguistic change only by studying written languages such as English. But that is not the case. Linguists can reconstruct changes that have occurred by comparing contemporary languages that are similar. Such languages show phonological, morphological, and syntactical similarities because they usually derive from a common ancestral language. For example, Romanian, Italian, French, Spanish, and Portuguese have many similarities. On the basis of these similarities, linguists can reconstruct what the ancestral language was like and how it changed into what we call the Romance languages. Of course, these reconstructions can easily be tested and confirmed because we know from many surviving writings what the ancestral language, Latin, was like; we also know from documents how Latin diversified as the Roman Empire expanded. Thus, common ancestry is frequently the reason why neighboring, and sometimes even separated, languages show patterns of similarity.

But languages can be similar for other reasons too. Contact between speech communities, often with one group dominant over another, may lead one language to borrow from the other. For example, English borrowed a lot of vocabulary from French after England was conquered by the French-speaking Normans in A.D. 1066. Languages may also show similarities even though they do not derive from a common ancestral language and even though there has been no contact or borrowing between them. Such similarities may reflect common or universal features of human cultures or human brains or both. (As we noted earlier in the chapter, the grammatical similarities exhibited by creole languages may reflect how the human brain is "wired.") Finally, even unrelated and separated languages may show some similarities because of the phenomenon of convergence; similarities can develop because some processes of linguistic change may have only a few possible outcomes.

Language Families and Culture History

Latin is the ancestral language of the Romance languages. We know this from documentary (written) records. But if the ancestral language of a set of similar languages is not known from written records, linguists still can reconstruct many features of that language by comparing the derived languages. (Such a reconstructed language is called a **protolanguage.**) That is, by comparing presumably related languages, linguists can become aware of the features that many of them have in common, features that were probably found in the common ancestral language. The languages that derive from the same protolanguage are called a *language family.* The language family that English belongs to is called *Indo-European* because it includes most of the languages of Europe and some of the languages of India. (Persian, spoken in Iran, and Kurdish also belong to this family.) About 50 percent of the world's population (now more than 6 billion people) speak Indo-European languages.[35] Another very large language family, now spoken by more than a billion people, is Sino-Tibetan, which includes the languages of northern and southern China as well as those of Tibet and Burma.[36]

The field of historical linguistics got its start in 1786, when a British scholar living in India, Sir William Jones, noticed similarities between Sanskrit, a language spoken and written in ancient India, and classical Greek, Latin, and more recent European languages.[37] In 1822, Jakob Grimm, one of the brothers Grimm of fairy tale fame, formulated rules to describe the sound shifts that had occurred when the various Indo-European languages diverged from each other. So, for example, in English and the other languages in the Germanic branch of the Indo-European family, *d* regularly shifted to *t* (compare the English *two* and *ten* with the Latin *duo* and *decem*), and *p* regularly shifted to *f* (compare the English *father* and *foot* to Latin's *pater* and *pes*). Scholars generally agree that the Indo-European languages derive from a language spoken 5,000–6,000 years ago.[38] The ancestral Indo-European language, many of whose features have now been reconstructed, is called *proto-Indo-European.*

The Bantu languages in Africa (spoken by perhaps 100 million people) form a subfamily of the larger Niger-Congo family of languages. Bantu speakers currently live in a wide band across the center of Africa and down the eastern and western sides of southern Africa. All of the Bantu languages presumably derive from people who spoke proto-Bantu. But where was their home-land? Most historical linguists now agree with Joseph Greenberg's suggestion that the origin of Bantu was in what is now the Middle Benue area of eastern Nigeria.[39] The point of origin is presumably where there is the greatest diversity of related languages and *dialects* (varying forms of a language); it is assumed that the place of origin has had the most time for linguistic diversity to develop, compared with an area only recently occupied by a related language. For example, England has more dialect diversity than New Zealand or Australia.

Why were the Bantu able to spread so widely over the last few thousand years? Anthro-pologists have only begun to guess.[40] Initially, the Bantu probably kept goats and practiced some form of agriculture and thereby were able to spread, displacing hunter-gatherers in the area. As the Bantu speakers expanded, they began to cultivate certain cereal crops and herd sheep and cattle. Around this time, after 1000 B.C., they also began to use and make iron tools, which may have given them significant advantages. In any case, by 1,500–2,000 years ago, Bantu speakers had spread throughout central Africa and into the northern reaches of southern Africa. But speakers of non-Bantu languages still live in eastern, southern, and southwestern Africa.

The Processes of Linguistic Divergence

Historical or comparative linguists hope to do more than record and date linguistic divergence. Just as physical anthropologists may attempt to develop explanations for human variation, so linguists investigate the possible causes of linguistic variation. Some of the divergence undoubtedly comes about gradually. When groups of people speaking the same language lose communication with one another because they become separated, either physically or socially, they begin to accumulate small changes in phonology, morphology, and syntax (which occur continuously in any language). These variant forms of language are considered **dialects** when the differences in phonology, morphology, and syntax are not great enough to produce unintelligibility. Eventually, if the separation continues, the former dialects of the same language will become separate languages; that is, they will become mutually unintelligible, as German and English now are. Just as culture change originates from individual changes, language change originates from individual speakers, either from spontaneous innovation or from borrowing. Only when innovative speech patterns are picked up by others does linguistic change occur.[41]

Geographic barriers, such as large bodies of water, deserts, and mountains, may separate speakers of what was once the same language, but distance by itself can also produce divergence. For example, if we compare dialects of English in the British Isles, it is clear that the regions farthest away from each other are the most different linguistically (compare the northeast of Scotland and London).[42]

Whereas isolation brings gradual divergence between speech communities, contact results in greater resemblance. This effect is particularly evident when contact between mutually unintelligible languages introduces borrowed words, which usually name some new item borrowed from the other culture—*tomato, canoe, sushi,* and so on. Bilingual groups within a culture may also introduce foreign words, especially when the mainstream language has no real equivalent. Thus, *salsa* has come into English, and *le weekend* into French.

Conquest and colonization often result in extensive and rapid borrowing, if not linguistic replacement. The Norman conquest of England introduced French as the language of the new aristocracy. It was 300 years before the educated classes began to write in English. During this time, the English borrowed words from French and Latin, and the two languages—English and French—became more alike than they would otherwise have been. About 50 percent of the English general vocabulary originated in French. In those 300 years of extensive contact, the grammar of English remained relatively stable. English lost most of its inflections or case endings, but it adopted little of the French grammar. In general, the borrowing of words, particularly free morphemes,[43] is much more common than the borrowing of grammar.[44] As we might expect, borrowing by one language from another can make the borrowing language more different from its *sibling languages* (those derived from a common ancestral language) than it would otherwise be. Partly as a result of the French influence, the English vocabulary looks

The Fledermaus cabaret bar in Vienna uses some English words in its sign out front.

quite different from the languages to which it is actually most similar in terms of phonology and grammar—German, Dutch, and the Scandinavian languages.

Relationships Between Language and Culture

Some attempts to explain the diversity of languages have focused on the possible interactions between language and other aspects of culture. On the one hand, if it can be shown that a culture can affect the structure and content of its language, then it would follow that linguistic diversity derives at least in part from cultural diversity. On the other hand, the direction of influence between culture and language might work in reverse: Linguistic features and structures might affect other aspects of the culture.

Cultural Influences on Language

One way a society's language may reflect its corresponding culture is in **lexical content,** or vocabulary. Which experiences, events, or objects are singled out and given words may be a result of cultural characteristics.

Basic Words for Colors, Plants, and Animals Early in the twentieth century, many linguists pointed to the lexical domain (vocabulary) of color words to illustrate the supposed truth that languages vary arbitrarily or without apparent reason. Different languages not only had different numbers of basic color words (from 2 to 12 or so; for example, the words *red, green,* and *blue* in English), but they also, it was thought, had no consistency in the way they classified or divided the colors of the spectrum. But findings from a comparative (cross-linguistic) study contradicted these traditional presumptions about variation in the number and meaning of basic color words. On the basis of their study of at first 20 and later over 100 languages, Brent Berlin and Paul Kay found that languages did not encode color in completely arbitrary ways.[45]

Although different languages do have different numbers of basic color words, most speakers of any language are very likely to point to the same color chips as the best representatives of particular colors. For example, people the world over mean more or less the same color when they are asked to select the best "red." Moreover, there appears to be a nearly universal sequence by which basic color words are added to a language.[46] If a language has just two basic color words, its speakers will always refer to "black" (or dark) hues and "white" (or light) hues. If a language has three basic color words, the third word will nearly always be "red." The next category to appear is either "yellow" or "grue" (green/blue), then different words for green and blue, and so on. To be sure, we usually do not see the process by which basic color words are added to a language. But we can infer the usual sequence because, for example, if a language has a word for "yellow," it will almost always have a word for "red," whereas having a word for "red" does not mean that the language will have a word for "yellow."

What exactly is a *basic* color word? All languages, even the ones with only two basic color terms, have many different ways of expressing how color varies. For example, in English, we have words such as *turquoise, blue-green, scarlet, crimson,* and *sky blue.* Linguists do not consider these to be basic color words. In English, the basic color words are *white, black, red, green, yellow, blue, brown, pink, purple, orange,* and *gray.* One feature of a basic color word is that it consists of a single morph; it cannot include two or more units of meaning. This feature eliminates combinations such as *blue-green* and *sky blue.* A second feature of a basic color word is that the color it represents is not generally included in a higher-order color term. For example, scarlet and crimson are usually considered variants of red, turquoise a variant of blue. A third feature is that basic terms tend to be the first-named words when people are asked for color words. Finally, for a word to be considered a basic color word, many individual speakers of the language have to agree on the central meaning (in the color spectrum) of the word.[47]

Why do different societies (languages) vary in number of basic color terms? Berlin and Kay suggest that the number of basic color terms in a language increases with technological specialization as color is used to decorate and distinguish objects.[48] There may also be many basic color terms because of a biological factor.[49] Peoples with darker (more pigmented) eyes seem to have more trouble distinguishing colors at the dark (blue-green) end of the spectrum than do peoples with lighter eyes. It might be expected, then, that peoples who live nearer the equator (who tend to have darker eyes, presumably for protection against damaging ultraviolet radiation) would tend to have fewer basic color terms. And they do.[50] Moreover, it seems that both cultural and biological factors are required to account for cross-linguistic variation in the number of basic color terms. Societies tend to have six or more such terms (with separate terms for blue and green) only when they are relatively far from the equator and only when their cultures are more technologically specialized.[51]

Cecil Brown has found what seem to be developmental sequences in other lexical domains. Two such domains are general, or *life-form,* terms for plants and for animals. Life-form terms are higher-order classifications. All languages have lower-order terms for specific plants and animals. For example, English has words such as *oak, pine, sparrow,* and *salmon.* English speakers make finer distinctions too—*pin oak, white pine, white-throated sparrow,* and *red salmon.* But why, in some languages, do people have a larger number of general terms such as *tree, bird,* and *fish?* It seems that these general terms show a universal developmental sequence too. That is, general terms seem to be added in a somewhat consistent order. After "plant" comes a term for "tree"; then one for "grerb" (small, green, leafy, nonwoody plant); then "bush" (for plants between tree and grerb in size); then "grass"; then "vine."[52] The life-form terms for animals also seem to be added in sequence; after "animal" comes a term for "fish," then "bird," then "snake," then "wug" (for small creatures other than fish, birds, and snakes—for example, worms and bugs), then "mammal."[53]

More complex societies tend to have a larger number of general, or life-form, terms for plants and animals than do simpler societies, just as they tend to have a larger number of basic color terms. Do all realms or domains of vocabulary increase in size as social complexity increases? If we look at the total vocabulary of a language (as can be counted in a dictionary), more complex societies do have larger vocabularies.[54] But if we look instead at the nonspecialist, **core vocabulary** of languages, it seems that all languages have a core vocabulary of about the same size.[55] Indeed, although some domains increase in size with social complexity, some remain the same and still others decrease. An example of a smaller vocabulary domain in complex societies is that of specific names for plants. Urban North Americans may know general terms for plants, but they know relatively few names for specific plants. The typical individual in a small-scale society can commonly name 400–800 plant species; a typical person in our own and similar societies may be able to name only 40–80.[56] The number of life-form terms is larger in societies in which ordinary people know less about particular plants and animals.[57]

The evidence now available strongly supports the idea that the vocabulary of a language reflects the everyday distinctions that are important in the society. Those aspects of environment or culture that are of special importance will receive greater attention in the language. For example, many languages lack the possessive transitive verb we write as *have,* as in "I have." Instead, the language may say something such as "it is to me." A cross-cultural study has suggested that a language may develop the verb *have* after the speakers of that language have developed a system of private property or personal ownership of resources.[58]

Linguistic Influences on Culture: The Sapir-Whorf Hypothesis

There is general agreement that culture influences language. But there is less agreement about the opposite possibility—that language influences other aspects of culture. Edward Sapir and Benjamin Lee Whorf suggested that language is a force in its own right, that it affects how individuals in a society perceive and conceive reality. This suggestion is known as the *Sapir-Whorf hypothesis.*[59] In comparing the English language with Hopi, Whorf pointed out that English-language categories convey discreteness with regard to time and space, but Hopi does not. English has a discrete past, present, and future, and things occur at a definite time. Hopi expresses things with more of an idea of ongoing processes without time being apportioned into fixed segments. According to Ronald Wardhaugh, Whorf believed that these language differences lead Hopi and English speakers to see the world differently.[60]

As intriguing as that idea is, the relevant evidence is mixed. Linguists today do not generally accept the view that language coerces thought, but some suspect that particular features of language may facilitate certain patterns of thought.[61] The influences may be clearest in poetry and metaphors, where words and phrases are applied to other than their ordinary subjects, as in "all the world's a stage."[62] One of the serious problems in testing the Sapir-Whorf hypothesis is that researchers need to figure out how to separate the effects of other aspects of culture from the effects of language.

One approach that may reveal the direction of influence between language and culture is to study how children in different cultures (speaking different languages) develop concepts as they grow up. If language influences the formation of a particular concept, we might expect that children will acquire that concept earlier in societies where the languages emphasize that concept. For example, some languages make more of gender differences than others. Do children develop gender identity earlier when their language emphasizes gender? (Very young girls and boys seem to believe they can switch genders by dressing in opposite-sex clothes, suggesting that they have not yet developed a stable sense that they are unchangeably girls or boys.) Alexander Guiora and his colleagues have studied children growing up in Hebrew-speaking homes (Israel), English-speaking homes (the United States), and Finnish-speaking homes (Finland). Hebrew has the most gender emphasis of the three languages; all nouns are either masculine or feminine, and even second-person and plural pronouns are differentiated by gender. English emphasizes gender less, differentiating by gender only in the third-person singular (*she* or *her* or *hers; he* or *him* or *his*). Finnish emphasizes gender the least; although some words, such as *man* and *woman,* convey gender, differentiation by gender is otherwise lacking in the language. Consistent with the idea that language may influence thought, Hebrew-speaking children acquire the concept of stable gender identity the earliest on the average, Finnish-speaking children the latest.[63]

Another approach is to predict from language differences how people may be expected to perform in experiments. Comparing the Yucatec Mayan language and English, John Lucy predicted that English speakers might recall the *number* of things presented more than Yucatec Mayan speakers. For most classes of nouns, English requires a linguistic way of indicating whether something is singular or plural. You cannot say "I have dog" (no indication of number), but must say "I have a dog," "I have dogs," or "I have one (two, three, several, many) dogs." Yucatec Maya, like English, can indicate a plural, but allows the noun to be neutral with regard to number. For example, the translated phrase there-is-dog-over-there (*yàan pèek té'elo'*) can be left ambiguous about whether there is one or more than one dog. In English, the same ambiguity would occur in the sentence "I saw deer over there," but English does not often allow ambiguity for animate or inanimate nouns.[64] In a number of experiments, Yucatec Mayan and American English speakers were equally likely to recall the objects in a picture, but they differed in how

N E W   P E R S P E C T I V E S   O N   G E N D E R

Does the English Language Promote Sexist Thinking?

Does English promote sexist thinking, or does the language merely reflect gender inequalities that already exist? For those who wish to promote gender equality, the answers to these questions are important because, if language influences thought (along the lines put forward by Edward Sapir and Benjamin Whorf), then linguistic change will be necessary to bring about change in the culture of gender. If it is the other way around, that is, if language reflects inequality, then social, economic, and political changes have to come before we can expect substantial linguistic change to occur.

Leaving aside for the moment which changes first, how does English represent gender inequity? Consider the following written by Benjamin Lee Whorf: "Speech is the best show man puts on. . . . Language helps man in his thinking." Although *man* in English technically refers to all humans and *his* technically refers to the thinking of a single person of either gender, the frequent use of such words could convey the idea that males are more important. Similarly, do the words *chairman, policeman, businessman,* and *salesman* convey that males are supposed to have those jobs? What is conveyed when there are two words for the two genders, as in *actor* and *actress* and *hero* and *heroine*? Usually the base word is male and the suffix is added for the female form. Does the suffix convey that the female form is an afterthought or less important?

It is not just the structure of the language that may convey gender inequality. How come in the pairs *sir/madam, master/mistress, wizard/witch,* the female version has acquired negative connotations? Men might be called animal names, such as wolves, rats, or pigs. But more animal images seem to be applied to women. They can be *chicks, henpeckers, cows, dogs, bitches, kittens,* or *birds.* Coming back to the original question, how would we know whether language promotes sexism or sexism influences language? One way to find out is to do experimental studies, such as the one conducted by Fatemeh Khosroshashi. Some individuals were asked to read texts written with *man, he,* and *his* referring to people; others were asked to read texts with more gender-neutral phrasing. Individuals were subsequently asked to draw pictures to go with the texts. The

ones who read the texts with more male terminology drew more accompanying pictures of men, strongly suggesting that the use of the terms *man, he,* and *his* conveyed the thought that the people in the text were men, not women, *because* of the vocabulary used. We need more such studies to help address the intellectual question of which comes first, linguistic or nonlinguistic culture.

It would be important to know whether societies with more "male-oriented" language are more male-dominated than are societies without such distinctions. We don't have that kind of comparative research yet. But one study by Robert and Ruth Munroe looked at the *proportion* of female and male nouns in 10 languages (six Indo-European, four other than Indo-European) in which nouns have gender. Although none of those societies could be described as having a female bias, the Munroes were able to ask whether those societies with less male bias in social customs (e.g., all children are equally likely to inherit property) have a higher proportion of female nouns than male nouns (more female than male nouns). The answer appears to be yes. Although this study does not reveal what came first, studies like it are important if we want to discover how language differences may be related to other aspects of culture. If male-oriented languages are not related to male dominance, then it is not likely that sexist thinking is a consequence of language.

On the assumption that language may influence thought, many are pushing for changes in the way English is used, if not structured. It is hard to get English speakers to adopt a gender-neutral singular pronoun to replace *he.* Attempts to do so go back to the eighteenth century and include suggestions of *tey, thon, per,* and *s/he.* Although these efforts have not succeeded, the way English is written and spoken has begun to change. Words or phrases such as *chair* (or *chairperson*), *police officer,* and *sales assistant* (*salesperson*) have begun to replace their former *man* versions. If Whorf were writing his sentence now, it probably would be written: "Speech is the best show humans put on. . . . Language helps people think."

Sources: Holmes 2001, 305–16; Khosroshashi 1989; Lakoff 1973; Munroe and Munroe 1969; Romaine 1994, 105–16; Wardhaugh 2002, 317.

often they described the number of a particular object in the picture. Yucatec Mayan speakers did so less often, consistent with their language's lack of insistence on indicating number.[65] So the salience of number in the experiments was probably a consequence of how the languages differ.

The Ethnography of Speaking

Many are concerned with the *ethnography of speaking*—that is, with cultural and subcultural patterns of speech variation in different social contexts.[66] The sociolinguist might ask, for example, what kinds of things one talks about in casual conversation with a stranger. A foreigner may know English vocabulary and grammar well but may not know that one typically chats with a stranger about the weather or where one comes from, and not about what one ate that day or how much money one earns. A foreigner may be familiar with much of the culture of a North American city, but if that person divulges the real state of his or her health and feelings to the first person who says, "How are you?" he or she has much to learn about "small talk" in North American English.

Similarly, North Americans tend to get confused in societies where greetings are quite different from ours. People in some other societies may ask as a greeting, "Where are you going?" or "What are you cooking?" Some Americans may think such questions are rude; others may try to answer in excruciating detail, not realizing that only vague answers are expected, just as we don't really expect a detailed answer when we ask people how they are.

Social Status and Speech

That a foreign speaker of a language may know little about the small talk of that language is but one example of the sociolinguistic principle that what we say and how we say it are not wholly predictable by the rules of our language. Who we are socially and whom we are talking to may greatly affect what we say and how we say it.

In a study interviewing children in a New England town, John Fischer noted that, in formal interviews, children were likely to pronounce the ending in words such as *singing* and *fishing,* but in

Strangers shake hands when they meet; friends may touch each other more warmly. How we speak to others also differs according to the degree of friendship.

informal conversations, they said *singin'* and *fishin'*. Moreover, he noted that the phenomenon also appeared to be related to social class; children from higher-status families were less likely to drop the ending than were children from lower-status families. Subsequent studies in English-speaking areas tend to support Fischer's observations with regard to this speech pattern.[67]

Status relationships between people can also influence the way they speak to each other. Terms of address are a good example. In English, forms of address are relatively simple. One is called either by a first name or by a title (such as *Doctor, Professor, Ms.,* or *Mister*) followed by a last name. A study by Roger Brown and Marguerite Ford indicates that terms of address in English vary with the nature of the relationship between the speakers.[68] The reciprocal use of first names generally signifies an informal or intimate relationship between two people. A title and last name used reciprocally usually indicates a more formal or businesslike relationship between individuals who are roughly equal in status. Nonreciprocal use of first names and titles in English is reserved for speakers who recognize a marked difference in status between them. This status difference can be a function of age, as when a child refers to her mother's friend as Mrs. Miller and is in turn addressed as Sally, or can be due to occupational hierarchy, as when a person refers to his boss as Ms. Ramirez and is in turn addressed as Joe.

Gender Differences in Speech

In many societies, the speech of men differs from the speech of women. The variation can be slight, as in our own society, or more extreme, as with the Carib Indians in the Lesser Antilles of the West Indies, among whom women and men use different words for the same concepts.[69] In Japan, males and females use entirely different words for numerous concepts (e.g., the male word for water is *mizu;* the female version is *ohiya*), and females often add the polite prefix *o-* (females will tend to say *ohasi* for chopsticks; males will tend to say *hasi*).[70] In the United States and other Western societies, there are differences in the speech of females and males, but they are not as dramatic as in the Carib and Japanese cases. For example, earlier we noted the tendency for the *g* to be dropped in words such as *singing* when the situation is informal and when the social class background is lower. But there is also a gender difference. Gender differences occur in intonation and in phrasing of sentences as well. Robin Lakoff found that, in English, women tend to answer questions with sentences that have rising inflections at the end instead of a falling intonation associated with a firm answer. Women also tend to add questions to statements, such as "They caught the robber last week, didn't they?"[71]

One explanation for the gender differences, particularly with regard to pronunciation, is that women in many societies may be more concerned than men with being "correct."[72] In societies with social classes, what is considered more correct by the average person may be what is associated with the upper class. In other societies, what is older may be considered more correct. Gender differences in speech may parallel some of the gender differences noted in other social behavior (as we will see in the chapter on sex and gender): Girls are more likely than boys to behave in ways that are acceptable to adults.

There are not enough studies to know just how common it is for women to exhibit more linguistic "correctness." We do know of some instances where it is not the case. For example, in a community in Madagascar where people speak Merina, a dialect of Malagasy, it is considered socially correct to avoid explicit directives. So, instead of directly ordering an action, a Merina speaker will try to say it indirectly. Also, it is polite to avoid negative remarks, such as expressing anger toward someone. In this community, however, women, not men, often break the rules; women speak more directly and express anger more often.[73] This difference may be related to the fact that women are more involved in buying and selling in the marketplace.

Men and women typically differ in what they talk about, or do not talk about. Deborah Tannen offers some examples. When women hear about someone else's troubles, they are likely to express understanding of the other's feelings; in contrast, men are likely to offer solutions. Men tend not to ask for directions; women do. Women tend to talk a lot in private settings; men talk more in public settings. These and other differences can cause friction and misunderstanding between the genders. When women express their troubles and men offer solutions, women feel that their feelings are not understood; men are frustrated that the women do not take their solutions seriously. Men may prefer to sit at home quietly and feel put upon to have to engage in conversation; women feel slighted when men avoid extended conversations with them. Why these differences? Tannen suggests that misunderstanding between men and women arises because boys and girls grow up in somewhat different cultures. Girls typically play in small groups, talk frequently, and are intimate with others. Boys more often play in large groups in which jockeying for status and attention are more of a concern. Higher-status individuals give directions and solutions; they do not seek directions or solutions. So asking for directions is like acknowledging lower status. But large play groups resemble public settings, and so later in life, men feel more comfortable speaking in public. Women, in contrast, are more comfortable speaking in small, intimate groups.[74]

Multilingualism and Code-Switching

For many people, the ability to speak more than one language is a normal part of life. One language may be spoken at home and another in school, the marketplace, or government. Or more than one language may be spoken at home if family members come from different cultures and still other languages are spoken outside. Some countries explicitly promote multilingualism. For example, Singapore has four official languages—English, Mandarin (one of the Chinese languages), Tamil, and Malay. English is stressed for trade, Mandarin as the language of communication with most of China, Malay as the language of the general region, and Tamil as the language of an important ethnic group. Moreover, most of the population speaks Hokkien, another Chinese language. Education is likely to be in English and Mandarin.[75]

What happens when people who know two or more languages communicate with each other? Very often you find them **code-switching,** using more than one language in the course of conversing.[76] Switching can occur in the middle of a Spanish–English bilingual sentence, as in "No van a bring it up in the meeting" ("They are not going to bring it up in the meeting").[77] Or switching can occur when the topic or situation changes, such as from social talk to schoolwork. Why do speakers of more than one language sometimes switch? Although speakers switch for a lot of different reasons, what is clear is that the switching is not a haphazard mix that comes from laziness or ignorance. Code-switching involves a great deal of knowledge of two or more languages and an awareness of what is considered appropriate or inappropriate in the community. For example, in the Puerto Rican community in New York City, code-switching within the same sentence seems to be common in speech among friends, but if a stranger who looks like a Spanish speaker approaches, the language will shift entirely to Spanish.[78]

Code-switching may need to be understood in terms of the broader political and historical context. For example, German speakers in Transylvania, where Romanian is the national language, hardly ever code-switch to Romanian. Perhaps the reason is that, before the end of World War II, German speakers were a privileged economic group who looked down upon landless Romanians and their language. Under socialism, the German speakers lost their economic privilege, but they continued to speak German among themselves. In the rare cases that Romanian is used among German speakers, it tends to be associated with low-status speech, such as singing bawdy songs. The opposite situation occurred in a Hungarian region of German-speaking Austria. The people of this agricultural region, annexed to Austria in 1921, were fairly poor peasant farmers. After World War II, business expansion began to attract labor from rural areas, so many Hungarians eagerly moved into jobs in industry. Younger generations saw German as a symbol of higher status and upward mobility; not surprisingly, code-switching between Hungarian and German became part of their conversations. Indeed, in the third generation, German has become the language of choice, except when speaking to the oldest Hungarians. The Hungarian–Austrian situation is fairly common in many parts of the world, where the language of the politically dominant group ends up being "linguistically dominant."[79]

Writing and Literacy

Most of us have come to depend on writing for so many things that it is hard to imagine a world without it. Yet humans spent most of their history on earth without written language and many, if not most, important human achievements predate written language. Parents and other teachers passed on their knowledge by oral instruction and demonstration. Stories, legends, and myths abounded—the stuff we call oral literature—even in the absence of writing. This is not to say that writing is not important. Far more information and far more literature can be preserved for a longer period of time with a writing system. The earliest writing systems are only about 6,000 years old and are associated with early cities and states. Early writing is associated with systematic record-keeping—keeping of ledgers for inventorying goods and transactions. In early times, probably only the elite could read and write—indeed only recently has universal literacy (the ability to read and write) become the goal of most countries. But in most countries, the goal of universal literacy is far from achieved. Even in countries with universal education, the quality of education and the length of education varies considerably between subcultures and genders. Just as some ways of speaking are considered superior to others, a high degree of literacy is usually considered superior to illiteracy.[80] But literacy in what language or languages? Recent efforts to preserve languages have encouraged writing of texts in languages that were only spoken previously. Obviously, there will be few texts in those languages; other languages have vast numbers of written texts. As more accumulated knowledge is written and stored in books, journals, and databases, attainment of literacy in those written languages will be increasingly critical to success. And texts do not only convey practical knowledge—they may also convey attitudes, beliefs, and values that are characteristic of the culture associated with the language in which the texts are written.

Children do not need help learning the language spoken in their homes. However, reading and writing cannot usually be learned without instruction. Nowadays, children in most cultures are expected to learn to read and write in school. These Trobriand children from Papua New Guinea are allowed to wear their traditional clothes to school once a week.

✓•⫯Study and **Review** on **myanthrolab.com**

Summary

1. The essential function language plays in all societies is that of communication. Although human communication is not limited to spoken language, such language is of overriding importance because it is the primary vehicle through which culture is shared and transmitted.

2. Systems of communication are not unique to humans. Other animal species communicate in a variety of ways—by sound, odor, body movement, and so forth. The ability of chimpanzees and gorillas to learn and use sign language suggests that symbolic communication is not unique to humans. Still, human language is distinctive as a communication system in that its spoken and symbolic nature permits an infinite number of combinations and recombinations of meaning.

3. Nonverbal human communication includes posture, mannerisms, body movement, facial expressions, and signs and gestures. Nonverbal human communication also includes tone of voice, accent, nonword sounds, and all the optional vocal features that communicate meaning apart from the language itself.

4. Descriptive (or structural) linguists try to discover the rules of phonology (the patterning of sounds), morphology (the patterning of sound sequences and words), and syntax (the patterning of phrases and sentences) that predict how most speakers of a language talk.

5. By comparing related languages, historical linguists try to reconstruct the features of the protolanguage, the linguistic changes over time (such as sound shifts), how the offspring languages separated from the protolanguage or from each other, and to establish the approximate dates of such separations.

6. When two groups of people speaking the same language lose communication with each other because they become separated either physically or socially, they begin to accumulate small changes in phonology, morphology, and syntax. If the separation continues, the two former dialects of the same language will eventually become separate languages—that is, they will become mutually unintelligible.

7. Whereas isolation brings about divergence between speech communities, contact results in greater resemblance. This effect is particularly evident when contact between people who speak mutually unintelligible languages introduces borrowed words, most of which name some new item borrowed from the other culture.

8. Some attempts to explain the diversity of languages have focused on the possible interaction between language and other aspects of culture. On the one hand, if it can be shown that a culture can affect the structure and content of its language, then it would follow that linguistic diversity derives at least in part from cultural diversity. On the other hand, the direction of influence between culture and language might work in reverse; the linguistic structures might affect other aspects of the culture.

9. In recent years, some linguists have begun to study variations in how people actually use language when speaking. This type of linguistic study, called sociolinguistics, is concerned with the ethnography of speaking—that is, with cultural and subcultural patterns of speaking in different social contexts.

10. In bilingual or multilingual populations, code-switching (using more than one language in the course of conversing) has become increasingly common.

11. Written language dates back only about 6,000 years, but writing and written records have become increasingly important; literacy is now a major goal of most countries.

Glossary Terms

accent (p. 224)
code-switching (p. 243)
core vocabulary (p. 238)
dialects (p. 236)
historical linguistics (p. 233)
lexical content (p. 237)

lexicon (p. 232)
morph (p. 232)
morpheme (p. 232)
morphology (p. 230)
phoneme (p. 230)
phones (p. 230)

phonology (p. 230)
protolanguage (p. 235)
syntax (p. 230)
symbolic communication
  (p. 225)

Critical Questions

1. Why might natural selection have favored the development of true language in humans but not in apes?

2. Would the world be better off with many different languages spoken or with just one universal language? Why do you think so?

3. How does some aspect of your speech differ from your parents or others of the previous generation? Why do you think it has changed?

Read the Original Source on myanthrolab.com

Read the chapter by Jane H. Hill, "Do Apes Have Language?" on MyAnthroLab and answer the following questions.

1. Jane Hill raises the question of whether apes have language. Briefly, what is her answer to the question?

2. Chimpanzees have learned signs from American Sign Language but they have not been able to learn to speak words. Why not?

Economics

((•─[Listen to the **Chapter Audio** on **myanthrolab.com**   [□]─[Read on **myanthrolab.com**

When we think of economics, we think of things and activities involving money. We think of the costs of goods and services, such as food, rent, haircuts, and movie tickets. We may also think of factories, farms, and other enterprises that produce the goods and services we need, or think we need. In industrial societies, workers may stand before a moving belt for 8 hours, tightening identical bolts that glide by. For this task, they are given bits of paper that may be exchanged for food, shelter, and other goods or services. But many societies—indeed, most that are known to anthropology—did not have money or the equivalent of the factory worker until relatively recently. Still, all societies have economic systems, whether or not they involve money. All societies have customary ways of getting food. They also have customs specifying how people gain access to natural resources; customary ways of transforming or converting those resources, through labor, into necessities and other desired goods and services. Finally, all societies have customs for distributing and perhaps exchanging goods and services.

As we shall see in this chapter, a great deal of the cross-cultural variation in economic systems is related to how a society primarily gets its food. However, other aspects of the culture also affect the economies. These other influences, which we cover in subsequent chapters, include the presence or absence of social (class and gender) inequality, family and kinship groups, and the political system.

Getting Food

For most people in our society, getting food consists of a trip to the supermarket. Within an hour, we can gather enough food from the shelves to last us a week. Seasons don't daunt us. Week after week, we know food will be there. But we do not think of what would happen if the food were not delivered to the supermarket. We wouldn't be able to eat, and without eating for a while, we would die. Despite the old adage "Man [or woman] does not live by bread alone," we could not live at all without bread or the equivalent. Food-getting activities, then, take precedence over other activities important to survival. Reproduction, social control (the maintenance of peace and order within a group), defense against external threat, and the transmission of knowledge and skills to future generations—none could take place without energy derived from food. But it is not merely energy that is required for survival and long-term reproduction. Food-getting strategies need to provide the appropriate combination of nutrients throughout varying seasons and changing environmental conditions.

In this chapter, we look at the ways different societies get food and discuss some of the features associated with the different patterns.

Foraging

Foraging or *food collection* may be generally defined as a food-getting strategy that obtains wild plant and animal resources through gathering, hunting, scavenging, or fishing. Although this was the way humans got their food for most of human history, foragers in the world today, also commonly referred to as **hunter-gatherers,** are not very numerous, and most of them live in what have been called the *marginal areas* of the earth—deserts, the Arctic, and dense tropical forests—habitats that do not allow easy exploitation by modern agricultural technologies. In the last few hundred years, only about 5 million people are or were foragers.[1]

Anthropologists are interested in studying the relatively few foraging societies still available for observation because these groups may help us understand some aspects of human life in the past, when all people were foragers. But we must be cautious in drawing inferences about the past from our observations of recent and contemporary foragers, for three reasons. First, early foragers lived in almost all types of environments, including some very bountiful ones. Therefore, what we observe among recent and contemporary foragers—who generally live in deserts, the Arctic, and tropical forests—may not be comparable to what would have been observable in more favorable environments in the past.[2] Second, contemporary foragers are not relics of the past. Like all contemporary societies, they have evolved and are still evolving. Indeed, recent research reveals considerable variation in economic behavior as well as in social structure in foraging groups that share common ancestry; this implies that recent foragers have responded to differences in local environmental conditions.[3] Third, recent and contemporary foragers have been interacting with kinds of societies that did not exist until after 10,000 years ago—agriculturalists, pastoralists, and intrusive, powerful state societies.[4] For example, evidence from South Asia and Southeast Asia suggests that trade with agriculturalists was probably an important component of foragers' economic strategies for millennia.[5] And, in the recent past, foraging people have increasingly depended on agriculture and commercial activities as well as trade, so what we see recently may be very different from the distant past when foraging was the only means of subsistence. Let us examine one area of the world where recent foragers were the only inhabitants until about 200 years ago.

Australian Aborigines Before Europeans came to the Australian continent, all the aboriginal people who lived there depended on foraging. Although the way of life of Australian aborigines is now considerably altered, we consider the life of the Ngatatjara as described by Richard Gould in the 1960s, when they still lived by gathering wild plants and hunting wild animals in the Gibson Desert of western Australia.[6]

The desert environment of the Ngatatjara averages less than 8 inches of rain per year, and the temperature in summer may rise to 118°F. The few permanent water holes are separated by hundreds of square miles of sand, scrub, and rock. Even before Europeans arrived in Australia, the area was sparsely populated—fewer than one person per 35–40 square miles. Now there are even fewer people because the aboriginal population was decimated by introduced diseases and mistreatment after the Europeans arrived.

On a typical day, the camp begins to stir just before sunrise, while it is still dark. Children are sent to fetch water, and the people breakfast on water and food left over from the night before. In the cool of the early morning, the adults talk and make plans for the day. The talking goes on for a while. Where should they go for food—to places they have been to recently or to new places? Sometimes there are other considerations. For example, one woman may want to search for plants whose bark she needs to make new sandals. When the women decide which plants they want to gather and where they think those plants are most likely to be found, they take up their digging sticks and set out with large wooden bowls of drinking water on their heads. Their children ride on their hips or walk alongside. Meanwhile, the men may have decided to hunt emus, 6-foot-tall ostrichlike birds that do not fly. The men go to a creek bed where they will wait to ambush any game that may come along. They lie patiently behind a screen of brush they have set up, hoping for a chance to throw a spear at an emu or even a kangaroo. They can throw only once because the game will run away if they miss.

By noon, the men and women are usually back at camp, the women with their wooden bowls each filled with up to 15 pounds of fruit or other plant foods, the men more often than not with only some small game, such as lizards and rabbits. The men's food-getting is less certain of success than the women's, so most of the Ngatatjara aborigines' diet is plant food. The daily cooked meal is eaten toward evening, after an afternoon spent resting, gossiping, and making or repairing tools.

The aborigines traditionally were nomadic, moving their campsites fairly frequently. The campsites were isolated and inhabited by only a small number of people, or they were clusters of groups including as many as 80 people. The aborigines never established a campsite right next to a place with water. If they were too close, their presence would frighten away game and might cause tension with neighboring bands, who would also wait for game to come to the scarce watering spots.

Today, many aborigines live in small settled villages. For example, in the 1980s, Victoria Burbank worked in a village she calls "Mangrove" in the Northern Territory of Australia. The once-nomadic aborigines now live in a village of about 600, which was founded in the 1950s around a Protestant mission. Their houses have stoves, refrigerators, toilets, washing machines, and even television sets. Their children attend school full time, and there is a health clinic for their medical needs. They still do some foraging, but most of their food comes from the store. Some earn wages, but many subsist on government welfare checks.[7]

General Features of Foragers Despite the differences in terrain and climate under which they live and the different food-collecting technologies they use, Australian aborigines and most other recent foragers have certain characteristic cultural patterns (see Table 11.1). Most live in small communities in sparsely populated territories and follow a nomadic lifestyle, forming no permanent settlements. As a rule, they do not recognize individuals' land rights. Their communities generally do not have different classes of people and tend to have no specialized or

TABLE 11.1 Variation in Food-Getting and Associated Features

	Food Collectors	Food Producers		
	Foragers	Horticulturalists	Pastoralists	Intensive Agriculturalists
Population density	Lowest	Low to moderate	Low	Highest
Maximum community size	Small	Small to moderate	Small	Large (towns and cities)
Nomadism/ permanence of settlements	Generally nomadic or seminomadic	More sedentary: communities may move after several years	Generally nomadic or seminomadic	Permanent communities
Food shortages	Infrequent	Infrequent	Frequent	Frequent
Trade	Minimal	Minimal	Very important	Very important
Full-time craft specialists	None	None or few	Some	Many (high degree of craft specialization)
Individual differences in wealth	Generally none	Generally minimal	Moderate	Considerable
Political leadership	Informal	Some part-time political officials	Part- and full-time political officials	Many full-time political officials

full-time political officials.[8] Division of labor in foraging societies is based largely on age and gender: Men exclusively hunt large marine and land animals and usually do most of the fishing, and women usually gather wild plant foods.[9]

Is there a typical pattern of food-getting among foragers? Many anthropologists have assumed that foragers typically get their food more from gathering than from hunting, and that women contribute more than men to subsistence, because women generally do the gathering.[10] Although gathering is the most important food-getting activity for some foragers (e.g., the Ngatatjara aborigines and the San of southern Africa), this is not true for most food-collecting societies known to us. A survey of 180 such societies indicates that there is a lot of variation with regard to which food-getting activity is most important to the society. Gathering is the most important activity for 30 percent of the surveyed societies, hunting for 25 percent, and fishing for 38 percent. (That is why we prefer the term *foragers* rather than the often-used *hunter-gatherers*; the term "foragers" allows us to recognize the importance of fishing.) In any case, because men generally do the fishing as well as the hunting, the men usually contribute more to food-getting than do the women among recent foragers.[11]

Because foragers move their camps often and walk great distances, it may seem that the food-collecting way of life is difficult. Although we do not have enough quantitative studies to tell us what is typical of most foragers, studies of two Australian aborigine groups[12] and of one San group[13] indicate that those foragers do not spend many hours getting food. For example, San adults spend an average of about 17 hours per week collecting food. Even when you add the time spent making tools (about 6 hours a week) and doing housework (about 19 hours a week), the San seem to have more leisure time than many agriculturalists, as we discuss later.

When we say that foragers tend to have certain traits, this does not mean that all of them have those traits. There is considerable variability among societies that depend on foraging. Foraging societies that depend heavily on fishing (such as on the Pacific Coast of the northwestern United States and Canada or on the south coast of New Guinea) are more likely to have bigger and more permanent communities and more social inequality than foraging societies elsewhere who mostly depend on game and plants.[14] The Pacific Coast and New Guinea coastal people also tend to have higher population densities, food storage,[15] occupational specialization, resource ownership, slavery, and competitiveness.[16] Two foraging groups that depended heavily on annual salmon runs were the Tlingit of southeastern Alaska and the Nimpkish of British Columbia. Both groups had a three-tiered class system with a high class, commoners, and slaves. The high-status individuals were obliged to stage competitive elaborate feasts and distributions of valuables.[17] This type of inequality and competitiveness was very different from what we find in typical foragers, who generally show little social differentiation. In New Guinea, Paul Roscoe has found that the amount of dependence upon fishing is strongly associated with density of population and settlement size. For example, societies with more than 75 percent dependence upon fishing have average community sizes of about 350 people, as compared with community size of about 50 for those with less than 25 percent dependence upon fishing. Some villages were much larger. One Asmat village had over 1,400 people and a Waropen village over 1,700.[18]

Food Production

Beginning about 10,000 years ago, certain peoples in widely separated geographic locations made the revolutionary changeover to **food production.** That is, they began to cultivate and then domesticate plants and animals. (Domesticated plants and animals are different from the ancestral wild forms.) With domestication of these food sources, people acquired control over certain natural processes, such as animal breeding and plant seeding. Today, most peoples in the world depend for their food on some combination of domesticated plants and animals.

Anthropologists generally distinguish three major types of food production systems: *horticulture, intensive agriculture,* and *pastoralism*.

Horticulture   The word **horticulture** may conjure up visions of people with "green thumbs" growing orchids and other flowers in greenhouses. But to anthropologists, the word means the growing of crops of all kinds with relatively simple tools and methods, in the absence of permanently cultivated fields. The tools are usually hand tools, such as the digging stick or hoe, not plows or other equipment pulled by animals or tractors. And the methods used do not include fertilization, irrigation, or other ways to restore soil fertility after a growing season.

There are two kinds of horticulture. The more common one involves a dependence on **extensive (shifting) cultivation.** The land is worked for short periods and then left idle for some years. During the years when the land is not cultivated, wild plants and brush grow; when the fields are later cleared by *slash-and-burn techniques,* nutrients are returned to the soil. The other kind of horticulture involves a dependence on long-growing tree crops. The two kinds of horticulture may be practiced in the same society, but in neither case is there permanent cultivation of field crops.

Most horticultural societies do not rely on crops alone for food. Many also hunt or fish; a few are nomadic for part of the year. For example, the Kayapo of the Brazilian Amazon leave their villages for as long as 3 months at a time to trek through the forest in search of game. The entire village participates in a trek, carrying large quantities of garden produce and moving their camp every day.[19] Other horticulturalists raise domestic animals, but these are usually not large animals, such as cattle and camels.[20] More often than not, horticulturalists raise smaller animals, such as pigs, chickens, goats, and sheep.

Let us look now at a horticultural society, the Yanomamö of the Brazilian–Venezuelan Amazon.

The Yanomamö   Dense tropical forest covers most of Yanomamö territory. From the air, the typical village is located in a forest clearing and looks like a single, large, circular lean-to with its inner side open to the central plaza. Each individual family has its own portion of the lean-to under a common roof and each has a back wall (part of the closed back wall around the circular village structure), but the portions are open on the sides to each other as well as onto the central plaza of the village. The Yanomamö get most of their calories from garden produce, but according to Raymond Hames, the Yanomamö actually spend most of their time foraging.[21]

Before the people can plant, the forest must be cleared of trees and brush. Like most shifting cultivators, the Yanomamö use a combination of techniques: slashing the undergrowth, felling trees, and using controlled burning to clear a garden spot—in other words, **slash-and-burn** horticulture. Before the

A Yanomamö boy peels cassava.

1950s, the Yanomamö had only stone axes, so felling trees was quite difficult. Now they have steel machetes and axes given or traded to them by missionaries.

Because of the work involved in clearing a garden, the Yanomamö prefer to make use of forest patches that have little thorny brush and not too many large trees.[22] After the ground is cleared, the Yanomamö plant plantains, manioc, sweet potatoes, taro, and a variety of plants for medicine, condiments, and craft materials. Men do the heavy clearing work to prepare a garden, and they as well as women plant the crops. Women usually go to the gardens daily to weed and harvest. After two or three years, the yields diminish and the forest starts growing back, making continued cultivation less desirable and more difficult, so they abandon the garden and clear a new one. If they can, they clear adjacent forest, but if gardens are far from the village, they will move the village to a new location. Villages are moved about every 5 years because of gardening needs and warfare. There is a great deal of intervillage raiding, so villages are often forced to flee to another location.

Extensive cultivation requires a lot of territory because new gardens are not cleared until the forest grows back. What is often misunderstood is why it is so important to shift gardens. Not only is a burned field easier to plant, but the organic matter that is burned provides necessary nutrients for a good yield. If horticulturalists come back too quickly to a spot with little plant cover, a garden made there will not produce a satisfactory yield.

The Yanomamö crops do not provide much protein, so hunting and fishing are important to their diet. Men hunt birds, peccaries, monkeys, and tapir with bows and arrows. Women, men, and children enjoy fishing. They catch fish by hand, with small bows and arrows, and by stream poisoning. Everybody gathers honey, hearts of palm, Brazil nuts, and cashews, although the men usually climb trees to shake down the nuts. Much of the foraging is done from the village base, but the Yanomamö, like the Kayapo, may go on treks to forage from time to time.

General Features of Horticulturalists In most horticultural societies, simple farming techniques have tended to yield more food from a given area than is generally available to foragers. Consequently, horticulture is able to support larger, more densely populated communities. The way of life of horticulturalists is more sedentary than that of foragers, although communities may move after some years to farm a new series of plots. (Some horticulturalists have permanent villages because they depend mostly on food from trees that keep producing for a long time.) In contrast with most recent food-collecting groups, horticultural societies exhibit the beginnings of social differentiation. For example, some individuals may be part-time craftworkers or part-time political officials, and certain members of a kin group may have more status than other individuals in the society.

Intensive Agriculture People engaged in **intensive agriculture** use techniques that enable them to cultivate fields permanently. Essential nutrients may be put back in the soil through the use of fertilizers, which may be organic material (most commonly dung from humans or other animals) or inorganic (chemical) fertilizers. But there are other ways to restore nutrients. The Luo of western Kenya plant beans around corn plants. Bacteria growing around the roots of the bean plant replace lost nitrogen, and the corn plant conveniently provides a pole for the bean plant to wind around as it grows. Some intensive agriculturalists use irrigation from streams and rivers to ensure an adequate supply of waterborne nutrients. Crop rotation and plant stubble that has been plowed under also restore nutrients to the soil.

In general, the technology of intensive agriculturalists is more complex than that of horticulturalists. Plows rather than digging sticks are generally employed. But there is enormous variation in the degree to which intensive agriculturalists rely on mechanization rather than hand labor. In some societies, the most complex machine is an animal-drawn plow; in the corn and wheat belts of the United States, huge tractors till, seed, and fertilize 12 rows at a time.[23]

Let's look at one group of intensive agriculturalists, those of the Mekong Delta in Vietnam.

Rural Vietnam: The Mekong Delta The village of Khanh Hau, situated along the flat Mekong Delta, comprised about 600 families when Gerald Hickey described it in the late 1950s, before the Vietnam War.[24] The delta area has a tropical climate, with a rainy season that lasts from May to November. As a whole, the area has been made habitable only through extensive drainage.

Wet rice cultivation is the principal agricultural activity of Khanh Hau. It is part of a complex, specialized arrangement that involves three interacting components: (1) a complex system of irrigation and water control; (2) a variety of specialized equipment, including plows, waterwheels, threshing sledges, and winnowing machines; and (3) a clearly defined set of socioeconomic roles—from those of landlord, tenant, and laborer to those of rice miller and rice merchant.

In the dry season, the farmer decides what sort of rice crop to plant, whether of long (120 days) or short (90 days) maturation. The choice depends on the capital at his disposal, the current cost of fertilizer, and the anticipated demand for rice. The seedbeds are prepared as soon as the rains have softened the ground in May. The soil is turned over (plowed) and broken up (harrowed) as many as six separate times, with two-day intervals for "airing" between operations. During this time, the rice seeds are soaked in water for at least 2 days to stimulate sprouting. Before the seedlings are planted, the paddy is plowed once more and harrowed twice in two directions at right angles.

Planting is a delicate, specialized operation that must be done quickly and is performed most often by hired male laborers. But efficient planting is not enough to guarantee a good crop. Proper fertilization and irrigation are equally important. In the irrigating, steps must be taken to ensure that the water level remains at exactly the proper depth over the entire paddy. Water is distributed by means of scoops, wheels, and mechanical pumps. Successive crops of rice ripen

Vietnamese farmers in the Mekong Delta working in a flooded rice paddy. Much of the delta was originally tropical forest.

from late September to May; all members of the family may be called upon to help with the harvest. After each crop is harvested, it is threshed, winnowed, and dried. Normally, the rice is sorted into three portions: one is set aside for use by the household in the following year; one is for payment of hired labor and other services (such as loans from agricultural banks); and one is for cash sale on the market. Aside from the harvesting, women do little work in the fields, spending most of their time on household chores. In families with little land, however, young daughters help in the fields and older daughters may hire themselves out to other farmers.

The villagers also cultivate vegetables; raise pigs, chickens, and other animals; and frequently engage in fishing. The village economy usually supports three or four implement makers and a much larger number of carpenters.

General Features of Intensive Agricultural Societies Societies with intensive agriculture are more likely than horticulturalists to have towns and cities, a high degree of craft specialization, complex political organization, and large differences in wealth and power. Studies suggest that intensive agriculturalists work longer hours than horticulturalists.[25] For example, men engaged in intensive agriculture average 9 hours of work a day, 7 days a week; women average almost 11 hours of work per day. Most of the work for women in intensive agricultural societies involves food processing and work in and around the home, but they also spend a lot of time working in the fields. We discuss some of the implications of the work patterns for women in the chapter on sex and gender.

Intensive agricultural societies are more likely than horticultural societies to face famines and food shortages, even though intensive agriculture is generally more productive than horticulture.[26] Why, if more food can be produced per acre, is there more risk of shortage among intensive agriculturalists? Intensive agriculturalists may be more likely to face food shortages because they are often producing crops for a market. Producing for a market pushes farmers to cultivate plants that give them the highest yield rather than cultivating plants that are drought-resistant or that require fewer nutrients. Farmers producing for a market also tend to concentrate on one crop. Crop diversity is often a protection against total crop failure because fluctuations in weather, plant diseases, or insect pests are not likely to affect all the crops. There are also fluctuations in market demand. If the market demand drops and the price falls for a particular crop, farmers may not have enough cash to buy the other food they need.

The Commercialization and Mechanization of Agriculture Some intensive agriculturalists produce very little for sale; most of what they produce is for their own use. But there is a worldwide trend for intensive agriculturalists to produce more and more for a market. This trend is called **commercialization,** which may occur in any area of life and which involves increasing dependence on buying and selling, usually with money as the medium of exchange. Some of the push toward commercialization comes from external pressures, from governments that impose taxes that must be paid by money. But some of the shift occurs when subsistence farmers choose to plant a cash crop to earn money for various reasons. For example, the Malaiyali farmers of India grow a cash crop, tapioca (cassava), as a way of responding to unpredictable rainfall. Tapioca is fairly drought-tolerant, grows in poor soils, and can be planted later in the year when the rainfall has become more predictable.[27]

The increasing commercialization of agriculture is associated with several other trends. One is that farm work is becoming more mechanized as hand labor becomes scarce, because of migration to industrial and service jobs in towns and cities, or because hired hand labor has become too expensive. A second trend is the emergence and spread of *agribusiness,* large corporation-owned farms that may be operated by multinational companies and worked entirely by hired, as opposed to family, labor. For example, consider how cotton farming has changed in the southeastern United States. In the 1930s, tractors replaced mules and horses used in plowing. This change allowed some landowners to evict their sharecroppers and expand their holdings. After World War II, mechanical cotton pickers replaced most of the harvest laborers. But a farmer had to have a good deal of money to acquire those machines, each of which cost many tens of thousands of dollars.[28] So the mechanization of cotton farming sent many rural farm laborers off to the cities of the North in search of employment, and the agricultural sector increasingly became big business. A third trend associated with the commercialization of agriculture, including animal raising, is a reduction in the proportion of the population engaged in food production. In the United States today, for example, less than 1 percent of the total population work on farms.[29] A fourth trend is that much of what people produce for sale nowadays is shipped to or received from markets in other countries. For example, in the summer months, fruits and vegetables are often shipped to markets where consumers have little local fresh produce.

Pastoralism Most agriculturalists keep and breed some animals (practice animal husbandry), but a small number of societies depend mostly for their living on domesticated herds of animals that feed on natural pasture.[30] We call such a system **pastoralism.** We might assume that pastoralists breed animals to eat their meat, but most do not. Pastoralists more often get their animal protein from live animals in the form of milk, and some pastoralists regularly take blood, which is rich in protein, from their animals to mix with other foods. The herds often indirectly provide food because many pastoralists trade animal products for plant foods and other necessities. In fact, a large proportion of their food may actually come from trade with agricultural groups.[31] For example, some pastoral groups in the Middle East derive much of their livelihood from the sale of what we call oriental rugs, which are made from the wool of their sheep on hand looms. One pastoral society we examine are the Saami or Lapps of Scandinavia.

The Saami The Saami practice reindeer herding in northwestern Scandinavia where Finland, Sweden, and Norway share common frontiers. It is a typical Arctic habitat: cold, windswept, with long, dark days for half the year. Considerable change has occurred recently, so we first discuss the food-getting strategy in the 1950s, as described by Ian Whitaker and T. I. Itkonen.[32]

The Saami herd their reindeer either intensively or, more often, extensively. In the *intensive system*, the herd is constantly under observation within a fenced area for the whole year. Intensively herded reindeer and other animals are accustomed to human contact. Hence, the summer corralling of the females for milking and the breaking-in of the oxen for use as work animals are not difficult

A Saami reindeer herder feeds two of her animals in the snow.

tasks. The *extensive system* involves allowing the animals to migrate over a large area. It requires little surveillance and encompasses large herds. Under this system, the reindeer are allowed to move through their seasonal feeding cycles watched by only one or two scouts. The other Saami stay with the herd only when it has settled in its summer or winter habitat. But milking, breaking-in, and corralling are harder in the extensive than in the intensive system because the animals are less accustomed to humans.

Even under the extensive system, which theoretically permits Saami to engage in subsidiary economic activities such as hunting and fishing, the reindeer herd is the essential, if not the only, source of income. A family might possess as many as 1,000 reindeer, but usually the figure is half that number. Studies show 200 to be the minimum number of reindeer needed to provide for a family of four or five adults. Women may have shared the herding chores in the past under the intensive system, but now, under the extensive system, men do the herding. Women still do the milking. The Saami eat the meat of the bull reindeer; the female reindeer are kept for breeding purposes. Bulls are slaughtered in the fall, after the mating season. Meat and hides are frequently sold or bartered for other food and necessities.

Reindeer are still herded nowadays, but snowmobiles, all-terrain vehicles, and even helicopters have replaced sleds for herding. Ferries move reindeer to and from different pastures, and the herders communicate by field telephones. With faster transportation, many Saami now live in permanent homes and can still get to their herds in hours. Saami children spend much of their time in school and, consequently, do not learn much of the herding ways. The Norwegian government now regulates pastoralism, licensing pastoralists and trying to limit the number of reindeer they can herd.[33] And many Saami no longer have reindeer.

General Features of Pastoralism In recent times, pastoralism has been practiced mainly in grassland and other semiarid habitats that are not especially suitable for cultivation without some significant technological input such as irrigation. Most pastoralists are nomadic, moving camp fairly frequently to find water and new pasture for their herds. But other pastoralists have somewhat more sedentary lives. They may move from one settlement to another in different seasons, or they may send some people out to travel with the herds in different seasons. Pastoral communities are usually small, consisting of a group of related families.[34] Individuals or families may own their own animals, but the community makes decisions about when and where to move the herds. There is a great deal of interdependence between pastoral and agricultural groups. That is, trade is usually necessary for pastoral groups to survive. Like agriculturalists, pastoralists are more vulnerable than foragers and horticulturalists to famine and food shortages. Pastoralists usually inhabit drought-prone regions, but recent pastoralists have had their access to grazing lands reduced, and political pressures have pushed them to decrease their movement over large areas. Mobility kept the risk of overgrazing to a minimum, but overgrazing in small territories has increased the risk of desertification.[35]

The Origin, Spread, and Intensification of Food Production

We see the first evidence of a changeover to food production—the cultivation and domestication of plants and animals—in the Near East about 8000 B.C. This shift occurred, probably independently, in other areas as well. There is evidence of cultivation some time around 6000 B.C. in China, Southeast Asia (what is now Malaysia, Thailand, Cambodia, and Vietnam), and Africa. In the New World, there appear to have been several places of original cultivation and domestication. The highlands of Mexico (about 7000 B.C.) and the central Andes around Peru (by about 6000 B.C.) were probably the most important in terms of food plants used today.

There are many theories of why food production developed; most have tried to explain the origin of domestication in the Near East. The possible reasons include the following:

1. Population growth in regions of bountiful wild resources pushed people to move to marginal areas, where they tried to reproduce their former abundance.

2. Global population growth filled up most of the world's habitable regions and forced people to utilize a broader spectrum of wild resources and to domesticate plants and animals.

3. Climatic change—hotter, drier summers and colder winters—favored settling near seasonal stands of wild grain; population growth in such areas would force people to plant crops and raise animals.

Whatever the reasons for the switch to food production, we still need to explain why food production has supplanted foraging as the primary mode of subsistence. We cannot assume that collectors would automatically adopt production as a superior way of life once they understood the process of domestication. After all, as we have noted, domestication may entail more work and provide less security than the food-collecting way of life.

The spread of agriculture may be linked to the need for territorial expansion. As a sedentary, food-producing population grew, it may have been forced to expand into new territory. Some of this territory may have been vacant, but foragers probably already occupied much of it. Although food production is not necessarily easier than collection, it is generally more productive per unit of land. Greater productivity enables more people to be supported in a given territory. In the competition for land between the faster-expanding food producers and the foragers, the food producers may have had a significant advantage: They had more people in a given area. Thus, the foraging groups may have been more likely to lose out in the competition for land. Some groups may have adopted cultivation, abandoning the foraging way of life to survive. Other groups, continuing as foragers, may have been forced to retreat into areas not desired by the cultivators. Today, as we have seen, the small number of remaining foragers inhabit areas not particularly suitable for cultivation—dry lands, dense tropical forests, and polar regions.

Just as prior population growth might account for the origins of domestication, further population growth and ensuing pressure on resources at later periods might also at least

This area of Montana is cultivated now. In the past, only foraging was practiced.

partly explain the transformation of horticultural systems into intensive agricultural systems. Ester Boserup suggested that intensification of agriculture, with a consequent increase in yield per acre, is not likely to develop naturally out of horticulture because intensification requires much more work.[36] She argued that people will be willing to intensify their labor only if they have to. Where emigration is not feasible, the prime mover behind intensification may be prior population growth. The need to pay taxes or tribute to a political authority may also stimulate intensification.

The Effect of Food-Getting on the Environment

Many people are now aware of industrial pollution—the dumping of industrial wastes in the ground or into rivers, the spewing of chemicals into the air through smokestacks—but we don't often realize how much humans have altered the environment by the ways they collect and produce food. Consider irrigation. Irrigation has made agriculture productive in arid or unpredictable rainfall environments. There are various ways to capture water for irrigation. Water can be channeled from rivers; rainwater can be caught in terraces carved out of hillsides; ancient water can be pumped up from vast underground reservoirs called aquifers. But much of the water use is wasteful, seeping into the channels or evaporating into the air before reaching the plants. Plants absorb water and leave behind the salts. But the extensive evaporation of water during irrigation mostly leads to higher concentration of minerals and salts. If drainage is poor and if the water table rises, the salt concentrations are not washed away. Often, the more a piece of land has been irrigated, the saltier the ground becomes. Eventually, the soil becomes too salty to grow crops effectively and crops have to be grown elsewhere.

Some archaeologists have suggested that the accumulation of toxic salts in the soil at least partly explains the doom or decline of various groups in the past. For example, salinization probably contributed to the decline of Sumer, an early empire in Mesopotamia, and other early states in what is now southern Iraq and southwestern Iran. Over time, the concentration of people shifted from the lower portion of the Tigris-Euphrates river system to the upper portion as irrigated land lower down became unusable for farming. Today, much of the soil is still too salty for cultivation. Recent irrigation schemes during Saddam Hussein's regime have seriously degraded the downstream Iraqi marshes. Less than 10 percent of the marsh wetlands remain, putting over 60 bird species at risk. In addition, the loss of the marshlands has reduced the ability of the marshland to filter the water before it reaches the Persian Gulf, which has led to declines in productivity of the coastal fisheries. The severity of the degradation in the region has been compared with the deforestation of the Amazon.

The lessons of history have not yet been learned. The San Joaquin Valley of California, perhaps the most productive agricultural area in the world, now has a serious salinization problem. One solution in many of the areas of the Great American Desert is to pump water up from underground. Indeed, in many places there is a great deal of water underground. For example, the Ogallala aquifer, which underlies parts of Nebraska, Kansas, Texas, Oklahoma, Colorado, and New Mexico, contains water left from the ice ages. But the pumping solution, if it is a solution, is only a short-term fix, for the huge Ogallala aquifer is also the fastest-disappearing aquifer. The only question is how long it will take to disappear totally.

Too many people raising too many animals can also have serious effects on the environment. We can easily imagine how the possibility of profit might inspire people to try to raise more animals than the land will support. For example, 300 years ago the Great American Desert was a vast grassland. It supported large herds of buffalo, which were all but exterminated by overhunting in the next 200 years. The European-American settlers soon discovered they could raise cattle and sheep on this grassland, but many parts of it were overgrazed. It took the swirling dust storms of the 1930s to make people realize that overgrazing as well as poor farming practices could be disastrous. The problems are not just recent ones. The Norse colonized Greenland and Iceland around A.D. 800; but overgrazing of pasture undoubtedly contributed to soil erosion and the disappearance or decline of the colonies by A.D. 1500.

Are environmental problems associated only with food production? Although food producers may be the worst offenders, there is reason to think that foragers may also have sometimes overfished, overgathered, or overhunted. For example, some scholars suspect that the movement of humans into the New World was mainly responsible for the disappearance of the mammoth. Unfortunately, there is little evidence that humans have been good conservers in the past. That does not mean that humans cannot do better in the future—but they have to want to.

Sources: Curtis et al. 2005; Dirks 2009; *Los Angeles Times* 1994; Hillel 2000; Reisner 1993.

However, Boserup's assumption that more work is required with intensive agriculture has recently been questioned. Comparing horticultural (swidden or shifting) rice production with rice produced on permanent fields using irrigation, Robert Hunt found that *less,* not more, labor is required with irrigation.[37] Still, population increase may generally provide the impetus to intensify production to increase yields to support the additional people.

Intensive agriculture has not yet spread to every part of the world. Horticulture continues to be practiced in certain tropical regions, and there are still some pastoralists and foragers. Some environments may make it somewhat more difficult to adopt certain subsistence practices. For example, intensive agriculture cannot supplant horticulture in some tropical environments without tremendous investments in chemical fertilizers and pesticides, not to mention the additional labor required.[38] And enormous amounts of water may be required to make agriculturalists out of foragers and pastoralists who now exploit semiarid environments. However, difficulty is not impossibility. Anna Roosevelt points out that, although horticulture was a common food-getting strategy in Amazonia in recent times, archaeological evidence indicates that there were complex societies practicing intensive agriculture on raised, drained fields in the past.[39] The physical environment does not completely control what can be done with it.

The Allocation of Resources

Natural Resources: Land

Every society has access to natural resources—land, water, plants, animals, minerals—and every society has cultural rules for determining who has access to particular resources and what can be done with them. In societies like the United States, where land and many other things may be bought and sold, land is divided into precisely measurable units, the borders of which may be visible or invisible. Individuals usually own relatively small plots of land and the resources on them. Large plots of land are generally owned collectively. The owner may be a government agency, such as the National Park Service, which owns land on behalf of the entire population of the United States (referred to as public ownership). Or the owner may be a corporation—a private collective of shareholders. In the United States, property ownership entails a more or less exclusive right to use land or other resources (called *usufruct*) in whatever ways the owner wishes, including the right to withhold or prevent use by others. In the United States and many other societies, property ownership also includes the right to "alienate" property—that is, to sell, give away, bequeath, or destroy the resources owned. This type of property ownership by individuals, families, or private corporations is often referred to as a *private property* system.

Society specifies what is considered property and the rights and duties associated with that property.[40] These specifications are social in nature, for they may be changed over time. For example, France declared all its beaches to be public, thereby stating, in effect, that the ocean shore is not a resource that an individual can own. As a result, all the hotels and individuals that had fenced-off portions of the best beaches for their exclusive use had to remove the barriers. Even in countries with private property, such as the United States, people cannot do anything that they want with their property. Federal, state, and local governments have adopted legislation to prevent the pollution of the air and the water supply. Such regulation may be new, but the rights of ownership in the United States have been limited for some time. For example, government may take land for use in the construction of a highway; compensation is paid, but the individual cannot prevent confiscation. Similarly, people are not allowed to burn their houses or to use them as brothels or munitions arsenals. In short, even with an individualistic system of ownership, property is not entirely private.

How societies differ in their rules for access to land and other natural resources seems to be related in part to how they differ in food-getting. Let us now examine how foragers, horticulturalists, pastoralists, and intensive agriculturalists structure rights to land in different ways. We look at traditional patterns first. As we shall see later, traditional rights to land have been considerably affected by state societies that have spread to and colonized native societies in the New World, Africa, and Asia.

Foragers Members of food-collecting societies generally do not have private ownership of land. If there is collective ownership, it is always by groups of related people (kinship groups) or by territorial groups (bands or villages). Land is not bought and sold. The reason is probably that land itself generally has no intrinsic value for foragers; what is of value is the presence of game and wild plant life on the land. If game moves away or food resources become less plentiful, the land is less valuable. Therefore, the greater the possibility that the wild food supply in a particular locale will fluctuate, the less desirable it is to parcel out small areas of land to individuals and the more advantageous it is to make land ownership communal. This is not to say that private ownership of land does not exist among foragers. Among foragers heavily dependent on fishing in rivers, individual or family ownership is more common,[41] perhaps because the fishing in rivers is more predictable than other kinds of foraging. And, in some foraging societies, individuals and families have private rights to trees.[42] It is more common in food-collecting societies for a group of individuals, usually kin, to "own" land. To be sure, such ownership is not usually exclusive; typically, some degree of access is provided to members of neighboring bands.[43]

Horticulturalists Like foragers, most horticulturalists do not have individual or family ownership of land. This may be because rapid depletion of the soil necessitates letting some of the land lie fallow for a period of years or abandoning an area after a few years and moving to a new

A Surui village in the Amazon with cleared land for horticulture in the foreground and the surrounding rain forest in the background.

location. There is no reason for individuals or families to claim permanent access to land that, given available technology, is not usable permanently. But, in contrast to foragers, horticulturalists are more likely to allocate particular plots of land to individuals or families for their use, although these individuals or families do not commonly own the land in our sense of potentially permanent ownership. For example, among the Mundurucú of Brazil, the village controls the rights to use land. People in the community can hunt and fish where they like, and they have the right to clear a garden plot wherever land belonging to the community is not being used. Gardens can be cultivated for only 2 years before the soil is exhausted, then the land reverts to the community. The Mundurucú distinguish between the land and the produce on the land, so that a person who cultivates the land owns the produce. Similarly, the person who kills an animal or catches a fish owns it, no matter where it was obtained. But because all food is shared with others, it does not really matter who owns it. Rights to land became more individualized when Mundurucú men began to tap rubber trees for sale. Rights to a particular path in the forest where trees were tapped could not be bought and sold, but the rights could be inherited by a son or son-in-law.[44]

Pastoralists The territory of pastoral nomads usually far exceeds that of most horticultural societies. Because their wealth ultimately depends on mobile herds, uncultivated pasture for grazing, and water for drinking, pastoralists often combine the adaptive potential of both foragers and horticulturalists. Like foragers, they generally need to know the potential of a large area of land. For example, the Basseri of southern Iran moved over an area of 15,000 square miles to obtain supplies of grass and water. And, like horticulturalists, pastoralists must move on when a resource is exhausted (in this case, until grass renews itself). Also like horticulturalists, they depend for subsistence on human manipulation of a natural resource—animals—as opposed to the horticulturalists' land.

Because land is only good if there is sufficient pasture and water, there would be considerable risk to individuals or families to own land that did not predictably have grass and water. So, like most foragers and horticulturalists, community members generally have free access to pasture land.[45] Although grazing land tends to be communally held, it is customary for pastoralist individuals to own animals.[46]

As among hunter-gatherers, pastoralists vary in how much a group actually has ownership rights to the territories through which they move their animals. The Basseri have rights to pass through certain areas, including agricultural areas and even cities, but they do not own the entire territory. The Baluch, another pastoralist group in the border region between Iran, Pakistan, and Afghanistan, claim a "tribal" territory, which they defend by force, if necessary.[47]

Intensive Agriculturalists Individual ownership of land resources—including the right to use the resources and the right to sell or otherwise dispose of them—is common among intensive agriculturalists. The development of such ownership is partly a result of the possibility of using land season after season, which gives the land more or less permanent value. But the concept of individual ownership is also partly a political and social matter. So, for example, the occupation and cultivation of frontier land in the United States was transformed by law into individual ownership. Under the Homestead Act of 1862, if a person cleared a 160-acre piece of land and farmed it for five years, the federal government would consider that person the owner of the land. This practice is similar to the custom in some societies by which a kin group, a chief, or a community is obligated to assign a parcel of land to anyone who wishes to farm it. The difference is that, once the American homesteader had become the owner of the land, the laws of the country gave the homesteader the right to dispose of it at will by selling or giving it away. Once individual ownership of land has become established, property owners may use their economic, and hence political, power to pass laws that favor themselves. In the early years of the United States, only property owners could vote.

Colonialism, the State, and Land Rights Almost universally around the world, colonial conquerors and settlers have taken land away from the natives or aborigines. Even if the natives were given other land in exchange, as in Brazil and the United States, these reservations were often, if not always, poorer in potential than the original land. (If the reservation land hadn't been poorer in quality,

Colonial governments have often taken land away from the natives to establish plantations. A family in Guatemala works on a coffee plantation.

the settlers would have taken it for themselves.)[48] In addition, the new centralized governments often tried to change how the natives owned the land, almost always in the direction of individual or private ownership. If kin groups or larger social entities owned the land, it would be more difficult for the settlers to get the natives to give it up, either by sale or threat. Individual owners could be dispossessed more easily.[49]

This is not to say that native peoples in Africa, Asia, and the New World were never guilty of conquering and exploiting others on their continents or elsewhere. They were. The Aztecs in Mexico and Central America, the native kingdoms in West Africa after about 800 years ago, and the Arabs after the rise of Islam were just some of the expanding state societies of the past, before the rise of the West. Wherever there have been "civilized" (urban) societies, there have been imperialism and colonialism.

The taking of land by state authorities does not just happen with colonialism and imperialism. Indigenous revolutionary movements have collectivized land, as in Russia, or broken up large private landholdings, as in Mexico. Typically, state authorities do not like communal land-use systems. State authorities particularly view mobile pastoralists unfavorably because their mobility makes them difficult to control. Governments usually try to settle pastoralists or break up communally held pasture into small units.[50]

The Conversion of Resources

In all societies, resources have to be transformed or converted through labor into food, tools, and other goods. These activities constitute what economists call *production*. In this section, after briefly reviewing different types of production, we examine how societies divide up the work to be done.

Types of Economic Production

At the times they were first described, most of the societies known to anthropology had a *domestic*—family or kinship—mode of production. People labored to get food and to produce shelter and implements for themselves and their kin. Usually families had the right to exploit productive resources and control the products of their labor. Even part-time specialists, such as potters, could still support themselves without that craft if they needed to. At the other extreme are *industrial* societies, where much of the work is based on mechanized production, as in factories but also in mechanized agriculture. Because machines and materials are costly, only some individuals (capitalists), corporations, or governments can afford the expenses of production. Therefore, most people in industrial societies labor for others as wage earners. Although wages can buy food, people out of work lose their ability to support themselves, unless they are protected by welfare payments or unemployment insurance. Then there is the *tributary* type of production system, found in nonindustrial societies in which most people still produce their own food but an elite or aristocracy controls a portion of production (including the products of specialized crafts). The feudal societies of medieval western Europe were examples of tributary production, as was czarist Russia under serfdom.[51]

Many people have suggested that our own and other developed economies are now moving from *industrialism* to *postindustrialism.* In many areas of commerce, computers have radically transformed the workplace. Computers "drive" machines and robots, and much of the manual work required in industry is disappearing. Businesses are now more knowledge- and service-oriented. Information is more accessible with telecommunication, so much so that *telecommuting* has entered our vocabulary to describe how people can now work (for wages) at home. With inexpensive home computers and speedy data transmission by telephone and other means, more people are able to work at home. In addition, when information and knowledge become more important than capital equipment, more people can own and have access to the productive resources of society.[52]

Forced and Required Labor

Thus far, we have mostly discussed *voluntary labor*—voluntary in the sense that no formal organization within the society compels people to work and punishes them for not working. Social training and social pressure are powerful enough to persuade an individual to perform some useful task. In both food-collecting and horticultural societies, individuals who can stand being the butt of jokes about laziness will still be fed. At most, the other members of the group will ignore them. There is no reason to punish them and no way to coerce them to do the work expected of them.

More complex societies have ways of forcing people to work for the authorities, whether those authorities are kings or presidents. An indirect form of forced labor is taxation. The average tax in the United States (local, state, and federal) is about 33 percent of income, which means that the average person works 4 months out of the year for the various levels of government. If a person decides not to pay the tax, the money will be taken forcibly or the person may be put in prison.

Money is the customary form of tax payment in a commercial society. In a politically complex but nonmonetary society, people may pay their taxes in other ways—by performing a certain number of hours of labor or by giving up a certain percentage of what they produce. The **corvée,** a system of required labor, existed in the Inca Empire in the central Andes before the Spanish conquest. Each male commoner was assigned three plots of land to work: a temple plot, a state plot, and his own plot. The enormous stores of food that went into state warehouses were used to supply the nobles, the army, the artisans, and all other state employees. If labor became overabundant, the people were still kept occupied; it is said that one ruler had a hill moved to keep some laborers busy. In addition to subsistence work for the state, Inca commoners were subject to military service, to duty as personal servants for the nobility, and to other "public" service.[53] Elderly villagers in the Chiang Mai area of Thailand describe corvée this way: "Villagers had to work one *rai* [*rai myong* or 0.1 acre] per person for them for nothing. And one had to do it properly. The lord's underlings would take a banana tree trunk and stick it upright in the field after it was plowed. If it fell over, that meant it was well plowed. Otherwise, one would have to keep on plowing until the ground was soft."[54]

Conscription or the draft, or compulsory military service, is also a form of corvée, in that a certain period of service is required, and failure to

The Great Wall of China, like many monumental works in ancient societies, was built with forced labor.

serve can be punished by a prison term or involuntary exile. Emperors of China had soldiers drafted to defend their territory and to build the Great Wall along the northern borders of the empire. The wall extends over 1,500 miles, and thousands were drafted to work on it. Slavery is the most extreme form of forced work, in that slaves have little control over their labor. Because slaves constitute a category or class of people in many societies, we discuss slavery more fully in the chapter on social stratification.

Division of Labor

All societies have some division of labor, some customary assignment of different kinds of work to different kinds of people. Universally, males and females and adults and children do not do the same kinds of work. In a sense, then, division of labor by gender and age is a kind of universal specialization of labor. Many societies known to anthropology divide labor only by gender and age; other societies have more complex specialization.

By Gender and Age All societies make use of gender differences to some extent in their customary assignment of labor. In the chapter on sex and gender, we discuss the division of labor by gender in detail.

Age is also a universal basis for division of labor. Clearly, children cannot do work that requires a great deal of strength. But, in many societies, girls and boys contribute much more in labor than do children in our own society. For example, they help in animal tending, weeding, and harvesting and do a variety of domestic chores such as child care, fetching water and firewood, and cooking and cleaning. In agricultural communities in the Ivory Coast, children's tasks mirror the tasks of same-sex adults (see Figure 11.1). In some societies, a child that is 6 years old is considered old enough to be responsible for a younger sibling for a good part of the day.[55] Animal tending is often important work for children. Children in some societies spend more time at this task than adults.[56]

Beyond Gender and Age In societies with relatively simple technologies, there is little specialization of labor beyond that of gender and age. But as a society's technology becomes more complex and it is able to produce large quantities of food, more of its people are freed from subsistence work to become specialists in some other tasks.

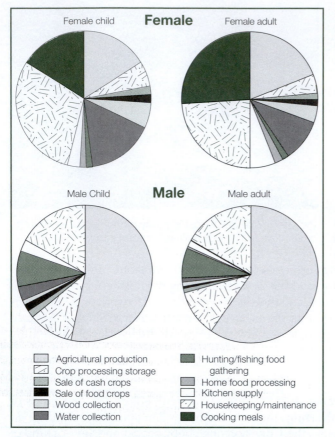

Figure 11.1 A Comparison of the Proportion of Work Tasks Done by Adults and Children

Source: From James A. Levine, Robert Weisell, Simon Chevassus, Claudio D. Martinez, and Barbara Burlingame, "The Distribution of Work Tasks for Male and Female Children and Adults Separated by Gender," in "Looking at Child Labor," *Science,* 296 (May 10, 2002): 1025.

In contrast with foragers, horticultural societies may have some part-time specialists. Some people may devote special effort to perfecting a particular skill or craft—pottery making, weaving, house building, doctoring—and in return for their products or services be given food or other gifts. Among some horticultural groups, the entire village may specialize part time in making a particular product, which can then be traded to neighboring people. With the development of intensive agriculture, full-time specialists—potters, weavers, blacksmiths—begin to appear.

The Distribution of Goods and Services

Goods and services are distributed in all societies by systems that, however varied, can be classified under three general types: reciprocity, redistribution, and market or commercial exchange.[57] The three systems often coexist in a society, but one system usually predominates. The predominant system seems to be associated with the society's food-getting technology and, more specifically, its level of economic development.

Reciprocity

Reciprocity consists of giving and taking without the use of money; it mainly takes the form of gift giving or generalized reciprocity. There may also be exchanges of equal value (barter or nonmonetary trade) or balanced reciprocity, without the use of money.[58]

Generalized Reciprocity When goods or services are given to another, without any apparent expectation of a return gift, we call it **generalized reciprocity.** Generalized reciprocity sustains the family in all societies. Parents give food, clothing, and labor to children because they want to or perhaps feel obliged to, but they do not usually calculate exactly how their children will reciprocate years later. These gifts are one-way transfers. In this sense, all societies have some kind of generalized reciprocity. But some societies depend on it almost entirely to distribute goods and services.

Lorna Marshall recounted how the San in the Nyae Nyae area divided an eland brought to a site where five bands and several visitors were camping—more than 100 people in all. The owner of the arrow that had first penetrated the eland was, by custom, the owner of the meat.

He first distributed the forequarters to the two hunters who had aided him in the kill. After that, the distribution depended on kinship: Each hunter shared with his wives' parents, wives, children, parents, and siblings, and they in turn shared with their kin. Sixty-three gifts of raw meat were recorded, after which further sharing of raw and cooked meat was begun.[59] The Nyae Nyae distribution of large game—clearly, generalized reciprocity—is common among foragers.

Parent–child giving may seem easy to understand, but why do some societies rely more on generalized reciprocity than others, particularly beyond the family? Sharing may be most likely if resources are unpredictable. So a Nyae Nyae band may share its water with other bands because they may have water now but not in the future. A related group of San in the Kalahari, the G//ana,[60] has been observed to share less than other groups. It turns out that the resources available to the G//ana are more predictable, because the G//ana supplement their hunting and gathering with plant cultivation and goat herding. Cultivated melons (which store water) appear to buffer the G//ana against water shortages, and goats buffer them against shortages of game. Thus, whereas the Nyae Nyae distribute the meat right after a kill, the G//ana dry it and then store it in their houses.[61]

Does food-sharing increase the food supply for an individual? Calculations for the Aché of eastern Paraguay, who get most of their food from hunting when they go on food-collecting trips, suggest that the average individual gets more food when food is shared. Even the males who actually do the hunting get more, although the benefits are greater for the females and children on the trip.[62] Mathematically, the risk that an individual food collector will not find enough food on a particular day will be appreciably reduced if at least six to eight adult collectors share the food they collect. Food-collecting bands may often contain only 25–30 people, which is about the size that is needed to ensure that there are six to eight adult collectors.[63]

What happens to a system of generalized reciprocity when resources are scarce because of a drought or other disaster? Does the ethic of giving break down? Evidence from a few societies suggests that the degree of sharing may actually *increase* during the period of food shortage.[64] For example, in describing the Netsilik Inuit, Asen Balikci said, "Whenever game was abundant, sharing among non-relatives was avoided, since every family was supposedly capable of obtaining the necessary catch. In situations of scarcity, however, caribou meat was more evenly distributed throughout camp."[65] Sharing may increase during mild scarcity because people can minimize their deprivation, but generalized reciprocity may be strained by extreme scarcity such as famine.[66]

Researchers generally have difficulty explaining sharing because they assume that, other things being equal, individuals would tend to be selfish. But experimental evidence suggests that sharing is likely even with people who do not know each other or who have no expectation of any return in the future from that person. Experimenters set up "games" in which they can control for or eliminate certain responses. For example, in one game, a particular player is given a certain amount of money and the player decides how much of the money to offer to the second player in the game. The second player can accept or reject the offer. If the division is rejected, no one gets any money. If the division is accepted, both players receive the proposed division. If selfishness were normal, one would expect that the proposer of the division would try to give away as little as possible and the second player should always accept whatever is offered because otherwise noth-ing is gained. Surprisingly, equal divisions are commonly proposed and low offers are commonly rejected because they are viewed as unfair. If a person views the offer as unfair and forfeits any money, that player seems willing to "punish" the greedy individual. Although such experiments were mostly done at first in Western societies, we now have results from over 15 other societies that largely confirm the earlier results.[67] And there is now evidence suggesting that cooperation may even evoke pleasure. Researchers studying brain activity in women, who are playing a game

The Inuit of Baffin Island, Canada are collecting their shares of whale meat. Hunting societies commonly share meat from larger animals.

allowing either cooperative or greedy strategies, found to their surprise that cooperation made certain areas of the brain light up. These areas are normally associated with pleasure, such as when eating desserts. So cooperation may be more "natural" than some people think.[68]

Balanced Reciprocity **Balanced reciprocity** is explicit and short term in its expectations of return. In contrast to generalized reciprocity or a one-way transfer, which has no expectation of a return, balanced reciprocity involves either an immediate exchange of goods or services or an agreed-upon exchange over a limited period of time. *Barter* is the term used most often for this type of nonmonetary exchange of goods and services. In the 1600s, the Iroquois of the North American Northeast traded deerskin to Europeans for brass kettles, iron hinges, steel axes, woven textiles, and guns.[69] The Iroquois acquired trade goods by balanced reciprocity, but such exchanges were not crucial to their economies.

Sometimes the line between generalized and balanced reciprocity is not so clear. Consider our gift giving at Christmas. Although such gift giving may appear to be generalized reciprocity, and it often is in the case of gift giving from parents to children, there may be strong expectations of balance. Two friends or relatives may try to exchange presents of fairly equal value, based on calculations of what last year's gift cost. If a person receives a $5 present when he or she gave a $25 present, that person may be hurt and perhaps angry. On the other hand, a person who receives a $500 present when he or she gave a $25 present may well also be dismayed.

Redistribution

Redistribution is the accumulation of goods or labor by a particular person, or in a particular place, for the purpose of subsequent distribution. Although redistribution is found in all societies, it becomes an important mechanism only in societies that have political hierarchies—that is, chiefs or other specialized officials and agencies. In all societies, there is some redistribution, at least within the family. Members of the family pool their labor, products, or income for the common good. But in many societies, there is little or no redistribution beyond the family. It seems that redistribution on a territorial basis emerges when there is a political apparatus to coordinate centralized collection and distribution of goods or to mobilize labor for some public purpose.

Why do redistribution systems develop? Elman Service suggested that they develop in agricultural societies that contain subregions suited to different kinds of crops or natural resources. Foragers can take advantage of environmental variation by moving to different areas. With agriculture, the task is more difficult; it might be easier to move different products across different regions.[70] If the demand for different resources or products becomes too great, reciprocity between individuals might become awkward. So it might be more efficient to have someone—a chief, perhaps—coordinate the exchanges.

Marvin Harris agreed that redistribution becomes more likely with agriculture, but for a somewhat different reason. He argued that competitive feasting, as in New Guinea, is adaptive because it encourages people to work harder to produce somewhat more than they need. Why would this feature be adaptive? Harris argued that, with agriculture, people really have to produce more than they need so that they can protect themselves against crises such as crop failure. The groups that make feasts may be indirectly ensuring themselves against crises by storing up social credit with other villages, who will reciprocate by making feasts for them in the future. On the other hand, inducements to collect more than they need may not be advantageous to food-collecting groups, who might lose in the long run by overcollecting.[71]

Market or Commercial Exchange

When we think of markets, we usually think of bustling, colorful places where goods are bought and sold. The exchanges usually involve money. In our own society, we have supermarkets and the stock market and other places for buying and selling that we call shops, stores, and malls. In referring to **market** or **commercial exchange,** economists and economic anthropologists are referring to exchanges or transactions in which the "prices" are subject to supply and demand, whether or not the transactions actually occur in a marketplace.[72] Market exchange involves not only the exchange (buying and selling) of goods but also transactions of labor, land, rentals, and credit.

Kinds of Money Although market exchange need not involve money, most commercial transactions, particularly nowadays, do involve what we call money. Some anthropologists define money according to the functions and characteristics of the **general-purpose money** used in our own and other complex societies, for which nearly all goods, resources, and services can be exchanged. According to this definition, money performs the basic functions of serving as an accepted medium of exchange, a standard of value, and a store of wealth. As a medium of exchange, it allows all goods and services to be valued in the same objective way; we say that an object or service is worth so much money. Also, money is nonperishable, and therefore savable or storable, and almost always transportable and divisible, so transactions can involve the buying and selling of goods and services that differ in value. Money has little or no intrinsic value; rather, it is society that determines its value. In the United States today, paper bills, bank checks, and credit and debit cards are fully accepted as money, and money is increasingly transferred electronically.

The Worldwide Trend Toward Commercialization

Most societies were not commercialized at all, or only barely so, when first described in the ethnographic record by explorers, missionaries, and anthropologists. That is, most societies as first described did not rely on market or commercial exchange to distribute goods and services. But commercial exchange has become the dominant form of distribution in the modern world. Most societies of the ethnographic past are now incorporated into larger nation-states; for example, the Trobriand Islands, where the Trobriand Islanders of Melanesia now live, is now a district in the nation of Papua New Guinea. Selling today goes far beyond the nation-state. The world is now a multinational market.[73]

However, there is considerable variation in the degree to which societies today depend on market or commercial exchange. Many societies still allocate land without purchase and distribute food and other goods primarily by reciprocity and redistribution, participating only peripherally in market exchange. These are societies in transition; their traditional subsistence economies are becoming commercialized.

What anthropologists call *peasant economies* are somewhat more commercialized than transitional subsistence economies. Although **peasants** also produce food largely for their own consumption, they regularly sell part of their surplus (food, other goods, or labor) to others, and land is one of the commodities they buy, rent, and sell. However, although their production is somewhat commercialized, peasants are still not like the fully commercialized farmers in industrialized societies, who rely on the market to exchange all or almost all of their crops for all or almost all of the goods and services they need.

In fully commercialized societies such as our own, market or commercial exchange dominates the economy; prices and wages are regulated, or at least significantly affected, by the forces of supply and demand. A modern industrial or postindustrial economy may involve international as well as national markets in which everything—natural resources, labor, goods, services, prestige items, religious and ceremonial items—has a price, stated in the same money terms. Reciprocity is reserved for family members and friends or remains behind the scenes in business transactions. Redistribution, however, is an important mechanism. It is practiced in the form of taxation and the use of public revenue for transfer payments and other benefits to low-income families—welfare, Social Security, health care, and so on. But commercial exchange is the major way goods and services are distributed.

Many anthropologists have noted that, with the introduction of money, customs of sharing seem to change dramatically. Money, perhaps because it is nonperishable and largely hideable, tends to invoke feelings of not wanting to share. The plight of a man from the central highlands of New Guinea is typical. He agrees that it is not good manners to refuse a request from a relative or village friend; nonetheless, to keep his income from being "eaten," he tries to conceal some of his income. Some of the strategies include opening a savings account into which his pay is deposited, purchasing a semipermanent house, or joining a revolving credit association.[74] A recent series of experiments in the United States, where money has always been fundamental to the economic system, suggests that even the mere reminder of money causes people to behave more independently and to be less helpful to others.[75]

Types of Commercialization

Migratory Labor One way commercialization can occur is for some members of a community to move to a place that offers the possibility of working for wages. This happened in Tikopia, an island near the Solomon Islands in the South Pacific. In 1929, when Raymond Firth first studied the island, its economy was still essentially noncommercial—simple, self-sufficient, and largely self-contained.[76] Some Western goods were available but, with the exception of iron and steel in limited quantities, not sought after. Their possession and use were associated solely with Europeans. This situation changed dramatically with World War II. During the war, military forces occupied neighboring islands, and people from Tikopia migrated to those islands to find employment. In the period following the war, several large commercial interests extended their activities in the Solomons, thus creating a continued demand for labor. As a result, when Firth revisited Tikopia in 1952, he found the economic situation already significantly altered. More than 100 Tikopians had left the island to work for varying periods. The migrants wanted to earn money because they aspired to standards of living previously regarded as appropriate only to Europeans. Already, living conditions on Tikopia were changing. Western cooking and water-carrying utensils, mosquito nets, kerosene storm lamps, and so forth had come to be regarded as normal items in a Tikopia household.

In many areas of the world, the money sent back home has become a major factor in the economy. Often remittances are not sent through the formal banking system, but rather through an informal network of brokers. In the Middle East and South Asia, the system is called *hawala* and is based on an honor system. For instance, the Hazara, the third largest ethnic group in Afghanistan, have migrated throughout the twentieth century to cities in Afghanistan as well as to Pakistan and Iran. The banks in Afghanistan are not functioning and the Hazara often do not have official identification papers, so they use *hawala* brokers to transfer money back home.[77] The money from remittances often far exceeds the money spent by development efforts.[78] But unlike development efforts, usually supported by wealthier countries, money received by remittances can be channeled where families want. Migration becomes part of a family's economic strategy. Of course, not all families can employ that strategy—the poorest families cannot afford the costs of long-distance migration.[79]

Nonagricultural Commercial Production Commercialization can also occur when a self-sufficient society comes to depend more and more on trading for its livelihood. Such a change is exemplified by the Mundurucú of the Amazon Basin, who largely abandoned

Navajo women weave rugs for sale.

general horticulture for commercial rubber production. They did this to obtain other industrially made objects.[80] The primary socioeconomic change that occurred among the Mundurucú and the Montagnais was a shift from cooperative labor and community autonomy to individualized economic activity and a dependence on an external market.

Among the Mundurucú, for example, before close trading links were established, the native population and the Europeans had been in contact for some 80 years without the Mundurucú way of life being noticeably altered. Some trading took place with Brazilians, with the chief acting as agent for the village. Barter was the method of exchange. Traders first distributed their wares, ranging from cheap cottons to iron hatchets, trinkets, and so on; they returned about 3 months later to collect manioc, India rubber, and beans from the Mundurucú. At this time (1860), however, rubber was only a secondary item of commerce.

The rapidly growing demand for rubber from the 1860s onward increased the importance of Mundurucú-trader relationships. Traders now openly began to appoint agents, called *capitoes,* whose job it was to encourage greater rubber production. *Capitoes* were given economic privileges and hence power, both of which began to undercut the position of the traditional chief. In addition, the process of rubber collection itself began to alter Mundurucú social patterns by moving people away from their jungle-based communities. The Mundurucú man who elected to gather rubber had to separate himself from his family for about half the year. The Mundurucú became increasingly dependent on goods the trader supplied. Firearms were useless without regular quantities of gun powder and lead or shot; clothing required needles and thread for repairs. But these items could be earned only through increased rubber production, which in turn led to greater dependency on the outside world. Metal pots took the place of clay ones, and manufactured hammocks replaced homemade ones. Gradually, the village agricultural cycle ceased to be followed by all in the community so that rubber production would not suffer. The authority of the traditional chiefs was weakened as that of the *capitoes* was enhanced.

Apricots laid out in flat baskets are drying in the Himalayan sun and are sold to the world market.

The point of no return was reached when significant numbers of Mundurucú abandoned the villages for permanent settlements near their individual territories of trees. These new settlements lacked the unity, the sense of community, of former village life. Nuclear families held and carefully maintained property in the interest of productivity.

With the discovery of gold, many Mundurucú young men have turned to panning for gold in rivers. The required equipment is simple, and gold is easier to transport and trade than rubber. Because gold can be sold for cash, which is then used for purchases, trading relationships are no longer so important. Cash is now used to buy transistor radios, tape recorders, watches, bicycles, and new kinds of clothing, in addition to firearms, metal pots, and tools. With money as a medium of exchange, the traditional emphasis on reciprocity has declined. Even food may now be sold to fellow Mundurucú, a practice that would have been unthinkable in the 1950s.[81]

Supplementary Cash Crops   A third way commercialization occurs is when people cultivating the soil produce a surplus above their subsistence requirements, which is then sold for cash. In many cases, this cash income must be used to pay rent or taxes. Under these circumstances, commercialization may be said to be associated with the formation of a peasantry.

What changes does the development of a peasantry entail? In some respects, there is little disturbance of the cultivator's (now peasant's) former way of life. The peasant still has to produce enough food to meet family needs, to replace what has been consumed, to cover a few ceremonial obligations (e.g., the marriage of a child, village festivals, and funerals). But in other respects, the peasant's situation is radically altered. For, in addition to the traditional obligations—indeed, often in conflict with them—the peasant now has to produce extra crops to meet the requirements of a group of outsiders—landlords or officials of the state. These outsiders expect to be paid rent or taxes in produce or currency, and they are able to enforce their expectations because they control the military and the police.

Introduction of Commercial and Industrial Agriculture   Commercialization can come about through the introduction of commercial agriculture, cultivation for sale rather than personal consumption. The system of agriculture may come to be industrialized. In other words, some of the production processes, such as plowing, weeding, irrigation, and harvesting, can be done by machine. Commercial agriculture is, in fact, often as mechanized as any manufacturing industry. Land is worked for the maximum return it will yield, and labor is hired and fired just as impersonally as in other industries.

The introduction of commercial agriculture brings several important social consequences. Gradually, a class polarization develops. Farmers and landlords become increasingly separated from laborers and tenants, just as the employer in town becomes socially separated from the employees. Gradually, too, manufactured items of all sorts are introduced into rural areas.

Laborers migrate to urban centers in search of employment, often meeting even less sympathetic conditions there than exist in the country.

The changeover to commercial agriculture may result in an improved standard of living in the short and long run. But sometimes the switch is followed by a decline in the standard of living if the market price for the commercial crop declines. For example, the changeover of the farmer-herders of the arid *sertão* region of northeastern Brazil after 1940 to the production of sisal (a plant whose fibers can be made into twine and rope) seemed to be a move that could provide a more secure living in their arid environment. But when the world price for sisal dropped and the wages of sisal workers declined, many workers were forced to curtail the caloric intake of their children. The poorer people were obliged to save their now more limited food supplies for the money earners, at the expense of the children.[82]

Commercialization can start in various ways: People can begin to sell and buy because they begin to work near home or away for wages, or because they begin to sell nonagricultural products, surplus food, or **cash crops** (crops grown deliberately for sale). One type of commercialization does not exclude another; all types can occur in any society. However commercialization begins, it seems to have predictable effects on traditional economics. The ethic of generalized reciprocity declines, particularly with respect to giving away money. (Perhaps because it is nonperishable and hideable, money seems more likely than other goods to be kept for one's immediate family rather than shared with others.) Property rights become individualized rather than collective when people begin to buy and sell. Even in societies that were previously egalitarian, commercialization usually results in more unequal access to resources and hence a greater degree of social stratification.

✓●—[Study and **Review** on **myanthrolab.com**

Summary

1. All societies have economic systems, whether or not these involve the use of money. All societies have customs specifying access to natural resources; customary ways of transforming or converting those resources, through labor, into necessities and other desired goods and services; and customs for distributing and perhaps exchanging goods and services.

2. Foraging—hunting, gathering, and fishing—depends on wild plants and animals and is the oldest human food-getting technology. Today, only a small number of societies depend largely on foraging and they tend to inhabit marginal environments.

3. Foragers tend to be nomadic or seminomadic, have low population density, small bands or communities, limited personal possessions, little recognition of individuals' land rights, division of labor along age and gender lines, and no class differences.

4. Beginning about 10,000 years ago, certain peoples in widely separated geographic locations began to make the revolutionary changeover to food production—the cultivation and raising of plants and animals.

5. Horticulturalists farm with relatively simple tools and methods and do not cultivate fields permanently. They generally have larger, more densely populated communities than can be fed by foraging. Their way of life is generally sedentary, although communities may move after some years to farm a new series of plots.

6. Intensive agriculture is characterized by techniques such as fertilization and irrigation that allow fields to be cultivated permanently. In contrast with horticultural societies, intensive agriculturalists are more likely to have towns and cities, a high degree of craft specialization, large differences in wealth and power, and more complex political organization. They are also more likely to face food shortages. In the modern world, intensive agriculture is increasingly mechanized and geared to production for a market.

7. Pastoralism is a subsistence technology involving principally the raising of large herds of animals. It is generally found in low-rainfall areas. Pastoralists tend to be nomadic, to have small communities consisting of related families, and to depend significantly on trade because they do not produce items (including certain types of food) they need.

8. Anthropologists generally agree that the physical environment normally exercises a restraining rather than a determining influence on how people in an area get their food; technology as well as social and political factors may be more important.

9. We see the first evidence of a changeover to food production in the Near East about 8000 B.C. Most archaeologists think that certain conditions must have pushed people to switch from collecting to producing food. Some possible causal factors include (1) population growth in regions of bountiful wild resources, which may have pushed people to move to marginal areas where they tried to reproduce their former abundance; (2) global population growth; and (3) the emergence of hotter and drier summers and colder winters.

10. Individual or private ownership of land—including the right to use its resources and the right to sell or otherwise dispose of them—is common among intensive agriculturalists and is generally lacking amongst foragers, horticulturalists, and pastoralists.

11. Resources are transformed or converted through labor into food, tools, and other goods. Production systems vary from domestic (family and kin), tributary, to industrial and post-industrial systems. More complex societies may have various forms of forced labor.

12. Division of labor by gender is universal.

13. Goods and services are distributed in all societies by systems that can be classified under three types: reciprocity, redistribution, and market or commercial exchange.

14. Redistribution becomes an important mechanism of distribution only in societies with political hierarchies.

15. Market or commercial exchange usually involves an all-purpose medium of exchange—money. Most societies today are at least partly commercialized; the world is becoming a single market system.

16. One of the principal changes resulting from the expansion of Western culture is the increasing dependence of much of the world on commercial exchange.

17. Subsistence economies transition to more commercialization in the following ways: (1) members of the community travel far to engage in migratory work; (2) greater dependence on trading; (3) producing surpluses to sell (in many instances, this cash income must be used to pay rent or taxes; under such circumstances, commercialization may be said to be associated with the formation of a peasantry); and (4) the introduction of commercial agriculture, in which all the cultivated commodities are produced for sale rather than for personal consumption.

Glossary Terms

balanced reciprocity (p. 268)
cash crops (p. 273)
commercialization (p. 255)
corvée (p. 264)
extensive (shifting)
   cultivation (p. 252)
food production (p. 251)
foraging (p. 248)

generalized
   reciprocity (p. 266)
general-purpose
   money (p. 269)
horticulture (p. 252)
hunter-gatherers (p. 248)
intensive agriculture (p. 253)

market or commercial
   exchange (p. 269)
pastoralism (p. 256)
peasants (p. 270)
reciprocity (p. 266)
redistribution (p. 268)
slash-and-burn (p. 252)

Critical Questions

1. Why might meat be valued more than plant foods in many societies?

2. Why might foragers be less likely than intensive agriculturalists to suffer from food shortages?

3. What are the possible effects of a postindustrial economy in which a large proportion of the population has inexpensive access to computers and information?

4. Do you expect any appreciable change in the amount of resources privately owned in the future? State your reasons.

5. We tend to emphasize the negative consequences of the worldwide trend toward commercialization. Have there been any beneficial consequences?

Read the Original Source on myanthrolab.com

Read the chapter by Burton Pasternak, "Han: Pastoralists and Farmers on a Chinese Frontier," on MyAnthroLab and answer the following questions.

1. The Han Chinese traditionally depended on intensive agriculture. The Mongols traditionally depended on pastoralism. What happened to the Han when they moved beyond the Great Wall to a grassland environment?

2. How has the change to more pastoralism affected marriage and family among the Han?

3. How have the Mongols changed?

12 Social Stratification: Class, Ethnicity, and Racism

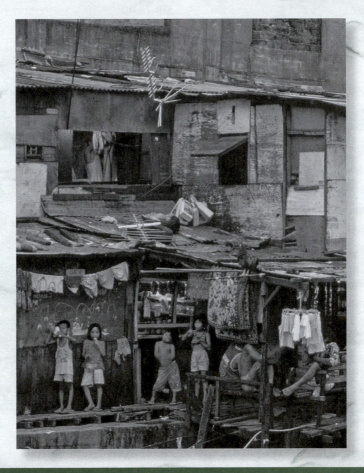

((•─[Listen to the **Chapter Audio** on **myanthrolab.com**   ▢•─[Read on **myanthrolab.com**

A long-enduring value in the United States is the belief that "all men are created equal." These famous words from the American Declaration of Independence do not mean that all people are equal in wealth or status but rather that all (including women nowadays) are supposed to be equal before the law. Equality before the law is the ideal. But the ideal is not always the actuality. Some people have advantages in legal treatment, and they generally also tend to have advantages of other kinds, including economic advantages. Without exception, recent and modern industrial and postindustrial societies such as our own are *socially stratified*—that is, they contain social groups such as families, classes, or ethnic groups that have unequal access to important advantages such as economic resources, power, and prestige.

Hasn't such inequality always existed? Anthropologists, based on firsthand observations of recent societies, would say not. To be sure, even the simplest societies (in the technological sense) have some differences in advantages based on age, ability, or gender—adults have higher status than children, the skilled more than the unskilled, men more than women (we discuss this topic in the chapter on sex and gender). But anthropologists would argue that *egalitarian* societies exist where *social groups* (e.g., families) have more or less the same access to rights or advantages. As we noted in the last chapter, the economic systems of many food collectors and horticulturalists promote equal access to economic resources for all families in the community. Moreover, such societies also tend to emphasize the sharing of food and other goods, which tends to equalize any small inequalities in resources between families. Until about 10,000 years ago, all human societies depended on food they hunted, gathered, and/or fished. And so we might expect that egalitarianism characterized most of human history. That is indeed what archaeologists suggest. Substantial inequality generally appears only with permanent communities, centralized political systems, and intensive agriculture, which are cultural features that began to appear in the world only in the last 10,000 years. Before that time, then, most societies were probably egalitarian. In the world today, egalitarian societies have all but disappeared because of two processes: the global spread of commercial or market exchange and the voluntary or involuntary incorporation of many diverse people into large, centralized political systems. In modern societies, some groups have more advantages than others. These groups may include *ethnic* groups. That is, ethnic diversity is almost always associated with differential access to advantages. When ethnic diversity is also associated with differences in physical features such as skin color, the social stratification may involve *racism,* the belief that some "racial" groups are inferior.

Systems of social stratification are strongly linked to the customary ways in which economic resources are allocated, distributed, and converted through labor into goods and services. So we would not expect much inequality if all people had relatively equal access to economic resources. But stratification cannot be understood solely in terms of economic resources; there are other benefits such as prestige and power that may be unequally distributed. We first examine how societies vary in their systems of stratification. Then we turn to possible explanations of why they vary.

Variation in Degree of Social Inequality

Societies vary in the extent to which social groups, as well as individuals, have unequal access to advantages. In this chapter, we are concerned with differential or unequal access to three types of advantages: (1) wealth or economic resources, (2) power, and (3) prestige. **Economic resources** are things that have value in a culture; they include land, tools and other technology, goods, and money. **Power**, a second and usually related advantage, is the ability to make others do what they do not want to do; power is influence based on the threat of force. When groups in a society have rules or customs that give them unequal access to wealth or resources, they generally also have unequal access to power. So, for example, when we speak of a "company town" in the United States, we are referring to the fact that the company that employs most of the residents of the town usually has considerable control over them. Finally, there is the advantage of **prestige**. When we speak of prestige, we mean that someone or some group is accorded particular respect or honor. Even if it is true that there is always unequal access by individuals to prestige (because of differences in age, gender, or ability), some societies in the ethnographic record have no social groups with unequal access to prestige.

Thus, anthropologists conventionally distinguish three types of society in terms of the degree to which different social groups have unequal access to advantages: *egalitarian, rank,* and *class societies* (see Table 12.1). Some societies in the ethnographic record do not fit easily into any of these three types; as with any classification scheme, some cases seem to straddle the line between types.[1] **Egalitarian societies** contain no social groups with greater or lesser access to economic resources, power, or prestige. **Rank societies** do not have very unequal access to economic resources or to power, but they do contain social groups with unequal access to prestige. Rank societies, then, are partly stratified. **Class societies** have unequal access to all three advantages—economic resources, power, and prestige.

Egalitarian Societies

Egalitarian societies can be found not only among foragers such as the San, Mbuti, Australian aborigines, Inuit, and Aché, but also among horticulturalists such as the Yanomamö and pastoralists such as the Saami. An important point to keep in mind is that egalitarian does not mean that all people within such societies are the same. There will always be differences among individuals in age and gender and in such abilities or traits as hunting skill, perception, health, creativity, physical prowess, attractiveness, and intelligence. According to Morton Fried, egalitarian means that, within a given society, "there are as many positions of prestige in any given age/sex grade as there are persons capable of filling them."[2] For instance, if a person can achieve high status by fashioning fine spears, and if many people in the society fashion such spears, then many acquire high status as spear makers. If high status is also acquired by carving bones into artifacts, and if only three people are considered expert carvers of bones, then only those three achieve high status as carvers. But the next generation might produce eight spear makers and 20 carvers. In an egalitarian society, the number of prestigious positions is adjusted to fit the number of qualified candidates. We would say, therefore, that such a society is not socially stratified.

TABLE 12.1 Stratification in Three Types of Societies

Some Social Groups Have Greater Access To:				
Type of Society	Economic Resources	Power	Prestige	Examples
Egalitarian	No	No	No	San, Mbuti, Australian aborigines, Inuit, Aché, Yanomamö
Rank	No	No	Yes	Samoans, Tahiti, Trobriand Islanders, Ifaluk
Class/caste	Yes	Yes	Yes	United States, Canada, Greece, India, Inca

There are, of course, differences in position and prestige arising out of differences in ability. Even in an egalitarian society, differential prestige exists. But, although some people may be better hunters or more skilled artists than others, there is still *equal access* to status positions for people of the same ability. Any prestige gained by achieving high status as a great hunter, for instance, is neither transferable nor inheritable. Because a man is a great hunter, it is not assumed that his sons are also great hunters. There also may be individuals with more influence, but it cannot be inherited, and there are no groups with appreciably more influence over time. An egalitarian society keeps inequality at a minimal level.

Any differences in prestige that do exist are not related to economic differences. Egalitarian groups depend heavily on *sharing*, which ensures equal access to economic resources despite differences in acquired prestige. For instance, in some egalitarian communities, some members achieve higher status through hunting. But even before the hunt begins, how the animal will be divided and distributed among the members of the band has already been decided according to custom. The culture works to separate the status that members achieve—recognition as great hunters—from actual possession of the wealth, which in this case would be the slain animal.

Just as egalitarian societies do not have social groups with unequal access to economic resources, they also do not have social groups with unequal access to power. As we will see later in the chapter on political life, unequal access to power by social groups seems to occur only in state societies, which have full-time political officials and marked differences in wealth. Egalitarian societies use a number of customs to keep leaders from dominating others. Criticism and ridicule can be very effective. The Mbuti of central Africa shout down an overassertive leader. When a Hadza man (in Tanzania) tried to get people to work for him, other Hadza made fun of him. Disobedience is another strategy. If a leader tries to command, people just ignore the command. In extreme cases, a particularly domineering leader may be killed by community agreement; this behavior was reported among the San and the Hadza. Finally, particularly among more nomadic groups, people may just move away from a leader they don't like. The active attempts to put down upstarts in many egalitarian societies prompts Christopher Boehm to suggest that dominance comes naturally to humans. Egalitarian societies work hard to reverse that tendency.[3] The Mbuti provide an example of a society almost totally equal: "Neither in ritual, hunting, kinship nor band relations do they exhibit any discernible inequalities of rank

In egalitarian societies, such as among the Mbuti hunter-gatherers, houses tend to look the same.

or advantage."[4] Their hunting bands have no leaders, and recognition of the achievement of one person is not accompanied by privilege of any sort. Economic resources such as food are communally shared, and even tools and weapons are frequently passed from person to person. Only within the family are rights and privileges differentiated.

Rank Societies

Most societies with social *ranking* practice agriculture or herding, but not all agricultural or pastoral societies are ranked. Ranking is characterized by social groups with unequal access to prestige or status but *not* significantly unequal access to economic resources or power. Unequal access to prestige is often reflected in the position of chief, a rank that only some members of a specified group in the society can achieve.

Unusual among rank societies were the 19th-century Native Americans who lived along the northwestern coast of the United States and the southwestern coast of Canada. An example were the Nimpkish, a Kwakiutl group.[5] These societies were unusual because their economy was based on food-collecting. But huge catches of salmon—which were preserved for year-round consumption—enabled them to support fairly large and permanent villages. These societies were similar to food-producing societies in many ways, not just in their development of social ranking. Still, the principal means of proving one's high status was to give away wealth. The tribal chiefs celebrated solemn rites by grand feasts called **potlatches,** at which they gave gifts to every guest.[6]

In rank societies, the position of chief is at least partly hereditary. The criterion of superior rank in some Polynesian societies, for example, was genealogical. Usually the eldest son succeeded to the position of chief, and different kinship groups were differentially ranked according to their genealogical distance from the chiefly line. In rank societies, chiefs are often treated with deference by people of lower rank. For example, among the Trobriand Islanders of Melanesia, people of lower rank must keep their heads lower than a person of higher rank. So, when a chief is standing, commoners must bend low. When commoners have to walk past a chief who happens to be sitting, he may rise and they will bend. If the chief chooses to remain seated, they must crawl.[7]

Although there is no question that chiefs in a rank society enjoy special prestige, there is some controversy over whether they really do not also have material advantages. Chiefs may sometimes look as if they are substantially richer than commoners, for they may receive many gifts and have larger storehouses. In some instances, the chief may even be called the "owner" of the land. However, Marshall Sahlins maintains that the chief's storehouses only house temporary accumulations for feasts or other redistributions. And although the chief may be designated the "owner" of the land, others have the right to use the land. Furthermore, Sahlins suggests that the chief in a rank society lacks power because he usually cannot make people give him gifts or force them to work on communal projects. Often the chief can encourage production only by working furiously on his own cultivation.[8]

This picture of economic equality in rank societies is beginning to be questioned. Laura Betzig studied patterns of food-sharing and labor on Ifaluk, a small atoll in the Western Carolines.[9] Chiefly status is inherited geneaologically in the female line, although most chiefs are male. (In the chapter on sex and gender, we discuss why political leaders are usually male, even in societies structured around women.) As in other chiefly societies, Ifaluk chiefs are accorded deference. For example, during collective meals prepared by all the island women, chiefs were served first and were bowed to. The Ifaluk chiefs are said to control the fishing areas. Were the catches equitably distributed? Betzig measured the amount of fish each household got. All the

In societies with rank and class, deference is usually shown to political leaders. Among the Nso of northwestern Cameroon, people bow to the Fon or cheif of a village, shown here in his courtyard.

commoners received an equal share, but the chiefs got extra fish; their households got twice as much per person as other households. Did the chiefs give away more later?

Theoretically, generosity is supposed to even things out, but Betzig found that the gifts from chiefs to other households did not equal the amount the chiefs received from others. Furthermore, although everyone gave to the chiefs, the chiefs gave mostly to their close relatives. On Ifaluk, the chiefs did not work harder than others; in fact, they worked less. Is this true in other societies conventionally considered to be rank societies? We do not know. However, we need to keep in mind that the chiefs in Ifaluk were not noticeably better off either. If they lived in palaces with servants, had elaborate meals, or were dressed in fine clothes and jewelry, we would not need measures of food received or a special study to see if the chiefs had greater access to economic resources because their wealth would be obvious. But rank societies may not have had as much economic equality as we used to think.

Class Societies

In class societies, as in rank societies, there is unequal access to prestige. But, unlike rank societies, class societies are characterized by groups of people that have substantially greater or lesser access to economic resources and power. That is, not every social group has the same opportunity to obtain land, animals, money, or other economic benefits or the same opportunity to exercise power that other groups have. Fully stratified or class societies range from somewhat open to virtually closed class, or *caste,* systems.

Open Class Systems

A **class** is a category of people who all have about the same opportunity to obtain economic resources, power, and prestige. Different classes have differing opportunities. We call class

People of the same social class tend to socialize together, where they live, where they vacation, or through shared activities. Debutantes and their escorts are presented at the Krewe of Rex ball during Mardi Gras in New Orleans.

systems *open* if there is some possibility of moving from one class to another. Although class status is not fully determined at birth in open class societies, there is a high probability that most people will stay close to the class into which they were born and will marry within that class. Classes tend to perpetuate themselves through the inheritance of wealth. John Brittain suggested that, in the United States, the transfer of money through bequests accounts for much of the wealth of the next generation. As we might expect, the importance of inheritance seems to increase at higher levels of wealth. That is, the wealth of richer people comes more from inheritance than does the wealth of not-so-rich people.[10]

Other mechanisms of class perpetuation may be more subtle, but they are still powerful. In the United States, many institutions make it possible for an upper-class person to have little contact with other classes. Private day and boarding schools put upper-class children in close contact mostly with others of their class. Attending these schools makes it more likely they will get into universities with higher prestige. Debutante balls and exclusive private parties ensure that young people meet the "right people." Country clubs, exclusive city clubs, and service in particular charities continue the process of limited association. People of the same class also tend to live in the same neighborhoods. Before 1948, explicit restrictions kept certain groups out of particular neighborhoods, but after the U.S. Supreme Court ruled such discrimination unconstitutional, more subtle methods were developed. For instance, zoning restrictions may prohibit multiple-family dwellings in a town or neighborhood and lots below a certain acreage.[11]

Identification with a social class begins early in life. In addition to differences in occupation, wealth, and prestige, social classes vary in many other ways, including religious affiliation, closeness to kin, ideas about childrearing, job satisfaction, leisure-time activities, style of clothes and furniture, and (as noted in the chapter on language and communication) even in styles of speech.[12] People from each class tend to be more comfortable with those from the same class; they talk similarly and are more likely to have similar interests and tastes.

Degree of Openness Some class systems are more open than others; that is, it is easier in some societies to move from one class position to another. Social scientists typically compare the class of people with the class of their parent or parents to measure the degree of mobility. Although most people aspire to move up, mobility also includes moving down. Obtaining more education, particularly a university education, is one of the most effective ways to move upward in contemporary societies. For example, in the United States, individuals with a college bachelor's degree average 75 percent more income than those with only a high school diploma. And individuals with professional degrees earn on average 119 percent more than those with a bachelor's degree.[13] In many countries, educational attainment predicts one's social class better than parents' occupation does.[14]

How do the United States and Canada compare with other countries in degree of class mobility? Canada, Finland, and Sweden have more mobility than the United States and Britain. Mexico and Peru have less mobility than the United States and Brazil, and Colombia considerably less.[15]

Class openness also varies over time. In "Paradise," Ontario, Barrett found that the rigid stratification system of the 1950s opened up considerably as new people moved into the community. No one disputed who belonged to the elite in the past. They were of British background, lived in the largest houses, had new cars, and vacationed in Florida. Moreover, they controlled all the leadership positions in the town. By the 1980s, though, the leaders came mostly from the middle and working classes.[16]

Degree of Inequality Degree of class mobility, however, is not the same as degree of economic inequality. For example, Japan, Italy, and Germany have less mobility than the United States, but less inequality. Degree of inequality can vary considerably over time. In the United States, inequality has fluctuated considerably from the 1900s to the present. The greatest inequality was just before the 1929 stock market crash, when the top 1 percent had 42.6 percent of all the wealth. The least inequality was in the mid-1970s, after the stock market declined by 42 percent. Then the top 1 percent controlled 17.6 percent of the wealth.

Change over time in the degree of inequality sometimes appears to have economic causes; for example, the 1929 crash made the wealthy less wealthy. But some of the change over time is due to shifts in public policy. During the New Deal of the 1930s, tax changes and work programs shifted more income to ordinary people; in the 1980s, tax cuts for the wealthy helped the rich get richer. In the 1990s, the rich continued to get richer and the poor got poorer.[17] By 2006, inequality was more concentrated at the top than since the 1929 crash. Only since the severe recession between 2007 and 2009 have the rich gotten somewhat less rich.[18] One way of calculating the disparity between rich and poor is to use the ratio of income held by the top fifth of the households divided by the income held by the bottom fifth. Comparatively speaking, the United States has more inequality than any of the countries in western Europe, with a ratio of 8.5 to 1 (see Figure 12.1). That is, the top 20 percent of U.S. households controls 8.5 times the wealth controlled by the bottom 20

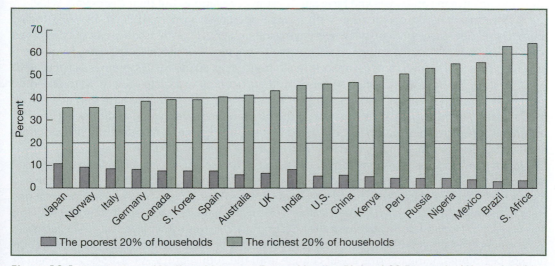

Figure 12.1 Proportion of National Income Earned by the Richest 20 Percent of Households Compared with the Poorest 20 Percent: Selected Country Comparisons

Source: These data are abstracted from World Bank 2004, 60–62.

percent. Norway, on the other hand, has a ratio of about 4 to 1. And Germany has a ratio of about 4.3 to 1. The degree of inequality in the United States exceeds that of India, with a ratio of about 4.7 to 1. Brazil is one of the most unequal countries, with ratios of 32 to 1.

Recognition of Class

Societies that have open class systems vary in the degree to which members of the society recognize that there are classes, albeit somewhat open classes. The United States is unusual in that, despite objective evidence of multiple social classes, many people deny their existence. The ideology that hard work and strong character can transform anyone into a success appears to be so powerful that it masks the realities of social inequality.[19] When we were growing up, we were told that "Anyone can be President of the United States." As "proof," people pointed to a few individuals who rose from humble beginnings. But consider the odds. How many presidents have come from poor families? How many were not European in background? How many were not Protestant? (And, as we discuss in the chapter on sex and gender, how many were not male?) So far, almost all of the presidents of the United States have been mainly European in ancestry, all but one have been Protestant, and all have been male. And only a handful came from humble beginnings. The paradox of an open class system is that, to move up in the social ladder, people seem to have to believe that it is possible to do so. However, it is one thing to believe in mobility; it is another thing to deny the existence of classes. Why might people need to deny that classes exist?

Caste Systems

Some societies have classes (called castes) that are virtually closed. A **caste** is a ranked group in which membership is determined at birth, and marriage is restricted to members of one's own caste. The only way you can belong is by being born into the group; and because you cannot marry outside the group, your children cannot acquire another caste status either. In India, for example, there are several thousand hereditary castes. Although the precise ranking of these thousands of groups is not clear, there appear to be four main levels of hierarchy. The castes in India are often thought to be associated with different occupations, but that is not quite true. Most Indians live in rural areas and have agricultural occupations, but their castes vary widely.[20]

Castes may exist in conjunction with a more open class system. Indeed, in India today, members of a low caste who can get wage-paying jobs, chiefly those in urban areas, may improve their social standing in the same ways available to people in other class societies. In general, however, they still cannot marry someone in a higher caste, so the caste system is perpetuated.

Questions basic to all stratified societies, and particularly to a caste society, were posed by John Ruskin, a 19th-century British essayist: "Which of us . . . is to do the hard and dirty work for the rest—and for what pay? Who is to do the pleasant and clean work, and for what pay?"[21] In India, those questions have been answered by the caste system, which mainly dictates how goods and services are exchanged, particularly in rural areas.[22]

Japan also had a caste group within a class society. Now called *burakumin* (instead of the pejorative *eta*), this group traditionally had occupations that were considered unclean.[23] Comparable to India's Untouchables, they were a hereditary, endogamous (in-marrying) group. Their occupations were traditionally those of farm laborer, leatherworker, and basket weaver; their standard of living was very low. The burakumin are physically indistinguishable from other Japanese.[24] The Japanese government officially abolished discrimination against the burakumin in 1871, but the burakumin did not begin organizing to bring about change until the 20th century. As of 1995, 73 percent of burakumin marriages were with non-burakumin. In public opinion polls, two-thirds of burakumin now said that they had not encountered discrimination. However, most burakumin still live in segregated neighborhoods where unemployment, crime, and alcoholism rates are high.[25]

In a considerable number of sub-Saharan African societies, some occupational specialties are only performed by certain castes. The specialties usually involve metalworking, pottery, woodworking, leatherworking, playing musical instruments, and praise-singing. In some cases, the caste consists of people who traditionally hunted and gathered. These castes usually constituted only a small minority of the society's population and were not the lowest ranking groups in society. Only slaves had a lower rank. The caste vocational distinctions have weakened in recent times as people have become more educated.[26]

Caste is somewhat less important in India, but has not disappeared. In Mumbai, the washers of the Dhobi caste process laundry.

In Rwanda, long before the ethnic division arose between the Hutu and Tutsi (see discussion later in the ethnicity section), the Twa, who comprised less than 1 percent of the population, were subject to serious discrimination. Their bodies were viewed as dangerous and polluting and they were avoided whenever possible. For example, if a Twa were present while others were eating or drinking, separate utensils were reserved only for Twa. The Twa traditional occupations were foraging, making pottery, entertaining, and serving as torturers or executioners for the Rwandan king. Mutton was considered a Twa food and other Rwandans would not eat mutton.[27]

In the United States, African Americans used to have more of a castelike status determined partly by the inherited characteristic of skin color. Until recently, some states had laws prohibiting an African American from marrying a European American. When interethnic marriage did occur, children of the union were often regarded as having lower status than European American children, even though they may have had blond hair and light skin. In the South, where treatment of African Americans as a caste was most apparent, European Americans refused to eat with African Americans or sit next to them at lunch counters, on buses, and in schools. Separate drinking fountains and toilets reinforced the idea of ritual uncleanness. The economic advantages and gains in prestige that European Americans enjoyed are well documented.[28] In the following sections on slavery, racism, and inequality, we discuss the social status of African Americans in more detail.

Slavery

Slavery has existed in some form in almost every part of the world at one time or another, in simpler as well as in more complex societies. Slaves are often obtained from other cultures directly: kidnapped, captured in war, or given as tribute. Or they may be obtained indirectly as payment in barter or trade. Slaves sometimes come from the same culture; one became a slave as payment of a debt, as a punishment for a crime, or even as a chosen alternative to poverty. Slave societies vary in the degree to which it is possible to become freed from slavery.[29] Sometimes the slavery system has been a closed class, or caste, system, sometimes a relatively open class system. In different slave-owning societies, slaves have had different, but always some, legal rights.[30] Because of the variability of slavery systems, the meaning of a slave is hard to define, but a common definition is that **slaves** are people who do not own their own labor, and as such they represent a class.

In the United States, slavery originated as a means of obtaining cheap labor, but the slaves soon came to be regarded as deserving of their low status because of their alleged inherent inferiority. Because the slaves were from Africa and were dark-skinned, some European Americans justified slavery and the belief in "black" people's inferiority by quoting scripture out of context ("They shall be hewers of wood and drawers of water"). Slaves could not marry or make any other contracts, nor could they own property. In addition, their children were also slaves, and the master had sexual rights over the female slaves. Because the status of slavery was determined by birth in the United States, slaves constituted a caste. During the days of slavery, therefore, the United States had both a caste and a class system. It is widely assumed that slavery occurred only in the southern United States, but although not on as large a scale, slavery existed in the northern states as well. New Jersey was the last northern state to legally give up slavery around the time of the U.S. Civil War.[31]

Among the Nupe, a society in central Nigeria, slavery was of quite another type.[32] The methods of obtaining slaves—as part of the booty of warfare and, later, by purchase—were similar to those of Europeans, but the position of the slaves was very different. Mistreatment was rare. Male slaves were given the same opportunities to earn money as other dependent males in the household—younger brothers, sons, or other relatives. A slave might be given a garden plot of his own to cultivate, or he might be given a commission if his master was a craftsman or a tradesman. Slaves could acquire property, wealth, and even slaves of their own. But all of a slave's belongings went to the master at the slave's death.

Manumission—the granting of freedom to slaves—was built into the Nupe system. If a male slave could afford the marriage payment for a free woman, the children of the resulting marriage were free; the man himself, however, remained a slave. Marriage and concubinage were the easiest ways out of bondage for a slave woman. Once she had produced a child by her master, both she and the child had free status. The woman, however, was only figuratively free; if a concubine, she had to remain in that role. As might be expected, the family trees of the nobility and the wealthy were liberally grafted with branches descended from slave concubines.

The most fortunate slaves among the Nupe were the house slaves. They could rise to positions of power in the household as overseers and bailiffs, charged with law enforcement and judicial duties. (Recall the Old Testament story of Joseph, who was sold into slavery by his brothers. Joseph became a household slave of the pharaoh and rose to the position of second in the kingdom because he devised an ingenious system of taxation.) There was even a titled group of Nupe slaves, the Order of Court Slaves, who were trusted officers of the king and members of an elite. Slave status in general, though, placed one at the bottom of the social ladder. In the Nupe system, few slaves, mainly princes from their own societies, ever achieved membership in the titled group. Nupe slavery was abolished at the beginning of the 20th century.

As for why slavery may have developed in the first place, cross-cultural research is as yet inconclusive. We do know, however, that slavery is not an inevitable stage in economic development, contrary to what some have assumed. In other words, slavery is not found mainly in certain economies, such as those dependent on intensive agriculture. Unlike the United States until the Civil War, many societies with intensive agriculture did not develop any variety of slavery. Also, the theory that slavery develops where available resources are plentiful but labor is scarce is not supported by the cross-cultural evidence. All we can say definitely is that slavery does not occur in developed or industrial economies; either it disappears or it was never present in them.[33]

Racism and Inequality

Racism is the belief that some "races" are inferior to others. In a society composed of people with noticeably different physical features, such as differences in skin color, racism is almost invariably associated with social stratification. Those "races" considered inferior make up a larger proportion of the lower social classes or castes. Even in more open class systems, where individuals from all backgrounds can achieve higher status positions, individuals from groups deemed inferior may be subject to discrimination in housing or may be more likely to be searched or stopped by the police.

In some societies, such as the United States, the idea that humans are divided into "races" is taken so much for granted that people are asked for their "race" on the census. Most Americans probably assume that the classification of people into categories such as "white" or "black" reflects important biological categories. But that is not so. We discussed the inapplicability of the "race" concept to humans more thoroughly in the human variation chapter, which is why we put "race" in quotes to reflect the fact that most anthropologists are now persuaded that the biological concept of "race" is not scientifically useful when applied to humans. However, "race" is a social concept that is important as a classifier in some societies.

Race as a Social Category

Racial classifications are social categories to which individuals are assigned, by themselves and others, to separate "our" group from others. We have seen that people tend to be *ethnocentric,* to view their culture as better than other cultures. Racial classifications may reflect the same tendency to divide "us" from "them," except that the divisions are supposedly based on biological differences.[34] The "them" are almost always viewed as inferior to "us."

We know that racial classifications have often been, and still are, used by certain groups to justify discrimination, exploitation, or genocide. The "Aryan race" was supposed to be the group

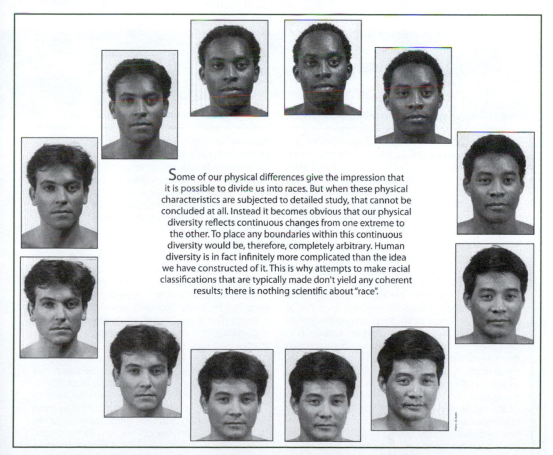

Some of our physical differences give the impression that it is possible to divide us into races. But when these physical characteristics are subjected to detailed study, that cannot be concluded at all. Instead it becomes obvious that our physical diversity reflects continuous changes from one extreme to the other. To place any boundaries within this continuous diversity would be, therefore, completely arbitrary. Human diversity is in fact infinitely more complicated than the idea we have constructed of it. This is why attempts to make racial classifications that are typically made don't yield any coherent results; there is nothing scientific about "race".

It is an illusion that there are races. The diversity of human beings is so great and so complicated that it is impossible to classify 5.8 billion individuals into discrete "races."

of blond-haired, blue-eyed, white-skinned people whom Adolf Hitler wanted to dominate the world, to which end he and others attempted to destroy as many members of the Jewish "race" as they could. (An estimated 6 million Jews and others were murdered in what is now called the Holocaust.[35]) But who were the Aryans? Technically, Aryans are any people, including the German-speaking Jews in Hitler's Germany, who speak one of the Indo-European languages. The Indo-European languages include such disparate modern tongues as Greek, Spanish, Hindi, Polish, French, Icelandic, German, Gaelic, and English. And many Aryans speaking these languages have neither blond hair nor blue eyes. Similarly, all kinds of people may be Jews, whether or not they descend from the ancient Near Eastern population that spoke the Hebrew language. There are light-skinned Danish Jews and darker Jewish Arabs. One of the most orthodox Jewish groups in the United States is based in New York City and is composed entirely of African Americans.

The arbitrary and social basis of most racial classifications becomes apparent when you compare how they differ from one place to another. Consider, for example, what used to be thought about the "races" in South Africa. Under apartheid, which was a system of racial segregation and discrimination, someone with mixed "white" and "black" ancestry was considered "colored." However, when important people of African ancestry (from other countries) would visit South Africa, they were often considered "white." Chinese were considered "Asian"; but the Japanese, who were important economically to South Africa, were considered "white."[36] In some parts of the United States, laws against interracial marriage continued in force through the 1960s. You

---

APPLIED ANTHROPOLOGY • • • • • • • •

Unequal in Death: African Americans Compared with European Americans

Everyone dies of something. Yet, if you consider cardiovascular disease, the leading cause of death in the United States, it turns out that after controlling for the effects of age and gender, African Americans die more often from that disease than European Americans. The same kind of disparity occurs also with almost every other major cause of death—cancer, cirrhosis of the liver, kidney disease, diabetes, injuries, infant mortality, and homicide. Medical anthropologists and health policy researchers want to know why. Without such understanding, it is hard to know how to reduce the disparity.

One reason may be subtle discrimination by the medical profession itself. For example, a European American with chest pain in the United States is more likely than an African American to be given an angiogram, a medical procedure that injects radioactive dye into the heart to look for deficits in blood flow through the coronary arteries that supply blood to the heart. And even if coronary heart disease is detected by an angiogram, an African American is less likely to receive bypass surgery. Thus, the death rate from cardiovascular disease may be higher for African Americans than for European Americans because of unequal medical care. Seeing a patient physically appears to make a difference. When heart specialists reviewed cases to make decisions about subsequent treatment after catheterization, recommendations did not differ by "race" when the doctors did not know the "race" of the patient.

Yet, although some difference in mortality may be due to disparity in medical treatment, this could only be part of the picture. African Americans may be more prone to cardiovascular disease because they are about twice as likely as European Americans to have high rates of hypertension (high blood pressure). But why the disparity in hypertension? Three possible explanations, not mutually exclusive, are discussed in the research literature. The first is a possible difference in genetics. The second is a difference in lifestyle. The third is class difference.

Most of the Africans that came to the Americas were forcibly taken as slaves between the 16th and 19th centuries, largely from West Africa. In one comparative study of hypertension, African Americans had much higher blood pressure than Africans in Nigeria and Cameroon, even in urban areas. People with African ancestry in the Caribbean were in the middle of the range. Lifestyle differences were also vast—the West Africans had

uld be considered a "negro" if you had an eighth or more "negro" ancestry (if one or more of ur eight grandparents were "negro").[37] In some states, an even smaller proportion made you egro." Some refer to this concept as the "one-drop" rule—just a tiny bit of "negro" (now called ack") ancestry was sufficient to determine your "racial" classification.[38] So only a small amount 'negro" ancestry made a person "negro." But a small amount of "white" ancestry did not make erson "white." Biologically speaking, this makes no sense, but socially it was another story.[39]

In much of Latin America and the Caribbean, the reverse rule is the case. A small amount European blood can make you "white." When people from Dominica, Haiti, or Cuba come the United States, they often find that their "race" has changed. They might have been con- ered "white" at home, but they are considered "black" in the United States. In contrast to United States, with a two-part division of "white" and "black," concepts of race in Latin erica are on more of a continuum from light to dark, with important middle positions (such "mestizo"). Wealth makes a difference too—if you are dark-skinned but wealthy, you will d to be considered "whiter."[40]

If people of different "races" are viewed as inferior, they are more likely going to end up on lower rungs of the social ladder in a socially stratified society. Discrimination will keep them of the better-paying or higher-status jobs and in neighborhoods that are poorer. As the box nequal in Death" shows, people of different "races" also suffer from differential access to lth care and have more health problems.

plenty of exercise, were lean, and ate low-fat and low-salt diets. Any possible difference in genes would seem to be insignificant. Jared Diamond has suggested that individuals who could retain salt would have been most likely to survive the terrible conditions of the sailing ships that brought slaves to the New World. Many died from diar- rhea and dehydration (salt-depleting conditions) on those voyages. Retention of salt would have been a genetic advantage then, but disadvan- tageous in places such as the United States with high-salt, high-fat diets. Critics of this theory sug- gest that salt-depleting diseases were not the leading causes of death in the slave voyages; tuberculosis and violence were more frequent causes of death. Furthermore, critics say that the slave ship theory would predict little genetic diver- sity in African American populations with respect to hypertension, but in fact there is great diversity.

Hypertension could be related also to differ- ences in lifestyle and wealth. As we noted in the section on racism and inequality, African Ameri- cans in the United States are disproportionately poorer. Study after study has noted that healthier lifestyle habits are generally correlated with higher positions on the socioeconomic ladder. Moreover,

individuals from higher social positions are more likely to have health insurance and access to care in superior hospitals. But even after correct- ing for factors such as obesity, physical activity, and social class, the health differential persists— African Americans still have a much higher inci- dence of hypertension than European Americans.

William Dressler suggests that stress is another possible cause of higher rates of hypertension. Despite increased economic mobility in recent years, African Americans are still subject to preju- dice and may consequently have more stress even if they have higher income. Stress is related to higher blood pressure. In a color-conscious society, a very dark-skinned individual walking in a wealthy neighborhood at night may be thought not to live there and may be stopped by the police. If Dressler is correct, darker-skinned African Ameri- cans who have objective indicators of higher sta- tus should have much higher blood pressure than would be expected from their relative education, age, body mass, or social class alone. And that seems to be true. Racism may affect health.

Sources: Cooper, Rotimi, and Ward 1999, 56–63; Diamond 1991; Dressler 1993; Geiger 2003; Smedley, Stith, and Nelson 2003, 3.

Ethnicity and Inequality

If "race" is not a scientifically useful category because people cannot be clearly divided into different "racial" categories based on sets of physical traits, then racial classifications such as "black" and "white" in the United States might better be described as *ethnic* classifications. How else can we account for the following facts? Groups that are thought of as "white" now in the United States were earlier thought of as belonging to inferior "races." For example, in the latter half of the 19th century, newspapers would often talk about the new immigrants from Ireland as belonging to the Irish "race." Similarly, before World War II, Jews were thought of as a separate "racial" group, and only became "white" afterward.[41] It is hard to escape the idea that changes in "racial" classification occurred as the Irish, Jews, and other immigrant groups became more accepted by the majority in the United States.[42]

It is apparent that *ethnic groups* and *ethnic identities* emerge as part of a social and political process. The process of defining **ethnicity** usually involves a group of people emphasizing common origins and language, shared history, and selected cultural differences such as a difference in religion. Those doing the defining can be outside or inside the ethnic group. Outsiders and insiders often perceive ethnic groups differently. In a country with one large core majority group, often the majority group doesn't think of itself as an ethnic group. Rather, they consider only the minority groups to have ethnic identities. For example, in the United States, it is not common for the majority to call themselves European Americans, but other groups may be called African Americans, Asian Americans, or Native Americans. The minority groups, on the other hand, may also have different named identities.[43] Asian Americans may identify themselves more specifically as Japanese Americans, Korean Americans, Chinese Americans, or Hmong. The majority population often uses derogatory names to identify people who are different. The majority may also tend to lump people of diverse ethnicities together. Naming a group establishes a boundary between it and other ethnic groups.[44]

Ethnic identity may be manipulated, by insiders and by outsiders, in different situations. A particularly repressive regime that emphasizes nationalism and loyalty to the state may not only suppress the assertiveness of ethnic claims; it may also act to minimize communication among people who might otherwise embrace the same ethnic identity.[45] More democratic regimes may allow more expression of difference and celebrate ethnic difference. However, manipulation of ethnicity does not come just from the top. It may be to the advantage of minority groups to lobby for more equal treatment as a larger entity, such as Asian American, rather than as Japanese, Chinese, Hmong, Filipino, or Korean American. Similarly, even though there are hundreds of Native American groups, originally speaking different languages, there may be political advantages for all if they are treated as Native Americans.

In many multiethnic societies, ethnicity and diversity are things to be proud of and celebrated. Shared ethnic identity often makes people feel comfortable with similar people and gives them a strong sense of belonging. Still, ethnic differences in multiethnic societies are usually associated with inequities in wealth, power, and prestige. In other words, ethnicity is part of the system of *stratification.*

Although some people believe that inequities are deserved, the origins of ethnic stereotypes, prejudice, and discrimination usually follow from historical and political events that give some groups dominance over others. For example, even though there were many early stories of help given by native peoples to the English settlers in the 17th century in the land now known as North America, the English were the invaders, and negative stereotypes about native peoples developed to justify taking their land and their lives. Referring to the negative stereotypes of

Members of minority ethnic groups are more often at the bottom of the socioeconomic "ladder," but not always, as these pictures from the United States illustrate.

Native Americans that developed, J. Milton Yinger said, "One would almost think that it had been the Indian who had invaded Europe, driven back the inhabitants, cut their population to one-third of its original size, unilaterally changed treaties, and brought the dubious glories of firewater and firearms."[46]

Similarly, as we noted in the section on slavery, African slaves were initially acquired as cheap labor, but inhumane treatment of slaves was justified by beliefs about their inferiority. Unfortunately, stereotypes can become self-fulfilling prophesies, especially if those discriminated against come to believe the stereotypes. It is easy to see how this can happen. If there is a widespread belief that a group is inferior, and that group is given inferior schools and little chance for improvement or little chance for a good job, the members of that group may acquire few skills and not try hard. The result is often a vicious cycle.[47]

And yet, the picture is not all bleak. Change has occurred. The ethnic identity a minority group forges can help promote political activism, such as the nonviolent civil rights movement in the United States in the 1960s. That activism, helped by some people in the more advantaged groups, helped break down many of the legal barriers and segregationist practices that reinforced inequality.

The traditional barriers in the United States have mostly been lifted in recent years, but the "color line" has not disappeared. African Americans are found in all social classes, but they remain underrepresented in the wealthiest group and overrepresented at the bottom. Discrimination may be lessened, but it is still not gone. In research done with matched pairs of "whites" and "blacks" applying for jobs or for housing, discrimination is still evident.[48] Thus, African Americans may have to be better than others to get promoted, or it may be assumed that they got ahead just because they were African American and were hired because of affirmative action programs. European Americans often expect African Americans to be "ambassadors," to be called on mainly for knowledge about how to handle situations involving other African Americans. African Americans may work with others, but they usually go home to African American neighborhoods. Or they may live in mixed neighborhoods and experience considerable isolation. Few African Americans can completely avoid the anguish of racism.[49]

The Emergence of Stratification

Anthropologists are not certain why social stratification developed. Nevertheless, they are reasonably sure that higher levels of stratification emerged relatively recently in human history. Archaeological sites dating before about 8,000 years ago do not show extensive evidence of inequality. Houses do not appear to vary much in size or content, and different communities of the same culture are similar in size and otherwise. Signs of inequality appear first in the Near East, about 2,000 years after agriculture emerged in that region. Inequality in burial suggests inequality in life. Particularly telling are unequal child burials. It is unlikely that children could achieve high status by their own achievements. So, when archaeologists find statues and ornaments only in some children's tombs, as at the 7,500-year-old site of Tell es-Sawwan in Iraq,[50] the grave goods suggest that those children belonged to a higher-ranking family or a higher class.

Another indication that stratification is a relatively recent development in human history is the fact that certain cultural features associated with stratification also developed relatively recently. For example, most societies that depend primarily on agriculture or herding have social classes.[51] Agriculture and herding developed within the past 10,000 years, so we may assume that most food collectors in the distant past lacked social classes. Other recently developed cultural features associated with class stratification include fixed settlements, political integration beyond the community level, the use of money as a medium of exchange, and the presence of at least some full-time specialization.[52]

In 1966, comparative sociologist Gerhard Lenski suggested that the trend toward increasing inequality since 8,000 years ago was reversing. He argued that inequalities of power and privilege in industrial societies—measured in terms of the concentration of political power and the distribution of income—are less pronounced than inequalities in complex preindustrial societies. Technology in industrialized societies is so complex, he suggested, that those in power are compelled to delegate some authority to subordinates if the system is to work. In addition, a decline in the birth rate in industrialized societies, coupled with the need for skilled labor, has pushed the average wage of workers far above the subsistence level, resulting in greater equality in the distribution of income. Finally, Lenski also suggested that the spread of the democratic ideology, and particularly its acceptance by elites, has significantly broadened the political power of the lower classes.[53] A few studies have tested and supported Lenski's hypothesis that inequality has decreased with industrialization. In general, nations that are highly industrialized exhibit a lower level of inequality than nations that are only somewhat industrialized.[54] But, as we have seen, even the most industrialized societies may still have an enormous degree of inequality.

Why did social stratification develop in the first place? On the basis of his study of Polynesian societies, Marshall Sahlins suggested that an increase in agricultural productivity results in social stratification.[55] According to Sahlins, the degree of stratification is directly related to the production of a surplus, which is made possible by greater technological efficiency. The higher the level of productivity and the larger the agricultural surplus, the greater the scope and complexity of the distribution system. The status of the chief, who serves as redistributing agent, is enhanced. Sahlins argued that the differentiation between distributor and producer inevitably gives rise to differentiation in other aspects of life:

First, there would be a tendency for the regulator of distribution to exert some authority over production itself—especially over productive activities which necessitate subsidization, such as communal labor or specialist labor. A degree of control of production implies a degree of control over the utilization of resources, or, in other words, some preeminent property rights. In turn, regulation of these economic processes necessitates the exercise of authority in interpersonal affairs; differences in social power emerge.[56]

Sahlins later rejected the idea that a surplus leads to chiefships, postulating instead that the relationship may be the other way around—that is, leaders encourage the development of a surplus so as to enhance their prestige through feasts, potlatches, and other redistributive events.[57] Of course, both trajectories are possible—surpluses may generate stratification, and stratification may generate surpluses; they are not mutually exclusive.

Lenski's theory of the causes of stratification is similar to Sahlins's original idea. Lenski, too, argued that production of a surplus is the stimulus in the development of stratification, but he focused primarily on the conflict that arises over control of that surplus. Lenski concluded that the distribution of the surplus will be determined on the basis of power. Thus, inequalities in power promote unequal access to economic resources and simultaneously give rise to inequalities in privilege and prestige.[58]

The "surplus" theories of Sahlins and Lenski do not really address the question of why the redistributors or leaders will want, or be able, to acquire greater control over resources. After all, the redistributors or leaders in many rank societies do not have greater wealth than others, and custom seems to keep things that way. One suggestion is that, as long as followers have mobility, they can vote with their feet by moving away from leaders they do not like. But when people start to make more permanent "investments" in land or technology (e.g., irrigation systems or weirs for fishing), they are more likely to put up with a leader's aggrandizement in exchange for protection.[59] Another suggestion is that access to economic resources becomes unequal only when there is population pressure on resources in rank or chiefdom societies.[60] Such pressure may be what induces redistributors to try to keep more land and other resources for themselves and their families.

C. K. Meek offered an example of how population pressure in northern Nigeria may have led to economic stratification. At one time, a tribal member could obtain the right to use land by asking permission of the chief and presenting him with a token gift in recognition of his higher status. But, by 1921, the reduction in the amount of available land had led to a system under which applicants offered the chief large payments for scarce land. As a result of these payments, farms came to be regarded as private property, and differential access to such property became institutionalized.[61]

Future research by archaeologists, sociologists, historians, and anthropologists should provide more understanding of the emergence of social stratification in human societies and how and why it may vary in degree.

✔•⌈Study and **Review** on **myanthrolab.com**

Summary

1. Without exception, recent and modern industrial and postindustrial societies such as our own are socially stratified—that is, they contain social groups such as families, classes, or ethnic groups that have unequal access to important advantages, such as economic resources, power, and prestige. Anthropologists, based on firsthand observations, would

say that such inequality has not always existed among the societies they have studied. Although even the simplest societies (in the technological sense) have some differences in advantages based on age, ability, or gender—adults have higher status than children, the skilled more than the unskilled, men more than women—anthropologists would argue that egalitarian societies exist where social groups (e.g., families) have more or less the same access to rights or advantages.

2. The presence or absence of customs or rules that give certain groups unequal access to economic resources, power, and prestige can be used to distinguish three types of societies. In egalitarian societies, social groups do not have unequal access to economic resources, power, or prestige; they are unstratified. In rank societies, social groups do not have very unequal access to economic resources or power, but they do have unequal access to prestige. Rank societies, then, are partially stratified. In class societies, social groups have unequal access to economic resources, power, and prestige. They are more completely stratified than are rank societies.

3. Stratified societies range from somewhat open class systems to caste systems, which are extremely rigid because caste membership is fixed permanently at birth.

4. Slaves are people who do not own their own labor; as such, they represent a class and sometimes even a caste. Slavery has existed in various forms in many times and places, regardless of "race" and culture. Sometimes slavery is a rigid and closed, or caste, system; sometimes it is a relatively open class system.

5. Within a society composed of people from widely divergent backgrounds and different physical features, such as skin color, racism is almost invariably associated with social stratification. Those "races" considered inferior make up a larger proportion of the lower social classes or castes. In the opinion of many biological anthropologists, "race" is not a scientifically useful device for classifying humans. "Racial" classifications should be recognized for what they mostly are—social categories to which individuals are assigned, by themselves and others, on the basis of supposedly shared biological traits.

6. In multiethnic societies, ethnic differences are usually associated with inequities in wealth, power, and prestige. In other words, ethnicity is part of the system of stratification.

7. Social stratification appears to have emerged relatively recently in human history, about 8,000 years ago. This conclusion is based on archaeological evidence and on the fact that certain cultural features associated with stratification developed relatively recently.

8. One theory suggests that social stratification developed as productivity increased and surpluses were produced. Another suggestion is that stratification can develop only when people have "investments" in land or technology and therefore cannot move away from leaders they do not like. A third theory suggests that stratification emerges only when there is population pressure on resources in rank societies.

Glossary Terms

caste (p. 284)
class (p. 281)
class societies (p. 278)
economic resources (p. 277)

egalitarian societies (p. 278)
ethnicity (p. 290)
manumission (p. 286)
potlatch (p. 280)

power (p. 277)
prestige (p. 278)
rank societies (p. 278)
slaves (p. 285)

Critical Questions

1. What might be some of the social consequences of large differences in wealth? Explain your reasoning.

2. Is an industrial or a developed economy incompatible with a more egalitarian distribution of resources? Why or why not?

3. In a multiethnic society, does ethnic identity help or hinder social equality? Explain your answer.

4. Why do you suppose the degree of inequality has decreased in some countries in recent years?

Read the Original Source on myanthrolab.com

Read "Haitians: From Political Repression to Chaos" by Robert Lawless on MyAnthroLab. Answer the questions below.

1. In what ways does Lawless suggest that the elite in Haiti maintain their power?
2. Why does Lawless say that "Voodoo" is an egalitarian religion?
3. Explain what role slavery played in Haitian history.

13 Sex and Gender

(◄•─ Listen to the **Chapter Audio** on **myanthrolab.com**　　　　📖─ Read on **myanthrolab.com**

Humans come in two major varieties or sexes: female and male. Each has different reproductive organs. The contrast between them is one of the facts of life shared with most animal species. But having different organs of reproduction does not explain why males and females may also differ in other physical ways. There are some animal species—such as pigeons, gulls, and laboratory rats—in which the two sexes differ little in appearance.[1] The fact that we are a species with two sexes does not explain why human females and males typically look different, nor why human males and females should differ in behavior or be treated differently by society. Yet, no society we know of treats females and males in exactly the same way; indeed, females usually have fewer advantages than males. That is why in the last chapter we were careful to say that egalitarian societies have no *social groups* with unequal access to resources, power, and prestige. But within social groups (e.g., families), even egalitarian societies usually allow males greater access to economic resources, power, and prestige.

Because many of the differences between females and males may reflect cultural expectations and experiences, many researchers now prefer to speak of those as **gender differences**, reserving the term **sex differences** for purely biological differences.[2] Unfortunately, biological and cultural influences are not always clearly separable, so it is sometimes hard to know which term to use. As long as societies treat males and females differently, we may not be able to separate the effects of biology from the effects of culture, and both may be present. As we discuss differences and similarities between females and males, keep in mind that not all cultures conceive of gender as including just two categories. Sometimes "maleness" and "femaleness" are thought of as opposite ends of a continuum, or there might be three or more categories of gender, such as "female," "male," and "other."[3]

In this chapter, we discuss what we know cross-culturally about how and why females and males may differ physically, in gender roles, and in personality. We also discuss how and why sexual behavior and attitudes about sex vary from culture to culture. First, we focus on how concepts about gender vary cross-culturally.

Gender Concepts

In the United States and many Western societies, there are only two genders: female or male. Your gender is assigned at birth based on external biological attributes. However, not all individuals feel comfortable with their gender assignment. The term *transgender* is now used to describe people who don't feel that their assigned gender fits them well.

The division into just two genders—male/female—is very common cross-culturally. But a strict dichotomy is far from universal. Some societies, like the Cheyenne Native Americans of the Great Plains, recognized male, female, and a third gender, referred to by the Cheyennes as "two-spirits." "Two-spirit" people were usually biological males. The gender status of "two-spirit" was often recognized after a boy finished his vision quest, usually in his preadolescent years. A two-spirit person would wear women's dress and take on many of the activities of women. A two-spirit might even be taken as a second wife by a man, but whether the man and the two-spirit person engaged in sex is unknown. The role of a "two-spirit" person was not equivalent to becoming a woman, because two-spirits played special roles at weddings and childbirth. Europeans referred to a two-spirit individual as a *berdache*.[4] Accounts of "two-spirit" biological females who take on the role of men are relatively rare, but they do occur in a number of native North American societies, such as the Kaska of Yukon Territory, the Klamath of southern Oregon, and the Mohave of the Colorado River area in the southwestern United States. These biological female "two-spirits" could marry women, and such relationships were known to be lesbian relationships.[5]

In Oman, there is a third gender role called *xanith*. Anatomically male, *xaniths* speak of themselves as "women." However, *xaniths* have their own distinctive dress—they wear clothes that are neither male nor female. In fact, their clothes and dress seem in-between. Men wear white clothes, women bright patterns, and *xaniths* wear unpatterned pastels. Men have short hair, women long, and *xaniths* are medium-length. Women are generally secluded in their houses and can only go out with permission from their husbands, but the *xanith* is free to come and go and works as a servant and/or a homosexual prostitute. But the *xanith* gender role is not necessarily forever. A *xanith* may decide to marry, and if he is able to have intercourse with his bride, he becomes a "man." An older *xanith* who is no longer attractive may decide to become an "old man."[6]

Physique and Physiology

As we noted earlier, males and females cannot readily be distinguished in some animal species. Although they differ in chromosome makeup and in their external and internal organs of reproduction, they do not differ otherwise. In contrast, humans are *sexually dimorphic*—that is, the two sexes of our species are generally different in size and appearance. Females have proportionately wider pelvises. Males typically are taller and have heavier skeletons. Females have a larger proportion of their body weight in fat; males have a larger proportion of body weight in muscle. Males typically have greater grip strength, proportionately larger hearts and lungs, and greater aerobic capacity (greater intake of oxygen during strenuous activity).

North American culture tends to view "taller" and "more muscled" as better, which may reflect a bias toward males. But how did these differences come about? Natural selection may have favored these traits in males but selected against them in females. Because females bear children, selection may have favored earlier cessation of growth, and therefore less ultimate height so that the nutritional needs of a fetus would not compete with a growing mother's needs.[7] (Females achieve their ultimate height shortly after puberty, but boys continue to grow for years after puberty.) Similarly, there is some evidence that females are less affected than males by nutritional shortages, presumably because they tend to be shorter and have proportionately more fat.[8] Natural selection may have favored more proportionate "fatness" in females because that resulted in greater reproductive success.

Athletes can build up their muscle strength and increase their aerobic work capacity through training. Given that fact, cultural factors, such as how much a society expects and allows males and females to engage in muscular activity, could influence the degree to which females and males differ muscularly and in aerobic capacity. Similar training may account for the recent trend toward decreasing differences between females and males in certain athletic events, such as marathons and swim meets. Even when it comes to female and male physique and physiology, then, what we see may be the result of both culture and genes.[9]

Gender Roles
Productive and Domestic Activities

In the chapter on economics, we noted that all societies assign or divide labor somewhat differently between females and males. Because role assignments have a clear cultural component, we speak of them as **gender roles**. What is of particular interest here about the gender division of labor is not so much that every society has different work for males and females but rather that so many societies divide up work in similar ways. The question, then, is: Why are there universal or near-universal patterns in such assignments?

Table 13.1 summarizes the worldwide patterns indicating which activities are performed by one gender in all or almost all societies, which activities are usually performed by one gender, and which activities are commonly assigned to either gender or both. Do the other distributions of activities in the table suggest why females and males generally do different things? Scholars have suggested four explanations or theories that we label: *strength theory, compatibility-with-child-care theory, economy-of-effort theory,* and *expendability theory.*

The *strength theory* focuses on the generally greater strength of males and their superior capacity to mobilize their strength in quick bursts of energy (because of greater aerobic work capacity). Certainly, males may generally best perform activities that require lifting heavy

TABLE 13.1 Worldwide Patterns in the Division of Labor by Gender

Type of Activity	Males Almost Always	Males Usually	Either Gender or Both	Females Usually	Females Almost Always
Primary subsistence activities	Hunt and trap animals, large and small	Fish Herd large animals Collect wild honey Clear land and prepare soil for planting	Collect shellfish Care for small animals Plant crops Tend crops Harvest crops Milk animals	Gather wild plants	
Secondary subsistence and household activities		Butcher animals	Preserve meat and fish	Care for children Cook Prepare vegetable foods, drinks, and dairy products Launder Fetch water Collect fuel	Care for infants
Other	Lumber Mine and quarry Make boats, musical instruments, and bone, horn, and shell objects Engage in combat	Build houses Make nets and rope Exercise political leadership	Prepare skins Make leather products, baskets, mats, clothing, and pottery	Spin yarn	

Source: Mostly adapted from Murdock and Provost 1973, 203–25. The information on political leadership and warfare comes from Whyte 1978a, 217. The information on child care comes from Weisner and Gallimore 1977, 169–80.

Hmong women carry large loads of firewood to market.

objects (hunting large animals, butchering, clearing land, or working with stone, metal, or lumber), throwing weapons, and running with great speed (as in hunting). And none of the activities females usually perform, with the possible exception of collecting firewood, seem to require the same degree of physical strength or quick bursts of energy. But the strength theory is not completely convincing, if only because it cannot readily explain all the observed patterns. For example, it is not clear that the male activities of trapping small animals, collecting wild honey, or making musical instruments require much physical strength. Moreover, as we will see shortly, women do hunt in some societies, suggesting that differences in strength cannot play a very important role.

The *compatibility-with-child-care theory* emphasizes that women's tasks need to be compatible with child care. Although males can take care of infants, most traditional societies rely on breast-feeding of infants, which men cannot do. (In most societies, women breast-feed their children for 2 years on the average.) Women's tasks may be those that do not take them far from home for long periods, that do not place children in potential danger if they are taken along, and that can be stopped and resumed if an infant needs care.[10]

The compatibility theory may explain why *no* activities other than infant care are listed in the right-hand column of Table 13.1. That is, it may be that there are practically no universal or near-universal women-only activities because until recently most women have had to devote much of their time to nursing and caring for infants, as well as caring for other children. This theory may also explain why men usually perform tasks such as hunting, trapping, fishing, collecting honey, lumbering, and mining. Those tasks are dangerous for infants to be around, and in any case, would be difficult to coordinate with infant care.[11]

Finally, the compatibility theory may also explain why men seem to take over certain crafts in societies with full-time specialization. Although the distinction is not shown in Table 13.1, crafts such as making baskets, mats, and pottery are women's activities in noncommercial societies but tend to be men's activities in societies with full-time craft specialists.[12] Similarly, weaving tends to be a female activity unless it is produced for trade.[13] Full-time specialization and production for trade may increase incompatibility with child care. Cooking is a good example in our own society. Many women are excellent cooks and traditionally did most of the cooking at home, but chefs and bakers tend to be men. Women might be more likely to work as chefs if they could leave their babies and young children in safe places to be cared for by other people or if the hours chefs and bakers work were not so long.

But the compatibility theory does not explain why men usually prepare soil for planting, make objects out of wood, or work bone, horn, and shell. All of those tasks could probably be stopped to tend to a child, and none of them is any more dangerous to children nearby than is cooking. Why, then, do males tend to do them? The *economy-of-effort theory* may help explain patterns that cannot readily be explained by the strength and compatibility theories. For example, it may be advantageous for men to make wooden musical instruments because men generally lumber.[14] Lumbering may give men more knowledge about the physical properties of various woods and make it more likely that they know how to work with different woods. The economy-of-effort interpretation also suggests that it would be advantageous for one gender to perform tasks that are physically located near each other. If women have to be near home to take care of nursing and young children, it would be economical for them to perform other chores in or near the home.

In many farming societies, women can do some agriculture and take care of their young children at the same time, as this mother in Zambia demonstrates.

Expendability theory suggests that men, rather than women, will tend to do the dangerous work in a society because the loss of men is less disadvantageous reproductively than the loss of women. If some men lose their lives in hunting, deep-water fishing, mining, quarrying, lumbering, and the like, reproduction need not suffer as long as most fertile women have sexual access to men—for example, if the society permits two or more women to be married to the same man.[15] If something is dangerous, why would anybody, male or female, be willing to do it? Perhaps only when society glorifies those roles and endows them with high prestige and other rewards.

Although the various theories, singly or in combination, seem to explain much of the division of labor by gender, there are some unresolved problems. Critics of the strength theory have pointed out that women in some societies do engage in very heavy labor.[16] If women in some societies can develop the strength to do such work, perhaps strength is more a function of training than traditionally has been believed.

The compatibility theory also has some problems. It suggests that labor is divided to conform to the requirements of child care. But sometimes it seems the other way around. For example, women who spend a good deal of time in agricultural work outside the home often ask others to watch and feed their infants while they are unavailable to nurse.[17] Consider, too, the mountain areas of Nepal, where agricultural work is incompatible with child care; heavy loads must be carried up and down steep slopes, fields are far apart, and labor takes up most of the day. Yet women do this work anyway and leave their infants with others for long stretches of time.[18]

Furthermore, in some societies, women hunt—one of the activities most incompatible with child care and generally not done by women. Many Agta women of the Philippines regularly hunt wild pig and deer; women alone or in groups kill almost 30 percent of the large game.[19] Women take nursing babies on hunting trips, and the women who hunt do not have lower reproductive rates than the women who choose not to hunt. Agta women may find it possible to hunt because the hunting grounds are only about a half hour from camp, the dogs that accompany the women assist in the hunting and protect the women and babies, and the women generally hunt in groups, so others can help carry babies as well as carcasses. Hunting by women is also fairly common among the Aka, forest foragers in the Central African Republic. Aka women participate in and sometimes lead in organizing cooperative net-hunting, in which an area is circled and animals are flushed out and caught in nets. Women spend approximately 18 percent of their time net-hunting, which is more than men do.[20] In the Canadian subarctic, teams of Chipewyan women would hunt small animals such as muskrats or rabbits, and would commonly join their husbands to hunt large animals such as moose. Women did not participate in long-distance hunts,[21] which also suggests that compatibility with child care was a consideration.

As the cases just described suggest, we need to know a lot more about labor requirements. More precisely, we need to know exactly how much strength is required in particular tasks, how dangerous those tasks are, and whether a person could stop working at a task to care for a child. So far, we have mostly guesses. When there is more systematically collected evidence on aspects of particular tasks, we will be in a better position to evaluate the various theories. In any case, none of the available theories implies that the worldwide patterns of division of labor shown in Table 13.1 will persist. As we know from our own and other industrial societies, a strict gender division of labor begins to disappear when machines replace human strength, when women have fewer children, and when women can assign child care to others.

Relative Contributions to Work

In the United States, there is a tendency to equate "work" with a job earning income. Until relatively recently, being a "homemaker" was not counted as an occupation. Anthropologists also tended to ignore household work; indeed, most of the research on division of labor by gender focuses on **primary subsistence activities**—gathering, hunting, fishing, herding, and farming—and relatively less attention is paid to gender contributions to **secondary subsistence activities**, those that involve the processing and preparation of food for eating or storing.

Overall Work

If we count all the kinds of economic activities shown in Table 13.1, women typically work more total hours per day than men in intensive agricultural and horticultural societies.[22] We do not know if this is a truly cross-cultural universal. However, we do know that, in many societies where women earn wages, they are still responsible for the bulk of the household work as well as the child care at home.

Subsistence Work

If we focus on contribution to primary subsistence activities, which are generally located further from the home, female and male contributions are more variable cross-culturally. Estimates of time actually working are not generally available, so most comparisons estimate how much each gender contributes to the diet in terms of caloric intake from primary subsistence activities.

In some societies, women have traditionally contributed more to the economy than men by any measure. For example, among the Tchambuli of New Guinea in the 1930s, the women did all the fishing—going out early in the morning by canoe to their fish traps and returning when the sun was hot. Some of the catch was traded for sago (a starch) and sugarcane, and it was the women who went on the long canoe trips to do the trading.[23]

In contrast, men did almost all of the primary subsistence work among the Toda of India. As they were described early in the twentieth century, they depended for subsistence almost entirely on the dairy products of their water buffalo, either by using the products directly or by selling them for grain. Women were not allowed to have anything to do with dairy work; only men tended the buffalo and prepared the dairy products. Women's work was largely household work. Women prepared the purchased grain for cooking, cleaned house, and decorated clothing.[24]

A survey of a wide variety of societies has revealed that both women and men contribute a good deal to primary food-getting activities, but men usually contribute more in most societies.[25] Because women are almost always occupied with infant and child care responsibilities, it is not surprising that men usually do most of the primary subsistence work, which generally has to be done away from the home.

Some of the variation is explained by the type of food-getting activities in the society. In societies that depend on hunting, fishing, and herding for most of their calories—generally male activities—men usually contribute more than women.[26] For example, among the Inuit who traditionally depended mostly on hunting and fishing, as well as among the Toda who depended mostly on herding, men did most of the primary subsistence work. In societies that depend on gathering, primarily women's work, women tend to do most of the food-getting.[27] The San are an example. But the predominant type of food-getting is not always predictive. For example, among the Tchambuli who depended mostly on fishing, women did most of the work. Most societies depend upon some form of food production, rather than foraging. With the exception of clearing land, preparing the soil, and herding large animals, which are usually men's tasks, men, women, or both do the work of planting, crop tending (weeding, irrigating), and harvesting (see Table 13.1). So we need some explanation of why women do most of the farming work in some societies but men do it in others. Different patterns predominate in different areas of the world. In Africa, south of the Sahara, women generally do most of the farming. In much of Asia and Europe and the areas around the Mediterranean, men do more.[28]

The type of agriculture may help explain some of the variation. Many have pointed out that men's contribution to primary subsistence tends to be much higher than women's in intensive agricultural societies, particularly with plow agriculture. In contrast, women's contribution is relatively high compared with men's and sometimes higher in horticultural societies. According to Ester Boserup, when population increases and there is pressure to make more intensive use of the land, cultivators begin to use the plow and irrigation, and males start to do more.[29] But it is not clear why.

Why should women not contribute a lot to farming just because plows are used? In trying to answer this question, most researchers shift to considering how much time males and females spend in various farming tasks, rather than estimating the total caloric contribution of females versus males. The reason for this shift is that gender contribution to farming varies substantially over the various phases of the production sequence, as well as from one crop to another. Thus, the total amount of time females versus males work at farming tasks is easier to estimate than how much each gender contributes to the diet in terms of calories. How would caloric contribution be judged, for example, if men do the clearing and plowing, women do the planting and weeding, and both do the harvesting?

Perhaps plow agriculture increases male contribution to subsistence because plowing takes longer and minimizes weeding time. Cross-culturally, men usually clear land. It has been estimated that, in one district in Nigeria, 100 days of work are required to clear one acre of virgin land for plowing by tractor; only 20 days are required to prepare the land for shifting cultivation.

Grinding corn is very time-consuming hard work. A woman in the highlands of Guatemala is grinding corn for tortillas.

Weeding is a task that probably can be combined with child care, and perhaps women may have mostly performed it previously for that reason.[30] But the fact that men do the plowing, which may take a lot of time, does not explain why women do relatively fewer farming tasks, including weeding, in societies that have the plow.[31]

Another explanation is that household chores increase substantially with intensive agriculture and limit the time women can spend in the fields. Intensive agriculturalists rely heavily on grain crops (such as corn, wheat, and oats) that are usually dried before storing. To make these dried foods edible, they either have to be cooked in water for a long time or they have to be processed first to make cooking faster. Cooking usually requires collecting water and firewood, neither usually close by, and both tasks are usually done by women. In addition, there is more cleaning of pots and utensils. Soaking, grinding, or pounding can reduce cooking time for hard grains, but the process that speeds up cooking the most—grinding—is itself very time-consuming unless done by machine.[32] Finally, household work may increase substantially with intensive agriculture because women in such societies have *more* children than women in horticultural societies.[33] If household work increases in these ways, it is easy to understand why women cannot contribute more time than men, or as much time as men, to intensive agriculture. But women's contribution, although less than men's, is nonetheless substantial; they seem to work outside the home 4½ hours a day, 7 days a week, on the average.[34]

We still have not explained why women contribute so much to horticulture in the first place. They may not have as much household work as intensive agricultural women, but neither do the men. Why, then, don't men do relatively more in horticulture also? Men in horticultural societies are often drawn away from cultivation into other types of activities. One of the most common is warfare, in which all able-bodied men are expected to participate. There is evidence that, if males are engaged in warfare when primary subsistence work has to be done, the women must do that subsistence work.[35] Men may also be withdrawn from primary subsistence work if they have to work in distant towns and cities for wages or if they periodically go on long-distance trading trips.[36]

When women contribute a lot to primary food-getting activities, we might expect effects on their childrearing. Several cross-cultural studies suggest that this expectation is correct. In societies with a high female contribution to primary subsistence (in terms of contributing calories), infants are fed solid foods earlier (so that other people besides mothers can feed them) than in societies with a low female contribution.[37] Girls are likely to be trained to be industrious (probably to help their mothers), and girl babies are more valued.[38]

Political Leadership and Warfare

In almost every known society, men rather than women are generally the leaders in the political arena. One cross-cultural survey found that, in about 88 percent of the surveyed societies, only men were leaders. In 10 percent of societies in which some women occupied leadership positions, the women were either outnumbered by or less powerful than the male leaders.[39] In the remaining 2 percent, leadership was fairly evenly distributed between men and women. If we look at countries, not cultures, women on the average make up only around 16 percent of the representatives in national parliaments or legislative bodies.[40] Whether or not we consider warfare to be part of the political sphere of life, we find an almost universal dominance of males in that arena. In 87 percent of the world's societies, women never participate actively in war.[41]

Even in *matrilineal* societies, which seem to be oriented around women (see the chapter on marriage, family, and kinship), men usually occupy formal political positions. Among the Iroquois of what is now New York State, women had control over resources, but men, not women, held political office. The highest political body among the League of the Iroquois, which comprised five societies, was a council of 50 male chiefs. Nonetheless, women could nominate, elect, and impeach their male representatives. Women also could decide between life and death for prisoners of war, forbid the men of their households to go to war, and intervene to bring about peace.[42]

Women in some societies engage in combat, as this Israeli helicopter gunner does.

Why have men (at least so far) almost always dominated the political sphere of life? Some scholars have suggested that men's role in warfare gives them the edge in all kinds of political leadership, particularly because they control weapons, an important resource.[43] But evidence suggests that force is rarely used to obtain leadership positions;[44] superior strength is not the deciding factor. Still, warfare may be related to political leadership for another reason. Warfare clearly affects survival, and it occurs regularly in most societies. Therefore, decision making about war may be among the most important kinds of politics in most societies. If so, then the people who know the most about warfare should be making the decisions about it.

To explain why males and not females usually engage in fighting, let us refer to three of the possible explanations of the worldwide patterns in the gender division of labor. Warfare, like hunting, probably requires strength (for throwing weapons) and quick bursts of energy (for running). And certainly combat is one of the most dangerous and uninterruptible activities imaginable, hardly compatible with child care. Also, even if they do not at the time have children, women may generally be kept out of combat because their potential fertility is more important to a population's reproduction and survival than their potential usefulness as warriors.[45] So the strength theory, the compatibility theory, and the expendability theory might all explain the predominance of men in warfare.

Two other factors may be involved in male predominance in politics. One is the generally greater height of men. Why height should be a factor in leadership is unclear, but studies suggest that taller people are more likely to be leaders.[46] Finally, there is the possibility that men dominate politics because they get around more in the outside world than do women. Men's activities typically take them farther from home; women tend to work more around the home. If societies choose leaders at least in part because of what they know about the larger world, then men will generally have some advantage. In support of this reasoning, Patricia Draper found that, in settled San groups, women no longer engaged in long-distance gathering, and they seemed to have lost much of their former influence in decision making.[47] Involvement in child care may also detract from influence in decision making. In a study of village leadership among the Kayapo of Brazil, Dennis Werner found that women with heavy child care burdens were less influential than women not as involved in child care; he suggests that they had fewer friends and missed many details of what was going on in the village.[48]

These various explanations suggest why men generally dominate politics, but we still need to explain why women participate in politics more in some societies than in others. Marc Ross investigated this question in a cross-cultural survey of 90 societies.[49] In that sample, the degree of female participation in politics varied considerably. For example, among the Mende of Sierra Leone, women regularly held high office, but among the Azande of Zaire, women took no part in public life. One factor that predicts the exclusion of women from politics is the organization of communities around male kin. As we will see later, when they marry, women usually have to leave their communities and move to their husband's place. If women are "strangers" in a community with many related males, then the males will have political advantages because of their knowledge of community members and past events.

The Relative Status of Women

There are probably as many definitions of status as there are researchers interested in the topic. To some, the relative status of the sexes means how much importance society confers on females versus males. To others, it means how much power and authority men and women have relative to each other. And to still others, it means what kinds of rights women and men possess to do what they want to do. In any case, many social scientists ask why the status of women appears to vary from one society to another. Why do women have few rights and little influence in some societies and more of each in other societies? In other words, why is there variation in degree of **gender stratification**?

In the small Iraqi town of Daghara, women and men live very separate lives.[50] In many respects, women appear to have very little status. Like women in some other parts of the Islamic world, women in Daghara live their lives mostly in seclusion, staying in their houses and interior courtyards. If women must go out, which they can do only with male approval, they must shroud their faces and bodies in long black cloaks. These cloaks must be worn in mixed company, even at home. Women are essentially excluded from political activities. Legally, they are considered to be under the authority of their fathers and husbands. Even the sexuality of women is controlled. There is strict emphasis on virginity before marriage. Because women are not permitted even casual conversations with strange men, the possibilities for extramarital or even premarital relationships are very slight. In contrast, hardly any sexual restrictions are imposed on men.

But some societies such as the Mbuti seem to approach equal status for males and females. Like most food collectors, the Mbuti have no formal political organization to make decisions or to settle disputes. Public disputes occur, and both women and men take part in the uproar that is part of such disputes. Not only do women make their positions known, but their opinions are often heeded. Even in domestic quarrels involving physical violence between husband and wife, others usually intervene to stop them, regardless of who hit whom first.[51] Women control the use of dwellings; they usually have equal say over the disposal of resources they or the men collect, over the upbringing of their children, and about whom their children should marry. One of the few signs of inequality is that women are somewhat more restricted than men with respect to extramarital sex.[52]

There are many theories about why women have relatively high or low status. One of the most common is that women's status will be high when they contribute substantially to primary subsistence activities. This theory would predict that women should have very little status when food-getting depends largely on hunting, herding, or intensive agriculture. A second theory suggests that men will be more valued and esteemed than women where warfare is particularly important. A third theory suggests that men will have higher status where there are centralized political hierarchies. The reasoning in this theory is essentially the same as the reasoning in the warfare theory: Men usually play the dominant role in political behavior, so men's status should be higher wherever political behavior is more important or frequent. Finally, there is the theory that women will have higher status where kin groups and couples' places of residence after marriage are organized around women.

One of the problems in evaluating these theories is that decisions have to be made about the meaning of *status*. Does it mean value? Rights? Influence? And do all these aspects of status vary together? Cross-cultural research by Martin Whyte suggests that they do not. For each sample society in his study, Whyte rated 52 items that might be used to define the relative status of the sexes. These items included such things as which sex can inherit property, who has final authority over disciplining unmarried children, and whether the gods in the society are male, female, or both. The results of the study indicate that very few of these items are related. Therefore, Whyte concluded, we cannot talk about status as a single concept. Rather, it seems more appropriate to talk about the relative status of women in different spheres of life.[53]

Women as well as men serve on political councils in many Coast Salish communities. Here, we see a swearing-in ceremony for the Special Chiefs' Council in Sardis, British Columbia.

Even though Whyte found no necessary connection between one aspect of status and another, he decided to ask whether some of the theories correctly predict why some societies have many, as opposed to few, areas in which the status of women is high. Let us turn first to the ideas *not* supported by the available cross-cultural evidence. The idea that generally high status stems from a greater caloric contribution to primary subsistence activities is not supported.[54] For example, women seem to have higher status the more a society depends on hunting, but women do little of the primary subsistence work in hunting societies. And it is commonly thought that warfare should bolster male status, but there is no consistent evidence that a high frequency of warfare generally lowers women's status in different spheres of life.[55]

What does predict higher status for women in many areas of life? Although the results are not strong, there is some support in Whyte's study for the theory that women have somewhat higher status where kin groups and marital residence are organized around women. (We discuss these features of society more fully in the chapter on marriage, family, and kinship.) The Iroquois are a good example. Even though Iroquois women could not hold formal political office, they had considerable authority within and beyond the household. Related women lived together in longhouses with husbands who belonged to other kin groups. In the longhouse, the women's authority was clear, and they could ask objectionable men to leave. The women controlled the allocation of the food they produced. Allocation could influence the timing of war parties because men could not undertake a raid without provisions. Women were involved in the selection of religious leaders, half of whom were women. Even in politics, although women could not speak or serve on the council, they largely controlled the selection of councilmen and could institute impeachment proceedings against those to whom they objected.[56]

In preindustrial societies, women have generally lower status in societies with more political hierarchy.[57] Lower status for women is also associated with other indicators of cultural complexity—social stratification, plow and irrigation agriculture, large settlements, private property, and craft specialization. Only one type of influence for women increases with cultural complexity: informal influence. However, informal influence may simply reflect a lack of *real* influence.[58] Why cultural complexity in preindustrial societies is associated with women having less authority in the home, less control over property, and more restricted sexual lives is not yet understood. However, the relationship between cultural complexity and gender equality appears to be reversed in industrial and postindustrial societies. Judging by a comparative study of gender attitudes in 61 countries, it seems that countries relying on agriculture such as Nigeria and Peru have the least favorable attitudes toward gender equality, industrial societies such as Russia and Taiwan have moderately favorable attitudes, and postindustrial societies such as Sweden and the United States have the most favorable attitudes toward gender equality.[59]

Western colonialism appears to have been generally detrimental to women's status. Although the relative status of men and women may not have been equal before the Europeans arrived, colonial influences seem generally to have undermined the position of women. There are plenty of examples of Europeans restructuring landownership around men and teaching men modern farming techniques, even in places where women were usually the farmers. In addition, men more often than women could earn cash through wage labor or through sales of goods (such as furs) to Europeans.[60] We are beginning to understand some of the conditions that may enhance or decrease certain aspects of women's status. If we can understand which of these conditions are most important, society may be able to reduce gender inequality if it wants to.[61]

Economic Development and Women's Status

Based on the writings of Ester Boserup and subsequent scholarship on women in development, the prevailing opinion was that development usually made things worse for women. Development agents commonly targeted men for learning new technology and how to produce crops for sale. Today, women in developing countries are still largely left out and women still face difficulties, but recent research has documented how women often find creative solutions to participating in commercial enterprises. In many cases, involvement in commercial activity leads to improvement in women's lives, at least as judged from material and status benefits they receive. Producing for a market might range in scale from raising a few extra pigs for sale in southwestern China, to more complex involvement such as contract farming for crop exports in Kenya, or market trading in Ghana.

Some of the creative strategies women use in Kenya to get around their structural disadvantages include buying or renting land with their proceeds, "pooling" small pieces of land to meet minimum requirements for commercial growers, joining women's rotating credit associations, and looking to the private sector for training and materials for contract agriculture.

Almost everywhere, women in developing countries use money from their commercial enterprise to purchase things for their households. At first the money might go to food purchases, household goods, and education for their children. If their incomes or savings grow, women may pay for large appliances, furniture, and farm machinery and vehicles. Women, in contrast to men, tend to plow all their earnings into household expenditures.

Most of these recent studies suggest that bringing money into the household generally translates into lasting changes, including increased educational opportunities, greater say in household decisions, and higher social status in the community.

Some opportunities for women open up when men move into other domains. For example, among the Asante of Ghana, many men moved out of market trading to take advantage of more lucrative cocoa production. Women had long been traders along with men, but with the departure of men, women took over many of men's former market niches and began to engage in longer-distance trade. And, in Kenya, male migration has increased the number of women who manage the farm and head households.

The places we have discussed so far are largely agricultural. Women's work is primarily in or near the household. Commercial involvement gets women more into the public sector. But what about industrial societies, where only a small proportion of people engage in farming? According to a survey of 61 countries, gender equality is more favored in industrializing countries than in agricultural societies. With industrialization, infant and child mortality decline, lessening the pressure on women to reproduce. Perhaps this frees them to pursue education and work outside the home. Postindustrial countries, with even lower fertility rates, are even more accepting of gender equality. As women learn more and get out in the world more, gender inequality appears to decline.

Sources: Bossen 2000; G. Clark 2000; Doyle 2005; Spring 2000a; 2000b; 2000c.

Personality Differences

Much of the research on gender differences in personality has taken place in the United States and other Western countries where psychology is a major field of study. Although such studies are informative, they do not tell us whether the observed differences hold true in cultures very different from our own. Fortunately, we now have systematic observational studies for various non-Western societies. These studies recorded the minute details of behavior of substantial numbers of males and females. Any conclusions about female–male differences in aggressiveness, for example, are based on actual counts of the number of times a particular individual tried to hurt or injure another person during a given amount of observation time. Almost all of these differences are subtle and a matter of degree, not a matter of a behavior being present or absent in females or males.

Which differences in personality are suggested by these systematic studies? Most of them have observed children in different cultural settings. The most consistent difference is in the area of aggression; boys try to hurt others more frequently than girls do. In an extensive comparative study of children's behavior, the Six Cultures project, this difference showed up as early as 3–6 years of age.[62] In the Six Cultures project, six different research teams observed children's behavior in Kenya (among the Gusii), Mexico, India, the Philippines, Okinawa, and the United States. A more recent cross-cultural comparison of four other cultures (the Logoli of Kenya, Nepal, Belize, and American Samoa) supports the sex difference in aggression.[63] Studies in the United States are consistent with the cross-cultural findings: In a large number of observation and experimental studies, boys exhibited more aggression than girls.[64]

Other female–male differences have turned up with considerable consistency, but we have to be cautious in accepting them, either because they have not been documented as well or because there are more exceptions. There seems to be a tendency for girls to exhibit more responsible behavior, including nurturance (trying to help others). Girls seem more likely to conform to adult wishes and commands. Boys try more often to exert dominance over others to get their own way. In play, boys and girls show a preference for their own gender. Boys seem to play in large groups, girls in small ones. And boys seem to maintain more distance between each other than girls do.[65]

If we assume that these differences are consistent across cultures, how can we explain them? Many writers and researchers believe that because certain female–male differences are so consistent, they are probably rooted in the biological differences between the two sexes. Aggression is one of the traits talked about most often in this connection, particularly because this male–female difference appears so early in life.[66] But an alternative argument is that societies bring up boys and girls differently because they almost universally require adult males and females to perform different types of roles. If most societies expect adult males to be warriors or to be prepared to be warriors, shouldn't we expect most societies to encourage or idealize aggression in males? And if females are almost always the caretakers of infants, shouldn't we also expect societies generally to encourage nurturant behaviors in females?

Researchers tend to adopt either the biological or the socialization view, but it is possible that both kinds of causes are important in the development of gender differences. For example, parents might turn a slight genetic difference into a large gender difference by maximizing that difference in the way they socialize boys versus girls.

It is difficult for researchers to distinguish the influence of genes and other biological conditions from the influence of socialization. We have research indicating that parents treat boy and girl infants differently as early as birth.[67] In spite of the fact that objective observers can see no major "personality" differences between girl and boy infants, parents often claim to.[68] But parents may unconsciously want to see differences and may therefore produce them in socialization. So even early differences could be learned rather than genetic. Remember, too, that researchers cannot do experiments with people; for example, parents' behavior cannot be manipulated to find out what would happen if boys and girls were treated in exactly the same ways.

However, there is considerable experimental research on aggression in nonhuman animals. These experiments suggest that the hormone androgen is partly responsible for higher levels of aggression. For example, in some experiments, females injected with androgen at about the time the sexual organs develop (before or shortly after birth) behave more aggressively when they are older than do females without the hormone. These results may or may not apply to humans, of course, but some researchers have investigated human females who were "androgenized" in the womb because of drugs given to their mothers to prevent miscarriage. By and large, the results of these studies are similar to the experimental studies—androgenized human females show similar patterns of higher aggression.[69] Some scholars take these results to indicate that biological differences between males and females are responsible for the male–female difference in aggression;[70] others suggest that even these results are not conclusive because females who get more androgen show generally disturbed metabolic systems, and general metabolic disturbance may itself increase aggressiveness. Furthermore, androgen-injected females may look more like males because they develop male-like genitals; therefore, they may be treated like males.[71]

Is there any evidence that socialization differences may account for differences in aggression? Although a cross-cultural survey of ethnographers' reports on 101 societies does show that more societies encourage aggression in boys than in girls, most societies show no difference in aggression training.[72] The few societies that do show differences in aggression training can hardly account for the widespread sex differences in actual aggressiveness. But the survey does not necessarily mean that there are no consistent differences in aggression training for boys and girls. All it shows is that there are no *obvious* differences. For all we know, the learning of aggression and other "masculine" traits by boys could be produced by subtle types of socialization.

One possible type of subtle socialization that could create gender differences in behavior is the chores children are assigned. It is possible that little boys and girls learn to behave differently because their parents ask them to do different kinds of work. Beatrice and John Whiting reported from the Six Cultures project that, in societies where children were asked to do a great deal of work, they generally showed more responsible and nurturant behavior. Because girls are almost always asked to do more work than boys, they may be more responsible and nurturant for this reason alone.[73] If this reasoning is correct, we should find that, if boys are asked to do girls' work, they will learn to behave more like girls.

A study of Luo children in Kenya by Carol Ember supports this view.[74] Girls were usually asked to babysit, cook, clean house, and fetch water and firewood. Boys were usually asked to do very little because boys' traditional work was herding cattle, and most families in the community studied had few cattle. But for some reason, more boys than girls had been born, and many mothers without girls at home asked their sons to do girls' chores. Systematic behavior observations showed that much of the behavior of the boys who did girls' work was intermediary between the behavior of other boys and the behavior of girls. The boys who did girls' work were more like girls in that they were less aggressive, less domineering, and more responsible than other boys, even when they weren't working. So it is possible that task assignment has an important influence on how boys and girls learn to behave. These and other subtle forms of socialization need to be investigated more thoroughly.

Misconceptions about Differences in Behavior

Before we leave the subject of behavior differences, we should note some widespread beliefs about them that research does not support. Some of these mistaken beliefs are that girls are more dependent than boys, that girls are more sociable, and that girls are more passive. The results obtained by the Six Cultures project cast doubt on all these notions.[75] First, if we think of dependency as seeking help and emotional support from others, girls are generally no more likely to behave this way than boys. To be sure, the results do indicate that boys and girls have somewhat

Cross-culturally, girls more often play in small, intimate groups, boys in larger groups.

different styles of dependency. Girls more often seek help and contact; boys more often seek attention and approval. As for sociability, which means seeking and offering friendship, the Six Cultures results showed no reliable differences between the sexes. Of course, boys and girls may be sociable in different ways because boys generally play in larger groups than girls. As for the supposed passivity of girls, the evidence is also not particularly convincing. Girls in the Six Cultures project did not consistently withdraw from aggressive attacks or comply with unreasonable demands. The only thing that emerged as a female–male difference was that older girls were less likely than boys to respond to aggression with aggression. But this finding may not reflect passivity as much as the fact that girls are less aggressive than boys, which we already knew.

So some of our common ideas about female–male differences are unfounded. Others, such as those dealing with aggression and responsibility, cannot be readily dismissed and should be investigated further.

As we noted, an observed difference in aggression does not mean that males are aggressive and females are not. Perhaps because males are generally more aggressive, aggression in females has been studied less often. For that reason, Victoria Burbank focused on female aggression in an Australian aborigine community she calls Mangrove. During the 18 months that she was there, Burbank observed some act of aggression almost every other day. Consistent with the cross-cultural evidence, men initiated aggression more often than women, but women were initiators about 43 percent of the time. The women of Mangrove engaged in almost all the same kinds of aggression as men did, including fighting, except that it tended not to be as lethal as male violence. Men most often used lethal weapons; when women fought with weapons, they mostly used sticks, not spears, guns, or knives. Burbank points out that, in contrast to Western cultures, female aggression is not viewed as unnatural or deviant but rather as a natural expression of anger.[76]

Sexuality

In view of the way the human species reproduces, it is not surprising that sexuality is part of our nature. But no society we know of leaves sexuality to nature; all have at least some rules governing "proper" conduct. There is much variation from one society to another in the degree of sexual activity permitted or encouraged before marriage, outside marriage, and even within marriage. And societies vary markedly in their tolerance of nonheterosexual sexuality.

Cultural Regulations of Sexuality: Permissiveness versus Restrictiveness

All societies seek to regulate sexual activity to some degree, and there is a lot of variation cross-culturally. Some societies allow premarital sex; others forbid it. The same is true for extramarital sex. In addition, a society's degree of restrictiveness is not always consistent throughout the life span or for all aspects of sex. For example, a number of societies ease sexual restrictions somewhat for adolescents, and many become more restrictive for adults.[77] Then, too, societies change over time. The United States has traditionally been restrictive, but until recently—before the emergence of the AIDS epidemic—more permissive attitudes were gaining acceptance.

Premarital Sex The degree to which sex before marriage is approved or disapproved of varies greatly from society to society. The Trobriand Islanders, for example, approved of and encouraged premarital sex, seeing it as an important preparation for later marriage roles. Both girls and boys were given complete instruction in all forms of sexual expression at the onset of puberty and were allowed plenty of opportunity for intimacy. Some societies not only allow premarital sex on a casual basis but specifically encourage trial marriages between adolescents. Among the Ila-speaking peoples of central Africa, at harvest time, girls were given houses of their own where they could play at being wife with the boys of their choice.[78]

On the other hand, premarital sex was discouraged in many societies. For example, among the Tepoztlan Indians of Mexico, a girl's life became "crabbed, cribbed, confined" from the time of her first menstruation. She was not to speak to or encourage boys in the least way. To do so would be to court disgrace, to show herself to be crazy. The responsibility of guarding the chastity and reputation of one or more daughters of marriageable age was often a burden for the mother. One mother said she wished her 15-year-old daughter would marry soon because it was inconvenient to "spy" on her all the time.[79] In many Muslim societies, a girl's premarital chastity was tested after her marriage. After the wedding night, blood-stained sheets were displayed as proof of the bride's virginity.

Cultures do not remain the same; attitudes and practices can change markedly over time, as in the United States. In the past, sex was generally delayed until after marriage; in the 1990s, most Americans accepted or approved of premarital sex.[80]

Sex in Marriage In most societies, some form of face-to-face sexual intercourse or coitus is the usual pattern, most preferring the woman on her back and the man on top. Couples in most cultures prefer privacy. This is easier in societies with single-family dwellings or separate rooms, but privacy is difficult to attain in the house in societies with unpartitioned dwellings and multiple families living there. For example, the Siriono of Bolivia had as many as 50 hammocks 10 feet apart in their houses. Not surprisingly, couples in such societies prefer to have sex outdoors in a secluded location.[81]

Night is often preferred for sex, but some cultures specifically opted for day. For example, the Chenchu of India believed that a child conceived at night might be born blind. In some societies, couples engage in sex quickly with little or no foreplay; in others, foreplay may take hours.[82] Attitudes toward marital sex and the frequency of it vary widely from culture to culture. In one cross-cultural survey, frequent marital sex is generally viewed as a good thing, but frequent sex is viewed as undesirable, causing weakness, illness, and sometimes death in 9 percent of the societies.[83] People in most societies abstain from intercourse during menstruation, during at least part of pregnancy, and for a period after childbirth. Some societies prohibit sexual relations before various activities, such as hunting, fighting, planting, brewing, and iron smelting. Our own society is among the most lenient regarding restrictions on intercourse within marriage, imposing only rather loose restraints during mourning, menstruation, and pregnancy.[84]

Extramarital Sex Extramarital sex is not uncommon in many societies. In about 69 percent of the world's societies, men have extramarital sex more than occasionally, and in about 57 percent of the societies women do so. The frequency of such sexual activity is higher than we might expect, given that only a slight majority of societies say they allow extramarital sex for men, and only a small number (11 percent) say they allow it for women.[85]

In quite a few societies, then, there is quite a difference between the restrictive code and actual practice. The Navajo of the 1940s were said to forbid adultery, but young married men under the age of 30 had about a quarter of their heterosexual contacts with women other than their wives.[86] And although people in the United States in the 1970s almost overwhelmingly rejected extramarital sex, 41 percent of married men and about 18 percent of married women had had extramarital sex. In the 1990s, proportionately more men and women reported that they had been faithful to their spouses.[87] Cross-culturally, most societies have a double standard with regard to men and women, with restrictions considerably greater for women.[88] A substantial number of societies openly accept extramarital relationships. The Chukchee of Siberia, who often traveled long distances, allowed a married man to engage in sex with his host's wife, with the understanding that he would offer the same hospitality when the host visited him.[89]

Although a society may allow extramarital sex, a recent cross-cultural study of individual reactions to extramarital sex finds that men and women try a variety of strategies to curtail such sex. Men are much more likely than women to resort to physical violence against their wives; women are more likely to distance themselves from their husbands. Gossip may be employed to shame the relationship and a higher authority may be asked to intervene in more complex societies. The researchers conclude that married women and men universally consider extramarital sex inappropriate, even in societies that permit it sometimes.[90]

Some cultures are more relaxed about sexuality than others. Does public sculpture reflect that? A park in Oslo, Norway, is dedicated to sculptures by Gustav Vigeland.

Homosexuality When most anthropologists discuss homosexuality, they usually refer to sex between males or sex between females. But although the biological male–female dichotomy corresponds to the gender male–female dichotomy in the West, other societies do not have the same gender concepts, so that the meaning of homosexuality may be different in different societies. For example, the Navajo of the American Southwest traditionally recognized four genders. Only relationships between people of the same gender would be considered homosexual, and they considered such relationships inappropriate.[91] Biologically speaking, some of the cross-gender relationships would be considered homosexual in the Western view. Most of the research to date has adopted the biological view that homosexuality is between people of the same biological sex.

The range in permissiveness or restrictiveness toward homosexual relations is as great as that for any other kind of sexual activity. Among the Lepcha of the Himalayas, a man was believed to become homosexual if he ate the flesh of an uncastrated pig. But the Lepcha said that homosexual behavior was practically unheard of, and they viewed it with disgust.[92] Perhaps because many societies deny that homosexuality exists, little is known about homosexual practices in the restrictive societies. Among the permissive ones, there is variation in the type and pervasiveness of homosexuality. In some societies, homosexuality is accepted but limited to certain times and certain individuals. For example, among the Papago of the southwestern United States, there were "nights of saturnalia" in which homosexual tendencies could be expressed. The Papago also had many male transvestites who wore women's clothing, did women's chores, and, if not married, could be visited by men.[93] A woman did not have the same freedom of expression. She could participate in the saturnalia feasts but only with her husband's permission, and female transvestites were nonexistent.

Homosexuality occurs even more widely in other societies. The Berber-speaking Siwans of North Africa expected all males to engage in homosexual relations. In fact, fathers made arrangements for their unmarried sons to be given to an older man in a homosexual arrangement. Siwan custom limited a man to one boy. Fear of the Egyptian government made this a secret matter, but before 1909, such arrangements were made openly. Almost all men were reported to have engaged in a homosexual relationship as boys; later, when they were between 16 and 20, they married girls.[94] Such prescribed homosexual relationships between people of different ages are a common form of homosexuality.[95] Among the most extremely pro-homosexual societies, the Etoro of New Guinea preferred homosexuality to heterosexuality. Heterosexuality was prohibited as many as 260 days a year and was forbidden in or near the house and gardens. Male homosexuality, on the other hand, was not prohibited at any time and was believed to make crops flourish and boys become strong.[96] Even among the Etoro, however, men were expected to marry women after a certain age.[97]

Only recently have researchers paid much attention to erotic relationships between females. Although early studies found relatively few societies with female–female sexual relationships, Evelyn Blackwood located reports of 95 societies with such practices, suggesting that it is more common than previously thought.[98] As with male homosexuality, some societies institutionalize same-sex sexual relationships—the Kaguru of Tanzania have female homosexual relationships between older and younger women as part of their initiation ceremonies, reminiscent of the male–male "mentor" relationships in ancient Greece.

Cross-culturally, it is extremely unusual to find "gays" or exclusive male or female homosexuals. In most societies, males and females are expected to marry, and homosexuality, if tolerated or approved, either occurs as a phase in one's life or occurs along with heterosexuality.[99]

Reasons for Restrictiveness

The research to date suggests that societies that are restrictive with regard to one aspect of heterosexual sex tend to be restrictive with regard to other aspects. Thus, societies that frown on sexual expression by young children also punish premarital and extramarital sex.[100] Furthermore, such societies tend to insist on modesty in clothing and are constrained in their talk about sex.[101] But societies that are generally restrictive about heterosexuality are not necessarily restrictive about homosexuality. Societies restrictive about premarital sex are neither more nor less likely to restrict homosexuality. In the case of extramarital sex, the situation is somewhat different. Societies that have a considerable amount of male homosexuality tend to disapprove of males having extramarital heterosexual relationships.[102] If we are going to explain restrictiveness, then, it appears we have to consider heterosexual and homosexual restrictiveness separately.

Let us consider homosexual restrictiveness first. Research so far has not yielded any clear-cut predictions, although several cross-cultural predictors about male homosexuality are intriguing. One such finding is that societies that forbid abortion and infanticide for married women (most societies permit these practices for illegitimate births) are likely to be intolerant of male homosexuality.[103] This and other findings are consistent with the point of view that homosexuality is less tolerated in societies that would like to increase population. Such societies may be intolerant of all kinds of behaviors that minimize population growth. Homosexuality would have this effect, if we assume that a higher frequency of homosexual relations is associated with a lower frequency of heterosexual relations. The less frequently heterosexual relations occur, the lower the number of conceptions there might be. Another indication that intolerance may be related to a desire for population growth is that societies with famines and severe food shortages are more likely to allow homosexuality. Famines and food shortages suggest population pressure on resources; under these conditions, homosexuality and other practices that minimize population growth may be tolerated or even encouraged.[104] Population pressure may also explain why our own society has become somewhat more tolerant of homosexuality recently. Of course, population pressure does not explain why certain individuals become homosexual or why most individuals in some societies engage in such behavior, but it might explain why some societies view such behavior more or less permissively.

Let us now turn to heterosexual behavior. Greater restrictiveness toward premarital sex tends to occur in more complex societies—societies that have hierarchies of political officials, part-time or full-time craft specialists, cities and towns, and class stratification.[105] It may be that, as social inequality increases and various groups come to have differential wealth, parents become more concerned with preventing their children from marrying "beneath them." Permissiveness toward premarital sexual relationships might lead a person to become attached to someone not considered a desirable marriage partner. Even worse, from the family's point of view, such "unsuitable" sexual liaisons might result in a pregnancy that could make it impossible for a girl to marry "well." Controlling mating, then, may be a way of trying to control property. Consistent with this view is the finding that virginity is emphasized in rank and stratified societies, in which families are likely to exchange goods and money in the course of arranging marriages.[106]

The biological fact that humans depend on sexual reproduction does not by itself help explain why females and males differ in so many ways across cultures, or why societies vary in the way they handle male and female roles. We are only beginning to investigate these questions. When we eventually understand more about how and why females and males are different or the same in roles, personality, and sexuality, we may be better able to decide how much we want the biology of sex to shape our lives.

✓•─Study and **Review** on **myanthrolab.com**

Summary

1. That humans reproduce sexually does not explain why males and females tend to differ in appearance and behavior, and to be treated differently, in all societies.

2. All or nearly all societies assign certain activities to females and other activities to males. These worldwide gender patterns of division of labor may be explained by male–female differences in strength, by differences in compatibility of tasks with child care, or by economy-of-effort considerations and/or the expendability of men.

3. Perhaps because women almost always have infant and child care responsibilities, men in most societies contribute more to primary subsistence activities, in terms of calories. When primary and secondary subsistence work is counted, women typically work more hours than men. In most societies, men are the leaders in the political arena, and warfare is almost exclusively a male activity.

4. The relative status of women compared with that of men seems to vary from one area of life to another. Whether women have relatively high status in one area does not necessarily indicate that they will have high status in another. Less complex societies, however, seem to approach more equal status for males and females in a variety of areas of life.

5. Field studies have suggested some consistent female–male differences in personality: Boys tend to be more aggressive than girls, and girls seem to be more responsible and helpful than boys.

6. Societies that are restrictive toward one aspect of heterosexual sex tend to be restrictive with regard to other aspects. And more complex societies tend to be more restrictive toward premarital heterosexual sex than less complex societies.

7. Societal attitudes toward homosexuality are not completely consistent with attitudes toward sexual relationships between the sexes. Societal tolerance of homosexuality is associated with tolerance of abortion and infanticide and with famines and food shortages.

Glossary Terms

gender differences (p. 297)
gender roles (p. 298)
gender stratification
 (p. 306)

primary subsistence
 activities (p. 302)
secondary subsistence
 activities (p. 302)

sex differences (p. 297)

Critical Questions

1. Would you expect female–male differences in personality to disappear in a society with complete gender equality in the workplace?

2. Under what circumstances would you expect male–female differences in athletic performance to disappear?

3. What conditions may make the election of a female head of state most likely?

Read the Original Source on myanthrolab.com

Read "Andean Mestizos: Growing Up Female and Male" by Lauris McKee in MyAnthroLibrary and answer the following questions.

1. Which of the Andean Mestizos' ideas about conception, pregnancy, and birth are different from those of your own culture? (Identify your own culture in your answer.)

2. According to McKee, what do the Mestizos say is the reason for the shorter breast-feeding of girls?

3. What are the consequences of the gender difference in breast-feeding? Are the parents aware of these consequences?

Marriage, Family, and Kinship

14

CHAPTER OUTLINE

Nearly all societies known to anthropology have had the custom of marriage. Why marriage is customary in nearly every society we know of is a classic and perplexing question, and one we attempt to deal with in this chapter. The near universality of marriage customs does not mean that everyone in a society gets married, nor that marriage and family customs are the same in all societies. On the contrary, there is much variation from society to society in how one marries, whom one marries, and even how many people a person can be married to simultaneously.

Families are universal; all societies have parent–child groups, but the form and size of the family can vary from society to society. Some societies have large extended families with two or more related parent–child groups; others have smaller independent families. Today, marriage is not always the basis for family life. One-parent families are becoming increasingly common in our own and other societies. Marriage has not disappeared in these places—it is still customary to marry—but more individuals are choosing now to have children without being married.

As we will see, kin groups that include hundreds or even thousands of related people are found in many societies and structure economic, social-political, and religious functions. In noncommercial societies, kin groups were probably the most important aspect of social organization.

Marriage

When anthropologists speak of marriage, they do not mean to imply that couples everywhere must get marriage certificates or have wedding ceremonies, as in our own society. **Marriage** merely means a socially approved sexual and economic union, usually between a woman and a man. It is presumed, by both the couple and others, to be more or less permanent, and it subsumes reciprocal rights and obligations between the two spouses and between spouses and their future children.[1] Marriage to more than one spouse at a time is quite common in many societies, as we shall see.

It is a socially approved sexual union in that a married couple does not have to hide the sexual nature of their relationship. A woman might say, "I want you to meet my husband," but

The bride's relatives arrive at the groom's home bearing gifts and Piki bread from the bride's family at a traditional Hopi engagement ceremony in Arizona.

she could not say, "I want you to meet my lover" without causing some embarrassment in most societies. Although the union may ultimately be dissolved by divorce, couples in all societies begin marriage with some idea of permanence in mind. Implicit too in marriage are reciprocal rights and obligations. These may be more or less specific and formalized regarding matters of property, finances, and childrearing. Marriage entails both a sexual and an economic relationship, as George Peter Murdock noted: "Sexual relations can occur without economic cooperation, and there can be a division of labor between men and women without sex. But marriage unites the economic and the sexual."[2]

Why is Marriage Nearly Universal?

Because virtually all societies practice female–male marriage as we have defined it, we can assume that the custom is adaptive. Several interpretations have traditionally been offered to explain why all human societies have the custom of marriage. Each suggests that marriage solves problems found in all societies: how to share the products of a gender division of labor; how to care for infants, who are dependent for a long time; and how to minimize sexual competition. To evaluate the plausibility of these interpretations, we must ask whether marriage provides the best or the only reasonable solution to each problem. After all, we are trying to explain a custom that is virtually universal. The comparative study of other animals, some of which have something like marriage, may help us to evaluate these explanations.

Gender Division of Labor We noted in the preceding chapter that males and females in every society perform different economic activities. This gender division of labor has often been cited as a reason for marriage because society has to have some mechanism by which women and men share the products of their labor.[3] But it seems unlikely that marriage is the only possible solution. The hunter-gatherer rule of sharing could be extended to include all the products brought in by both women and men. Thus, although marriage may solve the problem of sharing the fruits of a division of labor, it clearly is not the only possible solution.

Prolonged Infant Dependency Humans exhibit the longest period of infant dependency of any primate. The child's prolonged dependence places the greatest burden on the mother, who is the main child caregiver in most societies. Prolonged child care by human females may limit the kinds of work they can do. Also, they may need the help of a man to do certain types of work, such as hunting, that are incompatible with child care. Because of this prolonged dependency, it has been suggested that marriage is necessary.[4] But here the argument becomes essentially the same as the division-of-labor argument, and it has the same logical weakness. It is not clear why a group of women and men, such as a hunter-gatherer band, could not cooperate in providing for dependent children without marriage.

Sexual Competition Unlike most other female primates, the human female may engage in intercourse at any time throughout the year. Some scholars have suggested that more or less continuous female sexuality may have created a serious problem: considerable sexual competition between males for females. It is argued that society had to prevent such competition to survive, that it had to develop some way of minimizing the rivalry among males for females to reduce the chance of lethal and destructive conflict.[5]

There are several problems with this argument. First, why should continuous female sexuality make for more sexual competition in the first place? One might argue the other way around.

There might be more competition over the scarcer resources that would be available if females were less frequently interested in sex. Second, males of many animal species, even some that have relatively frequent female sexuality (as do many of our close primate relatives), do not show much aggression over females. Third, why couldn't sexual competition, even if it existed, be regulated by cultural rules other than marriage? For instance, society might have adopted a rule whereby men and women circulated among all the opposite-sex members of the group, each person staying a specified length of time with each partner. Such a system presumably would solve the problem of sexual competition. On the other hand, such a system might not work particularly well if individuals came to prefer certain other individuals. Jealousies attending those attachments might give rise to even more competition.

Other Mammals and Birds: Postpartum Requirements None of the theories we have discussed explains convincingly why marriage is the only or the best solution to a particular problem. Also, we have some comparative evidence on mammals and birds that casts doubt on those theories.[6] How can evidence from other animals help us evaluate theories about human marriage? If we look at the animals that, like humans, have some sort of stable female–male mating, as compared with those that are completely promiscuous, we can perhaps see what sorts of factors may predict male–female bonding ("marriage") in the warm-blooded animal species. Most species of birds, and some mammals such as wolves and beavers, have male-female bonding. Among 40 mammal and bird species, none of the three factors discussed previously—division of labor, prolonged infant dependency, and greater female sexuality—predicts or is correlated strongly with male–female bonding. With respect to division of labor by sex, most other animals have nothing comparable to a humanlike division of labor, but many have stable female–male matings anyway. The two other supposed factors—prolonged infant dependency and female sexuality—predict just the opposite of what we might expect. Mammal and bird species that have longer dependency periods or more female sexuality are less likely to have stable matings.

Does anything predict male–female bonding? One factor does among mammals and birds, and it may also help explain human marriage. Animal species in which females can simultaneously feed themselves and their babies after birth (*postpartum*) tend not to have stable matings;

Most birds, like these Canadian geese, have male-female bonding. Shortly after hatching, it would be difficult for a mother alone to feed herself, her babies, and protect the young without help.

species in which postpartum mothers cannot feed themselves and their babies at the same time tend to have stable matings. Among the typical bird species, a mother would have difficulty feeding herself and her babies simultaneously. Because the young cannot fly for a while and must be protected in a nest, the mother risks losing them to other animals if she goes off to obtain food. But if she has a male bonded to her (as most bird species do), he can bring back food or take a turn watching the nest. Among animal species that have no postpartum feeding problem, babies are able to travel with the mother almost immediately after birth as she moves about to eat (as do grazers such as horses), or the mother can transport the babies as she moves about to eat (as do baboons and kangaroos). We think the human female has a postpartum feeding problem. When humans lost most of their body hair, babies could not readily travel with the mother by clinging to her fur. And when humans began to depend on certain kinds of food-getting that could be dangerous (such as hunting), mothers could not engage in such work with their infants along.[7]

Recent research on the Hadza foragers of Tanzania appears to support this view. Frank Marlowe found that the caloric contribution of mothers and fathers depends on whether or not they have a nursing infant. Hadza women may generally contribute more calories than men to the diet, but married women who are nursing contribute substantially less than other married women. The lower contribution of nursing mothers appears to be made up by the Hadza father. Fathers with nursing children contribute significantly more food to the household than fathers with older children.[8]

Even if we assume that human mothers have a postpartum feeding problem, we still have to ask if marriage is the most likely solution to the problem. We think so, because other conceivable solutions probably would not work as well. For example, if a mother took turns babysitting with another mother, neither might be able to collect enough food for both mothers and the two sets of children dependent on them. But a mother and father share the same set of children, and therefore it would be easier for them to feed themselves and their children adequately. Another possible solution is no pair bonding at all, just a promiscuous group of males and females. But in that kind of arrangement, we think, a particular mother probably would not always be able to count on some male to watch her baby when she had to go out for food or to bring her food when she had to watch her baby. Thus, it seems to us that the problem of postpartum feeding by itself helps to explain why some animals, including humans, have relatively stable male–female bonds.[9] Of course, there is still the question of whether research on other animals can be applied to human beings. We think it can, but not everybody will agree.

How Does One Marry?

When we say that marriage is a socially approved sexual and economic union, we mean that all societies have some way of marking the onset of a marriage, but the ways of doing so vary considerably. For reasons that we don't fully understand, some cultures mark marriages by elaborate rites and celebrations; others mark marriages in much more informal ways. And most societies have economic transactions before, during, or even after the onset of the marriages.

Economic Aspects of Marriage
"It's not man that marries maid, but field marries field, vineyard marries vineyard, cattle marry cattle." In its down-to-earth way, this German peasant saying indicates that, in many societies, marriage involves economic considerations. In our culture, economic considerations may or may not be explicit. However, in about 75 percent of the societies known to anthropology,[10] one or more explicit economic transactions take place before or after the marriage.

Bride Price **Bride price** or **bride wealth** is a gift of money or goods from the groom or his kin to the bride's kin. Bride price is the most common form of transaction. In one cross-cultural sample, 44 percent of the societies with economic transactions at marriage practiced bride price; in almost all of those societies, the bride price was substantial.[11] Bride price occurs all over the world but is especially common in Africa and Oceania. Payment can be made in different currencies; livestock and food are two of the more common. With the increased importance of commercial exchange, money has increasingly become part of the bride price payments.

What kinds of societies are likely to have the custom of bride price? Cross-culturally, societies with bride price are likely to practice horticulture and lack social stratification. Bride price is also likely where women contribute a great deal to primary subsistence activities[12] and where they contribute more than men to all kinds of economic activities.[13] Although these findings might suggest that women are highly valued in such societies, recall that the status of women relative to men is not higher in societies in which women contribute a lot to primary subsistence activities. Indeed, bride price is likely to occur in societies in which men make most of the decisions in the household,[14] and decision making by men is one indicator of lower status for women.

Bride Service **Bride service**, which is the next most common type of economic transaction at marriage—occurring in about 19 percent of the societies with economic transactions—requires the groom to work for the bride's family, sometimes before the marriage begins, sometimes after. Bride service varies in duration. In some societies, it lasts for only a few months; in others, as long as several years. Native North and South American societies were likely to practice bride service, particularly if they were egalitarian food collectors.[15]

Exchange of Females Of the societies that have economic transactions at marriage, 6 percent have the custom whereby a sister or female relative of the groom is exchanged for the bride. These societies tend to be horticultural, egalitarian, and to have a relatively high contribution of women to primary subsistence.[16]

Gift Exchange Gift exchange, which involves the exchange of gifts of about equal value by the two kin groups about to be linked by marriage, occurs somewhat more often than the exchange of females (about 11 percent of those with economic transactions).[17] For example, among the Andaman Islanders, as soon as a boy and girl indicate their intention to marry, their respective sets of parents cease all communication and begin sending gifts of food and other objects to each other through a third party. This arrangement continues until the marriage is completed and the two kin groups are united.[18]

Dowry A **dowry** is usually a substantial transfer of goods or money from the bride's family to the bride, the groom, or the couple.[19] Unlike the types of transactions we have discussed so far, the dowry, which occurs in about 8 percent of the societies with economic transactions, is usually not a transaction between the kin of the bride and the kin of the groom. A family has to have wealth to give a dowry, but because the goods go to the new household, no wealth comes back to the family that gave the dowry. Payment of dowries was common in medieval and Renaissance Europe; the custom is still practiced in parts of eastern Europe and in sections of southern Italy and France, where land is often the major item the bride's family provides. Parts of India also practice the dowry. In contrast to societies with bride price, societies with dowry tend to be those in which women contribute relatively little to primary subsistence activities, there is a high

A young Iraqi couple in 2008 look at gold jewelry that will be part of her dowry. It is considered to be hers no matter what happens to the marriage.

degree of social stratification, and a man is not allowed to be married to more than one woman simultaneously.[20]

The dowry is provided by the bride's family to the bride, the groom, or the couple. But sometimes the payments to the bride originate from the groom's family. Because the goods are sometimes first given to the bride's father, who passes most if not all of them to her, this kind of transaction is called **indirect dowry**.[21] Indirect dowry occurs in about 12 percent of the societies in which marriage involves an economic transaction.

Whom Should One Marry or Not Marry?

Probably every child in our society knows the story of Cinderella—the poor, downtrodden, but lovely girl who accidentally meets, falls in love with, and eventually marries a prince. It is a charming tale, but it is misleading as a guide to mate choice in our society. All societies have rules restricting marriage with some other people, as well as preferences about which other people are the most desirable mates. Even in a modern, urbanized society such as ours, where theoretically mate choice is free, people tend to marry within their own class and geographic area.

Incest Taboo   Perhaps the most rigid regulation, found in *all* cultures, is the **incest taboo**, which prohibits sexual intercourse or marriage between some categories of kin.

The most universal aspect of the incest taboo is the prohibition of sexual intercourse or marriage between mother and son, father and daughter, and brother and sister. No society in recent times has permitted either sexual intercourse or marriage between those pairs. A few societies in the past, however, did permit incest, mostly within the royal and aristocratic families, though generally it was forbidden to the rest of the population. For example, the Incan and Hawaiian royal families allowed marriage within the family. Probably the best-known example of allowed incest involved Cleopatra of Egypt who was married to two of her younger brothers at different times.[22] The reasons seem to have been partly religious—a member of the family of the pharaoh, who was considered a god, could not marry any "ordinary" human—and partly economic, for marriage within the family kept the royal property undivided. In Egypt, between 30 B.C. and A.D. 324, incest was allowed not just in the royal family; an estimated 8 percent of commoner marriages were brother–sister marriages.[23] But, despite these exceptions, the fact remains that no culture we know of today permits or accepts incest within the nuclear family.

Arranged Marriages In an appreciable number of societies, marriages are arranged; immediate families or go-betweens handle the negotiations. Sometimes betrothals are completed while the future partners are still children. This was formerly the custom in much of Hindu India, China, Japan, and eastern and southern Europe. Implicit in the arranged marriage is the conviction that the joining together of two kin groups to form new social and economic ties is too important to be left to free choice and romantic love.

Arranged marriages are becoming less common in many places, and couples are beginning to have more say about their marriage partners. But in 1960, marriages were still arranged on the Pacific island of Rotuma, and sometimes the bride and groom did not meet until the wedding day. Today, weddings are much the same, but couples are allowed to "go out" and have a say about whom they wish to marry.[24]

Exogamy and Endogamy Marriage partners often must be chosen from outside one's own kin group or community; this is known as a rule of **exogamy**. Exogamy can take many forms. It may mean marrying outside a particular group of kin or outside a particular village or group of villages. When there are rules of exogamy, violations are often believed to cause harm. On the islands of Yap in Micronesia, people who are related through women are referred to as "people of one belly." The elders say that if two people from the same kinship group married, they would not have any female children and the group would die out.[25]

A study of foragers and horticulturalists found a clear relationship between population density and the distance between the communities of the husband and wife—the lower the density, the greater the marriage distance. Because foragers generally have lower densities than horticulturalists, they generally have further to go to find mates. Among the San, for instance, the average husband and wife had lived 40 miles (65 kilometers) from each other before they were married.[26]

A rule of **endogamy** obliges a person to marry within some group. The caste groups of India traditionally have been endogamous. The higher castes believed that marriage with lower castes would "pollute" them, and such unions were forbidden. Caste endogamy is also found in some parts of Africa.

These young South Asian Hindus in Great Britain are "speed dating." They talk with potential spouses for three minutes each. Traditionally, parents arrange marriages.

Cousin Marriages Kinship terminology for most people in the United States does not differ-entiate between types of cousins. In some other societies, such distinctions may be important, particularly with regard to first cousins; the terms for the different kinds of first cousins may indicate which cousins are suitable marriage partners (sometimes even preferred mates) and which are not. Although most societies prohibit marriage with all types of first cousins,[27] some societies allow and even prefer particular kinds of cousin marriage.

Cross-cousins are children of siblings of the opposite sex; that is, a person's cross-cousins are the father's sisters' children and the mother's brothers' children. **Parallel cousins** are chil-dren of siblings of the same sex; a person's parallel cousins, then, are the father's brothers' children and the mother's sisters' children. The Chippewa Indians used to practice cross-cousin marriage, as well as cross-cousin joking. With his female cross-cousins, a Chippewa man was expected to exchange broad, risqué jokes, but he would not do so with his parallel cousins, with whom severe propriety was the rule. In general, in any society in which cross-cousin marriage is allowed but parallel cousin is not, there is a joking relationship between a man and his female cross-cousins. This attitude contrasts with the formal and very respectful relationship the man maintains with female parallel cousins. Apparently, the joking relationship signifies the possi-bility of marriage, whereas the respectful relationship signifies the extension of the incest taboo to parallel cousins.

Parallel-cousin marriage is fairly rare, but Muslim societies usually prefer such marriages, allowing other cousin marriages as well. The Kurds, who are mostly Sunni Muslims, prefer a young man to marry his father's brother's daughter (for the young woman, this would be her father's brother's son). The father and his brother usually live near each other, so the woman will stay close to home in such a marriage. The bride and groom are also in the same kin group, so marriage in this case also entails kin group endogamy.[28]

There is evidence from cross-cultural research that cousin marriages are most apt to be permitted in relatively large and densely populated societies. Perhaps this is because the likelihood of such marriages, and therefore the risks of inbreeding, are minimal in those societies.[29]

How Many Does One Marry?

We are accustomed to thinking of marriage as involving just one man and one woman at a time—**monogamy**—but most societies known to anthropology have allowed a man to be married to more than one woman at the same time—**polygyny**. At any given time, however, the majority of men in societies permitting polygyny are married monogamously; few or no societies have enough women to permit most men to have at least two wives. Polygyny's mirror image—one woman being married to more than one man at the same time, called **polyandry**—is practiced in very few societies. Polygyny and polyandry are the two types of **polygamy**, or plural spouse marriage. **Group marriage**, in which more than one man is mar-ried to more than one woman at the same time, sometimes occurs but is not customary in any known society.

Polygyny The Old Testament has many references to men with more than one wife simulta-neously: King David and King Solomon are just two examples of men polygynously married. Polygyny in many societies is a mark of a man's great wealth or high status. In such societies, only the very wealthy can, and are expected to, support more than one wife. Some Muslim societies, especially Arabic-speaking ones, still view polygyny in this light. But a man does not always have to be wealthy to be polygynous; indeed, in some societies in which women are important

Polygyny is practiced by some in this country, even though it is prohibited by law.

contributors to the economy, it seems that men try to have more than one wife to become wealthier. For example, among the Siwai, a society in the South Pacific, status is achieved through feast giving. Pork is the main dish at these feasts, so the Siwai associate pig raising with prestige. This great interest in pigs sparks an interest in wives, because in Siwai society, women raise the food needed to raise pigs. Thus, although having many wives does not in itself confer status among the Siwai, the increase in pig herds that may result from polygyny is a source of prestige for the owner.[30]

Polygynously married Siwai men do seem to have greater prestige, but they complain that a household with multiple wives is difficult. Sinu, a Siwai, described his plight:

There is never peace for a long time in a polygynous family. If the husband sleeps in the house of one wife, the other one sulks all the next day. If the man is so stupid as to sleep two consecutive nights in the house of one wife, the other one will refuse to cook for him, saying, "So-and-so is your wife; go to her for food. Since I am not good enough for you to sleep with, then my food is not good enough for you to eat."[31]

Co-wife conflict seems not to be present in some societies. For example, Margaret Mead reported that married life among the Arapesh of New Guinea, even in the polygynous marriages, was "so even and contented that there is nothing to relate of it at all."[32] Why might there be little or no obvious jealousy between co-wives in a society? One possible reason is that a man is married to two or more sisters—**sororal polygyny**; it seems that sisters, having grown up together, are more likely to get along and cooperate as co-wives than are co-wives who are not also sisters—**nonsororal polygyny**. Indeed, a recent cross-cultural study confirms that endemic conflict and persistent resentment were virtually ubiquitous in societies with nonsororal polygyny.[33] The most commonly reported reason for the conflict and resentment was insufficient access to the husband for sex and emotional support. Perhaps because conflict is so common, polygynous societies have invented customs to try to lessen conflict and jealousy in co-wives:

1. Co-wives who are not sisters tend to have separate living quarters; sororal co-wives almost always live together.

2. Co-wives have clearly defined equal rights in matters of sex, economics, and personal possessions.

3. Senior wives often have special prestige, which may compensate the first wife for her loss of physical attractiveness.[34]

We must remember that, although jealousy and conflict are commonly mentioned in polygynous marriages, they are not always present. People who practice polygyny may think it has considerable advantages. In a study conducted by Philip and Janet Kilbride in Kenya, female as well as male married people agreed that polygyny had economic and political advantages. Polygynous families provide plenty of farm labor and extra food that can be marketed. They also tend to be influential in their communities and are likely to produce individuals who become government officials.[35] And in South Africa, Connie Anderson found that women choose to be married to a man with other wives because the other wives could help with child care and household work, provide companionship, and allow more freedom to come and go. Some women said they chose polygynous marriages because there was a shortage of marriageable males.[36]

How can we account for the fact that polygyny is allowed and often preferred in most of the societies known to anthropology? One theory is that polygyny will be permitted in societies that have a long **postpartum sex taboo**.[37] Recall that John Whiting suggested that couples, particularly in societies where staple foods have little protein, abstain from sexual intercourse for a long time to protect their child from *kwashiorkor*. If a child gets protein from mother's milk during its first few years, the likelihood of contracting kwashiorkor may be greatly reduced. Societies with long postpartum sex taboos also tend to be polygynous. Perhaps, then, a man's having more than one wife is a cultural adjustment to the taboo since men may seek other sexual relationships during the period of a long post-partum sex taboo. However, it is not clear why polygyny is the only possible solution to the problem. After all, it is conceivable that all of a man's wives might be subject to the postpartum sex taboo at the same time. Furthermore, there may be sexual outlets outside marriage.

Another explanation of polygyny is that it is a response to an excess of women over men, due largely to the prevalence of warfare in a society. Because men and not women are generally the warriors, warfare almost always takes a greater toll of men's lives. Given that almost all adults in noncommercial societies are married, polygyny may be a way of providing spouses for surplus women. Indeed, there is evidence that societies with imbalanced sex ratios in favor of women tend to have both polygyny and high male mortality in warfare. Conversely, societies with balanced sex ratios tend to have both monogamy and low male mortality in warfare.[38]

A third explanation is that a society will allow polygyny when men marry at an older age than women. The argument is similar to the sex ratio interpretation. Delaying the age of marriage for men would produce an artificial, though not an actual, excess of marriageable women. Why marriage for men is delayed is not clear, but the delay does predict polygyny.[39]

Is one of these explanations better than the others, or are all three factors—long postpartum sex taboo, an imbalanced sex ratio in favor of women, and delayed age of marriage for men— important in explaining polygyny? One way of trying to decide among alternative explanations is to do what is called a *statistical-control analysis*, which allows us to see if a particular factor still predicts when the effects of other possible factors are removed. In this case, when the possible effect of sex ratio is removed, a long postpartum sex taboo no longer predicts polygyny and hence is probably not a cause of polygyny.[40] But both an actual excess of women and a late age of marriage for men seem to be strong predictors of polygyny. Added together, these two factors predict even more strongly.[41]

Behavioral ecologists have also suggested ecological reasons why both men and women might prefer polygynous marriages. If there are enough resources, men might prefer polygyny because they can have more children if they have more than one wife. If resources are highly variable and men control resources, women might find it advantageous to marry a man with many resources even if she is a second wife. A recent study of foragers suggests that foraging societies in which men control hunting or fishing territories are more likely to be polygynous. The main problem with the theory of variable resources and their marital consequences is that many societies, particularly in the "modern" world, have great variability in wealth, but little polygyny. So behavioral ecologists have had to argue that polygyny is lacking because of socially imposed constraints. Degree of disease in the environment may also be a factor. Bobbi Low has suggested that a high incidence of disease may reduce the prevalence of "healthy" men. In such cases, it may be to a woman's advantage to marry a "healthy" man even if he is already married, and it may be to a man's advantage to marry several unrelated women to maximize genetic variation (and disease resistance) among his children. Indeed, societies with many pathogens are more likely to have polygyny.[42] A recent cross-cultural study compared the degree of disease explanation of polygyny with the imbalanced sex-ratio explanation. Both were supported. The number of pathogens predicted particularly well in more densely populated complex societies, where pathogen load is presumably greater. The sex-ratio explanation predicted particularly well in sparser, nonstate societies.[43] An excess of females and pathogen stress predicted polygyny in modern nations too.[44]

Polyandry   George Peter Murdock's "World Ethnographic Sample" included only four societies (less than 1 percent of the total) in which polyandry, or the marriage of several men to one woman, was practiced.[45] When the husbands are brothers we call it **fraternal polyandry**; if they are not brothers, it is **nonfraternal polyandry**. Some Tibetans, the Toda of India, and the Sinhalese of Sri Lanka have practiced fraternal polyandry. Among some Tibetans who practice fraternal polyandry, biological paternity seems to be of no particular concern; there is no attempt to link children biologically to a particular brother, and all children are treated the same.[46]

One possible explanation for the practice of polyandry is a shortage of women. The Toda practiced female infanticide[47]; the Sinhalese had a shortage of women but denied the practice of female infanticide.[48] A correlation between shortage of women and polyandry would account for why polyandry is so rare in the ethnographic record; an excess of men is rare cross-culturally.

Another possible explanation is that polyandry is an adaptive response to severely limited resources. Melvyn Goldstein studied Tibetans who live in the northwestern corner of Nepal, above 12,000 feet in elevation. Cultivable land is extremely scarce there, with most families having less than an acre. The people say they practice fraternal polyandry to prevent the division of a family's farm and animals. Instead of dividing up their land among them and each taking a wife, brothers preserve the family farm by sharing a wife. Although not recognized by the Tibetans, their practice of polyandry minimizes population growth. There are as many women as men of marriageable age. But about 30 percent of the women do not marry, and, although these women do have some children, they have far fewer than married women. Thus, the practice of polyandry minimizes the number of mouths to feed and therefore maximizes the standard of living of the polyandrous family.[49]

Family

All societies have families. A **family** is a social and economic unit consisting minimally of one or more parents (or parent substitute) and their children. Members of a family always have certain reciprocal rights and obligations, particularly economic ones. Family members usually live in one household, but common residence is not a defining feature of families. In simpler societies, the family and the household tend to be indistinguishable; only in more complex societies, and in societies becoming dependent on commercial exchange, may some members of a family live elsewhere.[50]

Variation in Family Form

The minimal family has one parent (or parent substitute). Single-parent families, usually headed by the mother, are common in some societies, but most societies typically have larger families. These larger family units usually include at least one **nuclear family** (a married couple and their children), but there is often polygamy, so there may be more than one spouse with more than one set of children. If a single-parent family, nuclear family, polygynous, or polyandrous family lives alone, each is an **independent family**. However, the **extended family** is the prevailing form of family in more than half the societies known to anthropology.[51] It may consist of two or more single-parent, monogamous, polygynous, or polyandrous families linked by a blood tie. Most commonly, the extended family consists of a married couple and one or more of the married children, all living in the same house or household. The constituent nuclear families are normally linked through the parent–child tie. An extended family, however, is sometimes composed of families linked through a sibling tie. Such a family might consist of two married brothers, their wives, and their children. Extended families may be very large, containing many relatives and including three or four generations. A diagram of these different types of family can be found in Figure 14.1.

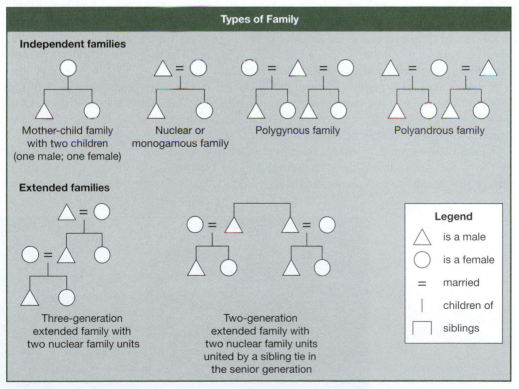

Figure 14.1
Anthropologists commonly use diagrams to represent family structures. At the top are four types of independent family assuming only two children (one male, one female) and only two spouses where multiple spouses are allowed. At the bottom are two types of extended family. These diagrams show only small extended families, but extended families can have many constituent family units if there are many children as well as plural marriages.

Extended-Family Households

In a society composed of extended-family households, marriage does not bring as pronounced a change in lifestyle as it does in our culture, where the couple typically moves to a new residence and forms a new, and basically independent, family unit. In extended families, the newlyweds are assimilated into an existing family unit. Margaret Mead described such a situation in Samoa:

> . . . the young couple live in the main household, simply receiving a bamboo pillow, a mosquito net and a pile of mats for their bed. . . . The wife works with all the women of the household and waits on all the men. The husband shares the enterprises of the other men and boys. Neither in personal service given or received are the two marked off as a unit.[52]

A young couple in Samoa, as in other societies with extended families, generally has little decision-making power over the governing of the household. Often the responsibility of running the household rests with the senior male. Nor can the new family accumulate its own property and become independent; it is a part of the larger corporate structure. Eventually the young people will have authority when the parents die.

Possible Reasons for Extended-Family Households

Why do most societies known to anthropology commonly have extended-family households? Extended-family households are found most frequently in societies with sedentary agricultural economies. M. F. Nimkoff and Russell Middleton suggested that the extended family may be a social mechanism that prevents the economically ruinous division of family property in societies in which property such as cultivated land is important.[53]

But agriculture is only a weak predictor of extended-family households. Many agriculturalists lack them, and many nonagricultural societies have them. A different theory is that extended-family households come to prevail in societies that have incompatible activity requirements—that is, requirements that cannot be met by a mother or a father in a one-family household. In other words, extended-family households are generally favored when the work a mother has to do outside the home (cultivating fields or gathering foods far away) makes it difficult for her to also care for her children and do other household tasks. Similarly, extended families may be favored when

The traditional houses of an extended family on Satawal Island in the Carolines, Micronesia.

the required outside activities of a father (warfare, trading trips, or wage labor far away) make it difficult for him to do the subsistence work required of males. There is cross-cultural evidence that societies with such incompatible activity requirements are more likely to have extended-family households than societies with compatible activity requirements, regardless of whether or not the society is agricultural. Even though they have incompatible activity requirements, however, societies with commercial or monetary exchange may not have extended-family households perhaps because a family may obtain the necessary help by "buying" the required services.[54]

In many societies, there are kin groups even larger than extended families. The rest of this chapter discusses the varieties of such groupings.

Marital Residence and Kinship

In the United States and Canada, as well as in many other industrial societies, a young man and woman usually establish a place of residence apart from their parents or other relatives when they marry, if they have not already moved away before that. Our society is so oriented toward this pattern of marital residence—*neolocal (new-place) residence*—that it seems to be the obvious and natural one to follow. Young adults may learn to live away from home most of the year if they join the armed forces or attend an out-of-town college. In any case, when young people marry, they generally live apart from family.

So familiar is neolocal residence to us that we tend to assume that all societies must practice the same pattern. On the contrary, of the 565 societies in George Peter Murdock's "World Ethnographic Sample," only about 5 percent followed this practice.[55] About 95 percent of the world's societies have had some other pattern of residence whereby a new couple settles within, or very close to, the household of the parents or some other close relative of either the groom or the bride. Marital residence largely predicts the types of kin groups found in a society, as well as how people refer to and classify their various relatives.

Patterns of Marital Residence

In societies in which newly married couples customarily live with or close to their kin, the pattern of residence varies. Children in all societies are required to marry outside the nuclear family because of the incest taboo and, with few exceptions, couples in almost all societies live together after they are married. Therefore, some children have to leave home when they marry. But which married children remain at home and which reside elsewhere? Societies vary in the way they deal with this question, but there are not many different patterns. The prevailing one could be one of the following (the percentages of each in the ethnographic record do not sum to 100 because of rounding):

1. **Patrilocal residence.** The son stays and the daughter leaves, so that the married couple lives with or near the husband's parents (67 percent of all societies).

2. **Matrilocal residence.** The daughter stays and the son leaves, so that the married couple lives with or near the wife's parents (15 percent of all societies).

3. **Bilocal residence.** Either the son or the daughter leaves, so that the married couple lives with or near either the wife's or the husband's parents (7 percent of all societies).

4. **Avunculocal residence.** Both son and daughter normally leave, but the son and his wife settle with or near his mother's brother (4 percent of all societies).[56]

In these definitions, we use the phrase "the married couple lives *with or near*" a particular set of in-laws. When couples live with or near the kin of a spouse, the couple may live in the same

In many societies known to anthropology, the bride goes to live with or near the husband's family. In a reenactment of a traditional Korean wedding ceremony, a bride is carried to the home of the groom.

household with those kin, creating an *extended-family* household, or they may live separately in an *independent-family* household, but nearby. (Because matrilocal, patrilocal, and avunculocal residence specify just one pattern, they are often called nonoptional or **unilocal residence** patterns.) A fifth pattern of residence is neolocal, in which the newly married couple does not live with or near kin.

5. **Neolocal residence.** Both son and daughter leave; married couples live apart from the relatives of both spouses (5 percent of all societies).

How does place of residence affect the social life of the couple? Because the pattern of residence governs with or near whom individuals live, it largely determines which people those individuals interact with and have to depend on. If the kin of the husband surrounds a married couple, for example, the chances are that those relatives will figure importantly in the couple's future. Whether the couple lives with or near the husband's or the wife's kin can also be expected to have important consequences for the status of the husband or wife. If married couples live patrilocally, as occurs in most societies, the wife may be far from her own kin. In any case, she will be an outsider among a group of male relatives who have grown up together. The feeling of being an outsider is particularly strong when the wife has moved into a patrilocal extended-family household.

Among the Tiv of central Nigeria,[57] the patrilocal extended family consists of the "great father," who is the head of the household, and his younger brothers, his sons, and his younger brothers' sons. Also included are the in-marrying wives and all unmarried children. (The sisters and daughters of the household head who have married would have gone to live where their husbands lived.) Authority is strongly vested in the male line, particularly the oldest of the household, who has authority over bride price, disputes, punishment, and plans for new buildings.

A somewhat different situation exists if the husband comes to live with or near his wife's parents. In this case, the wife and her kin take on somewhat greater importance, and the husband is the outsider. As we shall see, however, the matrilocal situation is not quite the mirror image of the patrilocal because the husband's kin in matrilocal societies often are not far away. Moreover, even though residence is matrilocal, women often do not have as much to say in decision making as their brothers do.

If the married couple does not live with or near the parents or close kin of either spouse, the situation is again quite different. It should not be surprising that relatives and kinship connections do not figure very largely in everyday life in neolocal residence situations. Toward the end of this chapter, we consider the factors that may explain residential variation; these same factors may also help explain the types of kinship groups that develop.

The Structure of Kinship

In noncommercial societies, kinship connections structure many areas of social life—from the kind of access an individual has to productive resources to the kind of political alliances formed between communities and larger territorial groups. In some societies, in fact, kinship connections have an important bearing on matters of life and death. In societies with feuding, any member of a kin group may be considered a suitable target to revenge a previous death. It is no wonder that anthropologists often speak of the web of kinship as providing the main structure of social action in noncommercial societies.

If kinship is important, there is still the question of which set of kin a person affiliates with and depends on. After all, if every single relative were counted as equally important, there would be an unmanageably large number of people in each person's kinship network. Consequently, in most societies in which kinship connections are important, rules allocate each person to a particular and definable set of kin.

Types of Affiliation with Kin We distinguish three main types of affiliation with kin: *unilineal descent, ambilineal descent,* and *bilateral kinship.* The first two types (unilineal descent and ambilineal descent) are based on **rules of descent**, which are rules that connect individuals with particular sets of kin because of known or presumed common ancestry.

Unilineal descent refers to the fact that a person is affiliated with a group of kin through descent links of one sex only—either males only or females only. Thus, unilineal descent can be either patrilineal or matrilineal.

1. **Patrilineal descent** affiliates individuals with kin of both sexes related to them *through men only.* As Figure 14.2 indicates, the children in patrilineal systems in each generation belong

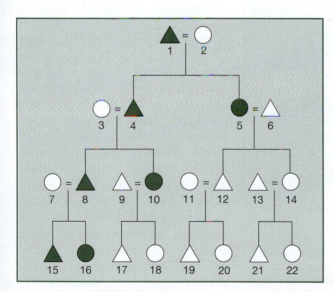

Note: A triangle represents a male; a circle represents a female; an equal sign (=) represents a marriage; vertical lines show descent; horizontal lines indicate siblings.

Figure 14.2 Patrilineal Descent
Individuals 4 and 5, who are the children of 1 and 2, affiliate with their father's patrilineal kin group, represented by the color blue. In the next generation, the children of 3 and 4 also belong to the blue kin group because they take their descent from their father, who is a member of that group. However, the children of 5 and 6 do not belong to this patrilineal group because they take their descent from their father, who is a member of a different group. That is, although the mother of 12 and 14 belongs to the blue patrilineal group, she cannot pass on her descent affiliation to her children, and because her husband (6) does not belong to her patrilineage, her children (12 and 14) belong to their father's group. In the fourth generation, only 15 and 16 belong to the blue patrilineal group because their father is the only male member of the preceding generation who belongs to the blue patrilineal group. In this diagram, then, 1, 4, 5, 8, 10, 15, and 16 are affiliated by the patrilineal descent; all the other individuals belong to other patrilineal groups.

to the kin group of their father; their father, in turn, belongs to the group of his father; and so on. Although a man's sons and daughters are all members of the same descent group, affiliation with that group is transmitted only by the sons to their children. Just as patrilo-cal residence is much more common than matrilocal residence, patrilineal descent is more common than matrilineal descent.

2.   **Matrilineal descent** affiliates individuals with kin of both sexes related to them *through women only*. In each generation, then, children belong to the kin group of their mother (see Figure 14.3). Although a woman's sons and daughters are all members of the same descent group, only her daughters can pass on their descent affiliation to their children.

Unilineal rules of descent affiliate an individual with a line of kin extending back in time and into the future. By virtue of this line of descent, whether it extends through males or females, some very close relatives are excluded. For example, in a patrilineal system, your mother and your mother's parents do not belong to your patrilineal group, but your father and his father (and their sisters) do. In your own generation in a matrilineal or patrilineal system, some cousins are excluded, and in your children's generation, some of your nieces and nephews are excluded.

Unilineal rules of descent can form clear-cut, and hence unambiguous, groups of kin, which can act as separate units even after the death of individual members. Referring again to Figures 14.2 and 14.3, we can see that the individuals in the highlight color belong to the same patrilineal or matrilineal descent group without ambiguity; individuals in the fourth generation belong to the group just as much as those in the first generation. In contrast to unilineal descent, **ambilineal descent** affiliates individuals with kin related to them through men *or* women. In other words, some people in the society affiliate with a group of kin through their fathers; others affiliate through their mothers. Consequently, the descent groups show both female and male genealogical links and they often if not usually overlap in membership.

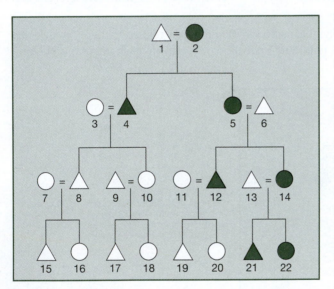

Figure 14.3 Matrilineal Descent

Individuals 4 and 5, who are the children of 1 and 2, affiliate with their mother's kin group, represented by the color blue. In the next generation, the children of 5 and 6 also belong to the blue kin group because they take their descent from their mother, who is a member of that group. However, the children of 3 and 4 do not belong to this matrilineal group because they take their descent from their mother, who is a member of a different group; their father, although a member of the blue matrilineal group, cannot pass his affiliation on to them under the rule of matrilineal descent. In the fourth generation, only 21 and 22 belong to the blue matrilineal group because their mother is the only female member of the preceding generation who belongs. Thus, individuals 2, 4, 5, 12, 14, 21, and 22 belong to the same matrilineal group.

These three rules of descent (patrilineal, matrilineal, and ambilineal) are usually, but not always, mutually exclusive. Most societies can be characterized as having only one rule of descent, but two principles are sometimes used to affiliate individuals with different sets of kin for different purposes. Some societies have, then, what is called **double descent** or **double unilineal descent**, whereby individuals affiliate for some purposes with a group of matrilineal kin and for other purposes with a group of patrilineal kin.

Many societies, including our own, do not have lineal (matrilineal, patrilineal, or ambilineal) descent groups—sets of kin who believe they descend from a common ancestor. These are societies with **bilateral kinship**. *Bilateral* means "two-sided," and in this case, it refers to the fact that one's relatives on both the mother's and father's sides are equal in importance or, more usually, in unimportance. Kinship reckoning in bilateral societies does not refer to common descent but rather is horizontal, moving outward from close to more distant relatives rather than upward to common ancestors (see Figure 14.4).

The term **kindred** describes a person's bilateral set of relatives who may be called upon for some purpose. Most bilateral societies have kindreds that overlap in membership. In North America, we think of the kindred as including the people we might invite to weddings, funerals, or some other ceremonial occasion; a kindred, however, is not usually a definite group. As anyone who has been involved in creating a wedding invitation list knows, a great deal of time may be spent deciding which relatives ought to be invited and which ones can legitimately be excluded. Societies with bilateral kinship differ in precisely how distant relatives have to be before they are lost track of or before they are not included in ceremonial activities.

The distinctive feature of bilateral kinship is that, aside from brothers and sisters, no two people belong to exactly the same kin group. Your kindred contains close relatives spreading out on both your mother's and father's sides, but the members of your kindred are affiliated only by way of their connection to you (**ego**, or the focus). Thus, the kindred is an *ego-centered* group of kin. Because different people (except for brothers and sisters) have different mothers and fathers,

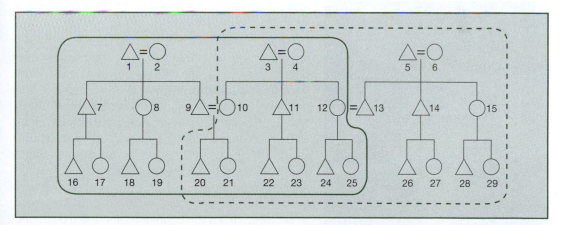

Figure 14.4 Bilateral Kinship
In a bilateral system, the kindred is ego-centered; hence, it varies with different points of reference (except for brothers and sisters). In any bilateral society, the kindred minimally includes parents, grandparents, aunts, uncles, and first cousins. So, if we look at the close kindred of the brother and sister 20 and 21 (enclosed by the solid line), it would include their parents (9 and 10), their aunts and uncles (7, 8, 11, 12), their grandparents (1, 2, 3, 4), and their first cousins (16–19, 22–25). But the kindred of the brother and sister 24 and 25 (shown by the dashed line) includes only some of the same people (3, 4, 10–12, 20–23); in addition, the kindred of 24 and 25 includes people not in the kindred of 20 and 21 (5, 6, 13–15, 26–29).

your first cousins will have different kindreds, and even your own children will have different kindred from yours. The ego-centered nature of the kindred makes it difficult for it to serve as a permanent or persistent group. The only thing the people in a kindred have in common is the ego or focal person who brings them together. A kindred usually has no name, no common purpose, and only temporary meetings centered around the ego.[58] Because everyone belongs to many different and overlapping kindreds, the society is not divided into clear-cut groups. This does not mean that the kindred cannot be turned to for help. Among the Chipewyan of sub-arctic Canada, for example, people would borrow a fishing net from a kindred member, or ask a kindred member to provide child care for a young person whose parent was ill. But recently, with the national and provincial governments providing resources such as housing and medical assistance, and with the increase in opportunities for wage labor, the kindred has ceased to be the main source of help for people in need. Aid from the state is making kinship less useful.[59]

Variation in Unilineal Descent Systems

In a society with unilineal descent, people usually refer to themselves as belonging to a particular unilineal group or set of groups because they believe they share common descent in either the male (patrilineal) or female (matrilineal) line. Anthropologists distinguish several types of unilineal descent groups: lineages, clans, phratries, and moieties.

Lineages   A **lineage** is a set of kin whose members trace descent from a common ancestor through known links. There may be **patrilineages** or **matrilineages**, depending on whether the links are traced through males only or through females only. Lineages are often designated by the name of the common male or female ancestor. In some societies, people belong to a hierarchy of lineages. That is, they first trace their descent back to the ancestor of a minor lineage, then to the ancestor of a larger and more inclusive major lineage, and so on.

Totem poles often symbolize the history of a descent group. A totem pole in Ketchikan, Alaska.

Clans   A **clan** (also sometimes called a **sib**) is a set of kin whose members believe themselves to be descended from a common ancestor, but the links back to that ancestor are not specified. In fact, the common ancestor may not even be known. Clans with patrilineal descent are called **patriclans**; clans with matrilineal descent are called **matriclans**. Clans often are designated by an animal name (Bear, Wolf), called a **totem**, which may have some special significance for the group and, at the very least, is a means of group identification. The word *totem* comes from the Ojibwa Indian word *ototeman*, "a relative of mine." In some societies, people have to observe taboos relating to their clan totem animal, such as being forbidden to kill or eat their totem.

Phratries   A **phratry** is a unilineal descent group composed of supposedly related clans or sibs. As with clans, the descent links in phratries are unspecified.

Moieties   When a whole society is divided into two unilineal descent groups, we call each group a **moiety**. (The word *moiety* comes from a French word meaning "half.") The people in each moiety believe themselves to be descended from a common ancestor, although they cannot specify how. Societies with moiety systems usually have relatively small populations (fewer than 9,000 people). Societies with phratries and clans tend to be larger.[60]

Combinations   Many societies have two or more types in various combinations. For example, some societies have lineages and clans; others may have clans and phratries but no lineages; and still others may have clans and moieties but neither phratries nor lineages. Even if societies have more than one type of unilineal kin group—for example, lineages and clans—there is no ambiguity about membership. Small groups are simply subsets of larger units; the larger units include people who say they are unilineally related further back in time.

Patrilineal Organization   Patrilineal organization is the most frequent type of descent system. The Kapauku Papuans, a people living in the central highlands of western New Guinea, are an example of a patrilineal society with various types of descent groups.[61] The male members of a patrilineage—all the living males who can trace their actual relationship through males to a common ancestor—constitute the male population of a single village or, more likely, a series of adjoining villages. The male members of the lineage live together by virtue of a patrilocal rule of residence and a fairly stable settlement pattern. A son stays near his parents and brings his wife to live in or near his father's house; the daughters leave home and go to live with their husbands. If the group lives in one place over a long period, the male descendants of one man will live in the same territory.

The members of the same patrilineage address each other affectionately and, within this group, a headman maintains law and order. Killing within the lineage is considered a serious offense, and any fighting that takes place is done with sticks rather than lethal weapons such as spears. The Kapauku also belong to larger and more inclusive patrilineal descent groups—clans and phratries. If a member of the patriclan eats the clan's plant or animal totem, it is believed that the person will become deaf. Kapauku are also forbidden to marry anyone from their clan. In other words, the clan is exogamous. Unlike the members of the patrilineage, the male members of the patriclan do not all live together. The lineage is also the largest group of kinsmen that acts together politically. Among clan members, there is no mechanism for resolving disputes, and members of the same patriclan (who belong to different lineages) may even go to war with one another.

The most inclusive patrilineal descent group among the Kapauku is the phratry, each of which is composed of two or more clans. The members of a phratry observe all the totemic taboos of the clans that belong to that phratry. Intermarriage of members of the same clan is forbidden, but members of the same phratry, if they belong to different clans, may marry.

Matrilineal Organization   Although societies with matrilineal descent seem in many respects like mirror images of their patrilineal counterparts, they differ in one important way. That difference has to do with who exercises authority. In patrilineal systems, descent affiliation is transmitted through males, and it is also the males who exercise authority. Consequently, in the patrilineal system, lines of descent and of authority converge. In a matrilineal system, however, although the line of descent passes through females, females rarely exercise authority in their kin groups. Usually males do. Thus, the lines of authority and descent do not converge.[62] Because males exercise authority in the kin group, an individual's mother's brother becomes an important authority figure because he is the individual's closest male matrilineal relative in the parental generation.

The individual's father does not belong to the individual's own matrilineal kin group and thus has no say in kin group matters.

The divergence of authority and descent in a matrilineal system has some effect on community organization and marriage. Most matrilineal societies practice matrilocal residence. Daughters stay at home after marriage and bring their husbands to live with them; sons leave home to join their wives. But the sons who are required to leave will be the ones who eventually exercise authority in their kin groups. This situation presents a problem. The solution that seems to have been realized in most matrilineal societies is that, although the males move away to live with their wives, they usually do not move too far away; indeed, they often marry women who live in the same village. Thus, matrilineal societies tend not to be locally exogamous—that is, members often marry people from inside the village—whereas patrilineal societies are often locally exogamous.[63]

N E W   P E R S P E C T I V E S   O N   G E N D E R

Variation in Residence and Kinship: What Difference Does It Make to Women?

When we say that residence and kinship have profound effects on people's lives, what exactly do we mean? We may imagine that it is hard for a woman in a patrilocal society to move at marriage into another village where her husband has plenty of relatives and she has few. But do we have evidence of that? Most ethnographies usually do not give details about people's feelings, but some do. For example, Leigh Minturn gives us the text of a letter that one new Rajput bride (who grew up in the village of Khalapur, India) sent to her mother shortly after she married into her husband's village. The letter was written when the bride had been gone 6 weeks, but she repeatedly asked if her mother, her father, and her aunts had forgotten her. She begged to be called home and said her bags were packed. She described herself as "a parrot in a cage" and complained about her in-laws. The bride's mother was not alarmed; she knew that such complaints were normal, reflections of her daughter's separation anxiety. Seven years later, when Minturn returned to India, the mother reported the daughter to be happy. Still, a few other brides did have more serious symptoms: ghost possession, 24- to 36-hour comas, serious depression, or suicide. What research has not told us is whether these serious symptoms are present more often in patrilocal, patrilineal societies than in other societies, particularly matrilocal, matrilineal societies.

Conversely, do men have some symptoms in matrilocal, matrilineal societies that they do not have in patrilocal societies? We do not know.

What about the status of women? Some research suggests that matrilocality and matrilineality enhance some aspects of women's status, but perhaps not as much as we might think. Even in matrilineal societies, men are usually the political leaders. The main effect of matrilocality and matrilineality appears to be that women control property, but they also tend to have more domestic authority in the home, more equal sexual restrictions, and more value placed on their lives. Alice Schlegel pointed out that women's status is not always relatively high in matrilineal societies, because they can be dominated by the husband or by brothers (because brothers play important roles in their kin groups). Only when neither the husband nor the brother dominates may women have considerable control over their own lives. Certainly the combination of matrilocality and matrilineality is better for women's status than patrilocality and patrilineality. Matrilocality and matrilineality might not enhance women's status because of the dominance of male matrilineal kin, but patrilocality and patrilineality are very likely to detract from women's status. Norma Diamond stated that, even after the Chinese Communist revolution, which abolished the landholding estates of patrilineages and gave women

The matrilineal organization on Chuuk, a group of small islands in the Pacific, illustrates the general pattern of authority in matrilineal systems.[64] The Chuukese have both matrilineages and matriclans. The matrilineage is a property-owning group whose members trace descent from a known common ancestor in the female line. The female lineage members and their husbands occupy a cluster of houses on the matrilineage's land. The property of the lineage group is administered by the oldest brother of the group, who allocates the productive property of his matrilineage and directs the work of the members. He also represents the group in dealings with the district chief and all outsiders, and he must be consulted on any matter that affects the group. There is also a senior woman of the lineage who exercises some authority, but only insofar as the activities of the women are concerned. She may supervise the women's cooperative work (they usually work separately from the men) and manage the household.

access to education as well as jobs outside the home, male dominance continued. The mode of production and labor changed, but patrilocality did not. Women were still usually the in-marrying strangers, and members of the patrilineage became a work team on the collective farm. Diamond pointed out that those few women who became local leaders were likely to have atypical marriages that allowed them to live in the villages of their birth.

Residence and descent also predict societal attempts to control reproduction. According to Suzanne Frayser, patrilineal societies have several sexual and reproductive dilemmas. One dilemma is the contradiction between the importance of males in kinship and women's role in reproduction. If patrilineal societies denigrate women too much, women may try to decrease their reproduction. If patrilineal societies exalt women too much, that exaltation may detract from the value of men. A second dilemma has to do with paternity, which is essential for patrilineal descent but harder than maternity to be certain of. Frayser argued that, because kin group links are traced through males in patrilineal societies, they will do more to ensure that the man a woman marries is the father. Frayser suggested that patrilineal societies therefore will be more restrictive about a woman's sexuality. Indeed, the results of her cross-cultural study indicate that patrilineal societies are more likely than

other societies to prohibit premarital and extramarital sex for women, and they are more likely to make it very difficult for a woman to divorce her husband.

Of course, we have to remember that there is considerable variation within patrilocal/patrilineal societies and matrilocal/matrilineal societies. In the patrilineal society that Audrey Smedley studied—the Birom of the Jos Plateau in Nigeria—women were formally barred from owning property, from holding political offices, and from major decision making. Yet, her fieldwork revealed that they had considerable autonomy in their personal lives in everyday life, including the legal right to take on lovers. Indeed, they had considerable indirect influence on decision making and were strong supporters of the patrilineal system. Smedley speculates that women support patrilineality in some environmental circumstances because it serves their interests and those of their children too. For example, male crops are highly valued, but such crops are grown on the more dangerous plains where men risked death at the hands of raiders from other groups. Food was scarce, so it may have been adaptive for everyone, including women, to give special status to men for growing crops in dangerous places.

Sources: N. Diamond 1975; Frayser 1985, 338–47; Minturn 1993, 54–71; Schlegel 2009; Smedley 2004; M. K. Whyte 1978b, 132–34.

Within the nuclear family, the father and mother have the primary responsibility for raising and disciplining their children. When a child reaches puberty, however, the father's right to discipline or exercise authority over the child ceases. The mother continues to exercise her right of discipline, but her brother may interfere. A woman's brother rarely interferes with his sister's child before puberty, but he may exercise some authority after puberty, especially because he is an elder in the child's own matrilineage. On Chuuk, men rarely move far from their birthplace. As Ward Goodenough pointed out, "Since matrilocal residence takes the men away from their home lineages, most of them marry women whose lineage houses are within a few minutes walk of their own."[65]

Functions of Unilineal Descent Groups

Unilineal descent groups exist in societies at all levels of cultural complexity.[66] Apparently, however, they are most common in noncommercial food-producing, as opposed to food-collecting, societies.[67] Unilineal descent groups often have important functions in the social, economic, political, and religious realms of life:

1. **Regulating Marriage.** In unilineal societies, individuals are not usually permitted to marry within their own unilineal descent groups. In general, the incest taboo in unilineal societies is extended to all presumed unilineal relatives.

2. **Economic Functions.** Members of a person's lineage or clan are often required to side with that person in any quarrel or lawsuit, to help him or her get established economically, to contribute to a bride price or fine, and to support the person in life crises. Mutual aid often extends to economic cooperation on a regular basis. The unilineal descent group may act as a corporate unit in landownership.

   The descent group sometimes views money earned—either by harvesting a cash crop or by leaving the community for a time to work for cash wages—as belonging to all. In recent times, however, young people in some places have shown an unwillingness to part with their money, viewing it as different from other kinds of economic assistance.

3. **Political Functions.** Headmen or elders may also have the right to settle disputes between two members within a lineage, although they generally lack power to force a settlement. And they may act as intermediaries in disputes between a member of their own clan and a member of an opposing kin group. One of the most important political functions of unilineal descent groups is their role in warfare—the attempt to resolve disputes within and outside the society by violent action. In societies without towns or cities, the organization of such fighting is often in the hands of descent groups.

4. **Religious Functions.** A clan or lineage may have its own religious beliefs and practices, worshiping its own gods or goddesses and ancestral spirits.

Ambilineal Systems

Societies with ambilineal descent groups are far less numerous than unilineal or even bilateral societies. Ambilineal societies, however, resemble unilineal ones in many ways. For instance, the members of an ambilineal descent group believe that they are descended from a common ancestor, although frequently they cannot specify all the genealogical links. The descent group is commonly named and may have an identifying emblem or even a totem; the descent group may own land and other productive resources; and myths and religious practices are often associated with the group. Marriage is often regulated by group membership, just as in unilineal systems, although kin group exogamy is not nearly as common as in unilineal systems. Moreover, ambilineal societies resemble unilineal ones in having various levels or types of descent groups. They may have lineages and higher orders of descent groups, distinguished (as in unilineal systems) by whether or not all the genealogical links to the supposed common ancestors are specified.[68]

Explaining Variation in Residence

If married couples in most societies live with or near kin, as in patrilocal, matrilocal, bilocal, and avunculocal patterns of residence, then why do couples in some societies, such as our own, typically live apart from kin? And, among the societies in which couples live with or near kin, why do most choose the husband's side (patrilocal residence), but some the wife's side (matrilocal residence)? Why do some non-neolocal societies allow a married couple to go to either the wife's or the husband's kin (bilocal residence), whereas most others do not allow a choice?

Neolocal Residence Many anthropologists have suggested that neolocal residence is related to the presence of a money or commercial economy. They argue that, when people can sell their labor or their products for money, they can buy what they need to live, without having to depend on kin. Indeed, neolocal residence tends to occur in societies with monetary or commercial exchange, whereas societies without money tend to have patterns of residence that locate a couple near or with kin.[69] The presence of money, then, partially accounts for neolocal residence: Money seems to allow couples to live on their own. Still, this fact does not quite explain why they choose to do so. One reason may be that couples in commercial societies do better on their own because the jobs available require physical or social mobility. Or perhaps couples prefer to live apart from kin because they want to avoid some of the interpersonal tensions and demands that may be generated by living with or near kin.

Matrilocal versus Patrilocal Residence It is traditionally assumed that, in societies in which married children live near or with kin, the pattern of residence will tend to be patrilocal if males contribute more to the economy and matrilocal if women contribute more. However plausible that assumption may seem, the cross-cultural evidence does not support it. Where men do most of the primary subsistence work, residence is patrilocal no more often than would be expected by chance. Conversely, where women do an equal amount or more of the subsistence work, residence is no more likely to be matrilocal than patrilocal.[70] And if we counted all work inside and outside the home, most societies should be matrilocal because women usually do more. But that is not true either; most societies are not matrilocal.

We can predict whether residence will be matrilocal or patrilocal, however, from the type of warfare practiced in the society. In most societies known to anthropology, neighboring

The Iroquois longhouses could house over 80 people. The female members of a matrilineage with their in-marrying husbands traditionally lived in one longhouse.

communities or districts are enemies. The type of warfare that breaks out periodically between such groups is called *internal* because the fighting occurs between groups that speak the same language. In other societies, the warfare is never within the same society but only with other language groups. This pattern of warfare is referred to as purely *external.* Cross-cultural evidence suggests that, in societies where warfare is at least sometimes internal, residence is almost always patrilocal rather than matrilocal. In contrast, residence is usually matrilocal when warfare is purely external.[71]

How can we explain this relationship between type of warfare and matrilocal versus patrilocal residence? One theory is that patrilocal residence tends to occur with internal warfare because there may be concern over keeping sons close to home to help with defense. Because women do not usually constitute the fighting force in any society, having sons reside at home after marriage might be favored as a means of maintaining a loyal and quickly mobilized fighting force in case of surprise attack from nearby. If warfare is purely external, however, people may not be so concerned about keeping their sons at home because families need not fear attack from neighboring communities or districts.[72]

With purely external warfare, then, the pattern of residence may be determined by other considerations, especially economic ones. If the women do most of the primary subsistence work in societies with purely external warfare, families might want their daughters to remain at home after marriage, so the pattern of residence might become matrilocal. If warfare is purely external but men still do more of the primary subsistence work, residence should still be patrilocal. Thus, the need to keep sons at home after marriage when there is internal warfare may take precedence over any considerations based on division of labor. Perhaps only when internal warfare is nonexistent may a female-dominant division of labor give rise to matrilocal residence.

The frequent absence of men because of long-distance trade or wage labor in distant places may also provide an impetus for matrilocal residence even after warfare ceases. For example, among the Miskito of eastern Central America, matrilocality allowed domestic and village life to continue without interruption when men were away from home for long periods of time, working as lumberers, miners, river transporters, and more recently as deep-sea divers for lobster, for which there is a lot of demand in the international economy. Even though some men would always be away from home, the Miskito continued to get food in their traditional ways, from farming (done mostly by the women) and from hunting and fishing (which was mostly men's work).[73]

Bilocal Residence In societies that practice bilocal residence, a married couple goes to live with or near either the husband's or the wife's parents. Although this pattern seems to involve a choice for the married couple, theory and research suggest that bilocal residence may occur out of necessity instead. Elman Service suggested that bilocal residence is likely to occur in societies that have recently suffered a severe and drastic loss of population because of the introduction of new infectious diseases.[74] Over the last 400 years, contact with Europeans in many parts of the world has resulted in severe population losses among non-European societies that lacked resistance to the Europeans' diseases. If couples need to live with some set of kin to make a living in noncommercial societies, it seems likely that couples in depopulated, noncommercial societies might have to live with whichever spouse's parents and other relatives are still alive. This interpretation is supported by cross-cultural evidence. Recently depopulated societies tend to have bilocal residence or frequent departures from unilocality, whereas societies that are not recently depopulated tend to have one pattern or another of unilocal residence.[75]

In hunter-gatherer societies, a few other circumstances may also favor bilocal residence. Bilocality tends to be found among those hunter-gatherers who have very small bands or unpredictable and low rainfall. Residential "choice" in these cases may be a question of adjusting marital residence to where the couple will have the best chance to survive or to find close relatives with whom to live and work.[76]

Avunculocal Residence Now that we have learned about matrilineal systems, the avunculocal pattern of residence, whereby married couples live with or near the husband's mother's brother, may become clearer. Although avunculocal residence is relatively rare, just about all avunculocal societies are matrilineal. As we have seen, the mother's brother plays an important role in decision making in most matrilineal societies. Aside from his brothers, who is a boy's closest male matrilineal relative? His mother's brother. Going to live with the mother's brother, then, provides a way of localizing male *matrilineal* relatives. But why should some matrilineal societies practice that form of residence? The answer may involve the prevailing type of warfare.

Avunculocal societies, in contrast with matrilocal societies, fight internally. Just as patrilocality may be a response to keep patrilineally related men home after marriage, avunculocality may also be a way of keeping related—in this case, matrilineally related—men together after marriage to provide for quick mobilization in case of surprise attack from nearby. Societies that already have strong, functioning matrilineal descent groups may choose initially, when faced with the emergence of fighting close to home, to switch to avunculocality rather than patrilocality. This is assuming that the close warfare results in high male mortality, which might make it more difficult to trace descent patrilineally than matrilineally. So such a society might begin to practice avunculocality rather than switch to patrilocality. Avunculocal residence would keep a higher number of related men together after marriage, compared with patrilocality, because there would be more possible links through women than through men if many men were dying relatively young in warfare.[77]

The Emergence of Unilineal Systems

Unilineal kin groups play very important roles in the organization of many societies. But not all societies have such groups. In societies that have complex systems of political organization, officials and agencies take over many of the functions that kin groups might perform, such as organizing work and warfare and allocating land. But not all societies that lack complex political organization have unilineal descent systems. Why, then, do some societies have unilineal descent systems, but others do not?

It is generally assumed that unilocal residence, patrilocal or matrilocal, is necessary for the development of unilineal descent. Patrilocal residence, if practiced for some time in a society, will generate a set of patrilineally related males who live in the same territory. Matrilocal residence over time will similarly generate a localized set of matrilineally related females. It is no wonder, then, that matrilocal and patrilocal residence are cross-culturally associated with matrilineal and patrilineal descent, respectively.[78]

But, although unilocal residence might be necessary for the formation of unilineal descent groups, it is apparently not the only condition required. For one thing, many societies with unilocal residence lack unilineal descent groups. For another, merely because related males or related females live together by virtue of a patrilocal or matrilocal rule of residence, it does not necessarily follow that the related people will actually view themselves as a descent group and function as such. Thus, it appears that other conditions are needed to supply the impetus for the formation of unilineal descent groups.

There is evidence that unilocal societies that engage in warfare are more apt to have unilineal descent groups than unilocal societies without warfare.[79] It may be, then, that the presence of fighting in societies lacking complex systems of political organization provides an impetus to the formation of unilineal descent groups. Unilineal descent groups provide individuals with unambiguous groups of people who can fight or form alliances as discrete units.[80] There is no ambiguity about an individual's membership. It is perfectly clear whether someone belongs to a particular clan, phratry, or moiety. This feature of unilineal descent groups enables them to act as separate and distinct units—mostly, perhaps, in warfare.

✓●—Study and Review on myanthrolab.com

Summary

1. All societies known today have the custom of marriage. Marriage is a socially approved sexual and economic union usually between a man and a woman that is presumed to be more or less permanent and that subsumes reciprocal rights and obligations between the two spouses and between the spouses and their children.

2. Marriage arrangements often include an economic element, including bride price (the most common form of economic transaction), bride service, female exchange, dowry, and indirect dowry.

3. Every society tells people whom they cannot marry, whom they can marry, and sometimes even whom they should marry. No society in recent times has allowed sex or marriage between brothers and sisters, mothers and sons, or fathers and daughters. In quite a few societies, marriages are arranged by the couple's kin. Some societies have rules of exogamy, which require marriage outside one's own kin group or community; others have rules of endogamy, requiring marriage within one's group. Although most societies prohibit all first-cousin marriages, some permit or prefer marriage with cross-cousins (children of siblings of the opposite sex) and parallel cousins (children of siblings of the same sex).

4. Most societies allow a man to be married to more than one woman at a time (polygyny). Polyandry, the marriage of one woman to several husbands, is rare.

5. The prevailing form of family in most societies is the extended family. It consists of two or more single-parent, monogamous (nuclear), polygynous, or polyandrous families linked by blood ties.

6. In our society, and in many other industrial societies, a newly married couple usually establishes a place of residence apart from parents or relatives (neolocal residence). But about 95 percent of the world's societies have some pattern of residence whereby the new couple settles within or very close to the household of the parents or some other close relative of the groom or bride. The four major patterns in which married couples live with or near kinsmen are the following: patrilocal residence (the most common), matrilocal residence, bilocal residence, and avunculocal residence.

7. In most societies where kinship is important, rules of affiliation allocate each person to a particular and definable set of kin. The three main types of affiliation with kin are: *unilineal descent* (patrilineal or matrilineal), *ambilineal descent,* and *bilateral kinship.*

8. With unilineal descent, people usually refer to themselves as belonging to a particular unilineal group or set of groups because they believe they share common descent in either the male or the female line. These people form what is called a unilineal descent group. There are several types, and a society may have more than one type: lineages, clans, phratries, and moieties.

Glossary Terms

ambilineal descent (p. 336)
avunculocal
   residence (p. 333)
bilateral kinship (p. 337)
bilocal residence (p. 333)
bride price (or bride
   wealth) (p. 324)
bride service (p. 324)
clan (or sib) (p. 338)
cross-cousins (p. 327)
double descent
   (or double unilineal
   descent) (p. 337)
dowry (p. 324)
ego (p. 337)
endogamy (p. 326)
exogamy (p. 326)
extended family (p. 331)

family (p. 330)
fraternal polyandry (p. 330)
group marriage (p. 327)
incest taboo (p. 325)
independent family (p. 331)
indirect dowry (p. 325)
kindred (p. 337)
lineage (p. 338)
marriage (p. 320)
matriclans (p. 338)
matrilineage (p. 338)
matrilineal descent (p. 336)
matrilocal residence (p. 333)
moiety (p. 339)
monogamy (p. 327)
neolocal residence (p. 334)
nonfraternal
   polyandry (p. 330)

nonsororal polygyny (p. 328)
nuclear family (p. 331)
parallel cousins (p. 327)
patriclans (p. 338)
patrilineage (p. 338)
patrilineal descent (p. 335)
patrilocal residence (p. 333)
phratry (p. 338)
polyandry (p. 327)
polygamy (p. 327)
polygyny (p. 327)
postpartum sex taboo
   (p. 329)
rules of descent (p. 335)
sororal polygyny (p. 328)
totem (p. 338)
unilineal descent (p. 335)
unilocal residence (p. 334)

Critical Questions

1. Will it remain customary in our society to marry? Why do you think it will or will not?

2. Why is polyandry so much less common than polygyny?

3. What other things about our society would change if we practiced other than neolocal residence?

4. Why might it be important for unilineal descent groups to be nonoverlapping in membership?

Read the Original Source on myanthrolab.com

Read Alan Howard and Jan Rensel's "Rotuma: Interpreting a Wedding" on MyAnthroLab and answer the following questions.

1. Howard and Rensel suggest that weddings among the Rotuma express their core values. What core values are expressed in their weddings?

2. How has courtship and marriage changed?

3. Compare the essential features of weddings in your culture (make sure to mention the name of your culture) with those described for the Rotuma.

15 Political Life

((•─Listen to the Chapter Audio on myanthrolab.com   ▭•─Read on myanthrolab.com

For people in the United States, the phrase *political life* has many connotations. It may call to mind the various branches of government: the executive branch, from the president on the national level to governors on the state level to mayors on the local level; legislative institutions, from Congress to state legislatures to city councils; and administrative bureaus, from federal government departments to local agencies.

Political life may also evoke thoughts of political parties, interest groups, lobbying, campaigning, and voting. In other words, when people living in the United States think of political life, they may think first of "politics," the activities (not always apparent) that influence who is elected or appointed to political office, what public policies are established, how they get established, and who benefits from those policies.

But in the United States and in many other countries, *political life* involves even more than government and politics. Political life also involves ways of preventing or resolving troubles and disputes both within and outside the society. Internally, a complex society such as ours may employ mediation or arbitration to resolve industrial disputes, a police force to prevent crimes or track down criminals, and courts and a penal system to deal with lawbreakers as well as with social conflict in general. Externally, such a society may establish embassies in other nations and develop and utilize its armed forces both to maintain security and to support domestic and foreign interests.

Formal governments have become more widespread around the world over the last 100 years, as powerful colonizing countries have imposed political systems upon others or as people less formally organized realized that they needed governmental mechanisms to deal with the larger world. But many societies known to anthropology did not have political officials, political parties, courts, or armies. Indeed, the band or village was the largest autonomous political unit in 50 percent of the societies in the ethnographic record, as of the times they were first described. And those units were only informally organized; that is, they did not have individuals or agencies formally authorized to make and implement policy or resolve disputes. Does this mean they did not have political life? If we mean political life as we know it in our own society, then the answer has to be that they did not. But if we look beyond our formal institutions and mechanisms—if we ask what functions these institutions and mechanisms perform—we find that all societies have had political activities and beliefs to create and maintain social order and cope with social disorder.

Many of the kinds of groups including descent groups have political functions. But when anthropologists talk about *political organization* or *political life,* they are focusing particularly on activities and beliefs pertaining to *territorial groups.* Territorial groups, on whose behalf political activities may be organized, range from small communities, such as bands and villages, to large communities, such as towns and cities, to multilocal groups, such as districts or regions, entire nations, or even groups of nations.

As we shall see, the different types of political organization, as well as how people participate in politics and how they cope with conflict, are often strongly linked to variation in food-getting, economy, and social stratification.

Types of Political Organization

Societies in the ethnographic record vary in *level of political integration*—that is, the largest territorial group on whose behalf political activities are organized—and in the degree to which political authority is centralized or concentrated in the integrated group. When we describe the political integration of particular societies, we focus on their traditional political systems.

Elman Service suggested that most societies can be classified into four principal types of political organization: bands, tribes, chiefdoms, and states.[1] Although Service's classification does not fit all societies, it is a useful way to show how societies vary in trying to create and maintain social order. We often use the present tense in our discussion because that is the convention in ethnographic writing, but readers should remember that most societies that used to be organized at the band, tribe, or chiefdom level are now incorporated into larger political entities. With a handful of exceptions, there are no politically autonomous bands or tribes or chiefdoms in the world anymore.

Band Organization

Some societies were composed of fairly small and usually nomadic groups of people. Each of these groups is conventionally called a **band** and is politically autonomous. That is, in **band organization,** the local group or community is the largest group that acts as a political unit. Because most recent foragers had band organization, some anthropologists contend that this type of political organization characterized nearly all societies before the development of agriculture, or until about 10,000 years ago. But we have to remember that almost all of the described food-collecting societies are or were located in marginal environments; and almost all were affected by more dominant societies nearby.[2] So it is possible that what we call "band organization" may not have been typical of foragers in the distant or prehistoric past.

Bands are typically small, with less than 100 people usually, often considerably less. Each small band occupies a large territory, so population density is low. Band size often varies by season, with the band breaking up or recombining according to the food resources available at a given time and place. Inuit bands, for example, are smaller in the winter, when food is hard to find, and larger in the summer, when there is sufficient food to feed a larger group.

Political decision making within the band is generally informal. The "modest informal authority"[3] that does exist can be seen in the way decisions affecting the group are made. Because the formal, permanent office of leader typically does not exist, decisions such as when camp has to be moved or how a hunt is to be arranged are either agreed upon by the community as a whole or made by the best qualified member. Leadership, when an individual exercises it, is not the consequence of bossing or throwing one's weight about. Each band may have its informal **headman,** or its most proficient hunter, or a person most accomplished in rituals. There may be one person with all these qualities, or several people, but such a person or people will have gained status through the community's recognition of skill, good sense, and humility. Leadership, in other words, stems not from power but from influence, not from office but from admired personal qualities. For example, among the Inglukik Inuit:

> Within each settlement . . . there is as a rule an older man who enjoys the respect of the others and who decides when a move is to be made to another hunting center, when a hunt is to be started, how the spoils are to be divided, when the dogs are to be fed. . . . He is called *isumaitoq,* "he who thinks." It is not always the oldest man, but as a rule an elderly man who is a clever hunter or, as head of a large family, exercises great authority. He cannot be called a chief; there is no obligation to follow his counsel; but they do so in most cases, partly because they rely on his experience, partly because it pays to be on good terms with this man.[4]

A summary of the general features of band organization can be found in Table 15.1. Note, however, that there are exceptions to these generalizations. For example, not all known foragers are organized at the band level or have all the features of a band type of society. Classic exceptions are the Native American societies of the Northwest Pacific coast, who had enormous resources of salmon and other fish, relatively large and permanent villages, and political organization beyond the level of the typical band societies in the ethnographic record.

TABLE 15.1 Suggested Trends in Political Organization and Other Social Characteristics

Type of Organization	Highest Level of Political Integration	Specialization of Political Officials	Predominant Mode of Subsistence	Community Size and Population Density	Social Differentiation	Major Form of Distribution
Band	Local group or band	Little or none; informal leadership	Foraging or food collecting	Very small communities; very low density	Egalitarian	Mostly reciprocity
Tribe	Sometimes multilocal group	Little or none; informal leadership	Extensive (shifting) agriculture and/or herding	Small communities; low density	Egalitarian	Mostly reciprocity
Chiefdom	Multilocal group	Some	Extensive or intensive agriculture and/or herding	Large communities; medium density	Rank	Reciprocity and redistribution
State	Multilocal group; often entire language group	Much	Intensive agriculture and herding	Cities and towns; high density	Class and caste	Mostly market exchange

Tribal Organization

When local communities mostly act autonomously but there are kinship groups (such as clans or lineages) or associations (such as age-sets—see page 352) that can potentially integrate several local groups into a larger unit (**tribe**), we say that the society has **tribal organization.** Unfortunately, the term *tribe* is sometimes used to refer to an entire society; that is, an entire language group may be called a tribe. But a tribal type of political system does not usually permit the entire society to act as a unit; all the communities in a tribal society may be linked only occasionally for some political (usually military) purpose. Thus, what distinguishes tribal from band political organization is the presence in the former of some multilocal, but not usually society-wide, integration. The multilocal integration, however, is *not permanent,* and it is *informal* in the sense that political officials do not head it. Frequently, the integration is called into play only when an outside threat arises; when the threat disappears, the local groups revert to self-sufficiency.[5] Tribal organization may seem fragile—and, of course, it usually is—but the fact that there are social ways to integrate local groups into larger political entities means that societies with tribal organization are militarily a good deal more formidable than societies with band organization.

Societies with tribal political organization are similar to band societies in their tendency to be egalitarian (see Table 15.1). At the local level, informal leadership is also characteristic. In those tribal societies where kinship provides the basic framework of social organization, the elders of the local kin groups tend to have considerable influence; where age-sets are important, a particular age-set is looked to for leadership. But, in contrast to band societies, societies with tribal organization generally are food producers. And because cultivation and animal husbandry are generally more productive than hunting and gathering, the population density of tribal societies is generally higher, local groups are larger, and the way of life is more sedentary than in hunter-gatherer bands.

Kinship Bonds Frequently communities are linked to each other by virtue of belonging to the same kin group, usually a unilineal group such as a lineage or clan. A **segmentary lineage system** is one type of tribal integration based on kinship. A society with such a system is composed of segments, or parts, each similar to the others in structure and function. Every local segment belongs to a hierarchy of lineages stretching farther and farther back genealogically. The hierarchy of lineages, then, unites the segments into larger and larger genealogical groups. The closer two groups are genealogically, the greater their general closeness. In the event of a dispute between members of different segments, people related more closely to one contestant than to another take the side of their nearest kinsman.

The Tiv of northern Nigeria offer a classic example of a segmentary lineage system, one that happens to link all the Tiv into a single genealogical structure or tribe. The Tiv are a large society, numbering more than 800,000. There are usually four levels of lineages. Each of the smallest lineages is in turn embedded in more inclusive lineages. Territorial organization follows lineage hierarchy. The most closely related lineages have territories near each other. All of Tivland is said to descend from one ancestor.[6]

Tiv lineage organization is the foundation of Tiv political organization. A dispute between the smallest neighboring lineages (and territories) remains minor, because no more than "brother" segments are involved. But a dispute between two small lineages from different larger lineages involves those larger lineages as well, with the requirement that smaller lineages within larger support each other. This process of mutual support, called **complementary opposition,** means that segments will unite only in a confrontation with some other group. Groups that will fight with each other in a minor dispute might coalesce at some later time against a larger group.

The segmentary lineage system was presumably very effective in allowing the Tiv to intrude into new territory and take land from other tribal societies with smaller descent groups. Individual Tiv lineage segments could call on support from related lineages when faced with border troubles. Conflicts within the society—that is, between segments—especially in border areas, were often turned outward, "releasing internal pressure in an explosive blast against other peoples."[7]

A segmentary lineage system may generate a formidable military force, but the combinations of manpower it produces are temporary, forming and dissolving as the occasion demands.[8] Tribal political organization does not make for a political system that more or less permanently integrates a number of communities.

Age-Set Systems Age-sets (groups of males of a certain age range) can function as the basis of a tribal type of political organization, as among the Karimojong of northeastern Uganda.[9] As herders, Karimojong adults are often separated from their usual settlements. Herders will meet, mingle for a while, then go their separate ways, but each may call upon other members of his age-set wherever he goes. The age-set system is important among the Karimojong because it immediately allocates to each individual a place in the system and thereby establishes for him an appropriate pattern of response. A quarrel in camp will be settled by the representatives of the senior age-set who are present, regardless of which section of the tribe they may belong to.

Among the Karimojong, political leaders are not elected from among the elders of a particular age-set, nor are they appointed; they acquire their positions informally. Usually a man's background, and the ability he has demonstrated in public debates over a period of time, will result in his being considered by the men of his neighborhood to be their spokesman. His function is to announce what course of action seems required in a particular situation, to initiate that action, and then to coordinate it after it has begun.

Chiefdom Organization

Whereas a tribe has some informal mechanism that can integrate more than one community, a **chiefdom** has some *formal* structure that integrates more than one community into a political unit. The formal structure could consist of a council with or without a chief, but most commonly there is a person—the **chief**—who has higher rank or authority than others. Most societies at the chiefdom level of organization contain more than one multicommunity political unit or chiefdom, each headed by a district chief or a council. There may also be more than one level of chief beyond the community, such as district chiefs and higher-level chiefs. Compared with tribal societies, societies with chiefdoms are more densely populated and their communities more permanent, partly as a consequence of their generally greater economic productivity (see Table 15.1).

The position of chief, which is sometimes hereditary and generally permanent, bestows high status on its holder. Most chiefdoms have social ranking and accord the chief and his family greater access to prestige. The chief may redistribute goods, plan and direct the use of public labor, supervise religious ceremonies, and direct military activities on behalf of the chiefdom. In South Pacific chiefdoms, the chiefs carried out most of these duties. In Fijian chiefdoms, for example, the chief was responsible for the redistribution of goods and the coordination of labor:

> [The chief] could summon the community's labor on his own behalf, or on behalf of someone else who requested it, or for general purposes. . . . Besides his right to summon labor he accumulated the greater proportion of the first fruits of the yam crop . . . and he benefited from other forms of food presentation, or by the acquisition of special shares in ordinary village distribution. . . . Thus, the paramount [chief] would collect a significant part of the surplus production of the community and redistribute it in the general welfare.[10]

Samoan chiefs gather at an open meeting house for a *saofa'i*, or entitlement ceremony, during which a new chief gains his position.

In contrast to leaders in tribal societies, who generally have to earn their privileges by their personal qualities, hereditary chiefs are said to have those qualities in their "blood." A high-ranking chief in Polynesia, a huge triangular area of islands in the South Pacific, inherited special religious power called *mana. Mana* sanctified his rule and protected him.[11] Chiefs in Polynesia had so much religious power that missionaries could convert people to Christianity only after their chiefs had been converted.[12]

In most chiefdoms, the chiefs did not have the power to compel people to obey them; people would act in accordance with the chief's wishes because the chief was respected and often had religious authority. But in the most complex paramount chiefdoms, such as those of Hawaii and Tahiti, the chiefs seemed to have more compelling sanctions than the "power" of respect or *mana.* Substantial amounts of goods and services collected by the chiefs were used to support subordinates, including specialists such as high priests, political envoys, and warriors who could be sent to quell rebellious factions.[13] When redistributions do not go to everybody—when chiefs are allowed to keep items for their own purposes—and when a chief begins to use armed force, the political system is on the way to becoming what we call a state.

State Organization

A state, according to one more or less standard definition, is "an autonomous political unit, encompassing many communities within its territory and having a centralized government with the power to collect taxes, draft men for work or war, and decree and enforce laws."[14] States, then, have a complex, centralized political structure that includes a wide range of permanent institutions with legislative, executive, and judicial functions and a large bureaucracy. Central to this definition is the concept of legitimate force used to implement policies both internally and externally. In states, the government tries to maintain a monopoly on the use of physical force.[15] This monopoly can be seen in the development of formal and specialized instruments of social control: a police force, a militia, or a standing army.

Just as a particular society may contain more than one band, tribe, or chiefdom, so may it contain more than one state. The contiguously distributed population speaking a single language may or may not be politically unified in a single state. Ancient Greece was composed of many city-states; so, too, was Italy until the 1870s. German speakers are also not politically unified; Austria and Germany are separate states, and Germany itself was not politically unified until the 1870s. We say that a society has **state organization** when it is composed of one or more political units that are states.

A state may include more than one society. Multisociety states are often the result of conquest or colonial control when the dominant political authority, itself a state, imposes a centralized government over a territory with many different societies and cultures, as the British did in Nigeria and Kenya. Colonialism is a common feature of state societies.

Nearly all of the multisociety states that emerged after World War II were the results of successful independence movements against colonial powers.[16] Most have retained their political unity despite the fact that they still contain many different societies. Multisociety or multiethnic states may also form voluntarily, in reaction to external threat. Switzerland comprises cantons, each of which speaks mainly French, German, Italian, or Romansch; the various cantons confederated originally to shake off control by the Holy Roman Empire. But some states have lost their unity recently, including the former Union of Soviet Socialist Republics (USSR) and much of Yugoslavia.

In addition to their strictly political features, intensive agriculture generally supports state-organized societies. The high productivity of the agriculture allows for the emergence of cities, a high degree of economic and other kinds of specialization, and market or commercial exchange. In addition, state societies usually have class stratification (see Table 15.1). Cities have grown tremendously in the last 100 years, largely as a result of migration and immigration.

When states come into existence, people's access to scarce resources is radically altered. So, too, is their ability not to listen to leaders: You usually cannot refuse to pay taxes or avoid labor or military conscription and go unpunished. Of course, the rulers of a state do not maintain the social

Popular will can change governments. Massive protest in the Ukraine led a newly elected president to resign.

order by force alone. The people must believe, at least to some extent, that those in power have a legitimate right to govern. If the people think otherwise, history suggests that those in power may eventually lose their ability to control. Witness the downfall of Communist parties throughout most of eastern Europe and the former Soviet Union and most recently the fall of some dictators in northern Africa.

A state society can retain its legitimacy, or at least its power, for a long time. For example, the Roman Empire was a complex state society that dominated the Mediterranean and Near East for hundreds of years. It began as a city-state that waged war to acquire additional territory. At its height, the Roman Empire embraced more than 55 million people[17]; the capital city of Rome had a population of well over a million.[18] The empire included parts of what are now Great Britain, France, Spain, Portugal, Germany, Romania, Turkey, Greece, Armenia, Egypt, Israel, and Syria.

Although all state societies employ coercion or the threat of it, some states are more autocratic than others. This is not just today, or in the recent past, but also in the distant past. The less autocratic states are characterized by more "collective action." They produce more public goods, such as transportation systems and redistribution systems, in times of need. The rulers do not live that luxuriously and the rulers must respond to grievances. The Lozi state of central southern Africa had considerable collective action. The Lozi built an extensive system of drainage canals. In hungry times, royal herds and the "state" gardens were used to feed distressed villages. And rulers were not that much more elevated in standard of living. In contrast, the Nupe state in western Africa financed very little in the way of public works, had little redistribution, and the rulers lived in elaborate palaces.[19] Collection action theorists suggest that, when the state relies more heavily on resources from taxpayers, the rulers must give the public more in return or else face noncompliance and rebellion. Richard Blanton and Lane Fargher's comparative study of premodern states supports collection action theory.[20]

Factors Associated with Variation in Political Organization

The kinds of political organization we call band, tribal, chiefdom, and state are points on a continuum of levels of political integration or unification, from small-scale local autonomy to large-scale regional unification. There also is variation in political authority, from a few temporary and informal political leaders to large numbers of permanent, specialized political officials, from the absence of coercive political power to the monopoly of public force by a central authority. These aspects of variation in political organization are generally associated with shifts from foraging to more intensive food production, from small communities to towns and cities, from low to high population densities, from an emphasis on reciprocity to redistribution to market exchange, and from egalitarian to rank to fully stratified class societies. The more important agriculture in a society and the bigger the community size, the larger the population that is politically unified and the greater the number and types of political officials.[21] These associations are summarized in Table 15.1.

Do these associations help explain why political organization varies? Clearly, the data indicate that several factors are associated with political development, but exactly why changes in organization occur is not yet understood. Although economic development may be a necessary condition for political development,[22] that relation does not fully explain why political organization should become more complex just because the economy can support it. Some theorists have suggested that competition between groups may be a more important reason for political consolidation. For example, Elman Service suggested competition as a reason why a society might change from a band level of political organization to a tribal level. Band societies are generally hunter-gatherers. With a changeover to agriculture, population density and competition between groups may increase. Service believed that such competition would foster the development of some informal organization beyond the community—namely, tribal organization—for offense and defense.[23] Indeed, both unilineal kinship groups and age-set systems seem to be associated with warfare.

Among agriculturalists, defensive needs might also be the main reason for switching from informal multivillage political organization to more formal chiefdom organization. Formally organized districts are probably more likely to defeat autonomous villages or even segmentary lineage systems.[24] In addition, there may be economic reasons for political development. With regard to chiefdoms, Service suggested that chiefdoms will emerge when redistribution between communities becomes important or when large-scale coordinated work groups are required. The more important these activities are, the more important—and hence more "chiefly"—the organizer and his family presumably become.[25] But redistribution is far from a universal activity of chiefs.[26]

Theory and research on the anthropology of political development have focused mostly on the high end of the scale of political complexity, and particularly on the origins of the first state societies. Those earliest states apparently rose independently of one another, after about 3500 B.C., in what are now southern Iraq, Egypt, northwestern India, northern China, and central Mexico. Several theories have been proposed to explain the rise of the earliest states, but no one theory seems to fit all the known archaeological sequences culminating in early state formation. The reason may be that different conditions in different places favored the emergence of centralized government. The state, by definition, implies the power to organize large populations for collective purposes. In some areas, the impetus may have been the need to organize necessary local or long-distance trade or both. In other areas, the state may have emerged as a way to control defeated populations that could not flee. In still other instances, other factors or a combination of factors may have fostered the development of states. It is still not clear what the specific conditions were that led to the emergence of the state in each of the early centers.[27]

The Spread of State Societies

The state level of political development has come to dominate the world. Societies with states have larger communities and higher population densities than do band, tribal, and chiefdom societies. They also have armies that are ready to fight at almost any time. State systems that have waged war against chiefdoms and tribes have almost always won, and the result has usually been the political incorporation of the losers. For example, the British and, later, the U.S. colonization of much of North America led to the defeat and incorporation of many Native American societies.

The defeat and incorporation of the Native Americans was at least partly due to the catastrophic depopulations they suffered because of epidemic diseases, such as smallpox and measles, brought by European travelers, traders, and colonists. Catastrophic depopulation was commonly the outcome of the first contacts between European Americans and the natives of North and South America, as well as the natives of the far islands in the Pacific. People in the New World and the Pacific had not been exposed, and therefore were not resistant, to the diseases the European Americans carried with them when they began to colonize the world. Before the expansion of Europeans, the people of the New World and the Pacific had been separated for a long time from the people and diseases on the geographically continuous landmass we separate into Europe, Africa, and Asia. Smallpox, measles, and the other former scourges of Europe had largely become childhood diseases that most individuals of European ancestry survived.[28]

Whether by depopulation, conquest, or intimidation, the number of independent political units in the world has decreased strikingly in the last 3,000 years, and especially in the last 200 years. Robert Carneiro estimated that in 1000 B.C., there may have been between 100,000 and 1 million separate political units in the world; today, there are fewer than 200.[29] In the ethnographic record, about 50 percent of the 2,000 or so societies described within the last 150–50 years ago had only local political integration. That is, the highest level of political integration in one out of two recent societies was the local community.[30] Thus, most of the decrease in the number of independent political units has occurred fairly recently.

But the recent secessions from the former Soviet Union and Yugoslavia and other separatist movements around the world suggest that ethnic rivalries may make for departures from the trend toward larger and larger political units. Ethnic groups that have been dominated by others in multinational states may opt for political autonomy, at least for a while. On the other hand,

A meeting of European Union heads of state and government in Rome. The EU is an organization encompassing many nation-states.

the separate nations of western Europe are becoming more unified every day, both politically and economically. So the trend toward larger political units may be continuing, even if there are departures from it now and then.

Extrapolating from past history, a number of investigators have suggested that the entire world will eventually come to be politically integrated, perhaps as soon as the twenty-third century and no later than A.D. 4850.[31] Only the future will tell if this prediction will come true. And only the future will tell if further political integration in the world will occur peacefully—with all parties agreeing—or by force or the threat of force, as has happened so often in the past.

Variation in Political Process

Anthropologists are increasingly interested in the politics, or political processes, of the societies they study: who acquires influence or power, how they acquire it, and how political decisions are made.

Getting to Be a Leader

In those societies that have hereditary leadership, which is common in rank societies and in state societies with monarchies, rules of succession usually establish how leadership is inherited. But for societies whose leaders are *chosen*, either as informal leaders or as political officials, we need a lot more research to understand why some kinds of people are chosen over others.

A few studies have investigated the personal qualities of leaders in tribal societies. One study, conducted among the Mekranoti-Kayapo of central Brazil, found that leaders, in contrast to followers, tend to be rated by their peers as higher in intelligence, generosity, knowledgeability, ambitiousness, and aggressiveness. Leaders also tend to be older and taller. And despite the egalitarian nature of Mekranoti society (at least with respect to sharing resources), sons of leaders are more likely than others to become leaders.[32]

Research in another Brazilian society, the Kagwahiv of the Amazon region, suggests another personal quality of leaders: They seem to have positive feelings about their fathers and mothers.[33] In many respects, studies of leaders in the United States show them to be not that different from their counterparts in Brazil. But there is one major difference: Mekranoti and Kagwahiv leaders are not wealthier than others; in fact, they give their wealth away. Leaders in the United States are generally wealthier than others.[34]

"Big Men" In some egalitarian tribal societies, the quest for leadership seems quite competitive. In parts of New Guinea and South America, "big men" compete with other ambitious men to attract followers. Men who want to compete must show that they have magical powers, success in gardening, and bravery in war. But, most important, they have to collect enough goods to throw big parties at which the goods are given away. Big men have to work very hard to attract and keep their followings, for dissatisfied followers can always join other aspiring men.[35] The wives of big men are often leaders too. Among the Kagwahiv, for example, a headman's wife is usually the leader of the women in the community; she is responsible for much of the planning for feasts and often distributes the meat at them.[36]

But how does a man get to be a big man? Among the Kumdi-Engamoi, a central Highlands group, a man who wants to be considered a *wua nium* (literally, a "great-important-wealthy man") needs to have many wives and daughters, because the amount of land controlled by a man and how much can be produced on that land depend on the number of women in his family. The more wives he has, the more land he is given to cultivate. He must also be a good speaker.

Everyone has the right to speak and give speeches, but to get to be known as a big man requires speaking well and forcefully and knowing when to sum up a consensus. It usually takes a man until his 30s or 40s to acquire more than one wife and to make his name through exchanges. When a man wants to inaugurate an exchange, he needs to get shells and pigs from his family and relatives. Once he has achieved a reputation as a *wua nium,* he can keep it only if he continues to perform well—that is, if he continues to distribute fairly, make wise decisions, speak well, and conduct exchanges.[37]

"Big Women"   In contrast to most of mainland New Guinea, the islands off the southeastern coast are characterized by matrilineal descent. But, like the rest of New Guinea, the islands also have a shifting system of leadership in which people compete for "big" status. Here, though, the people competing are women as well as men, and so there are "big women" as well as "big men." On the island of Vanatinai, for example, women and men compete with each other to exchange valuables. Women lead canoe expeditions to distant islands to visit male as well as female exchange partners, women mobilize relatives and exchange partners to mount large feasts, and the women get to keep the ceremonial valuables exchanged, at least for a while.[38]

The prominence of women on Vanatinai may be linked to the disappearance of warfare—the colonial powers imposed peace; we call this "pacification." Interisland exchanges became frequent when war became rarer in the early twentieth century, giving women and men more freedom to travel. For men, but not women, war provided a path to leadership; champion warriors would acquire great renown and influence. It is not that women did not participate in war; they did, which is unusual cross-culturally, but a woman could not become a war leader. Now, in the absence of war, women have an opportunity through exchanges to become leaders, or "big women."

Researchers continue to explore other features that may enhance a person's ability to become leaders where leadership is not hereditary. One fascinating new finding is that in the United States, after controlling for age and perceived attractiveness, individuals who are judged prior to the election to be more "competent" from photographs of their faces are more likely to win in congressional elections.[39] What makes a face look more "competent"? It has fewer "babyish" features—it is less round, has a bigger chin, smaller eyes, and a smaller forehead.[40] Whether these facial features also predict leadership cross-culturally is not yet known.

Political Participation

Political scientist Marc Ross conducted cross-cultural research on variation in degree of political participation. Ross phrased the research question: "Why is it that in some polities there are

In many egalitarian societies, leadership shifts informally from one person to another. In the highlands of New Guinea, leaders, such as the Huli man shown in the center of the photo, are commonly referred to as "big men." Achieving the status of "big man" is competitive and men have to work at becoming leaders and retaining their leadership.

relatively large numbers of persons involved in political life, while in others political action is the province of very few?"[41]

Political participation in preindustrial societies ranges from widespread to low or nonexistent. In 16 percent of the societies examined, there is widespread participation; decision-making forums are open to all adults. The forums may be formal (councils and other governing bodies) or informal. Next in degree of political participation are societies (37 percent) that have widespread participation by some but not all adults (men but not women, certain classes but not others). Next are societies (29 percent) that have some but not much input by the community. Finally, 18 percent of the societies have low or nonexistent participation, which means that leaders make most decisions, and involvement of the average person is very limited.

Degree of political participation seems to be high in small-scale societies, as well as in modern democratic nation-states, but not in between (feudal states and preindustrial empires). Why? In small-scale societies, leaders do not have the power to force people to act; thus, a high degree of political participation may be the only way to get people to go along with decisions. In modern democracies, which have many powerful groups outside the government—corporations, unions, and other associations are examples—the central authorities may only theoretically have the power to force people to go along; in reality, they rely mostly on voluntary compliance. For example, the U.S. government failed when it tried with force (Prohibition, 1920–1933) to stop the manufacture, transport, and sale of alcoholic beverages.

Another factor may be early family experiences. Some scholars recently have suggested that the type of family in which people are raised predicts the degree of political participation in a society. A large extended family with multiple generations tends to be hierarchical, with the older generations having more authority. Children may learn that they have to obey and subordinate their wishes to their elders. Societies with polygyny also seem to have less political participation. The ways of interacting in the family may carry over to the political sphere.[42]

A high degree of political participation seems to have an important consequence. In the modern world, democratically governed states rarely go to war with each other.[43] So, for example, the United States invaded three countries—Grenada, Panama, and Iraq—between 1980 and 1993, but no democracies. Similarly, it appears that more participatory, that is, more "democratic," political units in the ethnographic record fight with each other significantly less often than do less participatory political units, just as seems to be the case among modern nation-states.[44] Does this mean that democracies are more peaceful in general? Here there is more controversy. Judging by the frequency of war, modern democratic states do not look very different from autocratic states in their tendency to go to war. However, if you look at the severity of war as measured by casualty rates, democratic societies do look less warlike.[45] Exactly why more participation or more democracy is likely to lead to peace remains to be established. But there are policy implications of the relationship, which we explore in the chapter on global problems.

Resolution of Conflict

The resolution of conflict may be accomplished peacefully by avoidance, community action, mediation or the negotiation of compromises, apology, appeal to supernatural forces, or adjudication by a third party. As we shall see, the procedures used usually vary with degree of social complexity; decisions by third parties are more likely in hierarchical societies.[46] But peaceful solutions are not always possible, and disputes may erupt into violent conflict. When violence occurs within a political unit in which disputes are usually settled peacefully, we call such violence crime, particularly when committed by an individual. When the violence occurs between groups of people from separate political units—groups between which there is no procedure for settling disputes—we usually call such violence *warfare*. When violence occurs between subunits of a population that had been politically unified, we call it *civil war*.

Peaceful Resolution of Conflict

Most modern industrialized states have formal institutions and offices, such as police, district attorneys, courts, and penal systems, to deal with minor disputes and more serious conflicts that may arise in society. All these institutions generally operate according to **codified laws**—that is, a set of explicit, usually written rules stipulating what is permissible and what is not. Transgression of the law by individuals gives the state the right to take action against them. The state has a monopoly on the legitimate use of force in the society, for it alone has the right to coerce subjects into agreement with regulations, customs, political edicts, and procedures.

Many societies lack such specialized offices and institutions for dealing with conflict. Yet, because all societies have peaceful, regularized ways of handling at least certain disputes, some anthropologists speak of the *universality of law*. E. Adamson Hoebel, for example, stated the principle as follows:

> Each people has its system of social control. And all but a few of the poorest of them have as a part of the control system a complex of behavior patterns and institutional mechanisms that we may properly treat as law. For, "anthropologically considered, law is merely one aspect of our culture—the aspect which employs the force of organized society to regulate individual and group conduct and to prevent redress or punish deviations from prescribed social norms."[47]

Law, then, whether informal as in simpler societies, or formal as in more complex societies, provides a means of dealing peacefully with whatever conflicts develop. That does not mean that conflicts are always resolved peacefully. But that also does not mean that people cannot learn to resolve their conflicts peacefully. The fact that there are societies with little or no violent conflict means that it may be possible to learn from them; it may be possible to discover how to avoid violent outcomes of conflicts. How come South Africa could move relatively peacefully from a society dominated by people from Europe to one with government and civil rights shared by all groups? On the other hand, Bosnia had very violent conflict between ethnic groups and needed intervention by outside parties to keep the warring sides apart.[48]

Avoidance Violence can often be avoided if the parties to a dispute voluntarily avoid each other or are separated until emotions cool down. Anthropologists have frequently remarked that foragers are particularly likely to make use of this technique. People may move to other bands or move their dwellings to opposite ends of camp. Shifting horticulturalists may also split up when conflicts get too intense. Avoidance is obviously easier in societies, such as band societies, that are nomadic or seminomadic and in which people have temporary dwellings. And avoidance is more feasible when people live independently and self-sufficiently (e.g., in cities and suburbs).[49]

Community Action Societies have found various ways of resolving disputes peacefully. One such way involves action by a group or the community as a whole; collective action is common in simpler societies that lack powerful authoritarian leaders.[50] Many Inuit societies, for example, frequently resolve disputes through community action. An individual's failure to heed a taboo or to follow the suggestions of a shaman leads to expulsion from the group because the community cannot accept a risk to its livelihood. People who fail to share goods voluntarily will find them confiscated and distributed to the community, and they may be executed in the process. A single case of murder, as an act of vengeance (usually because of the abduction of a wife or as part of a blood feud), does not concern the community, but repeated murders do. Franz Boas gave a typical example:

> There was a native of Padli by the name Padlu. He had induced the wife of a native of Cumberland Sound to desert her husband and follow him. The deserted husband, meditating revenge . . . visited his friends in Padli, but before he could accomplish his intention of killing Padlu, the latter shot him. . . . A brother of the murdered man went to Padli to avenge the death . . . but he also was killed by Padlu. A third native of Cumberland Sound, who wished to avenge the death of his relatives, was also murdered by him.
>
> On account of these outrages the natives wanted to get rid of Padlu, but yet they did not dare to attack him. When the *pimain* (headman) of the Akudmurmuit learned of these events he started southward and *asked every man in Padli whether Padlu should be killed. All agreed;* so he went with the latter deer hunting . . . and . . . shot Padlu in the back.[51]

The killing of an individual is the most extreme action a community can take—we call it *capital punishment.* The community as a whole or a political official or a court may decide to administer such punishment, but capital punishment seems to exist in nearly all societies, from the simplest to the most complex.[52] It is often assumed that capital punishment deters crime. If it did, we would expect the abolition of capital punishment to be followed by an increase in homicide rates. But that does not seem to happen. A cross-national study indicates that the abolition of capital punishment tends to be followed by a decrease in homicide rates.[53]

Negotiation and Mediation In many conflicts, the parties to a dispute may come to a settlement themselves by **negotiation.** There aren't necessarily any rules for how they will do so, but any solution is "good" if it restores peace.[54] Sometimes an outside or third party is used to help bring about a settlement between the disputants. We call it **mediation** when the outside party tries to help bring about a settlement, but that third party does not have the formal authority to force a settlement. Both negotiation and mediation are likely when the society is relatively egalitarian and it is important for people to get along.[55]

Among the Nuer of East Africa, a pastoral and horticultural people, disputes within the community can be settled with the help of an informal mediator called the "leopard-skin chief." His position is hereditary, and makes

Although mediation is commonly used in relatively egalitarian societies, it is also used in societies with courts and other formal adjudication procedures for minor conflicts. A teacher in the United States tries to mediate a dispute between two boys.

its holder responsible for the social well-being of the district. Matters such as cattle stealing rarely come to the attention of the leopard-skin chief. But if, for example, a murder has been committed, the culprit will go at once to the house of the leopard-skin chief. Immediately the chief cuts the culprit's arm so that blood flows; until the cut has been made, the murderer may not eat or drink. If the murderer is afraid of vengeance by the slain man's family, he will remain at the house of the leopard-skin chief, which is considered sanctuary. Then, within the next few months, the chief attempts to mediate between the parties to the crime. The chief elicits from the slayer's kin that they are prepared to pay compensation to avoid a feud, and he persuades the dead man's kin that they ought to accept the compensation, usually in the form of cattle. The chief then collects the cattle—40 to 50—and takes them to the dead man's home, where he performs various sacrifices of cleansing and atonement.[56] Throughout the process, the chief acts as a go-between. He has no authority to force either party to negotiate, and he has no power to enforce a solution once it has been arrived at. However, he is able to take advantage of the fact that both disputants are anxious to avoid a blood feud.

Ritual Reconciliation—Apology The desire to restore a harmonious relationship may also explain ceremonial apologies. An apology is based on deference—the guilty party shows obeisance and asks for forgiveness. Such ceremonies tend to occur in recent chiefdoms.[57] Among the Fijians of the South Pacific, when a person offends someone of higher status, the offended person and other villagers begin to avoid, and gossip about, the offender. If offenders are sensitive to village opinion, they will perform a ceremony of apology called *i soro*. One of the meanings of *soro* is "surrender." In the ceremony, the offender bows the head and remains silent while an intermediary speaks, presents a token gift, and asks the offended person for forgiveness. The apology is rarely rejected.[58]

Oaths and Ordeals Still another way of peacefully resolving disputes is through oaths and ordeals, both of which involve appeals to supernatural power. An **oath** is the act of calling upon a deity to bear witness to the truth of what one says. An **ordeal** is a means used to determine guilt or innocence by submitting the accused to dangerous or painful tests believed to be under supernatural control.[59]

A common kind of ordeal, found in almost every part of the world, is scalding. Among the Tanala of Madagascar, the accused person, having first had his hand carefully examined for protective covering, has to reach his hand into a cauldron of boiling water and grasp, from underneath, a rock suspended there. He then plunges his hand into cold water, has it bandaged, and is led off to spend the night under guard. In the morning, his hand is unbandaged and examined. If there are blisters, he is guilty.

Oaths and ordeals have also been practiced in Western societies. Both were common in medieval Europe. Even today, in our own society, vestiges of oaths can be found. Children can be heard to say, "Cross my heart and hope to die," and witnesses in courts of law are obliged to swear to tell the truth.

Why do some societies use oaths and ordeals? John Roberts suggested that their use tends to be found in fairly complex societies in which political officials lack sufficient power to make and enforce judicial decisions or would make themselves unnecessarily vulnerable were they to attempt to do so. So the officials may use oaths and ordeals to let the gods decide guilt or innocence.[60] In contrast, smaller and less complex societies probably have no need for elaborate mechanisms such as courts, oaths, and ordeals to ascertain guilt. In such societies, everyone is aware of what crimes have been committed and who the guilty parties probably are.

Adjudication, Courts, and Codified Law We call it **adjudication** when a third party acting as judge makes a decision that the disputing parties have to accept. Judgment may be rendered by one person (a judge), a panel of judges, a jury, or a political agent or agency (a chief, a royal personage, a council). Judges and courts may rely on codified law and stipulated punishments, but codified law is not necessary for decisions to be made. Codified laws and courts are not limited to Western societies. From the late seventeenth century to the early twentieth century, for example, the Ashanti of West Africa had a complex political system with elaborate legal arrangements. The Ashanti state was a military-based empire possessing legal codes that resembled those of many ancient civilizations.[61] In Ashanti court procedure, elders examined and cross-examined witnesses as well as parties to the dispute. There were also quasi-professional advocates, and appeals against a verdict could be made directly to a chief. Particularly noteworthy was the emphasis on intent when assessing guilt. Drunkenness constituted a valid defense for all crimes except murder and cursing a chief, and a plea of insanity, if proved, was upheld for all offenses. Ashanti punishments could be severe. Fines were more frequent, however, and death sentences could often be commuted to banishment and confiscation of goods.

Why do some societies have codified systems and others do not? One explanation, advanced by E. Adamson Hoebel, A. R. Radcliffe-Brown, and others, is that there is little need for formal legal guidelines in small, closely knit communities because competing interests are minimal. Hence, simple societies need little codified law. There are relatively few matters to quarrel about, and the general will of the group is sufficiently well known and demonstrated frequently enough to deter transgressors.

This point of view is echoed in Richard Schwartz's study of two Israeli settlements. In one communal kibbutz, a young man aroused a good deal of community resentment because he had accepted an electric teakettle as a gift. The general opinion was that he had overstepped the code about not having personal possessions, and he was so informed. Accordingly, he gave the kettle to the communal infirmary. Schwartz observed that "no organized enforcement of the decision was threatened, but had he disregarded the expressed will of the community, his life . . . would have been made intolerable by the antagonism of public opinion."[62]

In this community, where people worked and ate together, not only did everyone know about transgressions, but a wrongdoer could not escape public censure. Thus, public opinion was an effective sanction. In another Israeli community, however, where individuals lived in widely separated houses and worked and ate separately, public opinion did not work as well. Not only were community members less aware of problems, but they had no quick way of making their feelings known. As a result, they established a judicial body to handle trouble cases.

Larger, more heterogeneous and stratified societies are likely to have more frequent disputes, which at the same time are less visible to the public. Individuals in stratified societies are generally not so dependent on community members for their well-being and hence are less likely to know of, or care about, others' opinions. In such societies, codified laws and formal authorities for resolving disputes develop—in order, perhaps, that disputes may be settled impersonally enough so that the parties can accept the decision and social order can be restored.

A good example of how more formal systems of law develop is the experience of towns in the American West during the gold rush period. These communities were literally swamped by total strangers. The townsfolk, having no control (authority) over these intruders because the strangers had no local ties, looked for ways to deal with the trouble cases that were continually flaring up. A first attempt at a solution was to hire gunslingers, who were also strangers, to act as peace officers or sheriffs, but this strategy usually failed. Eventually, towns succeeded in having federal authorities send in marshals backed by federal power.

Is there some evidence to support the theory that codified law is necessary only in larger, more complex societies? Data from a large, worldwide sample of societies suggest that codified law is associated with political integration beyond the local level. Murder cases, for example, are dealt with informally in societies that have only local political organization. In societies with multilocal political units, specialized political authorities tend to judge or adjudicate murder cases.[63] There is also some cross-cultural evidence that violence within a society tends to be less frequent when there are formal authorities (chiefs, courts) who have the power to punish murderers.[64] In general, adjudication or enforced decisions by outside authorities tend to occur in hierarchical societies with social classes and centralized power.[65]

Violent Resolution of Conflict

People often resort to violence when regular, effective alternative means of resolving a conflict are not available. Violence between individuals that is not considered legitimate is generally called **crime.** When violence occurs between territorial entities such as communities, districts, or nations, we call it **warfare.** The type of warfare varies in scope and complexity from society to society. Sometimes a distinction is made among feuding, raiding, and large-scale confrontations.[66]

Some scholars talk about a cultural pattern of violence. More often than not, societies with one type of violence have others. Societies with more war tend to have warlike sports, malevolent magic, severe punishment for crimes, high murder rates, feuding, and family violence.[67] More peaceful societies are not conflict-free, but they try more to resolve conflict nonviolently. What explains these more peaceful cultural patterns? Cross-cultural evidence supports the view that frequent warfare is the key to understanding all kinds of violence. Not only is war correlated with other kinds of aggression, but societies that are forced to stop fighting by more powerful societies appear to encourage aggression in their children less. It seems that, if war is frequent, the society encourages boys to be aggressive, so that they will grow up to be effective warriors. But socializing for aggression can spill over into other areas of life; high rates of crime and other violence may be inadvertent or unintended consequences of the encouragement of aggressiveness.[68] And societies with a lot of war commonly bestow high status on their warriors. Warriors are generally proud of their accomplishments, considering it an honor to be a brave and fierce warrior.[69]

Individual Violence Although it may seem paradoxical at first, violent behavior itself is often used to try to control behavior. In some societies, it is considered necessary for parents to beat children who misbehave. They don't consider this criminal behavior or child abuse; they consider it punishment (see the discussion of family violence in the chapter on global issues). Similar views may attach to interpersonal behavior between adults. If a person trespasses on your property or hurts someone in your family, some societies consider it appropriate or justified to kill or maim the trespasser. Is this social control, or is it just lack of control? Systems of individual self-help are characteristic of egalitarian societies.[70] How is this different from "community action," which earlier we classified under peaceful resolution of conflict? Because community action is explicitly based on obtaining a consensus, it is likely to lead to the ending of a particular dispute. Individual action, or self-help, particularly if it involves violence, is not.

Feuding Feuding is an example of how individual self-help may not lead to a peaceful resolution of conflict. **Feuding** is a state of recurring hostilities between families or groups of kin, usually motivated by a desire to avenge an offense—whether insult, injury, deprivation, or death—against a member of the group. The most common characteristic of the feud is that all members of the kin group carry the responsibility to avenge. The killing of any member of the offender's group is considered appropriate revenge because the kin group as a whole is regarded as responsible. Feuds are by no means limited to small-scale societies; they occur as frequently in societies with high levels of political organization.[71]

Raiding **Raiding** is a short-term use of force, planned and organized, to realize a limited objective. This objective is usually the acquisition of goods, animals, or other forms of wealth belonging to another, often neighboring community.

Raiding is especially prevalent in pastoral societies, in which cattle, horses, camels, or other animals are prized and an individual's own herd can be augmented by theft. Raids are often organized by temporary leaders or coordinators whose authority may not last beyond the planning and execution of the venture. Raiding may also be organized for the purpose of capturing people. Sometimes people are taken to marry—the capture of women to be wives or concubines is fairly common[72]—or to be slaves. Slavery has been practiced in about 33 percent of the world's known societies, and war has been one way of obtaining slaves either to keep or to trade for other goods.[73] Raiding, like feuding, is often self-perpetuating: The victim of a raid today becomes the raider tomorrow.[74]

Large-Scale Confrontations Individual episodes of feuds and raids usually involve relatively small numbers of people and almost always an element of surprise. Because they are generally attacked without warning, the victims are often unable to muster an immediate defense. Large-scale confrontations, in contrast, involve a large number of people and planning of strategies of attack and defense by both sides. Large-scale warfare is usually practiced among societies with intensive agriculture or industrialization. Only these societies possess a technology sufficiently advanced to support specialized armies, military leaders, strategists, and so on. But large-scale confrontations are not limited to state societies; they occur, for example, among the horticultural Dugum Dani of central New Guinea.

The military history of the Dani, with its shifting alliances and confederations, is reminiscent of that of Europe, although Dani battles involve far fewer fighters and less sophisticated weaponry. Among the Dani, long periods of ritual warfare are characterized by formal battles announced through a challenge sent by one side to the opposing side. If the challenge is accepted, the protagonists meet at the agreed-upon battle site to set up their lines. Fighting with spears, sticks, and bows and arrows begins at midmorning and continues either until nightfall or until rain intervenes. There may also be a rest period during the midday heat during which the two sides shout insults at each other or talk and rest among themselves.

The front line of battle is composed of about a dozen active warriors and a few leaders. Behind them is a second line, still within arrow range, composed of those who have just left the forward line or are preparing to join it. The third line, outside arrow range, is composed of noncombatants—males too old or too young to participate and those recovering from wounds. This third line merely watches the battle taking place on the grassy plain. On the hillsides far back from the front line, some of the old men help to direct ancestral ghosts to the battle by gouging a line in the ground that points in the direction of the battlefield.[75]

Yet, as total as large-scale confrontations may be, even such warfare has cultural rules. Among the Dani, for instance, no fighting occurs at night, and weapons are limited to simple spears and bows and arrows. Similarly, in state societies, governments will sign "self-denying" pacts restricting the use of poison gas, germ warfare, and so forth. Unofficially, private arrangements are common. One has only to glance through the memoirs of national leaders of the two

Large-scale confrontations occur in societies with armies, but they also occur in nonstate societies. The Masai of Kenya (shown here) battled with Kalenjin (not shown) over a land dispute following the 2008 disputed election.

world wars to become aware of locally arranged truces, visits to one another's front positions, exchanges of prisoners of war, and so on.

Explaining Warfare

Most societies in the anthropological record have had warfare between communities or larger territorial groups. The vast majority of the societies in a recent cross-cultural study had at least occasional wars when they were first described, unless they had been pacified or incorporated by more dominant societies.[76] Why have some people fought a great deal, and others only infrequently? Why in some societies does warfare occur internally, within the society or language group?

We have answers, based on cross-cultural studies, to some of those questions. There is evidence that people in nonstate preindustrial societies go to war mostly out of fear, particularly a fear of expectable but unpredictable natural disasters that will destroy food resources (e.g., droughts, floods, locust infestations). People may think they can protect themselves against such disasters ahead of time by taking things from defeated enemies. In any case, preindustrial societies with higher frequencies of war are very likely to have had a history of expectable but unpredictable disasters. The fact that chronic (annually recurring and therefore predictable) food shortages do not predict higher frequencies of war suggests that people go to war in an attempt to cushion the impact of the disasters they expect to occur in the future but cannot predict. Consistent with this tentative conclusion is the fact that the victors in war almost always take land or other resources from the defeated. And this is true for simpler as well as more complex preindustrial societies.[77] Might similar motives affect decisions about war and peace in the modern world?

We know that complex or politically centralized societies are likely to have professional armies, hierarchies of military authority, and sophisticated weapons.[78] But surprisingly, the frequency of warfare seems to be not much greater in complex societies than in simple band or tribal societies.[79] We have some evidence that warfare is unlikely to occur internally (within a society or territory) if it is small in population (21,000 or fewer people); in a larger society, there

Oil is a valuable resource in the world today. Iraq has more oil in the ground than most other countries.

is a high likelihood of warfare within the society, between communities or larger territorial divisions.[80] In fact, complex societies, even if they are politically unified, are not less likely than simpler societies to have internal warfare.[81]

What about the idea that men in band and tribal societies may mostly go to war over women?[82] If this were true, those band and tribal societies with the most frequent wars should have shortages of women, and those with little or no war—less often than once in 10 years—should have more equal numbers of women and men. But the cross-cultural evidence clearly contradicts this theory. Band and tribal societies with more wars do not have fewer women.[83]

What, if anything, do we know about recent warfare between nation-states? Although many people think that military alliances lessen the chance of war, it turns out that nations formally allied with other nations do not necessarily go to war less often than nations lacking formal alliances. Countries that are allies are, of course, less likely to go to war with each other; however, alliances can drag dependent allies into wars they don't want.[84] Countries that are economically interdependent, that trade with each other for necessities, are less likely to go to war with each other.[85] Finally, military equality between nations, particularly when preceded by a rapid military buildup, seems to increase rather than lessen the chance of war between those nations.[86]

Clearly, these findings contradict some traditional beliefs about how to prevent war. Military buildups do not make war less likely, but trade does. What else may? We have already noted that participatory ("democratic") political systems are less likely to go to war with each other than are authoritarian political systems. Later, in the chapter on global problems, we discuss how the results of cross-cultural and cross-national studies may translate into policies that could minimize the risk of war in the world. Although war may be common in the world, it is not inevitable. Societies change over time. The Vikings were extremely militaristic, but Norway today is now a peaceful society. A comparative study of Polynesian societies shows that, although all derive from a common cultural heritage, the size of the islands people settled on strongly influenced their patterns of interpersonal violence and warfare. The smallest islands had the lowest levels of violence and the least warfare. It appears that cooperation and harmony were more likely than violence in small "face-to-face" societies.[87]

Democracy and Economic Development

The subsistence economies that anthropologists traditionally study are becoming more commercialized as people increasingly produce goods and services for a market. And the pace of economic development is quickening, particularly in places that lacked industrial wage labor until recently, as their economies are increasingly integrated into the world system. What effect, if any, does economic development have on political participation? Can we speculate about the future on the basis of comparative research?

Most of the comparative research on the relationship between economic development and political participation has been cross-national, comparing data on different countries. Some countries are more democratic than others, with characteristics such as contested elections, an elected head of state, an elected powerful legislature, and the protection of civil liberties. In capitalist countries, more democracy is generally associated with higher levels of economic development, as measured by indicators such as per capita output; in countries that are not very industrialized, there is little democracy at the national level. Why should more democracy be associated with more economic development? The prevailing opinion is that economic development increases the degree of social equality in the country; and the more equality among interest groups, the more they demand participation in the political process, and hence the more democracy. Or, to put this theory another way, as the economy develops, the more what we might call the middle and working classes can demand rewards and power, and therefore the less power the elite can retain.

What about the societies usually studied by anthropologists, the ones in what we call the cross-cultural or ethnographic record? We know that some of the highest levels of political participation occur in the least complex societies, such as foraging societies. Many adults in such societies have a say in decisions, and leadership is informal; leaders can retain their roles only if people voluntarily go along with them. Concentrated power and less political participation are more likely in chiefdoms and states than in band and tribal societies. The more hierarchical chiefdoms and states usually depend on agriculture,

particularly intensive agriculture, which can produce more goods and services per capita than foraging economies can. So the relationship between economic development and political participation in the ethnographic record is *opposite* to what we find cross-nationally. That is, the more economic development, the less political participation in the societies studied by anthropologists. Why should this be so? It seems that social equality *decreases* as economic development increases in the ethnographic record (which does not include many industrialized societies). In that record, an economically developed society is likely to have features such as plowing, fertilizers, and irrigation, which make permanent cultivation of the fields and permanent communities possible. Such intensive agricultural activity is more conducive to concentrated wealth than is hunter-gatherer subsistence or shifting cultivation (horticulture). Thus, in the ethnographic record, the more economically developed societies have more social inequality and therefore less democracy.

The two sets of findings, the cross-national and the cross-cultural, are not that hard to reconcile. Social and economic inequality appears to work against democracy and extensive political participation. Social inequality increases with the switch from foraging to agriculture. But social inequality decreases with the switch from preindustrial agriculture to high (industrial) levels of economic development. Political participation decreases with the first switch and increases with the second because social inequality first increases and then decreases.

So what does comparative research suggest about the future? If the middle and working classes feel they are not getting a fair return on their labor, their demands should increase. The elite may be willing to satisfy those increased demands; if they do, their power will be reduced. In either case, unless the elite try to retain their power at any cost, there should be more political participation and more democracy, at least in the long run.

Sources: Bollen 1993; M. Ember, C. R. Ember, and Russett 1997; Muller 1997; Ross 2009b.

Political and Social Change In addition to commercialization and religious change brought about by the expansion of Western and other countries, political changes have often occurred when a foreign system of government has been imposed. But, as events in the former Soviet Union and South Africa indicate, dramatic changes in a political system can also occur more or less voluntarily. Perhaps the most striking type of political change in recent years is the spread of participatory forms of government, "democracy."

To political scientists, democracy is usually defined in terms of voting by a substantial proportion of the citizenry, governments brought to power by periodic contested elections, a chief executive either popularly elected or responsible to an elected legislature, and often also civil liberties such as free speech. Depending on which criteria are used, only 12–15 countries qualified as democracies as of the beginning of the twentieth century. The number decreased after World War I, as emerging dictatorships in Russia, Italy, Germany, central Europe, Japan, and elsewhere replaced democratic institutions. After World War II, despite all the rhetoric associated with the founding of the United Nations, the picture was not much different. Some members of the new North Atlantic Treaty Organization (NATO) were not democracies, and neither were many members of the wider Western alliance system, in Latin America, the Middle East, and Asia.

As of 1992, about half of the countries in the world had more or less democratic governments, and others were in transition to democracy.[88] Social scientists do not yet understand why this change is happening. But it is possible that the global communication of ideas has a lot to do with it. Authoritarian governments can censor their own newspapers and prevent group meetings, and sophisticated technology can block Internet use and cell phone connections, but ultimately authoritarian governments really cannot stop the movement of ideas. The movement of ideas, of course, does not explain the acceptance of those ideas. Why democracy has recently diffused to more countries than ever before still requires explanation, as does why some countries do not find it appealing.

✓•⌐Study and **Review** on **myanthrolab.com**

Summary

1. All societies have customs or procedures that, organized on behalf of territorial groups, result in decision making and the resolution of disputes. These ways of creating and maintaining social order and coping with social disorder vary from society to society.

2. Societies with a band type of political organization are composed of fairly small, usually nomadic groups. Each of these bands is politically autonomous, the band being the largest group that acts as a political unit. Authority within the band is usually informal. Societies with band organization generally are egalitarian hunter-gatherers. But band organization may not have been typical of foragers in the distant past.

3. Societies with tribal organization are similar to those with band organization in being egalitarian. But, in contrast with band societies, they generally are food producers, have a higher population density, and are more sedentary. Tribal organization is defined by the presence of groupings, such as clans and age-sets, that can integrate more than one local group into a larger whole.

4. The personal qualities of leaders in tribal societies seem to be similar to the qualities of leaders in the United States, with one major difference: U.S. leaders are generally wealthier than others in their society.

5. Chiefdom organization differs from tribal organization in having formal authority structures that integrate multicommunity political units. Compared with societies with tribal organization, societies with chiefdoms are more densely populated and their communities are more permanent. In contrast to "big men" in tribal societies, who generally have to earn their privileges by their personal qualities, chiefs generally hold their positions permanently. Most chiefdom societies have social ranking.

6. A state has been defined as a political unit composed of many communities and having a centralized government with the authority to make and enforce laws, collect taxes, and draft men for military service. In state societies, the government tries to maintain a monopoly on the use of physical force. In addition, states are generally characterized by class stratification, intensive agriculture (the high productivity of which presumably allows the emergence of cities), commercial exchange, a high degree of economic and other specialization, and extensive foreign trade.

7. Degree of political participation seems to be high in small-scale societies, as well as in modern democratic nation-states, but not in those in between, such as feudal states and preindustrial empires.

8. Many societies lack specialized offices and institutions for dealing with conflict. Yet all societies have peaceful, regularized ways of handling at least certain disputes. Avoidance, community action, and negotiation and mediation are more common in simpler societies. Ritual apology occurs frequently in chiefdoms. Oaths and ordeals tend to occur in complex societies in which political officials lack power to enforce judicial decisions. Adjudication is more likely in stratified, more complex societies. Capital punishment seems to exist in nearly all societies, from the simplest to the most complex.

9. People are likely to resort to violence when regular, effective alternative means of resolving a conflict are not available. Violence can occur between individuals, within communities, and between communities. Violence that occurs between political entities such as communities, districts, or nations is generally referred to as warfare. The type of warfare varies in scope and complexity from society to society. Preindustrial societies with higher warfare frequencies are likely to have had a history of unpredictable disasters that destroyed food supplies. More often than not, societies with one type of violence have others.

10. One of the most striking types of political change in recent years is the spread of participatory forms of government, "democracy."

Glossary Terms

adjudication (p. 364)
band (p. 350)
band organization (p. 350)
chief (p. 353)
chiefdom (p. 353)
codified laws (p. 361)
complementary opposition (p. 352)

crime (p. 365)
feuding (p. 365)
headman (p. 350)
mediation (p. 362)
negotiation (p. 362)
oath (p. 363)
ordeal (p. 363)

raiding (p. 366)
segmentary lineage system (p. 352)
state organization (p. 354)
tribal organization (p. 351)
tribe (p. 351)
warfare (p. 365)

Critical Questions

1. When, if ever, do you think the world will be politically unified? Why do you think so?

2. Why don't informal methods of social control work well in societies like our own? Why don't formal methods work better than they do?

3. What does research on war and violence suggest about how to reduce their likelihood?

Read the Original Source on myanthrolab.com

Read the chapter by Thomas Abler, "Iroquois: The Tree of Peace and the War Kettle" on MyAnthroLab and answer the following questions.

1. What was the Iroquois Confederacy? What kind of political organization was it?

2. What role did men and women play in making war and making peace?

3. What kinds of impacts did the Europeans have on the Iroquois?

Religion and Magic 16

((•—|Listen to the **Chapter Audio** on **myanthrolab.com** |□●|—|Read on **myanthrolab.com**

As far as we know, all societies have possessed beliefs that can be grouped under the term *religion.* These beliefs vary from culture to culture and from time to time. Yet, despite their variety, we shall define **religion** as any set of attitudes, beliefs, and practices pertaining to *supernatural power,* whether that power be forces, gods, spirits, ghosts, or demons.

In our society, we divide phenomena into the natural and the supernatural, but not all languages or cultures make such a neat distinction. Moreover, what is considered **supernatural**—powers believed to be not human or not subject to the laws of nature—varies from society to society. Some of the variation is determined by what a society regards as natural. For example, some illnesses commonly found in our society are believed to result from the natural action of bacteria and viruses. In other societies, and even among some people in our own society, illness is thought to result from supernatural forces, and thus it forms a part of religious belief.

Beliefs about what is, or is not, a supernatural occurrence also vary within a society at a given time or over time. In Judeo-Christian traditions, for example, floods, earthquakes, volcanic eruptions, comets, and epidemics were once considered evidence of supernatural powers intervening in human affairs. It is now generally agreed that they are simply natural occurrences—even though many still believe that supernatural forces may be involved. Thus, the line between the natural and the supernatural varies in a society according to what people believe about the causes of things and events in the observable world. Similarly, what is considered sacred in one society may not be so considered in another.

In many cultures, what we would consider religious is embedded in other aspects of everyday life. That is, it is often difficult to separate the religious, economic, or political from other aspects of the culture. Such cultures have little or no specialization of any kind; there are no full-time priests, no purely religious activities. So the various aspects of culture we distinguish (e.g., in the chapter titles of this book) are not separate and easily recognized in many societies, as they are in complex societies such as our own. After all, the categorizing of beliefs as religious, political, or social is a relatively new custom. The ancient Greeks, for instance, did not have a word for religion, but they did have many concepts concerning the behavior of their gods and their own expected duties to the gods.

Variation in Religious Beliefs

There is no general agreement among scholars as to why people need religion, or how spirits, gods, and other supernatural beings and forces come into existence. Yet there is general recognition of the enormous variation in the details of religious beliefs and practices. Societies differ in the kinds of supernatural beings or forces they believe in and the character of those beings. They also differ in the structure or hierarchy of those beings, in what the beings actually do, and in what happens to people after death. Variation exists also in the ways in which the supernatural is believed to interact with humans.

Types of Supernatural Forces and Beings

Supernatural Forces Some supernatural forces have no personlike character. For example, a supernatural, impersonal force called **mana,** after its Malayo-Polynesian name, is thought to inhabit some objects but not others, some people but not others. A farmer in Polynesia places stones around a field; the crops are bountiful; the stones have mana. During a subsequent year, the stones may lose their mana and the crops will be poor. People may also possess mana, as, for example, the chiefs in Polynesia were said to do. However, such power is not necessarily possessed permanently; chiefs who were unsuccessful in war or other activities were said to have lost their mana.

The word *mana* may be Malayo-Polynesian, but a similar concept is also found in our own society. We can compare mana to the power that golfers may attribute to some but, unhappily not all, of their clubs. A ballplayer might think a certain sweatshirt or pair of pants has supernatural power or force, and that more runs or points will be scored when they are worn. A four-leaf clover has mana; a three-leaf clover does not.

Objects, people, or places can be considered **taboo.** Anthony Wallace distinguished mana from taboo by pointing out that things containing mana are to be touched, whereas taboo things are not to be touched, for their power can cause harm.[1] Thus, those who touch them may themselves become taboo. Taboos surround food not to be eaten, places not to be entered, animals not to be killed, people not to be touched sexually, people not to be touched at all, and so on. An Australian aborigine could not normally kill and eat the animal that was his totem; Hebrew tribesmen were forbidden to touch a woman during menstruation or for 7 days afterward.

Supernatural Beings Supernatural beings fall within two broad categories: those of nonhuman origin, such as gods and spirits, and those of human origin, such as ghosts and ancestral spirits. Chief among the beings of nonhuman origin, **gods** are named personalities. They are often *anthropomorphic*—that is, conceived in the image of a person—although they are sometimes given the shapes of other animals or of celestial bodies, such as the sun or moon. Essentially, the gods are believed to have created themselves, but some of them then created, or gave birth to, other gods. Although some are seen as creator gods, not all peoples include the creation of the world as one of the acts of gods.

After their efforts at creation, many creator gods retire. Having set the world in motion, they are not interested in its day-to-day operation. Other creator gods remain interested in the ordinary affairs of human beings, especially the affairs of one small, chosen segment of humanity. Whether or not a society has a creator god, the job of running the creation is often left to lesser

A Guatemalan Maya family visits a cemetery on the Day of the Dead. It is believed that the spirits of the dead return for a visit on that day.

gods. The Maori of New Zealand, for example, recognize three important gods: a god of the sea, a god of the forest, and a god of agriculture. They call upon each in turn for help and try to get all three to share their knowledge of how the universe runs. The gods of the ancient Romans, on the other hand, specialized to a high degree. There were three gods of the plow, one god to help with the sowing, one for weeding, one for reaping, one for storing grain, one for manuring, and so on.[2]

Beneath the gods in prestige, and often closer to people, are multitudes of unnamed **spirits.** Some may be guardian spirits for people. Some, who become known for particularly efficacious work, may be promoted to the rank of named gods. Some spirits who are known to the people but are never invoked by them are of the hobgoblin type. Hobgoblins delight in mischief and can be blamed for any number of small mishaps; still other spirits take pleasure in deliberately working evil on behalf of people.

Many Native American groups believed in guardian spirits that had to be sought out, usually in childhood. For example, among the Sanpoil of northeastern Washington, boys and sometimes girls would be sent out on overnight vigils to acquire their guardians. Most commonly the spirits were animals, but they could also be uniquely shaped rocks, lakes, mountains, whirlwinds, or clouds. The vigil was not always successful. When it was, the guardian spirit appeared in a vision or dream, and always at first in human form. Conversation with the spirit would reveal its true identity.[3]

Ghosts are supernatural beings who were once human, and **ancestor spirits** are ghosts of dead relatives. The belief that ghosts or their actions can be perceived by the living is almost universal.[4] The near-universality of the belief in ghosts may not be difficult to explain. There are many cues in everyday experience that are associated with a loved one, and even after death, those cues might arouse the feeling that the dead person is still somehow present. The opening of a door or the smell of tobacco or cologne in a room may evoke the idea that the person is still present, if only for a moment. Then, too, loved ones live on in dreams. Small wonder, then, that most societies believe in ghosts. If the idea of ghosts is generated by these familiar associations, we might expect that ghosts in most societies would be close relatives and friends, not strangers—and they are.[5]

Although the belief in ghosts is nearly universal, the spirits of the dead do not play an active role in the life of the living in all societies. In his cross-cultural study of 50 societies, Swanson

A ghost festival in Thailand. The belief in ghosts is practically a cross-cultural universal.

found that people are likely to believe in active ancestral spirits where descent groups are important decision-making units. The descent group is an entity that exists over time, back into the past as well as forward into the future, despite the deaths of individual members.[6] The dead feel concern for the fortunes, the prestige, and the continuity of their descent group as strongly as the living. As a Lugbara elder (in northern Uganda in Africa) put it, "Are our ancestors not people of our lineage? They are our fathers and we are their children whom they have begotten. Those that have died stay near us in our homes and we feed and respect them. Does not a man help his father when he is old?"[7]

The Character of Supernatural Beings

Whatever type they may be, the gods or spirits venerated in a given culture tend to have certain personality or character traits. They may be unpredictable or predictable, aloof from or interested in human affairs, helpful or punishing. Why do the gods and spirits in a particular culture exhibit certain character traits rather than others?

We have some evidence from cross-cultural studies that the character of supernatural beings may be related to the nature of child training. Melford Spiro and Roy D'Andrade suggested that the god–human relationship is a projection of the parent–child relationship, in which case child-training practices might well be relived in dealings with the supernatural.[8] For example, if a child was nurtured immediately by her parents when she cried or waved her arms about or kicked, she might grow up expecting to be nurtured by the gods when she attracted their attention by performing a ritual. On the other hand, if her parents often punished her, she would grow up expecting the gods to punish her if she disobeyed them. William Lambert, Leigh Minturn Triandis, and Margery Wolf, in another cross-cultural study, found that societies with hurtful or punitive child-training practices are likely to believe that their gods are aggressive and malevolent; societies with less punitive child training are more likely to believe that the gods are benevolent.[9] These results are consistent with the Freudian notion that the supernatural world should parallel the natural. It is worth noting in this context that some peoples refer to the god as their father and to themselves as his children.

Structure or Hierarchy of Supernatural Beings

The range of social structures in human societies from egalitarian to highly stratified has its counterpart in the supernatural world. Some societies have gods or spirits that are not ranked; one god has about as much power as another. Other societies have gods or spirits that are ranked in prestige and power. For example, on the Pacific islands of Palau, which was a rank society, gods were ranked as people were. Each clan worshiped a god and a goddess that had names or titles similar to clan titles. Although a clan god was generally important only to the members of that clan, the gods of the various clans in a village were believed to be ranked in the same order that the clans were. Thus, the god of the highest-ranking clan was respected by all the clans of the village. Its shrine was given the place of honor in the center of the village and was larger and more elaborately decorated than other shrines.[10]

Although the Palauans did not believe in a high god or supreme being who outranked all the other gods, some societies do. Consider Judaism, Christianity, and Islam, which we call **monotheistic** religions. Although *monotheism* means "one god," most monotheistic religions actually include more than one supernatural being (e.g., demons, angels, the Devil). But the supreme being or high god, as the creator of the universe or the director of events (or both), is believed to be ultimately responsible for all events.[11] A **polytheistic** religion recognizes many important gods, no one of which is supreme.

Why do some societies have a belief in a high god and others do not? Recall Swanson's suggestion that people invent gods who personify the important decision-making groups in their society. He therefore hypothesized that societies with hierarchical political systems should be more likely to believe in a high god. In his cross-cultural study of 50 societies (none of which practiced any of the major world religions), he found that belief in a high god is strongly associated with three or more levels of "sovereign" (decision-making) groups. Of the 20 sample societies that had a hierarchy of three or more sovereign groups—for instance, family, clan, and chiefdom—17 possessed the idea of a high god. Of the 19 societies that had fewer than three levels of decision-making groups, only two had a high god.[12] Consistent with Swanson's findings, societies dependent on food production are more likely to have a belief in a high god than are food-collecting societies.[13] These results strongly suggest, then, that the realm of the gods parallels and may reflect the everyday social and political worlds. In the past, many state societies had state religions in which the political officials were also the officials of the temples (e.g., the pharaohs in Egypt). In recent times, most state societies have separated church and state, as in the United States and Canada.

Intervention of the Gods in Human Affairs

According to Clifford Geertz, when people face ignorance, pain, and the unjustness of life, they explain the events by the intervention of the gods.[14] Thus, in Greek religion, the direct intervention of Poseidon as ruler of the seas prevented Odysseus from getting home for 10 years. In the Old Testament, the direct intervention of Yahweh caused the great flood that killed most of the people in the time of Noah. In other societies, people may search their memories for a violated taboo that has brought punishment through supernatural intervention.

In addition to unasked-for divine interference, there are numerous examples of requests for divine intervention, either for good for oneself and friends or for evil for others. Gods are asked to intervene in the weather and to make the crops grow, to send fish to the fisherman and game to the hunter, to find lost things, and to accompany travelers and prevent accidents. They are asked to stop the flow of lava down the side of a volcano, to stop a war, or to cure an illness.

The gods do not intervene in all societies. In some, they intervene in human affairs; in others, they are not the slightest bit interested; and in still others, they interfere only occasionally. We have little research on why gods are believed to interfere in some societies and not in others. We do, however, have some evidence suggesting when the gods will take an interest in the morality or immorality of human behavior. Swanson's study suggests that the gods are likely to punish people for immoral behavior when there are considerable differences in wealth in the society.[15] His interpretation is that supernatural support of moral behavior is particularly useful where inequalities tax the ability of the political system to maintain social order and minimize social disorder. Envy of others' privileges may motivate some people to behave immorally; the belief that the gods will punish such behavior might deter it.

Variation in Religious Practices

Beliefs are not the only elements of religion that vary from society to society. Societies vary in the kinds of religious practitioners they have. There is also variation in how people interact with the supernatural. The manner of approach to the supernatural varies from supplication—requests, prayers, and so on—to manipulation. Many of these interactions are highly *ritualized.* **Rituals** are repetitive sets of behaviors that occur in essentially the same patterns every time they occur. Religious rituals involve the supernatural in some way. They are generally collective, follow customary patterns, and are thought to strengthen faith.[16]

Religion: A Force for Cooperation and Harmony?

Most social science theories about religion suggest that religious beliefs and rituals promote social cohesion and cooperation within the group that shares them. Some religions, including the major religions in the modern world (Buddhism, Christianity, Islam, Hinduism, Judaism), are more explicit than others in their direct concern with moral behavior. Moralizing religions believe that the gods will reward moral behavior and punish immoral behavior, and are generally found in large and complex societies. Such societies are likely to have towns or cities and less reliance on kinship and reciprocity to encourage moral behavior. Neighbors may not know each other well and although there may be codified law and courts, these mechanisms may not be sufficient to promote social order. Complex societies are also likely to have a large amount of social inequality, which increases the likelihood of property-related crime. The cross-cultural evidence is consistent with the theory that morality-based religions and collective rituals minimize antisocial behavior in groups of unrelated individuals. Perhaps to promote solidarity among unrelated people, religions in complex societies often extend kin terms to members of the religious communities, calling each other "brothers" and "sisters" or sometimes "God's children." Experimental evidence suggests individuals are more generous toward strangers if their religious feelings have been aroused. Religious communes are also four times as likely to survive compared with secular communes.

These studies raise important questions about exactly why and when moralizing religions came into existence and whether the spread of these religions had to do with their adaptive consequences. But there are also questions raised about mechanisms. For example, religious communes, as compared with secular communes, usually impose more requirements from members, such as food taboos, fasts, constraints on sex and possessions, and so on. A comparative study of communes suggests that the religious elements are more important than the commitments themselves. However, in experimental research, there are some hints that nonreligious conditions could also make people more cooperative. Experimental reminders of secular morality had as much effect as reminders of God. Also, there are examples of modern societies, especially in northern Europe, that are very cooperative, but not very religious.

However, even if religious belief and ritual promote greater in-group trust and cooperation, there is a dark side to strongly held religious belief—the potential for greater out-group conflict. History is replete with examples of people hurting others in the name of religion. Christianity and Islam are the two largest religions, possibly because of their zeal to convert others. Some of the biggest conflicts have occurred where the two largest religions meet. The Christian Crusades of the eleventh century through the thirteenth century were attempts to "liberate" sites in the Holy Land controlled by Muslims. Osama bin Laden cited the establishment of U.S. bases in Saudi Arabia, which "defiled" sacred lands in his view, as justification for the September 11, 2001, attacks on the United States. Religions or, more precisely, religious groups, do not necessarily promote violence. After all, some of the founders of various religions preached nonviolence and harmony. Exactly what persuades a religious group to commit violence is not well understood. There are five warning signs. One is when leaders act as if only they know the truth. A second is a call to blind obedience to a religious leader. A third is when the people believe it is possible to establish an "ideal world." A fourth is acting as if "the end justifies the means." Lastly, and perhaps the clearest, is a call for a "holy war."

In the globalized world today, there is more admixture of all types—heterogeneous cities full of people of different colors, dress, ethnicities, and religions. This situation has two potential outcomes: the potential for different groups to live together peacefully, or a greater potential for violence. Whether the major religions will adapt to create a new morality for the new global circumstances remains to be seen. Research has not told us enough yet about how to achieve more harmony across different religions or across different ethnicities. We can hope that simply learning more about other individuals and groups—their hopes, dreams, and expectations, how they have adapted to their environments—may enhance tolerance.

Sources: Norenzayan and Shariff 2008; Roes and Raymond 2003; Sosis and Bressler 2003; Stark 2001; Winkelman and Baker 2010, 259–65, 314–18.

Ways to Interact with the Supernatural

How to get in touch with the supernatural has proved to be a universal problem. Wallace identified a number of ways people the world over use, though not necessarily all together, including, but not limited to, prayer (asking for supernatural help), physiological experience (doing things to the body and mind), simulation (manipulating imitations of things), feasts, and sacrifices.[17]

Prayer can be spontaneous or memorized, private or public, silent or spoken. The Lugbara do not say the words of a prayer aloud, for doing so would be too powerful; they simply think about the things that are bothering them. The gods know all languages.

Doing things to the body or mind may involve drugs (hallucinogenics such as peyote or opiates) or alcohol; social isolation or sensory deprivation; dancing or running until exhausted; being deprived of food, water, and sleep; and listening to repetitive sounds such as drumming. Such behaviors may induce trances or altered states of consciousness.[18] Erika Bourguignon found that achieving these altered states, which she generally referred to as *trances,* is part of religious practice in 90 percent of the world's societies.[19] In some societies, trances are thought to involve the presence of a spirit or power inside a person that changes or displaces that person's personality or soul. These types are referred to as possession trances. Other types of trances may involve the journey of a person's soul, experiencing visions, or transmitting messages from spirits. Possession trances are especially likely in societies that depend on agriculture and have social stratification, slavery, and more complex political hierarchies. Nonpossession trances are most likely to occur in food-collecting societies. Societies with moderate levels of social complexity have both possession and nonpossession trances.[20]

One puzzle is why there is a preponderance of women thought to be possessed. Alice Kehoe and Dody Giletti suggested that women are more likely than men to suffer from nutritional deficiencies because of pregnancy, lactation, and men's priority in gaining access to food. Calcium deficiency in particular can cause muscular spasms, convulsive seizures, and disorientation, all of which may foster the belief that an individual is possessed.[21] Douglas Raybeck and his colleagues suggest that women's physiology makes them more susceptible to calcium deficiency even with an equivalent diet. In addition, women are subject to more stress because they are usually less able to control their lives. Higher levels of stress, they suggest, lower the body's reserves of calcium.[22] Bourguignon suggests a more psychological explanation of women's preponderance in possession trances. In many societies, women are brought up to be submissive. But when possessed, women are taken over by spirits and they are not responsible for what they do or say—therefore, they can unconsciously do what they are not able to do consciously.[23] Although intriguing, these suggestions need to be tested on individuals in field situations.

Voodoo employs simulation, or the imitation of things. Dolls are made in the likeness of an enemy and then are maltreated in hopes that the original enemy will experience pain and even death.

Divination seeks practical answers from the supernatural about anything that is troublesome—decisions to be made, interpersonal problems, or illness. Diviners use a variety of methods, including altered states of consciousness and simulation through the use of objects such as Ouija boards or tarot cards.[24]

Omar Moore suggested that, among the Naskapi hunters of Labrador, divination is an adaptive strategy for successful hunting. The Naskapi consult the diviner every 3 or 4 days when they have no luck in hunting. The diviner holds a caribou bone over the fire, as if the bone were a map, and the burns and cracks that appear in it indicate where the group should hunt. Moore, unlike the Naskapi, did not believe that the diviner really can find out where the animals will be; the cracks in the bones merely provide a way of randomly choosing where to hunt. Because humans are likely to develop customary patterns of action, they might be likely to look for game according to some plan. But game might learn to avoid hunters who operate according to a plan. Thus, any method of ensuring against patterning or predictable plans—any random strategy—may be advantageous. Divination by "reading" the bones would seem to be a random strategy. It also relieves any individual of the responsibility of deciding where to hunt, a decision that might arouse anger if the hunt failed.[25]

The eating of a sacred meal is found in many religions. For instance, Holy Communion is a simulation of the Last Supper. Australian aborigines, normally forbidden to eat their totem animal, have one totem feast a year at which they eat the totem. Feasts are often part of marriage and funeral ceremonies, as well as a fringe benefit of the sacrifice of food to the gods.

Some societies make sacrifices to a god in order to influence the god's action, either to divert anger or to attract goodwill. Characteristic of all sacrifices is that something of value is given up to the gods, whether it be food, drink, sex, household goods, or the life of an animal or person. Some societies feel that the god is obli-

A woman with offerings at a Hindu temple in Bali.

gated to act on their behalf if they make the appropriate sacrifice. Others use the sacrifice in an attempt to persuade the god, realizing there is no guarantee that the attempt will be successful.

Of all types of sacrifice, we probably think that the taking of human life is the ultimate. Nevertheless, human sacrifice is not rare in the ethnographic and historical records. Why have some societies practiced it? One cross-cultural study found that, among preindustrial societies, those with full-time craft specialists, slavery, and the corvée are most likely to practice human sacrifice. The suggested explanation is that the sacrifice mirrors what is socially important: Societies that depend mainly on human labor for energy (rather than animals or machines) may think of a human life as an appropriate offering to the gods when people want something very important.[26] Later studies found that societies with human sacrifice were at a mid-range level of political complexity, having alliances and confederacies with other polities, but only weak political integration. Such societies also seemed to be subject to population pressure and frequently carried out warfare for land and other resources. Human sacrifice, with humans from the outside groups, may have been an attempt to terrorize people from the other polities.[27]

Magic

All these modes of interacting with the supernatural can be categorized in various ways. One dimension of variation is how much people in society rely on pleading, asking, or trying to persuade the supernatural to act on their behalf, as opposed to whether they believe they can compel the supernatural to help by performing certain acts. For example, prayer is asking; performing voodoo is presumably compelling. When people believe their action can compel the supernatural to act in some particular and intended way, anthropologists often refer to the belief and related practice as **magic.**

Magic may involve manipulation of the supernatural for good or for evil. Many societies have magical rituals designed to ensure good crops, the replenishment of game, the fertility of domestic animals, and the avoidance and cure of illness in humans. We tend to associate the belief in magic with societies simpler than our own, but some people in complex societies take magic seriously and many follow some magical practices. People who engage in risky activities may try to ensure their safety by carrying or wearing lucky charms. They believe the charms protect them by invoking the help of supernatural beings or forces. We might also believe we can protect ourselves by not doing some things. For example, baseball players on a hitting streak may choose not to change their socks or sweatshirt for the next game (to continue their luck).

As we will see, the witch doctor and the shaman often employ magic to effect a cure. But the use of magic to bring about harm has evoked perhaps the most interest.

Sorcery and Witchcraft Sorcery and witchcraft are attempts to invoke the spirits to work harm against people. Although the words *sorcery* and *witchcraft* are often used interchangeably, they are also often distinguished. **Sorcery** may include the use of materials, objects, and medicines to invoke supernatural malevolence. **Witchcraft** may be said to accomplish the same ills by means of thought and emotion alone. Evidence of witchcraft can never be found. This lack of visible evidence makes an accusation of witchcraft both harder to prove and harder to disprove.

To the Azande of Zaire, in central Africa, witchcraft was part of everyday living. It was not used to explain events for which the cause was known, such as carelessness or violation of a taboo, but to explain the otherwise unexplainable. A man is gored by an elephant. He must have been bewitched because he had not been gored on other elephant hunts. A man goes to his beer hut at night, lights some straw, and holds it aloft to look at his beer. The thatch catches fire and the hut burns down. The man has been bewitched, for huts did not catch fire on hundreds of other nights when he and others did the same thing. Some of the pots of a skilled potter break; some of the bowls of a skilled carver crack. Witchcraft. Other pots, other bowls treated exactly the same have not broken.[28]

The witch craze in Europe during the 16th and 17th centuries and the witch trials in 1692 in Salem, Massachusetts, remind us that the fear of others, which the belief in witchcraft presumably represents, can increase and decrease in a society within a relatively short period of time. Many scholars have tried to explain these witch hunts. One factor often suggested is political turmoil, which may give rise to widespread distrust and a search for scapegoats. In the case of Europe during the 16th and 17th centuries, small regional political units were being incorporated into national states, and political allegiances were in flux. In addition, as Swanson noted, the commercial revolution and related changes were producing a new social class, the middle class, and "were promoting the growth of Protestantism and other heresies from Roman Catholicism."[29] In the case of Salem, the government of Massachusetts colony was unstable and there was much internal dissension. In 1692, the year of the witchcraft hysteria, Massachusetts was left without an English governor, and judicial practices broke down. These extraordinary conditions saw the accusation of a single person for witchcraft become the accusation of hundreds and the execution of 20 people. Swanson suggested that the undermining of legitimate political procedures may have generated the widespread fear of witches.[30]

It is also possible that epidemics of witchcraft accusation, like in Salem as well as other New England and European communities, may be the result of real epidemics—epidemics of disease. The disease implicated in Salem and elsewhere is the fungus disease called ergot, which can grow on rye plants. (The rye flour that went into the bread that the Salem people

ate may have been contaminated by ergot.) It is now known that people who eat grain products contaminated by ergot suffer from convulsions, hallucinations, and other symptoms,
such as crawling sensations in the skin. We also now know that ergot contains LSD, the drug
that produces hallucinations and other delusions that resemble those occurring in severe
mental disorders.

The presumed victims of bewitchment in Salem and other places had symptoms similar to
victims of ergot poisoning today. They suffered from convulsions and the sensations of being
pricked, pinched, or bitten. They had visions and felt as if they were flying through the air.
We cannot know for sure that ergot poisoning occurred during those times when witchcraft
accusations flourished. There is no direct evidence, of course, because the "bewitched" were
not medically tested. But we do have some evidence that seems to be consistent with the ergot
theory. Ergot is known to flourish on rye plants under certain climatic conditions—particularly
a very cold winter followed by a cool, moist spring and summer. Tree-ring growth indicates that
the early 1690s were particularly cold in eastern New England, and the outbreaks of witchcraft
accusation in Europe seem to have peaked with colder winter temperatures.[31] Interestingly, too,
when witchcraft hysteria was greatest in Europe, Europeans were using an ointment containing
a skin-penetrating substance that we now know produces hallucinations and a vivid sensation
of flying.[32] It may not be cause for wonder, then, that our popular image of witches is of people
flying through the air on broomsticks.

But whether or not epidemics of witchcraft hysteria are due to epidemics of ergot poisoning or episodes of political turmoil or both, we still have to understand why so many societies
in the ethnographic record believe in witchcraft and sorcery in the first place. Why do so many
societies believe that there are ways to invoke the spirits to work harm against people? One
possible explanation, suggested by Beatrice Whiting, is that sorcery or witchcraft will be found
in societies that lack procedures or judicial authorities to deal with crime and other offenses.
Her theory is that all societies need some form of social control—some way of deterring most
would-be offenders and of dealing with actual offenders. In the absence of judicial officials
who, if present, might deter and deal with antisocial behavior, sorcery may be a very effective
mechanism for social control. If you misbehave, the person you mistreated might cause you to
become ill or even die. The cross-cultural evidence seems to support this theory. Sorcery is more
important in societies that lack judicial authorities than in those that have them.[33]

Types of Practitioners

Individuals may believe that they can directly contact the supernatural, but almost all societies
also have part-time or full-time religious or magical practitioners. Research suggests there are
four major types of practitioners: shamans, sorcerers or witches, mediums, and priests. As we
shall see, the number of types of practitioners in a society seems to vary with degree of cultural
complexity.[34]

Shamans The word *shaman* may come from a language that was spoken in eastern Siberia.
The **shaman** is usually a part-time male specialist who has fairly high status in his community
and is often involved in healing.[35] We discuss the role of the shaman as healer in the chapter
on applied, practicing, and medical anthropology. More generally, the shaman deals with the
spirit world to try to get their help or to keep them from causing harm.[36] Here we focus on the
methods shamans use to help others.

The shaman enters into a trance, or some other altered state of consciousness, and then
journeys to other worlds to get help from guardians or other spirits. Dreams may be used

Shamans are usually male. Here, female shamans in Korea perform a healing ritual.

to provide insight or as a way for shamans to commune with spirits. People may seek help for practical matters, such as where to get food resources or whether to relocate, but solving a health problem is most often the goal of the shaman.[37] Shamans may also bring news from spirits, such as a warning about an impending disaster.[38]

Someone may receive a "call" to the role of shaman in recovering from an illness, through a vision quest, or in a dream. Shamans-in-training may enhance the vividness of their imagery by using hallucinogens, sleep or food deprivation, or engaging in extensive physical activity such as dancing. An important part of the process of being a shaman is learning to control the imagery and the spirit powers. Shamanistic training can take several years under the guidance of a master shaman.[39]

Sorcerers and Witches In contrast with shamans, who have fairly high status, sorcerers and witches of both sexes tend to have very low social and economic status in their societies.[40] Suspected sorcerers and witches are usually feared because they are thought to know how to invoke the supernatural to cause illness, injury, and death. Because sorcerers use materials for their magic, evidence of sorcery can be found, and suspected sorcerers are often killed for their malevolent activities. Because witchcraft supposedly is accomplished by thought and emotion alone, it may be harder to prove that someone is a witch, but the difficulty of proving witchcraft has not prevented people from accusing and killing others for being witches.

Mediums **Mediums** tend to be females. These part-time practitioners are asked to heal and divine while in possession trances—that is, when they are thought to be possessed by spirits. Mediums are described as having tremors, convulsions, seizures, and temporary amnesia.[41]

Priests **Priests** are generally full-time male specialists who officiate at public events. They have very high status and are thought to be able to relate to superior or high gods who are beyond the ordinary person's control. In most societies with priests, the people who get to be priests obtain their offices through inheritance or political appointment.[42] Priests are sometimes distinguished from other people by special clothing or a different hairstyle. The training of a priest can be vigorous and long, including fasting, praying, and physical labor, as well as learning the dogma and the religious rituals. Priests in the United States complete 4 years of theological school and sometimes serve first as apprentices under established priests. Priests do not receive a fee for their services but are supported by donations from parishioners or followers. Priests often have some political power as a result of their office—the chief priest is sometimes also the head of state or is a close adviser to the chief of state—and their material well-being is a direct reflection of their position in the priestly hierarchy.

The dependence on memorized ritual both marks and protects the priest. Shamans who repeatedly fail to effect cures will probably lose their followers. But if a priest performs a ritual and the gods choose not to respond, the nonresponse of the gods will be explained in terms of the people's unworthiness of supernatural favor.

Practitioners and Social Complexity More complex societies tend to have more types of religious or magical practitioners. If a society has only one type of practitioner, it is almost always a shaman; such societies tend to be nomadic or seminomadic food collectors. Societies with two types of practitioners (usually shaman healers and priests) have agriculture. Those with three types of practitioners are agriculturalists or pastoralists with political integration beyond the community (the additional practitioner type tends to be either a sorcerer or witch or a medium). Finally, societies with all four types of practitioners have agriculture, political integration beyond the community, and social classes.[43]

Religion and Adaptation

Following Malinowski, many anthropologists take the view that religions are adaptive because they reduce the anxieties and uncertainties that afflict all peoples. We do not really know that religion is the only means of reducing anxiety and uncertainty, or even that individuals or societies *have* to reduce their anxiety and uncertainty. Still, it seems likely that certain religious beliefs and practices have directly adaptive consequences. For example, the Hindu belief in the sacred cow has seemed to many to be the very opposite of a useful or adaptive custom. Their religion does not permit Hindus to slaughter cows. Why do the Hindus retain such a belief? Why do they allow all those cows to wander around freely, defecating all over the place, and not slaughter any of them? The contrast with our own use of cows could hardly be greater.

Marvin Harris suggested that the Hindu use of cows may have beneficial consequences that some other use of cows would not have. Harris pointed out that there may be a sound economic reason for not slaughtering cattle in India. The cows, and the males they produce, provide resources that could not easily be gotten otherwise. At the same time, their wandering around to forage is no strain on the food-producing economy.

The resources provided by the cows are varied. First, a team of oxen and a plow are essential for the many small farms in India. The Indians could produce oxen with fewer cows, but to do so, they would have to devote some of their food production to feeding those cows. In the present system, they do not feed the cows, and even though poor nutrition makes the cows relatively infertile, males, which are castrated to make oxen, are still produced at no cost to the economy. Second, cow dung is essential as a cooking fuel and fertilizer. The National Council of Applied Economic Research estimated that an amount of dung equivalent to 45 million tons of coal is burned annually. Moreover, it is delivered practically to the door each day at no cost. Alternative sources of fuel, such as wood, are scarce or costly. In addition, about 340 million tons of dung are used as manure—essential in a country obliged to derive three harvests a year from its intensively cultivated land. Third, although Hindus do not eat beef, cattle that die naturally or are butchered by non-Hindus are eaten by the lower castes, who, without the upper-caste taboo against eating beef, might not get this needed protein. Fourth, the hides and horns of the cattle that die are used in India's enormous leather industry. Therefore, because the cows do not themselves consume resources needed by people and it would be impossible to provide traction, fuel, and fertilizer as cheaply by other means, the taboo against slaughtering cattle may be very adaptive.[44]

A Catholic mass under open skies conducted by missionaries among the Karamojong of Uganda.

Religious Change

In any society, religious beliefs and practices change over time, but some types of change are quite dramatic. Perhaps the most dramatic is religious conversion, particularly when large numbers of people switch to a completely new religion presented by missionaries or other proselytizers. Changing religion so drastically is perplexing to many scholars of religion who believe that religious beliefs are deeply connected to one's sense of identity, one's family, one's community, and one's ideas about the world.[45] Within the last few centuries, conversion has sometimes followed Western expansion and exploration. In some native societies, contact has led to a breakdown of social structure and the growth of feelings of helplessness and spiritual demoralization. **Revitalization movements** have arisen as apparent attempts to restore such societies to their former confidence and prosperity. In recent times, religious *fundamentalist* movements have flourished.

Religious Conversion

The two world religions with the greatest interest now in obtaining converts have been Christianity and Islam. Christian missionaries, supported by their churches back home, have been some of the earliest Western settlers in interior regions and out-of-the-way places. Traders have been the main proselytizers of Islam. The presence of people from other religions does not necessarily mean that people convert to the new religion. For example, missionaries have not met with equal success in all parts of the world. In some places, large portions of the native population have converted to the new religion with great zeal. In others, missionaries have been ignored, forced to flee, or even killed. We do not fully understand why missionaries have been successful in some societies and not in others.

Christianity on Tikopia Tikopia was one of the few Polynesian societies to retain its traditional religious system into the first decades of the twentieth century. An Anglican mission was first established on the island in 1911. With it came a deacon and the founding of two schools for about 200 pupils. By 1929, approximately half the population had converted, and in the early 1960s, almost all of Tikopia gave at least nominal allegiance to Christianity.[46]

Traditional Tikopian belief embraced a great number of gods and spirits of various ranks who inhabited the sky, the water, and the land. One god in particular—the original creator and shaper of the culture—was given a place of special importance, but he was in no way comparable to the all-powerful God of Christianity. Unlike Christianity, Tikopian religion made no claim to universality. The Tikopian gods did not rule over all creation, only over Tikopia. It was thought that if one left Tikopia, one left the gods behind.

The people of Tikopia interacted with their gods and spirits primarily through religious leaders who were also the heads of descent groups. Clan chiefs presided over rituals associated with the everyday aspects of island life, such as house construction, fishing, planting, and harvesting.

The chief was expected to intercede with the gods on the people's behalf, to persuade them to bring happiness and prosperity to the group. Indeed, when conditions were good, it was assumed that the chief was doing his job well. When disaster struck, the prestige of the chief often fell in proportion. Why did the Tikopia convert to Christianity? Firth suggested several contributing factors.

First, the mission offered the people the prospect of acquiring new tools and consumer goods. Although conversion alone did not provide such benefits, attachment to the mission made them more attainable. Later, it became apparent that education, particularly in reading and writing English, was helpful in getting ahead in the outside world. Mission schooling became valued and provided a further incentive for adopting Christianity.

Second, conversion may have been facilitated by the ability of chiefs, as religious and political leaders, to bring over entire descent groups to Christianity. Should a chief decide to transfer his allegiance to Christianity, the members of his kin group usually followed him. In 1923, when Tafua, chief of the Faea district of Tikopia, converted to the new religion, he brought with him his entire group—nearly half the population of the island. The ability of the chiefs to influence their kin groups, however, was both an asset and a hindrance to missionary efforts because some chiefs steadfastly resisted conversion.

A final blow to traditional Tikopian religion came in 1955, when a severe epidemic killed at least 200 people in a population of about 1,700. According to Firth, "the epidemic was largely interpreted as a sign of divine discrimination," because three of the outstanding non-Christian religious leaders died.[47] Subsequently, the remaining non-Christian chiefs voluntarily converted to Christianity, and so did their followers. By 1966, all Tikopia, with the exception of one old woman, had converted to the new faith.

Although many Tikopians feel their conversion to Christianity has been a unifying, revitalizing force, the changeover from one religion to another has not been without problems. Christian missionaries on Tikopia have succeeded in eliminating the traditional Tikopian population-control devices of abortion, infanticide, and male celibacy. It is very possible that the absence of these controls will continue to intensify population pressure. The island, with its limited capacity to support life, can ill afford this outcome. Firth summed up the situation Tikopian society faced:

> In the history of Tikopia complete conversion of the people to Christianity was formerly regarded as a solution to their problems; it is now coming to be realized that the adoption and practice of Christianity itself represents another set of problems. As the Tikopia themselves are beginning to see, to be Christian Polynesians in the modern technologically and industrially dominated world, even in the Solomon Islands, poses as many questions as it supplies answers.[48]

Explaining Conversion Some of the motivation for switching to a new religion may have to do with economic and political advantages associated with converting to the new religion. With regard to the recent spread of Islam in Africa, Jean Ensminger suggests that Islam provided opportunities for those who wanted to engage in trade—"Islam brought a common language of trade (Arabic), a monetary system, an accounting system, and a legal code to adjudicate financial contracts and disputes."[49] These institutions were shared across ethnic groups, making it possible to engage in long-distance trade. Ensminger's study of the Orma, a pastoralist group in Kenya, suggests that the Orma only became interested in Islam after successful attacks by the Masai and Somali in the late 1800s almost decimated them and depleted their cattle. After 1920, as they began to recover their population somewhat and their cattle began to be replenished, there was rapid conversion to Islam, mostly led by the young, who perhaps were attracted by the economic opportunities.[50]

Loss of population may also have played a significant role in conversion to Christianity in the Roman Empire after A.D. 150 and in northern Mexico after A.D. 1593. In both situations, there were ravaging epidemics along with the presence of Christian personnel ready to help heal the sick.[51] Do epidemics play a role in other places? An exploratory cross-cultural study suggests that rapid population loss, usually from introduced diseases, predicts religious conversion, particularly when people believe that their traditional gods could help them.[52]

Revitalization Movements

The Seneca and the Religion of Handsome Lake
The Seneca reservation of the Iroquois on the Allegheny River in New York State was a place of "poverty and humiliation" by 1799.[53] Demoralized by whiskey and dispossessed from their traditional lands, unable to compete with the new technology because of illiteracy and lack of training, the Seneca were at an impasse. In this setting, Handsome Lake, the 50-year-old brother of a chief, had the first of a number of visions. In them, he met with emissaries of the Creator who showed him heaven and hell and commissioned him to revitalize Seneca religion and society. This he set out to do for the next decade and a half. As his principal text, he used the *Gaiwiio*, or "Good Word," a gospel that contains statements about the nature of religion and eternity and a code of conduct for the righteous. The *Gaiwiio* is interesting both for the influence of Quaker Christianity it clearly reveals,[54] and for the way the new material was merged with traditional Iroquois religious concepts.

Handsome Lake's teaching seems to have led to a renaissance among the Seneca. Temperance was widely accepted, as were schooling and new farming methods. By 1801, corn yields had been increased tenfold, new crops (oats, potatoes, flax) had been introduced, and public

A revitalization movement that became known as the Ghost Dance spread eastward from the Northwest from the 1870s to the 1890s. It was generally believed that, if people did the dance correctly, ghosts would come to life with sufficient resources to allow the people to return to their old ways and, as a result of some cataclysm, the people of European background would disappear.

Source: Ogallala Sioux performing the Ghost Dance at the Pine Ridge Indian Agency, South Dakota. Illustration by Frederic Remington, 1890.

health and hygiene had improved considerably. Handsome Lake himself acquired great power among his people. He spent the remainder of his life fulfilling administrative duties, acting as a representative of the Iroquois in Washington, and preaching his gospel to neighboring tribes. By the time of Handsome Lake's death in 1815, the Seneca clearly had undergone a dramatic rebirth, attributable at least in part to the new religion. Later in the century, some of Handsome Lake's disciples founded a church in his name that, despite occasional setbacks and political disputes, survives to this day.

Although many scholars believe cultural stress gives rise to these new religious movements, it is still important to understand exactly what the stresses are and how strong they have to become before a new movement emerges. Do different kinds of stresses produce different kinds of movements? And does the nature of the movement depend on the cultural elements already present?

Fundamentalism For some scholars, one of the main attributes of fundamentalism is the literal interpretation of a sacred scripture. But recent scholars have suggested that fundamentalist movements need to be understood more broadly as religious or political movements that appear in response to the rapidly changing environment of the modern world. In this broader view, fundamentalism occurs in many religions, including those of Christians, Jews, Islamics, Sikhs, Buddhists, and Hindus. Although each movement is different in content, Richard Antoun suggests that fundamentalist movements have the following elements in common: the selective use of scripture to inspire and assert proof of particular certainties; the quest for purity and traditional values in what is viewed as an impure world; active opposition to what is viewed as a permissive secular society and a nation-state that separates religion from the state; and an incorporation of selected modern elements such as television to promote the movements' aims.[55]

Fundamentalist religious movements do appear to be linked to the anxieties and uncertainties associated with culture change in general and globalization in particular. Many people in many countries are repelled by new behaviors and attitudes, and react in a way that celebrates the old. As Judith Nagata puts it, fundamentalism is a "quest for certainty in an uncertain world."[56] Protestant fundamentalism flourished at the end of the nineteenth century in the United States as immigrant groups came into the country in great numbers and the country became industrialized and increasingly urbanized. The fundamentalists denounced foreign influences, the decline of the Bible as a guide to moral behavior, the teaching of evolution, and they succeeded in getting the country to prohibit the sale of alcoholic beverages. Recent Islamic fundamentalist movements seem to be responses to a different kind of challenge to the social order—increasing Westernization. Westernization may have first arrived in conjunction with colonial rule. Later, it may have been promoted by Western-educated native elites.[57] Antoun suggests that fundamentalist movements deliberately push certain practices because the leaders know they will outrage the secular opposition. Examples in recent Islamic fundamentalist movements are the extreme punishment of cutting off a hand for theft and requiring women to be covered by veils or head-to-toe coverings in public.[58] Unfortunately, in present-day discourse, fundamentalism tends to be equated by Westerners with Islam itself. But, in historical perspective, all major religions have had fundamentalist movements in times of rapid culture change.

If the recent as well as distant past is any guide, we can expect religious belief and practice to be revitalized periodically, particularly during times of stress. Paradoxically, globalization has increased the spread of world religions but it has also increased the worldwide interest in shamanism and other features of religion that are different from the dominant religions. Thus, we can expect the world to continue to have religious variation.

✓●─Study and Review on myanthrolab.com

Summary

1. Religion is any set of attitudes, beliefs, and practices pertaining to supernatural power. Such beliefs may vary within a culture as well as among societies, and they may change over time.

2. There are wide variations in religious beliefs. Societies vary in the number and kinds of supernatural entities in which they believe. There may be impersonal supernatural forces (e.g., mana and taboo), supernatural beings of nonhuman origin (gods and spirits), and supernatural beings of human origin (ghosts and ancestor spirits). The religious belief system of a society may include any or all such entities.

3. Gods and spirits may be unpredictable or predictable, aloof from or interested in human affairs, helpful or punishing. In some societies, all gods are equal in rank; in others, there is a hierarchy of prestige and power among gods and spirits, just as among the humans in those societies.

4. A monotheistic religion is one in which there is one high god, as the creator of the universe or the director of events (or both); all other supernatural beings are either subordinate to, or function as alternative manifestations of, this god. A high god is generally found in societies with a high level of political development.

5. Faced with ignorance, pain, and injustice, people frequently explain events by claiming intervention by the gods. Such intervention has also been sought by people who hope it will help them achieve their own ends. The gods are likely to punish the immoral behavior of people in societies that have considerable differences in wealth.

6. Various methods have been used to attempt communication with the supernatural. Among them are prayer, taking drugs or otherwise affecting the body and mind, simulation, feasts, and sacrifices.

7. When people believe that their actions can compel the supernatural to act in a particular and intended way, anthropologists refer to the belief and related practice as magic. Sorcery and witchcraft are attempts to make the spirits work harm against people.

8. Almost all societies have part-time or full-time religious or magical practitioners. Recent cross-cultural research suggests that there are four major types of practitioners: shamans, sorcerers or witches, mediums, and priests. The number of types of practitioners seems to vary with degree of cultural complexity: The more complex the society, the more types of practitioners.

9. Perhaps the most dramatic type of religious change is religious conversion, particularly when large numbers of people switch to a completely new religion presented by missionaries or other proselytizers. In some native societies, contact has led to a breakdown of social structure and the growth of feelings of helplessness and spiritual demoralization. *Revitalization movements* have arisen as apparent attempts to restore such societies to their former confidence and prosperity. In recent times, religious *fundamentalist* movements have flourished.

Glossary Terms

ancestor spirits (p. 376)
divination (p. 380)
ghosts (p. 376)
gods (p. 375)
magic (p. 381)
mana (p. 374)
mediums (p. 384)

monotheistic (p. 377)
polytheistic (p. 377)
priests (p. 384)
religion (p. 374)
revitalization
   movements (p. 386)
rituals (p. 378)

shaman (p. 383)
sorcery (p. 382)
spirits (p. 376)
supernatural (p. 374)
taboo (p. 375)
witchcraft (p. 382)

Critical Questions

1. How does your conception of God compare with beliefs about supernatural beings in other religious systems?

2. What do you think is the future of religion? Explain your answer.

3. Could any of the religious practices you know about be classified as magic? Are they associated with anxiety-arousing situations?

📖 Read the Original Source on myanthrolab.com

Read the chapter by Debra Picchi titled "Bakairí: The Death of an Indian" on MyAnthroLab, and answer the following questions.

1. How come the Bakairí did not ask whether Western medicine works, but Westerners asked whether shamanism works?

2. Why would a shaman be able to settle disputes?

17

The Arts

((•–⌐Listen to the **Chapter Audio** on **myanthrolab.com**   ⌐◉⌐Read on **myanthrolab.com**

Most societies do not have a word for art.[1] Perhaps that is because art, particularly in societies with relatively little specialization, is often an integral part of religious, social, and political life.

The oldest art found so far comes from caves in South Africa. Pieces of red ochre were engraved there more than 77,000 years ago. Art is clearly an old feature of human cultures. What do we mean by "art"? A stone spear point and a bone fishhook obviously require skill and creativity to make. But we do not call them art. Why do we feel that some things are art and others are not?

Some definitions of art emphasize its evocative quality. From the viewpoint of the person who creates it, art expresses feelings and ideas; from the viewpoint of the observer or participant, it evokes feelings and ideas. The feelings and ideas on each side may or may not be exactly the same. And they may be expressed in a variety of ways—drawing, painting, carving, weaving, body decoration, music, dance, or story. An artistic work or performance is intended to excite the senses, to stir the emotions of the beholder or participant. It may produce feelings of pleasure, awe, repulsion, or fear, but usually not indifference.[2]

Artistic activities are always cultural in part, involving shared and learned patterns of behavior, belief, and feeling. What are some of the ideas about art in our own culture? We tend to think that anything useful is not art. If a basket has a design that is not necessary to its function, we may possibly consider it art, especially if we keep it on a shelf; but the basket with bread on the table would probably not be considered art. The fact that such a distinction is not made in other societies strongly suggests that our ideas about art are cultural. Among Native Americans in the Pacific Northwest, elaborately carved totem poles not only displayed the crests of the lineages of their occupants, they also supported the house.[3] The fact that artistic activities are partly cultural is evident when we compare how people in different societies treat the outsides of their houses. Most North Americans share the value of decorating the interiors of their homes with pictures—paintings, prints, or photographs hung on the walls. But they do not share the value of painting pictures on the outside walls of their houses, as Native Americans did in the Pacific Northwest.

In our society, we also insist that a work must be unique to be considered art. This aspect is clearly consistent with our emphasis on the individual. However, even though we require that artists be unique and innovative, the art they produce must still fall within some range of acceptable variation. Artists must communicate to us in a way we can relate to, or at least learn to relate to. Often, they must follow certain current styles of expression that other artists or critics have set, if they hope to have the public accept their art. The idea that an artist should be original is a cultural idea; in some societies, the ability to replicate a traditional pattern is more valued than originality.

Art seems to have several qualities. It expresses as well as communicates. It stimulates the senses, affects emotions, and evokes ideas. It is produced in culturally patterned ways and styles. It has cultural meaning. In addition, some people are thought to be better at it than others.[4] To illustrate the cross-cultural variation that exists in artistic expression, we consider first the art of body decoration and adornment.

Body Decoration and Adornment

In all societies, people decorate or adorn their bodies. The decorations may be permanent—scars, tattoos, or changes in the shape of a body part. Or they may be temporary, in the form of paint or objects such as feathers, jewelry, skins, and clothing that are not strictly utilitarian. Much of this decoration seems to be motivated by aesthetic considerations, which, of course, vary from culture to culture.

However, in addition to satisfying aesthetic needs, body decoration or adornment may be used to delineate social position, rank, sex, occupation, local and ethnic identity, or religion within a society. Along with social stratification come visual means of declaring status. The symbolic halo (the crown) on the king's head, the scarlet hunting jacket of the English gentleman, the eagle feathers of the Native American chief's bonnet, the gold-embroidered jacket of the Indian rajah—each mark of high status is recognized in its own society. Jewelry in the shape of a cross or the Star of David indicates Christian or Jewish inclinations. Clothes may set apart the priest, nun, or member of a sect such as the Amish.

The erotic significance of some body decoration is also apparent. Women draw attention to erogenous zones of the body by painting, as on the lips, and by attaching some object—an earring, a flower behind the ear, a necklace, bracelet, brooch, anklet, or belt. Men draw attention, too, by beards, tattoos, and penis sheaths (in some otherwise naked societies) that point upward. We have only to follow the fashion trends for women of Europe and North America during the past 300 years, with their history of pinched waists, ballooned hips, bustled rumps, exaggerated breasts, painted faces, and exposed bosoms, to realize the significance of body adornment for sexual provocation. Why some societies emphasize the erotic adornment of women and others emphasize it in men is not yet understood.

Type of body adornment may reflect politics. Polynesians decorate their bodies with tattoos, which are permanent. In Samoa, bands and stripes were restricted to people of high-status; low-status people could have tattoos only of solid black and only from waist to knees. Within the ruling class, the number of tattooed triangles down a man's leg indicated his relative rank. Because tattooing is permanent, it is a form of body decoration well suited to a society with inherited social stratification. On the other hand, in Melanesia, typically with "big men" type of leadership that is somewhat fluid, Melanesians paint their bodies, and the painting is ephemeral. It disappears within a short time, or after the first wash.[5]

Explaining Variation in the Arts

In our society, we stress the freedom of the artist, so it may seem to us that art is completely free to vary. But our emphasis on uniqueness obscures the fact that different cultures not only use or emphasize different materials and have different ideas of beauty, but they also may have characteristic styles and themes. It is easy to see styles when we look at art that is different from our own; it is harder to see similarity when we look at the art of our own culture. If we look at dance styles, for example, we may think that the dance style of the 1940s is completely different from the dance style of today. It might take an outsider to notice that, in our culture, we still generally see couples dancing as a pair rather than in a group line or circle, as in dances we call "folk dances." And, in our culture, females and males dance together rather than separately. Furthermore, our popular music still has a beat or combination of beats and is made by many of the same kinds of instruments as in the past.

But where do these similarities in form and style come from? Much of the research on variation in the arts supports the idea that form and style in visual art, music, dance, and folklore are very much influenced by other aspects of culture. Some psychological anthropologists would go even further, suggesting that art, like religion, expresses the typical feelings, anxieties, and experiences of people in a culture. And the typical feelings and anxieties in turn are influenced by basic institutions such as childrearing, economy, social organization, and politics.

Consider how the physical form of art a society prefers may reflect its way of life. For example, Richard Anderson pointed out that the art of traditionally nomadic people such as the !Kung, Inuit, and Australian aborigines is mostly carryable.[6] Song, dance, and oral literature are very important in those societies and are as portable as they can be. Those societies decorate useful objects that they carry with them—harpoons for the Inuit, boomerangs for the Australian aborigines, ostrich egg "canteens" for the !Kung. But they don't have bulky things such as sculpture or elaborate costumes.

Visual Art

Perhaps the most obvious way artistic creations reflect how we live is by mirroring the environment—the materials and technologies available to a culture. Stone, wood, bones, tree bark, clay, sand, charcoal, berries for staining, and a few mineral-derived ochers are generally available materials. In addition, depending on the locality, other resources are accessible: shells, horns, tusks, gold, copper, and silver. The way in which a society views its environment is sometimes apparent in its choice and use of artistic materials. Certain metals, for example, may be reserved for ceremonial objects of special importance. Or the belief in the supernatural powers of a stone or tree may cause a sculptor to be sensitive to that particular material.[7]

What is particularly meaningful to anthropologists is the realization that, although the materials available to a society may to some extent limit or influence what it can do artistically, the materials by no means determine what is done. Why does the artist in Japanese society rake sand into patterns, the artist in Navajo society paint sand, and the artist in Roman society melt sand to form glass? Moreover, even when the same material is used in the same way in different societies, the form or style of the work varies enormously from culture to culture.

A society may choose to represent objects or phenomena that are especially important to the people or elite. An examination of the art of the Middle Ages tells us something about the medieval preoccupation with theological doctrine. In addition to revealing the primary concerns of a society, the content of that society's art may also reflect the culture's social stratification. Authority figures may be represented in obvious ways. In the art of ancient Sumerian society,

The same materials may be used artistically in different ways. In Japan (on the left), sand is raked into patterns. In the Northern Territory of Australia (on the right), the Yuendumu paint the sand.

the sovereign was portrayed as being much larger than his followers, and the most prestigious gods were given oversized eyes. Also, differences in clothing and jewelry styles within a society usually reflect social stratification.

Art historians have always recognized certain possible relationships between the art of a society and other aspects of its culture. Much of this attention has been concentrated on the content of art, because European art has been representational for such a long time. But the style of the art may reflect other aspects of culture. John Fischer, for example, examined the stylistic features of art with the aim of discovering "some sort of regular connection between some artistic feature and some social situation."[8] He argued that the artist expresses a form of social fantasy. In other words, in a stable society, artists will respond to those conditions in the society that bring security or pleasure to them and the society.

Assuming that "pictorial elements in design are, on one psychological level, abstract, mainly unconscious representations of persons in the society,"[9] Fischer reasoned that egalitarian societies would tend to have different stylistic elements in their art as compared with stratified societies. Egalitarian societies are generally composed of small, self-sufficient communities that are structurally similar and have little differentiation between people. Stratified societies, on the other hand, generally have larger and more interdependent, and dissimilar, communities and great differences among people in prestige, power, and access to economic resources. Fischer hypothesized, and found in a cross-cultural study, that certain elements of design were strongly related to the presence of social hierarchy. His findings are summarized in Table 17.1.

Repetition of a simple element, for example, tends to be found in the art of egalitarian societies, which have little political organization and few authority positions. If each element unconsciously represents individuals within the society, the relative sameness of people seems to be reflected in the repetitiveness of design elements. Conversely, the combinations of different design elements in complex patterns that tend to be found in the art of stratified societies seem to reflect the high degree of social differentiation that exists in such societies.[10]

According to Fischer, the egalitarian society's empty space in a design represents the society's relative isolation. Because egalitarian societies are usually small and self-sufficient, they tend to shy away from outsiders, preferring to find security within their own group. In contrast, the art of stratified societies is generally crowded. The hierarchical society does not seek to isolate individuals or communities within the group because they must be interdependent, each social level ideally furnishing services for those above it and help for those beneath it.[11]

Symmetry, the third stylistic feature related to type of society, is similar to the first. Symmetry may suggest likeness or an egalitarian society; asymmetry suggests difference and perhaps stratification. The fourth feature of interest here, the presence or absence of enclosures or boundaries— "frames" in our art—may indicate the presence or absence of hierarchically imposed rules circumscribing individual behavior. An unenclosed design may reflect free access to most property in egalitarian societies; boundaries or enclosures may reflect the idea of private property. Or they may symbolically represent the real differences in dress, occupation, type of food allowed, and manners that separate the different classes of people.

Studies such as Fischer's offer anthropologists new tools with which to evaluate ancient societies that are known only by a few pieces

TABLE 17.1 Artistic Differences in Egalitarian and Stratified Societies

Egalitarian Society	Stratified Society
Repetition of simple elements	Integration of unlike elements
Much empty or irrelevant space	Little empty space
Symmetrical design	Asymmetrical design
Unenclosed figures	Enclosed figures

Source: Based on Fischer 1961.

of pottery or a few tools or paintings. If art reflects certain aspects of a culture, then the study of whatever art of a people has been preserved may provide a means of testing the accuracy of the guesses we make about their culture on the basis of more ordinary archaeological materials. For example, even if we did not know from classical Greek writings that Athens became much more socially stratified between 750 B.C. and 600 B.C., we might guess that such a transformation had occurred because of the changes we can see over time in the way the Athenians decorated vases. Consistent with Fischer's cross-cultural findings, as Athens became more stratified, its vase painting became more complex, more crowded, and more enclosed.[12]

Music

When we hear the music of another culture, we often don't know what to make of it. We may say it does not "mean" anything to us, not realizing that the "meaning" of music has been programmed into us by our culture. In music as well as in art, our culture largely determines what we consider acceptable variation, what we say has "meaning" to us. Even a trained musicologist, listening for the first time to music of a different culture, will not be able to hear the subtleties of tone and rhythm that members of the culture hear with ease. This predicament is similar to that of the linguist who, exposed to a foreign language, cannot at first distinguish phonemes, morphemes, and other regular patterns of speech.

Not only do instruments vary, but music itself varies widely in style from society to society. For example, in some societies, people prefer music with a regularly recurring beat; in others, they prefer changes in rhythm. There are also variations in singing styles. In some places, it is customary to have different vocal lines for different people; in other places, people all sing together in the same way.

Is variation in music, as in the other arts, related to other aspects of culture? On the basis of a cross-cultural study of more than 3,500 folk songs from a sample of the world's societies, Alan Lomax and his co-researchers found that song style seems to vary with cultural complexity.

Changes in Greek vases show how increasing stratification is associated with integration of unlike elements as well as more crowded design. The one on the left dates from around 1000 B.C. when there was less stratification. The vase on the right dates from the time period between 750 B.C. and 600 B.C., when stratification was at its maximum.

Lomax and his co-researchers found some features of song style to be correlated with cultural complexity. (The societies classified as more complex tend to have higher levels of food-production technology, social stratification, and higher levels of political integration.) For example, wordiness and clearness of enunciation were found to be associated with cultural complexity. Presumably the more a society depends on verbal information, as in giving complex instructions for a job or explaining different points of law, the more strongly will clear enunciation in transmitting information be a mark of its culture. Thus, hunter-gatherer bands, in which people know their productive role and perform it without ever being given complex directions, are more likely than we are to base much of their singing on lines of nonwords, such as our refrain line "tra-la-la-la-la." Their songs are characterized by lack of explicit information, by sounds that give pleasure in themselves, by much repetition, and by relaxed, slurred enunciation.[13]

CURRENT RESEARCH AND ISSUES — Do Masks Show Emotion in Universal Ways?

Face masks in rituals and performances not only hide the real face of the mask wearer but they often evoke powerful emotions in the audience—anger, fear, sadness, joy. You might think, because so many things vary cross-culturally, that the ways in which emotion is displayed and recognized in the face vary too. But apparently they do not vary that much.

Research on masks builds on work by Paul Ekman and Carroll Izard, who used photographs of individuals experiencing, or actors simulating, various emotions. They then showed photographs to members of different cultural groups and asked them to identify the emotions displayed. A particular emotion was identified correctly by most viewers, whatever the viewer's native culture. Coding schemes were developed to enable researchers to compare the detailed facial positions of individual portions of the face (eyebrows, mouth, etc.) for different emotions. When we scowl we contract the eyebrows and lower the corners of the mouth; in geometric terms, we make angles and diagonals on our faces. When we smile, we raise the corners of the mouth; we make it curved.

Psychologist Joel Aronoff and his colleagues compared two types of wooden face masks from many different societies—masks described as threatening (e.g., designed to frighten off evil spirits) versus masks associated with nonthreatening functions (a courtship dance). As suspected, the two sets of masks had significantly different proportions of certain facial elements. The threatening masks had eyebrows and eyes facing inward and downward and a downward-facing mouth. The threatening masks also were more likely to have pointed heads, chins, beards, and ears, as well as projections from the face such as horns. In more abstract or geometrical terms, threatening features generally tend to be angular or diagonal, and nonthreatening features tend to be curved or rounded. A face with a pointed beard is threatening; a baby's face is not. The theory—originally suggested by Charles Darwin, the evolutionist—is that humans express and recognize basic emotions in uniform ways because all human faces are quite similar, skeletally and muscularly.

Is it the facial features themselves that convey threat or is it the design elements of angularity and diagonality that convey threat? To help answer this question, students in the United States were asked to associate adjectives with drawings of abstract pairs of design features (e.g., a V shape and a U shape). Even with abstract shapes, the angular patterns were thought of as less "good," more "powerful," and "stronger" than the curved shapes. In subsequent studies, students recognized the V shape more quickly than other shapes, and this shape triggered more response in the brain in areas associated with threat.

We should not be surprised to discover that humans all over the world use their faces, and masks, to show emotions in the same ways. Aren't we all members of the same species? The universality of human emotion as expressed in the face becomes obvious only when we see faces (and

The most obvious, and universal, example of a song made entirely of repetition is the relaxed lullaby of a mother repeating a comforting syllable to her baby while improvising her own tune. But this type of song is not characteristic of our society. Although our songs sometimes have single lines of nonwords, it is rare for an entire song to be made of them. Usually, the nonwords act as respites from information.

In associating variation in music with cultural complexity, Lomax found that elaboration of song parts also corresponds to the complexity of a society. Societies in which leadership is informal and temporary seem to symbolize their social equality by an *interlocked* style of singing. Each person sings independently but within the group, and no one singer is differentiated from the others. Rank societies, in which there is a leader with prestige but no real power, are characterized by a song style in which one "leader" may begin the song, but the others soon

Masks with V shapes represent threat. There are many such shapes on the masked individual from Panama shown on the right—the placement of the horns, the spikes on the outside of the mask, over the eyes, the ears, the pointed chin, and of course the many pointed teeth. The nonthreatening Iroquois mask on the left has more curved lines and generally lacks angles.

masks) from elsewhere, showing emotions in ways that are unmistakable to us.

Thus, we become aware of universality (in masks as well as other cultural things) in the same way we become aware of variation—by exposure

through reading and direct experience with the ways cultures do and do not vary.

Sources: Aronoff, Barclay, and Stevenson 1988; Aronoff, Woike, and Hyman 1992; Larson, Aronoff, and Stearns 2007; Larson et al. 2009.

drown out his voice. In stratified societies, where leaders have the power of force, choral singing is generally marked by a clear-cut role for the leader and a secondary "answering" role for the others. Societies marked by elaborate stratification show singing parts that are differentiated and in which the soloist is deferred to by the other singers.

Lomax also found a relationship between **polyphony,** where two or more melodies are sung simultaneously, and a high degree of female participation in food-getting. In societies in which women's work is responsible for at least half of the food, songs are likely to contain more than one simultaneous melody, with the higher tunes usually sung by women.[14] In societies in which women do not contribute much to food production, the songs are more likely to have a single melody and to be sung by males.[15]

In some societies, survival and social welfare are based on a unified group effort; in those cultures, singing tends to be marked by cohesiveness. That is, cohesive work parties, teams of gatherers or harvesters, and kin groups, who work voluntarily for the good of the family or community, seem to express their interconnectedness in song by blending both tone and rhythm.

Some variations in music may be explained as a consequence of variation in childrearing practices. Barbara Ayres suggested that the importance of regular rhythm in the music of a culture is related to the rhythm's *acquired reward value*—that is, its associations with feelings of security or relaxation in infancy. In a cross-cultural study of this possibility, Ayres found a strong correlation between a society's method of carrying infants and the type of musical rhythm the society produced. In some societies, the mother or an older sister carries the child, sometimes for 2 or 3 years, in a sling, pouch, or shawl, so that the child is in bodily contact with her for much of the day and experiences the motion of her rhythmic walking. Ayres discovered that such societies tend to have a regularly recurring beat in their songs. Societies in which the child is put into a cradle or is strapped to a cradleboard tend to have music based either on irregular rhythm or on free rhythm.[16]

Cultural emphasis on obedience or independence in children is another variable that may explain some aspects of musical performance. In societies in which children are generally trained for compliance, cohesive singing predominates; where children are encouraged to be assertive, singing is mostly individualized. Moreover, assertive training of children is associated with a raspy voice or harsh singing. A raspy voice seems to be an indication of assertiveness and is most often a male voice quality. Interestingly enough, in societies in which women's work predominates in subsistence production, the women sing with harsher voices.

Other voice characteristics may also be associated with elements of culture. For example, sexual restrictions in a society seem to be associated with voice restrictions, especially with a nasalized or narrow, squeezed tone. These voice qualities are associated with anxiety and are especially noticeable in sounds of pain, deprivation, or sorrow. Restrictive sexual practices may be a source of pain and anxiety, and the nasal tone in song may reflect such emotions.[17]

Folklore

Folklore is a broad category comprising all the myths, legends, folktales, ballads, riddles, proverbs, and superstitions of a cultural group.[18] In general, folklore is transmitted orally, but it may also be written. Games are also sometimes considered folklore, although they may be learned by imitation as well as transmitted orally. All societies have a repertoire of stories that they tell to entertain each other and teach children. Examples of our folklore include fairy tales and the legends we tell about our folk heroes, such as George Washington's confessing that he chopped down the cherry tree. Folklore is not always clearly separable from the other arts, particularly music and dance; stories often are conveyed in those contexts.

Although some folklore scholars emphasize the traditional aspects of folklore and the continuity between the present and the past, more recently attention has been paid to the innovative and emergent aspects of folklore. In this view, folklore is constantly created by any social group that has shared experiences. So, for example, computer programmers may have their jokes and their own proverbs (e.g., "Garbage in, garbage out!").[19] Jan Brunvand compiled a set of recently arisen *urban legends.* One such legend is "The Hook." The story, which has many versions, is basically about a young couple parked on Lover's Lane with the radio on. There is an announcement that a killer with an artificial hand is loose, so the girl suggests that they leave. The boy starts the car and drives her home. When he walks around the car to open her door, he finds a bloody hook attached to the door handle.[20] There are even legends on college campuses. What is the answer to the question of how long students should wait for a tardy professor? Students have an answer, ranging from 10 to 20 minutes. Is this a rule, or only a legend? Brunvand reported that he never found a regulation about how long to wait for a professor on any campus that tells this story![21]

Some folklore scholars are interested in universal or recurrent themes. Clyde Kluckhohn suggested that five themes occur in the myths and folktales of all societies: catastrophe, generally through flood; the slaying of monsters; incest; sibling rivalry, generally between brothers; and castration, sometimes actual but more commonly symbolic.[22] Edward Tylor, who proposed that religion is born from the human need to explain dreams and death, suggested that hero myths follow a similar pattern the world over—the central character is exposed at birth, is subsequently saved by others (humans or animals), and grows up to become a hero.[23] Joseph Campbell argued that hero myths resemble initiations—the hero is separated from the ordinary world, ventures forth into a new world (in this case, the supernatural world) to triumph over powerful forces, and then returns to the ordinary world with special powers to help others.[24]

Myths may indeed have universal themes, but few scholars have looked at a representative sample of the world's societies, and therefore we cannot be sure that current conclusions about universality are correct. Indeed, most folklore researchers have not been interested in universal themes but in the particular folktales told in specific societies or regions. For example, some scholars have focused on the "Star Husband Tale," a common Native American story. Stith Thompson presented 84 versions of this tale; his goal was to reconstruct the original version and pinpoint its place of origin. By identifying the most common elements, Thompson suggested that the basic story (and probably the original) is the following:

> Two girls sleeping out of doors wish that stars would be their husbands. In their sleep the girls are taken to the sky where they find themselves married to stars, one of which is a young man and the other an old man. The women are warned not to dig, but they disregard the warning and accidentally open up a hole in the sky. Unaided they descend on a rope and arrive home safely.[25]

The tale, Thompson suggested, probably originated in the Plains and then spread to other regions of North America.

Alan Dundes has concentrated on the structure of folktales; he thinks that Native American folktales, including the "Star Husband Tale," have characteristic structures. One is a movement away from disequilibrium. Equilibrium is the desirable state; having too much or too little of anything is a condition that should be rectified as soon as possible. Disequilibrium, which Dundes calls *lack,* is indicated by the girls in the "Star Husband Tale" who do not have husbands. The lack is then corrected, in this case by marriage with the stars. This tale has another common

Native American structure, says Dundes—a sequence of prohibition, interdiction, violation, and consequence. The women are warned not to dig, but they do—and as a consequence, they escape for home.[26] It should be noted that the consequences in folktales are not always good. Icarus in the Greek tale is warned not to fly too high or too low. He flies too high; the sun melts the wax that holds his feathered wings, and he falls and drowns.

As useful as it might be to identify where certain tales originated, or what their common structures might be, many questions remain. What do the tales mean? Why did they arise in the first place? It is clearly not enough to suggest an interpretation. Why should we believe it? We should give it serious consideration only if some systematic test seems to support it.

One feature of folktale variation that has been investigated cross-culturally is aggression. George Wright found that variation in childrearing patterns predicted some aspects of how aggression is exhibited in folktales. Where children are severely punished for aggression, more intense aggression appears in the folktales. And in such societies, strangers are more likely than the hero or friends of the hero to be the aggressors in the folktales. It seems that where children may be afraid to exhibit aggression toward their parents or those close to them because of fear of punishment, the hero or close friends in folktales are also not likely to be aggressive.[27]

Other kinds of fears may be reflected in folktales. A cross-cultural study by Alex Cohen found that unprovoked aggression is likely in folktales of societies that are subject to unpredictable food shortages. Why? One possibility is that the folktales reflect reality; after all, a serious drought may seem capricious, not possibly provoked by any human activity, brought on by the gods or nature "out of the blue." Curiously, however, societies with a history of unpredictable food shortages hardly mention natural disasters in their folktales, perhaps because disasters are too frightening. In any case, the capriciousness of unpredictable disasters seems to be transformed into the capricious aggression of characters in the folktales.[28]

Folklore, just like other aspects of art, may at least partly reflect the feelings, needs, and conflicts that people acquire as a result of growing up in their culture.

Viewing the Art of Other Cultures

Sally Price raised some critical questions about how Western museums and art critics look at the visual art of less complex cultures. Why is it that when artworks from Western or Oriental civilizations are displayed in a museum here, they carry the artist's name? In contrast, art from less complex cultures, often labeled "primitive art," tends to be displayed without the name of the artist; instead, it is often accompanied by a description of where it came from, how it was constructed, and what it may be used for. More words of explanation seem to accompany displays of unfamiliar art. Price suggested that the art pieces that we consider the most worthy require the least labeling, subtly conveying that the viewer needs no help to judge a real work of art.[29] In addition, art acquired from less complex cultures tends to be labeled by the name of the Westerner who acquired it. It is almost as if the fame of the collector, not the art itself, sets the value of such art.[30]

Just as the art from less complex cultures tends to be nameless, it also tends to be treated as timeless. We recognize that Western art and the art from classical civilizations change over time, which is why it must be dated, but the art from other places seems to be viewed as representing a timeless cultural tradition.[31] Do we know that the art of peoples with simpler technology changes less, or is this assumption a kind of ethnocentrism? Price, who has studied the art of the Saramakas of Suriname, points out that although Westerners think of Saramakan art as still representing its African ancestry, Saramakans themselves can identify shifts in their art styles over time. For example, they describe how calabashes used to be decorated on the outside, then the style changed to decorating the inside. They can also recognize the artist who made particular carved calabashes as well as identify those who were innovators of designs and techniques.[32]

When Westerners do notice changes over time in the art of less complex societies, it seems to be because they are concerned about whether the art represents traditional forms or is "tourist art." Tourist art is often evaluated negatively, perhaps because of its association with money. But famous Western artists often also worked for fees or were supported by elite patrons, and yet the fact that they were paid does not seem to interfere with our evaluation of their art.[33]

Although it seems that individual artists can usually be recognized in any community, some societies do appear to be more "communal" than others in their art style. For example, let us compare the Puebloan peoples of the Southwest with native peoples of the Great Plains. Traditionally, women Puebloan potters did not sign their pots, and they largely followed their pueblo's characteristic style. In contrast, each Plains warrior stressed his individual accomplishments by painting representations of those accomplishments on animal hides. Either the warrior would do it himself or he would ask someone else to do it for him. These hides were worn by the warrior or displayed outside his tipi.[34]

Artistic Change and Culture Contact

It is unquestionably true that contact with the West did alter some aspects of the art of other cultures, but that does not imply that their art was changeless before. What kinds of things changed with contact? In some places, artists began to represent European contact itself. For example, in Australia, numerous rock paintings by aborigines portray sailing ships, men on horseback carrying pistols, and even cattle brands. With encouragement from Europeans, indigenous artists also began drawing on tree bark, canvas, and fiberboard to sell to Europeans. Interestingly, the art for sale mostly emphasizes themes displayed before contact and does not include representations of ships and guns.[35] As aboriginal populations were decimated by European contact, a lot of their traditional art forms disappeared, particularly legends and rock paintings that were associated with the sacred sites of each clan. The legends described the creation of the sacred places, and art motifs with painted human or animal heroes marked the sites.[36]

In North America, contact between native groups produced changes in art even before the Europeans came. Copper, sharks' teeth, and marine shells were traded extensively in precontact times and were used in the artwork of people who did not have access to those materials locally. Ceremonies were borrowed among groups, and with the new ceremonies came changes in artistic traditions. Borrowing from other native groups continued after European contact. The Navajo, who are well known today for their rug weaving, were not weavers in the seventeenth century. They probably obtained their weaving technology from the Hopi and then began to weave wool and herd sheep. European contact also produced material changes in art; new materials, including beads, wool cloth, and silver, were introduced. Metal tools such as needles and scissors could now be used to make more tailored and more decorated skin clothing. In the Northwest, the greater availability of metal tools made it possible to make larger totem poles and house posts.[37]

After they were placed on reservations, virtually all Native Americans had to change their ways of making a living. Selling arts and crafts earned some of them supplementary income. Most of these crafts used traditional techniques and traditional designs, altered somewhat to suit European expectations. Outsiders played important roles in encouraging changes in arts and crafts. Some storekeepers became patrons to particular artists who were then able to devote

Navajo rugs have changed over time. On the left are rugs from 1905; on the right, rugs from a modern trading post.

themselves full time to their craft. Traders would often encourage changes, such as new objects—for example, ashtrays and cups made of pottery. Scholars have played a role too. Some have helped artisans learn about styles of the past that had disappeared. For example, with the encouragement of anthropologists and others in the Santa Fe area, Maria and Julian Martinez of San Ildefonso Pueblo brought back a polished black-on-black pottery style originally produced by nearby ancient peoples.[38]

Some of the artistic changes that have occurred after contact with the West are partly predictable from the results of cross-cultural research on artistic variation. Remember that Fischer found that egalitarian societies typically had less complex designs and more symmetry than did stratified societies. With the loss of traditional ways of making a living and with the increase in wage labor and commercial enterprises, many Native American groups have become more socially stratified. Extrapolating from Fischer's results, we would predict that designs on visual art should become more complex and asymmetrical as social stratification increases. Indeed, if early reservation art (1870–1901) among the Shoshone-Bannock of southeastern Idaho is compared with their recent art (1973–1983), it is clear that the art has become more complex as social stratification has increased.[39] It could also be true that the art changed because the artists came to realize that more asymmetry and complexity would sell better to people who collect art.

✓•—Study and Review on **myanthrolab.com**

Summary

1. Not all societies have a word for art, but art universally seems to have several qualities. It expresses as well as communicates. It stimulates the senses, affects emotions, and evokes ideas. It is produced in culturally patterned ways and styles. It has cultural meaning. Some people are thought to be better at it than others.

2. All societies decorate or adorn the body, temporarily or permanently. But there is enormous cultural variation in the parts decorated and how. Body decoration may be used to delineate social position, gender, or occupation. It may also have an erotic significance, as, for example, in drawing attention to erogenous zones of the body.

3. The materials used to produce visual art, the way those materials are used, and the natural objects the artist may choose to represent all vary from society to society and reveal much about a particular society's relation to its environment. Some studies indicate a correlation between artistic design and social stratification.

4. Like the visual arts, music is subject to a remarkable amount of variation from society to society. Some studies suggest correlations between musical styles and cultural complexity. Other research shows links between childrearing practices and a society's preference for certain rhythmical patterns and voice quality.

5. Folklore is a broad category including all the myths, legends, folktales, ballads, riddles, proverbs, and superstitions of a cultural group. In general, folklore is transmitted orally, but it may also be written. Some anthropologists have identified basic themes in myths—catastrophe, slaying of monsters, incest, sibling rivalry, and castration. Myths may reflect a society's deepest preoccupations.

6. Art is always changing, but recent culture contact has had some profound effects on art in various parts of the world. With the decimation of many indigenous populations, many areas have lost some of their artistic traditions. But the art also changed as individuals began to sell arts and crafts.

Glossary Terms

folklore (p. 400)
polyphony (p. 400)

Critical Questions

1. How innovative or original can a successful artist be? Explain your answer.
2. What kind of art do you prefer, and why?
3. Do you think art made for tourists is inferior? Whatever you think, why do you think so?

Read the Original Source on myanthrolab.com

Read the chapter by Donald Mitchell titled "Nimpkish: Complex Foragers on the Northwest Coast of North America" on MyAnthroLab, and answer the following questions.

1. The art form of dance was important to the Nimpkish. Why do you think?
2. In what season were the dances held, and why do you think they occurred then?

18 Global Problems

((•–|Listen to the **Chapter Audio** on **myanthrolab.com** |▣–|Read on **myanthrolab.com**

The news on television and in the newspapers makes us aware every day that terrible social problems threaten people around the world. War, crime, family violence, natural disasters, poverty, famine—all these and more are the lot of millions of people in many places. And now there is an increasing threat of terrorism. Can anthropological and other research help us solve these global social problems? Many anthropologists and other social scientists think so.

High-tech communications have increased our awareness of problems all over the world, and we seem to be increasingly more aware of, and bothered by, problems in our own society. For these two reasons, and perhaps also because we know much more than we used to about human behavior, we may be more motivated now to try to solve those problems. We call them "social problems" not just because a lot of people worry about them but also because they have social causes and consequences, and treating or solving them requires changes in social behavior. Even AIDS, which we discuss in the next chapter, is partly a social problem. It may be caused by a virus, but it is mostly transmitted by social (sexual) contact with another person. And the main ways to avoid it—abstinence and "safe" sex—require changes in social behavior.

The idea that we can solve social problems, even the enormous ones such as war and family violence, is based on two assumptions. First, we have to assume that it is possible to discover the causes of a problem. And two, we have to assume that we may be able to do something about the causes, once they are discovered, and thereby eliminate or reduce the problem. Not everyone would agree with these assumptions. Some would say that our understanding of a social problem cannot ever be sufficient to suggest a solution guaranteed to work. To be sure, no understanding in science is perfect or certain; there is always some probability that even a well-supported explanation is wrong or incomplete. But the uncertainty of knowledge does not rule out the possibility of application. With regard to social problems, the possible payoff from even incomplete understanding could be a better and safer world. This possibility is what motivates many researchers who investigate social problems. After all, the history of the various sciences strongly supports the belief that scientific understanding can often allow humans to control nature, not just predict and explain it. Why should human behavior be any different?

So what do we know about some of the global social problems, and what policies or solutions are suggested by what we know?

Natural Disasters and Famine

Natural events such as floods, droughts, earthquakes, and insect infestations are usually but not always beyond human control, but their effects are not.[1] We call such events accidents or emergencies when only a few people are affected, but we call them disasters when large numbers of people or large areas are affected. The harm caused is not just a function of the magnitude of the natural event. Between 1960 and 1980, 43 natural disasters in Japan killed an average of 63 people per disaster. During the same period, 17 natural disasters in Nicaragua killed an average of 6,235 people per disaster. In the United States, between 1960 and 1976, the average flood or other environmental disturbance killed just one person, injured a dozen, and destroyed fewer than five buildings. These comparative figures demonstrate that climatic and other events in the physical environment become disasters because of events or conditions in the social environment.

If people live in houses that are designed to withstand earthquakes—if governing bodies require such construction and the economy is developed enough so that people can afford such construction—the effects of an earthquake will be minimized. If poor people are forced to live in deforested floodplains to be able to find land to farm (as in coastal Bangladesh), if the poor

Although earthquakes are not preventable, collapse of houses is mostly preventable by building houses to withstand earthquakes. In Bam, Iran, 20,000 people were killed during a 2003 earthquake and most of the houses collapsed. This woman sits amid the ruins of her house.

are forced to live in shanties built on precarious hillsides (like those of Rio de Janeiro), the floods and landslides that follow severe hurricanes and rainstorms can kill thousands and even hundreds of thousands.

Thus, natural disasters can have greater or lesser effects on human life, depending on social conditions. And therefore disasters are also social problems, problems that have social causes and possible social solutions. Legislating safe construction of a house is a social solution. The 1976 earthquake in Tangsham, China, killed 250,000 people, mostly because they lived in top-heavy adobe houses that could not withstand severe shaking, whereas the 1989 Loma Prieta earthquake in California, which was of comparable intensity, killed 65 people.

One might think that floods, of all disasters, are the least influenced by social factors. After all, without a huge runoff from heavy rains or snow melt, there cannot be a flood. But consider why so many people have died from Hwang River floods in China. (One such flood, in 1931, killed nearly 4 million people, making it the deadliest single disaster in history.) The floods in the Hwang River basin have occurred mostly because the clearing of nearby forests for fuel and farmland has allowed enormous quantities of silt to wash into the river, raising the riverbed and increasing the risk of floods that burst the dams that normally would contain them. The risk of disastrous flooding would be greatly reduced if different social conditions prevailed—if people were not so dependent on firewood for fuel, if they did not have to farm close to the river, or if the dams were higher and more numerous.

Famines, episodes of severe starvation and death, often appear to be triggered by physical events such as a severe drought or a hurricane that kills or knocks down food trees and plants. But famines do not inevitably follow such an event. Social conditions can prevent a famine or increase the likelihood of one. Consider what is likely to happen in Samoa after a hurricane.[2] Whole villages that have lost their coconut and breadfruit trees, as well as their taro patches, pick up and move for a period of time to other villages where they have relatives and friends. The visitors stay and are fed until some of their cultivated trees and plants start to bear food again, at which point they return home. This kind of intervillage reciprocity probably could occur only in a society that has relatively little inequality in wealth. Nowadays, the central government or international agencies may also help out by providing food and other supplies.

Researchers point out that famine rarely results from just one bad food production season. During one bad season, people can usually cope by getting help from relatives, friends, and neighbors or by switching to less desirable foods. The 1974 famine in the African Sahel occurred after 8 years of bad weather; a combination of drought, floods, and a civil war in 1983–1984 contributed to the subsequent famine in the Sahel, Ethiopia, and Sudan.[3] Famine almost always has some social causes. Who has rights to the available food, and do those who have more food distribute it to those who have less? Cross-cultural research suggests that societies with individual property rights rather than shared rights are more likely to suffer famine.[4] Nonetheless, government assistance can lessen the risk of famine in societies with individual property.

Relief provided by government may not always get to those who need it the most. In India, for example, the central government provides help in time of drought to minimize the risk of famine. But the food and other supplies provided to a village may end up being unequally distributed, following the rules of social and gender stratification. Members of the local elite arrange to function as distributors and find ways to manipulate the relief efforts to their advantage. Lower-class and lower-caste families still suffer the most. Within the family, biases against females, particularly young girls and elderly women, translate into their getting less food. It is no wonder, then, that in times of food shortage and famine, the poor and other socially disadvantaged people are especially likely to die.[5]

Thus, the people of a society may not all be equally at risk in case of disaster. In socially stratified societies, the poor particularly suffer. They are likely to be forced to overcultivate, overgraze, and deforest their land, making it more susceptible to degradation. A society most helps those it values the most.

People in the past, and even recently in some places, viewed disasters as divine retribution for human immorality. For example, the great flood described in the Old Testament was understood to be God's doing. But scientific research increasingly allows us to understand the natural causes of disasters, and particularly the social conditions that magnify or minimize their effects. To reduce the impact of disasters, then, we need to reduce the social conditions that magnify the effects of disasters. If humans are responsible for those social conditions, humans can change them. If earthquakes destroy houses that are too flimsy, we can build stronger houses. If floods caused by overcultivation and overgrazing kill people directly (or indirectly by stripping their soils), we can grow new forest cover and provide new job opportunities to floodplain farmers. If prolonged natural disasters or wars threaten famine, social distribution systems can lessen the risk. In short, we may not be able to do much about the weather or other physical causes of disasters, but we can do a lot—if we want to—about the social factors that make disasters disastrous.

Inadequate Housing and Homelessness

In most nations, those who are poor typically live in inadequate housing, in areas we call *slums*. The magnitude of the problem is made clear in some statistics. As of the 2000s, 32 percent of the population of urban areas live in slums, most of them in developing countries. In developing countries only 15 percent of the urban households have sewers, 37 have piped water, and 60 percent have electricity.[6]

In many of the developing nations, where cities are growing very rapidly, squatter settlements emerge as people build dwellings (often makeshift) that are typically declared illegal, either because the land is illegally occupied or because the dwellings violate building codes. Squatter settlements are often located in degraded environments that are subject to flooding and mudslides or have inadequate or polluted water.

But contrary to what some people have assumed, not all dwellers in illegal settlements are poor; all but the upper-income elite may be found in such settlements.[7] Moreover, although squatter settlements have problems, they are not chaotic and unorganized places that are full of crime. Most of the dwellers are employed, aspire to get ahead, live in intact nuclear families, and help each other.[8] People live in such settlements because they cannot find affordable housing and they house themselves as best they can. Many researchers think that such self-help tendencies should be assisted to improve housing because governments in developing countries can seldom afford costly public housing projects. But they could invest somewhat in infrastructure—sewers, water supplies, roads—and provide construction materials to those who are willing to do the work required to improve their dwellings.[9]

Housing in slum areas or shantytowns does provide shelter, minimal though it may be. But many people in many areas of the world have no homes at all. Even in countries such as the United States, which are affluent by world standards, large numbers of people are homeless. They sleep in parks, over steam vents, in doorways, subways, and cardboard boxes. Homelessness is difficult to measure. In 1987, more than 1 million people were estimated to be homeless in the United States.[10] Homelessness has increased in the last few decades. About 3.5 million people experienced homelessness in 2000, almost 40 percent of them children.[11]

Who are the homeless, and how did they get to be homeless? We have relatively little research on these questions, but what we do have suggests differences in the causes of homelessness in different parts of the world. In the United States, unemployment and the shortage of decent low-cost housing appear to be at least partly responsible for the large number of homeless people.[12] But there is also another factor: the deliberate policy to reduce the number of people hospitalized for mental illness and other disabilities. For example, from the mid-1960s to the mid-1990s, New York State released thousands of patients from mental hospitals. Many of these ex-patients had to live in cheap hotels or poorly monitored facilities with virtually no support network. With very little income, they found it especially hard to cope with their circumstances. Ellen Baxter and Kim Hopper, who studied the homeless in New York City, suggest that one event is rarely sufficient to render a person homeless. Rather, poverty and disability (mental or physical) seem to lead to one calamity after another and, finally, homelessness.[13]

Many people cannot understand why homeless individuals do not want to go to municipal shelters. But observations and interviews with the homeless suggest that violence pervades the municipal shelters, particularly the men's shelters. Many feel safer on the streets. Some private charities provide safe shelters and a caring environment. These shelters are filled, but the number of homeless they can accommodate is small.[14] Even single-room-occupancy hotels are hardly better. Many of them are infested with vermin, the common bathrooms are filthy, and they, like the shelters, are often dangerous.[15]

Some poor individuals may be socially isolated, with few or no friends and relatives and little or no social contact. But a society with many such individuals does not necessarily have much homelessness. Socially isolated individuals, even mentally ill individuals, could still have housing, or so the experience of Melbourne, Australia, suggests. Universal health insurance there pays for health care as well as medical practitioners' visits to isolated and ill individuals, wherever they live. Disabled individuals receive a pension or sickness benefits sufficient to allow them to live in a room or apartment. And there is still a considerable supply of cheap housing in Melbourne. Research in Melbourne suggests that a severe mental disorder often precedes living in marginal accommodations—city shelters, commercial shelters, and cheap single rooms. About 50 percent of the people living in such places were diagnosed as previously having some form of mental illness; this percentage is similar to what seems to be the case for homeless people and people living in marginal accommodations in the United States.

The contrast between the United States and Australia makes it clear that social and political policies cause homelessness. Individuals with similar characteristics live in both Australia and the United States, but a larger percentage of them are homeless in the United States.[16]

Because homelessness cannot occur if everybody can afford housing, some people would say that homelessness can happen only in a society with great extremes in income. Statistics on income distribution in the United States clearly show that, since the 1970s, the rich have gotten much richer and the poor have gotten much poorer.[17] The United States now has more income inequality than any country in western Europe and more than most high-income countries. In fact, the profile of inequality in the United States more closely resembles that of developing countries, such as Cambodia and Morocco[18] (see the discussion in the chapter on social stratification).

A homeless boy in Calcutta, India, with his belongings.

In the United States and many other countries, most homeless people are adults. Whereas adults are "allowed" to be homeless, public sensibilities in the United States appear to be outraged by the sight of children living in the streets; when authorities discover homeless children, they try to find shelters or foster homes for them. But many countries have "street children." In the late 1980s, 80 million of the world's children lived in the streets: 40 million in Latin America, 20 million in Asia, 10 million in Africa and the Middle East, and 10 million elsewhere.[19] In the 2000s, the estimated number grew to about 150 million worldwide.[20]

Lewis Aptekar, who studied street children in Cali, Colombia, reported some surprises.[21] Whereas many of the homeless in the United States and Australia are mentally disabled, the street children in Cali, ranging in age from 7 to 16, are mostly free of mental problems; by and large, they also test normally on intelligence tests. In addition, even though many street children come from abusive homes or never had homes, they usually seem happy and enjoy the support and friendship of other street children. They cleverly and creatively look for ways to get money, frequently through entertaining passersby.

Although observers might think that the street children must have been abandoned by their families, most of them in actuality have at least one parent they keep in touch with. Street life begins slowly, not abruptly; children usually do not stay on the streets full time until they are about 13 years old. Though street children in Cali seem to be in better physical and mental shape than their siblings who stay at home, they often are viewed as a "plague." The street children come from poor families and cope with their lives as best they can, so why are they not viewed with pity and compassion? Aptekar suggests that well-off families see the street children as a threat because a life independent of family may appeal to children, even those from well-off families, who wish to be free of parental constraint and authority.

Whether people become homeless, whether they have shantytowns, seems to depend on a society's willingness to share wealth and help those in need. The street children of Cali may remind us that children as well as adults need companionship and care. Addressing physical needs without responding to emotional needs may get people off the streets, but it won't get them a "home."

Family Violence and Abuse

In U.S. society, we hear regularly about the abuse of spouses and children, which makes us think that such abuse is increasing—but is it? This seems to be a simple question, but it is not so simple to answer. We have to decide what we mean by *abuse*.

Is physical punishment of a child who does something wrong child abuse? Not so long ago, teachers in public schools in the United States were allowed to discipline children by hitting them with rulers or paddles, and many parents used switches or belts. Many would consider these practices to be child abuse, but were they abusive when they were generally accepted? Some would argue that abuse is going beyond what a culture considers appropriate behavior. Others would disagree and would focus on the violence and severity of parents' or teachers' behavior, not the cultural judgment of appropriateness. And abuse need not involve physical violence. It could be argued that verbal aggression and neglect may be just as harmful as physical aggression. Neglect presents its own problems of definition. People from other cultures might argue that we act abusively when we put an infant or child alone in a room to sleep.[22] Few would disagree about severe injuries that kill a child or spouse or require medical treatment, but other disciplinary behaviors are more difficult to judge.

To avoid having to decide what is or is not abuse, many researchers focus their studies on variation in the frequencies of specific behaviors. For example, one can ask which societies have physical punishment of children without calling physical punishment abusive.

According to four national interview surveys of married or cohabiting couples in the United States conducted from 1975 to 1995, physical violence against children appears to have decreased in frequency over time, as did serious assaults by husbands against wives. But serious assaults by wives on husbands did not decrease.[23] The decreasing rates of abuse may be mostly due to reporting differences: wife and child beating is less acceptable now. For example, men report dramatically fewer assaults on their wives, but wives report only slight declines.[24] However, the United States remains a society with a lot of physical violence in families. In 1992 alone, one out of 10 couples had a violent assault episode and one out of 10 children was severely assaulted by a parent.[25] A survey conducted in the mid-1990s found that about 75 percent of the violence against women comes from a male intimate partner, such as a husband. In contrast, most of the violence men experience comes from strangers and acquaintances. Just as women face more risk from those close to them, so do children. When a child is the target of violence, it usually comes from the birth mother.[26]

Cross-culturally, if one form of family violence occurs, others are also likely. So, for example, wife beating, husband beating, child punishment, and fighting among siblings are all significantly associated with each other. But the relationships between these types of family violence are not that strong, which means that they cannot be considered as different facets of the same phenomenon. Indeed, somewhat different factors seem to explain different forms of family violence.[27] We focus here on two forms of violence that are most prevalent cross-culturally: violence against children and violence against wives.

Violence against Children

Cross-culturally, many societies practice and allow infanticide. Frequent reasons for infanticide include illegitimacy, deformity of the infant, twins, too many children, or that the infant is unwanted. Infanticide is usually performed by the mother, but this does not mean that she is uncaring; it may mean that she cannot adequately feed or care for the infant or that it has a poor chance to survive. The reasons for infanticide are similar to those given for abortion. Therefore, it seems that infanticide may be performed when abortion does not work or when unexpected qualities of the infant (e.g., deformity) force the mother to reevaluate her ability to raise the child.[28]

Physical punishment of children occurs at least sometimes in over 70 percent of the world's societies.[29] And physical punishment is frequent or typical in 40 percent of the world's societies. The finding that societies with class stratification and political hierarchy, either native or introduced (colonialism), are very likely to practice corporal punishment of children[30] suggests that parents are consciously or unconsciously preparing their children for a life of power inequality. Research in the United States is consistent with the cross-cultural finding: Those at the bottom of the socioeconomic hierarchy are more likely than those at the top to practice corporal punishment of children.[31] Unfortunately, parents probably do not realize that physical punishment may produce more violent behavior in their children, an outcome they probably do not want or intend.

Violence against Wives

Cross-culturally, wife beating is the most common form of family violence; it occurs at least occasionally in about 85 percent of the world's societies. In about half the societies, wife beating is sometimes serious enough to cause permanent injury or death.[32] It is often assumed that wife beating is common in societies in which males control economic and political resources. In a cross-cultural test of this assumption, David Levinson found that not all indicators of male dominance predict wife beating, but many do. Specifically, wife beating is most common when men control the products of family labor, when men have the final say in decision making in the home, when divorce is difficult for women, when remarriage for a widow is controlled by the husband's kin, and when women do not have any female work groups.[33] Similarly, in the United States, the more one spouse in the family makes the decisions and has the power, the more physical violence occurs in the family. Wife beating is even more likely when the husband controls the household and is out of work.[34]

Wife beating appears to be related to broader patterns of violence. Societies that have violent methods of conflict resolution within communities, physical punishment of criminals, high frequency of warfare, and cruelty toward enemies generally have more wife beating.[35] Corporal punishment of children may be related to wife beating. Research in the United States supports the idea that individuals (males and females) who were punished corporally as adolescents are more likely to approve of marital violence and are more likely to commit it.[36]

Reducing the Risk

What can be done to minimize family violence? First, we have to recognize that probably nothing can be done as long as people in a society do not acknowledge that a problem exists. If severe child punishment and wife beating are perfectly acceptable by almost everyone in a society, they are unlikely to be considered social problems that need solutions. In our own society, many programs are designed to take abused children or wives out of the family situation or to punish the abuser. (Of course, in these situations, the violence has already occurred and was serious enough to have been noticed.) Cross-culturally, at least with respect to wife beating, intervention by others seems to be successful only if the intervention occurs before violence gets serious. As one would expect, however, those societies most prone to a high rate of wife beating are the

MIGRANTS AND IMMIGRANTS

Refugees Are a Global Social Problem

The continuing turmoil in many countries throughout the world has created a flow of refugees that is much larger than ever before in world history. Refugees have become a worldwide social problem; their numbers are high. In the past, thousands of people might have had to flee persecution and war. Now the refugees number in the millions. They flee to other parts of the country, to neighboring countries, and to countries on the other side of the world. As many as an estimated 140 million people became refugees in the twentieth century. For example, the refugees from the civil wars in Somalia are not unusual; 10 percent of the Somali population is now living outside of Somalia, perhaps a million people altogether.

Conceivably, the problem could be handled with less suffering if countries were willing to accept any and all refugees. Shouldn't governments accept them for humanitarian reasons, just because the refugees could die otherwise? Or does there have to be an acknowledged or felt need in the accepting country for cheap labor? There is a fine line between people who want to migrate to have a better or safer life, and people who have to migrate because they would be killed if they don't flee. Refugees are a problem not just because they are suffering, and the world should do something. They are also a problem because countries may refuse to accept them, because their numbers are so large. Governments and charitable agencies have to provide support until the refugees acquire the skills for making a living on their own.

Compare how we think of refugees from different places. Some are accepted (however grudgingly), whereas others are not. The United States only half-heartedly tries to prevent poor Mexicans from entering the country. But people from Africa who are threatened with genocide are rejected much more. Why? Is it because

Mexicans and others from Latin America have skills that we need, and they are willing to take jobs that no one else wants because the pay is low and the benefits nil? Who benefits from this state of affairs? Too many! Think of the employers who would otherwise have to pay their workers more or invest in labor-saving machinery. Think of the Chinese "coolies" who were brought in 150 years ago to build the railroads that linked the eastern and western United States. And, of course, think of the refugee laborers. If they didn't "cross the border" looking for work, their children left at home would suffer or even die from malnutrition and other consequences of poverty.

So, what are countries to do? Should they throw open their doors to everyone who wants to come in? Humanitarians might say yes. But this too would make for problems. Some would say that we should not accept and support refugees when we already have lots of poor people. Don't we owe them more than we owe poor people from somewhere else? Shouldn't our tax money go to improve the lives of people already here? What are taxes for, anyway?

How to help refugees is clearly a complex issue. But if we don't do anything to help them, is that ethical? Refugees are the consequences of social inequality and persecution. They are a global social problem that won't go away, as long as the world contains governments that persecute their own citizens, or allow some groups to persecute others. If the solution is not to rely on those governments because they are not likely to change what they are doing, it would seem that we will have to rely for the near future on international organizations (like the United Nations and charitable foundations) if we want to reduce or eliminate the worldwide problem of refugees.

Sources: Harrell-Bond 1996; Van Hear 2004.

least likely to practice immediate intervention. More helpful perhaps, but admittedly harder to arrange, is the promotion of conditions of life that are associated with low family violence. Research so far suggests that promoting the equality of men and women and the sharing of childrearing responsibilities may go a long way toward lessening incidents of family violence.[37] And reducing the risk of corporal punishment of children may reduce the risk of violence when they have families.

Crime

What is a crime in one society is not necessarily a crime in another. Just as it is difficult to decide what constitutes abuse, it is difficult to define *crime.* In one society, it may be a crime to walk over someone's land without permission; in another, there might not be any concept of personal ownership, and therefore no concept of trespassing. In seeking to understand variation in crime, many researchers have not surprisingly preferred to compare those behaviors that are more or less universally considered crimes and that are reliably reported. For example, in a large-scale comparison of crime in 110 nations over a span of 70 years, Dane Archer and Rosemary Gartner concentrated on homicide rates. They argued that homicide is harder for the public to hide and for officials to ignore than are other crimes. A comparison of interviews about crime with police records suggests that homicide is the most reliably reported crime in official records.[38]

One of the clearest findings to emerge from comparative studies of crime is that war is associated with higher rates of homicide. Archer and Gartner compared changes in homicide rates of nations before and after major wars. Whether a nation is defeated or victorious, homicide rates tend to increase after a war. This result is consistent with the idea that a society or nation legitimizes violence during wartime. That is, during wartime, societies approve of killing the enemy; afterward, homicide rates may go up because inhibitions against killing have been relaxed.[39] Ted Gurr suggested that the long-term downtrend in crime in Western societies seems to be consistent with an increasing emphasis on humanistic values and nonviolent achievement of goals. But such goals may be temporarily suspended during wartime. In the United States, for example, surges in violent crime rates occurred during the 1860s and 1870s (during and after the Civil War), after World War I, after World War II, and during the Vietnam War.[40] Recently, however, the homicide rate in the United States has declined.[41]

In the types of societies that anthropologists have typically studied, homicide statistics were not usually available; so cross-cultural studies of homicide usually measure homicide rates by comparing and rank-ordering ethnographers' statements about the frequency of homicide. For example, the statement that murder is "practically unheard of" is taken to mean that the murder rate is lower than where it is reported that "homicide is not uncommon." Despite the fact that the data on cultural homicide rates are not quantitative, the cross-cultural results are consistent with the cross-national results; more war is usually associated with more homicide and assault, as well as with socially approved aggressive behaviors (as in aggressive games) and severe physical punishment for wrongdoing.[42] A cross-cultural study suggests that the more war a society has, the more the society socializes or trains boys in aggression, and such socialization strongly predicts higher rates of homicide and assault.[43]

Capital punishment—execution of criminals—is severe physical punishment for wrongdoing. It is commonly thought that the prospect of capital punishment deters would be murderers. Yet, cross-national research suggests otherwise. More countries show murder rates going down rather than up after capital punishment was abolished.[44] Capital punishment may legitimize violence rather than deter it.

Research conducted in the United States suggests that juvenile delinquents (usually boys) are likely to come from broken homes, with the father absent for much of the time the boy is growing up. The conclusion often drawn is that father absence somehow increases the likelihood of delinquency and adult forms of physical violence. But other conditions that may cause delinquency are also associated with broken homes, conditions such as the stigma of not having a "regular" family and the generally low standard of living of such families. It is therefore important to conduct research in other societies, in which father absence does not occur in concert with these other factors, to see if father absence by itself is related to physical violence.

For example, in many polygynous societies, children grow up in a mother–child household; the father lives separately and is seldom around the child. Does the father absence explanation of delinquency and violence fit such societies? The answer is apparently yes: Societies in which children are reared in mother–child households or the father spends little time caring for the child tend to have more physical violence by males than do societies in which fathers spend time with children.[45] The rate of violent crime is also more frequent in nations that have more women than men, which is consistent with the theory that father absence increases violence.[46]

More research is needed to discover exactly what accounts for these relationships. It is possible, as some suggest, that boys growing up without fathers are apt to act "supermasculine," to show how "male" they are. But it is also possible that mothers who rear children alone have more frustration and more anger, and therefore are likely to provide an aggressive role model for the child. In addition, high male mortality in war predicts polygyny, as we saw in the chapter on marriage, family, and kinship; therefore, boys in polygynous societies are likely to be exposed to a warrior tradition.[47]

Trying to act supermasculine, however, may be likely to involve violence only if aggression is an important component of the male gender role in society. If men were expected by society to be sensitive, caring, and nonviolent, boys who grew up without fathers might try to be super-sensitive and supercaring. So society's expectations for males probably shape how growing up in a mother–child household affects behavior in adolescence and later.[48] The media may also influence the expectations for males. Numerous studies in the United States show that, even controlling for other factors like parental neglect, family income, and mental illness, more television watching in childhood and adolescence predicts more overt aggression later. Estimates show that an hour of prime-time television depicts three to five violent acts, and an hour of children's television depicts 20 to 25 violent acts.[49]

One widely held idea is that poor economic conditions increase the likelihood of crime, but the relationship does not appear to be strong. Also, the findings are somewhat different for different types of crime. For example, hundreds of studies in this and other countries do not show a clear relationship between changes in economic well-being as measured by unemployment rates and changes in violent crime as measured by homicide. The rate of homicide does not appear to increase in bad times. Property crimes, however, do increase with increases in unemployment. Violent crime does appear to be associated with one economic characteristic: Homicide is usually highest in nations or societies with high income inequality.[50] Why income inequality predicts homicide but downturns in the economy do not is something of a puzzle.[51]

The fact that property crime is linked to unemployment is consistent with the cross-cultural finding that theft (but not violent crime) tends to occur less often in egalitarian societies than in stratified ones. Societies with equal access to resources usually have distribution mechanisms that offset any differences in wealth. Hence, theft should be less of a temptation and therefore less likely in an egalitarian society. Theft rates are higher in socially stratified societies despite the fact that

Evidence indicates that violence on TV encourages violence in real life.

they are more likely than egalitarian societies to have police and courts to punish crime. Societies may try to deter property and other crimes when the rates of such are high, but we do not know that these efforts actually reduce the rates.

So what does the available research suggest about how we might be able to reduce crime? The results so far indicate that homicide rates are highest in societies that socialize their boys for aggression. Such socialization is linked to war and other forms of socially approved violence—capital punishment, television and movie violence by heroes, violence in sports. The statistical evidence suggests that war encourages socialization for aggression, which in turn results unintentionally in high rates of violence. The policy implication of these results is that, if we can reduce socialization for aggression by reducing the risk of war and therefore the necessity to produce effective warriors, and if we can reduce other forms of socially approved violence, we may thereby reduce the rates of violent crime. The reduction of inequalities in wealth may also help to reduce crime, particularly theft. And although it is not yet clear why, it appears that raising boys with a male role model around may reduce the likelihood of male violence in adulthood.

War

War is an unfortunate fact of life in most societies known to anthropology, judging by the cross-cultural research we referred to in the chapter on political life. Almost every society had at least occasional wars when it was first described, unless it had been pacified (usually by Western colonial powers).[52] Since the Civil War, the United States has not had any wars on its territory, but it is unusual in that respect. Before pacification, most societies in the ethnographic record had frequent armed combat between communities or larger units that spoke the same language. That is, most warfare was internal to the society or language group. Even some wars in modern times involved speakers of the same language; recall the wars between Italian states before the unification of Italy and many of the "civil" wars of the last two centuries. Although people in some societies might fight against people in other societies, such "external" wars were usually not organized on behalf of the entire society or even a major section of it.[53] That is, warfare in the ethnographic record did not usually involve politically unified societies. The absolute numbers of people killed may have been small, but this does not mean that warfare in nonindustrial societies was a trivial matter. Indeed, it appears that nonindustrial warfare may have been even more lethal *proportionately* than modern warfare, judging by the fact that wars killed 25–30 percent of the males in some nonindustrial societies.[54]

Although warfare has occurred frequently in societies at all levels of complexity, changes over time tell us that war is not inevitable. For example, Norway is one of the world's most peaceful countries. The Viking age, as shown in this reenactment, was an era of militarism.

In the chapter on political life, we discussed the possibility that people in nonindustrial societies go to war mostly out of fear, particularly a fear of expectable but unpredictable natural disasters (droughts, floods, hurricanes, among others) that destroy food supplies.[55] People with more of a history of such disasters have more war. It seems as if people go to war to protect themselves ahead of time from disasters, inasmuch as the victors in war almost always take resources (land, animals, other things) from the defeated, even when the victors have no current resource problems. Another factor apparently making for more war is teaching children to mistrust others. People who grow up to be mistrustful of others may be more likely to go to war than to negotiate or seek conciliation with "enemies." Mistrust or fear of others seems to be partly caused by threat or fear of disasters.[56]

Is warfare in and between modern state societies explainable in much the same way that nonindustrial warfare seems to be explainable? If the answer to that question turns out to be yes, it will certainly be a modified yes, because the realities of industrialized societies require an expanded conception of disasters. In the modern world, with its complex economic and political dependencies among nations, we may not be worried only about weather or pest disasters that could curtail food supplies. Possible curtailments of other resources, particularly oil, may also scare us into going to war. According to some commentators, the decision in 1991 to go to war against Iraq after it invaded Kuwait fits this theory of war.

But even if the "threat-to-resources" theory is true, we may be coming to realize (since the end of the Cold War) that war is not the only way to ensure access to resources. There may be a better way in the modern world, a way that is more cost-effective as well as more preserving of human life. If it is true that war is most likely when people fear unpredictable disasters of any kind, the risk of war should lessen when people realize that the harmful effects of disasters could be reduced or prevented by international cooperation. Just as we have the assurance of disaster relief within our country, we could have the assurance of disaster relief worldwide. That is, the fear of unpredictable disasters and the fear of others, and the consequent risk of war, could be reduced by the assurance ahead of time that the world would help those in need in case of disaster. Instead of going to war out of fear, we could go to peace by agreeing to share. The certainty of international cooperation could compensate for the uncertainty of resources.

Consider how Germany and Japan have fared in the years since their "unconditional surrender" in World War II. They were forbidden to participate in the international arms race and could rely on others, particularly the United States, to protect them. Without a huge burden of armaments, Germany and Japan thrived. But countries that competed militarily, particularly the United States and the Soviet Union at the height of the Cold War, experienced economic difficulties. Doesn't that scenario at least suggest the wisdom of international cooperation, particularly the need for international agreements to ensure worldwide disaster relief? Compared with going to war and its enormous costs, going to peace would be a bargain!

Recent research in political science and anthropology suggests an additional way to reduce the risk of war. Among the societies known to anthropology, studies indicate that people in more participatory—that is, more "democratic"—political systems rarely go to war with each other.[57] Thus, if authoritarian governments were to disappear from the world because the powerful nations of the world stopped supporting them militarily and otherwise, the world could be more peaceful for this reason too.

Although democratically governed states rarely go to war with each other, it used to be thought that they are not necessarily more peaceful in general, that they are as likely to go to war as are other kinds of political systems, but not so much with each other. For example, the United States has gone to war with Grenada, Panama, and Iraq—all authoritarian states—but not with democratic Canada, with which the United States has also had disputes. But now a consensus is emerging among political scientists that democracies are not only unlikely to go to war with each other, they are also less warlike in general.[58] The theory suggested by the cross-national and cross-cultural results is that democratic conflict resolution within a political system generalizes to democratic conflict resolution between political systems, particularly if the systems are both democratic. If our participatory institutions and perceptions allow us to resolve our disputes peacefully, internally and externally, we may think that similarly governed people would also be disposed to settle things peacefully. Therefore, disputes between participatory political systems should be unlikely to result in war.

The understanding that participatory systems rarely fight each other, and knowing why they do not, would have important consequences for policy in the contemporary world. The kinds of military preparations believed necessary and the costs people would be willing to pay for them might be affected. On the one hand, understanding the relationship between democracy and peace might encourage war making against authoritarian regimes to overturn them—with enormous costs in human life and otherwise. On the other hand, understanding the consequences of democracy might encourage us to assist the emergence and consolidation of more participatory systems of government in the countries of eastern Europe, the former Soviet Union, and elsewhere. In any case, the relationship between democracy and peace strongly suggests that it is counterproductive to support any undemocratic regimes, even if they happen to be enemies of our enemies, if we want to minimize the risk of war in the world. The latest cross-national evidence suggests that extending democracy around the world would minimize the risk of war. Encouraging nations to be more interdependent economically, and encouraging the spread of international nongovernmental organizations (like professional societies and trade associations) to provide informal ways to resolve conflicts, would also minimize the risk of war, judging by results of recent research by political scientists.[59]

Terrorism

Ever since September 11, 2001, when terrorists crashed airliners into the World Trade Center towers in New York City and into the Pentagon in Arlington, Virginia, people all over the world realize that terrorism has become a social problem globally. It is now painfully clear that organized groups of terrorists can train their people to kill themselves and thousands of others half a world away, not only by hijacking airliners and flying them into skyscrapers, but also by using easily transported explosives and biological weapons. Social scientists are now actively trying to understand terrorism, in the hope that research may lead to ways to minimize the likelihood of future attacks. But there are lots of questions to answer. What is terrorism and how shall it be defined? How long has terrorist activity been around? What are the causes of terrorism? What kind of people are likely to become terrorists? And what are the consequences of terrorism?

Answering these questions is not so simple. Most people can point to instances that hardly anyone would have trouble calling terrorism—spraying nerve gas in a Japanese subway, Palestinian suicide bombers targeting Israeli civilians, and Ku Klux Klan members lynching African Americans.[60] It is harder to identify the boundaries between terrorism, crime, political repression, and warfare.[61] Most researchers agree that terrorism involves the threat or use of violence

A candlelight vigil after the terrorist attack in 2008 on the Taj Mahal Hotel in Mumbai, India.

against civilians. Terrorism is usually also politically or socially organized, in contrast to most crimes, which are usually perpetrated by individuals acting on their own. (To be sure, crime can be socially organized too, as, for example, in what we call "organized crime.") One marker of the difference between most crime and terrorism is that criminals rarely take public credit for their activities because they want to avoid being caught. In terrorism, the perpetrators usually proclaim their responsibility. In terrorism also, the violence is directed mostly at unarmed people, including women and children. It is intended to frighten the "enemy," to *terrorize* them, to scare them into doing something that the terrorists want to see happen. Generally, then, **terrorism** may be defined as the use or threat of violence to create terror in others, usually for political purposes.[62] Some define terrorism as perpetrated by groups that are not formal political entities. However, this criterion presents some difficulty. What are we to call it when governments support death squads and genocide against their own civilians? Some scholars call this "state terror."[63] And what are we to call the activities of some governments that support secret operations against other countries (often referred to as "state-sponsored terrorism")? Finally, although some nations conducting war explicitly try to avoid civilian casualties and focus primarily on combatants (armed soldiers), their weapons, and resources or "assets" such as factories, air strips, and fuel depots, many attacks in wartime throughout history have purposefully targeted civilians (e.g., the United States dropped atomic bombs on Hiroshima and Nagasaki to persuade the Japanese to end World War II).

One thing is certain about terrorism: It is not a new development. Some of the words we use for terrorists—for example, "zealots" and "assassins"—derive from terrorist movements in the past. The Zealots, Jewish nationalists who revolted against the Romans occupying Judea in the first century, would hide in crowds and stab officials and priests as well as soldiers. In the eleventh and twelfth centuries in southwest Asia, the Fedayeen (a group of Muslim Isma'ili Shi'ites) undertook to assassinate Sunni rulers despite the almost certainty of their own capture or death. The rulers said that the Fedayeen were under the influence of hashish and called them

"Hashshashin," which is the root of the later term *assassin*.[64] In the late eighteenth and early nineteenth centuries, the "reign of terror" occurred during and after the French Revolution. In the early and middle twentieth century, dictator Joseph Stalin ordered the execution of many millions of people who were considered enemies of the Soviet state. Six million Jews and millions of other innocents were exterminated by the German Third Reich in the 1930s and 1940s.[65] And many Latin American regimes, such as that in Argentina, terrorized and killed dissidents in the 1970s and 1980s.[66] Now there is a heightened fear of terrorists who may have access to weapons of mass destruction. In a world made smaller by global transportation, cell phones, and the Internet, terrorism is a greater threat than ever before.

We still lack systematic research that explains why terrorism occurs and why people are motivated to become terrorists. But there is a good deal of research about state terrorism. Political scientist R. J. Rummel estimates that governments have killed nearly 262 million people in the twentieth century (he calls this kind of terrorism "democide"). State terrorism has been responsible for four times more deaths than all the wars, civil and international, that occurred in the twentieth century. Regimes in the Soviet Union (1917–1987), China (1923–1987), and Germany (1933–1945) were responsible for killing more than a total of 190 million civilians. Proportionately the Khmer Rouge regime in Cambodia topped them all, killing over 30 percent of its population from 1975 to 1978.[67] What predicts state terrorism against one's own people? Rummel finds one clear predictor: totalitarian governments. By far, they have the highest frequencies of domestic state terrorism, controlling for factors such as economic wealth, type of religion, and population size. As Rummel puts it, "Power kills; absolute power kills absolutely."[68] Democratic countries are less likely to practice state terrorism, but when they do, it occurs during or after a rebellion or a war.[69]

We know relatively little so far about what predicts who will become a terrorist. We do know that terrorists often come from higher social statuses and generally have more education than the average person.[70] If state terrorism is more likely to occur in totalitarian regimes, terrorists and terrorist groups may be more likely to occur in such societies. If so, the spread of democracy may be our best hope of minimizing the risk of terrorism in the world, just as the spread of democracy seems to minimize the likelihood of war between countries.

Making the World Better

Many social problems afflict our world, not just the ones discussed in this chapter.[71] We don't have the space to discuss the international trade in drugs and how it plays out in violence, death, and corruption. We haven't talked about the negative effects of environmental degradations such as water pollution, ozone depletion, and destruction of forests and wetlands. We haven't said much, if anything, about overpopulation, the energy crisis, and a host of other problems we should care and do something about, if we hope to make this a safer world. But we have tried in this chapter to encourage positive thinking about global social problems; we have suggested how the results of past and future scientific research could be applied to solving some of those problems.

We may know enough now that we can do something about our problems, and we will discover more through future research. Social problems are mostly of human making and are therefore susceptible to human unmaking. There may be obstacles on the road to solutions, but we can overcome them if we want to. So let's go for it!

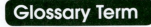 Study and Review on myanthrolab.com

Summary

1. We may be more motivated now to try to solve social problems because worldwide communication has increased our awareness of them elsewhere, because we seem to be increasingly bothered by problems in our own society, and because we know more than we used to about various social problems that afflict our world.

2. The idea that we can solve global social problems is based on two assumptions. We have to assume that it is possible to discover the causes of a problem, and we have to assume that we will be able to do something about the causes once they are discovered and thereby eliminate or reduce the problem.

3. Disasters such as earthquakes, floods, and droughts can have greater or lesser effects on human life, depending on social conditions. Therefore, disasters are partly social problems, with partly social causes and solutions.

4. Whether people become homeless, whether they have shantytowns, seems to depend on a society's willingness to share wealth and to help those in need.

5. Promoting the equality of men and women and the sharing of childrearing responsibilities may reduce family violence.

6. We may be able to reduce rates of violent crime if we can reduce socialization and training for aggression. To do that, we would have to reduce the likelihood of war, the high likelihood of which predicts more socialization for aggression and other forms of socially approved aggression. The reduction of inequalities in wealth may also help to reduce crime, particularly theft. And raising boys with a male role model around may reduce the likelihood of male violence in adulthood.

7. People seem to be most likely to go to war when they fear unpredictable disasters that destroy food supplies or curtail the supplies of other necessities. Disputes between more participatory (more "democratic") political systems are unlikely to result in war. Therefore, the more democracy spreads in the world, and the more people all over the world are assured of internationally organized disaster relief, the more they might go to peace rather than to war to solve their problems.

8. Terrorism has occurred throughout history. State terrorism has killed more than all wars in the twentieth century and seems to be predicted mostly by totalitarianism.

Glossary Term

terrorism (p. 420)

Critical Questions

1. What particular advantages do anthropologists have in trying to solve practical problems?
2. Select one of the social problems discussed in this chapter and suggest what you think could be done to reduce or eliminate it.
3. Do global problems require solutions by global agencies? If so, which?

Read the Original Source on myanthrolab.com

Read the chapter by Paul C. Rosenblatt titled "Human Rights Violations" on MyAnthroLab. Answer the following questions.

1. Rosenblatt states that human rights may be enhanced by "promoting more respectful, peaceful, and nonexploitive relations among different groups within countries." Explain why he thinks so.
2. Why does he say that "saints can be sinners and sinners can be saints"?
3. Rosenblatt asks: "Is it moral for the United States and a handful of other powerful nations to impose their will on other nations?" What do you think, and why do you think so?

19

Applied and Practicing Anthropology

((•─┤Listen to the **Chapter Audio** on **myanthrolab.com**   ┌◘─┤Read on **myanthrolab.com**

Anthropology is no longer a merely academic subject. A large number of anthropologists in the United States are applied and practicing anthropologists. Some estimates suggest that more than half of those with graduate degrees in anthropology are now employed outside of colleges and universities.[1] The fact that so many organizations hire anthropologists suggests an increasing realization that anthropology, what it has discovered and can discover about humans, is useful. Anthropologists who call themselves applied or practicing anthropologists work for a large variety of organizations, government agencies, international development agencies, private consulting firms, public health organizations, medical schools, public interest law firms, community development agencies, charitable foundations, and profit-seeking corporations.

Applied or **practicing anthropology** as a profession is explicitly concerned with making anthropological knowledge useful. Applied or practicing anthropologists may be involved in one or more phases of a project: assembling relevant knowledge, developing plans and policies, assessing the likely social and environmental impacts, implementation, and evaluating the project and its effects.[2] Anthropologists are most often involved in gathering information, rather than constructing policy or initiating action.[3] The organizations that hire the applied anthropologists usually set policy and have staff to execute projects. However, anthropologists are increasingly finding themselves involved in policymaking and action. The field of applied or practicing anthropology is very diverse. In this chapter, after focusing on general issues, we turn to some frequent types of applied work: *cultural resource management,* the "social impact" studies required in connection with many government or private programs, and *forensic anthropology,* the use of physical anthropology to help identify human remains and assist in solving crimes. The chapter concludes with an extensive discussion of the application of anthropological knowledge to the study of health and illness.

Ethics of Applied Anthropology

Anthropologists have usually studied people who are disadvantaged—by imperialism, colonialism, and other forms of exploitation—and so it is no wonder that we care about the people's lives we have shared. But caring is not enough to improve others' lives. We may need basic research that allows us to understand how a condition might be successfully treated since a particular proposed "improvement" might actually not be an improvement; well-meaning efforts have sometimes produced harmful consequences. And even if we know that a change would be an improvement, there is still the problem of how to make that change happen. The people to be affected may not want to change. Is it ethical to try to persuade them? And, conversely, is it ethical *not* to try? Applied anthropologists must take all of these matters into consideration in determining whether and how to act in response to a perceived need.

Anthropology as a profession has adopted certain principles of responsibility. Above all, an anthropologist's first responsibility is to those who are being studied; everything should be done to ensure that their welfare and dignity will be protected. Anthropologists also have a responsibility to those who will read about their research; research findings should be reported openly and truthfully.[4] But because applied anthropology often deals with planning and implementing changes in some population, ethical responsibilities can become complicated. Perhaps the most important ethical question is: Will the change truly benefit the potentially affected population?

In May 1946, the Society for Applied Anthropology established a committee to draw up a specific code of ethics for professional applied anthropologists. After many meetings and revisions, a statement on ethical responsibilities was finally adopted in 1948, and in 1983, the

Businesses and consulting companies are doing more ethnographic research. Such research in the United States among families during the morning suggests that "breakfast" has become an intermittent series of snacks throughout the morning as families struggle with their time schedules and finding the right foods for their children.

statement was revised.[5] According to the code, the targeted community should be included as much as possible in the formulation of policy, so that people in the community may know in advance how the program will affect them. Perhaps the most important aspect of the code is the pledge not to recommend or take any action that is harmful to the interests of the community. The National Association for the Practice of Anthropology goes further: If the work the employer expects of the employee violates the ethical principles of the profession, the practicing anthropologist has the obligation to try to change those practices or, if change cannot be brought about, to withdraw from the work.[6]

Ethical issues are often complicated. Thayer Scudder described the situation of Gwembe Tonga villagers who were relocated after a large dam was built in the Zambezi Valley of central Africa. Economic conditions improved during the 1960s and early 1970s, as the people increasingly produced goods and services for sale. But then conditions deteriorated. By 1980, the villagers were in a miserable state; rates of mortality, alcoholism, theft, assault, and murder were up. Why? One reason was that they had cut back on producing their own food in favor of producing for the world market. Such a strategy works well when world market prices are high; however, when prices fall, so does the standard of living.[7] The situation described by Scudder illustrates the ethical dilemma for many applied anthropologists. As he said: "So how is it that I can still justify working for the agencies that fund such projects?" He points out that large-scale projects are almost impossible to stop. The anthropologist can choose to stand on the sidelines and complain or try to influence the project to benefit the affected population as much as possible.[8]

The problem described by Scudder comes about in part because the anthropologist is not often involved until after a decision is made to go ahead with a change program. This situation has begun to change as applied anthropologists are increasingly asked to participate in earlier stages of the planning process. Anthropologists are also increasingly asked to help in projects initiated by the affected party. Such requests may range from help in solving problems in corporate organizations to helping Native Americans with land claims. Because the project is consistent with the wishes of the affected population, the results are not likely to put the anthropologist into an ethical dilemma.

Evaluating the Effects of Planned Change

The decision as to whether a proposed change would benefit the affected population is not always easy to make. In certain cases, as when improved medical care is involved, the benefits offered to the target group would seem to be unquestionable—we all feel sure that health is better than illness. However, what about the long-term effects? Consider a public health innovation such as inoculation against disease. Once the inoculation program was begun, the number of children surviving would probably increase. But will there be enough food for the additional population? Given the level of technology, capital, and land resources possessed by the population, there might not be enough resources to feed more people. Thus, the death rate, because of starvation, might rise to its previous level and perhaps even exceed it. Without additional changes to increase the food supply, the inoculation program in the long term might merely change the causes of death. This example shows that, even if a program of planned change has beneficial consequences in the short run, a great deal of thought and investigation has to be given to its long-term effects.

Debra Picchi raised questions about the long-term effects on the Bakairí Indians of a program by the Brazilian National Indian Foundation (FUNAI) to produce rice with machine technology.[9] The Bakairí of the Mato Grosso region largely practice slash-and-burn horticulture in gallery forests along rivers, with supplementary cattle raising, fishing, and hunting. In the early part of the twentieth century, their population had declined to 150 people and they were given a relatively small reserve, much of it parched and infertile (*cerrado*). When the Bakairí population began to increase, FUNAI introduced a scheme to plant rice on formerly unused *cerrado* land, using machinery, insecticides, and fertilizer. FUNAI paid the costs for the first year and expected that the scheme would be self-supporting by the third year. The project did not go so well because FUNAI did not deliver all the equipment needed and did not provide adequate advice. Only half the expected rice was produced. Still, it was more food than the Bakairí had previously, so the program should have been beneficial to them.

But there were unanticipated negative side effects. Using *cerrado* land for agriculture reduced the area on which cattle could be grazed; cattle are an important source of high-quality protein. Mechanization also makes the Bakairí more dependent on cash for fuel, insecticides, fertilizer, and repairs. But cash is hard to come by. Only some individuals can be hired—usually men with outside experience who have the required knowledge of machinery. So the cash earned in the now-mechanized agriculture goes mainly to a relatively small number of people, creating new inequalities of income.

These failures were not the fault of anthropologists—indeed, most instances of planned change by governments and other agencies usually have begun without the input of anthropologists at all. Applied anthropologists have played an important role in pointing out the problems with programs like these that fail to evaluate long-term consequences. Such evaluations are an important part of convincing governments and other agencies to ask for anthropological help in the first place.

Difficulties in Instituting Planned Change

After numerous reforestation projects failed in Haiti, an anthropologist, Gerald Murray, was asked to help design a program that would work.[10] Understanding why previous projects failed was the first step in helping Murray design an effective project. One problem seems to have been that previous projects were run through the government's Ministry of Agriculture. The seedling trees that were given away were referred to as the "state's trees." In the project proposed by Murray, private voluntary organizations rather than the Haitian government were used to distribute trees and the farmers were told that they were the tree owners. Ownership included the right to cut the trees and sell the wood, just as they could sell crops. In the new plan, the tree seedlings given away were fast-growing species that matured in as little as 4 years. In addition, the new seedlings were very small and could be planted quickly. Perhaps most important of all, the new trees could be planted in borders or interspersed with other crops, interfering little with traditional crop patterns. To Murray's great surprise, by the end of 2 years, 2,500 Haitian households had planted

People cut down trees in Haiti for firewood and to clear fields, resulting in severe deforestation. The need for reforestation is clear, but how to bring about change was not so clear.

3 million seedlings. Over 20 years, the estimate is that over a 100 million trees were planted and over 350,000 farm families were involved in the project, more than 40 percent of rural households.[11] Because growing trees do not spoil, farmers were postponing their cutting and sales until they needed cash. So even though farmers were told that it was all right to cut down trees, a statement contrary to the message of previous reforestation projects, the landscape was filling up with trees.

Whether a program of planned change can be successfully implemented depends largely on whether the people want the proposed change and like the proposed program. Before an attempt can be made at cultural innovation, the innovators must determine whether the population is aware of the benefits of the proposed change. Lack of awareness can be a temporary barrier to solving the problem at hand. For example, health workers have often had difficulty convincing people that they were becoming ill because something was wrong with their water supply. Many people do not believe that disease can be transmitted by water. At other times, the population is perfectly aware of the problem. A case in point involved Taiwanese women who were introduced to family-planning methods beginning in the 1960s. The women knew they were having more children than they wanted or could easily afford, and they wanted to control their birth rate. They offered no resistance—they merely had to be given the proper devices and instructions, and the birth rate quickly fell to a more desirable, and more manageable, level.[12]

Overcoming Resistance

Not all proposed change programs are beneficial to the recipients. Sometimes resistance is rational. Applied anthropologists have pointed to cases where the judgment of the affected population has been better than that of the agents of change. One such example occurred during a Venezuelan government–sponsored program to give infants powdered milk. The mothers rejected the milk, even though it was free, on the grounds that it implied that the mothers' milk was no good.[13] But who is to say that the resistance was not in fact intuitively smart, reflecting an awareness that such a milk program would not benefit the children? Medical research now indicates quite clearly that mothers' milk is far superior to powdered milk or formula. First, human milk best supplies the nutrients needed for human development. Second, it is now known that the mother, through her milk, is able to transmit antibodies (disease resistances) to the baby. And third, nursing delays ovulation and usually increases the spacing between births.[14]

The switchover to powdered milk and formula in many underdeveloped areas has been nothing short of a disaster, resulting in increased malnutrition and misery. For one thing, powdered milk must be mixed with water, but if the water and the bottles are not sterilized, more sickness is introduced. Then, too, if powdered milk has to be purchased, mothers without cash are forced to dilute the milk to stretch it. And if a mother feeds her baby formula or powder for even a short time, the process is tragically irreversible, for her own milk dries up and she cannot return to breast-feeding even if she wants to.

As the Venezuelan example suggests, individuals may be able to resist proposed medical or health projects because acceptance is ultimately a personal matter. Large development projects planned by powerful governments or agencies rarely are stoppable, but even they can be resisted successfully. The Kayapo of the Xingu River region of Brazil were able to cancel a plan by the Brazilian government to build dams along the river for hydroelectric power. The Kayapo gained international attention when some of their leaders appeared on North American and European television and then successfully organized a protest in 1989 by members of several tribal groups. Their success seemed to come in part from their ability to present themselves to the international community as guardians of the rain forest—an image that resonated with international environmental organizations that supported their cause. Although to outsiders it might seem that the Kayapo want their way of life to remain as it was, the Kayapo are not opposed to all change. In fact, they want greater access to medical care, other government services, and manufactured goods from outside.[15]

Even if a project is beneficial to a population, it may still meet with resistance. Factors that may hinder acceptance can be divided roughly into three, sometimes overlapping, categories: *cultural, social,* and *psychological* barriers.

Cultural barriers are shared behaviors, attitudes, and beliefs that tend to impede the acceptance of an innovation. For example, members of different societies may view gift giving in different ways. Particularly in commercialized societies, things received for nothing are often believed to be worthless. When we discuss approaches to AIDs prevention later in the chapter, we will see that certain beliefs about sex make it difficult for people to follow medical guidelines for safer sex. It is very important for agents of change to understand what the shared beliefs and attitudes are. For instance, in a program in Haiti to prevent child mortality from diarrhea, change agents used the terminology for traditional native herbal tea remedies (*rafrechi,* or cool refreshment) to identify the new oral rehydration therapy, which is a very successful medical treatment. In native belief, diarrhea is a "hot" illness and people believe that appropriate remedies have to have cooling properties.[16]

The acceptance of planned change may also depend on social factors. Research suggests that acceptance is more likely if the change agent and the target or potential adopter are similar socially. But change agents may have higher social status and more education than the people they are trying to influence. So change agents may work more with higher-status individuals because they are more likely to accept new ideas. If lower-status individuals also have to be reached, change agents of lower status may have to be employed.[17]

Finally, acceptance may depend on psychological factors—that is, how the individuals perceive both the innovation and the agents of change. In the course of

Medha Patkar leading a protest rally in New Delhi against Narmada dams.

trying to encourage women in the southeastern United States to breast-feed rather than bottle-feed their infants, researchers discovered a number of reasons why women were reluctant to breast-feed their infants, even though they heard it was healthier. Many women did not have confidence that they would produce enough milk for their babies; they were embarrassed about breast-feeding in public; and their family and friends had negative attitudes.[18] In designing an educational program, change agents may have to address such psychological concerns directly.

Discovering and Utilizing Local Channels of Influence

In planning a project involving cultural change, the administrator of the project should find out what the normal channels of influence are in the population. In most communities, there are preestablished networks for communication, as well as people of high prestige or influence who are looked to for guidance and direction. An understanding of such channels of influence is extremely valuable when deciding how to introduce a program of change. In addition, it is useful to know at what times, and in what sorts of situations, one channel is likely to be more effective in spreading information and approval than another.

An example of the effective use of local channels of influence occurred when an epidemic of smallpox broke out in the Kalahandi district of the state of Orissa in India. The efforts of health workers to vaccinate villagers against the disease were consistently resisted. The villagers, naturally suspicious and fearful of these strange men with their equally strange medical equipment, were unwilling to offer themselves, and particularly their babies, to the peculiar experiments the strangers wished to perform. Afraid of the epidemic, the villagers appealed for help to their local priest, whose opinions on such matters they trusted. The priest went into a trance, explaining that the illness was the result of the goddess Thalerani's anger with the people. She could be appeased, he continued, only by massive feasts, offerings, and other demonstrations of the villagers' worship of her. Realizing that the priest was the village's major opinion leader, at least in medical matters, the frustrated health workers tried to get the priest to convince his people to undergo vaccination. At first, the priest refused to cooperate with the strange men, but when his favorite nephew fell ill, he decided to try any means available to cure the boy. He thereupon went into another trance, telling the villagers that the goddess wished all her worshipers to be vaccinated. Fortunately, the people agreed, and the epidemic was largely controlled.[19]

If channels of influence are not stable, using influential people in a campaign can sometimes backfire. In the educational campaign in Haiti to promote the use of oral rehydration therapy to treat diarrhea in children, Madame Duvalier, the first lady of Haiti at the time, lent her name to the project. Because there were no serious social or cultural barriers to the treatment and mothers reported that children took to the solutions well, success was expected. But in the middle of the campaign, Haiti became embroiled in political turmoil and the first lady's husband was overthrown. Some of the public thought that the oral rehydration project was a plot by the Duvaliers to sterilize children, and this suspicion fueled resistance.[20] As the earlier discussion of Haiti deforestation shows, people in Haiti were suspicious of any government-sponsored program.

Cultural Resource Management

Large-scale programs of planned change have an impact not only on living people, they can also have an impact on the archaeological record left by the ancestors of living people. Recovering and preserving the archaeological record before programs of planned change disturb or destroy it is called **cultural resource management (CRM).** CRM work is carried out by archaeologists who are often called "contract archaeologists" because they typically work under contract to a government agency, a private developer, or a native group.

What kinds of impact can programs of planned change have on the archaeological record? In the 1960s, a large number of hydroelectric dam projects were initiated to provide flood control and to bring a stable source of electrical power to developing nations. In Egypt, a dam was built on the Nile River at a site called Aswan. Archaeologists realized that once the dam was in place a huge lake would form behind it, submerging thousands of archaeological sites, including the massive temple of Rameses II. Something needed to be done; the archaeological record had to be salvaged or protected. In the language of CRM, there needed to be a *mitigation plan* put into action. And there was. As the Aswan dam was being built, archaeologists went to work excavating sites that would be flooded. Archaeologists and engineers designed a way to take apart the temple of Rameses II and rebuild it, piece by piece, on higher ground where it would not be flooded. By the time the dam was completed in 1965, hundreds of sites had been investigated and two entire temple complexes moved.

Large-scale development projects are not the only projects that involve CRM archaeologists. In many nations, including the United States and Canada, historic preservation laws require any project receiving federal funds to ensure that archaeological resources are protected or their damage mitigated. Virtually all highway projects rely on federal funding, and before a highway can be built, a complete archaeological survey of the proposed right-of-way has to be made. A CRM archaeologist will work with the construction company, the state archaeologist, and perhaps a federal archaeologist to decide on the best course of action. In some cases, the archaeological site will be excavated. In others, the right-of-way may be moved. In still others, the decision is to allow the archaeological site to be destroyed because it would be too costly to excavate or the site may not be significant enough to warrant excavation.

CRM archaeologists do not work only for state or federal agencies. In many nations today, CRM archaeologists are also working with native peoples to protect, preserve, and manage archaeological materials for them. Indeed, archaeologist John Ravesloot recently stated that "the future of American archaeology is with Indian communities functioning as active, not passive, participants in the interpretation, management, and preservation of their rich cultural heritage."[21] One example of such a working relationship is the Zuni Heritage and Historic Preservation Office. During the 1970s, the Pueblo of Zuni decided it needed to train tribal members in archaeology to ensure that Zuni cultural resources and properties were managed properly. It hired three professional archaeologists and, with additional assistance from the National Park Service and the Arizona State Museum, initiated a program to train and employ tribal members in cultural resource management. Working with these non-Zuni archaeologists, the Pueblo of Zuni were able to establish their own historic preservation office that today manages and coordinates all historic preservation on the Zuni reservation, a task that the federal government managed until 1992. The Pueblo also established the Zuni Cultural Resource Enterprise, a Zuni-owned CRM business that employs both Zuni and non-Zuni archaeologists and carries out contract archaeology projects both on and off the Zuni reservation.[22]

Cultural resource management accounts for the majority of archaeology jobs in the United States.[23] As development and construction projects continue to affect the archaeological record, the need for well-trained CRM archaeologists is likely to persist.

Forensic Anthropology

Many of us are fascinated by detective stories. We are interested in crimes and why they occur, and we like to read about them, fictional or not. **Forensic anthropology** is the specialty in anthropology that is devoted to helping solve crimes and identifying human remains, usually by applying knowledge of physical anthropology.[24] It is attracting increasing attention by the public, and

A forensic anthropologist digs out a body, apparently a victim of state-sponsored violence in Argentina between 1976 and 1983.

an increasing number of practitioners. One forensic anthropologist says she is called "the bone lady" by law enforcement personnel.[25] Like others in her line of work, she is asked to dig up or examine human bones to help solve crimes. Narrowing down identification is one of the first priorities, but it is not as simple as on television shows. Are these the bones of a man or woman? How old was the person? How well the forensic anthropologist can answer these seemingly simple questions depends on whether the remains include most bones of the skeleton. Identification of an adult's sex from remains is easier if the pelvis is present, but establishing sex in nonadult remains is not reliable from skeletal remains.[26] With regard to estimating age, only a wide age range can be estimated for adults, but a much narrower range can be estimated for nonadult remains. Forensic anthropologists are often asked for "race" as well. As we discussed in earlier chapters, "race" is not a useful biological category when applied to humans, but it is a significant social category. Forensic anthropologists can estimate with fairly high accuracy whether a person's ancestors came from Asia, Europe, or Africa, but they cannot detect skin color.[27] The police files may suggest that an adult male with Asian ancestry disappeared 5 years ago. The forensic anthropologist could say with a high probability that the remains were of an Asian male adult. Dental, surgical, or hospital records from that individual might lead to unique features that could be matched for more precise identification. Sometimes the forensic anthropologist can suggest the cause of death when the law enforcement people are stumped.

Some cultural anthropologists have also done forensic work, often in connection with legal cases involving Native Americans. For example, in 1978, Barbara Joans was asked to advise the defense in a trial of six older Bannock-Shoshoni women from the Fort Hall reservation who were accused of fraud. They had received "supplemental security income (SSI)," which the social service agency claimed they had no right to receive because they had not reported receiving rent money on land that they owned. Joans presented evidence that the women, although they spoke some English, did not have enough proficiency to understand the nuances of what the SSI people told them. The judge agreed with the defense and ruled that the SSI would have to use a Bannock-Shoshoni interpreter in the future when they went to the reservation to describe the requirements of the program.[28]

In recent years, Clyde Snow and other forensic anthropologists have been called on to confirm horrendous abuses of human rights. Governments have been responsible for the systematic killing of their citizens, and forensic anthropologists have helped to bring the perpetrators to justice. For example, Snow and other forensic anthropologists helped to confirm that the military dictatorship in Argentina in the 1980s was responsible for the deaths of many Argentine civilians who had "disappeared." The forensic anthropologists were also able to determine the location of mass graves and the identity of victims of state-organized brutality in Guatemala. In addition to bringing the perpetrators to justice, confirming the massacres and identifying the victims help the families of the "disappeared" put their anguish behind them.

Medical Anthropology

Illness and death are significant events for people everywhere. No one is spared. So it should not be surprising that how people understand the causes of illness and death, how they behave, and what resources they marshal to cope with these events are extremely important parts of culture. Some argue that we will never completely understand how to treat illness effectively until we understand the cultural behaviors, attitudes, values, and the larger social and political milieu in which people live. Others argue that society and culture have little to do with the outcome of illness—the reason that people die needlessly is that they do not get the appropriate medical treatment.

But anthropologists, particularly those in **medical anthropology,** who are actively engaged in studying health and illness, are increasingly realizing that biological *and* social factors need to be considered if we are to reduce human suffering. For instance, some populations have an appalling incidence of infant deaths due to diarrhea. The origin of this situation is mostly biological, in the sense that the deaths are caused by bacterial infection. But why are so many infants exposed to those bacteria? Usually, the main reason is social. The affected infants are likely to be poor. Because they are poor, they are likely to live with infected drinking water. Similarly, malnutrition may be the biological result of a diet poor in protein, but such a diet is usually also a cultural phenomenon, reflecting a society with classes of people with very unequal access to the necessities of life. In many ways, therefore, medical anthropology, and anthropology in general, are developing in the direction of a "biocultural synthesis."[29]

Cultural Understandings of Health and Illness

Medical researchers and medical practitioners in the United States and other Western societies do not exist in a social vacuum. Many of their ideas and practices are influenced by the culture in which they live. We may think of medicine as purely based on "fact," but it is clear on reflection that many ideas stem from the culture in which the researchers reside. Consider the recent shift in attitudes toward birth. Not so long ago in the United States, fathers were excluded from the birth, hospitals whisked the baby away from the mother and only brought the baby to her infrequently, and visitors (but not attending nurses and doctors) had to wear masks when holding the baby. Rationalizations were given for those practices, but looking back at them, they do not appear to be based on scientific evidence. Many medical anthropologists now argue that the *biomedical paradigm* (the system in which physicians are trained) itself needs to be understood as part of the culture.

Discovering the health-related beliefs, knowledge, and practices of a cultural group—its **ethnomedicine**—is one of the goals of medical anthropology. How do cultures view health and illness? What are their theories about the causes of illness? Do those theories impact on how illnesses are treated? What is the therapeutic process? Are there specialized medical practitioners, and how do they heal? Are there special medicines, and how are they administered? These are just some of the questions asked by the anthropological study of ethnomedicine.

Concepts of Balance or Equilibrium Many cultures have the view that the body should be kept in equilibrium or balance. The balance may be between hot and cold, or wet and dry, as in many cultures of Latin America and the Caribbean.[30] The notion of balance is not limited to opposites. For example, the ancient Greek system of medicine, stemming from Hippocrates, assumed that there were four "humors"—blood, phlegm, yellow bile, and black bile—that must be kept in balance. These humors have hot and cold as well as wet and dry properties. The Greek medical system was widely diffused in Europe and spread to parts of the Islamic world.

In China and elsewhere, tai chi exercises are believed to bring harmony and balance.

In Europe, the humoral medical system was dominant until the germ theory replaced it in the 1900s.[31] In the Ayurvedic system, whose practice dates back 4,000 years in North India, Pakistan, Bangladesh, Sri Lanka, and in the Arab world, there are three humors (phlegm, bile, and flatulence), and a balance between hot and cold is also important.[32] The Chinese medical system, which dates back about 3,500 years, initially stressed the balance between the contrasting forces of *yin* and *yang* and later added the concept of humors, which were six in number in Chinese medicine.[33]

The concepts of hot and cold and *yin* and *yang* are illustrated in Emily Ahern's ethnographic description of the medical system of the Taiwanese Hokkien.[34] The body requires both hot and cold substances; when the body is out of balance, a lack of one substance can be restored by eating or drinking the missing substance. So, for example, when Ahern was faint with heat, she was told to drink some bamboo shoot soup because it was "cold." In the winter, you need more hot substances; in the summer, you want fewer. Some people can tolerate more imbalance than others; people who are older, for instance, can tolerate imbalance less than those who are young. A loss of blood means a loss of heat. So, for a month after childbirth, women eat mostly a soup made of chicken, wine, and sesame oil—all "hot" ingredients. Hot things to eat are generally oily, sticky, or come from animals; cold things tend to be soupy, watery, or made from plants.

Supernatural Forces The Taiwanese Hokkien believe that most illnesses have natural or physiological causes, but around the world, it is more common to believe that illnesses are caused by supernatural forces. In fact, in a cross-cultural study of 139 societies, George P. Murdock found that only two societies did not have the belief that gods or spirits could cause illness, making such a belief a near universal. And 56 percent of those sample societies thought that gods or spirits were the major causes of illness.[35] As we discussed in the chapter on religion and magic, sorcery and witchcraft are common in the world's societies. Although humans practice both sorcery and witchcraft for good or evil, making people ill is one of their major uses. Illness can also be thought of as caused by the loss of one's soul, fate, retribution for violation of a taboo, or contact with a polluting or tabooed substance or object. Sorcery is believed to be a cause of illness by most societies on all continents; retribution because of violation of a taboo is also very frequent in all but one region of the world. The belief that soul loss can cause illness is absent in the area around the Mediterranean, uncommon in Africa, infrequent in the New World and the Pacific, and has its highest frequency in Eurasia.[36]

On Chuuk (Truk), an atoll in the central Pacific, serious illnesses and death are mainly believed to be the work of spirits. Occasionally, the spirits of relatives are to blame, although they usually do not cause serious damage. More often, illness is caused by the spirit of a particular locality or a ghost on a path at night.[37] Nowadays, one of two therapeutic options or their combination is often chosen: hospital medicine or Chuuk medicine. Chuuk medical treatment requires a careful evaluation of symptoms by the patient and the patient's relatives, because different spirits inflict different symptoms. If the symptom match is clear, the patient may choose an appropriate Chuuk medical formula to cure the illness. The patient may also ask whether he or she has done something wrong, and if so, what might point to the appropriate spirit and countervailing formula. For example, there is a taboo on having sexual relations before going to sea. If a person who violated this prohibition becomes ill, the reef spirits will be suspected. The Chuuk medical formula is supposed to cure illness quickly and dramatically. For this reason, Chuuk patients ask for a discharge from a hospital if their condition does not improve quickly. If treatment fails, the Chuukese believe that they need to reevaluate the diagnosis, sometimes with the aid of a diviner.[38] In contrasting their theories of illness to the American germ theory, the people of Chuuk point out that, although they have seen ghosts, they have never seen the germs that Americans talk about. Using both methods, some people recover and some do not, so the ultimate cause is a matter of faith.[39]

The Biomedical Paradigm In most societies, people simply think that their ideas about health and illness are true. Often people are not aware that there may be another way of viewing things until they confront another medical system. Western medical practice has spread widely. People with other medical systems have had to recognize that Western practitioners may consider their ideas about health and illness to be deficient, so they often need to decide which course (Western or non-Western) to follow in dealing with illness. Change, however, is not entirely one-way. For example, for a long time, the Western medical profession disparaged the Chinese practice of acupuncture, but now more medical practitioners are recognizing that acupuncture may provide effective treatment of certain conditions.

Most medical anthropologists use the term **biomedicine** to refer to the dominant medical paradigm in Western cultures today, with the *bio* part of the word emphasizing the biological emphasis of this medical system. As Robert Hahn points out, biomedicine appears to focus on specific diseases and cures for those diseases. Health is not the focus, as it is thought to be the *absence* of disease. Diseases are considered to be purely natural, and there is relatively little interest in the person or the larger social and cultural systems. Doctors generally do not treat the whole body but tend to specialize, with the human body partitioned into zones that belong to different specialties. Death is seen as a failure, and biomedical practitioners do everything they can to prolong life, regardless of the circumstances under which the patient would live life.[40]

Treatment of Illness

Anthropologists who study diseases in this and other cultures can be roughly classified into two camps. First, there are those, the more relativistic, who think that the culture so influences disease symptoms, incidence, and treatment that there are few if any cultural universals about any illness. If each culture is unique, we should expect its conception and treatment of an illness to be unique too, not like beliefs and practices in other cultures. Second, there are those, the more universalistic, who see cross-cultural similarities in the conception and treatment of illness, despite the unique qualities of each culture. For example, native remedies may contain chemicals that are the same as, or similar in effect to, chemicals used in remedies by Western biomedicine.[41] The reality might be that a given culture is very much like other cultures in some respects but unique in other respects.

In their extensive research on Maya ethnomedicine, Elois Ann Berlin and Brent Berlin make a strong case that, although studies of the Maya have emphasized beliefs about illness that are based on supernatural causes, a good deal of Maya ethnomedicine is about natural conditions, their signs and symptoms, and the remedies used to deal with those conditions. In regard to

A Dayak woman in Malaysia collects herbal medicine.

gastrointestinal diseases, the Berlins found that the Maya have a wide-ranging and accurate understanding of anatomy, physiology, and symptoms. Furthermore, the remedies they use, including recommendations for food, drink, and herbal medicines, have properties that are not that different from those of the biomedical profession.[42]

Carole Browner also suggests that the emphasis on "hot-cold" theories of illness in Latin America has been over-emphasized, to the neglect of other factors that influence choices about reproductive health and female health problems. In a study of the medical system in a highland Oaxacan community, Browner finds that certain plants are used to expel substances from the uterus—to facilitate labor at full term, to produce an abortion, or to induce menstrual flow. Other plants are used to retain things in the uterus—to prevent excess blood loss during menstruation, to help healing after delivery, and to prevent miscarriage. Most of these plant remedies appear to work.[43]

The biomedical establishment has become increasingly aware of the value of studying the "traditional" medicinal remedies discovered or invented by people around the world. In studying the indigenous medicines of the Hausa of Nigeria, Nina Etkin and Paul Ross asked individuals to describe the physical attributes of more than 600 plants and their possible medicinal uses, more than 800 diseases and symptoms, and more than 5,000 prepared medicines. Although many medicines were used for treating sorcery, spirit aggression, or witchcraft, most medicines were used for illnesses regarded by the Hausa as having natural causes. Malaria is a serious endemic medical problem in the Hausa region, as in many areas of Africa. The Hausa use approximately 72 plant remedies for conditions connected with malaria—among them anemia, intermittent fever, and jaundice. Experimental treatment of malaria in laboratory animals supports the efficacy of many of the Hausa remedies. But perhaps the most important part of the Etkin and Ross findings is the role of diet. Although most medical research does not consider the possible medical efficacy of the *foods* that people eat in combating illness, food is, of course, consumed in much larger quantities and more often than medicine. It is noteworthy, therefore, that the Hausa eat many plants with antimalarial properties; in fact, dietary consumption of these plants appears to be greatest during the time of year when the risk of malarial infection is at its highest. Recent research has also discovered that foods and spices like garlic, onions, cinnamon, ginger, and pepper have antiviral or antibacterial properties.[44]

Medical Practitioners In our society, we may be so used to consulting a full-time medical specialist (if we do not feel better quickly) that we tend to assume that biomedical treatment is the only effective medical treatment. If we are given a medicine, we expect it to have the appropriate medical effect and make us feel better. Therefore, many in the biomedical system, practitioners and patients alike, are perplexed by the seeming effectiveness of other medical systems that are based in part on symbolic or ritual healing. Yet there is increasing evidence that the *form* of treatment may be just as important as the *content* of treatment.[45]

Illness may be viewed as being due to something in one's social life being out of order. The cause could be retribution for one's own bad behavior or thoughts, or the work of an angry individual practicing sorcery or witchcraft. Or a bad social situation or a bad relationship may be thought of as provoking physical symptoms because of anxiety or stress. In societies with occupational specialization, priests, who are formally trained full-time religious practitioners, may be asked to convey messages or requests for healing to higher powers.[46] Societies with beliefs in sorcery and witchcraft as causes of illness typically have practitioners who are believed to be able to use magic in reverse—that is, to undo the harm invoked by sorcerers and witches. Sometimes sorcerers or witches themselves may be asked to reverse illnesses caused by others. However, they may not be sought out because they are often feared and have relatively low status.[47] Shamans are perhaps the most important medical practitioners in societies lacking full-time occupational specialization.

After working with shamans in Africa, E. Fuller Torrey, a psychiatrist and anthropologist, concluded that they use the same mechanisms and techniques to cure patients as psychiatrists and achieve about the same results. He isolated four categories used by healers the world over:

1. **The naming process.** If a disease has a name—"neurasthenia" or "phobia" or "possession by an ancestral spirit" will do—then it is curable; the patient realizes that the doctor understands his case.

2. **The personality of the doctor.** Those who demonstrate some empathy, nonpossessive warmth, and genuine interest in the patient get results.

3. **The patient's expectations.** One way of raising the patient's expectations of being cured is the trip to the doctor; the longer the trip—to the Mayo Clinic, Menninger Clinic, Delphi, or Lourdes—the easier the cure. An impressive setting (the medical center) and impressive paraphernalia (the stethoscope, the couch, attendants in uniform, the rattle, the whistle, the drum, the mask) also raise the patient's expectations. The healer's training is important. And high fees also help to raise a patient's expectations. (The Paiute doctors always collect their fees before starting a cure; if they don't, it is believed that they will fall ill.)

4. **Curing techniques.** Drugs, shock treatment, conditioning techniques, and so on have long been used in many different parts of the world.[48]

Biomedical research is not unaware of the effect of the mind on healing. In fact, considerable evidence has accumulated that psychological factors can be very important in illness. Patients who believe that medicine will help them often recover quickly even if the medicine is only a sugar pill or a medicine not particularly relevant to their condition. Such effects are called *placebo effects*.[49] Placebos do not just have psychological effects. Although the mechanisms are not well understood, they may also alter body chemistry and bolster the immune system.[50]

Shamans may coexist with medical doctors. Don Antonio, a respected Otomi Indian shaman in central Mexico, has many patients, perhaps not as many as before modern medicine, but still plenty. In his view, when he was born, God gave him his powers to cure, but his powers are reserved for removing "evil" illnesses (those caused by sorcerers). "Good" illnesses can be cured by herbs and medicine, and he refers patients with those illnesses to medical doctors; he believes that doctors are more effective than he could be in those cases. The doctors, however, do not seem to refer any patients to Don Antonio or other shamans.[51]

The most important full-time medical practitioner in the biomedical system is the physician, and the patient-physician relationship is central. In the ideal scheme of things, the physician is viewed as having the ability, with some limits, of being able to treat illness, alleviate suffering, and

A Navajo medicine man performs a healing ceremony involving a snake painted on the ground.

prolong the life of the patient, as well as offering promises of patient confidentiality and privacy. The patient relies on the physician's knowledge, skill, and ethics. Consistent with the biomedical paradigm, doctors tend to treat patients as having "conditions" rather than as complete people. Because patients commonly go to physicians to solve a particular condition or sickness, physicians tend to try to do something about it even in the face of uncertainty. Physicians tend to rely on technology for diagnoses and treatment and place relatively low value on talking with patients. In fact, physicians tend to give patients relatively little information, and they may not listen very well.[52]

Despite the importance of physicians in biomedicine, patients do not always seek physician care. In fact, one-third of the population of the United States regularly consults with alternative practitioners, such as acupuncturists or chiropractors, often unbeknownst to the physician. Somewhat surprisingly, individuals with more education are more likely to seek alternative care.[53]

Political and Economic Influences on Health

People with more social, economic, and political power in a society are generally healthier.[54] Inequality in health in socially stratified societies is not surprising. The poor usually have more exposure to disease because they live in more crowded conditions. And the poor are more likely to lack the resources to get quality care. For many diseases, health problems, and death rates, incidence or relative frequency varies directly with social class. In the United Kingdom, for example, people in the higher social classes are less likely to have headaches, bronchitis, pneumonia, heart disease, arthritis, injuries, and mental disorders, to name just a few of the differences.[55] Ethnic differences also predict health inequities. In South Africa under apartheid, the 14 percent minority population, referred to as "white," controlled most of the income of the country and most of the high-quality land. "Blacks" were restricted to areas with shortages of housing, inadequate housing, and little employment. To get a job, families often had to be disrupted; usually the husband would have to migrate to find work. "Blacks" lived, on average, about 9 years less than "whites" in 1985, and "black" infants died at about seven times the rate of "white" infants. In the United States recently, the differences between African Americans and European Americans in health are not as stark as in South Africa, but those favoring European Americans are still substantial. As of 2001, the difference in life expectancy was about 5–6 years, and African American infant mortality was almost three times the rate for European American infants. Robert Hahn has estimated that poverty accounts for about 19 percent of the overall mortality in the United States.[56]

Inequities, because of class and ethnicity, are not limited to within-society differences. Power and economic differentials *between* societies also have profound health consequences. Over the course of European exploration and expansion, indigenous peoples died in enormous numbers from introduced diseases, wars, and conquests; they had their lands expropriated and diminished in size and quality. When incorporated into colonial territories or into countries, indigenous people usually become minorities and they are almost always very poor. These conditions of life not only affect the incidence of disease, they also tend to lead to greater substance abuse, violence, depression, and other mental pathologies.[57] Medical anthropologists have studied an enormous variety of conditions. What follows is only a small sampling.

AIDS

We may think that epidemics are a thing of the past. But the recent and sudden emergence of the disease we call **AIDS (acquired immune deficiency syndrome)** reminds us that new diseases, or new varieties of old diseases, can appear at any time. Like all other organisms, disease-causing organisms also evolve. The human immunodeficiency virus (HIV) that causes AIDS emerged only recently. Viruses and bacteria are always mutating, and new strains emerge that are initially a plague on our genetic resistance and on medical efforts to contain them.

Millions of people around the world already have the symptoms of AIDS, and millions more are infected with HIV but do not know they are infected. As of December 2007, 33 million adults and children in the world were living with HIV/AIDS.[58] There are a few signs of improvement since 2001. The percentage of people infected globally is now stable; some countries have improved with prevention efforts, and the number of new cases each year has gone down. However, AIDS is the major cause of death in sub-Saharan Africa and is still a leading cause of death worldwide.[59] There is still no cure. AIDS is a frightening epidemic not only because of its death toll. It is also frightening because it takes a long time (on average, 4 years) after exposure for symptoms to appear. This means that many people who have been infected by HIV but do not know they are infected may continue, unknowingly, to transmit the virus to others.[60]

Transmission occurs mostly via sexual encounters, through semen and blood. Drug users may also transmit HIV by way of contaminated needles. Transmission by blood transfusion has been virtually eliminated in this and other societies by medical screening of blood supplies. In many countries, however, there is still no routine screening of blood prior to transfusions. HIV may be passed from a pregnant woman to her offspring through the placenta and after birth through her breast milk. The rate of transmission between a mother and her baby is 20–40 percent. Children are also at great risk because they are likely to be orphaned by a parent's death from AIDS. At the turn of the twenty-first century, approximately 14 million children were parentless because of AIDS.[61]

Many people think of AIDS as only a medical problem that requires only a medical solution, without realizing that behavioral, cultural, and political issues need to be addressed as well. It is true that developing a vaccine or a drug to prevent people from getting AIDS and finding a permanent cure for those who have it will finally solve the problem. But, for a variety of reasons, we can expect that

Millions of children in sub-Saharan Africa are orphaned because of AIDS. These orphaned children in Uganda look on during a visit by Britain's Queen Elizabeth to their center.

the medical solution alone will not be sufficient, at least not for a while. First, to be effective worldwide, or even within a country, a vaccine has to be inexpensive and relatively easy to produce in large quantities; the same is true of any medical treatment. Second, governments around the world have to be willing and able to spend the money and hire the personnel necessary to manage an effective program.[62] Third, future vaccination and treatment will require the people at risk to be willing to get vaccinated and treated, which is not always the case. Witness the fact that the incidence of measles is on the rise in the United States because many people are not having their children vaccinated.

There are now expensive drug treatments that significantly reduce the degree of HIV infection, but we do not know if an effective and inexpensive vaccine or treatment will be developed soon. In the meantime, the risk of HIV infection can be reduced only by changes in social, particularly sexual, behavior. But to persuade people to change their sexual behavior, it is necessary to find out exactly what they do sexually, and why they do what they do.

Research so far suggests that different sexual patterns are responsible for HIV transmission in different parts of the world. In the United States, England, northern Europe, Australia, and Latin America, the recipients of anal intercourse, particularly men, are the most likely individuals to acquire HIV infection; vaginal intercourse can also transmit the infection, usually from the man to the woman. Needle sharing can transmit the infection, too. In Africa, the most common mode of transmission is vaginal intercourse, and so women get infected more commonly in Africa than elsewhere.[63] In fact, in Africa there are slightly more cases of HIV in women as compared with men.[64]

As of now, there are only two known ways to reduce the likelihood of sexual HIV transmission. One way is to abstain from sexual intercourse; the other is to use condoms. Male circumcision now appears to decrease the risk of HIV infection, but studies have not yet evaluated long-term effects.[65] Educational programs that teach how AIDS spreads and what one can do about it may reduce the spread somewhat, but such programs may fail where people have incompatible beliefs and attitudes about sexuality. For example, people in some central African societies believe that deposits of semen after conception are necessary for a successful pregnancy and generally enhance a woman's health and ability to reproduce. It might be expected then that people who have these beliefs about semen would choose not to use condoms; after all, condoms in their view are a threat to public health.[66] Educational programs may also emphasize the wrong message. Promiscuity may increase the risk of HIV transmission, so hardly anyone would question the wisdom of advertising to reduce the number of sexual partners. And, at least in the homosexual community in the United States, individuals report fewer sexual partners than in the past. What was not anticipated, however, was that individuals in monogamous relationships, who may feel safe, are less likely to use condoms or to avoid the riskiest sexual practices. Needless to say, sex with a regular partner who is infected is not safe![67] In what may seem like something of a paradox, the United Nations observed that, for most women in the world today, the major risk factor for being infected with HIV is being married.[68] It is not marriage, *per se,* that heightens the risk of HIV infection; rather, the proximate cause may be the lower likelihood of condom use or less abstinence by a married couple.

Undernutrition

What people eat is intrinsically connected to their survival and the ability of a population to reproduce itself, so we would expect that the ways people obtain, distribute, and consume food have been generally adaptive.[69] For example, the human body cannot synthesize eight amino acids. Meat can provide all of these amino acids, and combinations of particular plants can also provide them for a complete complement of protein. The combination of maize and beans in many traditional Native American diets, or *tortillas* and *frijoles* in Mexico, can provide all the needed amino acids. In places where wheat (often made into bread) is the staple, dairy products combined with wheat also provide complete protein.[70] Even the way that people have prepared for scarcity, such as breaking up into mobile bands, cultivating crops that can better withstand drought, and preserving food in case of famine, are probably adaptive practices in unpredictable environments. Geneticists have proposed that populations in famine-prone areas may have had genetic selection for "thrifty genes"—genes that allow individuals to need a minimum of food and store the extra in fatty tissue to get them past serious scarcity.[71] Customary diets and genetic changes may have been selected over a long stretch of time, but many serious nutritional problems observed today are due to rapid culture change. For instance, although "thrifty genes" may be adaptive during famine, they may become maladaptive when food is readily available. The high prevalence of diabetes and obesity in many populations today may be linked to such genes.

Often the switch to commercial or cash crops has harmful effects in another direction—creating undernutrition. For example, when the farmer-herders of the arid region in northeastern Brazil started growing sisal, a drought-resistant plant used for making twine and rope, many of them abandoned subsistence agriculture. The small landholders used most of their land for sisal growing and, when the price of sisal fell, they had to work as laborers for others to try to make ends meet. Food then had to be mostly bought, but if a laborer or sisal grower didn't earn enough, there was not enough food for the whole family.

Analysis of allocation of food in some households by Daniel Gross and Barbara Underwood suggests that the laborer and his wife received adequate nutrition, but the children often received much less than required. Lack of adequate nutrition usually results in retarded weight and height in children. As is commonly the case when there is substantial social inequality, the children from lower-income groups weigh substantially less than those from higher-income groups. But even though there were some economic differences before sisal production, the effects on nutrition appeared negligible before, judging from the fact that there was little or no difference in weight among adults from higher and lower socioeconomic positions who grew up prior to sisal production. But more recently, 45 percent of the children from lower economic groups were undernourished as compared with 23 percent of those children from the higher economic groups.[72]

This is not to say that commercialization is always deleterious to adequate nutrition. For example, in the Highlands of New Guinea, there is evidence that the nutrition of children improved when families started growing coffee for sale. However, in this case, the families still had land to grow some crops for consumption. The extra money earned from coffee enabled them to buy canned fish and rice, which provided children with higher amounts of protein than the usual staple of sweet potatoes.[73]

Nutritional imbalances for females have a far-reaching impact on reproduction and the health of the infants they bear. In some cultures, the lower status of women has a direct bearing on their access to food. Although the custom of feeding males first is well known, it is less often realized that females end up with less nutrient-dense food such as meat. Deprivation of food sometimes starts in infancy where girl babies, as in India, are weaned earlier than boy babies.[74] Parents may be unaware that their differential weaning practice has the effect of reducing the amount of high-quality protein that girl infants receive. Indeed, in Ecuador, Lauris McKee found that parents thought that earlier weaning of girls was helpful to them. They believed that mothers' milk transmitted sexuality and aggression, both ideal male traits, to their infants and so it was important that girl babies be weaned early. Mothers weaned their

Eating Disorders, Biology, and the Cultural Construction of Beauty

Cultures differ about what they consider beautiful, including people. In many cultures, fat people are considered more beautiful than thin people. Melvin Ember did fieldwork years ago on the islands of American Samoa. When he returned to the main island after 3 months on a distant island, he ran into a Samoan acquaintance, a prominent chief. The chief said: "You look good. You gained weight." In reality, he had lost 30 pounds! The chief may not have remembered how heavy the anthropologist had been, but he clearly thought that fat was better than thin. Among the Azawagh Arabs of Niger, fatness was not merely valued and considered beautiful; great care was taken to ensure that young girls became fat by insisting and sometimes forcing them to drink large quantities of milk-based porridge.

Around the world, fatness is generally considered more desirable than thinness, particularly for women. Fatness is widely valued in these cultures not only because it is considered more beautiful, but also because it is thought to be a marker of health, fertility, and higher status in societies with social stratification. This view is in strong contrast to the ideal in the United States and many other Western societies, where fatness is thought to be unattractive and to reflect laziness, a lack of self-control, and poor health. Thinness, particularly in the upper classes, is considered beautiful. How can we explain these differences in what is considered beautiful?

Recent cross-cultural research suggests that the picture is more complicated. It appears that societies with unpredictable resources actually value thinness, particularly in societies that have no way of storing food. At first glance, this seems puzzling. Shouldn't an individual who stores calories on the body be better off than an individual who is thin when facing starvation, particularly if there is no food storage? Perhaps. But 10 thin individuals will generally consume less than 10 heavier people, so perhaps there is a group advantage to being thin. Indeed, many societies with frequent episodes of famine encourage fasting or eating very light meals, as among the Gurage of Ethiopia. The strongest cross-cultural predictor of valuing fatness in women is what is often referred to as "machismo" or "protest masculinity." Societies with a strong emphasis on male aggression, strength,

and sexuality are the most likely to value fatness in women; those with little machismo value thinness. Why machismo is associated with valuing fatness in women is far from clear. One suggestion is that machismo actually reflects male insecurity and fear of women. Such men may not be looking for closeness or intimacy with their wives, but they may want to show how potent they are by having lots of children. If fatness suggests fertility, men may look for wives who are fatter. Consistent with this idea, the ideal of thinness in women became more common in North America with the rise of women's movements in the 1920s and late 1960s. Consider that Marilyn Monroe epitomized beauty in the 1950s; she was well rounded, not thin. Thin became more popular only when women began to question early marriage and having many children. Behaviors associated with machismo became less acceptable at those times.

Cultural beliefs about what is considered a beautiful body can impose enormous pressures on females to achieve the ideal body type—whether it be fat or thin. In the United States and other Western countries, the effort to be thin can be carried to an extreme, resulting in the eating disorders anorexia nervosa and bulimia. If you suffer from these often fatal illnesses, you may regularly eat little and you may regularly force yourself to throw up, thus depriving your body of nutrients in your quest to be thinner and thinner. The irony of "thinness" being idealized in the United States and other Western countries is that obesity is becoming more common in those societies. In 2001, the incidence of obesity increased in the United States to 31 percent, and medical researchers worried about the increase in heart disease and diabetes resulting from obesity. Whether or not obesity is a result of an eating disorder (in the psychological sense) is more debatable. Researchers are finding biological causes of obesity, such as resistance to the hormone leptin, which regulates appetite, suggesting that much of the obesity "epidemic" has biological causes. Still, fast food, increasing sedentariness, and extremely large portion sizes are probably contributing factors also.

Sources: J. L. Anderson et al. 1992; P. J. Brown 1997, 100; C. R. Ember et al. 2005: Friedman 2003; Loustaunau and Sobo 1997, 85; Popenoe 2004; N. Wolf 1991.

girls at about 11 months and their boys at about 20 months, a 9-month difference. McKee found that girl infants had a significantly higher mortality than boy infants in their second year of life, suggesting that the earlier weaning time for girls and their probable undernutrition may have been responsible.[75]

Applied and practicing anthropologists are not the only ones interested in solving problems. Many researchers in anthropology and the other social sciences do *basic research* on social problems. Such research may involve fieldwork to get a broad understanding of cultural ideas and practices about health, illness, or violence. Or basic research may involve testing theories about the possible causes of specific problems. The results of such tests could suggest solutions to the problems if the causes, once discovered, can be reduced or eliminated.

✓●—Study and **Review** on myanthrolab.com

Summary

1. Applied or practicing anthropology as a profession is explicitly concerned with making anthropological knowledge useful. Applied or practicing anthropologists may be involved in one or more phases of programs that are designed to change peoples' lives: assembling relevant knowledge, constructing alternative plans, assessing the likely social and environmental impact of particular plans, implementing the programs, and monitoring the programs and their effects.

2. Applied or practicing anthropologists work for a large variety of organizations, government agencies, international development agencies, private consulting firms, public health organizations, medical schools, public interest law firms, community development agencies, charitable foundations, and profit-seeking corporations.

3. The code of ethics for those who work professionally as applied anthropologists specifies that the target population should be included as much as possible in the formulation of policy, so that people in the community may know in advance how the program may affect them. But perhaps the most important aspect of the code is the pledge not to be involved in any plan whose effect will not be beneficial. It is often difficult to evaluate the effects of planned changes. Long-term consequences may be detrimental even if the changes are beneficial in the short run.

4. Even if a planned change will prove beneficial to the targeted population, the people may not accept it. And if the proposed innovation is not utilized by the intended population, the project cannot be considered a success. Affected populations may reject or resist a proposed innovation for cultural, social, or psychological reasons. It is important to understand what the reasons are. The population may also resist the proposed change because they unconsciously or consciously know it is not good for them. To be effective, change agents may have to discover and use the traditional channels of influence in introducing their projects.

5. Cultural resource management usually takes the form of "contract archaeology" to record and/or conserve the archaeology of a building site.

6. Forensic anthropology is the specialty in anthropology that is devoted to helping solve crimes and identifying human remains, usually by applying knowledge of physical anthropology.

7. Medical anthropologists suggest that biological and social factors need to be considered if we are to understand how to treat illness effectively and reduce the suffering in human life. Understanding ethnomedicine—the medical beliefs and practices of a society or cultural group—is one of the goals of medical anthropology.

8. Many cultures have the view that the body should be kept in equilibrium or balance. The balance may be between hot and cold, or wet and dry, or there may be other properties that need to be balanced. The belief that gods or spirits can cause illness is a near universal. The belief in sorcery or witchcraft as a cause of illness is also very common.

9. Some researchers are finding evidence that many of the plant remedies that indigenous peoples use contain chemicals that are the same as, or similar in effect to, chemicals used in Western biomedicine remedies.

10. People with more social, economic, and political power in a society are generally healthier. Power and economic differentials between societies also have had profound health consequences.

11. The enormous death toll of AIDS, the leading cause of adult death in many countries today, will be reduced when medical science develops effective and inexpensive medicines to treat victims of HIV or AIDS and a vaccine to prevent individuals from getting HIV. In the meantime, if the death toll from AIDS is to be reduced, changes in attitudes, beliefs, and practices regarding sexual activity are needed.

12. The ways that people obtain, distribute, and consume food have been generally adaptive. Geneticists have proposed that populations in famine-prone areas may have had genetic selection for "thrifty genes." Now these populations with regular food supplies may be prone to diabetes and obesity. Many of the serious nutritional problems of today are due to rapid culture change, particularly those making for an increasing degree of social inequality.

Glossary Terms

AIDS (acquired immune deficiency syndrome) (p. 439)
applied (or practicing) anthropology (p. 425)

biomedicine (p. 435)
cultural resource management (CRM) (p. 430)
ethnomedicine (p. 433)

forensic anthropology (p. 431)
medical anthropology (p. 433)

Critical Questions

1. What particular advantages do anthropologists have in trying to solve practical problems?

2. Is it ethical to try to influence people's lives when they have not asked for help? Explain your answer.

3. Why do native remedies often contain chemicals that are the same as, or similar in effect to, chemicals used in Western biomedicine remedies?

4. Why might people engage in sexual practices that increase their likelihood of contracting AIDS?

Read the **Original Source** on **myanthrolab.com**

Read the chapter by Andrew W. Miracle titled "A Shaman for Organizations" on MyAnthroLab. Answer the following questions.

1. Why does Miracle call himself a "shaman"?

2. According to Miracle, what skills are useful to an applied anthropologist? Why does he think so?

Glossary

Absolute dating A method of dating fossils in which the actual age of a deposit or specimen is measured. Also known as *chronometric dating*.

Accent Differences in pronunciation characteristic of a group.

Acclimatization Impermanent physiological changes that people make when they encounter a new environment.

Acculturation The process of extensive borrowing of aspects of culture in the context of superordinate–subordinate relations between societies; usually occurs as the result of external pressure.

Acheulian A stone toolmaking tradition dating from 1.5 million years ago. Compared with the Oldowan tradition, Acheulian assemblages have more large tools created according to standardized designs or shapes. One of the most characteristic and prevalent tools in the Acheulian tool kit is the so-called hand axe, which is a teardrop-shaped bifacially flaked tool with a thinned sharp tip. Other large tools might have been cleavers and picks.

Adapid A type of prosimian with many lemurlike features; appeared in the early Eocene.

Adaptation Refers to genetic changes that allow an organism to survive and reproduce in a specific environment.

Adaptive Traits that enhance survival and reproductive success in a particular environment.

Adaptive customs Cultural traits that enhance survival and reproductive success in a particular environment.

Adjudication The process by which a third party acting as judge makes a decision that the parties to a dispute have to accept.

Aegyptopithecus An Oligocene anthropoid and probably the best-known propliopithecid.

Agriculture The practice of raising domesticated crops.

AIDS (acquired immune deficiency syndrome) A disease caused by the HIV virus.

Allele One member of a pair of genes.

Allen's rule The rule that protruding body parts (particularly arms and legs) are relatively shorter in the cooler areas of a species' range than in the warmer areas.

Ambilineal descent The rule of descent that affiliates individuals with groups of kin related to them through men or women.

Ancestor spirits Supernatural beings who are the ghosts of dead relatives.

Anthropoids One of the two suborders of primates; includes monkeys, apes, and humans.

Anthropological linguistics The anthropological study of languages.

Anthropology A discipline that studies humans, focusing on the study of differences and similarities, both biological and cultural, in human populations. Anthropology is concerned with typical biological and cultural characteristics of human populations in all periods and in all parts of the world.

Applied (practicing) anthropology The branch of anthropology that concerns itself with applying anthropological knowledge to achieve practical goals, usually in the service of an agency outside the traditional academic setting.

Arboreal Adapted to living in trees.

Archaeology The branch of anthropology that seeks to reconstruct the daily life and customs of peoples who lived in the past and to trace and explain cultural changes. Often lacking written records for study, archaeologists must try to reconstruct history from the material remains of human cultures. See also **Historical archaeology**.

Archaic Time period in the New World during which food production first developed.

Ardipithecus ramidus Perhaps the first hominid, dating to about 4.5 million years ago. Its dentition combines apelike and australopithecine-like features, and its skeleton suggests it was bipedal.

Artifact Any object made by a human.

Atlatl Aztec word for "spear thrower."

Australopithecus Genus of Pliocene and Pleistocene hominids.

Australopithecus aethiopicus An early robust australopithecine.

Australopithecus afarensis A species of *Australopithecus* that lived 4 million to 3 million years ago in East Africa and was definitely bipedal.

Australopithecus africanus A species of *Australopithecus* that lived between about 3 million and 2 million years ago.

Australopithecus anamensis A species of *Australopithecus* that lived perhaps 4.2 million years ago.

Australopithecus bahrelghazali An early gracile australopithecine, dating to about 3 million years ago, and currently represented by only a single jaw. It is an interesting species because it is found in western Chad, distant from the East African Rift Valley where all other early australopithecines have been found.

Australopithecus boisei An East African robust australopithecine species dating from 2.2 million to 1.3 million years ago with somewhat larger cranial capacity than *A. africanus*. No longer thought to be larger than other australopithecines, it is robust primarily in the skull and jaw, most strikingly in the teeth. Compared with *A. robustus*, *A. boisei* has even more features that reflect a huge chewing apparatus.

Australopithecus garhi A gracile australopithecine, dating to about 2.5 million years ago.

Australopithecus robustus A robust australopithecine species found in South African caves dating from about 1.8 million to 1 million years ago. Not as large in the teeth and jaws as *A. boisei*.

Avunculocal residence A pattern of residence in which a married couple settles with or near the husband's mother's brother.

Balanced reciprocity Giving with the expectation of a straightforward immediate or limited-time trade.

Balancing selection A type of selection that occurs when a heterozygous combination of alleles is positively favored even though a homozygous combination is disfavored.

Band A fairly small, usually nomadic local group that is politically autonomous.

Band organization The kind of political organization where the local group or band is the largest territorial group in the society that acts as a unit. The local group in band societies is politically autonomous.

Bergmann's rule The rule that smaller-sized subpopulations of a species inhabit the warmer parts of its geographic range and larger-sized subpopulations the cooler areas.

Bifacial tool A tool worked or flaked on two sides.

Bilateral kinship The type of kinship system in which individuals affiliate more or less equally with their mother's and father's relatives; descent groups are absent.

Bilocal residence A pattern of residence in which a married couple lives with or near either the husband's parents or the wife's parents.

Bilophodont Having four cusps on the molars that form two parallel ridges. This is the common molar pattern of Old World monkeys.

Biological (physical) anthropology The study of humans as biological organisms, dealing with the emergence and evolution of humans and with contemporary biological variations among human populations.

Biomedicine The dominant medical paradigm in Western societies today.

Bipedalism Locomotion in which an animal walks on its two hind legs.

Blade A thin flake whose length is usually more than twice its width. In the blade technique of toolmaking, a core is prepared by shaping a piece of flint with hammerstones into a pyramidal or cylindrical form. Blades are then struck off until the core is used up.

Brachiators Animals that move through the trees by swinging hand over hand from branch to branch. They usually have long arms and fingers.

Bride price A substantial gift of goods or money given to the bride's kin by the groom or his kin at or before the marriage. Also called *bride wealth*.

Bride service Work performed by the groom for his bride's family for a variable length of time either before or after the marriage.

Burin A chisel-like stone tool used for carving and for making such artifacts as bone and antler needles, awls, and projectile points.

Carpolestes A mouse-sized arboreal creature living about 56 million years ago; a strong candidate for the common primate ancestor.

Cash crop A cultivated commodity raised for sale rather than for personal consumption by the cultivator.

Caste A ranked group, often associated with a certain occupation, in which membership is determined at birth and marriage is restricted to members of one's own caste.

Catarrhines The group of anthropoids with narrow noses and nostrils that face downward. Catarrhines include monkeys of the Old World (Africa, Asia, and Europe), as well as apes and humans.

Cercopithecoids Old World monkeys.

Cerebral cortex The "gray matter" of the brain; the center of speech and other higher mental activities.

Chief A person who exercises authority, usually on behalf of a multicommunity political unit. This role is generally found in rank societies and is usually permanent and often hereditary.

Chiefdom A political unit, with a chief at its head, integrating more than one community but not necessarily the whole society or language group.

Chromosomes Paired rod-shaped structures within a cell nucleus containing the genes that transmit traits from one generation to the next.

Chronometric dating See **Absolute dating**.

Civilization Urban society, from the Latin word for "city-state."

Clan A set of kin whose members believe themselves to be descended from a common ancestor or ancestress but cannot specify the links back to that founder; often designated by a totem. Also called a *sib*.

Class A category of people who have about the same opportunity to obtain economic resources, power, and prestige.

Class societies Societies containing social groups that have unequal access to economic resources, power, and prestige.

Cline The gradually increasing (or decreasing) frequency of a gene from one end of a region to another.

Code-switching Using more than one language in the course of conversing.

Codified laws Formal principles for resolving disputes in heterogeneous and stratified societies.

Commercial exchange See **Market (or commercial) exchange**.

Commercialization The increasing dependence on buying and selling, with money usually as the medium of exchange.

Complementary opposition The occasional uniting of various segments of a segmentary lineage system in opposition to similar segments.

Consanguineal kin One's biological relatives; relatives by birth.

Context The relationships between and among artifacts, ecofacts, fossils, and features.

Continental drift The movement of the continents over the past 135 million years. In the early Cretaceous (circa 135 million years ago), there were two "supercontinents": *Laurasia*, which included North America and Eurasia; and *Gondwanaland*, which included Africa, South America, India, Australia, and Antarctica. By the beginning of the Paleocene (circa 65 million years ago), Gondwanaland had broken apart, with South America drifting west away from Africa, India drifting east, and Australia and Antarctica drifting south.

Core vocabulary Nonspecialist vocabulary.

Corvée A system of required labor.

Cretaceous Geological epoch 135 million to 65 million years ago, during which dinosaurs and other reptiles ceased to be the dominant land vertebrates, and mammals and birds began to become important.

Crime Violence not considered legitimate that occurs within a political unit.

Cro-Magnons Humans who lived in western Europe about 35,000 years ago, they were once thought to be the earliest specimens of modern-looking humans, or *Homo sapiens sapiens*. But it is now known that modern-looking humans appeared earlier outside of Europe; the earliest so far found lived in Africa.

Cross-cousins Children of siblings of the opposite sex. One's cross-cousins are the father's sisters' children and mother's brothers' children.

Cross-cultural researcher An ethnologist who uses ethnographic data about many societies to test possible explanations of cultural variation to discover general patterns about cultural traits—what is universal, what is variable, why traits vary, and what the consequences of the variability might be.

Crossing-over Exchanges of sections of chromosomes from one chromosome to another.

Cultural anthropology The study of cultural variation and universals in the past and present. Also refers to the subfield **ethnology**, one of the three subfields of cultural anthropology (the other subfields are anthropological linguistics and archaeology).

Cultural relativism The attitude that a society's customs and ideas should be viewed within the context of that society's problems and opportunities.

Cultural resource management (CRM) The branch of applied anthropology that seeks to recover and preserve the archaeological record before programs of planned change disturb or destroy it.

Culture The set of learned behaviors, beliefs, attitudes, values, and ideals that are characteristic of a particular society or other social group.

Cuneiform Wedge-shaped writing invented by the Sumerians around 3000 B.C.

Descriptive (structural) linguistics The study of how languages are constructed.

Dialect A variety of a language spoken in a particular area or by a particular social group.

Diastema A gap between the canine and first premolar found in apes.

Diffusion The borrowing by one society of a cultural trait belonging to another society as the result of contact between the two societies.

Directional selection A type of natural selection that increases the frequency of a trait (the trait is said to be positively favored, or adaptive).

Diurnal Active during the day.

Divination Getting the supernatural to provide guidance.

DNA Deoxyribonucleic acid; a long, two-stranded molecule in the genes that directs the makeup of an organism according to the instructions in its genetic code.

Domestication Modification or adaptation of plants and animals for use by humans. When people plant crops, we refer to the process as cultivation. It is only when the crops cultivated and the animals raised have been modified—are different from wild varieties— that we speak of plant and animal domestication.

Dominant The allele of a gene pair that is always phenotypically expressed in the heterozygous form.

Double descent or double unilineal descent A system that affiliates individuals with a group of matrilineal kin for some purposes and with a group of patrilineal kin for other purposes.

Dowry A substantial transfer of goods or money from the bride's family to the bride.

Dryopithecus Genus of ape from the later Miocene found primarily in Europe. It had thin tooth enamel and pointed molar cusps very similar to those of the fruit-eating chimpanzees of today.

Ecofacts Natural items that humans have used; things such as the remains of animals eaten by humans or plant pollens found on archaeological sites are examples of ecofacts.

Economic resources Things that have value in a culture, including land, tools and other technology, goods, and money.

Egalitarian societies Societies in which all people of a given age-sex category have equal access to economic resources, power, and prestige.

Ego In the reckoning of kinship, the reference point or focal person.

Endogamy The rule specifying marriage to a person within one's own group (kin, caste, community).

Eocene A geological epoch 55 million to 34 million years ago during which the first definite primates appeared.

Epipaleolithic Time period during which food production first developed in the Near East.

Ethnicity The process of defining ethnicity usually involves a group of people emphasizing common origins and language, shared history, and selected aspects of cultural difference such as a difference in religion. Because different groups are doing the perceiving, ethnic identities often vary with whether one is inside or outside the group.

Ethnocentric Refers to judgment of other cultures solely in terms of one's own culture.

Ethnocentrism The attitude that other societies' customs and ideas can be judged in the context of one's own culture.

Ethnogenesis Creation of a new culture.

Ethnographer A person who spends some time living with, interviewing, and observing a group of people to describe their customs.

Ethnographic analogy Method of comparative cultural study that extrapolates to the past from recent or current societies.

Ethnography A description of a society's customary behaviors and ideas.

Ethnohistorian An ethnologist who uses historical documents to study how a particular culture has changed over time.

Ethnology The study of how and why recent cultures differ and are similar. The parent term "cultural anthropology" is usually used nowadays to refer to this subfield of cultural anthropology.

Ethnomedicine The health-related beliefs, knowledge, and practices of a cultural group.

Excavation The careful removal of the archaeological deposits; the recovery of artifacts, ecofacts, fossils, and features from the soil in which those deposits have been buried.

Exogamy The rule specifying marriage to a person from outside one's own group (kin or community).

Explanation An answer to a *why* question. In science, there are two kinds of explanation that researchers try to achieve: associations and theories.

Extended family A family consisting of two or more single-parent, monogamous, polygynous, or polyandrous families linked by a blood tie.

Extensive (shifting) cultivation A type of horticulture in which the land is worked for short periods and then left to regenerate for some years before being used again. Also called **shifting cultivation**.

Falsification Showing that a theory seems to be wrong by finding that implications or predictions derivable from it are not consistent with objectively collected data.

Family A social and economic unit consisting minimally of a parent and a child.

Features Artifacts of human manufacture that cannot be removed from an archaeological site. Hearths, storage pits, and buildings are examples of features.

Feuding A state of recurring hostility between families or groups of kin, usually motivated by a desire to avenge an offense against a member of the group.

Fieldwork Firsthand experience with the people being studied and the usual means by which anthropological information is obtained. Regardless of other methods that anthropologists may use (e.g., censuses, surveys), fieldwork usually involves participant-observation for an extended period of time, often a year or more. See **Participant-observation**.

Folklore Includes all the myths, legends, folktales, ballads, riddles, proverbs, and superstitions of a cultural group. Generally, folklore is transmitted orally, but it may also be written.

Food production The form of subsistence technology in which food-getting is dependent on the cultivation and domestication of plants and animals.

Foraging May be generally defined as a food-getting strategy that obtains wild plant and animal resources through gathering, hunting, scavenging, or fishing; also known as food collection.

Foramen magnum Opening in the base of the skull through which the spinal cord passes en route to the brain.

Forensic anthropology The application of anthropology, usually physical anthropology, to help identify human remains and assist in solving crimes.

Fossils The hardened remains or impressions of plants and animals that lived in the past.

Fraternal polyandry The marriage of a woman to two or more brothers at the same time.

Gender differences Differences between females and males that reflect cultural expectations and experiences.

Gender roles Roles that are culturally assigned to genders.

Gender stratification The degree of unequal access by the different genders to prestige, authority, power, rights, and economic resources.

Gene Chemical unit of heredity.

Gene flow The process by which genes pass from the gene pool of one population to that of another through mating and reproduction.

General-purpose money A universally accepted medium of exchange.

Generalized reciprocity Gift giving without any immediate or planned return.

Genetic drift The various random processes that affect gene frequencies in small, relatively isolated populations.

Genotype The total complement of inherited traits or genes of an organism.

Genus A group of related species; pl., genera.

Ghosts Supernatural beings who were once human; the souls of dead people.

Globalization The ongoing spread of goods, people, information, and capital around the world.

Gloger's rule The rule that populations of birds and mammals living in warm, humid climates have more melanin (and therefore darker skin, fur, or feathers) than populations of the same species living in cooler, drier areas.

Gods Supernatural beings of nonhuman origin who are named personalities; often anthropomorphic.

Gracile australopithecines The earliest group of australopithecines, usually differentiated from the robust australopithecines by their lighter dentition and smaller faces.

Group marriage Marriage in which more than one man is married to more than one woman at the same time; not customary in any known human society.

Half-life The time it takes for half of the atoms of a radioactive substance to decay into atoms of a different substance.

Handaxe A teardrop-shaped stone tool characteristic of Acheulian assemblages.

Hard hammer A technique of stone tool manufacture where one stone is used to knock flakes from another stone. Flakes produced through hard hammer percussion are usually large and crude.

Headman A person who holds a powerless but symbolically unifying position in a community within an egalitarian society; may exercise influence but has no power to impose sanctions.

Hermeneutics The study of meaning.

Heterozygous Possessing differing genes or alleles in corresponding locations on a pair of chromosomes.

Hieroglyphics "Picture writing," as in ancient Egypt and in Mayan sites in Mesoamerica (Mexico and Central America).

Historical linguistics The study of how languages change over time.

Holistic Refers to an approach that studies many aspects of a multifaceted system.

Hominids The group of hominoids consisting of humans and their direct ancestors. It contains at least two genera: *Homo* and *Australopithecus*.

Hominoids The group of catarrhines that includes both apes and humans.

Homo Genus to which modern humans and their ancestors belong.

Homo erectus The first hominid species to be widely distributed in the Old World. The earliest finds are possibly 1.8 million years old. The brain (averaging 895–1,040 cc) was larger than that found in any of the australopithecines or *H. habilis* but smaller than the average brain of a modern human.

Homo ergaster The African form of *Homo erectus*. Many paleoanthropologists do not make a formal distinction between *Homo ergaster* and *Homo erectus*.

Homo floresiensis A dwarf species of hominid that lived on the Indonesian island of Flores until about 12,000 years ago and probably descended from an isolated *Homo erectus* population.

Homo habilis Dating from about 2 million years ago, an early species belonging to our genus, *Homo*, with cranial capacities averaging about 630–640 cc, about 50 percent of the brain capacity of modern humans.

Homo heidelbergensis A transitional species between *Homo erectus* and *Homo sapiens.*

Homo neandertalensis The technical name for the Neandertals, a group of robust and otherwise anatomically distinct hominids that are close relatives of modern humans—so close that some believe they should be classified as *Homo sapiens neandertalensis.*

Homo rudolfensis Early species belonging to our genus, *Homo.* Similar enough to *Homo habilis* that some paleoanthropologists make no distinction between the two.

Homo sapiens All living people belong to one biological species, *Homo sapiens,* which means that all human populations on earth can successfully interbreed. The first *Homo sapiens* may have emerged about 200,000 years ago.

Homo sapiens sapiens Modern-looking humans, undisputed examples of which appeared about 50,000 years ago; may have appeared earlier.

Homozygous Possessing two identical genes or alleles in corresponding locations on a pair of chromosomes.

Horticulture Plant cultivation carried out with relatively simple tools and methods; nature is allowed to replace nutrients in the soil, in the absence of permanently cultivated fields.

Human paleontology The study of the emergence of humans and their later physical evolution. Also called *paleoanthropology.*

Human variation The study of how and why contemporary human populations vary biologically.

Hunter-gatherers People who collect food from naturally occurring resources, that is, wild plants, animals, and fish. The term *hunter-gatherers* minimizes sometimes heavy dependence on fishing. Also referred to as *foragers* or *food collectors.*

Hybridization The creation of a viable offspring from the mating of two different species.

Hylobates The family of hominoids that includes gibbons and siamangs; often referred to as the lesser apes (as compared with the great apes such as gorillas and chimpanzees).

Hypotheses Predictions, which may be derived from theories, about how variables are related.

Hypoxia A condition of oxygen deficiency that often occurs at high altitudes. The percentage of oxygen in the air is the same as at lower altitudes, but because the barometric pressure is lower, less oxygen is taken in with each breath. Often, breathing becomes more rapid, the heart beats faster, and activity is more difficult.

Incest taboo Prohibition of sexual intercourse or marriage between mother and son, father and daughter, and brother and sister; often extends to other relatives.

Independent family A family unit consisting of one monogamous (nuclear) family, or one polygynous or one polyandrous family.

Indicator artifacts Items that changed relatively rapidly and that, thus, can be used to indicate the relative age of associated items.

Indirect dowry Goods given by the groom's kin to the bride (or her father, who passes most of them to her) at or before her marriage.

Indirect percussion A toolmaking technique common in the Upper Paleolithic. After shaping a core into a pyramidal or cylindrical form, the toolmaker can put a punch of antler or wood or another hard material into position and strike it with a hammer. Using a hammer-struck punch enabled toolmakers to strike off consistently shaped blades.

Insectivore The order or major grouping of mammals, including modern shrews and moles, that is adapted to feeding on insects.

Intensive agriculture Food production characterized by the permanent cultivation of fields and made possible by the use of the plow, draft animals or machines, fertilizers, irrigation, water-storage techniques, and other complex agricultural techniques.

Kenyanthropus platyops A nearly complete 3.5-million-year-old skull found in western Kenya. It is thought by some scholars to be a species of gracile australopithecine (and hence should not be regarded as a separate genus).

Kenyapithecus An apelike primate from the middle Miocene found in East Africa. It had very thickly enameled teeth and robust jaws, suggesting a diet of hard, tough foods. Probably somewhat terrestrial.

Kindred A bilateral set of close relatives.

Knuckle walking A locomotor pattern of primates such as the chimpanzee and gorilla in which the weight of the upper part of the body is supported on the thickly padded knuckles of the hands.

Laws (scientific) Associations or relationships that almost all scientists accept.

Levalloisian method A method that allowed flake tools of a predetermined size to be produced from a shaped core. The toolmakers first shaped the core and prepared a "striking platform" at one end. Flakes of predetermined and standard sizes could then be knocked off. Although some Levallois flakes date from as far back as 400,000 years ago, they are found more frequently in Mousterian tool kits.

Lexical content Vocabulary or lexicon.

Lexicon The words and morphs, and their meanings, of a language; approximated by a dictionary.

Lineage A set of kin whose members trace descent from a common ancestor through known links.

Lithics The technical name for tools made from stone.

Lower Paleolithic The period of the Oldowan and Acheulian stone tool traditions.

Magic The performance of certain rituals that are believed to compel the supernatural powers to act in particular ways.

Maladaptive Traits that diminish the chances of survival and reproduction in a particular environment.

Maladaptive customs Cultural traits that diminish the chances of survival and reproduction in a particular environment.

Mana A supernatural, impersonal force that inhabits certain objects or people and is believed to confer success and/or strength.

Manumission The granting of freedom to a slave.

Market or commercial exchange Transactions in which the "prices" are subject to supply and demand, whether or not the transactions occur in a marketplace.

Marriage A socially approved sexual and economic union, usually between a man and a woman, that is presumed, both by the couple and by others, to be more or less permanent, and that subsumes reciprocal rights and obligations between the two spouses and their future children.

Matriclan A clan tracing descent through the female line.

Matrilineage A kin group whose members trace descent through known links in the female line from a common female ancestor.

Matrilineal descent The rule of descent that affiliates individuals with kin of both sexes related to them through women only.

Matrilocal residence A pattern of residence in which a married couple lives with or near the wife's parents.

Measure To describe how something compares with other things on some scale of variation.

Mediation The process by which a third party tries to bring about a settlement in the absence of formal authority to force a settlement.

Medical anthropology The application of anthropological knowledge to the study of health and illness.

Mediums Part-time religious practitioners who are asked to heal and divine while in a trance.

Meiosis The process by which reproductive cells are formed. In this process of division, the number of chromosomes in the newly formed cells is reduced by half, so that when fertilization occurs the resulting organism has the normal number of chromosomes appropriate to its species, rather than double that number.

Mesolithic The archaeological period in the Old World beginning about 12,000 B.C. Humans were starting to settle down in semipermanent camps and villages, as people began to depend less on big game (which they used to have to follow over long distances) and more on relatively stationary food resources such as fish, shellfish, small game, and wild plants rich in carbohydrates, proteins, and oils.

Messenger RNA (mRNA) A type of ribonucleic acid that is used in the cell to copy the DNA code for use in protein synthesis.

Microlith A small, razorlike blade fragment that was probably attached in a series to a wooden or bone handle to form a cutting edge.

Middle Paleolithic The time period of the Mousterian stone tool tradition.

Miocene The geological epoch from 24 million to 5.2 million years ago.

Mitosis Cellular reproduction or growth involving the duplication of chromosome pairs.

Moiety A unilineal descent group in a society that is divided into two such maximal groups; there may be smaller unilineal descent groups as well.

Monogamy Marriage between only one man and only one woman at a time.

Monotheistic Believing that there is only one high god and that all other supernatural beings are subordinate to, or are alternative manifestations of, this supreme being.

Morph The smallest unit of a language that has a meaning.

Morpheme One or more morphs with the same meaning.

Morphology The study of how sound sequences convey meaning.

Mousterian tool assemblage Named after the tool assemblage found in a rock shelter at Le Moustier in the Dordogne region of southwestern France. Compared with an Acheulian assemblage, the Middle Paleolithic (40,000–300,000 years ago) Mousterian has a smaller proportion of large core tools such as hand axes and cleavers and a bigger proportion of small flake tools such as scrapers. Flakes were often altered or "retouched" by striking small flakes or chips from one or more edges.

Mutation A change in the DNA sequence, producing an altered gene.

Natural selection The outcome of processes that affect the frequencies of traits in a particular environment.

Traits that enhance survival and reproductive success increase in frequency over time.

Neandertal The common name for the species *Homo neandertalensis*.

Negotiation The process by which the parties to a dispute try to resolve it themselves.

Neolithic Originally meaning "the new stone age," now meaning the presence of domesticated plants and animals. The earliest evidence of domestication comes from the Near East about 8000 B.C.

Neolocal residence A pattern of residence whereby a married couple lives separately, and usually at some distance, from the kin of both spouses.

Nocturnal Active during the night.

Nonfraternal polyandry Marriage of a woman to two or more men who are not brothers.

Nonsororal polygyny Marriage of a man to two or more women who are not sisters.

Normalizing selection The type of natural selection that removes harmful genes that arose by mutation.

Norms Standards or rules about acceptable behavior in a society. The importance of a norm usually can be judged by how members of a society respond when the norm is violated.

Nuclear family A family consisting of a married couple and their young children.

Oath The act of calling upon a deity to bear witness to the truth of what one says.

Obsidian A volcanic glass that can be used to make mirrors or sharp-edged tools.

Occipital torus A ridge of bone running horizontally across the back of the skull in apes and some hominids.

Oldowan The earliest stone toolmaking tradition, named after the tools found in Bed I at Olduvai Gorge, Tanzania, from about 2.5 million years ago. The stone artifacts include core tools and sharp-edged flakes made by striking one stone against another. Flake tools predominate. Among the core tools, so-called choppers are common.

Oligocene The geological epoch 34 million to 24 million years ago during which definite anthropoids emerged.

Omnivorous Eating both meat and vegetation.

Omomyid A type of prosimian with many tarsierlike features that appeared in the early Eocene.

Operational definition A description of the procedure that is followed in measuring a variable.

Opposable thumb A thumb that can touch the tips of all the other fingers.

Optimal foraging theory The theory that individuals seek to maximize the returns (in calories and nutrients)

on their labor in deciding which animals and plants they will go after.

Ordeal A means of determining guilt or innocence by submitting the accused to dangerous or painful tests believed to be under supernatural control.

Orrorin tugenensis An apparently bipedal primate dating to between 5.8 and 6 million years, making it possibly the earliest known hominid.

Paleoanthropology See **Human paleontology**.

Paleocene The geological epoch 65 million to 55 million years ago.

Parallel cousins Children of siblings of the same sex. One's parallel cousins are the father's brothers' children and the mother's sisters' children.

Parapithecids Small monkeylike Oligocene primates found in the Fayum area of Egypt.

Participant-observation Living among the people being studied—observing, questioning, and (when possible) taking part in the important events of the group. Writing or otherwise recording notes on observations, questions asked and answered, and things to check out later are parts of participant-observation.

Pastoralism A form of subsistence technology in which food-getting is based directly or indirectly on the maintenance of domesticated animals.

Patriclan A clan tracing descent through the male line.

Patrilineage A kin group whose members trace descent through known links in the male line from a common male ancestor.

Patrilineal descent The rule of descent that affiliates individuals with kin of both sexes related to them through men only.

Patrilocal residence A pattern of residence in which a married couple lives with or near the husband's parents.

Peasants Rural people who produce food for their own subsistence but who must also contribute or sell their surpluses to others (in towns and cities) who do not produce their own food.

Percussion flaking A toolmaking technique in which one stone is struck with another to remove a flake.

Phenotype The observable physical appearance of an organism, which may or may not reflect its genotype or total genetic constitution. Phenotype is usually affected by both genetic and environmental conditions.

Phone A speech sound in a language.

Phoneme A sound or set of sounds that makes a difference in meaning to the speakers of the language.

Phonology The study of the sounds in a language and how they are used.

Phratry A unilineal descent group composed of a number of supposedly related clans (sibs).

Physical (biological) anthropology See **Biological (physical) anthropology**.

Pierolapithecus A middle Miocene ape that has wrists and vertebrae that would have made it capable of brachiation, but also has relatively short fingers like modern monkeys.

Platyrrhines The group of anthropoids that have broad, flat-bridged noses, with nostrils facing outward; these monkeys are currently found only in the New World (Central and South America).

Pleistocene A geological epoch that started 1.6 million years ago and, according to some, continues into the present. During this period, glaciers have often covered much of the earth's surface and humans became the dominant life-form.

Plesiadapis The most well known of the plesiadapiforms, possibly an archaic primate.

Pliocene The geological epoch 5.2 million to 1.6 million years ago during which the earliest definite hominids appeared.

Polyandry The marriage of one woman to more than one man at a time.

Polygamy Plural marriage; one individual is married to more than one spouse simultaneously. **Polygyny** and **polyandry** are types of polygamy.

Polygyny The marriage of one man to more than one woman at a time.

Polyphony Two or more melodies sung simultaneously.

Polytheistic Recognizing many gods, none of whom is believed to be superordinate.

Pongids Hominoids whose members include both the living and extinct apes.

Postpartum sex taboo Prohibition of sexual intercourse between a couple for a period of time after the birth of their child.

Potassium-argon (K-Ar) dating A chronometric dating method that uses the rate of decay of a radioactive form of potassium (^{40}K) into argon (^{40}Ar) to date samples from 5,000 years to 3 billion years old. The K-Ar method dates the minerals and rocks in a deposit, not the fossils themselves.

Potlatch A feast among Pacific Northwest Native Americans at which great quantities of food and goods are given to the guests in order to gain prestige for the host(s).

Power The ability to make others do what they do not want to do or influence based on the threat of force.

Practicing anthropology See **Applied (practicing) anthropology**.

Prehensile Adapted for grasping objects.

Pressure flaking Toolmaking technique whereby small flakes are struck off by pressing against the core with a bone, antler, or wooden tool.

Prestige Being accorded particular respect or honor.

Priests Generally full-time specialists, with very high status, who are thought to be able to relate to superior or high gods beyond the ordinary person's access or control.

Primary subsistence activities The food-getting activities: gathering, hunting, fishing, herding, and agriculture.

Primate A member of the mammalian order Primates, divided into the two suborders of prosimians and anthropoids.

Primatologists Researchers who study primates.

Proconsul The best-known genus of proto-apes from the early Miocene.

Prognathic A physical feature that is sticking out or pushed forward, such as the faces in apes and some hominid species.

Propliopithecids Apelike anthropoids dating from the early Oligocene, found in the Fayum area of Egypt.

Prosimians Literally "pre-monkeys," one of the two suborders of primates; includes lemurs, lorises, and tarsiers.

Protolanguage A hypothesized ancestral language from which two or more languages seem to have derived.

Quadrupeds Animals that walk on all fours.

Race In biology, race refers to a subpopulation or variety of a species that differs somewhat in gene frequencies from other varieties of the species. All members of a species can interbreed and produce viable offspring. Many anthropologists do not think that the concept of race is usefully applied to humans because humans do not fall into geographic populations that can be easily distinguished in terms of different sets of biological or physical traits. Thus, race in humans is largely a culturally assigned category.

Rachis The seed-bearing part of a plant. In the wild variety of grain, the rachis shatters easily, releasing the seeds. Domesticated grains have a tough rachis, which does not shatter easily.

Racism The belief, without scientific basis, that some "races" are inferior to others.

Radiocarbon, or carbon-14 (^{14}C) dating A dating method uses the decay of carbon-14 to date organic remains. It is reliable for dating once-living matter up to 50,000 years old.

Raiding A short-term use of force, generally planned and organized, to realize a limited objective.

Rank societies Societies that do not have any unequal access to economic resources or power, but with social groups that have unequal access to status positions and prestige.

Recessive An allele phenotypically suppressed in the heterozygous form and expressed only in the homozygous form.

Reciprocity Giving and taking (not politically arranged) without the use of money.

Redistribution The accumulation of goods (or labor) by a particular person or in a particular place and their subsequent distribution.

Relative dating A method of dating fossils that determines the age of a specimen or deposit relative to a known specimen or deposit.

Religion Any set of attitudes, beliefs, and practices pertaining to supernatural power, whether that power rests in forces, gods, spirits, ghosts, or demons.

Revitalization movements New religious movements intended to save a culture by infusing it with a new purpose and life.

Revolution A usually violent replacement of a society's rulers.

Ribosome A structure in the cell used in making proteins.

Rituals Repetitive sets of behaviors that occur in essentially the same patterns every time they occur. Religious rituals involve the supernatural in some way.

Robust australopithecines A later group of australopithecines usually differentiated from the gracile australopithecines by their heavier dentition and larger faces.

Rules of descent Rules that connect individuals with particular sets of kin because of known or presumed common ancestry.

Sagittal crest A ridge of bone running along the top of the skull in apes and early hominids.

Sagittal keel An inverted V-shaped ridge running along the top of the skull in *Homo erectus*.

Sahelanthropus tchadensis A hominoid found in Chad dating to around 7 million years ago.

Savanna Tropical grassland.

Secondary subsistence activities Activities that involve the preparation and processing of food either to make it edible or to store it.

Sedentarism Settled life.

Segmentary lineage system A hierarchy of more inclusive lineages; usually functions only in conflict situations.

Segregation The random sorting of chromosomes in meiosis.

Sex differences The typical differences between females and males that are most likely due to biological differences.

Sexual dimorphism A marked difference in size and appearance between males and females of a species.

Shaman A religious intermediary, usually part time, whose primary function is to cure people through sacred songs, pantomime, and other means; sometimes called a witch doctor by Westerners.

Shifting cultivation See **Extensive cultivation**.

Sib See **Clan**.

Siblings A person's brothers and sisters.

Sickle-cell anemia (sicklemia) A condition in which red blood cells assume a crescent (sickle) shape when deprived of oxygen, instead of the normal (disk) shape. The sickle-shaped red blood cells do not move through the body as readily as normal cells, and thus cause damage to the heart, lungs, brain, and other vital organs.

Sites Locations where the material remains of human activity have been preserved in a way that archaeologists or paleoanthropologists can recover them.

Sivapithecus A genus of ape from the later Miocene known for its thickly enameled teeth, suggesting a diet of hard, tough, or gritty items. Found primarily in western and southern Asia and now thought to be ancestral to orangutans.

Slash-and-burn A form of shifting cultivation in which the natural vegetation is cut down and burned off. The cleared ground is used for a short time and then left to regenerate.

Slaves A class of people who do not own their own labor or the products thereof.

Society A group of people who occupy a particular territory and speak a common language not generally understood by neighboring peoples. By this definition, societies do not necessarily correspond to nations.

Sociolinguistics The study of cultural and subcultural patterns of speaking in different social contexts.

Soft hammer A technique of stone tool manufacture in which a bone or wood hammer is used to strike flakes from a stone.

Sorcery The use of certain materials to invoke supernatural powers to harm people.

Sororal polygyny The marriage of a man to two or more sisters at the same time.

Speciation The development of a new species.

Species A population that consists of organisms able to interbreed and produce viable and fertile offspring.

Spirits Unnamed supernatural beings of nonhuman origin who are beneath the gods in prestige and often closer to the people; may be helpful, mischievous, or evil.

State An autonomous political unit with centralized decision making over many communities with power to govern by force (e.g., to collect taxes, draft people for work and war, and make and enforce laws). Most states have cities with public buildings; full-time craft and religious specialists; an "official" art style; a hierarchical social structure topped by an elite class; and a governmental monopoly on the legitimate use of force to implement policies.

State organization A society is described as having state organization when it includes one or more states.

Statistical association A relationship or correlation between two or more variables that is unlikely to be due to chance.

Stratified An archaeological deposit that contains successive layers or strata.

Stratigraphy The study of how different rock formations and fossils are laid down in successive layers or strata. Older layers are generally deeper or lower than more recent layers.

Structural linguistics See **Descriptive (structural) linguistics**.

Subculture The shared customs of a subgroup within a society.

Subsistence economies Economies in which almost all able-bodied adults are largely engaged in getting food for themselves and their families.

Supernatural Believed to be not human or not subject to the laws of nature.

Symbolic communication An arbitrary (not obviously meaningful) gesture, call, word, or sentence that has meaning even when its *referent* is not present.

Syntax The ways in which words are arranged to form phrases and sentences.

Taboo A prohibition that, if violated, is believed to bring supernatural punishment.

Taurodontism Having teeth with an enlarged pulp cavity.

Terrestrial Adapted to living on the ground.

Terrorism The use or threat of violence to create terror in others, usually for political purposes.

Theoretical construct Something that cannot be observed or verified directly.

Theories Explanations of associations or laws.

Totem A plant or animal associated with a clan (sib) as a means of group identification; may have other special significance for the group.

Tribal organization The kind of political organization in which local communities mostly act autonomously but there are kin groups (such as clans) or associations (such as age-sets) that can temporarily integrate a number of local groups into a larger unit.

Tribe A territorial population in which there are kin or nonkin groups with representatives in a number of local groups.

Unifacial tool A tool worked or flaked on one side only.

Unilineal descent Affiliation with a group of kin through descent links of one sex only.

Unilocal residence A pattern of residence (patrilocal, matrilocal, or avunculocal) that specifies just one set of relatives that the married couple lives with or near.

Upper Paleolithic The time period associated with the emergence of modern humans and their spread around the world.

Variable A thing or quantity that varies.

Vertical clinging and leaping A locomotor pattern characteristic of several primates, including tarsiers and galagos. The animal normally rests by clinging to a branch in a vertical position and uses its hind limbs alone to push off from one vertical position to another.

Warfare Violence between political entities such as communities, districts, or nations.

Witchcraft The practice of attempting to harm people by supernatural means, but through emotions and thought alone, not through the use of tangible objects.

"Y-5" pattern Refers to the pattern of cusps on human molars. When looked at from the top, the cusps of the molars form a Y opening toward the cheek.

Notes

Chapter 1

1. Durham 1991, 228–37; Harrison 1975.
2. Chimpanzee Sequencing and Analysis Consortium 2005.
3. Nolan 2003, 2.
4. Van Willigen 2002, 7.
5. Kedia and van Willigen 2005; Miracle 2009.
6. Hempel 1965, 139.
7. J. Whiting 1964.
8. Nagel 1961, 83–90.
9. Ibid., 85. See also McCain and Segal 1988, 75–79.
10. McCain and Segal 1988, 62–64.
11. Caws 1969, 1378.
12. McCain and Segal 1988, 56–57, 131–32.
13. J. Whiting 1964, 519–20.
14. McCain and Segal 1988, 67–69.
15. Blalock 1972, 15–20; Thomas 1986, 18–28. See also M. Ember 1970, 701–03.
16. Ogburn 1922, 200–80.

Chapter 2

1. Bernard 2001, 323.
2. Peacock 1986, 54.
3. Lawless et al. 1983, xi–xxi; Peacock 1986, 54–65.
4. Romney et al. 1986.
5. Bernard 2001, 190.
6. See Murdock and White 1969 for a description of the SCCS sample; the HRAF Collection of Ethnography is described at www.yale.edu/hraf; for a description of many different cross-cultural samples, see C. R. Ember and M. Ember 2009.
7. Martin 1990, 42.
8. Isaac 1997.
9. F. H. Brown 1992.
10. Gentner and Lippolt 1963.
11. American Anthropological Association 1991.
12. Szklut and Reed 1991.
13. Lambert et al. 2000, 405.
14. Hill and Hurtado 2004.
15. Waldbaum 2005.

Chapter 3

1. Sagan 1975.
2. Lovejoy 1964, 58–63.
3. Lovejoy 1964, 63.
4. Mayr 1982, 339–60.
5. Wallace 1858/1970.
6. Mayr 1982, 423.
7. Darwin had a still longer title. It continued, *Or the Preservation of the Favoured Races in the Struggle for Life*. Darwin's notion of "struggle for life" is often misinterpreted to refer to a war of all against all. Although animals may fight with each other at times over access to resources, Darwin was referring mainly to their metaphorical "struggle" with the environment, particularly to obtain food.
8. Darwin 1970/1859.
9. Futuyma 1982 provides an overview of this long controversy.
10. Huxley 1970.
11. R. N. Brandon 1990, 6–7.
12. G. Williams 1992, 7.

13. J. M. Smith 1989, 42–45.
14. Hooper 2002.
15. Grant 2002.
16. Devilliers and Chaline 1993, 22–23.
17. Beadle and Beadle 1966, 216.
18. Golden et al. 2000; Hayden 2000; Marshall 2000; Pennisi 2000; Travis 2000.
19. Daiger 2005.
20. Olsen 2002.
21. Dobzhansky 1962, 138–40.
22. Relethford 1990, 94.
23. G. A. Harrison et al. 1988, 198–200.
24. Brace 1996.
25. Grant and Grant 2002.
26. Rice and Salt 1988, cited in Rennie 2002, 83.
27. Chatterjee 1997.
28. Paley 1810.
29. Center for Renewal of Science and Culture, "The Wedge Strategy," cited in Forrest 2001, 16.
30. McMullin 2001, 174.
31. Rennie 2002.
32. Barash 1977.
33. Krebs and Davies 1984; 1987.
34. Badcock 2000.
35. Boyd and Richerson 2005.
36. Schaller 1972.
37. Hare et al. 2002.
38. E. O. Wilson 1975.
39. B. Low 2009.
40. D. Campbell 1965.
41. Nissen 1958.
42. Boyd and Richerson 1985/1996.
43. Durham 1991.

Chapter 4

1. See Durham 1991, 154–225, for an extensive discussion of the relationship between genes and culture.
2. Stewart 1950.
3. *Genesis* 17: 9–15.
4. Hanna, Little, and Austin 1989, 133–36; G. A. Harrison et al. 1988, 504–07.
5. D. F. Roberts 1953, cited in Garn 1971, 73. See also Roberts 1978.
6. D. F. Roberts 1953.
7. G. A. Harrison et al. 1988, 308–10.
8. Polednak 1974, 49–57. See also Branda and Eaton 1978.
9. Loomis 1967.
10. Post, Daniels, and Binford 1975, 65–80.
11. Holden 2000; Jablonski and Chaplin 2000.
12. Stini 1975, 53.
13. Mazess 1975.
14. Greksa and Beall 1989, 223.
15. Greksa and Beall 1989, 226.
16. Frisancho and Greksa 1989, 204.
17. Eveleth and Tanner 1990, 176–79.
18. Eveleth and Tanner 1990, 205–06.
19. Bogin 1988, 105–06.
20. G. A. Harrison et al. 1988, 300.
21. G. A. Harrison et al. 1988, 198.

22. Huss-Ashmore and Johnston 1985, 482–83.
23. G. A. Harrison et al. 1988, 385–86.
24. Martorell 1980, 81–106.
25. Martorell et al. 1991.
26. Gray and Wolfe 1980; 2009; Gunders and Whiting 1968; Landauer and Whiting 1964; 1981.
27. Landauer and Whiting 1981.
28. Eveleth and Tanner 1990, 205.
29. Landauer 1973.
30. Motulsky 1971, 223.
31. Motulsky 1971, 226.
32. Motulsky 1971, 229.
33. Motulsky 1971, 230.
34. Motulsky 1971, 233.
35. Ibid.
36. Black 1992.
37. An examination of the epidemic diseases spread by Europeans can be found in Chapter 11 of J. Diamond 1997.
38. Neel et al. 1970; in his 2000 work, Patrick Tierney accused the Neel research team of fueling a measles outbreak among the Yanomamö by administering a harmful measles vaccine. However, the scientific evidence indicates that Tierney is wrong. The vaccine Neel and associates used was widely pretested and there was no way that the vaccine could have caused the epidemic. Measles was already spreading in the Amazon, which was why the vaccination program was initiated. See Gregor and Gross 2004.
39. Relethford 1990, 425–27.
40. Merbs 1992.
41. Durham 1991, 105–07.
42. Ibid.
43. Ibid.
44. G. A. Harrison et al. 1988, 231.
45. For a review of the early research, see Durham 1991, 123–27. The particular form of malaria that is discussed is caused by the species *Plasmodium falciparum*.
46. See Madigral 1989 for a report of her own research and a review of earlier studies.
47. Pennisi 2001b.
48. Durham 1991, 124–45.
49. Motulsky 1971, 238.
50. J. Diamond 1993.
51. Molnar 1998, 158; Pennisi 2001a.
52. Durham 1991, 230.
53. Brodey 1971.
54. Durham 1991, 233–35.
55. Relethford 1990, 127.
56. McCracken 1971; see also references to the work of F. J. Simoons as referred to in Durham 1991, 240–41.
57. Huang 2002; McCracken 1971.
58. Durham 1991, 263–69.
59. Marks 1994; Shanklin 1993, 15–17.
60. Molnar 1998, 19.
61. Brace et al. 1993.
62. Brooks et al. 1993.
63. Brace et al. 1993.
64. Brooks et al. 1993.
65. M. King and Motulsky 2002.
66. Goodrich 1959, 7–15.
67. Coe 1966, 74–76.
68. Thompson 1966, 89.
69. McNeill 1976.
70. Motulsky 1971, 232.
71. Ibid.
72. MacArthur and Wilson 1967.
73. Johanson and Edey 1981.
74. Peregrine et al. 2000; 2003.
75. Lieberman 1999.
76. Klineberg 1935; 1944.
77. Ibid.
78. Jensen 1969.
79. Herrnstein and Murray 1994.
80. Kamin 1995.
81. M. W. Smith 1974.
82. Dobzhansky 1973, 11.
83. Dobzhansky 1973, 14–15.
84. Research by Sandra Scarr and others reported in Boyd and Richerson 1985, 56.
85. Nisbett 2009.
86. Dobzhansky 1962, 243.
87. Haldane 1963.
88. Simpson 1971, 297–308.

Chapter 5

1. The classic description of common primate traits is from Napier and Napier 1967. For primate social organization, see Smuts et al. 1987.
2. Bearder 1987, 14.
3. Richard 1985, 22ff.
4. Doyle and Martin 1979; Tattersall 1982.
5. Richard 1987, 32.
6. Bearder 1987, 13.
7. MacKinnon and MacKinnon 1980.
8. Cartmill 1992a, 28; Fleagle 1999, 118–22.
9. Napier and Napier 1967, 32–33.
10. Richard 1985, 164–65.
11. Cartmill 1992a, 29; Goldizen 1987, 34; see also Eisenberg 1977; Fleagle 1999, 168–74; Sussman and Kinzey 1984.
12. Eisenberg 1977, 15–17.
13. Crockett and Eisenberg 1987; Robinson and Janson 1987; Robinson, Wright, and Kinzey 1987.
14. Hrdy 1977, 18.
15. Napier 1970, 80–82.
16. Fedigan 1982, 11.
17. Fleagle 1999, 302.
18. Clark Le Gros 1964, 184.
19. Pennisi 2007.
20. Preuschoft et al. 1984.
21. Carpenter 1940; Chivers 1974.
22. Rijksen 1978, 22.
23. Fossey 1983, xvi.
24. Tuttle 1986, 99–114.
25. Schaller 1963; 1964.
26. Fossey 1983, 47.
27. Harcourt 1979, 187–92.
28. Susman 1984; F. J. White 1996.
29. Goodall 1963; van Lawick-Goodall 1971.
30. Teleki 1973.
31. Stanford 2009.
32. Stanford 2009.
33. Falk 1987.
34. Female bonobos, or pygmy chimpanzees, engage in sexual intercourse nearly as often as human females—see Thompson-Handler et al. 1984.

35. By male–female bonding, we mean that at least one of the sexes is "faithful," that is, typically has intercourse with just one opposite-sex partner throughout at least one estrus or menstrual cycle or breeding season. Note that the bonding may not be monogamous; an individual may be bonded to more than one individual of the opposite sex. See M. Ember and C. R. Ember 1979.
36. C. R. Ember and M. Ember 1984, 207.
37. C. R. Ember and M. Ember 1984, 208–09.
38. de Waal and Lanting 1997.
39. Rumbaugh 1970, 52–58.
40. Boesche et al. 1994.
41. Observation by others cited by A. Jolly 1985, 53.
42. Hannah and McGrew 1987.
43. Seyfarth, Cheney, and Marler 1980.
44. Gardner and Gardner 1969.
45. Gardner and Gardner 1980.
46. Greenfield and Savage-Rumbaugh 1990.
47. Gingerich 1986; Szalay 1972; Szalay, Tattersall, and Decker 1975.
48. Cartmill 2009; Ciochon and Etler 1994, 41; Fleagle 1994.
49. Block and Boyer 2002.
50. Conroy 1990, 49–53.
51. Conroy 1990, 53.
52. Habicht 1979.
53. Sussman 1991.
54. Cartmill 1974; Richard 1985, 31.
55. Szalay 1968.
56. Cartmill 1974; for more recent statements, see Cartmill 1992b; 2009.
57. Fleagle 1994, 22–23.
58. Conroy 1990, 119.
59. Radinsky 1967.
60. Conroy 1990, 105; Fleagle 1994, 21.
61. Alexander 1992; Conroy 1990, 111.
62. Kay, Ross, and Williams 1997.
63. Conroy 1990, 46; Martin 1990, 46.
64. Fleagle and Kay 1985, 25; Kay, Ross, and Williams 1997.
65. Jaeger et al. 1999.
66. Simons 1995; Simons and Rassmussen 1996.
67. Kay 2000, 441.
68. Conroy 1990, 156; Kay 2000, 441–42.
69. Fleagle 1999, 404–09.
70. Rosenberger 1979.
71. Fleagle and Kay 1987.
72. Aiello 1993; Hartwig 1994.
73. Andrews 2000b, 486.
74. Conroy 1990, 160–61; Fleagle and Kay 1985, 25, 30.
75. Fleagle 1999, 413–15; Fleagle and Kay 1983, 205.
76. Begun 2002.
77. Conroy 1990, 206–11.
78. Begun 2002.
79. Andrews 2000a, 485.
80. Begun 2002.
81. Ward et al. 1999; Zimmer 1999.
82. Begun 2002; Kelley 1992, 225.
83. Moyà-Solà et al. 2004.
84. T. Harrison 1986; T. Harrison and Rook 1997.
85. Ward 1997.
86. Begun 2002.
87. Begun 2002.
88. Fleagle 1999, 480–83.
89. Bilsborough 1992, 65.
90. Simons 1992, 207.

Chapter 6

1. Thorpe, Holder, and Crompton 2007.
2. Rose 1984.
3. Bilsborough 1992, 64–65.
4. Oakley 1964.
5. Kingston, Marino, and Hill 1994.
6. Hewes 1961.
7. Shipman 1986; Trinkaus 1987.
8. Lovejoy 1981.
9. C. Jolly 1970.
10. Washburn 1960.
11. Pilbeam 1972, 153.
12. Wolpoff 1971.
13. Savage-Rumbaugh 1994.
14. Wolpoff 1983.
15. Zimmer 2004.
16. Zihlman 1992.
17. Wheeler 1984; 1991.
18. Falk 1988.
19. Zihlman 1992, 414.
20. Lovejoy 1988.
21. Aiello and Dean 1990, 268–74.
22. Aiello and Dean 1990, 507–08.
23. Gibbons 2002.
24. Brunet et al. 2002; Wong 2003.
25. Aiello and Collard 2001; Pickford et al. 2002; Wong 2003.
26. Richmond and Jungers 2008.
27. T. D. White, Suwa, and Asfaw 1995.
28. T. D. White, Suwa, and Asfaw 1994.
29. Hailie-Selassie 2001.
30. Rose 1984; Susman et al. 1985.
31. Conroy 1990, 274; Culotta 1995; Wilford 1995.
32. Culotta 1995.
33. Leakey et al. 1995.
34. Tattersall and Schwartz 2000, 93.
35. Johanson and White 1979; Simpson 2009; T. D. White et al. 1981.
36. Johanson and Edey 1981, 17–18.
37. Johanson and White 1979.
38. Lewin 1983.
39. Conroy 1990, 291–92; Simpson 2009.
40. Fleagle 1999, 515–18.
41. Fleagle 1999, 515, 520.
42. Grine 1988a.
43. Kimbel et al. 1984.
44. Clarke and Tobias 1995; Jungers 1988b.
45. Lovejoy 1988.
46. Clarke and Tobias 1995; Tattersall and Schwartz 2000, 88–89.
47. Conroy 1990, 280–82.
48. Pilbeam 1972, 107.
49. Holloway 1974.
50. Szalay and Delson 1979, 504.
51. Asfaw et al. 1999.
52. Brunet et al. 1995.
53. Ibid.
54. Leakey et al. 2001.
55. Szalay and Delson 1979, 504; B. Wood 1992.
56. Jungers 1988a; McHenry 1988.
57. Grine 1993; Walker and Leakey 1988.

58. Broom 1950.

59. Fleagle 1999, 522.

60. McHenry 2009.

61. Ibid.

62. Grine 1988b.

63. Stringer 1985.

64. McHenry 2009.

65. Fleagle 1999, 529.

66. McHenry 2009.

67. Fleagle 1999, 511–15.

68. B. Wood 1992.

69. McHenry 2009; Tobias 1994.

70. Simpson 2009.

71. Susman 1994.

72. Ibid.

73. Holden 1997.

74. Leakey 1960.

75. Clark 1970, 68; Schick and Toth 1993, 97–99.

76. Schick and Toth 1993, 153–70.

77. Ibid., 129.

78. Ibid., 157–59.

79. Isaac 1984.

80. Schick and Toth 1993, 175–76.

81. Speth 2009.

82. Shipman 1986. For the idea that scavenging may have been an important food-getting strategy even for protohominids, see Szalay 1975.

83. M. Leakey 1971.

84. Potts 1988, 253–58.

85. Potts 1984.

86. Potts 1988, 278–81.

87. Boyd and Silk 2000, 249–50.

88. Dobzhansky 1962, 196.

89. Bromage and Dean 1985; Gibbons 2008; B. H. Smith 1986.

90. Chapais 2008.

91. Gowlett 2008.

92. McHenry 1982.

93. McHenry 1982.

94. Dunbar and Shultz 2007; Herrmann et al. 2007; Silk 2007.

95. Simpson et al. 2008.

96. Pilbeam and Gould 1974.

97. Leonard 2002.

98. Stedman et al. 2004.

99. Rightmire 2000.

100. Swisher et al. 1994.

101. Balter and Gibbons 2000; Gabunia et al. 2000.

102. Vekua et al. 2002; Gore 2002.

103. Wolpoff and Nkini 1985; see also Balter 2001; Rightmire 2000.

104. Day 1986, 409–12; Fleagle 1999, 534–35; Kramer 2009.

105. Rightmire 2000; Tobias 1994.

106. Franciscus and Trinkaus 1988.

107. Feibel and Brown 1993.

108. Ruff and Walker 1993.

109. Brown et al. 2004; Morwood et al. 2004.

110. Falk et al. 2005.

111. Weston and Lister 2009; Wong 2005.

112. Fleagle 1999, 306.

113. M. Ember and C. R. Ember 1979; cf. Lovejoy 1981.

114. Clayman 1989, 857–58.

115. Bordes 1968, 51–97.

116. Phillipson 1993, 57.

117. Schick and Toth 1993, 227, 233.

118. Ibid., 231–33; Whittaker 1994, 27.

119. Schick and Toth 1993, 258–60; Whittaker 1994, 27.

120. Lawrence Keeley's analysis reported in Schick and Toth 1993, 260; see that page for their analysis of tool use.

121. Calvin 1983.

122. Yamei, Potts, and Baoyin 2000.

123. Ciochon, Olson, and James 1990, 178–83; Pope 1989.

124. Howell 1966.

125. Binford 1987; Klein 1987.

126. L. G. Freeman 1994.

127. A good example of this problem is the ongoing debate about fire use at Zhoukoudian cave, as reported by Weiner et al. 1998.

128. Isaac 1984, 35–36. Other evidence for deliberate use of fire comes from the Swartkrans cave in South Africa and is dated 1 million to 1.5 million years ago; see Brain and Sillen 1988.

129. Goren-Inbar et al. 2004.

130. Binford and Ho 1985.

131. Leonard 2002.

132. Clark 1970, 94–95.

133. Ibid., 96–97.

134. de Lumley 1969.

Chapter 7

1. Stringer 1985.

2. Ibid.

3. Rightmire 1997.

4. Carbonell et al. 2008.

5. Fleagle 1999, 535–37; Rightmire 1997.

6. Spencer 1984.

7. Trinkaus 1985.

8. Stringer 2000.

9. Trinkaus and Shipman 1993a; 1993b.

10. Krings et al. 1997.

11. Ibid.

12. Green et al. 2008; Ovchinnikov et al. 2000.

13. Krause et al. 2007.

14. Lalueza-Fox et al. 2007.

15. Pennisi 2009.

16. Hodgson and Driscoll 2008; Serre et al. 2004.

17. Gibbons 2001; Tattersall 1999, 115–16.

18. Mellars 1996: 405–19.

19. Mellars 1998.

20. Strauss 1989.

21. Schick and Toth 1993, 288–92.

22. Klein 1989, 291–96.

23. Schick and Toth 1993, 288–92; Whittaker 1994, 30–31.

24. Klein 1989, 421–22.

25. Binford and Binford 1969.

26. Fish 1981, 377.

27. Butzer 1982, 42.

28. Phillipson 1993, 63.

29. For the controversy about whether the inhabitants of the Dordogne Valley lived in their homesites year-round, see Binford 1973.

30. Schick and Toth 1993, 292.

31. Klein 1977.

32. Klein 1974.

33. Bordes 1961.

34. T. Patterson 1981.

35. Phillipson 1993, 64.

36. Klein 1983, 38–39.

37. Binford 1984, 195–97. To explain the lack of complete skeletons of large animals, Klein (1983) suggests that the hunters

may have butchered the large animals elsewhere because they could carry home only small cuts.
38. Wilford 1997.
39. Chase and Dibble 1987.
40. Stringer, Hublin, and Vandermeersch 1984, 107.
41. Singer and Wymer 1982, 149.
42. Gibbons 2003.
43. Bräuer 1984, 387–89, 394; Rightmire 1984, 320.
44. Valladas et al. 1988.
45. Stringer et al. 1984, 121.
46. For arguments supporting the single-origin theory, see the chapters by Günter Bräuer, F. Clark Howell, and C. B. Stringer et al., in F. Smith and Spencer 1984. For arguments supporting the multiregional theory, see the chapters by C. L. Brace et al., David W. Frayer, Fred H. Smith, and Milford H. Wolpoff et al. in the same volume.
47. Cann 1988.
48. Cann 1988.
49. Vigilant et al. 1991.
50. Cann, Stoneking, and Wilson 1987.
51. Vigilant et al. 1991.
52. Stoneking 1997.
53. Hammer and Zegura 1996.
54. Hammer and Zegura 2002.
55. Cavalli-Sforza and Feldman 2003.
56. Stringer 2003.
57. Frayer et al. 1993; Wolpoff 1999, 501–04, 727–31.
58. Frayer et al. 1993; Wolpoff 1999, 735–43.
59. D. Lieberman 1995.
60. Templeton 1993.
61. Trinkaus 1986.
62. Eswaran 2002.
63. Templeton 1996; see also Ayala 1995; 1996.
64. Reed et al. 2004.
65. Duarte et al. 1999.
66. Bahn 1998.
67. Tattersall 1999, 198–203.
68. Trinkaus 1986; see also Trinkaus and Howells 1979.
69. Culotta 2005.
70. Klein 2003.
71. R. White 1982.
72. Strauss 1982.
73. Dawson 1992, 24–71.
74. COHMAP 1988.
75. Martin and Wright 1967.
76. Mellars 1994.
77. T. Patterson 1981.
78. Klima 1962.
79. Schick and Toth 1993, 293–99; Whittaker 1994, 33.
80. Whittaker 1994, 31.
81. Bordaz 1970, 68.
82. Whittaker 1994, 33.
83. Phillipson 1993, 60.
84. Bordaz 1970.
85. Ibid.
86. We thank Robert L. Kelly (personal communication) for bringing this possibility to our attention. See also J. D. Clark 1977, 136.
87. Ascher 1961.
88. Semenov 1970, 103. For a more recent discussion of research following this strategy, see Keeley 1980.
89. Klein 1994, 508.
90. Soffer 1993, 38–40.
91. Phillipson 1993, 74.
92. Morell 1995.
93. Henshilwood et al. 2002.
94. Ucko and Rosenfeld 1967.
95. Rice and Paterson 1985; 1986.
96. Rice and Paterson 1985, 98.
97. Hawkins and Kleindienst 2001.
98. Jayaswal 2002.
99. Peregrine and Bellwood 2001.
100. McDonald 1998.
101. Hoffecker, Powers, and Goebel 1993.
102. Gibbons 1995; Roosevelt et al. 1996.
103. Goebel, Waters, and O'Rourke 2008.
104. Dillehay 2000.
105. Gilbert et al. 2008.
106. Greenberg and Ruhlen 1992, 94–99.
107. Turner 1989; see also Kitchen, Miyamoto, and Mulligan (2008) for a more recent reanalysis of genetic and linguistic evidence for a three-stage colonization of the Americas.
108. McDonald 1998; Turner 2005.
109. Wheat 1967.
110. Fagan 1991, 79.
111. Hoffecker et al. 1993.
112. Jennings 1968, 72–88.
113. Judge and Dawson 1972.
114. Wheat 1967.
115. Fagan 1989, 221.
116. Wheat 1967.
117. Ibid.
118. Fagan 1989, 227.
119. Fagan 1991, 192.
120. Fagan 1989, 227.
121. Collins 1976, 88–125.
122. Chard 1969, 171.
123. G. Clark 1975, 101–61.
124. Petersen 1973, 94–96.
125. Daniel 2001.
126. Sassaman 1996, 58–83.
127. Ibid.
128. J. Brown 1983, 5–10.

Chapter 8

1. N. Miller 1992.
2. Crawford 1992; MacNeish 1991, 256; 268; Phillipson 1993, 118.
3. Flannery 1986, 6–8; Pearsall 1992; B. Smith 1992a.
4. Hole 1992.
5. Binford 1971.
6. Flannery 1973a.
7. Simcha, Gopher, and Abbo 2000.
8. Harlan 1967.
9. Flannery 1971.
10. Mellaart 1961.
11. Henry 1989, 214–15.
12. J. A. Brown and Price 1985.
13. Henry 1989, 38–39, 209–10; 1991. See Olszewski 1991 for some questions about the degree of social complexity in Natufian sites.
14. Martin and Wright 1967.
15. A recent analysis of these changes can be found in Kuehn 1998; see also J. A. Brown 1985.
16. Marcus and Flannery 1996, 49–50.
17. Ibid., 50–53.

18. Balter 2007; Jones and Liu 2009.
19. Gorman 1970.
20. Chang 1970; Gorman 1970.
21. J. Clark 1970, 171–72.
22. Phillipson 1993, 111–12.
23. Alroy 2001.
24. Martin 1973.
25. Grayson 1977; 1984. See also Barnosky et al. 2004; Guthrie 1984; L. G. Marshall 1984.
26. Holdaway and Jacomb 2000.
27. M. N. Cohen 1977b, 12, 85.
28. M. N. Cohen 1989, 112–13.
29. M. N. Cohen 1989, 113–15.
30. Flannery 1973b.
31. Patterson 1971.
32. D. Harris 1977; G. Johnson 1977.
33. Lee 1972; Sussman 1972.
34. For some examples of societies that have practiced infanticide, see D. Harris 1977.
35. Howell 1979; Lee 1979.
36. Frisch 1980; Howell 1979.
37. Zohary 1969.
38. Flannery 1965.
39. Hole 1992; MacNeish 1991, 127–28.
40. Chessa et al. 2009; Clutton-Brock 1992.
41. Redman 1978, 167–169.
42. Zeder and Hesse 2000.
43. Hole, Flannery, and Neely 1969.
44. Ibid.
45. Flannery 1986, 3–5; Pringle 1998.
46. Marcus and Flannery 1996, 64–66.
47. Flannery 1986, 6–8.
48. Fedoroff 2003.
49. Flannery 1986, 8–9; Marcus and Flannery 1996, 66–67.
50. Marcus and Flannery 1996, 66–68.
51. Piperno and Stothert 2003.
52. Hole 1992; MacNeish 1991, 37, 47.
53. B. Smith 1992b, 163, 287.
54. Asch and Asch 1978.
55. Clutton-Brock 1992.
56. Müller-Haye 1984.
57. Wenke 1984, 350, 397–98.
58. Chang 1981; MacNeish 1991, 159–63.
59. MacNeish 1991, 267–68.
60. Denham et al. 2003; Neumann 2003.
61. Hole 1992.
62. Phillipson 1993, 118.
63. MacNeish 1991, 314.
64. Clutton-Brock 1992; Hanotte et al. 2002.
65. Cited in MacNeish 1991, 6.
66. Braidwood 1960.
67. Wright 1971.
68. Flannery 1986, 10–11.
69. M. N. Cohen 1977a; 1977b, 279.
70. Byrne 1987, referred to in Blumler and Byrne 1991; see also Henry 1989, 30–38; McCorriston and Hole 1991.
71. Henry 1989, 41.
72. McCorriston and Hole 1991.
73. Henry 1989, 54.
74. Speth and Spielmann 1983.
75. B. White 1973; see also Kasarda 1971.
76. C. R. Ember 1983.
77. Konner and Worthman 1980.

78. Roosevelt 1984; see also Cohen 1987; 2009; M. N. Cohen and Armelagos 1984, 585–602. For evidence suggesting that the transition to food production was not generally associated with declining health, see Starling and Stock 2007; Wood et al. 1992.
79. Roosevelt 1984.
80. Renfrew 1969.
81. Connah 1987; Service 1975; Wenke 1990.
82. Flannery 1972.
83. Flannery 1972; Redman 1978, 215–16.
84. Wright and Johnson 1975.
85. The discussion in the remainder of this section draws from Wright and Johnson 1975; see also G. Johnson 1987.
86. Wright and Johnson 1975.
87. Service 1975.
88. Flannery 1972.
89. Service 1975, 207.
90. Flannery 1972; Service 1975.
91. This description of Sumerian civilization is based on Kramer 1963.
92. Diamond 1989.
93. Helms 1975, 34–36, 54–55; Sanders, Parsons, and Santley 1979.
94. Millon 1967.
95. Millon 1976.
96. Millon 1967.
97. Helms 1975, 61–63; Weaver 1993.
98. Wenke 1984, 289.
99. Connah 1987, 67.
100. Fagan 1989, 428–30.
101. Connah 1987, 216–17.
102. Vogel 2009.
103. Wenke 1984, 305–20.
104. Chang 1981.
105. Chang 1968, 235–55.
106. Haas, Creamer, and Ruiz 2004; Solis, Haas, and Creamer 2001.
107. For an overview, see Lumbreras 1974.
108. M. Fowler 1975.
109. For a more complete review of the available theories, see various chapters in R. Cohen and Service 1978; see also Chapter 1 in Zeder 1991.
110. Wittfogel 1957.
111. Adams 1960; H. T. Wright 1986.
112. Wheatley 1971, 291.
113. Adams 1960.
114. Adams 1981, 244.
115. Adams 1981, 243; Service 1975, 274–75.
116. Carneiro 1970; Sanders and Price 1968, 230–32.
117. M. Harris 1979, 101–02.
118. T. C. Young 1972.
119. Sanders and Price 1968, 141.
120. Blanton et al. 1981, 224. For the apparent absence of population pressure in the Teotihuacàn Valley, see Brumfiel 1976. For the Oaxaca Valley, see Feinman et al. 1985.
121. Wright and Johnson 1975. Carneiro (1988), however, argued the opposite, that the population grew just before the states emerged in southwestern Iran. Whether or not population declined, Frank Hole (1994) has suggested that climate change around that time may have forced local populations to relocate, some to centers that became cities.
122. Polanyi, Arensberg, and Pearson 1957, 257–62; Sanders 1968.
123. Wright and Johnson 1975.
124. Rathje 1971.
125. Chang 1986, 234–94.

126. For a discussion of how political dynamics may play an important role in state formation, see Brumfiel 1983.
127. Johnson and Earle 1987, 324–26.
128. Childe 1950.
129. Service 1975, 12–15, 89–90.
130. J. Diamond 1997, 205–07.
131. Dirks 1993.
132. Johnson and Earle 1987, 243–48, 304–06.
133. Ferguson and Whitehead 1992.
134. Weiss et al. 1993.
135. Grossman 2002; Kerr 1998.
136. Haug et al. 2003.
137. DeMenocal 2001; Haug et al. 2003; Hodell et al. 2001.
138. Holden 1996.

Chapter 9

1. Linton 1945, 30.
2. Sapir 1938, cited by Pelto and Pelto 1975, 1.
3. Pelto and Pelto 1975, 14–15.
4. de Waal 2001, 269.
5. M. F. Brown 2008, 372.
6. Hewlett 2004.
7. Miner 1956, 504–05, reproduced by permission of the American Anthropological Association. Although Miner is not a foreign visitor, he wrote this description in a way that shows how these behaviors might be seen from an outside perspective.
8. Lee 1972.
9. Hatch 1997.
10. Durkheim 1938/1895, 3.
11. Asch 1956.
12. Bond and Smith 1996.
13. Berns et al. 2005.
14. Hall 1966, 159–60.
15. Ibid., 120.
16. R. Brown 1965, 549–609.
17. Chibnik 1981, 256–68.
18. Linton 1936, 306.
19. Ibid., 310–11.
20. Silver 1981.
21. Greenfield, Maynard, and Childs 2000.
22. Rogers 1983, 263–69.
23. Valente 1995, 21.
24. Linton 1936, 326–27.
25. G. M. Foster 1962, 26.
26. Bodley 1990: 7–11.
27. Pelto and Müller-Wille 1987, 207–43.
28. Aporta and Higgs 2005.
29. Bodley 1990: 38–41.
30. Schrauf 1999.
31. Roth 2001.
32. Boyd and Richerson 1996/1985, 106.
33. D. T. Campbell 1965. See also Boyd and Richerson 1996/1985; Durham 1991.
34. The historical information we refer to comes from a book by Nevins (1927). For how radical the American Revolution was, see G. Wood 1992.
35. Paige 1975.
36. Bestor 2001, 76.
37. Trouillot 2001, 128.
38. Durrenberger 2001a; see also Hannerz 1996.
39. Traphagan and Brown 2002.
40. Trouillot 2001, 128.

41. Bradsher 2002, 3.
42. Guest and Jones 2005.
43. Yergin 2002, A29.
44. G. Thompson 2002, A3.
45. Sengupta 2002, A3.
46. J. D. Hill 1996, 1.
47. Bilby 1996, 127–28, referring to Hoogbergen 1990, 23–51.
48. Bilby 1996, 128–37.
49. Kottak 1996, 136, 153.
50. Roosens 1989, 9.
51. Cashdan 2001.
52. C. R. Ember and Levinson 1991.

Chapter 10

1. Keller 1974/1902, 34.
2. Wilden 1987, 124, referred to in Christensen, Hockey, and James 2001.
3. Lambert 2001.
4. Ekman and Keltner 1997, 32.
5. von Frisch 1962.
6. Gibson and Jessee 1999, 189–90; King 1999.
7. Hockett and Ascher 1964; the vervet monkey example is described in Seyfarth, Cheney, and Marler 1980.
8. T. S. Eliot 1963.
9. Snowdon 1999, 81.
10. Pepperberg 1999.
11. Mukerjee 1996, 28.
12. Savage-Rumbaugh 1992, 138–41.
13. J. H. Hill 1978, 94; 2009.
14. Ibid.
15. Senner 1989.
16. Chomsky 1975.
17. Southworth and Daswani 1974, 312. See also Boas 1911/1964, 121–23.
18. Akmajian et al. 2001, 296.
19. Bickerton 1983.
20. Ibid., 122.
21. B. Berlin 1992; Hays 1994.
22. G. Miller 2004.
23. Blount 1981; Gleitman and Wanner 1982.
24. R. Brown 1980, 93–94.
25. de Villiers and de Villiers 1979, 48; see also Wanner and Gleitman 1982.
26. Bickerton 1983, 122.
27. E. Bates and Marchman 1988, as referred to by Snowdon 1999, 88–91.
28. Crystal 1971, 168.
29. Ibid., 100–01.
30. Barinaga 1992, 535.
31. M. Ember and C. R. Ember 1999; R. L. Munroe, Munroe, and Winters 1996. The theory about the effect of baby-holding on consonant–vowel alternation is an extension of the theory that regular baby-holding encourages a preference for regular rhythm in music; see Ayres 1973.
32. Sapir and Swadesh 1964, 103.
33. Akmajian et al. 2001, 149–54.
34. Chaucer 1926, 8. Our modern English translation is based on the glossary in this book.
35. Katzner 2002, 10.
36. Akmajian et al. 2001, 334.
37. Baldi 1983, 3.
38. Ibid., 12.
39. Greenberg 1972; see also Phillipson 1976, 71.

40. Phillipson 1976, 79.
41. Holmes 2001, 194–95.
42. Trudgill 1983, 34.
43. Weinreich 1968: 31.
44. But see Thomason and Kaufman (1988) for a discussion of how grammatical changes due to contact may be more important than was previously assumed.
45. Berlin and Kay 1969.
46. Ibid.
47. Ibid., 5–6.
48. Ibid., 104; Witkowski and Brown 1978.
49. Bornstein 1973, 41–101.
50. M. Ember 1978, 364–67.
51. Ibid.
52. C. H. Brown 1977.
53. C. H. Brown 1979.
54. Witkowski and Burris 1981.
55. Ibid.
56. C. H. Brown and Witkowski 1980, 379.
57. C. H. Brown 1984, 106.
58. Webb 1977, 42–49; see also Rudmin 1988.
59. Sapir 1931, 578; see also J. B. Carroll 1956.
60. Wardhaugh 2002, 222.
61. Denny 1979, 97.
62. Friedrich 1986.
63. Guiora et al. 1982.
64. Lucy 1992, 46.
65. Ibid., 85–148.
66. Hymes 1974, 83–117.
67. Fischer 1958; Wardhaugh 2002, 160–88.
68. R. Brown and Ford 1961.
69. Wardhaugh 2002, 315.
70. Shibamoto 1987, 28.
71. Lakoff 1973; 1990.
72. Holmes 2001, 158–59; Trudgill 1983, 87–88; Wardhaugh 2002, 328.
73. Keenan 1989.
74. Tannen 1990, 49–83.
75. Wardhaugh 2002, 100.
76. Heller 1988, 1.
77. Pfaff 1979.
78. Wardhaugh 2002, 108.
79. Gal 1988, 249–55.
80. Collins and Blot 2003, 1–3.

Chapter 11

1. Hitchcock and Beisele 2000, 5.
2. C. R. Ember 1978.
3. Kent 1996.
4. Myers 1988; Schrire 1984a.
5. Morrison and Junker 2002.
6. The discussion of the Australian aborigines is based on R. A. Gould 1969.
7. Burbank 1994, 23; 2009.
8. Data from Textor 1967 and Service 1979.
9. Murdock and Provost 1973, 207.
10. DeVore and Konner 1974; R. B. Lee 1968.
11. C. R. Ember 1978.
12. McCarthy and McArthur 1960.
13. R. B. Lee 1979, 256–58, 278–80.
14. Palsson 1988; Roscoe 2002.
15. Keeley 1991.
16. R. L. Kelly 1995, 293–315.
17. Mitchell 2009; Tollefson 2009.
18. Roscoe 2002.
19. D. Werner 1978.
20. Textor 1967.
21. This section is largely based on Hames 2009.
22. Chagnon 1983, 60.
23. S. S. King 1979.
24. Hickey 1964, 135–65.
25. C. R. Ember 1983, 289.
26. Dirks 2009; Messer 1996, 244; Textor 1967.
27. Finnis 2006.
28. Barlett 1989, 253–91.
29. U.S. Environmental Protection Agency 2009.
30. Salzman 1996.
31. A. L. Johnson 2002; Lees and Bates 1974.
32. Itkonen 1951; Whitaker 1955.
33. Paine 1994.
34. Textor 1967.
35. Dirks 2009.
36. Boserup 1993/1965.
37. R. C. Hunt 2000.
38. Janzen 1973.
39. Roosevelt 1992.
40. Hoebel 1968/1954, 46–63.
41. Pryor 2005, 36.
42. Ibid.
43. Leacock and Lee 1982; Pryor 2005, 36.
44. R. Murphy 1960, 69, 142–43.
45. Salzman 1996.
46. Not all pastoralists have individual ownership. For example, the Tungus of northern Siberia have kin group ownership of reindeer. See Dowling 1975, 422.
47. Salzman 2002.
48. Fratkin 2008, 86–89.
49. Bodley 1990, 77–93; Wilmsen 1989, 1–14.
50. Salzman 1996, 904–05.
51. Plattner 1989, 379–96.
52. Hage and Powers 1992.
53. Steward and Faron 1959, 122–25.
54. Bowie 2006, 251.
55. B. B. Whiting and Edwards 1988, 164.
56. Nag, White, and Peet 1978, 295–96.
57. Polanyi 1957.
58. Sahlins 1972, 188–96.
59. L. Marshall 1961, 239–41.
60. The "//" sign in the name for the G//ana people symbolizes a click sound not unlike the sound we make when we want a horse to move faster.
61. Cashdan 1980, 116–20.
62. H. Kaplan, Hill, and Hurtado 1990.
63. Winterhalder 1990.
64. Mooney 1978.
65. Balikci 1970, quoted in Mooney 1978, 392.
66. Mooney 1978, 392.
67. Ensminger 2002; Fehr and Fischbacher 2003; Henrich et al. 2004, as cited by Ensminger 2002.
68. Angier 2002, F1, F8.
69. Abler 2009.
70. Service 1962, 145–46.
71. M. Harris 1975, 118–21.
72. Plattner 1985, viii.

73. Plattner 1985, xii.
74. Pollier 2000.
75. Vohs, Mead, and Goode 2006.
76. The description of Tikopia is based on Firth 1959, Chapters 5, 6, 7, and 9, passim.
77. Monsutti 2004.
78. Eversole 2005; Monsutti 2004.
79. Eversole 2005.
80. Most of this discussion is based on R. F. Murphy and Steward 1956.
81. Burkhalter and Murphy 1989.
82. Gross and Underwood 1971.

Chapter 12

1. In an analysis of many native societies in the New World, Gary Feinman and Jill Neitzel argue that egalitarian and rank societies ("tribes" and "chiefdoms," respectively) are not systematically distinguishable. See Feinman and Neitzel (1984, 57).
2. Fried 1967, 33.
3. Boehm 1993, 230–31; 1999.
4. M. G. Smith 1966, 152.
5. D. Mitchell 2009.
6. Drucker 1965, 56–64.
7. Service 1978, 249.
8. Sahlins 1958, 80–81.
9. Betzig 1988.
10. Brittain 1978.
11. Higley 1995, 1–47.
12. Argyle 1994.
13. U.S. Census Bureau 2002.
14. Featherman and Hauser 1978, 4, 481; Treiman and Ganzeboom 1990, 117.
15. Behrman, Gaviria, and Székely, 2001; Solon 2002.
16. S. R. Barrett 1994, 17, 41.
17. Johnston 1999, 16; *New York Times International,* Tuesday, September 30, 1997, p. A26; K. Phillips 1990; U.S. Census Bureau 1993.
18. Leonhardt and Fabrikant 2009.
19. Durrenberger 2001b, who refers to Goldschmidt 1999 and Newman 1988; 1993.
20. Klass 2009.
21. Ruskin 1963, 296–314.
22. O. Lewis 1958.
23. Kristof 1995, A18.
24. For more information about caste in Japan, see Berreman 1972, 403–14; 1973.
25. Kristof 1995; 1997.
26. Tamari 1991; 2005.
27. Taylor 2005.
28. Berreman 1960, 120–27.
29. O. Patterson 1982, vii–xiii, 105.
30. Pryor 1977, 219.
31. Harper 2003.
32. Nadel 1942.
33. Pryor 1977, 217–47.
34. M. D. Williams 2009.
35. S. S. Friedman 1980, 206.
36. M. H. Ross 2009a.
37. Marks 1994, 32.
38. Fluehr-Lobban 2006, 12.
39. Marks 1994, 32.
40. Fluehr-Lobban 2006, 12.

41. Armelagos and Goodman 1998, 365.
42. O. Patterson 2000.
43. M. Nash 1989, 2.
44. Ibid., 10.
45. Barth 1994, 27.
46. Yinger 1994, 169.
47. Ibid., 169–71.
48. Ibid., 216–17.
49. Benjamin 1991; see also M. D. Williams 2009.
50. Flannery 1972.
51. Data from Textor 1967.
52. Ibid.
53. Lenski 1984/1966, 308–18.
54. Cutright 1967, 564; Treiman and Ganzeboom 1990, 117.
55. Sahlins 1958.
56. Ibid., 4.
57. Sahlins 1972.
58. Lenski 1984/1966.
59. Gilman 1990.
60. Fried 1967, 201ff; Harner 1975.
61. Meek 1940, 149–50.

Chapter 13

1. Leibowitz 1978, 43–44.
2. Chafetz 1990, 28; Epstein 1988, 5–6; Schlegel 1989, 266.
3. Jacobs and Roberts 1989.
4. Segal 2004; Segal also cites the work of W. Williams 1992.
5. Blackwood 1984b; Lang 1999, 93–94.
6. Wikan 1982, 168–86.
7. Stini 1971.
8. Frayer and Wolpoff 1985, 431–32.
9. For reviews of theories and research on sexual dimorphism and possible genetic and cultural determinants of variation in degree of dimorphism over time and place, see Frayer and Wolpoff 1985 and Gray 1985, 201–09, 217–25.
10. J. K. Brown 1970b, 1074.
11. Among the Aché hunter-gatherers of Paraguay, women collect the type of honey produced by stingless bees (men collect other honey); this division of labor is consistent with the compatibility theory. See Hurtado et al. 1985, 23.
12. Byrne 1994; Murdock and Provost 1973, 213.
13. R. O'Brian 1999.
14. D. R. White, Burton, and Brudner 1977, 1–24.
15. Mukhopadhyay and Higgins 1988, 473.
16. J. K. Brown 1970b, 1073–78; D. R. White et al. 1977.
17. Nerlove 1974.
18. N. E. Levine 1988.
19. M. J. Goodman et al. 1985.
20. Noss and Hewlett 2001.
21. Brumbach and Jarvenpa 2006; Jarvenpa and Brumbach 2006.
22. C. R. Ember 1983, 288–89.
23. Mead 1950 [originally published 1935], 180–84.
24. Rivers 1967 [originally published 1906], 567.
25. M. Ember and Ember 1971, 573, Table 1.
26. Schlegel and Barry 1986.
27. Wood and Eagly 2002, 706, drawing on data from H. Kaplan et al. 2000.
28. Boserup 1970, 22–25; see also Schlegel and Barry 1986, 144–45.
29. Boserup 1970, 22–25.
30. Bossen 2000, 31–34.
31. C. R. Ember 1983, 286–87; data from Murdock and Provost 1973, 212; Bradley 1995.

32. C. R. Ember 1983.
33. Ibid.
34. Ibid., 287–93.
35. M. Ember and Ember 1971, 579–80.
36. Ibid., 581; see also Sanday 1973, 1684.
37. Nerlove 1974.
38. Schlegel and Barry 1986.
39. Whyte 1978a, 217.
40. *Human Development Report 2010*.
41. D. B. Adams 1983; Whyte 1978a.
42. J. K. Brown 1970a.
43. Divale and Harris 1976; Sanday 1974.
44. Quinn 1977, 189–90.
45. Graham 1979.
46. D. Werner 1982; Stogdill 1974, cited in Ibid.; see also Handwerker and Crosbie 1982.
47. Draper 1975, 103.
48. D. Werner 1984.
49. M. H. Ross 1986.
50. This description is based on the fieldwork of Elizabeth and Robert Fearnea (1956–1958), as reported in M. K. Martin and Voorhies 1975, 304–31.
51. Begler 1978.
52. Ibid. See also Whyte 1978a, 229–32.
53. Whyte 1978b, 95–120; see also Quinn 1977.
54. Whyte 1978b, 124–29, 145; see also Sanday 1973.
55. Whyte 1978b, 129–30.
56. J. K. Brown 1970a.
57. Whyte 1978b, 135–36.
58. Ibid., 135.
59. Doyle 2005.
60. Quinn 1977, 85; see also Etienne and Leacock 1980, 19–20.
61. Chafetz 1990, 11–19.
62. B. B. Whiting and Edwards 1973.
63. R. L. Munroe et al. 2000, 8–9.
64. Maccoby and Jacklin 1974.
65. For a more extensive discussion of behavior differences and possible explanations of them, see C. R. Ember 1981.
66. B. B. Whiting and Edwards 1973.
67. For references to this research, see C. R. Ember 1981, 559.
68. Rubin, Provenzano, and Haskett 1974.
69. For a discussion of this evidence, see Ellis 1986, 525–27; C. R. Ember 1981.
70. For example, Ellis (1986) considers the evidence for the biological view of aggression "beyond reasonable dispute."
71. For a discussion of other possibilities, see C. R. Ember 1981.
72. Rohner 1976.
73. B. B. Whiting and Whiting 1975; see also B. B. Whiting and Edwards 1988, 273.
74. C. R. Ember 1973, 424–39.
75. B. B. Whiting and Edwards 1973, 175–79; see also Maccoby and Jacklin 1974.
76. Burbank 1994.
77. Heise 1967.
78. C. S. Ford and Beach 1951, 191.
79. O. Lewis 1951, 397.
80. Farley 1996, 60.
81. C. S. Ford and Beach 1951, 23–25, 68–71.
82. Ibid., 40–41, 73.
83. Broude 2009.
84. C. S. Ford and Beach 1951, 82–83.
85. Broude and Greene 1976.

86. Kluckhohn 1948, 101.
87. M. Hunt 1974, 254–57; Lewin 1994.
88. Broude 1980, 184.
89. C. S. Ford and Beach 1951, 114.
90. Jankowiak, Nell, and Buckmaster 2002.
91. Lang 1999, 97, citing Thomas 1993.
92. J. Morris 1938, 191.
93. Underhill 1938, 117, 186.
94. 'Abd Allah 1917, 7, 20.
95. Cardoso and Werner 2004.
96. R. C. Kelly 1974.
97. Cardoso and Werner 2004.
98. Blackwood 1984a; Blackwood and Wieringa 1999, 49.
99. Cardoso and Werner 2004, 207.
100. Data from Textor 1967.
101. W. N. Stephens 1972, 1–28.
102. Broude 1976, 243.
103. D. Werner 1975; 1979.
104. D. Werner 1979, 345–62; see also D. Werner 1975, 36.
105. Data from Textor 1967.
106. Schlegel 1991.

Chapter 14

1. Stephens 1963, 5.
2. Murdock 1949, 8.
3. Murdock 1949, 7–8.
4. Ibid., 9–10.
5. See, for example, Linton 1936, 135–36.
6. M. Ember and C. R. Ember 1979.
7. Ibid.
8. Marlowe 2003, 221–23.
9. M. Ember and C. R. Ember 1979.
10. Schlegel and Eloul 1987, 119.
11. Schlegel and Eloul 1988, 295, Table 1. We used the data to calculate the frequency of various types of economic transactions in a worldwide sample of 186 societies.
12. Schlegel and Eloul 1988, 298–99.
13. Pryor 1977, 363–64.
14. Ibid.
15. Schlegel and Eloul 1988, 296–97.
16. Ibid.
17. Ibid.
18. Radcliffe-Brown 1922, 73.
19. Goody 1973, 17–21; Murdock 1967.
20. Pryor 1977, 363–65; Schlegel and Eloul 1988, 296–99.
21. Schlegel and Eloul 1988, following Goody 1973, 20.
22. R. Middleton 1962, 606.
23. Durham 1991, 293–94, citing research by Hopkins 1980.
24. Howard and Rensel 2009.
25. Lingenfelter 2009.
26. Macdonald and Hewlett 1999, 504–06.
27. M. Ember 1975, 262, Table 3.
28. Busby 2009.
29. M. Ember 1975, 260–69; see also Durham 1991, 341–57.
30. Oliver 1955, 352–53.
31. Ibid., 223–24, quoted in W. Stephens 1963, 58.
32. Mead 1950/1935, 101.
33. Jankowiak, Sudakov, and Wilreker 2005.
34. The discussion of these customs is based on W. Stephens 1963, 63–67.
35. Kilbride and Kilbride 1990, 202–06.
36. C. Anderson 2000, 102–03.

37. J. W. M. Whiting 1964.
38. M. Ember 1974b.
39. M. Ember 1984–1985. The statistical relationship between late age of marriage for men and polygyny was first reported by Witkowski 1975.
40. M. Ember 1974b, 202–05.
41. M. Ember 1984–1985. For other predictors of polygyny, see D. R. White and Burton 1988.
42. Low 1990.
43. M. Ember, C. R. Ember, and Low 2007.
44. Barber 2008.
45. Coult and Habenstein 1965; Murdock 1957.
46. M. C. Goldstein 1987, 39.
47. Stephens 1963, 45.
48. Hiatt 1980.
49. M. Goldstein 1987. Formerly, in feudal Tibet, a class of serfs who owned small parcels of land also practiced polyandry. Goldstein suggests that a shortage of land would explain their polyandry too. See M. C. Goldstein 1971.
50. Pasternak 1976, 96.
51. Coult and Habenstein 1965.
52. Mead 1961/1928, quoted in Stephens 1963, 134–35.
53. Nimkoff and Middleton 1960.
54. Pasternak, C. R. Ember, and M. Ember 1976, 109–23.
55. Coult and Habenstein 1965; Murdock 1957.
56. Percentages calculated from Coult and Habenstein 1965.
57. L. Bohannan and P. Bohannan 1953.
58. J. D. Freeman 1961.
59. Jarvenpa 2004.
60. C. R. Ember, M. Ember, and Pasternak 1974, 84–89.
61. Pospisil 1963.
62. Schneider 1961a.
63. M. Ember and C. R. Ember 1971, 581.
64. Schneider 1961b.
65. Goodenough 1951, 145.
66. Coult and Habenstein 1965.
67. Data from Textor 1967.
68. Davenport 1959.
69. M. Ember 1967.
70. M. Ember and C. R. Ember 1971. See also Divale 1974.
71. Divale 1974; M. Ember and Ember 1971, 583–85.
72. M. Ember and Ember 1971. For a different theory—that matrilocal residence precedes, rather than follows, the development of purely external warfare—see Divale 1974.
73. Helms 2009; Herlihy 2007; see also M. Ember and Ember 1971.
74. Service 1962, 137.
75. C. R. Ember and M. Ember 1972.
76. C. R. Ember 1975.
77. M. Ember 1974a.
78. Data from Textor 1967.
79. C. R. Ember et al. 1974.
80. The importance of warfare and competition as factors in the formation of unilineal descent groups is also suggested by Sahlins 1961, 332–45 and Service 1962.

Chapter 15

1. Service 1962.
2. Schrire 1984b; see also Leacock and Lee 1982, 8.
3. Service 1962, 109.
4. Mathiassen 1928, 213.
5. Service 1962, 114–15.
6. Bohannan 1954, 3.

7. Sahlins 1961, 342.
8. Sahlins 1961, 345.
9. N. Dyson-Hudson 1966, Chapters 5 and 6.
10. Sahlins 1962, 293–94.
11. Sahlins 1963, 295.
12. Sahlins 1983, 519.
13. Sahlins 1963, 297.
14. Carneiro 1970, 733.
15. Weber 1947, 154.
16. Wiberg 1983.
17. Finley 1983.
18. Carcopino 1940, 18–20.
19. Blanton and Fargher 2008.
20. Ibid.
21. M. Ember 1963; Naroll 1961; Textor 1967. See also Ross 1981.
22. M. Ember 1963, 244–46.
23. Service 1962; see also Braun and Plog 1982; Haas 1990.
24. Carneiro 1990; A. Johnson and Earle 1987, 158.
25. Service 1962, 112, 145.
26. Feinman and Nietzel 1984.
27. For a more detailed description and evaluation of the available theories, see Chapter 13 in C. Ember, M. Ember, and Peregrine 2011. *Anthropology*. Upper Saddle River, NJ: Prentice Hall. See also R. Cohen and Service 1978.
28. McNeill 1976.
29. Carneiro 1978, 215.
30. Textor 1967.
31. Carneiro 1978; Hart 1948; Marano 1973, 35–40; Naroll 1967; cf. Peregrine, C. R. Ember, and M. Ember 2004 and other articles in Graber 2004.
32. D. Werner 1982.
33. Kracke 1979, 232.
34. D. Werner 1982.
35. Sahlins 1963.
36. Kracke 1979, 41.
37. Brandewie 1991.
38. Lepowsky 1990.
39. Todorov et al. 2005.
40. Zebrowitz and Montepare 2005.
41. Ross 1988, 73. The discussion in this section draws mostly from Zebrowitz and Montepare 2005, 73–89, and from Ross 2009b.
42. Bondarenko and Korotayev 2000; Korotayev and Bondarenko 2000.
43. Russett and Oneal 2001.
44. C. R. Ember, Ember, and Russett 1992.
45. Rummel 2002b.
46. Scaglion 2009.
47. Hoebel 1968/1954, 4, quoting S. P. Simpson and Field 1946, 858.
48. Fry and Björkqvist 1997.
49. D. Black 1993, 79–83.
50. Ross 1988.
51. Boas 1888, 668.
52. Otterbein 1986, 107.
53. Archer and Gartner 1984, 118–39.
54. D. Black 1993, 83–86; Scaglion 2009.
55. Ibid.
56. Evans-Pritchard 1940, 291. The discussion of the Nuer follows this source.
57. Hickson 1986.
58. Ibid.; Koch et al. 1977, 279.

59. J. M. Roberts 1967, 169.
60. Ibid., 192.
61. Hoebel 1968/1954, Chapter 9.
62. Schwartz 1954, 475.
63. Textor 1967.
64. Masumura 1977, 388–99.
65. D. Black 1993; Newman 1983, 131; Scaglion 2009.
66. Otterbein and Otterbein (1965) and Fry (2006, 88) do not consider feuding to be warfare.
67. See summaries of the evidence in C. R. Ember and Ember 1994; see also Fry 2006.
68. C. R. Ember and Ember 1994.
69. Chacon and Mendoza 2007.
70. Ericksen and Horton 1992; Newman 1983, 131.
71. Otterbein and Otterbein 1965, 1476.
72. D. R. White 1988.
73. Patterson 1982, 345–52.
74. Gat 1999, 373, as referred to in Wadley 2003.
75. Heider 1970, 105–11; 1979, 88–99.
76. M. Ember and Ember 1992, 188–89.
77. C. R. Ember and Ember 1992; M. Ember 1982. For a discussion of how Dani warfare seems to be motivated mainly by economic considerations, see Shankman 1991. B. W. Kang (2000, 878–79) finds a strong correlation between environmental stress and warfare frequency in Korean history.
78. Otterbein 1970.
79. C. R. Ember and Ember 1992; see also Loftin 1971; Otterbein 1970.
80. C. R. Ember 1974.
81. Otterbein 1968, 283; Ross 1985.
82. Divale and Harris 1976, 521–38; see also Gibbons 1993.
83. C. R. Ember and Ember 1992, 251–52.
84. Singer 1980.
85. Russett and Oneal 2001, 89.
86. Ibid., 145–48.
87. Younger 2008.
88. Russett 1993, 10–11, 14, 138.

Chapter 16

1. Wallace 1966, 60–61.
2. Malefijt 1968, 153.
3. Ray 1954, 172–89.
4. Rosenblatt, Walsh, and Jackson 1976, 51.
5. Ibid., 55.
6. Swanson 1969, 97–108; see also Sheils 1975.
7. Middleton 1971, 488.
8. Spiro and D'Andrade 1958.
9. Lambert, Triandis, and Wolf 1959; Rohner 1975, 108.
10. Barnett 1960, 79–85.
11. Swanson 1969, 56.
12. Ibid., 55–81; see also W. D. Davis 1971. Peregrine (1996, 84–112) replicated Swanson's finding for North American societies.
13. Textor 1967; Underhill 1975.
14. Geertz 1966.
15. Swanson 1969, 153–74.
16. Stark and Finke 2000, 107–08.
17. Wallace 1966, 52–67.
18. Winkelman 1986b, 178–83.
19. Bourguignon 1973.
20. Bourguignon and Evascu 1977; Winkelman 1986b, 196–98.
21. Kehoe and Giletti 1981.

22. Raybeck 1998, referring to Raybeck, Shoobe, and Grauberger 1989.
23. Bourguignon 2004, 572.
24. Winkelman and Peck 2004.
25. O. K. Moore 1957.
26. Sheils 1980.
27. Winkelman and Baker 2010, 293–96 and references therein.
28. Evans-Pritchard 1979, 362–66.
29. Swanson 1969, 150; see also H. R. Trevor-Roper 1971, 444–49.
30. Swanson 1969, 150–51.
31. Caporael 1976; Matossian 1982; 1989, 70–80. For possible reasons to dismiss the ergot theory, see Spanos 1983.
32. Harner 1972.
33. B. B. Whiting 1950, 36–37; see also Swanson 1969, 137–52, 240–41.
34. Winkelman 1986a.
35. Ibid., 28–29.
36. Knecht 2003, 11.
37. Harner and Doore 1987, 3, 8–9; Krippner 1987, 128; Noll 1987, 49.
38. De Laguna 1972, 701C.
39. See Krippner 1987, 126–27; Noll 1987, 49–50.
40. Winkelman 1986a, 27–28.
41. Ibid., 28.
42. Ibid., 27.
43. Ibid., 35–37.
44. M. Harris 1966.
45. Buckser and Glazier 2003; Rambo 2003.
46. Discussion is based on Firth 1970.
47. Ibid., 387.
48. Ibid., 418.
49. Ensminger 1997, 7.
50. Ibid.
51. Reff 2005; see also McNeill 1998; Stark 1996.
52. C. R. Ember 1982.
53. Wallace 1970/1858, 239.
54. The Quakers, long-time neighbors and trusted advisers of the Seneca, took pains not to interfere with Seneca religion, principles, and attitudes.
55. Antoun 2001.
56. Nagata 2001.
57. Antoun 2001, 17–18.
58. Ibid., 45.

Chapter 17

1. Maquet 1986, 9.
2. R. P. Armstrong 1981, 11.
3. Malin 1986, 27.
4. R. L. Anderson 1989, 11.
5. Steiner 1990.
6. R. L. Anderson 1990, 225–26.
7. Sweeney 1952, 335.
8. Fischer 1961, 80.
9. Ibid., 81.
10. Peregrine 2007 also finds that the ceramics of complex societies tend toward nonrepetition and complex designs.
11. Ibid., 83.
12. Dressler and Robbins 1975, 427–34.
13. Lomax 1968, 117–28.
14. Lomax 1968, 166–67.
15. Ibid., 167–69.
16. Ayres 1973.
17. E. Erickson 1968.

18. Dundes 1989.
19. Bauman 1992.
20. Brunvand 1993, 14.
21. Ibid., 296.
22. Kluckhohn 1965.
23. As discussed in Segal 1987, 1–2.
24. J. Campbell 1949, 30, as quoted in Segal 1987, 4.
25. S. Thompson 1965, 449.
26. Dundes 1965, reported in F. W. Young 1970.
27. G. O. Wright 1954.
28. A. Cohen 1990.
29. Price 1989, 82–85.
30. Ibid., 102–03.
31. Ibid., 56–67.
32. Ibid., 112.
33. Ibid., 77–81.
34. Warner 1986, 172–75.
35. Layton 1992, 93–94.
36. Ibid., 31, 109.
37. J. C. H. King 1986.
38. Warner 1986, 178–86.
39. Merrill 1987.

Chapter 18

1. The discussion in this section draws extensively from Aptekar 1994.
2. Information collected during Melvin Ember's fieldwork in American Samoa, 1955–1956.
3. Mellor and Gavian 1987.
4. Dirks 1993.
5. Torry 1986.
6. United Nations Human Settlements Programme 2003, xi, 16, 59.
7. Rodwin and Sanyal 1987.
8. Mangin 1967.
9. Rodwin and Sanyal 1987; for a critique of self-help programs, see Ward 1982.
10. A. Cohen and Koegel 2009.
11. National Coalition for the Homeless 2008.
12. A. Cohen and Koegel 2009.
13. Baxter and Hopper 1981, 30–33, 50–74.
14. Ibid.
15. A. Cohen and Koegel 2009.
16. H. Herrman 1990.
17. Barak 1991, 63–65.
18. World Bank 2004.
19. Aptekar 1991, 326.
20. UN Works n.d.
21. Aptekar 1988; 1991, 326–49.
22. Korbin 1981, 4.
23. Straus 2001, 195–96.
24. Straus and Kantor 1994.
25. Straus 1995, 30–33; Straus and Kantor 1995.
26. Straus 1991; U.S. Department of Justice 1988; 1994; 2000.
27. Levinson 1989, 11–12, 44.
28. Minturn and Stashak 1982. Using a sociobiological orientation, a study by Daly and Wilson (1988, 43–59) also suggests that infanticide is largely due to the difficulty of raising the infant successfully.
29. Levinson 1989, 26–28.
30. C. R. Ember and Ember 2005; see also Petersen, Lee, and Ellis 1982, as cited in Levinson 1989, 63.
31. Lareau 2003, 230.

32. Levinson 1989, 31.
33. Ibid., 71.
34. Gelles and Straus 1988, 78–88.
35. Erchak 2009; Levinson 1989, 44–45.
36. Straus and Yodanis 1996.
37. Levinson 1989, 104–07.
38. Archer and Gartner 1984, 35.
39. Archer and Gartner 1984, 63–97.
40. Gurr 1989, 47–48.
41. U.S. Department of Justice n.d.
42. Eckhardt 1975; Russell 1972; Sipes 1973.
43. C. R. Ember and Ember 1994.
44. Archer and Gartner 1984, 118–39.
45. Bacon, Child, and Barry 1963; Barry 2007; B. B. Whiting 1965.
46. Barber 2000.
47. C. R. Ember and Ember 1994, 625.
48. C. R. Ember and Ember 1993, 227.
49. C. A. Anderson and Bushman 2002, 2377; J. G. Johnson et al. 2002.
50. In preindustrial societies, homicide and assault are similarly predicted by the presence of indigenous money, almost always associated with wealth concentration—see Barry 2007.
51. Gartner 2009; Krahn, Hartnagel, and Gartrell 1986, as referred to in Daly and Wilson 1988, 287–88; Loftin, McDowall, and Boudouris 1989.
52. C. R. Ember and Ember 1997.
53. Most of the discussion in this section comes from C. R. Ember and M. Ember 1992, 204–06.
54. Gat 1999, 563–83; Meggitt 1977, 201.
55. Data from Korea is consistent with this explanation of war: More environmental stress strongly predicts higher frequencies of warfare in Korea between the 1st century B.C. and the 8th century A.D. See B. W. Kang 2000, 878.
56. For the cross-cultural results suggesting the theory of war described here, see C. R. Ember and M. Ember 1992.
57. For the results on political participation and peace in the ethnographic record, see C. R. Ember, M. Ember, and Russett 1992. For the results on political participation and peace in the modern world, see Russett and Oneal 2001.
58. Russett and Oneal 2001, 49.
59. Ibid., 125ff.
60. Some of these examples are from Henderson 2001.
61. See the discussions in Ibid., 3–9, and S. K. Anderson and Sloan 2002, 1–5.
62. S. K. Anderson and Sloan 2002, 465.
63. This definition is adapted from Chomsky, who is quoted in Henderson 2001, 5.
64. S. K. Anderson and Sloan 2002, 6–7.
65. Ibid., 6–8.
66. Suárez-Orozco 1992.
67. R. J. Rummel 2002a.
68. R. J. Rummel 2002c.
69. R. J. Rummel 2002d.
70. S. K. Anderson and Sloan 2002, 422.
71. *Scientific American,* Crossroads for Planet Earth 2005.

Chapter 19

1. Nolan 2003, 2.
2. Kushner 1991.
3. Van Willigen 2002, 10.
4. "Appendix C: Statements on Ethics . . . " 1971. 1991; "Appendix I: Revised Principles . . . " 1990. 1991.

5. Appendix A: Report of the Committee on Ethics . . . 2002; Appendix F: Professional and Ethical Responsibilities . . . 2002.
6. Appendix H: National Association of Practicing Anthropologists' Ethical Guidelines . . . 1988. 1991.
7. Scudder 1978.
8. Ibid., 204ff.
9. Picchi 1991, 26–38; for a more general description of the Bakairí, see Picchi 2009.
10. Murray and Bannister 2004; Wulff and Fiste 1987.
11. Ibid.
12. Niehoff 1966, 255–67.
13. G. M. Foster 1969, 8–9.
14. Jelliffe and Jelliffe 1975.
15. W. H. Fisher 1994.
16. Coreil 1989, 149–50.
17. Rogers 1983, 321–31.
18. Bryant and Bailey 1990.
19. Niehoff 1966, 219–24.
20. Coreil 1989, 155.
21. Ravesloot 1997, 174.
22. Anyon and Ferguson 1995.
23. Society for American Archaeology 2009.
24. Komar and Buikstra 2008, 11–12.
25. Manhein 1999.
26. Komar and Buikstra 2008, 126–45.
27. Brace 1995.
28. Joans 1997.
29. A. H. Goodman and Leatherman 1998; Kleinman, Das, and Lock, 1997.
30. Loustaunau and Sobo 1997, 80–81; Rubel and Haas 1996, 120.
31. Loustaunau and Sobo 1997, 82–83, referring to Magner 1992, 93.
32. Loustaunau and Sobo 1997, referring to Gesler 1991, 16.
33. Loustaunau and Sobo 1997, referring to G. M. Foster 1994, 11; C. Leslie 1976, 4.
34. Ahern 1975, 92–97, as appearing in eHRAF World Cultures, 2000.
35. Murdock 1980, 20.
36. C. C. Moore 1988.
37. T. Gladwin and Sarason 1953, 64–66.
38. Mahony 1971, 34–38, as seen in eHRAF World Cultures, 2000.
39. Gladwin and Sarason 1953, 65.
40. Hahn 1995, 133–39.
41. For an exhaustively documented presentation of the more universalistic approach, see E. A. Berlin and Berlin 1996; see also Browner 1985, 13–32; Rubel et al. 1984.
42. E. A. Berlin and B. Berlin 1996.
43. Browner 1985; Ortiz de Montellano and Browner 1985.
44. Etkin and Ross 1997.
45. Moerman 1997, 240–41.
46. Loustaunau and Sobo 1997, 98–101.
47. Winkelman 1986a.
48. Torrey 1972.
49. Loustaunau and Sobo 1997, 101–02; Moerman 1997.
50. Loustaunau and Sobo 1997, 102.
51. Dow 1986, 6–9, 125.
52. Hahn 1995, 131–72.
53. Ibid., 165.
54. For a discussion of some of the relevant research, see Hahn 1995, 80–82.
55. Mascie-Taylor 1990, 118–21.
56. See references in Hahn 1995, 82–87; for more recent statistics: Shrestha 2006; Singh and van Dyck. n.d.
57. A. Cohen 1999.
58. UNAIDS 2007, 1.
59. Ibid., 4–6.
60. Bolton 1989.
61. Reported in Carey et al. 2004, 462.
62. Bolton 1989.
63. Carrier and Bolton 1991; Schoepf 1988, 625, cited in Carrier and Bolton 1991.
64. Simmons, Farmer, and Schoepf, 1996, 64.
65. Altman 2008.
66. Schoepf 1988, 637–38.
67. Bolton 1992.
68. Farmer 1997, 414. Married men in Thailand are gradually turning away from commercial sex and having affairs with married women who are believed to be safe; see Lyttleton 2000, 299.
69. Quandt 1996, 272–89.
70. McElroy and Townsend 2002.
71. See discussion in Leslie Lieberman 2004.
72. Gross and Underwood 1971.
73. McElroy and Townsend 2002, 187, referring to Harvey and Heywood 1983, 27–35.
74. Quandt 1996, 277.
75. McKee 1984, 96.

Bibliography

'Abd Allah, Mahmud M. 1917. Siwan customs. *Harvard African Studies* 1:1–28.

Abler, Thomas S. 2009. Iroquois: The tree of peace and the war kettle. In MyAnthroLibrary, eds. C. R. Ember, M. Ember, and P. N. Peregrine. MyAnthroLibrary.com. Pearson.

Adams, David B. 1983. Why there are so few women warriors. *Behavior Science Research* 18:196–212.

Adams, Robert McCormick. 1960. The origin of cities. *Scientific American* (September):153–68.

Adams, Robert McCormick. 1981. *Heartland of cities: Surveys of ancient settlement and land use on the central floodplain of the Euphrates.* Chicago: University of Chicago Press.

Ahern, Emily M. 1975. Sacred and secular medicine in a Taiwan village: A study of cosmological disorders. In *Medicine in Chinese cultures: Comparative studies of health care in Chinese and other societies,* eds. A. Kleinman et al. Washington, DC: U.S. Department of Health, Education, and Welfare, National Institutes of Health.

Aiello, Leslie C. 1993. The origin of the New World monkeys. In *The Africa–South America connection,* eds. W. George and R. Lavocat, 100–18. Oxford, UK: Clarendon Press.

Aiello, Leslie C., and Mark Collard, 2001. Our newest oldest ancestor? *Nature* 410 (November 29):526–27.

Aiello, Leslie C., and Christopher Dean. 1990. *An introduction to human evolutionary anatomy.* London: Academic Press.

Akmajian, Adrian, Richard A. Demers, Ann K. Farmer, and Robert M. Harnish. 2001. *Linguistics: An introduction to language and communication.* Cambridge, MA: MIT Press.

Alexander, John P. 1992. Alas, poor *Notharctus. Natural History* (August):55–59.

Alroy, John. 2001. A multispecies overkill simulation of the End-Pleistocene megafaunal mass extinction. *Science* 292 (June 8):1893–96.

Alvarez, L. W., W. Alvarez, F. Asara, and H. V. Michel. 1980. Extra-terrestrial cause for the Cretaceous–Tertiary extinction. *Science* 208 (4448):1095–108.

Altman, Lawrence K. 2008. Protective effects of circumcision are shown to continue after trials' end. *New York Times,* August 12. http://www.nytimes.com.

American Anthropological Association. 1991. Revised principles of professional responsibility, 1990. In *Ethics and the profession of anthropology: Dialogue for a new era,* ed. Carolyn Fluehr-Lobban, 274–79. Philadelphia: University of Pennsylvania Press.

Anderson, Connie M. 2000. The persistence of polygyny as an adaptive response to poverty and oppression in apartheid South Africa. *Cross-Cultural Research* 34:99–112.

Anderson, Craig A., and Brad J. Bushman. 2002. The effects of media violence on society. *Science* 295 (March 29):2377–79.

Anderson, J. L., C. B. Crawford, J. Nadeau, and T. Lindberg. 1992. Was the Duchess of Windsor right? A cross-cultural review of the socioecology of ideal female body shape. *Ethnology and Sociobiology* 13:197–227.

Anderson, Richard L. 1989. *Art in small-scale societies.* 2nd ed. Englewood Cliffs, NJ: Prentice Hall.

Anderson, Richard L. 1990. *Calliope's sisters: A comparative study of philosophies of art.* Upper Saddle River, NJ: Prentice Hall.

Anderson, Sean K., and Stephen Sloan. 2002. *Historical dictionary of terrorism.* 2nd ed. Lanham, MD: Scarecrow Press.

Andrews, Peter. 2000a. Proconsul. In *Encyclopedia of human evolution and prehistory,* eds. I. Tattersall, E. Delson, and J. van Couvering. New York: Garland.

Andrews, Peter. 2000b. Propliopithecidae. In *Encyclopedia of human evolution and prehistory,* eds. I. Tattersall, E. Delson, and J. van Couvering. New York: Garland.

Angier, Natalie. 2002. Why we're so nice: We're wired to cooperate. *New York Times,* Science Times, July 23, pp. F1, F8.

Antoun, Richard T. 2001. *Understanding fundamentalism: Christian, Islamic, and Jewish movements.* Walnut Creek, CA: AltaMira Press.

Anyon, Roger, and T. J. Ferguson. 1995. Cultural resources management at the Pueblo of Zuni, New Mexico, USA. *Antiquity* 69:913–30.

Aporta, Claudio, and Eric Higgs. 2005. Satellite culture: Global positioning systems, Inuit wayfinding, and the need for a new account of technology. *Current Anthropology* 46:729–46.

Appendix A: Report of the Committee on Ethics, Society for Applied Anthropology. 2002. In *Ethics and the profession of anthropology,* ed. C. Fluehr-Lobban. Philadelphia: University of Pennsylvania Press.

Appendix C: Statements on Ethics: Principles of Professional Responsibility, Adopted by the Council of the American Anthropological Association, May 1971. 1991. In *Ethics and the profession of anthropology,* ed. C. Fluehr-Lobban. Philadelphia: University of Pennsylvania Press.

Appendix F: Professional and Ethical Responsibilities, SfAA. 2002. In *Ethics and the profession of anthropology,* ed. C. Fluehr-Lobban. Philadelphia: University of Pennsylvania Press.

Appendix H: National Association of Practicing Anthropologists' Ethical Guidelines for Practitioners, 1988. 1991. In *Ethics and the profession of anthropology,* ed. C. Fluehr-Lobban. Philadelphia: University of Pennsylvania Press.

Appendix I: Revised Principles of Professional Responsibility, 1990. 1991. In *Ethics and the profession of anthropology,* ed. C. Fluehr-Lobban. Philadelphia: University of Pennsylvania Press.

Aptekar, Lewis. 1988. *Street children of Cali.* Durham, NC: Duke University Press.

Aptekar, Lewis. 1991. Are Colombian street children neglected? The contributions of ethnographic and ethnohistorical approaches to the study of children. *Anthropology and Education Quarterly* 22:326–49.

Aptekar, Lewis. 1994. *Environmental disasters in global perspective.* New York: G. K. Hall/Macmillan.

Archer, Dane, and Rosemary Gartner. 1984. *Violence and crime in cross-national perspective.* New Haven, CT: Yale University Press.

Argyle, Michael. 1994. *The psychology of social class.* New York: Routledge.

Armelagos, George J., and Alan H. Goodman. 1998. Race, racism, and anthropology. In *Building a new biocultural synthesis: Political-economic perspectives on human biology,* eds. A. H. Goodman and T. L. Leatherman. Ann Arbor: University of Michigan Press.

Armstrong, Robert P. 1981. *The powers of presence.* Philadelphia: University of Pennsylvania Press.

Aronoff, Joel, Andrew M. Barclay, and Linda A. Stevenson. 1988. The recognition of threatening facial stimuli. *Journal of Personality and Social Psychology* 54:647–55.

Aronoff, Joel, Barbara A. Woike, and Lester M. Hyman. 1992. Which are the stimuli in facial displays of anger and happiness? Configurational bases of emotion recognition. *Journal of Personality and Social Psychology* 62:1050–66.

Asch, Nancy B., and David L. Asch. 1978. The economic potential of *Iva annua* and its prehistoric importance in the Lower Illinois Valley. In *The nature and status of ethnobotany,* ed. R. Ford. Anthropological Papers No 67, Museum of Anthropology. Ann Arbor: University of Michigan.

Asch, Solomon. 1956. Studies of independence and conformity: A minority of one against a unanimous majority. *Psychological Monographs* 70:1–70.

471

Ascher, Robert. 1961. Analogy in archaeological interpretation. *Southwestern Journal of Anthropology* 17:317–25.

Asfaw, Berhane, Tim White, Owen Lovejoy, Bruce Latimer, Scott Simpson, and Glen Suwa. 1999. *Australopithecus garhi:* A new species of early hominid from Ethiopia. *Science* 284 (April 23):629–36.

Ayala, Francisco J. 1995. The myth of Eve: Molecular biology and human origins. *Science* 270 (December 22):1930–36.

Ayala, Francisco J. 1996. Communication. *Science* 274 (November 29):1354.

Ayres, Barbara C. 1973. Effects of infant carrying practices on rhythm in music. *Ethos* 1:387–404.

Bacon, Margaret, Irvin L. Child, and Herbert Barry III. 1963. A cross-cultural study of correlates of crime. *Journal of Abnormal and Social Psychology* 66:291–300.

Badcock, Christopher R. 2000. *Evolutionary psychology: A critical introduction.* Cambridge, UK: Blackwell.

Bahn, Paul. 1998. Neanderthals emancipated. *Nature* 394 (August 20):719–20.

Baldi, Philip. 1983. *An introduction to the Indo-European languages.* Carbondale: Southern Illinois University Press.

Balikci, Asen. 1970. *The Netsilik Eskimo.* Garden City, NY: Natural History Press.

Balter, Michael. 2001. In search of the first Europeans. *Science* 291 (March 2):1722–25.

Balter, Michael. 2007. Seeking agriculture's ancient roots. *Science* 316 (June 29):1830–35.

Balter, Michael, and Ann Gibbons. 2000. A glimpse of humans' first journey out of Africa. *Science* 288 (May 12):948–50.

Barak, Gregg. 1991. *Gimme shelter: A social history of homelessness in contemporary America.* New York: Praeger.

Barash, David P. 1977. *Sociobiology and behavior.* New York: Elsevier.

Barber, Nigel. 2000. The sex ratio as a predictor of cross-national variation in violent crime. *Cross-Cultural Research* 34:264–82.

Barber, Nigel. 2008. Explaining cross-national differences in polygyny intensity: Resource-defense, sex-ratio, and infectious diseases. *Cross-Cultural Research* 42:103–17.

Barinaga, Maria. 1992. Priming the brain's language pump. *Science* 255 (January 31):535.

Barlett, Peggy F. 1989. Industrial agriculture. In *Economic anthropology,* ed. S. Plattner. Stanford, CA: Stanford University Press.

Barnett, Homer G. 1960. *Being a Palauan.* New York: Holt, Rinehart & Winston.

Barnosky, Anthony, Paul Koch, Robert Feranec, Scott Wing, and Alan Shabel. 2004. Assessing the causes of Late Pleistocene extinctions on the continents. *Science* 306 (October 1):70–75.

Barrett, Stanley R. 1994. *Paradise: Class, commuters, and ethnicity in rural Ontario.* Toronto: University of Toronto Press.

Barry, Herbert III. 2007. Wealth concentration associated with frequent violent crime in diverse communities. *Social Evolution and History* 6:29–38.

Barth, Fredrik. 1994. Enduring and emerging issues in the analysis of ethnicity. In *The anthropology of ethnicity,* eds. H. Vermeulen and C. Govers. Amsterdam: Het Spinhuis.

Bates, Elizabeth, and V. A. Marchman, 1988. What is and is not universal in language acquisition. In *Language, communication, and the brain,* ed. F. Plum, 19–38. New York: Raven Press.

Bauman, Richard. 1992. Folklore. In *Folklore, cultural performances, and popular entertainments,* ed. R. Bauman. New York: Oxford University Press.

Baxter, Ellen, and Kim Hopper. 1981. *Private lives/public spaces: Homeless adults on the streets of New York City.* New York: Community Service Society of New York.

Beadle, George, and Muriel Beadle. 1966. *The language of life.* Garden City, NY: Doubleday.

Bearder, Simon K. 1987. Lorises, bushbabies, and tarsiers: Diverse societies in solitary foragers. In *Primate societies,* eds. B. Smuts et al. Chicago: University of Chicago Press.

Begler, Elsie B. 1978. Sex, status, and authority in egalitarian society. *American Anthropologist* 80:571–88.

Begun, David. 2002. Miocene apes. In *Physical anthropology: Original readings in method and practice,* eds. P. N. Peregrine, C. R. Ember, and M. Ember. Upper Saddle River, NJ: Prentice Hall.

Behrman, Jere R., Alejandro Gaviria, and Miguel Székely. 2001. Intergenerational mobility in Latin America. Inter-American Development Bank, Working Paper #45. http://www.iadb.org/res/publications/pubfiles/pubWP-452.pdf (accessed June 2009).

Benjamin, Lois. 1991. *The black elite: Facing the color line in the twilight of the twentieth century.* Chicago: Nelson-Hall.

Berggren, William A., Dennis V. Kent, John D. Obradovich, and Carl C. Swisher III. 1992. Toward a revised paleogene geochronology. In *Eocene-Oliocene climatic and biotic evolution,* eds. D. R. Prothero and W. A. Berggren. Princeton, NJ: Princeton University Press.

Berlin, Brent. 1992. *Ethnobiological classification: Principles of categorization of plants and animals in traditional societies.* Princeton, NJ: Princeton University Press.

Berlin, Brent, and Paul Kay. 1969. *Basic color terms: Their universality and evolution.* Berkeley: University of California Press.

Berlin, Elois A. 1996. General overview of Maya ethnomedicine. In *Medical ethnobiology of the highland Maya of Chiapas, Mexico,* eds. E. A. Berlin and B. Berlin, 52–53. Princeton, NJ: Princeton University Press.

Berlin, Elois Ann, and Brent Berlin. 1996. *Medical ethnobiology of the highland Maya of Chiapas, Mexico: The gastrointestinal diseases.* Princeton, NJ: Princeton University Press.

Bernard, H. Russell. 2001. *Research methods in cultural anthropology: Qualitative and quantitative approaches.* 3rd ed. Walnut Creek, CA: AltaMira Press.

Berns, G., J. Chappelow, C. Zink, G. Pagnoni, M. Martin-Skurski, and J. Richards. 2005. Neurobiological correlates of social conformity and independence during mental rotation. *Biological Psychiatry* 58:245–53.

Berreman, Gerald D. 1960. Caste in India and the United States. *American Journal of Sociology* 66:120–27.

Berreman, Gerald D. 1972. Race, caste and other invidious distinctions in social stratification. *Race* 13:403–14.

Berreman, Gerald D. 1973. *Caste in the modern world.* Morristown, NJ: General Learning Press.

Bestor, Theodore C. 2001. Supply-side sushi: Commodity, market, and the global city. *American Anthropologist* 103:76–95.

Betzig, Laura. 1988. Redistribution: Equity or exploitation? In *Human reproductive behavior,* eds. L. Betzig, M. B. Mulder, and P. Turke, 49–63. Cambridge, UK: Cambridge University Press.

Bickerton, Derek. 1983. Creole languages. *Scientific American* (July):116–22.

Bilby, Kenneth. 1996. Ethnogenesis in the Guianas and Jamaica: Two Maroon cases. In *Ethnogenesis in the Americas,* ed. J. D. Hill, 119–41. Iowa City: University of Iowa Press.

Bilsborough, Alan. 1992. *Human evolution.* New York: Blackie Academic & Professional.

Binford, Lewis R. 1971. Post-Pleistocene adaptations. In *Prehistoric agriculture,* ed. S. Struever. Garden City, NY: Natural History Press.

Binford, Lewis R. 1973. Interassemblage variability: The Mousterian and the "functional" argument. In *The explanation of culture change,* ed. C. Renfrew. Pittsburgh, PA: University of Pittsburgh Press.

Binford, Lewis R. 1984. *Faunal remains from Klasies River mouth.* Orlando, FL: Academic Press.

Binford, Lewis R. 1987. Were there elephant hunters at Torralba? In *The evolution of human hunting,* eds. M. Nitecki and D. Nitecki. New York: Plenum Press.

Binford, Lewis R., and Chuan Kun Ho. 1985. Taphonomy at a distance: Zhoukoudian, "The cave home of Beijing Man"? *Current Anthropology* 26:413–42.

Binford, Sally R., and Lewis R. Binford. 1969. Stone tools and human behavior. *Scientific American* (April):70–84.

Black, Donald. 1993. *The social structure of right and wrong.* San Diego, CA: Academic Press.

Black, Francis L. 1992. Why did they die? *Science* 258 (December 11):1739–40.

Blackwood, Evelyn. 1984a. *Cross-cultural dimensions of lesbian relations.* Master's thesis, San Francisco State University.

Blackwood, Evelyn. 1984b. Sexuality and gender in certain Native American tribes: The case of cross-gender females. *Signs* 10:27–42.

Blackwood, Evelyn, and Saskia E. Wieringa. 1999. Sapphic shadows: Challenging the silence in the study of sexuality. In *Female desires: Same-sex relations and transgender practices across cultures,* eds. Evelyn Blackwood and Saskia E. Weiringa, 39–63. New York: Columbia University Press.

Blalock, Hubert M. 1972. *Social statistics.* 2nd ed. New York: McGraw-Hill.

Blanton, Richard E., and Lane Fargher. 2008. *Collective action in the formation of pre-modern states.* New York: Springer.

Blanton, Richard E., Stephen A. Kowalewski, Gary Feinman, and Jill Appel. 1981. *Ancient Mesoamerica: A comparison of change in three regions.* New York: Cambridge University Press.

Block, Jonathan I., and Doug M. Boyer. 2002. Grasping primate origins. *Science* 298 (November 22):1606–10.

Blount, Ben G. 1981. The development of language in children. In *Handbook of cross-cultural human development,* eds. R. H. Munroe, R. L. Munroe, and B. B. Whiting. New York: Garland.

Blumler, Mark A., and Roger Byrne. 1991. The ecological genetics of domestication and the origins of agriculture. *Current Anthropology* 32:23–35.

Boas, Franz. 1888. *Central Eskimos.* Bureau of American Ethnology Annual Report No. 6. Washington, DC.

Boas, Franz. 1964/1911. On grammatical categories. In *Language in culture and society,* ed. D. Hymes. New York: Harper & Row.

Boaz, Noel T., and Alan J. Almquist. 1997. *Biological anthropology: A synthetic approach to human evolution.* Upper Saddle River, NJ: Prentice Hall.

Boaz, Noel T., and Alan J. Almquist. 1999. *Essentials of biological anthropology.* Upper Saddle River, NJ: Prentice Hall.

Bodley, John H. 1990. *Victims of progress,* 3rd edition. Mountain View CA: Mayfield Publishing Company.

Boehm, Christopher. 1993. Egalitarian behavior and reverse dominance hierarchy. *Current Anthropology* 34:230–31.

Boehm, Christopher. 1999. *Hierarchy in the forest: The evolution of egalitarian behavior.* Cambridge, MA: Harvard University Press.

Boesche, Christophe, P. Marchesi, N. Marchesi, B. Fruth, and F. Joulian. 1994. Is nut cracking in wild chimpanzees a cultural behavior? *Journal of Human Evolution* 26:325–38.

Bogin, Barry. 1988. *Patterns of human growth.* Cambridge, UK: Cambridge University Press.

Bohannan, Laura, and Paul Bohannan. 1953. *The Tiv of central Nigeria.* London: International African Institute.

Bohannan, Paul. 1954. The migration and expansion of the Tiv. *Africa* 24:2–16.

Bollen, Kenneth A. 1993. Liberal democracy: Validity and method factors in cross-national measures. *American Journal of Political Science* 37:1207–30.

Bolton, Ralph. 1989. Introduction: The AIDS pandemic, a global emergency. *Medical Anthropology* 10:93–104.

Bolton, Ralph. 1992. AIDS and promiscuity: Muddled in the models of HIV prevention. *Medical Anthropology* 14:145–223.

Bond, Rod, and Peter B. Smith. 1996. Culture and conformity: A meta-analysis of studies using Asch's (1952b, 1956) line judgment task. *Psychological Bulletin* 11:111–37.

Bondarenko, Dmitri, and Andrey Korotayev. 2000. Family size and community organization: A cross-cultural comparison. *Cross-Cultural Research* 34:152–89.

Bordaz, Jacques. 1970. *Tools of the old and new stone age.* Garden City, NY: Natural History Press.

Bordes, François. 1961. Mousterian cultures in France. *Science* 134 (September 22):803–10.

Bordes, François. 1968. *The old stone age.* New York: McGraw-Hill.

Bornstein, Marc H. 1973. The psychophysiological component of cultural difference in color naming and illusion susceptibility. *Behavior Science Notes* 8:41–101.

Boserup, Ester. 1970. *Woman's role in economic development.* New York: St. Martin's Press.

Boserup, Ester. 1993/1965. *The conditions of agricultural growth: The economics of agrarian change under population pressure.* Toronto: Earthscan.

Bossen, Laurel. 2000. Women farmers, small plots, and changing markets in China. In *Women farmers and commercial ventures: Increasing food security in developing countries,* ed. Anita Spring, 171–89. Boulder, CO: Lynne Rienner Press.

Bourguignon, Erika. 1973. Introduction: A framework for the comparative study of altered states of consciousness. In *Religion, altered states of consciousness, and social change,* ed. E. Bourguignon. Columbus: Ohio State University Press.

Bourguignon, Erika. 2004. Suffering and healing, subordination and power: Women and possession trance. *Ethos* 32:557–74.

Bourguignon, Erika, and Thomas L. Evascu. 1977. Altered states of consciousness within a general evolutionary perspective: A holocultural analysis. *Behavior Science Research* 12:197–216.

Bowie, Katherine A. 2006. Of corvée and slavery: Historical intricacies of the division of labor and state power in northern Thailand. In *Labor in cross-cultural perspective,* eds. E. Paul Durrenberger and Judith E. Martí, 245–64. Lanham, MD: Roman & Littlefield.

Boyd, Robert, and Peter J. Richerson. 1996/1985. *Culture and the evolutionary process.* Chicago: University of Chicago Press.

Boyd, Robert, and Peter J. Richerson. 2005. *The origin and evolution of cultures.* New York: Oxford University Press.

Boyd, Robert, and Joan Silk. 2000. *How humans evolved.* 2nd ed. New York: Norton.

Brace, C. Loring. 1995. Region does not mean "race"—reality versus convention in forensic anthropology. *Journal of Forensic Sciences* 40:171–75.

Brace, C. Loring. 1996. A four-letter word called race. In *Race and other misadventures: Essays in honor of Ashley Montague in his ninetieth year,* eds. Larry T. Reynolds and Leonard Leiberman. New York: General Hall.

Brace, C. Loring, David P. Tracer, Lucia Allen Yaroch, John Robb, Kari Brandt, and A. Russell Nelson. 1993. Clines and clusters versus "race": A test in ancient Egypt and the case of a death on the Nile. *Yearbook of Physical Anthropology* 36:1–31.

Bradley, Candice. 1995. Keeping the soil in good heart: Weeding, women and ecofeminism. In *Ecofeminism,* ed. K. Warren. Bloomington: Indiana University Press.

Bradsher, Keith. 2002. Pakistanis fume as clothing sales to U.S. tumble. *New York Times,* June 23, p. 3.

Braidwood, Robert J. 1960. The agricultural revolution. *Scientific American* (September):130–48.

Brain, C. K., and A. Sillen. 1988. Evidence from the Swartkrans Cave for the earliest use of fire. *Nature,* 336 (December 1):464–66.

Branda, Richard F., and John W. Eaton. 1978. Skin color and nutrient photolysis: An evolutionary hypothesis. *Science* 201 (August 18):625–26.

Brandewie, Ernest. 1991. The place of the big man in traditional Hagen society in the central highlands of New Guinea. In *Anthropological approaches to political behavior,* eds. F. McGlynn and A. Tuden. Pittsburgh, PA: University of Pittsburgh Press.

Brandon, Robert N. 1990. *Adaptation and environment.* Princeton, NJ: Princeton University Press.

Bräuer, Günter. 1984. A craniological approach to the origin of anatomically modern *Homo sapiens* in Africa and implications for the appearance of modern Europeans. In *The origins of modern humans,* eds. F. Smith and F Spencer. New York: Alan R. Liss.

Braun, David P., and Stephen Plog. 1982. Evolution of "tribal" social networks: Theory and prehistoric North American evidence. *American Antiquity* 47:504–25.

Brittain, John A. 1978. *Inheritance and the inequality of material wealth.* Washington, DC: Brookings Institution.

Brodey, Jane E. 1971. Effects of milk on blacks noted. *New York Times,* October 15, p. 15.

Bromage, Timothy G., and M. Christopher Dean. 1985. Reevaluation of the age at death of immature fossil hominids. *Nature* 317 (October 10):525–27.

Brooks, Alison S., Fatimah Linda Collier Jackson, and R. Richard Grinker. 1993. Race and ethnicity in America. *Anthro Notes* (National Museum of Natural History Bulletin for Teachers) 15, no. 3 (Fall):1–3, 11–15.

Broom, Robert. 1950. *Finding the missing link.* London: Watts.

Broude, Gwen J. 1976. Cross-cultural patterning of some sexual attitudes and practices. *Behavior Science Research* 11:227–62.

Broude, Gwen J. 1980. Extramarital sex norms in cross-cultural perspective. *Behavior Science Research* 15:181–218.

Broude, Gwen J. 2009. Variations in sexual attitudes, norms, and practices. In MyAnthroLibrary, eds. C. R. Ember, M. Ember, and P. N. Peregrine. MyAnthroLibrary.com. Pearson.

Broude, Gwen J., and Sarah J. Greene. 1976. Cross-cultural codes on twenty sexual attitudes and practices. *Ethnology* 15:409–29.

Brown, Cecil H. 1977. Folk botanical life-forms: Their universality and growth. *American Anthropologist* 79:317–42.

Brown, Cecil H. 1979. Folk zoological life-forms: Their universality and growth. *American Anthropologist* 81:791–817.

Brown, Cecil H. 1984. World view and lexical uniformities. *Reviews in Anthropology* 11:99–112.

Brown, Cecil H., and Stanley R. Witkowski. 1980. Language universals. In *Toward explaining human culture,* eds. D. Levinson and M. J. Malone, Appendix B. New Haven, CT: HRAF Press.

Brown, Frank H. 1992. Methods of dating. In *The Cambridge encyclopedia of human evolution,* eds. S. Jones, R. Martin, and D. Pilbeam. New York: Cambridge University Press.

Brown, James A. 1983. Summary. In *Archaic hunters and gatherers in the American Midwest,* eds. J. L. Phillips and J. A. Brown, 5–10. New York: Academic Press.

Brown, James A. 1985. Long-term trends to sedentism and the emergence of complexity in the American Midwest. In *Prehistoric hunter-gatherers,* eds. T. Price and J. Brown, 201–31. Orlando, FL: Academic Press.

Brown, James A., and T. Douglas Price. 1985. Complex hunter-gatherers: Retrospect and prospect. In *Prehistoric hunter-gatherers,* eds. T. Price and J. Brown. Orlando, FL: Academic Press.

Brown, Judith K. 1970a. Economic organization and the position of women among the Iroquois. *Ethnohistory* 17:151–67.

Brown, Judith K. 1970b. A note on the division of labor by sex. *American Anthropologist* 72:1073–78.

Brown, Michael F. 2008. Cultural relativism 2.0. *Current Anthropology* 49:363–83.

Brown, Peter J. 1997. Culture and the evolution of obesity. In *Applying cultural anthropology,* eds. A. Podolefsky and P. J. Brown. Mountain View, CA: Mayfield.

Brown, Peter J., T. Sutikna, M. J. Morwood, R. P. Soejono, Jatmiko, E. Wayhu Saptomo, and Rokus Awe Due. 2004. A new small-bodied hominin from the Late Pleistocene of Flores, Indonesia. *Nature* 431 (October 28):1055–061.

Brown, Roger. 1965. *Social psychology.* New York: Free Press.

Brown, Roger. 1980. The first sentence of child and chimpanzee. In *Speaking of apes,* eds. T. A. Sebeok and J. Umiker-Sebeok. New York: Plenum Press.

Brown, Roger, and Marguerite Ford. 1961. Address in American English. *Journal of Abnormal and Social Psychology* 62:375–85.

Browner, Carole H. 1985. Criteria for selecting herbal remedies. *Ethnology* 24:13–32.

Brues, Alice. 1992. Forensic diagnosis of race—General race versus specific populations. *Social Science and Medicine* 34:125–28.

Brumbach, Hetty Jo, and Robert Jarvenpa. 2006. Chipewyan society and gender relations. In *Circumpolar lives and livelihood: A comparative ethnoarchaeology of gender and subsistence,* eds. R. Jarvenpa and H. J. Brumbach, 24–53. Lincoln: University of Nebraska Press.

Brumfiel, Elizabeth M. 1976. Regional growth in the eastern Valley of Mexico: A test of the "population pressure" hypothesis.

In *The early Mesoamerican village,* ed. K. Flannery. New York: Academic Press.

Brumfiel, Elizabeth M. 1983. Aztec state making: Ecology, structure, and the origin of the state. *American Anthropologist* 85:261–84.

Brunet, Michel, Alain Beauvilain, Yves Coppens, Elile Heintz, Aladji H. E. Moutaye, and David Pilbeam. 1995. The first australopithecine 2,500 kilometers west of the Rift Valley (Chad). *Nature* 378:273–75.

Brunet, Michel, Franck Guy, David Pilbeam, Hassane Taisso Mackaye, Andossa Likius, Djimdoumalbaye Ahounta, Alain Beauvilain, Cécile Blondel, Hervé Bocherens, Jean-Renaud Boisserie, Louis De Bonis, Yves Coppens, Jean Dejax, Christiane Denys, Philippe Duringer, Véra Eisenmann, Gongdibé Fanone, Pierre Fronty, Denis Geraads, Thomas Lehmann, Fabrice Lihoreau, Antoine Louchart, Adoum Mahamat, Gildas Merceron, Guy Mouchelin, Olga Otero, Pablo Pelaez Campomanes, Marcia Ponce De Leon, Jean-Claude Rage, Michel Sapanet, Mathieu Schuster, Jean Sudre, Pascal Tassy, Xavier Valentin, Patrick Vignaud, Laurent Viriot, Antoine Zazzo, and Christoph Zollikofer. 2002. A new hominid from the upper Miocene of Chad, Central Africa. *Nature* 418 (July 11):145–51.

Brunvand, Jan Harold. 1993. *The baby train: And other lusty urban legends.* New York: Norton.

Bryant, Carol A., and Doraine F. C. Bailey. 1990. The use of focus group research in program development. In *Soundings,* eds. J. van Willigen and T. L. Finan. NAPA Bulletin No. 10. Washington, DC: American Anthropological Association.

Buckser, Andrew, and Stephen D. Glazier, eds. 2003. Preface. In *The anthropology of religious conversion,* eds. Andrew Buckser and Stephen D. Glazier. Lanham, MD: Roman & Littlefield.

Buettner-Janusch, John. 1973. *Physical anthropology: A perspective.* New York: Wiley.

Burbank, Victoria K. 1994. *Fighting women: Anger and aggression in aboriginal Australia.* Berkeley: University of California Press.

Burbank, Victoria K. 2009. Australian Aborigines: An adolescent mother and her family. In MyAnthroLibrary, eds. C. R. Ember, M. Ember, and P. N. Peregrine. MyAnthroLibrary.com. Pearson.

Burkhalter, S. Brian, and Robert F. Murphy. 1989. Tappers and sappers: Rubber, gold and money among the Mundurucú. *American Ethnologist* 16:100–16.

Busby, Annette. 2009. Kurds: A culture straddling national borders. In MyAnthroLibrary, eds. C. R. Ember, M. Ember, and P. N. Peregrine. MyAnthroLibrary.com. Pearson.

Butzer, Karl W. 1982. Geomorphology and sediment stratigraphy. In *The Middle Stone Age at Klasies River Mouth in South Africa,* eds. R. Singer and J. Wymer. Chicago: University of Chicago Press.

Byrne, Bryan. 1994. Access to subsistence resources and the sexual division of labor among potters. *Cross-Cultural Research* 28:225–50.

Byrne, Roger. 1987. Climatic change and the origins of agriculture. In *Studies in the Neolithic and urban revolutions,* ed. L. Manzanilla. British Archaeological Reports International Series 349. Oxford: British Archaeological Reports.

Calvin, William H. 1983. *The throwing Madonna: Essays on the brain.* New York: McGraw-Hill.

Campbell, Donald T. 1965. Variation and selective retention in socio-cultural evolution. In *Social change in developing areas,* eds. H. Barringer, G. Blankstein, and R. Mack. Cambridge, MA: Schenkman.

Campbell, Joseph. 1949. *The hero with a thousand faces.* New York: Pantheon.

Cann, Rebecca. 1988. DNA and human origins. *Annual Review of Anthropology* 17:127–43.

Cann, Rebecca, M. Stoneking, and A. C. Wilson. 1987. Mitochondrial DNA and human evolution. *Nature* 325 (January 1):31–36.

Caporael, Linnda R. 1976. Ergotism: The Satan loosed in Salem? *Science* (April 2):21–26.

Carbonell, Eudald, José M. Bermúdez de Castro, Josep M. Parés, Alfredo Pérez-González, Gloria Cuenca-Bescós, Andreu Ollé, Marina Mosquera, Rosa Huguet, Jan van der Made,

Antonio Rosas, Robert Sala, Josep Vallverdú, Nuria García, Darryl E. Granger, María Martinón-Torres, Xosé P. Rodríguez, Greg M. Stock, Josep M. Vergès, Ethel Allué, Francesc Burjachs, Isabel Cáceres, Antoni Canals, Alfonso Benito, Carlos Díez, Marina Lozano, Ana Mateos, Marta Navazo, Jesús Rodríguez, Jordi Rosell, Juan L. Arsuaga. 2008. The first hominin of Europe. *Nature* 452 (March 27):465–69.

Carcopino, Jerome. 1940. *Daily life in ancient Rome: The people and the city at the height of the empire.* Edited with bibliography and notes by Henry T. Rowell. Translated from the French by E. O. Lorimer. New Haven, CT: Yale University Press.

Cardoso, Fernando Luis and Dennis Werner. 2004. Homosexuality. In *Encyclopedia of sex and gender: Men and women in the world's cultures*, vol 1., eds. C. Ember and M. Ember, 204–15. New York: Kluwer Academic/Plenum Press.

Carey, James W., Erin Picone-DeCaro, Mary Spink Neumann, Devorah Schwartz, Delia Easton, and Daphne Cobb St. John. 2004. HIV/AIDS research and prevention. In *Encyclopedia of medical anthropology: Health and illness in the world's cultures*, vol. 1, eds. C. R. Ember and M. Ember, 462–79. New York: Kluwer Academic/Plenum Press.

Carneiro, Robert L. 1970. A theory of the origin of the state. *Science* 169 (August 21):733–38.

Carneiro, Robert L. 1978. Political expansion as an expression of the principle of competitive exclusion. In *Origins of the state*, eds. R. Cohen and E. R. Service. Philadelphia: Institute for the Study of Human Issues.

Carneiro, Robert L. 1988. The circumscription theory: Challenge and response. *American Behavioral Scientist* 31:497–511.

Carneiro, Robert L. 1990. Chiefdom-level warfare as exemplified in Fiji and the Cauca Valley. In *The anthropology of war*, ed. J. Haas. New York: Cambridge University Press.

Carpenter, Clarence R. 1940. A field study in Siam of the behavior and social relations of the gibbon (*Hylobates lar*). *Comparative Psychology Monographs* 16(5):1–212.

Carrier, Joseph, and Ralph Bolton. 1991. Anthropological perspectives on sexuality and HIV prevention. *Annual Review of Sex Research* 2:49–75.

Carroll, John B., ed. 1956. *Language, thought, and reality: Selected writings of Benjamin Lee Whorf.* New York: Wiley.

Cartmill, Matt. 1974. Rethinking primate origins. *Science* (April 26):436–37.

Cartmill, Matt. 1992a. New views on primate origins. *Evolutionary Anthropology* 1:105–11.

Cartmill, Matt. 1992b. Non-human primates. In *The Cambridge encyclopedia of human evolution*, eds. S. Jones, R. Martin, and D. Pilbeam. New York: Cambridge University Press.

Cartmill, Matt. 2009. Explaining primate origins. In MyAnthroLibrary, eds. C. R. Ember, M. Ember, and P. N. Peregrine. MyAnthroLibrary.com. Pearson.

Cashdan, Elizabeth. 1980. Egalitarianism among hunters and gatherers. *American Anthropologist* 82:116–20.

Cashdan, Elizabeth. 2001. Ethnic diversity and its environmental determinants: Effects of climate, pathogens, and habitat diversity. *American Anthropologist* 103:968–91.

Cavalli-Sforza, L. Luca, and Marcus W. Feldman. 2003. The application of molecular genetic approaches to the study of human evolution. *Nature Genetics Supplement* 33:266–75.

Caws, Peter. 1969. The structure of discovery. *Science* 166 (December 12):1375–80.

Center for Renewal of Science and Culture. 2001. The wedge strategy, cited in Barbara Forrest, "The wedge at work." In *Intelligent design creationism and its critics*. ed. Robert Pennock, 16. Boston, IT Press.

Chacon, Richard J., and Rubén G. Mendoza. 2007. Ethical considerations and conclusions regarding indigenous warfare and ritual violence in Latin America. In *Latin American indigenous warfare and ritual violence*, eds. Richard J. Chacon and Rubén G. Mendoza. Tucson: University of Arizona Press.

Chafetz, Janet Saltzman. 1990. *Gender equity: An integrated theory of stability and change.* Sage Library of Social Research No. 176. Newbury Park, CA: Sage.

Chagnon, Napoleon. 1983. *Yanomamö: The fierce people.* 3rd ed. New York: Holt, Rinehardt, and Winston.

Chang, Kwang-Chih. 1968. *The archaeology of ancient China.* New Haven, CT: Yale University Press.

Chang, Kwang-Chih. 1970. The beginnings of agriculture in the Far East. *Antiquity* 44:175–85.

Chang, Kwang-Chih. 1981. In search of China's beginnings: New light on an old civilization. *American Scientist* 69:148–60.

Chang, Kwang-Chih. 1986. *Archaeology of ancient China.* 4th ed. New Haven, CT: Yale University Press.

Chapais, Bernard. 2008. *Primeval kinship: How pair-bonding gave birth to human society.* Cambridge, MA: Harvard University Press.

Chard, Chester S. 1969. *Man in prehistory.* New York: McGraw-Hill.

Chase, Philip, and Harold Dibble. 1987. Middle Paleolithic symbolism: A review of current evidence and interpretations. *Journal of Anthropological Archaeology* 6:263–69.

Chatterjee, Sankar. 1997. *The rise of birds: 225 million years of evolution.* Baltimore: Johns Hopkins University Press.

Chaucer, Geoffrey. 1926. *The prologue to the Canterbury Tales, the Knights Tale, the Nonnes Prestes Tale*, ed. Mark H. Liddell. New York: Macmillan.

Chessa, Bernardo, Filipe Pereira, Frederick Arnaud, Antonio Amorim, Félix Goyache, Ingrid Mainland, Rowland R. Kao, Josephine M. Pemberton, Dario Beraldi, Michael J. Stear, Alberto Alberti, Marco Pittau, Leopoldo Iannuzzi, Mohammad H. Banabazi, Rudovick R. Kazwala, Ya-ping Zhang, Juan J. Arranz, Bahy A. Ali, Zhiliang Wang, Metehan Uzun, Michel M. Dione, Ingrid Olsaker, Lars-Erik Holm, Urmas Saarma, Sohail Ahmad, Nurbiy Marzanov, Emma Eythorsdottir, Martin J. Holland, Paolo Ajmone-Marsan, Michael W. Brutord, Juha Kantanen, Thomas E. Spencer, and Massimo Palmarini. 2009. Revealing the history of sheep domestication using retrovirus integrations. *Science* 324 (April 24):532–36.

Chibnik, Michael. 1981. The evolution of cultural rules. *Journal of Anthropological Research* 37:256–68.

Childe, V. Gordon. 1950. The urban revolution. *Town Planning Review* 21:3–17.

Chimpanzee Sequencing and Analysis Consortium. 2005. Initial sequence of the chimpanzee genome and comparison with the human genome. *Nature* 437 (September 1):69–87.

Chivers, David J. 1974. *The siamang in Malaya.* Basel, Switzerland: Karger.

Chomsky, Noam. 1975. *Reflections on language.* New York: Pantheon.

Christensen, Pia, Jenny Hockey, and Allison James, 2001. Talk, silence and the material world: Patterns of indirect communication among agricultural farmers in northern England. In *An anthropology of indirect communication*, eds. J. Hendry and C. W. Watson, 68–82. London: Routledge.

Ciochon, Russell, John Olsen, and Jamie James. 1990. *Other origins: The search for the giant ape in human prehistory.* New York: Bantam.

Ciochon, Russell L., and Dennis A. Etler. 1994. Reinterpreting past primate diversity. In *Integrative paths to the past*, eds. R. Corruccini and R. Ciochon. Upper Saddle River, NJ: Prentice Hall.

Claassen, Cheryl. 1991. Gender, shellfishing, and the Shell Mound Archaic. In *Engendering Archaeology*, eds. J. Gero and M. Conkey. Oxford, UK: Blackwell.

Claassen, Cheryl. 2009. Gender and archaeology. In MyAnthroLibrary, eds. C. R. Ember, M. Ember, and P. N. Peregrine. MyAnthroLibrary.com. Pearson.

Clark, J. Desmond. 1970. *The prehistory of Africa.* New York: Praeger.

Clark, J. Desmond. 1977. Interpretations of prehistoric technology from ancient Egyptian and other sources. Pt. II: Prehistoric arrow forms in Africa as shown by surviving examples of the traditional arrows of the San Bushmen. *Paleorient* 3:127–50.

Clark, Gracia. 2000. Small-scale traders' key role in stabilizing and diversifying Ghana's rural communities and livelihoods. In *Women farmers and commercial ventures: Increasing food security in developing countries,* ed. Anita Spring, 253–70. Boulder, CO: Lynne Rienner.

Clark, Grahame. 1975. *The earlier stone age settlement of Scandinavia.* Cambridge, UK: Cambridge University Press.

Clark, W. E. Le Gros. 1964. *The fossil evidence for human evolution.* Chicago: University of Chicago Press.

Clarke, Ronald J., and P. V. Tobias. 1995. Sterkfontein member 2 foot bones of the oldest South African hominid. *Science* 269 (July 28):521–24.

Clayman, Charles B., ed. 1989. *American Medical Association encyclopedia of medicine.* New York: Random House.

Clutton-Brock, Juliet. 1992. Domestication of animals. In *The Cambridge encyclopedia of human evolution,* eds. S. Jones, R. Martin, and D. Pilbeam. New York: Cambridge University Press.

Coale, Ansley J. 1974. The history of the human population. *Scientific American* (September):41–51.

Coe, Michael D. 1966. *The Maya.* New York: Praeger.

Cohen, Alex. 1990. A cross-cultural study of the effects of environmental unpredictability on aggression in folktales. *American Anthropologist* 92:474–79.

Cohen, Alex. 1999. *The mental health of indigenous peoples: An international overview.* Geneva: Department of Mental Health, World Health Organization.

Cohen, Alex, and Paul Koegel. 2009. Homelessness. In MyAnthroLibrary, eds. C. R. Ember, M. Ember, and P. N. Peregrine. MyAnthroLibrary.com. Pearson.

Cohen, Mark N. 1977a. *The food crisis in prehistory: Overpopulation and the origins of agriculture.* New Haven, CT: Yale University Press.

Cohen, Mark N. 1977b. Population pressure and the origins of agriculture. In *Origins of agriculture,* ed. C. A. Reed. The Hague: Monton.

Cohen, Mark N. 1987. The significance of long-term changes in human diet and food economy. In *Food and evolution,* eds. M. Harris and E. Ross. Philadelphia: Temple University Press.

Cohen, Mark N. 1989. *Health and the rise of civilization.* New Haven, CT: Yale University Press.

Cohen, Mark N. 2009. Were early agriculturalists less healthy than food collectors? In MyAnthroLibrary, eds. C. R. Ember, M. Ember, and P. N. Peregrine. MyAnthroLibrary.com. Pearson.

Cohen, Mark N., and George J. Armelagos. 1984. Paleopathology at the origins of agriculture: Editors' summation. In *Paleopathology at the origins of agriculture,* eds. M. N. Cohen and G. J. Armelagos. Orlando, FL: Academic Press.

Cohen, Ronald, and Elman R. Service, eds. 1978. *Origins of the state: The anthropology of political evolution.* Philadelphia: Institute for the Study of Human Issues.

COHMAP (Cooperative Holocene Mapping Project) Personnel. 1988. Climatic changes of the last 18,000 years. *Science* 241 (August 26):1043–52.

Collins, Desmond. 1976. Later hunters in Europe. In *The origins of Europe,* ed. D. Collins. New York: Thomas Y. Crowell.

Collins, James, and Richard Blot. 2003. *Literacy and literacies.* Cambridge, UK: Cambridge University Press.

Connah, Graham. 1987. *African civilizations: Precolonial cities and states in tropical Africa.* Cambridge, UK: Cambridge University Press.

Conroy, Glenn C. 1990. *Primate evolution.* New York: Norton.

Cooper, Richard S., Charles N. Rotimi, and Ryk Ward. 1999. The puzzle of hypertension in African Americans. *Scientific American* (February):56–63.

Coreil, Jeannine. 1989. Lessons from a community study of oral rehydration therapy in Haiti. In *Making our research useful,* eds. J. van Willigen, B. Rylko-Bauer, and A. McElroy. Boulder, CO: Westview Press.

Coult, Allan D., and Robert W. Habenstein. 1965. *Cross tabulations of Murdock's "World ethnographic sample."* Columbia: University of Missouri Press.

Crawford, Gary W. 1992. Prehistoric plant domestication in East Asia. In *The origins of agriculture,* eds. C. Cowan and P. Watson. Washington, DC: Smithsonian Institution Press.

Crockett, Carolyn, and John F. Eisenberg. 1987. Howlers: Variations in group size and demography. In *Primate societies,* eds. B. Smuts et al. Chicago: University of Chicago Press.

Crystal, David. 1971. *Linguistics.* Middlesex, UK: Penguin.

Culotta, Elizabeth. 1995. New hominid crowds the field. *Science* 269 (August 18):918.

Culotta, Elizabeth. 2005. Calorie count reveals Neandertals out-ate hardiest modern humans. *Science* 307 (February 11):840.

Cutright, Phillips. 1967. Inequality: A cross-national analysis. *American Sociological Review* 32:562–78.

Daiger, Stephen. 2005. Was the human genome project worth the effort? *Science* 308 (April 15):362–64.

Daly, Martin, and Margo Wilson. 1988. *Homicide.* New York: Aldine.

Daniel, I. Randolph. 2001. Early Eastern Archaic. In *Encyclopedia of prehistory,* vol. 6: North America, eds. P. N. Peregrine and M. Ember. New York: Kluwer Academic/Plenum Press.

Darwin, Charles. 1970/1859. The origin of species. In *Evolution of man,* ed. L. B. Young. New York: Oxford University Press.

Davenport, William. 1959. Nonunilinear descent and descent groups. *American Anthropologist* 61:557–72.

Davis, William D. 1971. Societal complexity and the nature of primitive man's conception of the supernatural. Doctoral dissertation, University of North Carolina, Chapel Hill.

Dawson, Alistair. 1992. *Ice age earth.* London: Routledge.

Day, Michael. 1986. *Guide to fossil man.* 4th ed. Chicago: University of Chicago Press.

De Laguna, Frederica. 1972. *Under Mount Saint Elias: The history and culture of the Yakutat Tlingit.* Washington, DC: Smithsonian Institution Press, as seen in the eHRAF Collection of Ethnography on the Web, 2000.

de Lumley, Henry. 1969. A Paleolithic camp at Nice. *Scientific American* (May):42–50.

DeMenocal, Peter. 2001. Cultural responses to climate change during the late Holocene. *Science* 292 (April 27):667–73.

de Villiers, Peter A., and Jill G. de Villiers. 1979. *Early language.* Cambridge, MA: Harvard University Press.

de Waal, Frans. 2001. *The ape and the sushi master: Cultural reflections of a primatologist.* New York: Basic Books.

De Waal, Frans, and Frans Lanting. 1997. *Bonobo: The forgotten ape.* Berkeley: University of California Press.

Deacon, Terrence. 1992. Primate brains and senses. In *The Cambridge encyclopedia of human evolution,* eds. S. Jones, R. Martin, and D. Pilbeam. New York: Cambridge University Press.

Denham, Tim P., S. G. Haberle, C. Lentfer, R. Fullagar, J. Field, M. Therin, N. Porch, and B. Winsborough. 2003. Origins of agriculture at Kuk Swamp in the highlands of New Guinea. *Science* 301 (July 11):189–93.

Denny, J. Peter. 1979. The "extendedness" variable in classifier semantics: Universal features and cultural variation. In *Ethnolinguistics,* ed. M. Mathiot. The Hague: Mouton.

Devilliers, Charles, and Jean Chaline. 1993. *Evolution: An evolving theory.* New York: Springer.

DeVore, Irven, and Melvin J. Konner. 1974. Infancy in hunter-gatherer life: An ethological perspective. In *Ethology and psychiatry,* ed. N. F. White. Toronto: Ontario Mental Health Foundation and University of Toronto Press.

Diamond, Jared. 1989. The accidental conqueror. *Discover* (December):71–76.

Diamond, Jared. 1991. The saltshaker's curse—Physiological adaptations that helped American Blacks survive slavery may now be predisposing their descendants to hypertension. *Natural History* (October):20–27.

Diamond, Jared. 1993. Who are the Jews? *Natural History* (November):12–9.

Diamond, Jared. 1997. *Guns, germs, and steel.* New York: Norton.

Diamond, Norma. 1975. Collectivization, kinship, and the status of women in rural China. In R. R. Reiter, *Toward an anthropology of women.* New York: Monthly Review Press.

Dillehay, Thomas. 2000. *The settlement of the Americas.* New York: Basic Books.

Dirks, Robert. 1993. Starvation and famine. *Cross-Cultural Research* 27:28–69.

Dirks, Robert. 2009. Hunger and famine. In MyAnthroLibrary, eds. C. R. Ember, M. Ember, and P. N. Peregrine. MyAnthroLibrary .com. Pearson.

Divale, William T. 1974. Migration, external warfare, and matrilocal residence. *Behavior Science Research* 9:75–133.

Divale, William T., and Marvin Harris. 1976. Population, warfare, and the male supremacist complex. *American Anthropologist* 78:521–38.

Dobzhansky, Theodosius. 1962. *Mankind evolving: The evolution of the human species.* New Haven, CT: Yale University Press.

Dobzhansky, Theodosius. 1973. *Genetic diversity and human equality.* New York: Basic Books.

Dow, James. 1986. *The shaman's touch: Otomi Indian symbolic healing.* Salt Lake City: University of Utah Press.

Dowling, John H. 1975. Property relations and productive strategies in pastoral societies. *American Ethnologist* 2:419–26.

Doyle, Rodger. 2005. Leveling the playing field: Economic development helps women pull even with men. *Scientific American* (June):32.

Doyle, Gerald A., and R. D. Martin, eds. 1979. *The study of prosimian behavior.* New York: Academic Press.

Draper, Patricia. 1975. !Kung women: Contrasts in sexual egalitarianism in foraging and sedentary contexts. In *Toward an anthropology of women,* ed. R. R. Reiter. New York: Monthly Review Press.

Dressler, William W. 1993. Health in the African American community: Accounting for health inequalities. *Medical Anthropology Quarterly* 7:325–45.

Dressler, William W., and Michael C. Robbins. 1975. Art styles, social stratification, and cognition: An analysis of Greek vase painting. *American Ethnologist* 2:427–34.

Drucker, Philip. 1965. *Cultures of the north Pacific coast.* San Francisco: Chandler.

Duarte, Cidalia, J. Mauricio, P. B. Pettitt, P. Souto, E. Trinkaus, H. van der Plicht, and J. Zilhao. 1999. The early Upper Paleolithic human skeleton from the Abrigo do Lagar Velho (Portugal) and modern human emergence in Iberia. *Proceedings of the National Academy of Sciences of the United States* 96:7604–09.

Dunbar, Robin, and Susanne Shultz. 2007. Evolution of the social brain. *Science* 317 (September 7):1344–47.

Dundes, Alan. 1965. Structural typology in North American Indian folktales. In *The study of folklore,* ed. A. Dundes. Upper Saddle River, NJ: Prentice Hall.

Dundes, Alan. 1989. *Folklore matters.* Knoxville: University of Tennessee Press.

Durham, William H. 1991. *Coevolution: Genes, culture and human diversity.* Stanford, CA: Stanford University Press.

Durkheim, Émile. 1938/1895. *The rules of sociological method.* 8th ed. trans. Sarah A. Soloway and John H. Mueller. ed. George E. Catlin. New York: Free Press.

Durrenberger, E. Paul. 2001a. Anthropology and globalization. *American Anthropologist* 103:531–35.

Durrenberger, E. Paul. 2001b. Explorations of class and consciousness in the U.S. *Journal of Anthropological Research* 57:41–60.

Dyson-Hudson, Neville. 1966. *Karimojong politics.* Oxford, UK: Clarendon Press.

Eckhardt, William. 1975. Primitive militarism. *Journal of Peace Research* 12:55–62.

eHRAF World Cultures. http://ehrafworldcultures.yale.edu. Accessed 2000.

Eisenberg, John F. 1977. Comparative ecology and reproduction of New World monkeys. In *The biology and conservation of the Callitrichidae.* ed. Devra Kleinman. Washington, DC: Smithsonian Institution Press.

Ekman, Paul, and Dachner Keltner. 1997. Universal facial expressions of emotion: An old controversy and new findings. In *Nonverbal communication: Where nature meets culture,* eds. U. Segerstrale and P. Molnar. Mahwah, NJ: Erlbaum.

Eldredge, Niles, and S. J. Gould. 1972. Punctuated equilibria: An alternative to phyletic gradualism. In *Models in Paleobiology,* ed. TJM Schopf, 82–115. San Francisco: Freeman, Cooper & Co.

Eliot, Thomas Sterns. 1963. The love song of J. Alfred Prufrock. In *Collected poems, 1909–1962.* New York: Harcourt, Brace & World.

Ellis, Lee. 1986. Evidence of neuroandrogenic etiology of sex roles from a combined analysis of human, nonhuman primate and nonprimate mammalian studies. *Personality and Individual Differences* 7:519–52.

Ember, Carol R. 1973. Feminine task assignment and the social behavior of boys. *Ethos* 1:424–39.

Ember, Carol R. 1974. An evaluation of alternative theories of matrilocal versus patrilocal residence. *Behavior Science Research* 9:135–49.

Ember, Carol R. 1975. Residential variation among hunter-gatherers. *Behavior Science Research* 9:135–49.

Ember, Carol R. 1978. Myths about hunter-gatherers. *Ethnology* 17:439–48.

Ember, Carol R. 1981. A cross-cultural perspective on sex differences. In *Handbook of cross-cultural human development,* eds. R. H. Munroe, R. L. Munroe, and B. B. Whiting. New York: Garland.

Ember, Carol R. 1982. The conditions favoring religious conversion. Paper presented at the annual meeting of the Society for Cross-Cultural Research, February. Minneapolis, Minnesota.

Ember, Carol R. 1983. The relative decline in women's contribution to agriculture with intensification. *American Anthropologist* 85:285–304.

Ember, Carol R., and Melvin Ember. 1972. The conditions favoring multilocal residence. *Southwestern Journal of Anthropology* 28:382–400.

Ember, Carol R., and Melvin Ember. 1984. The evolution of human female sexuality: A cross-species perspective. *Journal of Anthropological Research* 40:202–10.

Ember, Carol R., and Melvin Ember. 1992. Resource unpredictability, mistrust, and war: A cross-cultural study. *Journal of Conflict Resolution* 36:242–62.

Ember, Carol R., and Melvin Ember. 1993. Issues in cross-cultural studies of interpersonal violence. *Violence and Victims* 8:217–33.

Ember, Carol R., and Melvin Ember. 1994. War, socialization, and interpersonal violence: A cross-cultural study. *Journal of Conflict Resolution* 38:620–46.

Ember, Carol R., and Melvin Ember. 1997. Violence in the ethnographic record: Results of cross-cultural research on war and aggression. In *Troubled times,* eds. D. Martin and D. Frayer. Langhorn, PA: Gordon and Breach.

Ember, Carol R., and Melvin Ember. 2005. Explaining corporal punishment of children: A cross-cultural study. *American Anthropologist* 107:609–19.

Ember, Carol R. and Melvin Ember. 2009a. On Cross-Cultural Research. In MyAnthroLibrary, eds. C. R. Ember, M. Ember, and P. N. Peregrine. MyAnthroLibrary.com. Pearson.

Ember, Carol R., and Melvin Ember. 2009b. *Cross-cultural research methods.* 2nd ed. Lanham, CA: AltaMira Press.

Ember, Carol R., Melvin Ember, Andrey Korotayev, Victor de Munck. 2005. Valuing thinness or fatness in women: Reevaluating the effect of resource scarcity. *Evolution and Human Behavior* 26:257–70.

Ember, Carol R., Melvin Ember, and Burton Pasternak. 1974. On the development of unilineal descent. *Journal of Anthropological Research* 30:69–94.

Ember, Carol R., Melvin Ember, and Peter N. Peregrine. 2011. *Anthropology.* 13th ed. Upper Saddle River, NJ: Prentice Hall.

Ember, Carol R., Melvin Ember, and Bruce Russett. 1992. Peace between participatory polities: A cross-cultural test of the "democracies rarely fight each other" hypothesis. *World Politics* 44:573–99.

Ember, Carol R., and David Levinson. 1991. The substantive contributions of worldwide cross-cultural studies using secondary data. *Behavior Science Research* [Special issue: Cross-cultural and comparative research: Theory and method], 25:79–140.

Ember, Melvin. 1963. The relationship between economic and political development in nonindustrialized societies. *Ethnology* 2:228–48.

Ember, Melvin. 1967. The emergence of neolocal residence. *Transactions of the New York Academy of Sciences* 30:291–302.

Ember, Melvin. 1970. Taxonomy in comparative studies. In *A handbook of method in cultural anthropology*, eds. R. Naroll and R. Cohen. Garden City, NY: Natural History Press.

Ember, Melvin. 1974a. The conditions that may favor avunculocal residence. *Behavior Science Research* 9:203–09.

Ember, Melvin. 1974b. Warfare, sex ratio, and polygyny. *Ethnology* 13:197–206.

Ember, Melvin. 1975. On the origin and extension of the incest taboo. *Behavior Science Research* 10:249–81.

Ember, Melvin. 1978. Size of color lexicon: Interaction of cultural and biological factors. *American Anthropologist* 80:364–67.

Ember, Melvin. 1982. Statistical evidence for an ecological explanation of warfare. *American Anthropologist* 84:645–49.

Ember, Melvin. 1984–1985. Alternative predictors of polygyny. *Behavior Science Research* 19:1–23.

Ember, Melvin, and Carol R. Ember. 1971. The conditions favoring matrilocal versus patrilocal residence. *American Anthropologist* 73:571–94.

Ember, Melvin, and Carol R. Ember. 1979. Male-Female bonding: A cross-species study of mammals and birds. *Behavior Science Research* 14:37–56.

Ember, Melvin, and Carol R. Ember. 1992. Cross-cultural studies of war and peace: Recent achievements and future possibilities. In *Studying war*, eds. S. P. Reyna and R. E. Downs. New York: Gordon and Breach.

Ember, Melvin, and Carol R. Ember. 1999. Cross-language predictors of consonant-vowel syllables. *American Anthropologist* 101:730–42.

Ember, Melvin, Carol R. Ember, and Bobbi S. Low. 2007. Comparing explanations of polygyny. *Cross-Cultural Research* 41:428–40.

Ensminger, Jean. 1997. Transaction costs and Islam: Explaining conversion in Africa. *Journal of Institutional and Theoretical Economics* 153:4–29.

Ensminger, Jean. 2002. Experimental economics: A powerful new method for theory testing in anthropology. In *Theory in economic anthropology*, ed. J. Ensminger, 59–78. Walnut Creek, CA: AltaMira Press.

Epstein, Cynthia Fuchs. 1988. *Deceptive distinctions: Sex, gender, and the social order*. New York: Russell Sage Foundation.

Erchak, Gerald M. 2009. Family violence. In MyAnthroLibrary, eds. C. R. Ember, M. Ember, and P. N. Peregrine. MyAnthroLibrary .com. Pearson.

Ericksen, Karen Paige, and Heather Horton. 1992. "Blood feuds": Cross-cultural variations in kin group vengeance. *Behavior Science Research* 26:57–85.

Erickson, Clark. 1988. Raised field agriculture in the Lake Titicaca basin. *Expedition* 30(1):8–16.

Erickson, Clark. 1989. Raised fields and sustainable agriculture in the Lake Titicaca basin of Peru. In *Fragile lands of Latin America*, ed. John Browder, 230–48. Boulder: Westview Press.

Erickson, Clark. 1998. Applied archaeology and rural development. In *Crossing currents: Continuity and change in Latin America*, eds. Michael Whiteford and Scott Whiteford, 34–45. Upper Saddle River, NJ: Prentice Hall.

Erickson, Clark. 2003. Agricultural landscapes as world heritage: Raised field agriculture in Bolivia and Peru. In *Managing Change: Sustainable Approaches to the Conservation of the Built Environment*, eds. Jeanne-Marie Teutonico and Frank Matero, 181–204. Los Angeles: Getty Conservation Institute.

Erickson, Edwin. 1968. Self-assertion, sex role, and vocal rasp. In *Folk song style and culture*, ed. A. Lomax. Washington, DC: American Association for the Advancement of Science.

Eswaran, Vinayak. 2002. A diffusion wave out of Africa. *Current Anthropology* 43:749–74.

Etienne, Mona, and Eleanor Leacock, eds. 1980. *Women and colonization: Anthropological perspectives*. New York: Praeger.

Etkin, Nina L., and Paul J. Ross. 1997. Malaria, medicine, and meals: A biobehavioral perspective. In *The anthropology of medicine*, eds. L. Romanucci-Ross, D. E. Moerman, and L. R. Tancredi, 169–209. Westport, CT: Bergin & Garvey.

Evans-Pritchard, Edward E. 1940. The Nuer of the Southern Sudan. In *African political systems*, eds. M. Fortes and E. E. Evans-Pritchard. New York: Oxford University Press.

Evans-Pritchard, Edward E. 1979. Witchcraft explains unfortunate events. In *Reader in comparative religion*. 3rd ed. eds. W. A. Lessa and E. Z. Vogt. New York: Harper & Row.

Eveleth, Phyllis B., and James M. Tanner. 1990. *Worldwide variation in human growth*. 2nd ed. Cambridge, UK: Cambridge University Press.

Eversole, Robyn. 2005. "Direct to the poor": Revisited: Migrant remittances and development assistance. In *Migration and economy: Global and local dynamics*, ed. Lillian Trager, 289–322. Walnut Creek, CA: AltaMira Press.

Fagan, Brian M. 1989. *People of the earth: An introduction to world prehistory*. 6th ed. Glenview, IL: Scott, Foresman.

Fagan, Brian M. 1991. *Ancient North America: The archaeology of a continent*. London: Thames and Hudson.

Falk, Dean. 1987. Hominid paleoneurology. *Annual Review of Anthropology* 16:13–30.

Falk, Dean. 1988. Enlarged occipital/marginal sinuses and emissary foramina: Their significance in hominid evolution. In *Evolutionary history of the "robust" australopithecines*, ed. F. E. Grine. New York: Aldine.

Falk, Dean, C. Hildebolt, K. Smith, M. J. Morwood, T. Sutikna, P. Brown, Jatmiko, E. W. Saptomo, B. Brunsden, F. Prior. 2005. The brain of LBI, *Homo floresiensis*. *Science* 308 (April 8):242–45.

Farley, Reynolds. 1996. *The new American reality: Who we are, how we got here, where we are going*. New York: Russell Sage Foundation.

Farmer, Paul. 1997. Ethnography, social analysis, and the prevention of sexually transmitted HIV infection among poor women in Haiti. In *The anthropology of infectious disease*, eds. M. C. Inhorn and P. J. Brown, 413–38. Amsterdam: Gordon and Breach.

Featherman, David L., and Robert M. Hauser. 1978. *Opportunity and change*. New York: Academic Press.

Fedigan, Linda Marie. 1982. *Primate paradigms: Sex roles and social bonds*. Montreal: Eden Press.

Fedoroff, Nina. 2003. Prehistoric GM corn. *Science* 302 (November 14):1158–59.

Fehr, Ernst, and Urs Fischbacher. 2003. The nature of human altruism. *Nature* (October 23):785–91.

Feibel, Craig S., and Francis H. Brown. 1993. Microstratigraphy and paleoenvironments. In *The Nariokotome* Homo erectus *Skeleton*, eds. A. Walker and R. Leakey. Cambridge, MA: Harvard University Press.

Feinman, Gary M., Stephen A. Kowalewski, Laura Finsten, Richard E. Blanton, and Linda Nicholas. 1985. Long-term demographic change: A perspective from the Valley of Oaxaca, Mexico. *Journal of Field Archaeology* 12:333–62.

Feinman, Gary, and Jill Neitzel. 1984. Too many types: An overview of sedentary prestate societies in the Americas. In *Advances in archaeological methods and theory*, vol. 7, ed. M. B. Schiffer. Orlando, FL: Academic Press.

Ferguson, R. Brian, and Neil L. Whitehead. 1992. Violent edge of empire. In *War in the tribal zone*, eds. R. B. Ferguson and N. Whitehead, 1–30. Santa Fe, NM: School of American Research Press.

Finley, Moses I. 1983. *Politics in the ancient world*. Cambridge, UK: Cambridge University Press.

Finnis, Elizabeth. 2006. Why grow cash crops? Subsistence farming and crop commercialization in the Kolli Hills, South India. *American Anthropologist* 108:363–69.

Firth, Raymond. 1959. *Social change in Tikopia*. New York: Macmillan.

Firth, Raymond. 1970. *Rank and religion in Tikopia*. Boston: Beacon Press.

Fischer, John L. 1958. Social influences on the choice of a linguistic variant. *Word* 14:47–56.

Fischer, John. 1961. Art styles as cultural cognitive maps. *American Anthropologist* 63:80–83.

Fish, Paul R. 1981. Beyond tools: Middle Paleolithic debitage analysis and cultural inference. *Journal of Anthropological Research* 37:374–86.

Fisher, William H. 1994. Megadevelopment, environmentalism, and resistance: The institutional context of Kayapo indigenous politics in central Brazil. *Human Organization* 53:220–32.

Flannery, Kent V. 1965. The ecology of early food production in Mesopotamia. *Science* 147 (March 12):1247–56.

Flannery, Kent V. 1971. The origins and ecological effects of early domestication in Iran and the Near East. In *Prehistoric agriculture,* ed. S. Struever. Garden City, NY: Natural History Press.

Flannery, Kent V. 1972. The cultural evolution of civilizations. *Annual Review of Ecology and Systematics* 3:399–426.

Flannery, Kent V. 1973a. The origins of agriculture. *Annual Review of Anthropology* 2:271–310.

Flannery, Kent V. 1973b. The origins of the village as a settlement type in Mesoamerica and the Near East: A comparative study. In *Territoriality and proxemics,* ed. R. Tringham. Andover, MA: Warner.

Flannery, Kent V., ed. 1986. *Guila Naquitz: Archaic foraging and early agriculture in Oaxaca, Mexico.* Orlando, FL: Academic Press.

Fleagle, John G. 1994. Anthropoid origins. In *Integrative paths to the past,* eds. R. Corruccini and R. Ciochon. Upper Saddle River, NJ: Prentice Hall.

Fleagle, John G. 1999. *Primate adaptation and evolution.* 2nd ed. San Diego, CA: Academic Press.

Fleagle, John G., and Richard F. Kay. 1983. New interpretations of the phyletic position of Oligocene hominoids. In *New Interpretations of ape and human ancestry,* eds. R. Ciochon and R. Corruccini. New York: Plenum Press.

Fleagle, John G., and Richard F. Kay. 1985. The paleobiology of catarrhines. In *Ancestors,* ed. E. Delson. New York: Alan R. Liss.

Fleagle, John G., and Richard F. Kay. 1987. The phyletic position of the *Parapithecidae. Journal of Human Evolution* 16:483–531.

Fluehr-Lobban, Carolyn. 2006. *Race and racism: An introduction.* Lanham: AltaMira Press.

Ford, Clellan S., and Frank A. Beach. 1951. *Patterns of sexual behavior.* New York: Harper.

Forrest, Barbara, 2001. The wedge at work. In *Intelligent design creationism and its critics,* ed. Robert Pennock. Boston: MIT Press.

Fossey, Dian. 1983. *Gorillas in the mist.* Boston: Houghton Mifflin.

Foster, George M. 1962. *Traditional cultures and the impact of technological change.* New York: Harper & Row.

Foster, George M. 1969. *Applied anthropology.* Boston: Little, Brown.

Foster, George M. 1994. *Hippocrates' Latin American legacy: Humoral medicine in the New World.* Amsterdam: Gordon and Breach.

Fowler, Melvin L. 1975. A pre-Columbian urban center on the Mississippi. *Scientific American* (August):92–101.

Franciscus, Robert G., and Erik Trinkaus. 1988. Nasal morphology and the emergence of *Homo erectus. American Journal of Physical Anthropology* 75:517–27.

Fratkin, Elliot. 2008. Pastures lost: The decline of mobile pastoralism among Maasai and Rendille in Kenya, East Africa. In *Economies and the transformation of landscape,* eds. Lisa Cliggett and Christopher A. Pool, 149–68. Lanham, MD: AltaMira Press.

Frayer, David W. 2009. Testing theories and hypotheses about modern human origins. In MyAnthroLibrary, eds. C. R. Ember, M. Ember, and P. N. Peregrine. MyAnthroLibrary.com. Pearson.

Frayer, David W., and Milford H. Wolpoff. 1985. Sexual dimorphism. *Annual Review of Anthropology* 14:429–73.

Frayer, David W., M. Wolpoff, A. Thorne, F. Smith, and G. Pope. 1993. Theories of modern human origins: The paleontological test. *American Anthropologist* 95:24–27.

Frayser, Suzanne G. 1985. *Varieties of sexual experience.* New Haven, CT: HRAF Press.

Freeman, J. D. 1961. On the concept of the kindred. *Journal of the Royal Anthropological Institute* 91:192–220.

Freeman, Leslie G. 1994. Torralba and Ambrona: A review of discoveries. In *Integrative paths to the past,* eds. R. Corruccini and R. Ciochon. Upper Saddle River, NJ: Prentice Hall.

Freyman, R. 1987. The first technology. *Scientific American* (April):112.

Fried, Morton H. 1967. *The evolution of political society: An essay in political anthropology.* New York: Random House.

Friedman, Jeffrey M. 2003. A war on obesity, not the obese. *Science* 299 (February 7):856–58.

Friedman, Saul S. 1980. Holocaust. In *Academic American Encyclopedia,* vol. 10. Princeton, NJ: Areté.

Friedrich, Paul. 1986. *The language parallax.* Austin: University of Texas Press.

Frisancho, A. Roberto, and Lawrence P. Greksa. 1989. Development responses in the acquisition of functional adaptation to high altitude. In *Human population biology,* eds. M. Little and J. Haas. New York: Oxford University Press.

Frisch, Rose. E. 1980. Fatness, puberty, and fertility. *Natural History* (October):16–27.

Fry, Douglas P. 2006. *The human potential for peace: An anthropological challenge to assumptions about war and violence.* New York: Oxford University Press.

Fry, Douglas P., and Kaj Björkvist, eds. 1997. *Cultural variation in conflict resolution: Alternatives to violence.* Mahwah, NJ: Erlbaum.

Futuyma, Douglas. 1982. *Science on trial.* New York: Pantheon.

Gabunia, Leo, A. Vekua, D. Lordkipanidze, et al. 2000. Earliest Pleistocene hominid cranial remains from Dmanisi, Republic of Georgia: Taxonomy, geological setting, and age. *Science* 288 (May 12):1019–25.

Gal, Susan. 1988. The political economy of code choice. In *Codeswitching,* ed. M. Heller, 245–64. Berlin: Mouton de Gruyter.

Gardner, Beatrice T., and R. Allen Gardner. 1980. Two comparative psychologists look at language acquisition. In *Children's language,* vol. 2, ed. K. Nelson. New York: Halsted Press.

Gardner, R. Allen, and Beatrice T. Gardner. 1969. Teaching sign language to a chimpanzee. *Science* 165 (August 15):664–72.

Garn, Stanley M. 1971. *Human races.* 3rd ed. Springfield, IL: Charles C Thomas.

Gartner, Rosemary. 2009. Crime variations across cultures and nations. In MyAnthroLibrary, eds. C. R. Ember, M. Ember, and P. N. Peregrine. MyAnthroLibrary.com. Pearson.

Gat, Azar. 1999. The pattern of fighting in simple, small-scale, prestate societies. *Journal of Anthropological Research* 55:563–83.

Geertz, Clifford. 1966. Religion as a cultural system. In *Anthropological approaches to the study of religion,* ed. M. Banton. New York: Praeger.

Geiger, H. Jack. 2003. Racial and ethnic disparities in diagnosis and treatment: A review of the evidence and a consideration of causes. In *Unequal treatment: confronting racial and ethnic disparities in health care,* eds. Brian D. Smedley, Adrienne Y. Stith, and Alan R. Nelson, 417–54. Washington, DC: National Academy Press.

Gelles, Richard J., and Murray A. Straus. 1988. *Intimate violence.* New York: Simon & Schuster.

Gentner, Wolfgang, and H. J. Lippolt. 1963. The potassium-argon dating of upper tertiary and Pleistocene deposits. In *Science in archaeology,* eds. D. Brothwell and E. Higgs. New York: Basic Books.

Gesler, Wilbert. 1991. *The cultural geography of health care.* Pittsburgh, PA: University of Pittsburgh Press.

Gibbons, Ann. 1993. Warring over women. *Science* 261 (August 20):987–88.

Gibbons, Ann. 1995. First Americans: Not mammoth hunters, but forest dwellers? *Science* 268 (April 19):346–47.

Gibbons, Ann. 2001. The riddle of co-existence. *Science* 291(March 2):1725–29.

Gibbons, Ann. 2002. One scientist's quest for the origin of our species. *Science* 298 (November 29):1708–11.

Gibbons, Ann. 2003. Oldest members of *Homo sapiens* discovered in Africa. *Science* 300 (June 13):1641.

Gibbons, Ann. 2008. The birth of childhood. *Science* 322 (November 14):1040–43.

Gibson, Kathleen R., and Stephen Jessee. 1999. Language evolution and expansions of multiple neurological processing areas. In *The origins of language,* ed. B. J. King, 189–227. Santa Fe, NM: School of American Research Press.

Gilbert, M. Thomas P., Dennis L. Jenkins, Anders Götherstrom, Nuria Naveran, Juan J. Sanchez, Michael Hofreiter, Philip Francis Thomsen, Jonas Binladen, Thomas F. G. Higham, Robert M. Yohe, II, Robert Parr, Linda Scott Cummings, and Eske Willerslev. 2008. DNA from pre-Clovis human coprolites in Oregon, North America. *Science* 320 (May 9):786–89.

Gilman, Antonio. 1990. The development of social stratification in Bronze Age Europe. *Current Anthropology* 22:1–23.

Gingerich, Philip D. 1986. *Pleisiadipis* and the delineation of the order primates. In *Major topics in primate evolution,* eds. B. Wood, L. Martin, and P. Andrews, 32–46. Cambridge, UK: Cambridge University Press.

Gladwin, Thomas, and Seymour B. Sarason. 1953. *Truk: Man in paradise.* New York: Wenner-Gren Foundation for Anthropological Research.

Gleitman, Lila R., and Eric Wanner. 1982. Language acquisition: The state of the art. In *Language acquisition,* eds. E. Wanner and L. R. Gleitman. Cambridge, UK: Cambridge University Press.

Goebel, Ted, Michael Waters, and Dennis O'Rourke. 2008. The late Pleistocene dispersal of modern humans in the Americas. *Science* 319 (March 14):1479–1502.

Golden, Frederic, Michael Lemonick, and Dick Thompson. 2000. The race is over. *Time* (July 3):18–23.

Goldizen, Anne Wilson. 1987. Tamarins and marmosets: Communal care of offspring. In *Primate societies,* eds. B. Smuts et al. Chicago: University of Chicago Press.

Goldschmidt, Walter. 1999. Dynamics and status in America. *Anthropology Newsletter* 40(5):62, 64.

Goldstein, Melvyn C. 1971. Stratification, polyandry, and family structure in central Tibet. *Southwestern Journal of Anthropology* 27:65–74.

Goldstein, Melvyn C. 1987. When brothers share a wife. *Natural History* (March):39–48.

Goodall, Jane. 1963. My life among wild chimpanzees. *National Geographic* (August):272–308.

Goodenough, Ward H. 1951. *Property, kin, and community on Truk.* New Haven, CT: Yale University Press.

Goodman, Alan H., and Thomas L. Leatherman, eds. 1998. *Building a new biocultural synthesis: Political-economic perspectives on human biology.* Ann Arbor: University of Michigan Press.

Goodman, Madeleine J., P. Bion Griffin, Agnes A. Estioko-Griffin, and John S. Grove. 1985. The compatibility of hunting and mothering among the Agta hunter-gatherers of the Philippines. *Sex Roles* 12:1199–209.

Goodrich, L. Carrington. 1959. *A short history of the Chinese people.* 3rd ed. New York: Harper & Row.

Goody, Jack. 1973. Bridewealth and dowry in Africa and Eurasia. In *Bridewealth and dowry,* eds. J. Goody and S. H. Tambiah. Cambridge, UK: Cambridge University Press.

Gore, Rick. 2002. The first pioneer? *National Geographic* (August).

Goren-Inbar, Naama, N. Alperson, M. Kislev, O. Simchoni, Y. Melamed, A. Ben-Nun, and E. Werker. 2004. Evidence of hominid control of fire at Gesher Benot Ya'aqov, Israel. *Science* 304 (April 30):725–27.

Gorman, Chester. 1970. The Hoabinhian and after: Subsistence patterns in Southeast Asia during the Late Pleistocene and early recent periods. *World Archaeology* 2:315–19.

Gould, Richard A. 1969. *Yiwara: Foragers of the Australian desert.* New York: Scribner's.

Gowlett, John A. J. 2008. Deep roots of kin: Developing the evolutionary perspective from prehistory. In *Early human kinship: From sex to social reproduction,* eds. Nicholas Allen, Hilary Callan, Robin Dunbar, and Wendy James, 41–57. Oxford, UK: Blackwell.

Graber, Robert, ed. 2004. Special issue. The future state of the world: An anthropological symposium. *Cross-Cultural Research* 38:95–207.

Graham, Susan Brandt. 1979. Biology and human social behavior: A response to van den Berghe and Barash. *American Anthropologist* 81:357–60.

Grant, Bruce S. 2002. Sour grapes of wrath. *Science* 297 (August 9):940–41.

Grant, Peter R., and Rosemary Grant. 2002. Unpredictable evolution in a 30-year study of Darwin's finches. *Science* 296 (April 26):707–11.

Grant, Peter R., and Rosemary Grant. 2008. *How and why species multiply: The radiation of Darwin's finches.* Princeton, NJ: Princeton University Press.

Gray, J. Patrick. 1985. *Primate sociobiology.* New Haven, CT: HRAF Press.

Gray, J. Patrick, and Linda D. Wolfe. 1980. Height and sexual dimorphism of stature among human societies. *American Journal of Physical Anthropology* 53:446–52.

Gray, J. Patrick, and Linda Wolfe. 2009. What accounts for population variation in height? In MyAnthroLibrary, eds. C. R. Ember, M. Ember, and P. N. Peregrine. MyAnthroLibrary.com. Pearson.

Grayson, Donald K. 1977. Pleistocene avifaunas and the overkill hypothesis. *Science* 195 (February 18):691–92.

Grayson, Donald K. 1984. Explaining Pleistocene extinctions: Thoughts on the structure of a debate. In *Quaternary extinctions,* eds. P. S. Martin and R. Klein. Tucson: University of Arizona Press.

Green, Richard E., Anna-Sapfo Malaspinas, Johannes Krause, Adrian W. Briggs, Philip L.F. Johnson, Caroline Uhler, Matthias Meyer, Jeffrey M. Good, Tomislav Maricic, Udo Stenzel, Kay Prüfer, Michael Siebauer, Hernán A. Burbano, Michael Ronan, Jonathan M. Rothberg, Michael Egholm, Pavao Rudan, Dejana Brajković, Željko Kućan, Ivan Gušić, Mårten Wikström, Liisa Laakkonen, Janet Kelso, Montgomery Slatkin, and Svante Pääbo. 2008. A complete Neandertal mitochondrial genome sequence determined by high-throughput sequencing. *Cell* 134:416–26.

Greenberg, Joseph H. 1972. Linguistic evidence regarding Bantu origins. *Journal of African History* 13:189–216.

Greenberg, Joseph H., and Merritt Ruhlen. 1992. Linguistic origins of Native Americans. *Scientific American* (November):94–99.

Greenfield, Patricia M., Ashley E. Maynard, and Carla P. Childs. 2000. History, culture, learning, and development. *Cross-Cultural Research* 34:351–74.

Greenfield, Patricia Marks, and E. Sue Savage-Rumbaugh. 1990. Grammatical combination in *Pan paniscus:* Processes of learning and invention in the evolution and development of language. In *"Language" and intelligence in monkeys and apes,* eds. S. Parker and K. Gibson. New York: Cambridge University Press.

Gregor, Thomas A., and Daniel R. Gross. 2004. Guilt by association: The culture of accusation and the American Anthropological Association's investigation of *Darkness in El Dorado. American Anthropologist* 106:687–98.

Greksa, Lawrence P., and Cynthia M. Beall. 1989. Development of chest size and lung function at high altitude. In *Human population biology,* eds. M. Little and J. Haas. New York: Oxford University Press.

Grine, Frederick E. 1988a. Evolutionary history of the 'robust' australopithecines: A summary and historical perspective. In *Evolutionary history of the "robust" australopithecines,* ed. F. E. Grine. New York: Aldine.

Grine, Frederick E., ed. 1988b. *Evolutionary history of the "robust" australopithecines.* New York: Aldine.

Grine, Frederick E. 1993. Australopithecine taxonomy and phylogeny: Historical background and recent interpretation. In *The Human evolution source book,* eds. R. Ciochon and J. Fleagle. Upper Saddle River, NJ: Prentice Hall.

Gross, Daniel R., and Barbara A. Underwood. 1971. Technological change and caloric costs: Sisal agriculture in northeastern Brazil. *American Anthropologist* 73:725–40.

Grossman, Daniel. 2002. Parched turf battle. *Scientific American* (December):32–33.

Guest, Greg, and Eric C. Jones. 2005. Globalization, health, and the environment: An introduction. In *Globalization, health, and the environment: An integrated perspective,* ed. Greg Guest, 3–26. Lanham, MD: Roman & Littlefield.

Guiora, Alexander Z., Benjamin Beit-Hallahmi, Risto Fried, and Cecelia Yoder. 1982. Language environment and gender identity attainment. *Language Learning* 32:289–304.

Gunders, S., and J. W. M. Whiting. 1968. Mother–infant separation and physical growth. *Ethnology* 7:196–206.

Gurr, Ted Robert. 1989. Historical trends in violent crime: Europe and the United States. In *Violence in America,* vol. 1: *The history of crime,* ed. T. R. Gurr. Newbury Park, CA: Sage.

Guthrie, Dale R., 1984. Mosaics, allelochemics, and nutrients: An ecological theory of Late Pleistocene megafaunal extinctions. In *Quaternary extinctions,* eds. P. S. Martin and R. Klein. Tucson: University of Arizona Press.

Haas, Jonathan. 1990. Warfare and the evolution of tribal polities in the prehistoric Southwest. In *The anthropology of war,* ed. J. Haas. New York: Cambridge University Press.

Haas, Jonathan, Winifred Creamer, and Alvaro Ruiz. 2004. Dating the late Archaic occupation of the Norte Chico region in Peru. *Nature* 432 (December 23):1020–23.

Habicht, Johann K. A. 1979. *Paleoclimate, paleomagnetism, and continental drift.* Tulsa, OK: American Association of Petroleum Geologists.

Hage, Jerald, and Charles H. Powers. 1992. *Post-industrial lives: Roles and relationships in the 21st century.* Newbury Park, CA: Sage.

Hahn, Robert A. 1995. *Sickness and healing: An anthropological perspective.* New Haven, CT: Yale University Press.

Hailie-Selassie, Yohannes. 2001. Late Miocene hominids from the Middle Awash, Ethiopia. *Nature* 412 (July 12):178–81.

Haldane, John B. S. 1963. Human evolution: Past and future. In *Genetics, paleontology, and evolution,* eds. G. Jepsen, E. Mayr, and G. Simpson. New York: Atheneum.

Hall, Edward T. 1966. *The hidden dimension.* Garden City, NY: Doubleday.

Hames, Raymond. 2009. Yanomamö: Varying adaptations of foraging horticulturalists. In MyAnthroLibrary, eds. C. R. Ember, M. Ember, and P. N. Peregrine. MyAnthroLibrary.com. Pearson.

Hammer, Michael F., and Stephen L. Zegura. 1996. The role of the Y chromosome in human evolutionary studies. *Evolutionary Anthropology* 5:116–34.

Hammer, Michael F., and Stephen L. Zegura. 2002. The human Y chromosome haplogroup tree. *Annual Review of Anthropology* 31:303–21.

Handwerker, W. Penn, and Paul V. Crosbie. 1982. Sex and dominance. *American Anthropologist* 84:97–104.

Hanna, Joel M., Michael A. Little, and Donald M. Austin. 1989. Climatic physiology. In *Human population biology,* eds. M. Little and J. Haas. New York: Oxford University Press.

Hannah, Alison C., and W. C. McGrew. 1987. Chimpanzees using stones to crack open oil palm nuts in Liberia. *Primates* 28:31–46.

Hannerz, Ulf. 1996. *Transnational connections: Culture, people, places.* London: Routledge.

Hanotte, Olivier, et al. 2002. African pastoralism: Genetic imprints of origins and migrations. *Science* 296 (April 12):336–43.

Harcourt, Alexander H. 1979. The social relations and group structure of wild mountain gorillas. In *The great apes.* eds. D. Hamburg and E. McCown. Menlo Park, CA: Benjamin/Cummings.

Hare, Brian, Michelle Brown, Christina Williamson, and Michael Tomasello. 2002. The domestication of social cognition in dogs. *Science,* 298 (November 22):1634–36.

Harlan, Jack R. 1967. A wild wheat harvest in Turkey. *Archaeology* 20:197–201.

Harner, Michael. 1972. The role of hallucinogenic plants in European witchcraft. In *Hallucinogens and shamanism,* ed. M. Harner. New York: Oxford University Press.

Harner, Michael J. 1975. Scarcity, the factors of production, and social evolution. In *Population, ecology, and social evolution,* ed. S. Polgar. The Hague: Mouton.

Harner, Michael, and Gary Doore. 1987. The ancient wisdom in shamanic cultures. In *Shamanism,* comp. S. Nicholson. Wheaton, IL: Theosophical Publishing House.

Harper, Douglas. 2003. Slavery in the North. http://www.slave-north.com (accessed June, 2009).

Harrell-Bond, Barbara. 1996. Refugees. In *Encyclopedia of cultural anthropology,* vol. 3, eds. D. Levinson and M. Ember, 1076–81. New York: Henry Holt.

Harris, David R. 1977. Settling down: An evolutionary model for the transformation of mobile bands into sedentary communities. In *The evolution of social systems,* eds. J. Friedman and M. Rowlands. London: Duckworth.

Harris, Marvin. 1966. The cultural ecology of India's sacred cattle. *Current Anthropology* 7:51–63.

Harris, Marvin. 1975. *Cows, pigs, wars and witches: The riddles of culture.* New York: Random House, Vintage.

Harris, Marvin. 1979. *Cultural materialism: The struggle for a science of culture.* New York: Random House.

Harrison, Geoffrey A., James M. Tanner, David R. Pilbeam, and P. T. Baker. 1988. *Human biology: An introduction to human evolution, variation, growth, and adaptability.* 3rd ed. Oxford, UK: Oxford University Press.

Harrison, Gail G. 1975. Primary adult lactase deficiency: A problem in anthropological genetics. *American Anthropologist* 77:812–35.

Harrison, Terry. 1986. A reassessment of the phylogenetic relationships of *Oreopithecus bamboli. Journal of Human Evolution* 15:541–84.

Harrison, Terry, and L. Rook. 1997. Enigmatic anthropoid or misunderstood ape? The phylogenetic status of *Oreopithecus bamboli* reconsidered. In *Function, phylogeny and fossils: Miocene hominoid evolution and adaptation,* eds. D. R. Begun, C. V. Ward, and M. D. Rose, 327–62. New York: Plenum Press.

Hart, Hornell. 1948. The logistic growth of political areas. *Social Forces* 26:396–408.

Hartwig, Walter C. 1994. Pattern, puzzles and perspectives on platyrrhine origins. In *Integrative paths to the past,* eds. R. Corruccini and R. Ciochon, 69–93. Upper Saddle River, NJ: Prentice Hall.

Harvey, Philip W., and Peter F. Heywood. 1983. Twenty-five years of dietary change in Simbu Province, Papua New Guinea. *Ecology of Food and Nutrition* 13:27–35.

Hatch, Elvin. 1997. The good side of relativism. *Journal of Anthropological Research* 53:371–81.

Haug, Gerald, et al. 2003. Climate and the collapse of Maya civilization. *Science* 299 (March 14):1731–35.

Hawkins, Alicia, and M. Kleindienst. 2001. Aterian. In *Encyclopedia of prehistory,* vol. 1: *Africa,* eds. P. N. Peregrine and M. Ember, 23–45. New York: Kluwer Academic/Plenum Press.

Hayden, Thomas. 2000. A genome milestone. *Newsweek* (July 3):51–52.

Hays, Terence E. 1994. Sound symbolism, onomatopoeia, and New Guinea frog names. *Journal of Linguistic Anthropology* 4:153–74.

Heider, Karl. 1970. *The Dugum Dani.* Chicago: Aldine.

Heider, Karl. 1979. *Grand Valley Dani: Peaceful warriors.* New York: Holt, Rinehart & Winston.

Heise, David R. 1967. Cultural patterning of sexual socialization. *American Sociological Review* 32:726–39.

Heller, Monica, ed. 1988. *Codeswitching: Anthropological and sociolinguistic perspectives.* Berlin: Mouton de Gruyter.

Helms, Mary W. 1975. *Middle America.* Upper Saddle River, NJ: Prentice Hall.

Helms, Mary W. 2009. Miskito: Adaptations to colonial empires, past and present. In MyAnthroLibrary, eds. C. R. Ember, M. Ember, and P. N. Peregrine. MyAnthroLibrary.com. Pearson.

Henderson, Harry. 2001. *Global terrorism: The complete reference guide.* New York: Checkmark Books.

Henrich, Joseph, Robert Boyd, Samuel Bowles, Colin Camerer, Ernst Fehr, and Herbert Gintis, eds. 2004. *Foundations of human sociality: Economic experiments and ethnographic evidence from fifteen small-scale societies.* Oxford, UK: Oxford University Press.

Henry, Donald O. 1989. *From foraging to agriculture: The Levant at the end of the ice age.* Philadelphia: University of Pennsylvania Press.

Henry, Donald O. 1991. Foraging, sedentism, and adaptive vigor in the Natufian: Rethinking the linkages. In *Perspectives on the past*, ed. G. A. Clark. Philadelphia: University of Pennsylvania Press.

Henshilwood, Christopher, et al. 2002. Emergence of modern human behavior: Middle Stone Age engravings from South Africa. *Science* 295 (February 15):1278–80.

Herlihy, Laura Hobson. 2007. Matrifocality and women's power on the Miskito Coast. *Ethnology* 46:133–49.

Herrmann, Esther, Joseph Call, Maria Victoria Herandez-Lloreda, Brain Hare, and Michael Tomasello. 2007. Humans have evolved specialized skills in social cognition: The cultural intelligence hypothesis. *Science* 317 (September 7):1360–65.

Herrman, Helen. 1990. A survey of homeless mentally ill people in Melbourne, Australia. *Hospital and Community Psychiatry* 41:1291–92.

Herrnstein, Richard J., and Charles Murray. 1994. *The bell curve: Intelligence and class structure in American life*. New York: Free Press.

Hewes, Gordon W. 1961. Food transport and the origin of hominid bipedalism. *American Anthropologist* 63:687–710.

Hewlett, Barry S. 2004. Diverse contexts of human infancy. In MyAnthroLibrary, eds. C. R. Ember, M. Ember, and P. N. Peregrine. MyAnthroLibrary.com. Pearson.

Hiatt, Lester R. 1980. Polyandry in Sri Lanka: A test case for parental investment theory. *Man* 15:583–98.

Hickey, Gerald Cannon. 1964. *Village in Vietnam*. New Haven, CT: Yale University Press.

Hickson, Letitia. 1986. The social contexts of apology in dispute settlement: A cross-cultural study. *Ethnology* 25:283–94.

Higley, Stephen Richard. 1995. *Privilege, power, and place: The geography of the American upper class*. Lanham, MD: Rowman & Littlefield.

Hill, Jane H. 1978. Apes and language. *Annual Review of Anthropology* 7:89–112.

Hill, Jane H. 2009. Do apes have language? In MyAnthroLibrary, eds. C. R. Ember, M. Ember, and P. N. Peregrine. MyAnthroLibrary.com. Pearson.

Hill, Jonathan D. 1996. Introduction: Ethnogenesis in the Americas, 1492–1992. In *Ethnogenesis in the Americas*, ed. J. D. Hill, 1–19. Iowa City: University of Iowa Press.

Hill, Kim, and A. Magdalena Hurtado. 2004. The ethics of anthropological research with remote tribal populations. In *Lost paradises and the ethics of research and publication*, eds. F. M. Salzano and A. M. Hurtado, 193–210. Oxford, UK: Oxford University Press.

Hillel, Daniel. 2000. *Salinity management for sustainable irrigation: Integrating science, environment, and economics*. Washington, DC: World Bank.

Hinkes, Madeleine. 1993. Race, ethnicity, and forensic anthropology. *National Association for Applied Anthropology Bulletin* 13:48–54.

Hitchcock, Robert K. and Megan Beisele. 2000. Introduction. In *Hunters and gatherers in the modern world: Conflict, resistance, and self-determinations*, eds. P. P. Schweitzer, M. Biesele, and R. K. Hitchcock, 1–27. New York: Berghahn Books.

Hockett, Charles F., and R. Ascher. 1964. The human revolution. *Current Anthropology* 5:135–68.

Hodell, David, M. Brenner, J. Curtis, and T. Guilderson. 2001. Solar forcing and of drought frequency in the Maya lowlands. *Science* 292 (May 18):1367–70.

Hodgson, Jason, and Todd Driscoll. 2008. No evidence of a Neandertal contribution to modern human diversity. *Genome Biology* 9:206.1–206.7.

Hoebel, E. Adamson. 1968/1954. *The law of primitive man*. New York: Atheneum.

Hoffecker, John F., W. Roger Powers, and Ted Goebel. 1993. The colonization of Beringia and the peopling of the New World. *Science* 259 (January 1):46–53.

Holdaway, R. N., and C. Jacomb. 2000. Rapid extinction of the moas (*Aves: Dinornithiformes*): Model, test, and implications. *Science* 287 (March 24):2250–57.

Holden, Constance. 1996. "Last of the Cahokians." *Science* 272 (April 19):351–54.

Holden, Constance. 1997. Tooling around—Dates show early Siberian settlement. *Science* 275 (February 28):1268.

Holden, Constance. 2000. Selective power of UV. *Science* 289 (September 1):1461.

Hole, Frank. 1992. Origins of agriculture. In *The Cambridge encyclopedia of human evolution*, eds. S. Jones, R. Martin, and D. Pilbeam. New York: Cambridge University Press.

Hole, Frank. 1994. Environmental shock and urban origins. In *Chiefdoms and early states in the Near East*, eds. G. Stein and M. Rothman. Madison, WI: Prehistory Press.

Hole, Frank, Kent V. Flannery, and James A. Neely. 1969. Prehistory and human ecology of the Deh Luran Plain. *Memoirs of the Museum of Anthropology*, No. 1. Ann Arbor: University of Michigan.

Holloway, Ralph L. 1974. The casts of fossil hominid brains. *Scientific American* (July):106–15.

Holmes, Janet. 2001. *An introduction to sociolinguistics*. 2nd ed. London: Longman.

Hoogbergen, Wim. 1990. *The Boni Maroon Wars in Suriname*. Leiden: E. J. Brill.

Hooper, Judith. 2002. *Of moths and men: The untold story of science and the peppered moth*. New York: Norton.

Hopkins, Keith. 1980. Brother-sister marriage in Roman Egypt. *Comparative Studies in Society and History* 22:303–54.

Howard, Alan, and Jan Rensel. 2009. Rotuma: Interpreting a wedding. In MyAnthroLibrary, eds. C. R. Ember, M. Ember, and P. N. Peregrine. MyAnthroLibrary.com. Pearson.

Howell, F. Clark. 1966. Observations on the earlier phases of the European Lower Paleolithic. In *Recent studies in paleoanthropology. American anthropologist*. Special publication, April, 88–200.

Howell, Nancy. 1979. *Demography of the Dobe !Kung*. New York: Academic Press.

Hrdy, Sarah Blaffer. 1977. *The langurs of Abu: Female and male strategies of reproduction*. Cambridge, MA: Harvard University Press.

Huang, Hsing T. 2002. Hypolactasia and the Chinese diet. *Current Anthropology* 43:809–19.

Human Development Report 2010. Statistical Tables. http://hdr.undp.org/en/statistics/gii/ (accessed March 12, 2011).

Hunt, Morton. 1974. *Sexual behavior in the 1970s*. Chicago: Playboy Press.

Hunt, Robert C. 2000. Labor productivity and agricultural development: Boserup revisited. *Human Ecology* 28:251–77.

Hurtado, Ana M., Kristen Hawkes, Kim Hill, and Hillard Kaplan. 1985. Female subsistence strategies among the Aché hunter-gatherers of eastern Paraguay. *Human Ecology* 13:1–28.

Huss-Ashmore, Rebecca, and Francis E. Johnston. 1985. Bioanthropological research in developing countries. *Annual Review of Anthropology* 14:475–527.

Huxley, Thomas H. 1970. Man's place in nature. In *Evolution of man*, ed. L. Young. New York: Oxford University Press.

Hymes, Dell. 1974. *Foundations in sociolinguistics: An ethnographic approach*. Philadelphia: University of Pennsylvania Press.

Isaac, Glynn. 1971. The diet of early man: Aspects of archaeological evidence from Lower and Middle Pleistocene sites in Africa. *World Archaeology* 2:277–99.

Isaac, Glynn. 1984. The archaeology of human origins: Studies of the Lower Pleistocene in East Africa, 1971–1981. In *Advances in world archaeology*, eds. F. Wendorf and A. Close. Orlando, FL: Academic Press.

Itkonen, Toivo I. 1951. The Lapps of Finland. *Southwestern Journal of Anthropology* 7:32–68.

Jablonski, Nina G., and George Chaplin. 2000. The evolution of human skin color. *Journal of Human Evolution* 39:57–106.

Jacobs, Sue-Ellen, and Christine Roberts. 1989. Sex, sexuality, gender and gender variance. In *Gender and anthropology*, ed. S. Morgen. Washington, DC: American Anthropological Association.

Jaeger, Jean-Jacques, T. Thein, M. Benammi, Y. Chaimanee, A. N. Soe, T. Lwin, T. Tun, S. Wai, and S. Ducrocq. 1999. A new primate from the middle Eocene of Myanmar and the Asian early origins of anthropoids. *Science* 286 (October 15):528–30.

Jankowiak, William, M. Diane Nell, and Ann Buckmaster. 2002. Managing infidelity: A cross-cultural perspective. *Ethnology* 41:85–101.

Jankowiak, William, Monica Sudakov, and Benjamin C. Wilreker. 2005. Co-wife conflict and co-operation. *Ethnology* 44:81–98.

Janzen, Daniel H. 1973. Tropical agroecosystems. *Science* 182 (December 21):1212–19.

Jarvenpa, Robert. 2004. Silot'ine: An insurance perspective on Northern Dene kinship networks in recent history. *Journal of Anthropological Research* 60:153–78.

Jarvenpa, Robert, and Hetty Jo Brumbach. 2006. Chipewyan hunters: A task differentiation analysis. In *Circumpolar lives and livelihood: A comparative ethnoarchaeology of gender and subsistence,* eds. Robert Jarvenpa and Hetty Jo Brumbach, 54–78. Lincoln: University of Nebraska Press.

Jayaswal, Vidula. 2002. South Asian Upper Paleolithic. In *Encyclopedia of prehistory,* vol. 8: *South and Southwest Asia,* eds. P. N. Peregrine and M. Ember. New York: Kluwer Academic/Plenum Press.

Jelliffe, Derrick B., and E. F. Patrice Jelliffe. 1975. Human milk, nutrition, and the world resource crisis. *Science* 188 (May 9):557–61.

Jennings, Jesse D. 1968. *Prehistory of North America.* New York: McGraw-Hill.

Jensen, Arthur. 1969. How much can we boost IQ and scholastic achievement? *Harvard Educational Review* 29:1–123.

Joans, Barbara. 1997. Problems in Pocatello: A study in linguistic misunderstanding. In *Applying cultural anthropology: An introductory reader.* 3rd ed. eds. A. Podolefsky and P. J. Brown, 51–54. Mountain View, CA: Mayfield.

Johanson, Donald C., and Maitland Edey. 1981. *Lucy: The beginnings of humankind.* New York: Simon & Schuster.

Johanson, Donald C., and Tim D. White. 1979. A systematic assessment of early African hominids. *Science* 203 (January 26):321–30.

Johnson, Allen, and Timothy Earle. 1987. *The evolution of human societies: From foraging group to agrarian state.* Stanford, CA: Stanford University Press.

Johnson, Amber Lynn. 2002. Cross-cultural analysis of pastoral adaptations and organizational states: A preliminary study. *Cross-Cultural Research* 36:151–80.

Johnson, Gregory A. 1977. Aspects of regional analysis in archaeology. *Annual Review of Anthropology* 6:479–508.

Johnson, Gregory A. 1987. The changing organization of Uruk administration on the Susiana Plain. In *Archaeology of western Iran,* ed. F. Hole. Washington, DC: Smithsonian Institution Press.

Johnson, Jeffrey G., Patricia Cohen, Elizabeth M. Smailies, Stephanie Kasen, and Judith S. Brook. 2002. Television viewing and aggressive behavior during adolescence and adulthood. *Science* 295 (March 29):2468–70.

Johnston, David Cay. 1999. Gap between rich and poor found substantially wider. *New York Times,* National, September 5, p. 16.

Jolly, Alison. 1985. *The evolution of primate behavior.* 2nd ed. New York: Macmillan.

Jolly, Clifford. 1970. The seed-eaters: A new model of hominid differentiation based on a baboon analogy. *Man* 5:5–28.

Jones, Martin, and Xinyi Liu. 2009. Origins of agriculture in East Asia. *Science* 324 (May 8):730–31.

Jones, Steve, Robert Martin, and David Pilbeam, eds. 1992. *The Cambridge encyclopedia of human evolution.* New York: Cambridge University Press.

Judge, W. James, and Jerry Dawson. 1972. Paleo-Indian settlement technology in New Mexico. *Science* 176 (June 16):1210–16.

Jungers, William L. 1988a. New estimates of body size in australopithecines. In *Evolutionary history of the "robust" australopithecines,* ed. F. Grine. New York: Aldine.

Jungers, William L. 1988b. Relative joint size and hominoid locomotor adaptations with implications for the evolution of hominid bipedalism. *Journal of Human Evolution* 17:247–65.

Kamin, Leon J. 1995. Behind the curve. *Scientific American* (February):99–103.

Kang, Bong W. 2000. A reconsideration of population pressure and warfare: A protohistoric Korean case. *Current Anthropology* 41:873–81.

Kaplan, Hillard, Kim Hill, and A. Magdalena Hurtado. 1990. Risk, foraging and food sharing among the Aché. In *Risk and uncertainty in tribal and peasant economies,* ed. E. Cashdan. Boulder, CO: Westview Press.

Kaplan, Hillard, Kim Hill, Jane Lancaster, and A. Magdalena Hurtado. 2000. A theory of human life history evolution, diet, intelligence, and longevity. *Evolutionary Anthropology* 9:156–84.

Kasarda, John D. 1971. Economic structure and fertility: A comparative analysis. *Demography* 8, no. 3 (August):307–18.

Katzner, Kenneth. 2002. *Languages of the world.* London: Routledge.

Kay, Richard F. 2000. Teeth. In *Encyclopedia of human evolution and prehistory,* eds. I. Tattersall, E. Delson, and J. van Couvering. New York: Garland.

Kay, Richard F., C. Ross, and B. A. Williams. 1997. Anthropoid origins. *Science* 275 (February 7):797–804.

Kedia, Satish, and John van Willigen, eds. 2005. *Applied anthropology: Domains of application.* Wesport, CT: Praeger.

Keeley, Lawrence H. 1980. *Experimental determination of stone tool uses: A microwear analysis.* Chicago: University of Chicago Press.

Keeley, Lawrence H. 1991. Ethnographic models for late glacial hunter-gatherers. In *The late glacial in north-west Europe: Human adaptation and environmental change at the end of the Pleistocene,* eds. N. Barton, A. J. Roberts, and D. A. Roe. London: Council for British Archaeology. *CBA Research Report* 77:179–90.

Keenan, Elinor. 1989. Norm-makers, norm-breakers: Uses of speech by men and women in a Malagasy community. In *Explorations in the ethnography of speaking.* 2nd ed. eds. R. Bauman and J. Sherzer. New York: Cambridge University Press.

Kehoe, Alice B., and Dody H. Giletti. 1981. Women's preponderance in possession cults: The calcium-deficiency hypothesis extended. *American Anthropologist* 83:549–61.

Keller, Helen. 1974/1902. *The story of my life.* New York: Dell.

Kelley, Jay. 1992. The evolution of apes. In *The Cambridge encyclopedia of human evolution,* eds. S. Jones, R. Martin, and D. Pilbeam. New York: Cambridge University Press.

Kelly, Raymond C. 1974. Witchcraft and sexual relations: An exploration in the social and semantic implications of the structure of belief. Paper presented at the annual meeting of the American Anthropological Association, Mexico City (November).

Kelly, Robert L. 1995. *The foraging spectrum: Diversity in hunter-gatherer lifeways.* Washington, DC: Smithsonian Institution Press.

Kent, Susan, ed. 1996. *Cultural diversity among twentieth-century foragers: An African perspective.* Cambridge, UK: Cambridge University Press.

Kerr, Richard A. 1998. Sea-floor dust shows drought felled Akkadian empire. *Science* 299 (January 16):325–26.

Khosroshashi, Fatemeh. 1989. Penguins don't care, but women do: A social identity analysis of a Whorfian problem. *Language in Society* 18:505–25.

Kilbride, Philip L., and Janet C. Kilbride. 1990. Polygyny: A modern contradiction? In P. L. Kilbride and J. C. Kilbride, *Changing family life in East Africa: Women and children at risk.* University Park: Pennsylvania State University Press.

Kimbel, William H., T. D. White, and D. C. Johansen. 1984. Cranial morphology of *Australopithecus afarensis:* A comparative study based on composite reconstruction of the adult skull. *American Journal of Physical Anthropology* 64:337–88.

King, Barbara J. 1999. Introduction. In *The origins of language,* ed. B. J. King, 3–19. Santa Fe, NM: School of American Research Press.

King, Jonathan C. H. 1986. Tradition in Native American art. In *The arts of the North American Indian,* ed. E. L. Wade. New York: Hudson Hills Press.

King, Marie-Claire, and Arno Motulsky. 2002. Mapping human history. *Science* 298 (December 20):2342–43.

King, Seth S. 1979. Some farm machinery seems less than human. *New York Times,* April 8, p. E9.

Kingston, John D., Bruno D. Marino, and Andrew Hill. 1994. Isotopic evidence for Neogene hominid paleoenvironments in the Kenya Rift Valley. *Science* 264 (May 13):955–59.

Kitchen, Andrew, Michael Miyamoto, and Connie Mulligan. 2008. A three-stage colonization model for the peopling of the Americas. *PLoS ONE* 3(2):e1596.

Klass, Morton. 2009. Is there "caste" outside of India? In *MyAnthroLibrary,* eds. C. R. Ember, M. Ember, and P. N. Peregrine. MyAnthroLibrary.com. Pearson.

Klein, Richard G. 1974. Ice-Age hunters of the Ukraine. *Scientific American* (June):96–105.

Klein, Richard G. 1977. The ecology of early man in Southern Africa. *Science* 197 (July 8):115–26.

Klein, Richard G. 1983. The Stone Age prehistory of Southern Africa. *Annual Review of Anthropology* 12:25–48.

Klein, Richard G. 1987. Reconstructing how early people exploited animals: Problems and prospects. In *The evolution of human hunting,* eds. M. Nitecki and D. Nitecki. New York: Plenum Press.

Klein, Richard G. 1989. *The human career: Human biological and cultural origins.* Chicago: University of Chicago Press.

Klein, Richard G. 1994. Southern Africa before the ice age. In *Integrative paths to the past,* eds. R. Corruccini and R. Ciochon. Upper Saddle River, NJ: Prentice Hall.

Klein, Richard G. 2003. Whither the Neanderthals? *Science* 299 (March 7):1525–28.

Kleinman, Arthur, Veena Das, and Margaret Lock, eds. 1997. *Social suffering.* Berkeley: University of California Press.

Klima, Bohuslav. 1962. The first ground-plan of an Upper Paleolithic loess settlement in Middle Europe and its meaning. In *Courses toward urban life,* eds. R. Braidwood and G. Willey. Chicago: Aldine.

Klineberg, Otto. 1935. *Negro intelligence and selective migration.* New York: Columbia University Press.

Klineberg, Otto, ed. 1944. *Characteristics of the American Negro.* New York: Harper & Brothers.

Kluckhohn, Clyde. 1948. As an anthropologist views it. In *Sex habits of American men,* ed. A. Deutsch. Upper Saddle River, NJ: Prentice Hall.

Kluckhohn, Clyde. 1965. Recurrent themes in myths and mythmaking. In *The study of folklore,* ed. A. Dundes. Upper Saddle River, NJ: Prentice Hall.

Knecht, Peter. 2003. Aspects of shamanism: An introduction. In *Shamans in Asia,* eds. C. Chilson and P. Knecht, 1–30. London: RoutledgeCurzon.

Koch, Klaus-Friedrich, Soraya Altorki, Andrew Arno, and Letitia Hickson. 1977. Ritual reconciliation and the obviation of grievances: A comparative study in the ethnography of law. *Ethnology* 16:269–84.

Komar, Debra A., and Jane E. Buikstra. 2008. *Forensic anthropology: Contemporary theory and practice.* New York: Oxford University Press.

Konner, Melvin, and Carol Worthman. 1980. Nursing frequency, gonadal function, and birth spacing among !Kung hunter-gatherers. *Science* 267 (February 15):788–91.

Korbin, Jill E. 1981. Introduction. In *Child abuse and neglect,* ed. J. E. Korbin. Berkeley: University of California Press.

Korotayev, Andrey, and Dmitri Bondarenko. 2000. Polygyny and democracy: A cross-cultural comparison. *Cross-Cultural Research* 34:190–208.

Kottak, Conrad Phillip. 1996. The media, development, and social change. In *Transforming societies, transforming anthropology,* ed. E. F. Moran. Ann Arbor: University of Michigan Press.

Kracke, Waud H. 1979. *Force and persuasion: Leadership in an Amazonian society.* Chicago: University of Chicago Press.

Krahn, Harvey, T. F. Hartnagel, and J. W. Gartrell. 1986. Income inequality and homicide rates: Cross-national data and criminological theories. *Criminology* 24:269–95.

Kramer, Andrew. 2009. The natural history and evolutionary fate of *Homo erectus.* In *MyAnthroLibrary,* eds. C. R. Ember, M. Ember, and P. N. Peregrine. MyAnthroLibrary.com. Pearson.

Kramer, Samuel Noel. 1963. *The Sumerians: Their history, culture, and character.* Chicago: University of Chicago Press.

Krause, Johannes, Carles Lalueza-Fox, Ludovic Orlando, Wolfgang Enard, Richard E. Green, Hernán A. Burbano, Jean-Jacques Hublin, Catherine Hänni, Javier Fortea, Marco de la Rasilla, Jaume Bertranpetit, Antonio Rosas, and Svante Pääbo. 2007. The derived FOXP2 variant of modern humans was shared with Neandertals. *Current Biology* 17(21):1908–12.

Krebs, John R., and N. B. Davies, eds. 1984. *Behavioural ecology: An evolutionary approach.* 2nd ed. Sunderland, MA: Sinauer.

Krebs, John R., and N. B. Davies. 1987. *An introduction to behavioural ecology.* 2nd ed. Sunderland, MA: Sinauer.

Krings, Matthias, A. Stone, R. W. Schmitz, H. Krainitzki, M. Stoneking, and S. Paabo. 1997. Neandertal DNA sequences and the origin of modern humans. *Cell* 90:19–30.

Krippner, Stanley. 1987. Dreams and shamanism. In *Shamanism,* comp. S. Nicholson, 125–32. Wheaton, IL: Theosophical Publishing House.

Kristof, Nicholas D. 1995. Japan's invisible minority: Better off than in past, but still outcasts. *New York Times,* International, November 30, p. A18.

Kristof, Nicholas D. 1997. Japan's invisible minority: Burakumin. *Britannica Online,* December.

Kuehn, Steven. 1998. New evidence for Late Paleoindian—early Archaic subsistence behavior in the western Great Lakes. *American Antiquity* 63:457–76.

Kushner, Gilbert. 1991. Applied anthropology. In *Career explorations in human services,* eds. W. G. Emener and M. Darrow. Springfield, IL: Charles C Thomas.

Lakoff, Robin. 1973. Language and woman's place. *Language in Society* 2:45–80.

Lakoff, Robin. 1990. Why can't a woman be less like a man? In *Talking power,* ed. R. Lakoff. New York: Basic Books.

Lalueza-Fox, Carles, Holger Römpler, David Caramelli, Claudia Stäubert, Giulio Catalano, David Hughes, Nadin Rohland, Elena Pilli, Laura Longo, Silvana Condemi, Marco de la Rasilla, Javier Fortea, Antonio Rosas, Mark Stoneking, Torsten Schöneberg, Jaume Bertranpetit, and Michael Hofreiter. 2007. A melanocortin 1 receptor allele suggests varying pigmentation among Neandertals. *Science* 318 (November 30):1453–55.

Lambert, Helen. 2001. Not talking about sex in India: Indirection and the communication of bodily intention. In *An anthropology of indirect communication,* eds. J. Hendry and C. W. Watson, 51–67. London: Routledge.

Lambert, Patricia M., Banks L. Leonard, Brian R. Billman, Richard A. Marlar, Margaret E. Newman, and Karl J. Reinhard. 2000. Response to critique of the claim of cannibalism at Cowboy Wash. *American Antiquity* 65(2):397–406.

Lambert, William W., Leigh Minturn Triandis, and Margery Wolf. 1959. Some correlates of beliefs in the malevolence and benevolence of supernatural beings: A cross-societal study. *Journal of Abnormal and Social Psychology* 58:162–69.

Landauer, Thomas K. 1973. Infantile vaccination and the secular trend in stature. *Ethos* 1:499–503.

Landauer, Thomas K., and John W. M. Whiting. 1964. Infantile stimulation and adult stature of human males. *American Anthropologist* 66:1007–28.

Landauer, Thomas K., and John W. M. Whiting. 1981. Correlates and consequences of stress in infancy. In *Handbook of cross-cultural human development.* eds. R. H. Munroe, R. Munroe, and B. Whiting. New York: Garland.

Lang, Sabine. 1999. Lesbians, men-women and two-spirits: Homosexuality and gender in Native American cultures. In *Female desires: Same-sex relations and transgender practices across cultures,* eds. Evelyn Blackwood and Saskia E. Weiringa, 91–116. New York: Columbia University Press.

Lareau, Annette. 2003. *Unequal childhoods: Class, race, and family life.* Berkeley: University of California Press.

Larson, Christine L., J. Aronoff, I. C. Sarinopoulos, and D. C. Zhu. 2009. Recognizing threat: A simple geometric shape activates neural circuitry for threat detection. *Journal of Cognitive Neuroscience* 21:1523–35.

Lawless, Robert, Vinson H. Sutlive, Jr., and Mario D. Zamora, eds. 1983. *Fieldwork: The human experience.* New York: Gordon and Breach.

Layton, Robert. 1992. *Australian rock art: A new synthesis.* Cambridge, UK: Cambridge University Press.

Leacock, Eleanor, and Richard Lee. 1982. Introduction. In *Politics and history in band societies,* eds. E. Leacock and R. Lee. Cambridge, UK: Cambridge University Press.

Leakey, Louis S. B. 1960. Finding the world's earliest man. *National Geographic* (September):420–35.

Leakey, Meave, C. S. Feibel, I. McDougall, and A. Walker. 1995. New four-million-year-old hominid species from Kanapoi and Allia Bay, Kenya. *Nature* 376 (August 17):565–71.

Leakey, Meave, Fred Spoor, Frank Brown, Patrick Gathogo, Christopher Kiarie, Louise Leakey, Ian McDougall. 2001. New Hominin genus from Eastern Africa shows diverse middle Pliocene lineages. *Nature* 410 (March 22):433–51.

Leakey, Mary. 1971. *Olduvai Gorge: Excavations in Beds I and II.* Cambridge, UK: Cambridge University Press.

Lee, Richard B. 1968. What hunters do for a living, or, how to make out on scarce resources. In *Man the hunter,* eds. R. B. Lee and I. DeVore. Chicago: Aldine.

Lee, Richard B. 1972. Population growth and the beginnings of sedentary life among the !Kung bushmen. In *Population growth,* ed. B. Spooner. Cambridge, MA: MIT Press.

Lee, Richard B. 1979. *The !Kung San: Men, women, and work in a foraging society.* Cambridge, UK: Cambridge University Press.

Lees, Susan H., and Daniel G. Bates. 1974. The origins of specialized nomadic pastoralism: A systemic model. *American Antiquity* 39:187–93.

Leibowitz, Lila. 1978. *Females, males, families: A biosocial approach.* North Scituate, MA: Duxbury.

Lenski, Gerhard. 1984/1966. *Power and privilege: A theory of social stratification.* Chapel Hill: University of North Carolina Press.

Leonard, William R. 2002. Food for thought: Dietary change was a driving force in human evolution. *Scientific American* (December):108–15.

Leonhardt, David, and Geraldine Fabrikant. 2009. Rise of the super-rich hits a sobering wall. *New York Times,* New York Edition, August 20, p. A1.

Lepowsky, Maria. 1990. Big men, big women and cultural autonomy. *Ethnology* 29:35–50.

Leslie, Charles. 1976. Introduction. In *Asian medical systems: A comparative study,* ed. C. Leslie. Los Angeles: University of California Press.

Levine, James A., Robert Weisell, Simon Chevassus, Claudio D. Martinez, and Barbara Burlingame. 2002. The distribution of work tasks for male and female children and adults separated by gender. In *Science* 296 (May 10):1025.

Levine, Nancy E. 1988. Women's work and infant feeding: A case from rural Nepal. *Ethnology* 27:231–51.

Levinson, David. 1989. *Family violence in cross-cultural perspective.* Newbury Park, CA: Sage.

Levinson, David, and Melvin Ember, eds., 1997. *American immigrant cultures: Builders of a nation,* 2 vols. New York: Macmillan Reference.

Lewin, Roger. 1983. Fossil Lucy grows younger, again. *Science* 219 (January 7):43–44.

Lewin, Tamar. 1994. Sex in America: Faithfulness in marriage is overwhelming. *New York Times,* National, October 7, pp. A1, A18.

Lewis, Oscar. 1951. *Life in a Mexican village: Tepoztlan revisited.* Urbana: University of Illinois Press.

Lewis, Oscar (with the assistance of Victor Barnouw). 1958. *Village life in northern India.* Urbana: University of Illinois Press.

Lieberman, Daniel E. 1995. Testing hypotheses about recent human evolution from skulls: Integrating morphology, function, development, and phylogeny. *Current Anthropology* 36:159–97.

Lieberman, Leonard. 1999. Scientific insignificance. *Anthropology Newsletter* 40:11–12.

Lieberman, Leonard, Rodney Kirk, and Alice Littlefield. 2003. Perishing paradigm: Race 1931–99. *American Anthropologist* 105:110–13.

Lieberman, Leslie Sue. 2004. Diabetes mellitus and medical anthropology. In *Encyclopedia of medical anthropology: Health and illness in the world's cultures,* vol. I, eds. Carol R. Ember and Melvin Ember, 335–53. New York: Kluwer Academic Press/Plenum Press.

Lingenfelter, Sherwood G. 2009. Yap: Changing roles of men and women. In MyAnthroLibrary, eds. C. R. Ember, M. Ember, and P. N. Peregrine. MyAnthroLibrary.com. Pearson.

Linton, Ralph. 1936. *The study of man.* New York: Appleton-Century-Crofts.

Linton, Ralph. 1945. *The cultural background of personality.* New York: Appleton-Century-Crofts.

Loftin, Colin K. 1971. *Warfare and societal complexity: A cross-cultural study of organized fighting in preindustrial societies.* Doctoral dissertation, University of North Carolina at Chapel Hill.

Loftin, Colin, David McDowall, and James Boudouris. 1989. Economic change and homicide in Detroit, 1926–1979. In *Violence in America,* vol. 1: *The history of crime,* ed. T. R. Gurr. Newbury Park, CA: Sage.

Lomax, Alan, ed. 1968. *Folk song style and culture.* American Association for the Advancement of Science Publication No. 88. Washington, DC.

Loomis, W. Farnsworth. 1967. Skin-pigment regulation of vitamin-D biosynthesis in man. *Science* 157 (August 4):501–06.

Los Angeles Times. 1994. Plundering earth is nothing new. News Service, as reported in the *New Haven Register,* June 12, pp. A18–A19.

Loustaunau, Martha O., and Elisa J. Sobo. 1997. *The cultural context of health, illness, and medicine.* Westport, CT: Bergin & Garvey.

Lovejoy, Arthur O. 1964. *The great chain of being: A study of the history of an idea.* Cambridge, MA: Harvard University Press.

Lovejoy, C. Owen. 1981. The origin of man. *Science* 211 (January 23):341–50.

Lovejoy, C. Owen. 1988. Evolution of human walking. *Scientific American* (November):118–25.

Low, Bobbi. 1990. Marriage systems and pathogen stress in human societies. *American Zoologist* 30:325–39.

Low, Bobbi S. 2009. Behavioral ecology, "sociobiology" and human behavior. In MyAnthroLibrary, eds. C. R. Ember, M. Ember, and P. N. Peregrine. MyAnthroLibrary.com. Pearson.

Lucy, John A. 1992. *Grammatical categories and cognition: A case study of the linguistic relativity hypothesis.* Cambridge, UK: Cambridge University Press.

Lumbreras, Luis. 1974. *The peoples and cultures of ancient Peru.* Washington, DC: Smithsonian Institution Press.

Lyttleton, Chris. 2000. *Endangered relations: Negotiating sex and AIDS in Thailand.* Bangkok: White Lotus Press.

MacArthur, Robert H., and E. O. Wilson. 1967. *Theory of island biogeography.* Princeton, NJ: Princeton University Press.

Maccoby, Eleanor E., and Carol N. Jacklin. 1974. *The psychology of sex differences.* Stanford, CA: Stanford University Press.

Macdonald, Douglas H., and Barry S. Hewlett. 1999. Reproductive interests and forager mobility. *Current Anthropology* 40:501–23.

MacKinnon, John, and Kathy MacKinnon. 1980. The behavior of wild spectral tarsiers. *International Journal of Primatology* 1:361–79.

MacNeish, Richard S. 1991. *The origins of agriculture and settled life.* Norman: University of Oklahoma Press.

Madrigal, Lorena. 1989. Hemoglobin genotype, fertility, and the malaria hypothesis. *Human Biology* 61:311–25.

Magner, Lois. 1992. *A history of medicine.* New York: Marcel Dekker.

Mahony, Frank Joseph. 1971. *A Trukese theory of medicine.* Ann Arbor, MI: University Microfilms.

Malefijt, Annemarie De Waal. 1968. *Religion and culture: An introduction to anthropology of religion.* New York: Macmillan.

Malin, Edward. 1986. *Totem poles of the Pacific Northwest coast.* Portland, OR: Timber Press.

Mangin, William. 1967. Latin American squatter settlements: A problem and a solution. *Latin American Research Review* 2:65–98.

Manhein, Mary H. 1999. *The bone lady: Life as a forensic anthropologist.* Baton Rouge: Louisiana State University Press.

Maquet, Jacques. 1986. *The aesthetic experience: An anthropologist looks at the visual arts.* New Haven, CT: Yale University Press.

Marano, Louis A. 1973. A macrohistoric trend toward world government. *Behavior Science Notes* 8:35–40.

Marcus, Joyce, and Kent V. Flannery. 1996. *Zapotec civilization.* London: Thames and Hudson.

Marks, Jonathan. 1994. Black, white, other: Racial categories as cultural constructs masquerading as biology. *Natural History* (December):32–35.

Marlowe, Frank W. 2003. A critical period for provisioning by Hadza men: Implications for pair bonding. *Evolution and Human Behavior* 24:217–29.

Marshall, Eliot. 2000. Rival genome sequencers celebrate a milestone together. *Science* 288 (June 30):2294–95.

Marshall, Larry G. 1984. Who killed cock robin? An investigation of the extinction controversy. In *Quaternary extinctions,* eds. P. Martin and R. Klein. Tucson: University of Arizona Press.

Marshall, Lorna. 1961. Sharing, talking and giving: Relief of social tensions among !Kung Bushmen. *Africa* 31:239–42.

Martin, M. Kay, and Barbara Voorhies. 1975. *Female of the species.* New York: Columbia University Press.

Martin, Paul S. 1973. The discovery of America. *Science* 179 (March 9):969–74.

Martin, Paul S., and H. E. Wright, eds. 1967. *Pleistocene extinctions: The search for a cause.* New Haven, CT: Yale University Press.

Martin, Robert D. 1990. *Primate origins and evolution: A phylogenetic reconstruction.* Princeton, NJ: Princeton University Press.

Martorell, Reynaldo. 1980. Interrelationships between diet, infectious disease and nutritional status. In *Social and biological predictors of nutritional status, physical growth and neurological development,* eds. L. Greene and F. Johnston. New York: Academic Press.

Martorell, Reynaldo, Juan Rivera, Haley Kaplowitz, and Ernesto Pollitt. 1991. Long-term consequences of growth retardation during early childhood. Paper presented at the Sixth International Congress of Auxology, September 15–19, Madrid.

Mascie-Taylor, C. G. Nicholas. 1990. The biology of social class. In *Biosocial aspects of social class,* ed. C. G. N. Mascie-Taylor, 117–42. Oxford, UK: Oxford University Press.

Masumura, Wilfred T. 1977. Law and violence: A cross-cultural study. *Journal of Anthropological Research* 33:388–99.

Mathiassen, Therkel. 1928. *Material culture of Iglulik Eskimos.* Copenhagen: Glydendalske.

Matossian, Mary K. 1982. Ergot and the Salem witchcraft affair. *American Scientist* 70:355–57.

Matossian, Mary K. 1989. *Poisons of the past: Molds, epidemics, and history.* New Haven, CT: Yale University Press.

Mayr, Ernst. 1982. *The growth of biological thought: Diversity, evolution, and inheritance.* Cambridge, MA: Belknap Press of Harvard University Press.

Mazess, Richard B. 1975. Human adaptation to high altitude. In *Physiological Anthropology,* ed. A. Damon. New York: Oxford University Press.

McCain, Garvin, and Erwin M. Segal. 1988. *The game of science.* 5th ed. Monterey, CA: Brooks/Cole.

McCarthy, Frederick D., and Margaret McArthur. 1960. The food quest and the time factor in Aboriginal economic life. In *Records of the Australian-American scientific expedition to Arnhem Land,* ed. C. P. Mountford, vol. 2: *Anthropology and Nutrition.* Melbourne: Melbourne University Press.

McCorriston, Joy, and Frank Hole. 1991. The ecology of seasonal stress and the origins of agriculture in the Near East. *American Anthropologist* 93:46–69.

McCracken, Robert D. 1971. Lactase deficiency: An example of dietary evolution. *Current Anthropology* 12:479–500.

McDonald, Kim A. 1998. New evidence challenges traditional model of how the New World was settled. *Chronicle of Higher Education* (March 13):A22.

McElroy, Ann, and Patricia Townsend. 2002. *Medical anthropology in ecological perspective.* 3rd ed. Boulder, CO: Westview Press.

McHenry, Henry M. 1982. The pattern of human evolution: Studies on bipedalism, mastication, and encephalization. *Annual Review of Anthropology* 11:151–73.

McHenry, Henry M. 1988. New estimates of body weight in early hominids and their significance to encephalization and megadontia in "robust" australopithecines. In *Evolutionary history of the "robust" australopithecines,* ed. F. E. Grine. New York: Aldine.

McHenry, Henry M. 2009. Robust australopithecines. Our family tree, and homoplasy. In MyAnthroLibrary, eds. C. R. Ember, M. Ember, and P. N. Peregrine. MyAnthroLibrary.com. Pearson.

McKee, Lauris. 1984. Sex differentials in survivorship and the customary treatment of infants and children. *Medical Anthropology* 8:91–108.

McMullin, Ernan. 2001. Plantinga's defense of special creation. In *Intelligent design creationism and its critics,* ed. R. Pennock, 174. Boston: MIT Press.

McNeill, William H. 1976. *Plagues and peoples.* Garden City, NY: Doubleday/Anchor.

McNeill, William H. 1998. *Plagues and peoples.* New York: Anchor Books/Doubleday.

Mead, Margaret. 1950/1935. *Sex and temperament in three primitive societies.* New York: Mentor.

Mead, Margaret. 1961/1928. *Coming of age in Samoa.* 3rd ed. New York: Morrow.

Meek, Charles K. 1940. *Land law and custom in the colonies.* London: Oxford University Press.

Meggitt, Mervyn J. 1977. *Blood is their argument: Warfare among the Mae Enga tribesmen of the New Guinea highlands.* Palo Alto, CA: Mayfield.

Mellaart, James. 1961. Roots in the soil. In *The dawn of civilization,* ed. S. Piggott. London: Thomas & Hudson.

Mellars, Paul. 1994. The Upper Paleolithic revolution. In *The Oxford illustrated prehistory of Europe,* ed. B. Cunliffe, 42–78. Oxford, UK: Oxford University Press.

Mellars, Paul. 1996. *The Neanderthal legacy.* Princeton, NJ: Princeton University Press.

Mellars, Paul. 1998. The fate of the Neaderthals. *Nature* 395 (October 8):539–40.

Mellor, John W., and Sarah Gavian. 1987. Famine: Causes, prevention, and relief. *Science* 235 (January 30):539–44.

Meltzer, David J. 1993. Pleistocene peopling of the Americas. *Evolutionary Anthropology* 1(1):157–69.

Merbs, Charles F. 1992. A new world of infectious disease. *Yearbook of Physical Anthropology* 35:3–42.

Merrill, Elizabeth Bryant. 1987. Art styles as reflections of sociopolitical complexity. *Ethnology* 26:221–30.

Messer, Ellen. 1996. Hunger vulnerability from an anthropologist's food system perspective. In *Transforming societies, transforming anthropology,* ed. E. F. Moran. Ann Arbor: University of Michigan Press.

Middleton, John. 1971. The cult of the dead: Ancestors and ghosts. In *Reader in comparative religion.* 3rd ed. eds. W. A. Lessa and E. Z. Vogt. New York: Harper & Row.

Middleton, Russell. 1962. Brother-sister and father-daughter marriage in ancient Egypt. *American Sociological Review* 27:603–11.

Miller, Greg. 2004. Listen, baby. *Science* 306 (November 12):1127.

Miller, Naomi. 1992. The origins of plant cultivation in the Near East. In C. W. Cowan and P. J. Watson, eds. *The Origins of agriculture.* Washington, DC: Smithsonian Institution Press.

Millon, René. 1967. Teotihuacán. *Scientific American* (June):38–48.

Millon, René. 1976. Social relations in ancient Teotihuacán. In *The valley of Mexico,* ed. E. Wolf. Albuquerque: University of New Mexico Press.

Miner, Horace. 1956. Body rituals among the Nacirema. *American Anthropologist* 58:504–05.

Minturn, Leigh. 1993. *Sita's daughters: Coming out of Purdah: The Rajput women of Khalapur revisited.* New York: Oxford University Press.

Minturn, Leigh, and Jerry Stashak. 1982. Infanticide as a terminal abortion procedure. *Behavior Science Research* 17:70–85.

Miracle, Andrew W. 2009. A shaman to organizations. In MyAnthroLibrary, eds. C. R. Ember, M. Ember, and P. N. Peregrine. MyAnthroLibrary.com. Pearson.

Mitchell, Donald. 2009. Nimpkish: Complex foragers on the northwest coast of North America. In MyAnthroLibrary, eds. C. R. Ember, M. Ember, and P. N. Peregrine. MyAnthroLibrary.com. Pearson.

Moerman, Daniel E. 1997. Physiology and symbols: The anthropological implications of the placebo effect. In *The anthropology of medicine*. 3rd ed. eds. L. Romanucci-Ross, D. E. Moerman, and L. R. Tancredi, 240–53. Westport, CT: Bergin & Garvey.

Molnar, Stephen. 1998. *Human variation: Races, types, and ethnic groups*. 4th ed. Upper Saddle River, NJ: Prentice Hall.

Monsutti, Alessandro. 2004. Cooperation, remittances, and kinship among the Hazaras. *Iranian Studies* 37:219–40.

Mooney, Kathleen A. 1978. The effects of rank and wealth on exchange among the coast Salish. *Ethnology* 17:391–406.

Moore, Carmella C. 1988. An optimal scaling of Murdock's theories of illness data—An approach to the problem of interdependence. *Behavior Science Research* 22:161–79.

Moore, Omar Khayyam. 1957. Divination: A new perspective. *American Anthropologist* 59:69–74.

Morell, Virginia. 1995. The earliest art becomes older—and more common. *Science,* 267 (March 31):1908–09.

Morris, John. 1938. *Living with Lepchas: A book about the Sikkim Himalayas*. London: Heinemann.

Morrison, Kathleen D., and Laura L. Junker. 2002. *Forager-traders in South and Southeast Asia: Long-term histories*. Cambridge, UK: Cambridge University Press.

Morwood, Michael J., R. Soejono, R. Roberts, T. Sutikna, C. Turney, K. Westaway, W. Rink, J. Zhao, G. van den Bergh, R. Due, D. Hobbs, M. Moore, M. Bird, and L. Fifield. 2004. Archaeology and age of a new hominin from Flores in Eastern Indonesia. *Nature* 431 (October 28):1087–91.

Moser, Stephanie. 1998. *Ancestral images: The iconography of human origins*. Ithaca, NY: Cornell University Press.

Motulsky, Arno. 1971. Metabolic polymorphisms and the role of infectious diseases in human evolution. In *Human populations, genetic variation, and evolution*, ed. L. N. Morris. San Francisco: Chandler.

Moyá-Solá, Salvador, et al. 2004. *Pierolapithecus catalaunicus*. A new middle Miocene great ape from Spain. *Science* 306 (November 19):1339–44.

Mukerjee, Madhusree. 1996. Field notes: Interview with a parrot. *Scientific American* (April):28.

Mukhopadhyay, Carol C., and Patricia J. Higgins. 1988. Anthropological studies of women's status revisited: 1977–1987. *Annual Review of Anthropology* 17:461–95.

Muller, Edward N. 1997. Economic determinants of democracy. In *Inequality, democracy, and economic development*, ed. M. Midlarsky, 133–55. Cambridge, UK: Cambridge University Press.

Müller-Haye, B. 1984. Guinea pig or cuy. In *Evolution of domesticated animals*, ed. I. Mason. New York: Longman.

Munroe, Robert L., Robert Hulefeld, James M. Rodgers, Damon L. Tomeo, and Steven K. Yamazaki. 2000. Aggression among children in four cultures. *Cross-Cultural Research* 34:3–25.

Munroe, Robert L., and Ruth H. Munroe. 1969. A cross-cultural study of sex, gender, and social structure. *Ethnology* 8:206–11.

Munroe, Robert L., Ruth H. Munroe, and Stephen Winters. 1996. Cross-cultural correlates of the consonant-vowel (cv) syllable. *Cross-Cultural Research* 30:60–83.

Murdock, George P. 1949. *Social structure*. New York: Macmillan.

Murdock, George P. 1957. World ethnographic sample. *American Anthropologist* 59:664–87.

Murdock, George P. 1967. Ethnographic atlas: A summary. *Ethnology* 6:109–236.

Murdock, George P. 1980. *Theories of illness: A world survey*. Pittsburgh, PA: University of Pittsburgh Press.

Murdock, George P., and Caterina Provost. 1973. Factors in the division of labor by sex: A cross-cultural analysis. *Ethnology* 12:203–25.

Murdock, George P., and Douglas R. White. 1969. Standard cross-cultural sample. *Ethnology* 8:329–69.

Murphy, Robert F. 1960. *Headhunter's heritage: Social and economic change among the Mundurucú*. Berkeley: University of California Press.

Murphy, Robert F., and Julian H. Steward. 1956. Tappers and trappers: Parallel process in acculturation. *Economic Development and Cultural Change* 4 (July):335–55.

Murray, Gerald F., and M. E. Bannister. 2004. Peasants, agroforesters, and anthropologists: A 20-year venture in income-generating trees and hedgerows in Haiti. *Agroforestry Systems* 61:383–97.

Myers, Fred R. 1988. Critical trends in the study of hunter-gatherers. *Annual Review of Anthropology* 17:261–82.

Nadel, Siegfried F. 1942. *A black Byzantium: The kingdom of Nupe in Nigeria*. London: Oxford University Press.

Nag, Moni, Benjamin N. F. White, and R. Creighton Peet. 1978. An anthropological approach to the study of the economic value of children in Java and Nepal. *Current Anthropology* 19:293–301.

Nagata, Judith. 2001. Beyond theology: Toward an anthropology of "fundamentalism." *American Anthropologist* 103:481–98.

Nagel, Ernest. 1961. *The structure of science: Problems in the logic of scientific explanation*. New York: Harcourt, Brace & World.

Napier, John R. 1970. Paleoecology and catarrhine evolution. In *Old World monkeys: Evolution, systematics, and behavior*. eds. J. R. Napier and P. H. Napier. New York: Academic Press.

Napier, John R., and P. H. Napier. 1967. *A handbook of living primates*. New York: Academic Press.

Naroll, Raoul. 1961. Two solutions for Galton's problem. In *Readings in cross-cultural methodology*, ed. Frank Moore, 221–45. New Haven, CT: HRAF Press.

Naroll, Raoul. 1967. Imperial cycles and world order. *Peace Research Society: Papers* 7:83–101.

Nash, Manning. 1989. *The cauldron of ethnicity in the modern world*. Chicago: University of Chicago Press.

National Coalition for the Homeless. 2008. How many people experience homelessness? NCH Fact Sheet #2. http://www.nationalhomeless.org/factsheets/How_Many.html (accessed September 3, 2009).

Neel, James V., Willard R. Centerwall, Napoleon A. Chagnon, and Helen L. Casey. 1970. Notes on the effect of measles and measles vaccine in a virgin-soil population of South American Indians. *American Journal of Epidemiology* 91:418–29.

Nerlove, Sara B. 1974. Women's workload and infant feeding practices: A relationship with demographic implications. *Ethnology* 13:207–14.

Neumann, Katharina. 2003. New Guinea: A cradle of agriculture. *Science* 301 (July 11):180–81.

Nevins, Allan. 1927. *The American states during and after the revolution*. New York: Macmillan.

Newman, Katherine S. 1983. *Law and economic organization: A comparative study of preindustrial societies*. Cambridge, MA: Cambridge University Press.

Newman, Katherine S. 1988. *Falling from grace: The experience of downward mobility in the American middle class*. New York: Free Press.

Newman, Katherine S. 1993. *Declining fortunes: The withering of the American dream*. New York: Basic Books.

Niehoff, Arthur H. 1966. *A casebook of social change*. Chicago: Aldine.

Nimkoff, Meyer F., and Russell Middleton. 1960. Types of family and types of economy. *American Journal of Sociology* 66:215–25.

Nisbett, Richard E. 2009. Education is all in your mind. *New York Times*. Sunday Opinion, February 8, p. 12.

Nissen, Henry W. 1958. Axes of behavioral comparison. In *Behavior and evolution*, eds. A. Roe and G. G. Simpson. New Haven, CT: Yale University Press.

Nolan, Riall W. 2003. Anthropology in practice: Building a career outside the academy. Boulder: Lynne Rienner.

Noll, Richard. 1987. The presence of spirits in magic and madness. In *Shamanism*, comp. S. Nicholson, 47–61. Wheaton, IL: Theosophical Publishing House.

Norenzayan, Ara, and Azim F. Shariff. 2008. The origin and evolution of religious prosociality. *Science* 322 (October 3):58–62.

Noss, Andrew J., and Barry S. Hewlett. 2001. The contexts of female hunting in central Africa. *American Anthropologist* 103:1024–40.

Oakley, Kenneth. 1964. On man's use of fire, with comments on tool-making and hunting. In *Social life of early man*, ed. S. L. Washburn. Chicago: Aldine.

O'Brian, Robin. 1999. Who weaves and why? Weaving, loom complexity, and trade. *Cross-Cultural Research* 33:30–42.

Ogburn, William F. 1922. *Social change*. New York: Huebsch.

Oliver, Douglas L. 1955. *A Solomon Island society*. Cambridge, MA: Harvard University Press.

Olsen, Steve. 2002. Seeking the signs of selection. *Science* 298 (November 15):1324–25.

Olszewski, Deborah I. 1991. Social complexity in the Natufian? Assessing the relationship of ideas and data. In *Perspectives on the past*, ed. G. Clark. Philadelphia: University of Pennsylvania Press.

Ortiz de Montellano, Bernard R., and C. H. Browner. 1985. Chemical bases for medicinal plant use in Oaxaca, Mexico. *Journal of Ethnopharmacology* 13:57–88.

Osti, Roberto. 1994. The eloquent bones of Abu Hureyra. *Scientific American* (August):1.

Otterbein, Keith. 1968. Internal war: A cross-cultural study. *American Anthropologist* 70:277–89.

Otterbein, Keith. 1970. *The evolution of war*. New Haven, CT: HRAF Press.

Otterbein, Keith. 1986. *The ultimate coercive sanction: A cross-cultural study of capital punishment*. New Haven, CT: HRAF Press.

Otterbein, Keith, and Charlotte Swanson Otterbein. 1965. An eye for an eye, a tooth for a tooth: A cross-cultural study of feuding. *American Anthropologist* 67:1470–82.

Ovchinnikov, Igor V., et al. 2000. Molecular analysis of Neanderthal DNA from the Northern Caucasus. *Nature* 404 (March 30):490–94.

Paige, Jeffery M. 1975. *Agrarian revolution: Social movements and export agriculture in the underdeveloped world*. New York: Free Press.

Paine, Robert. 1994. *Herds of the tundra*. Washington, DC: Smithsonian Institution Press.

Paley, William. 1810. *Natural theology*. Boston: Joshua Belcher.

Palsson, Gisli. 1988. Hunters and gatherers of the sea. In *Hunters and gatherers. 1. History, evolution and social change*, eds. T. Ingold, D. Riches, and J. Woodburn. New York: St. Martin's Press.

Pasternak, Burton. 1976. *Introduction to kinship and social organization*. Upper Saddle River, NJ: Prentice Hall.

Pasternak, Burton, Carol R. Ember, and Melvin Ember. 1976. On the conditions favoring extended family households. *Journal of Anthropological Research* 32:109–23.

Patterson, Orlando. 1982. *Slavery and social death: A comparative study*. Cambridge, MA: Harvard University Press.

Patterson, Orlando. 2000. Review of *One drop of blood: The American misadventure of race*, by Scott L. Malcomson. *New York Times Book Review*, October 22, pp. 15–16.

Patterson, Thomas C. 1971. Central Peru: Its population and economy. *Archaeology* 24:316–21.

Patterson, Thomas C. 1981. *The evolution of ancient societies: A world archaeology*. Upper Saddle River, NJ: Prentice Hall.

Peacock, James L. 1986. *The anthropological lens: Harsh light, soft focus*. Cambridge, UK: Cambridge University Press.

Pearsall, Deborah. 1992. The origins of plant cultivation in South America. In *The origins of agriculture*, eds. C. Cowan and P. Watson. Washington, DC: Smithsonian Institution Press.

Pelto, Pertti J., and Ludger Müller-Wille. 1987. Snowmobiles: Technological revolution in the Arctic. In *Technology and social change*. 2nd ed. eds. H. R. Bernard and P. J. Pelto. Prospect Heights, IL: Waveland Press.

Pelto, Pertti J., and Gretel H. Pelto. 1975. Intra-cultural diversity: Some theoretical issues. *American Ethnologist* 2:1–18.

Pennisi, Elizabeth. 2000. Finally, the book of life and instructions for navigating it. *Science* 288 (June 30):2304–07.

Pennisi, Elizabeth. 2001a. Genetic change wards off malaria. *Science* 294 (November 16):1439.

Pennisi, Elizabeth. 2001b. Malaria's beginnings: On the heels of hoes? *Science* 293 (July 20):416–17.

Pennisi, Elizabeth. 2007. Genomicists tackle the primate tree. *Science* 316 (April 13):218–21.

Pennisi, Elizabeth. 2009. Tales of a prehistoric human genome. *Science* 323 (February 13):866–71.

Pepperberg, Irene Maxine. 1999. *The Alex studies: Cognitive and communicative abilities of grey parrots*. Cambridge, MA: Harvard University Press.

Peregrine, Peter N. 1996. The birth of the gods revisited: A partial replication of Guy Swanson's (1960) cross-cultural study of religion. *Cross-Cultural Research* 30:84–112.

Peregrine, Peter N. 2007. Cultural correlates of ceramic styles. *Cross-Cultural Research* 41:223–35.

Peregrine, Peter N., and Peter Bellwood. 2001. Southeast Asia Upper Paleolithic. In *Encyclopedia of prehistory*, vol. 3: *East Asia and Oceania*, eds. P. N. Peregrine and M. Ember, 307–09. New York: Kluwer Academic/Plenum Press.

Peregrine, Peter N., Carol R. Ember, and Melvin Ember. 2000. Teaching critical evaluation of Rushton. *Anthropology Newsletter* 41 (February):29–30.

Peregrine, Peter N., Carol R. Ember, and Melvin Ember. 2003. Cross-cultural evaluation of predicted associations between race and behavior. *Evolution and Human Behavior* 24:357–64.

Peregrine, Peter N., Melvin Ember, and Carol R. Ember. 2004. Predicting the future state of the world using archaeological data: An exercise in archaeomancy. *Cross-Cultural Research* 38:133–46.

Petersen, Erik B. 1973. A survey of the Late Paleolithic and the Mesolithic of Denmark. In *The Mesolithic in Europe*, ed. S. K. Kozlowski. Warsaw: Warsaw University Press.

Petersen, Larry R., G. R. Lee, and G. J. Ellis. 1982. Social structure, socialization values, and disciplinary techniques: A cross-cultural analysis. *Journal of Marriage and the Family* 44:131–42.

Pfaff, Carol. 1979. Constraints on language mixing. *Language* 55:291–318, as cited in *An introduction to sociolinguistics*. 2nd ed. ed. R. Wardhaugh. Oxford, UK: Blackwell.

Phillips, Kevin. 1990. *The politics of rich and poor: Wealth and the American electorate in the Reagan aftermath*. New York: Random House.

Phillipson, David W. 1976. Archaeology and Bantu linguistics. *World Archaeology* 8:65–82.

Phillipson, David W. 1993. *African archaeology*. 2nd ed. New York: Cambridge University Press.

Picchi, Debra. 1991. The impact of an industrial agricultural project on the Bakairí Indians of central Brazil. *Human Organization* 50:26–38.

Picchi, Debra. 2009. Bakairí: The death of an Indian. In MyAnthroLibrary, eds. C. R. Ember, M. Ember, and P. N. Peregrine. MyAnthroLibrary.com. Pearson.

Pickford, Martin, Brigette Senut, Dominique Gommery, and Jacques Treil. 2002. Bipedalism in *Orrorin tugenensis* revealed by its femora. *Comptes Rendu de l'Académie des Science des Paris*, Palevol 1, 1–13.

Pilbeam, David. 1972. *The ascent of man*. New York: Macmillan.

Pilbeam, David, and Stephen Jay Gould. 1974. Size and Scaling in Human Evolution. *Science* 186 (December 6):892–900.

Piperno, Dolores, and Karen Stothert. 2003. Phytolith evidence for early holocene cucurbita domestication in southwest Ecuador. *Science* 299 (February, 14):1054–57.

Plattner, Stuart, ed. 1985. *Markets and marketing*. Monographs in Economic Anthropology, No. 4. Lanham, MD: University Press of America.

Plattner, Stuart. 1989. Marxism. In *Economic anthropology*, ed. S. Plattner. Stanford, CA: Stanford University Press.

Polanyi, Karl. 1957. The economy as instituted process. In *Trade and market in the early empires*, eds. K. Polanyi, C. M. Arensberg, and H. W. Pearson. New York: Free Press.

Polanyi, Karl, Conrad M. Arensberg, and Harry W. Pearson, eds. 1957. *Trade and market in the early empires.* New York: Free Press.

Polednak, Anthony P. 1974. Connective tissue responses in negroes in relation to disease. *American Journal of Physical Anthropology* 41:49–57.

Pollier, Nicole. 2000. Commoditization, cash, and kinship in post-colonial Papua New Guinea. In *Commodities and globalization: Anthropological perspectives,* eds. Angelique Haugerud, M. Priscilla Stone, and Peter D. Little, 197–217. Lanham, MD: Rowman & Littlefield.

Pope, Geoffrey G. 1989. Bamboo and human evolution. *Natural History* (October):49–57.

Popenoe, Rebecca. 2004. *Feeding desire: Fatness, beauty, and sexuality among a Saharan people.* London: Routledge.

Pospisil, Leopold. 1963. *The Kapauku Papuans of West New Guinea.* New York: Holt, Rinehart & Winston.

Post, Peter W., Farrington Daniels, Jr., and Robert T. Binford, Jr. 1975. Cold injury and the evolution of "white" skin. *Human Biology* 47:65–80.

Potts, Richard. 1984. Home bases and early hominids. *American Scientist* 72:338–47.

Potts, Richard. 1988. *Early hominid activities at Olduvai.* New York: Aldine.

Prag, John, and Richard Neave. 1997. *Making faces: Using forensic and archaeological evidence.* College Station: Texas A&M University Press.

Preuschoft, Holger, David J. Chivers, Warren Y. Brockelman, and Norman Creel, eds. 1984. *The lesser apes: Evolutionary and behavioural biology.* Edinburgh, UK: Edinburgh University Press.

Price, Sally. 1989. *Primitive art in civilized places.* Chicago: University of Chicago Press.

Pringle, Heather. 1998. The slow birth of agriculture. *Science* 282 (November 20):1446–50.

Pryor, Frederic L. 1977. *The origins of the economy: A comparative study of distribution in primitive and peasant economies.* New York: Academic Press.

Pryor, Frederic L. 2005. *Economic systems of foraging, agricultural, and industrial societies.* Cambridge, UK: Cambridge University Press.

Quandt, Sara A. 1996. Nutrition in anthropology. In *Handbook of medical anthropology,* rev. ed., eds. C. F. Sargent and T. M. Johnson, 272–89. Westport, CT: Greenwood Press.

Quinn, Naomi. 1977. Anthropological studies on women's status. *Annual Review of Anthropology* 6:181–225.

Radcliffe-Brown, Alfred R. 1922. *The Andaman Islanders: A study in social anthropology.* Cambridge, UK: Cambridge University Press.

Radinsky, Leonard. 1967. The oldest primate endocast. *American Journal of Physical Anthropology* 27:358–88.

Rambo, Lewis R. 2003. Anthropology and the study of conversion. In *The anthropology of religious conversion,* eds. Andrew Buckser and Stephen D. Glazier, 211–22. Lanham, MD: Roman & Littlefield.

Rasmussen, D. Tab. 1990. Primate origins: Lessons from a neotropical marsupial. *American Journal of Primatology* 22:263–77.

Rathje, William L. 1971. The origin and development of lowland classic Maya civilization. *American Antiquity* 36:275–85.

Ravesloot, John. 1997. Changing Native American perceptions of archaeology and archaeologists. In *Native Americans and archaeologists,* eds. N. Swidler, et al. Walnut Creek, CA: AltaMira Press.

Ray, Verne F. 1954. *The Sanpoil and Nespelem: Salishan peoples of northeastern Washington.* New Haven, CT: Human Relations Area Files.

Raybeck, Douglas. 1998. Toward more holistic explanations: Cross-cultural research and cross-level analysis. *Cross-Cultural Research* 32:123–42.

Raybeck, Douglas, J. Shoobe, and J. Grauberger. 1989. Women, stress and participation in possession cults: A reexamination of the calcium deficiency hypothesis. *Medical Anthropology Quarterly* 3:139–61.

Redman, Charles L. 1978. *The rise of civilization: From early farmers to urban society in the ancient Near East.* San Francisco: W. H. Freeman.

Reed, David, V. Smith, S. Hammond, A. Rogers, and D. Clayton. 2004. Genetic analysis of lice supports direct contact between modern and archaic humans. *PLoS Biology* 2 (November):1972–83.

Reff, Daniel T. 2005. *Plagues, priests, and demons: Sacred narratives and the rise of Christianity in the Old World and the New.* Cambridge, UK: Cambridge University Press.

Reisner, Marc. 1993. *Cadillac desert: The American West and its disappearing water.* Rev. ed. New York: Penguin.

Relethford, John. 1990. *The human species: An introduction to biological anthropology.* Mountain View, CA: Mayfield.

Renfrew, Colin. 1969. Trade and culture process in European history. *Current Anthropology* 10:156–69.

Rennie, John. 2002. 15 answers to creationist nonsense. *Scientific American* (July):78–85.

Rhine, Stanley. 1993. Skeletal criteria for racial attribution. *National Association for Applied Anthropology Bulletin* 13:54–67.

Rice, Patricia C., and Ann L. Paterson. 1985. Cave art and bones: Exploring the interrelationships. *American Anthropologist* 87:94–100.

Rice, Patricia C., and Ann L. Paterson. 1986. Validating the cave art—Archeofaunal relationship in Cantabrian Spain. *American Anthropologist* 88:658–67.

Rice, William. R., and G. W. Salt. 1988. Speciation via disruptive selection on habitat preference: experimental evidence. *American Naturalist* 129:911–17.

Richard, Alison F. 1985. *Primates in nature.* New York: W. H. Freeman.

Richard, Alison F. 1987. Malagasy prosimians: Female dominance. In *Primate societies,* eds. B. Smuts, et al. Chicago: University of Chicago Press.

Richmond, Brian G., and William L. Jungers. Orrorin tugenensis femoral morphology and the evolution of human bipedalism. *Science* 319 (21, March 2008):1662–65.

Rightmire, G. Philip. 1984. Homo sapiens in sub-Saharan Africa. In *The origins of modern humans,* eds. F. H. Smith and F. Spencer. New York: Alan R. Liss.

Rightmire, G. Philip. 1997. Human evolution in the Middle Pleistocene: The role of Homo heidelbergensis. *Evolutionary Anthropology* 6:218–27.

Rightmire, G. Philip. 2000. Homo erectus. In *Encyclopedia of human evolution and prehistory,* eds. I. Tattersall, E. Delson, and J. van Couvering. New York: Garland.

Rijksen, Herman D. 1978. *A field study on Sumatran Orang Utans (Pongo Pygmaeus Abelii Lesson 1827): Ecology, Behaviour and Conservation.* Wageningen, The Netherlands: H. Veenman and Zonen.

Rivers, William H. R. 1967/1906. *The Todas.* Oosterhout, N.B., The Netherlands: Anthropological Publications.

Roberts, Derek F. 1953. Body weight, race, and climate. *American Journal of Physical Anthropology,* 533–58.

Roberts, Derek F. 1978. *Climate and human variability.* 2nd ed. Menlo Park, CA: Cummings.

Roberts, John M. 1967. Oaths, autonomic ordeals, and power. In *Cross-cultural approaches,* ed. C. S. Ford. New Haven, CT: HRAF Press.

Robins, Ashley H. 1991. *Biological perspectives on human pigmentation.* New York: Cambridge University Press.

Robinson, John G., and Charles H. Janson. 1987. Capuchins, squirrel monkeys, and atelines: Socioecological convergence with Old World primates. In *Primate societies.* eds. B. Smuts, et al. Chicago: University of Chicago Press.

Robinson, John G., Patricia C. Wright, and Warren G. Kinzey. 1987. Monogamous cebids and their relatives: Intergroup calls and spacing. In *Primate societies,* eds. B. Smuts, et al. Chicago: University of Chicago Press.

Rodwin, Lloyd, and Bishwapriya Sanyal. 1987. Shelter, settlement, and development: An overview. In *Shelter, settlement, and development,* ed. L. Rodwin. Boston: Allen & Unwin.

Roes, Frans L., and Michel Raymond. 2003. Belief in moralizing gods. *Evolution and Human Behavior* 24:126–35.

Rogers, Everett M. 1983. *Diffusion of innovations.* 3rd ed. New York: Free Press.

Rohner, Ronald P. 1975. *They love me, they love me not: A worldwide study of the effects of parental acceptance and rejection.* New Haven, CT: HRAF Press.

Rohner, Ronald P. 1976. Sex differences in aggression: Phylogenetic and enculturation perspectives. *Ethos* 4:57–72.

Romaine, Suzanne. 1994. *Language in society: An introduction to sociolinguistics.* Oxford, UK: Oxford University Press.

Romney, A. Kimball, Susan C. Weller, and William H. Batchelder. 1986. Culture as consensus: A theory of culture and informant accuracy. *American Anthropologist* 88:313–38.

Roosens, Eugeen E. 1989. *Creating ethnicity: The process of ethnogenesis.* Newbury Park, CA: Sage.

Roosevelt, Anna C. 1984. Population, health, and the evolution of subsistence: Conclusions from the conference. In *Paleopathology at the origins of agriculture,* eds. M. Cohen and G. Armelagos. Orlando, FL: Academic Press.

Roosevelt, Anna C. 1992. Secrets of the forest. *The Sciences* (November/December):22–28.

Roosevelt, Anna C., et al. 1996. Paleoindian cave dwellers in the Amazon: The peopling of the Americas. *Science* 272 (April 19):373–84.

Roscoe, Paul. 2002. The hunters and gatherers of New Guinea. *Current Anthropology* 43:153–62.

Rose, M. D. 1984. Food acquisition and the evolution of positional behaviour: The case of bipedalism. In *Food acquisition and processing in primates,* eds. D. Chivers, B. Wood, and A. Bilsborough. New York: Plenum Press.

Rosenberger, Alfred L. 1979. Cranial anatomy and implications of *Dolichocebus,* a late Oligocene ceboid primate. *Nature* 279 (May 31):416–18.

Rosenblatt, Paul C., R. Patricia Walsh, and Douglas A. Jackson. 1976. *Grief and mourning in cross-cultural perspective.* New Haven, CT: HRAF Press.

Ross, Marc Howard. 1981. Socioeconomic complexity, socialization, and political differentiation: A cross-cultural study. *Ethos* 9:217–47.

Ross, Marc Howard. 1985. Internal and external conflict and violence. *Journal of Conflict Resolution* 29:547–79.

Ross, Marc Howard. 1986. Female political participation: A cross-cultural explanation. *American Anthropologist* 88:843–58.

Ross, Marc Howard. 1988. Political organization and political participation: Exit, voice, and loyalty in preindustrial societies. *Comparative Politics* 21:73–89.

Ross, Marc Howard. 2009a. Ethnocentrism and ethnic conflict. In MyAnthroLibrary, eds. C. R. Ember, M. Ember, and P. N. Peregrine. MyAnthroLibrary.com. Pearson.

Ross, Marc Howard. 2009b. Political participation. In MyAnthroLibrary, eds. C. R. Ember, M. Ember, and P. N. Peregrine. MyAnthroLibrary.com. Pearson.

Roth, Eric Abella. 2001. Demise of the sepaade tradition: Cultural and biological explanations. *American Anthropologist* 103:1014–23.

Rubel, Arthur J., and Michael R. Hass. 1996. Ethnomedicine. In *Medical anthropology,* rev. ed., eds. C. F. Sargent and T. M. Johnson. Westport, CT: Praeger.

Rubel, Arthur J., Carl O'Nell, and Rolando Collado-Ardón (with the assistance of John Krejci and Jean Krejci). 1984. *Susto: A folk illness.* Berkeley: University of California Press.

Rubin, Jeffrey Z., F. J. Provenzano, and R. F. Haskett. 1974. The eye of the beholder: Parents' views on the sex of newborns. *American Journal of Orthopsychiatry* 44:512–19.

Rudmin, Floyd Webster. 1988. Dominance, social control, and ownership: A history and a cross-cultural study of motivations for private property. *Behavior Science Research* 22:130–60.

Ruff, Christopher B., and Alan Walker. 1993. Body size and body shape. In *The Nariokotome* Homo erectus *skeleton,* eds. A. Walker and R. Leakey. Cambridge, MA: Harvard University Press.

Rumbaugh, Duane M. 1970. Learning skills of anthropoids. In *Primate behavior,* vol. 1., ed. L. Rosenblum. New York: Academic Press.

Rummel, Rudolf J. 2002a. Death by government. Chapter 1. http://www.hawaii.edu/powerkills/DBG.CHAP1.HTM.

Rummel, Rudolf J. 2002b. Democracies are less warlike than other regimes. http://www.hawaii.edu/powerkills/DP95.htm.

Rummel, Rudolf J. 2002c. Statistics of democide. Chapter 17. http://www.hawaii.edu/powerkills/SOD.CHAP17.HTM.

Rummel, Rudolf J. 2002d. Statistics of democide. Chapter 21. http://www.hawaii.edu/powerkills/SOD.CHAP21.HTM.

Ruskin, John. 1963. Of king's treasures. In *The genius of John Ruskin,* ed. J. D. Rosenberg. New York: Braziller.

Russell, Elbert W. 1972. Factors of human aggression. *Behavior Science Notes* 7:275–312.

Russett, Bruce (with the collaboration of William Antholis, Carol R. Ember, Melvin Ember, and Zeev Maoz). 1993. *Grasping the democratic peace: Principles for a post–cold war world.* Princeton, NJ: Princeton University Press.

Russett, Bruce, and John R. Oneal. 2001. *Triangulating peace: Democracy, interdependence, and international organizations.* New York: Norton.

Sagan, Carl. 1975. A cosmic calendar. *Natural History* (December):70–73.

Sahlins, Marshall D. 1958. *Social stratification in Polynesia.* Seattle: University of Washington Press.

Sahlins, Marshall D. 1961. The segmentary lineage: An organization of predatory expansion. *American Anthropologist* 63:332–45.

Sahlins, Marshall D. 1962. *Moala: Culture and nature on a Fijian island.* Ann Arbor: University of Michigan Press.

Sahlins, Marshall D. 1963. Poor man, rich man, big-man, chief: Political types in Melanesia and Polynesia. *Comparative Studies in Society and History* 5:285–303.

Sahlins, Marshall D. 1972. *Stone Age economics.* Chicago: Aldine.

Sahlins, Marshall D. 1983. Other times, other customs: The anthropology of history. *American Anthropologist* 85:517–44.

Salzman, Philip Carl. 1996. Pastoralism. In *Encyclopedia of cultural anthropology,* vol. 3, eds. D. Levinson and M. Ember, 899–905. New York: Henry Holt.

Salzman, Philip Carl. 2002. Pastoral nomads: Some general observations based on research in Iran. *Journal of Anthropological Research* 58:245–64.

Sanday, Peggy R. 1973. Toward a theory of the status of women. *American Anthropologist* 75:1682–700.

Sanday, Peggy R. 1974. Female status in the public domain. In *Woman, culture, and society,* eds. M. Z. Rosaldo and L. Lamphere. Stanford, CA: Stanford University Press.

Sanders, William T. 1968. Hydraulic agriculture, economic symbiosis, and the evolution of states in central Mexico. In *Anthropological archaeology in the Americas,* ed. B. Meggers. Washington, DC: Anthropological Society of Washington.

Sanders, William T., Jeffrey R. Parsons, and Robert S. Santley. 1979. *The basin of Mexico: Ecological processes in the evolution of a civilization.* New York: Academic Press.

Sanders, William T., and Barbara J. Price. 1968. *Mesoamerica.* New York: Random House.

Sapir, Edward. 1931. Conceptual categories in primitive languages. Paper presented at the autumn meeting of the National Academy of Sciences, New Haven, CT. Published in *Science* 74.

Sapir, Edward. 1938. Why cultural anthropology needs the psychiatrist. *Psychiatry* 1:7–12.

Sapir, Edward, and M. Swadesh. 1964. American Indian grammatical categories. In *Language in culture and society,* ed. D. Hymes. New York: Harper & Row.

Sassaman, Kenneth. 1996. Early Archaic settlement in the South Carolina coastal plain. In *The Paleoindian and early Archaic Southeast,* eds. D. G. Anderson and K. E. Sassaman, 58–83. Tuscaloosa: University of Alabama Press.

Savage-Rumbaugh, E. Sue. 1992. Language training of apes. In *The Cambridge encyclopedia of human evolution,* eds. S. Jones, R. Martin, and D. Pilbeam. New York: Cambridge University Press.

Savage-Rumbaugh, E. Sue. 1994. Hominid evolution: Looking to modern apes for clues. In *Hominid culture in primate perspective*, eds. D. Quiatt and J. Itani. Niwot: University Press of Colorado.

Scaglion, Richard. 2009. Law and society. In MyAnthroLibrary, eds. C. R. Ember, M. Ember, and P. N. Peregrine. MyAnthroLibrary .com. Pearson.

Schaller, George. 1963. *The mountain gorilla: Ecology and behavior.* Chicago: University of Chicago Press.

Schaller, George. 1964. *The year of the gorilla.* Chicago: University of Chicago Press.

Schaller, George. 1972. *The Serengeti lion: A study of predator-prey relations.* Chicago: University of Chicago Press.

Schick, Kathy D., and Nicholas Toth. 1993. *Making silent stones speak.* New York: Simon & Schuster.

Schlegel, Alice. 1989. Gender issues and cross-cultural research. *Behavior Science Research* 23:265–80.

Schlegel, Alice. 1991. Status, property, and the value on virginity. *American Ethnologist* 18:719–34.

Schlegel, Alice. 2009. The status of women. In MyAnthroLibrary, eds. C. R. Ember, M. Ember, and P. N. Peregrine. MyAnthroLibrary.com. Pearson.

Schlegel, Alice, and Herbert Barry III. 1986. The cultural consequences of female contribution to subsistence. *American Anthropologist* 88:142–50.

Schlegel, Alice, and Rohn Eloul. 1987. A new coding of marriage transactions. *Behavior Science Research* 21:118–40.

Schlegel, Alice, and Rohn Eloul. 1988. Marriage transactions: Labor, property, and status. *American Anthropologist* 90:291–309.

Schneider, David M. 1961a. Introduction: The distinctive features of matrilineal descent groups. In *Matrilineal kinship*, eds. D. M. Schneider and K. Gough, 1–29. Berkeley: University of California Press.

Schneider, David M. 1961b. Truk. In *Matrilineal kinship*, eds. D. M. Schneider and K. Gough, 202–33. Berkeley: University of California Press.

Schoepf, Brooke. 1988. Women, AIDS and economic crisis in central Africa. *Canadian Journal of African Studies* 22:625–44.

Schrauf, Robert W. 1999. Mother tongue maintenance among North American ethnic groups. *Cross-Cultural Research* 33:175–92.

Schrire, Carmel, ed. 1984a. *Past and present in hunter-gatherer studies.* Orlando, FL: Academic Press.

Schrire, Carmel. 1984b. Wild surmises on savage thoughts. In *Past and present in hunter-gatherer studies*, ed. C. Schrire. Orlando, FL: Academic Press.

Schwartz, Richard D. 1954. Social factors in the development of legal control: A case study of two Israeli settlements. *Yale Law Journal* 63 (February):471–91.

Scientific American. 2005. Crossroads for Planet Earth. *Scientific American.* Special Issue, September.

Scudder, Thayer. 1978. Opportunities, issues and achievements in development anthropology since the mid-1960s: A personal view. In *Applied anthropology in America*. 2nd ed. eds. E. M. Eddy and W. L. Partridge. New York: Columbia University Press.

Segal, Edwin S. 2004. Cultural constructions of gender. In *Encyclopedia of sex and gender: Men and women in the world's cultures*, vol. 1, eds. C. Ember and M. Ember, 3–10. New York: Kluwer Academic/Plenum Press.

Segal, Robert A. 1987. *Joseph Campbell: An introduction.* New York: Garland.

Semenov, Sergei A. 1970. *Prehistoric technology.* Trans. M. W. Thompson. Bath, UK: Adams & Dart.

Sengupta, Somini. 2002. Money from kin abroad helps Bengalis get by. *New York Times*, June 24, p. A3.

Senner, Wayne M. 1989. Theories and myths on the origins of writing: A historical overview. In *The origins of writing*, ed. W. M. Senner. Lincoln: University of Nebraska Press.

Serre, David, André Langaney, Mario Chech, Maria Teschler-Nicola, Maja Paunovic, Philippe Mennecier, Michael Hofreiter, Göran Possnert, and Svante Pääbo. 2004. No evidence of Neandertal mtDNA contribution to early modern humans. *PLoS Biology* 2:313–17.

Service, Elman R. 1962. *Primitive social organization: An evolutionary perspective.* New York: Random House.

Service, Elman R. 1975. *Origins of the state and civilization: The process of cultural evolution.* New York: Norton.

Service, Elman R. 1978. *Profiles in ethnology.* 3rd ed. New York: Harper & Row.

Service, Elman R. 1979. *The hunters.* 2nd ed. Upper Saddle River, NJ: Prentice Hall.

Seyfarth, Robert M., Dorothy L. Cheney, and Peter Marler. 1980. Monkey response to three different alarm calls: Evidence of predator classification and semantic communication. *Science* 210 (November 14):801–03.

Shanklin, Eugenia. 1993. *Anthropology and race.* Belmont, CA: Wadsworth.

Shankman, Paul. 1991. Culture contact, cultural ecology, and Dani warfare. *Man* 26:299–321.

Sheils, Dean. 1975. Toward a unified theory of ancestor worship: A cross-cultural study. *Social Forces* 54:427–40.

Sheils, Dean. 1980. A comparative study of human sacrifice. *Behavior Science Research* 15:245–62.

Shibamoto, Janet S. 1987. The womanly woman: Japanese female speech. In *Language, gender, and sex in comparative perspective*, eds. S. U. Philips, S. Steele, and C. Tanz. Cambridge, UK: Cambridge University Press.

Singh, Gopal K., and Peter C. van Dyck. n.d. Infant Mortality in the United States, 1935-2007: Over Seven Decades of Progress and Disparities. Retrieved from: http://www.hrsa.gov/healthit/images/mchb_infantmortality_pub.pdf on September 17, 2011.

Shipman, Pat. 1986. Scavenging or hunting in early hominids: Theoretical framework and tests. *American Anthropologist* 88:27–43.

Shrestha, Laura B. 2006. Life Expectancy in the United States. CRS Report for Congress. Retrieved from: http://aging.senate.gov/crs/aging1.pdf on September 17, 2011.

Silk, Joan. 2007. Social components of fitness in primate groups. *Science* 317 (September 7):1347–51.

Silver, Harry R. 1981. Calculating risks: The socioeconomic foundations of aesthetic innovation in an Ashanti carving community. *Ethnology* 20:101–14.

Simcha, Lev-Yadun, Avi Gopher, and Shahal Abbo, 2000. The cradle of agriculture. *Science* 288 (June 2):1602–03.

Simmons, Janie, Paul Farmer, and Brooke G. Schoepf. 1996. A global perspective. In *Women, poverty, and AIDS: Sex, drugs, and structural violence*, eds. P. Farmer, M. Connors, and J. Simmons, 39–90. Monroe, ME: Common Courage Press.

Simons, Elwyn L. 1992. The primate fossil record. In *The Cambridge encyclopedia of human evolution*, eds. S. Jones, R. Martin, and D. Pilbeam. New York: Cambridge University Press.

Simons, Elwyn L. 1995. Skulls and anterior teeth of *Catopithecus* (Primates: Anthropoidea) from the Eocene shed light on anthropoidean origins. *Science* 268 (June 30):1885–88.

Simons, Elwyn L., and D. T. Rassmussen. 1996. Skull of *Catopithecus browni*, an early tertiary catarrhine. *American Journal of Physical Anthropology* 100:261–92.

Simpson, George Gaylord. 1971. *The meaning of evolution.* New York: Bantam.

Simpson, S. P., and Ruth Field. 1946. Law and the social sciences. *Virginia Law Review* 32:858.

Simpson, Scott W. 2009. *Australopithecus afarensis* and human evolution. In MyAnthroLibrary, eds. C. R. Ember, M. Ember, and P. N. Peregrine. MyAnthroLibrary.com. Pearson.

Simpson, Scott W., Jay Quade, Naomi Levin, Robert Butler, Guillaume Dupont-Nivet, Melanie Everett, and Sileshi Semaw. 2008. A female *Homo erectus* pelvis from Gona, Ethiopia. *Science* 322 (November 14):1089–91.

Singer, J. David. 1980. Accounting for international war: The state of the discipline. *Annual Review of Sociology* 6:349–67.

Singer, Ronald, and John Wymer. 1982. *The Middle Stone Age at Klasies River mouth in South Africa*. Chicago: University of Chicago Press.

Sipes, Richard G. 1973. War, sports, and aggression: An empirical test of two rival theories. *American Anthropologist* 75:64–86.

Smay, Diana, and George Armelagos. 2000. Galileo wept: A critical assessment of the use of race in forensic anthropology. *Transforming Anthropology* 9 (2):19–29.

Smedley, Audrey. 2004. *Women creating patrilyny*. Walnut Creek, CA: AltaMira Press.

Smedley, Brian D., Adrienne Y. Stith, and Alan R. Nelson, eds. 2003. *Unequal treatment: Confronting racial and ethnic disparities in health care*. Washington, DC: National Academy Press.

Smith, B. Holly. 1986. Dental development in *Australopithecus* and early *Homo*. *Nature* 323 (September 25):327–30.

Smith, Bruce D. 1992a. Prehistoric plant husbandry in eastern North America. In *The origins of agriculture*, eds. C. Cowan and P. Watson. Washington, DC: Smithsonian Institution Press.

Smith, Bruce D. 1992b. *Rivers of change*. Washington, DC: Smithsonian Institution Press.

Smith, Fred H., and Frank Spencer, eds. 1984. *The origins of modern humans: A world survey of the fossil evidence*. New York: Alan R. Liss.

Smith, John Maynard. 1989. *Evolutionary genetics*. New York: Oxford University Press.

Smith, Michael G. 1966. Preindustrial stratification systems. In *Social structure and mobility in economic development*, eds. N. J. Smelser and S. M. Lipset. Chicago: Aldine.

Smith, Margot W. 1974. Alfred Binet's remarkable questions: A cross-national and cross-temporal analysis of the cultural biases built into the Stanford-Binet Intelligence Scale and other Binet Tests. *Genetic Psychology Monographs* 89:307–34.

Smuts, Barbara B., Dorothy L. Cheney, Robert M. Seyfarth, Richard W. Wrangham, and Thomas T. Struhsaker, eds. 1987. *Primate societies*. Chicago: University of Chicago Press.

Snowdon, Charles T. 1999. An empiricist view of language evolution and development. In *The origins of language*, ed. B. J. King, 79–114. Santa Fe, NM: School of American Research Press.

Society for American Archaeology. 2009. FAQs for students. http://www.saa.org/ForthePublic/FAQs/ForStudents/tabid/101/Default.aspx (accessed August 26, 2009).

Soffer, Olga. 1993. Upper Paleolithic adaptations in central and eastern Europe and man-mammoth interactions. In *From Kostenki to Clovis*, eds. O. Soffer and N. D. Praslov. New York: Plenum Press.

Solis, Ruth Shady, Jonathan Haas, and Winifred Creamer. 2001. Dating Caral, a preceramic site in the Supe Valley of the central coast of Peru. *Science* 292 (April 27):723–26.

Solon, Gary. 2002. Cross-country differences in intergenerational earnings mobility. *Journal of Economic Perspectives* 16:59–66.

Sosis, Richard, and Eric R. Bressler. 2003. Cooperation and commune longevity: A test of the costly signaling theory of religion. *Cross-Cultural Research* 37:211–39.

Southworth, Franklin C., and Chandler J. Daswani. 1974. *Foundations of linguistics*. New York: Free Press.

Spanos, Nicholas P. 1983. Ergotism and the Salem witch panic: A critical analysis and an alternative conceptualization. *Journal of the History of the Behavioral Sciences* 19:358–69.

Spencer, Frank. 1984. The Neandertals and their evolutionary significance: A brief historical survey. In *The origins of modern humans*, eds. F. H. Smith and F. Spencer. New York: Alan R. Liss.

Speth, John D. 2009. Were our ancestors hunters or scavengers? In MyAnthroLibrary, eds. C. R. Ember, M. Ember, and P. N. Peregrine. MyAnthroLibrary.com. Pearson.

Speth, John D., and Katherine A. Spielmann. 1983. Energy source, protein metabolism, and hunter-gatherer subsistence strategies. *Journal of Anthropological Archaeology* 2:1–31.

Spiro, Melford E., and Roy G. D'Andrade. 1958. A cross-cultural study of some supernatural beliefs. *American Anthropologist* 60:456–66.

Spring, Anita. 1995. *Agricultural development and gender issues in Malawi*. Lanham, MD: University Press of America.

Spring, Anita. 2000a. Agricultural commercialization and women farmers in Kenya. In *Women farmers and commercial ventures: Increasing food security in developing countries*, ed. Anita Spring, 317–41. Boulder, CO: Lynne Rienner.

Spring, Anita. 2000b. Commercialization and women farmers: Old paradigms and new themes. In *Women farmers and commercial ventures: Increasing food security in developing countries*, ed. Anita Spring, 1–37. Boulder, CO: Lynne Rienner.

Spring, Anita, ed., 2000c. *Women farmers and commercial ventures: Increasing food security in developing countries*. Boulder, CO: Lynne Rienner.

Stanford, Craig. 2009. Chimpanzee hunting behavior and human evolution. In MyAnthroLibrary, eds. C. R. Ember, M. Ember, and P. N. Peregrine. MyAnthroLibrary.com. Pearson.

Stark, Rodney. 1996. *The rise of Christianity: A sociologist reconsiders history*. Princeton, NJ: Princeton University Press.

Stark, Rodney. 2001. Gods, rituals and the moral order. *Journal for the Scientific Study of Religion* 40:619–36.

Stark, Rodney, and Roger Finke. 2000. *Acts of faith: explaining the human side of religion*. Berkeley: University of California Press.

Starling, Anne, and Jay Stock. 2007. Dental indicators of health and stress in early Egyptian and Nubian agriculturalists: A difficult transition and gradual recovery. *American Journal of Physical Anthropology* 134(4):520–28.

Stedman, Hansell, B. Kozyak, A. Nelson, D. Thesier, L. Su, D. Low, C. Bridges, J. Shrager, N. Minugh-Purvis, and M. Mitchell. 2004. Myosin gene mutation correlates with anatomical changes in the human lineage. *Nature* 428 (March 25):415–18.

Steiner, Christopher B. 1990. Body personal and body politic: Adornment and leadership in cross-cultural perspective. *Anthropos* 85:431–45.

Stephens, William N. 1963. *The family in cross-cultural perspective*. New York: Holt, Rinehart & Winston.

Stephens, William N. 1972. A cross-cultural study of modesty. *Behavior Science Research* 7:1–28.

Steward, Julian H., and Louis C. Faron. 1959. *Native peoples of South America*. New York: McGraw-Hill.

Stewart, Thomas D. 1950. Deformity, trephanating, and mutilation in South American Indian skeletal remains. In *Handbook of South American Indians*, vol. 6: *Physical anthropology, linguistics, and cultural geography* ed. J. A. Steward. Bureau of American Ethnology Bulletin 143. Washington, DC: Smithsonian Institution Press.

Stini, William A. 1971. Evolutionary implications of changing nutritional patterns in human populations. *American Anthropologist* 73:1019–30.

Stini, William A. 1975. *Ecology and human adaptation*. Dubuque, IA: Wm. C. Brown.

Stogdill, Ralph M. 1974. *Handbook of leadership: A survey of theory and research*. New York: Macmillan.

Stoneking, Mark. 1997. Recent African origin of human mitochondrial DNA. In *Progress in population genetics and human evolution*, eds. P. Donnelly and S. Tavaré, 1–13. New York: Springer.

Straus, Murray A. 1991. Physical violence in American families: Incidence rates, causes, and trends. In *Abused and battered*, eds. D. D. Knudsen and J. L. Miller. New York: Aldine.

Straus, Murray A. 1995. Trends in cultural norms and rates of partner violence: An update to 1992. In *Understanding partner violence: Prevalence, causes, consequences, and solutions*, eds. S. M. Stith and M. A. Straus, 30–33. Minneapolis, MN: National Council on Family Relations. http://pubpages.unh.edu/~mas2/v56.pdf/ (accessed August 2002).

Straus, Murray A. 2001. Physical aggression in the family: Prevalence rates, links to non-family violence, and implications for primary prevention of societal violence. In *Prevention and control of aggression and the impact on its victims*, ed. M. Martinez, 181–200. New York: Kluwer Academic/Plenum Press.

Straus, Murray A., and Glenda Kaufman Kantor. 1994 (July). Change in Spouse assault rates from 1975 to 1992: A comparison of three national surveys in the United States. Paper presented at the 13th World Congress of Sociology, Bielefeld, Germany. http://pubpages.unh.edu/~mas2/v55. pdf/ (accessed August 2002).

Straus, Murray A., and Glenda Kaufman Kantor. 1995. Trends in physical abuse by parents from 1975 to 1992: A comparison of three national surveys. Paper presented at the annual meeting of the American Society of Criminology, Boston, November 18. http://pubpages.unh.edu/~mas2/V57.pdf/ (accessed August 2002).

Straus, Murray A., and Carrie L. Yodanis. 1996. Corporal punishment in adolescence and physical assaults on spouses in later life: What accounts for the link? *Journal of Marriage and the Family* 58:825–41.

Strauss, Lawrence Guy. 1982. Comment on White. *Current Anthropology* 23:185–86.

Strauss, Lawrence Guy. 1989. On early hominid use of fire. *Current Anthropology* 30:488–91.

Stringer, Christopher B. 1985. Evolution of a species. *Geographical Magazine* 57:601–07.

Stringer, Christopher B. 2000. Neandertals. In *Encyclopedia of human evolution and prehistory*, eds. I. Tattersall, E. Delson, and J. van Couvering. New York: Garland.

Stringer, Christopher. B. 2003. Out of Ethiopia. *Nature* 423 (June 12):692–95.

Stringer, Christopher B., J. J. Hublin, and B. Vandermeersch. 1984. The origin of anatomically modern humans in western Europe. In *The origins of modern humans*, eds. F. H. Smith and F. Spencer. New York: Alan R. Liss.

Suárez-Orozco, Marcelo. 1992. A grammar of terror: Psychocultural responses to state terrorism in dirty war and post-dirty war Argentina. In *The paths to domination, resistance, and terror*, eds. C. Nordstrom and J. Martin, 219–59. Berkeley: University of California Press.

Susman, Randall L., ed. 1984. *The pygmy chimpanzee: Evolutionary biology and behavior.* New York: Plenum Press.

Susman, Randall L. 1994. Fossil evidence for early hominid tool use. *Science* 265 (September 9):1570–73.

Susman, Randall L., Jack T. Stern, Jr., and William L. Jungers. 1985. Locomotor adaptations in the Hadar hominids. In *Ancestors: The hard evidence*, ed. E. Delson, 184–92. New York: Alan R. Liss.

Sussman, Robert W. 1972. Child transport, family size, and the increase in human population size during the Neolithic. *Current Anthropology* 13:258–67.

Sussman, Robert W. 1991. Primate origins and the evolution of angiosperms. *American Journal of Primatology* 23:209–23.

Sussman, Robert W., and W. G. Kinzey. 1984. The ecological role of the callitrichidae: A review. *American Journal of Physical Anthropology* 64:419–49.

Swanson, Guy E. 1969. *The birth of the gods: The origin of primitive beliefs.* Ann Arbor: University of Michigan Press.

Sweeney, James J. 1952. African negro culture. In *African folktales and sculpture*, ed. P. Radin. New York: Pantheon.

Swisher, Carl C., III, G. H. Curtis, T. Jacob, A. G. Getty, A. Suprijo, and Widiasmoro. 1994. Age of the earliest known hominids in Java, Indonesia. *Science* 263 (February 25):1118–21.

Szalay, Frederick S. 1968. The beginnings of primates. *Evolution* 22:32–33.

Szalay, Frederick S. 1972. Paleobiology of the earliest primates. In *The functional and evolutionary biology of the primates*, ed. R. Tuttle, 3–35. Chicago: University of Chicago Press.

Szalay, Frederick S. 1975. Hunting-scavenging protohominids: A model for hominid origins. *Man* 10:420–29.

Szalay, Frederick S., and Eric Delson. 1979. *Evolutionary history of the primates.* New York: Academic Press.

Szalay, Frederick S., I. Tattersall, and R. Decker. 1975. Phylogenetic relationships of *Plesiadipis*—Postcranial evidence. *Contributions to Primatology* 5:136–66.

Szklut, Jay, and Reed, Robert Roy. 1991. Community anonymity in anthropological research: A reassessment. In *Ethics and the profession of anthropology: Dialogue for a new era*, ed. Carolyn

Fluehr-Lobban, 97–116. Philadelphia: University of Pennsylvania Press.

Tamari, Tal. 1991. The development of caste systems in West Africa. *Journal of African History* 32:221–50.

Tamari, Tal. 2005. Kingship and caste in Africa: History, diffusion and evolution. In *The character of kingship*, ed. Declan Quigley, 141–70. Oxford, UK: Berg.

Tannen, Deborah. 1990. *You just don't understand: Women and men in conversation.* New York: William Morrow.

Tattersall, Ian. 1982. *The primates of Madagascar.* New York: Columbia University Press.

Tattersall, Ian. 1997 (April). Out of Africa again...and again? *Scientific American* 276:60–68.

Tattersall, Ian. 1999. *The last Neanderthal.* Boulder, CO: Westview Press.

Tattersall, Ian. 2009. Paleoanthropology and evolutionary theory. In MyAnthroLibrary, eds. C. R. Ember, M. Ember, and P. N. Peregrine. MyAnthroLibrary.com. Pearson.

Tattersall, Ian, and Jeffrey Schwartz. 2000. *Extinct humans.* Boulder, CO: Westview Press.

Tattersall, Ian, Eric Delson, and John Van Couvering, eds. 2000. *Encyclopedia of Human Evolution and Prehistory.* New York: Garland.

Taylor, Christopher C. 2005. Mutton, mud, and runny noses: A hierarchy of distaste in early Rwanda. *Social Analysis* 49:213–30.

Taylor, Robert E., and M. J. Aitken, eds. 1997. *Chronometric Dating in Archaeology.* New York: Plenum Press.

Teleki, Geza. 1973. The omnivorous chimpanzee. *Scientific American* (January):32–42.

Templeton, Alan R. 1993. The "Eve" hypotheses: A genetic critique and reanalysis. *American Anthropologist* 95:51–72.

Templeton, Alan R. 1996. Gene lineages and human evolution. *Science* 272 (May 31):1363.

Textor, Robert B., comp. 1967. *A cross-cultural summary.* New Haven, CT: HRAF Press.

Thomas, David Hurst. 1986. *Refiguring anthropology: First principles of probability and statistics.* Prospect Heights, IL: Waveland.

Thomas, Wesley. 1993. *A traditional Navajo's perspectives on the cultural construction of gender in the Navajo world.* Paper presented at the University of Frankfurt, Germany. As referred to in Lang 1999.

Thomason, Sarah Grey, and Terrence Kaufman. 1988. *Language contact, creolization, and genetic linguistics.* Berkeley: University of California Press.

Thompson, Elizabeth Bartlett. 1966. *Africa, past and present.* Boston: Houghton Mifflin.

Thompson, Ginger. 2002. Mexico is attracting a better class of factory in its south. *New York Times*, June 29, p. A3.

Thompson, Stith. 1965. Star Husband Tale. In *The study of folklore*, ed. A. Dundes. Upper Saddle River, NJ: Prentice Hall.

Thompson-Handler, Nancy, Richard K. Malenky, and Noel Badrian. 1984. Sexual behavior of *Pan paniscus* under natural conditions in the Lomako Forest, Equateur, Zaire. In *The pygmy chimpanzee*, ed. R. Susman. New York: Plenum Press.

Thorpe, Susannah K. S, R. L. Holder, and R. H. Compton. 2007. Origin of human bipedalism as an adaptation for locomotion on flexible branches. *Science* 316 (June 2007):1328–31.

Tierney, Patrick. 2000. *Darkness in El Dorado.* New York: Norton.

Tobias, Philip V. 1994. The craniocerebral interface in early hominids: Cerebral impressions, cranial thickening, paleoneurobiology, and a new hypothesis on encephalization. In *Integrative paths to the past*, eds. R. Corruccini and R. Ciochon. Upper Saddle River, NJ: Prentice Hall.

Todorov, Alexander, Anesu N. Mandisodza, Amir Goren, and Crystal C. Hall. 2005. Inference of competence from faces predict election outcomes. *Science* 308 (June 10):1623–26.

Tollefson, Kenneth D. 2009. Tlingit: Chiefs past and present. In MyAnthroLibrary, eds. C. R. Ember, M. Ember, and P. N. Peregrine. MyAnthroLibrary.com. Pearson.

Torrey, E. Fuller. 1972. *The mind game: Witchdoctors and psychiatrists.* New York: Emerson Hall.

Torry, William I. 1986. Morality and harm: Hindu peasant adjustments to famines. *Social Science Information* 25:125–60.

Traphagan, John W., and L. Keith Brown. 2002. Fast food and intergenerational commensality in Japan: New styles and old patterns. *Ethnology* 41:119–34.

Travis, John. 2000. Human genome work reaches milestone. *Science News* (July 1):4–5.

Treiman, Donald J., and Harry B. G. Ganzeboom. 1990. Cross-national comparative status-attainment research. *Research in Social Stratification and Mobility* 9:117.

Trevor-Roper, Hugh R. 1971. The European witch-craze of the sixteenth and seventeenth centuries. In *Reader in comparative religion.* 3rd ed. eds. W. A. Lessa and E. Z. Vogt. New York: Harper & Row.

Trinkaus, Erik. 1985. Pathology and the posture of the La Chapelle-aux-Saints Neandertal. *American Journal of Physical Anthropology* 67:19–41.

Trinkaus, Erik. 1986. The Neandertals and modern human origins. *Annual Review of Anthropology* 15:193–218.

Trinkaus, Erik. 1987. Bodies, brawn, brains and noses: Human ancestors and human predation. In *The evolution of human hunting,* eds. M. Nitecki and D. Nitecki. New York: Plenum Press.

Trinkaus, Erik, and William W. Howells. 1979. The Neanderthals. *Scientific American* (December):118–33.

Trinkaus, Erik, and Pat Shipman. 1993a. *The Neandertals: Changing the image of mankind.* New York: Knopf.

Trinkaus, Erik, and Pat Shipman. 1993b. Neandertals: Images of ourselves. *Evolutionary Anthropology* 1:194–201.

Trouillot, Michel-Rolph. 2001. The anthropology of the state in the age of globalization: Close encounters of the deceptive kind. *Current Anthropology* 42:125–38.

Trudgill, Peter. 1983. *Sociolinguistics: An introduction to language and society.* Rev. ed. New York: Penguin.

Turner, Christy G., II. 1987. Telltale teeth. *Natural History* (January):6–9.

Turner, Christy G., II. 1989. Teeth and prehistory in Asia. *Scientific American* (February):88–95.

Turner, Christy. G., II. 2005. A synoptic history of physical anthropological studies on the peopling of Alaska and the Americas. *Alaska Journal of Anthropology* 3:157–70.

Tuttle, Russell H. 1986. *Apes of the world: Their social behavior, communication, mentality, and ecology.* Park Ridge, NJ: Noyes.

Ucko, Peter J., and Andrée Rosenfeld. 1967. *Paleolithic cave art.* New York: McGraw-Hill.

UNAIDS. 2007 (December). *AIDS epidemic update.* http://data.unaids.org/pub/EPISlides/2007/2007_epiupdate_en.pdf

UN Works. n.d. http://www.un.org/works/goingon/mongolia/lessonplan_homelessness.html.

Underhill, Ralph. 1975. Economic and political antecedents of monotheism: A cross-cultural study. *American Journal of Sociology* 80:841–61.

Underhill, Ruth M. 1938. *Social organization of the Papago Indians.* New York: Columbia University Press.

United Nations Human Settlements Programme. 2003. The challenge of slums: Global report on human settlements, 2003. Nairobi, Kenya: Author.

U.S. Census Bureau. 1993. *Statistical abstract of the United States: 1993,* 113th ed. Washington, DC: U.S. Government Printing Office.

U.S. Census Bureau. 2002. The big payoff: Educational entertainment and synthetic estimates of work-life earnings. *Statistical abstract of the United States: 1993,* 113th ed. Washington, DC: U.S. Government Printing Office. http://www.census.gov/prod/2002pubs/p23-210.pdf.

U.S. Department of Justice. 1988 (November). Prevalence, incidence, and consequences of violence against women: Findings from the National Violence against Women Survey. Washington, DC.

U.S. Department of Justice. 1994 (April). Violent crime. NCJ-147486. Washington, DC: Author

U.S. Department of Justice. 2000. Children as victims. *Juvenile Justice Bulletin 1999.* National Report Series. Washington, DC: Author.

U.S. Department of Justice. n.d. Bureau of Justice statistics homicide trends in the U.S: Long-term trends and patterns. http://www.ojp.gov/bjs/homicide/hmrt.htm (accessed Sept. 5, 2009).

U.S. Environmental Protection Agency. 2009. http://epa.gov/oecaagct/ag101/demographics.html (accessed October 15, 2009).

Valente, Thomas W. 1995. *Network models of the diffusion of innovations.* Cresskill, NJ: Hampton Press.

Valladas, Helene, J. L. Joron, G. Valladas, O. Bar-Yosef, and B. Vandermeersch. 1988. Thermoluminescence dating of Mousterian "Proto-Cro-Magnon" remains from Israel and the origin of modern man. *Nature* 337 (February 18):614–16.

Van Hear, Nicholas. 2004. Refugee diasporas or refugees in diaspora. In *Encyclopedia of diasporas: Immigrant and refugee cultures around the world,* vol. 1, eds. M. Ember, C. R. Ember, and I. Skoggard, 580–89. New York: Kluwer Academic/Plenum Press.

Van Lawick-Goodall, Jane. 1971. *In the shadow of man.* Boston: Houghton Mifflin.

Van Willigen, John. 2002. *Applied anthropology: An introduction.* 3rd ed. Westport, CT: Bergin & Garvey.

Vekua, Abesalom, David Lordkipanidze, G. Philip Rightmire, Jordi Agusti, Reid Ferring, Givi Maisuradze, Alexander Mouskhelishvili, Medea Nioradze, Marcia Ponce de Leon, Martha Tappen, Merab Tvalchrelidze, and Christoph Zollikofer. 2002. A new skull of early *Homo* from Dmanisi, Georgia. *Science* 297 (July 5):85–89.

Vigilant, Linda, Mark Stoneking, Henry Harpending, Kristen Hawkes, and Allan C. Wilson. 1991. African populations and the evolution of human mitochrondrial DNA. *Science* 253 (September 27):1503–07.

Vogel, Joseph O. 2009. De-mystifying the past: Great Zimbabwe, King Solomon's mines, and other tales of Old Africa. In MyAnthroLibrary, eds. C. R. Ember, M. Ember, and P. N. Peregrine. MyAnthroLibrary.com. Pearson.

Vohs, Kathleen D., Nicole L. Mead, and Miranda R. Goode. 2006. The psychological consequences of money. *Science* 314 (November 17):1154–56.

von Frisch, Karl. 1962. Dialects in the language of the bees. *Scientific American* (August):78–87.

Wadley, Reed L. 2003. Lethal treachery and the imbalance of power in warfare and feuding. *Journal of Anthropological Research* 59:531–54.

Waldbaum, Jane C. 2005. Helping hand for China. *Archaeology* 58:6.

Walker, Alan, and R. Leakey. 1988. The evolution of *Australopithecus boisei.* In *Evolutionary history of the "robust" australopithecines,* ed. F. Grine, 247–58. New York: Aldine.

Wallace, Alfred Russell. 1970/1858. On the tendency of varieties to depart indefinitely from the original type. (Originally published in 1858.) In *Evolution of man,* ed. L. B. Young. New York: Oxford University Press.

Wallace, Anthony. 1966. *Religion: An anthropological view.* New York: Random House.

Wanner, Eric, and Lila R. Gleitman, eds. 1982. *Language acquisition: The state of the art.* Cambridge, UK: Cambridge University Press.

Ward, Peter M. 1982. Introduction and purpose. In *Self-help housing,* ed. P. M. Ward. London: Mansell.

Ward, Steve. 1997. The taxonomy and phylogenetic relationships of *Sivapithecus* revisited. In *Function, phylogeny and fossils: Miocene hominoid evolution and adaptation,* eds. D. R. Begun, C. V. Ward, and M. D. Rose, 269–90. New York: Plenum Press.

Ward, Steve, B. Brown, A. Hill, J. Kelley, and W. Downs. 1999. *Equatorius:* A new hominoid genus from the middle Miocene of Kenya. *Science* 285 (August 27):1382–86.

Wardhaugh, Ronald. 2002. *An introduction to sociolinguistics.* 4th ed. Oxford, UK: Blackwell.

Warner, John Anson. 1986. The individual in Native American art: A sociological view. In *The arts of the North American Indian,* ed. E. L. Wade. New York: Hudson Hills Press.

Washburn, Sherwood. 1960. Tools and human evolution. *Scientific American* (September):62–75.

Weaver, Muriel Porter. 1993. *The Aztecs, Maya, and their predecessors.* 3rd ed. San Diego, CA: Academic Press.

Webb, Karen E. 1977. An evolutionary aspect of social structure and a verb "have." *American Anthropologist* 79:42–49.

Weber, Max. 1947. *The theory of social and economic organization.* Trans. A. M. Henderson and Talcott Parsons. New York: Oxford University Press.

Weiner, Jonathan. 1994. *Beak of the finch.* New York: Vintage.

Weiner, Steve, Q. Xi, P. Goldberg, J. Liu, and O. Bar-Yousef. 1998. Evidence for the use of fire at Zhoukoudian, China. *Science,* 281 (July 10):251–53.

Weinreich, Uriel. 1968. *Languages in contact.* The Hague: Mouton.

Weisner, Thomas S., and Ronald Gallimore. 1977. My brother's keeper: Child and sibling caretaking. *Current Anthropology* 18:169–90.

Weiss, Harvey, M. A. Courty, W. Wetterstrom, F. Guichard, L. Senior, R. Meadow, and A. Curnow. 1993. The genesis and collapse of third millennium north Mesopotamian civilization. *Science* 261 (August 20):995–1004.

Wenke, Robert J. 1984. *Patterns in prehistory: Humankind's first three million years.* 2nd ed. New York: Oxford University Press.

Wenke, Robert. 1990. *Patterns in prehistory: Humankind's first three million years.* 3rd ed. New York: Oxford University Press.

Werner, Dennis. 1975. *On the societal acceptance or rejection of male homosexuality.* Master's thesis, Hunter College of the City University of New York.

Werner, Dennis. 1978. Trekking in the Amazon forest. *Natural History* (November):42–54.

Werner, Dennis. 1979. A cross-cultural perspective on theory and research on male homosexuality. *Journal of Homosexuality* 4:345–62.

Werner, Dennis. 1982. Chiefs and presidents: A comparison of leadership traits in the United States and among the Mekranoti-Kayapo of central Brazil. *Ethos* 10:136–48.

Werner, Dennis. 1984. Child care and influence among the Mekranoti of central Brazil. *Sex Roles* 10:395–404.

Weston, Eleanor, and Adrian Lister. 2009. Insular dwarfism in hippos and a model for brain size reduction in *Homo floresiensis. Nature* 459 (May 7):85–88.

Wheat, Joe B. 1967. A Paleo-Indian bison kill. *Scientific American* (January):44–52.

Wheatley, Paul. 1971. *The pivot of the four quarters.* Chicago: Aldine.

Wheeler, Peter. 1984. The evolution of bipedality and loss of functional body hair in hominids. *Journal of Human Evolution* 13:91–98.

Wheeler, Peter. 1991. The influence of bipedalism in the energy and water budgets of early hominids. *Journal of Human Evolution* 23:379–88.

Whitaker, Ian. 1955. *Social relations in a nomadic Lappish community.* Oslo: Utgitt av Norsk Folksmuseum.

White, Benjamin. 1973. Demand for labor and population growth in colonial Java. *Human Ecology* 1, no. 3 (March):217–36.

White, Douglas R. 1988. Rethinking polygyny: Co-wives, codes, and cultural systems. *Current Anthropology* 29:529–88.

White, Douglas R., and Michael L. Burton. 1988. Causes of polygyny: Ecology, economy, kinship, and warfare. *American Anthropologist* 90:871–87.

White, Douglas R., Michael L. Burton, and Lilyan A. Brudner. 1977. Entailment theory and method: A cross-cultural analysis of the sexual division of labor. *Behavior Science Research* 12:1–24.

White, Frances J. 1996. *Pan paniscus* 1973 to 1996: Twenty-three years of field research. *Evolutionary Anthropology* 5:11–17.

White, Randall. 1982. Rethinking the Middle/Upper Paleolithic transition. *Current Anthropology* 23:169–75.

White, Timothy D., Donald C. Johanson, and William H. Kimbel. 1981. *Australopithecus africanus:* Its phyletic position reconsidered. *South African Journal of Science* 77:445–70.

White, Timothy D., G. Suwa, and B. Asfaw. 1994. *Australopithecus ramidus,* a new species of early hominid from Aramis, Ethiopia. *Nature* 371 (September 22):306–33.

White, Timothy D., G. Suwa, and B. Asfaw. 1995. Corrigendum: *Australopithecus ramidus,* a new species of early hominid from Aramis, Ethiopia. *Nature* 375 (May 4):88

Whiting, Beatrice B. 1950. *Paiute sorcery.* Viking Fund Publications in Anthropology No. 15. New York: Wenner-Gren Foundation.

Whiting, Beatrice B. 1965. Sex identity conflict and physical violence. *American Anthropologist* 67:123–40.

Whiting, Beatrice B., and Carolyn Pope Edwards. 1973. A cross-cultural analysis of sex differences in the behavior of children aged three through eleven. *Journal of Social Psychology* 91:171–88.

Whiting, Beatrice B., and Carolyn Pope Edwards (in collaboration with Carol R. Ember, Gerald M. Erchak, Sara Harkness, Robert L. Munroe, Ruth H. Munroe, Sara B. Nerlove, Susan Seymour, Charles M. Super, Thomas S. Weisner, and Martha Wenger). 1988. *Children of different worlds: The formation of social behavior.* Cambridge, MA: Harvard University Press.

Whiting, Beatrice B., and John W. M. Whiting (in collaboration with Richard Longabaugh). 1975. *Children of six cultures: A psycho-cultural analysis.* Cambridge, MA: Harvard University Press.

Whiting, John W. M. 1964. Effects of climate on certain cultural practices. In *Explorations in cultural anthropology,* ed. W. Goodenough. New York: McGraw-Hill.

Whittaker, John C. 1994. *Flintknapping: Making and understanding stone tools.* Austin: University of Texas Press.

Whyte, Martin K. 1978a. Cross-cultural codes dealing with the relative status of women. *Ethnology* 17:211–37.

Whyte, Martin K. 1978b. *The status of women in preindustrial societies.* Princeton, NJ: Princeton University Press.

Wiberg, Hakan. 1983. Self-determination as an international issue. In *Nationalism and self-determination in the Horn of Africa,* ed. I. M. Lewis. London: Ithaca Press.

Wikan, Unni. 1982. *Beyond the veil in Arabia.* Baltimore: Johns Hopkins University Press.

Wilden, Anthony. 1987. *The rules are no game: The strategy of communication.* London: Routledge and Kegan Paul.

Wilford, John Noble. 1995. The transforming leap, from 4 legs to 2. *New York Times,* September 5, p. C1ff.

Wilford, John Noble. 1997. Ancient German spears tell of mighty hunters of Stone Age. *New York Times,* March 4, p. C6.

Williams, George C. 1992. *Natural selection: Domains, levels, and challenges.* New York: Oxford University Press.

Williams, Melvin D. 2009. Racism: The production, reproduction, and obsolescence of social inferiority. In MyAnthroLibrary, eds. C. R. Ember, M. Ember, and P. N. Peregrine. MyAnthroLibrary.com. Pearson.

Williams, Walter L. 1992. *The spirit and the flesh.* Boston: Beacon Press.

Wilmsen, Edwin N., ed. 1989. *We are here: Politics of Aboriginal land tenure.* Berkeley: University of California Press.

Wilson, Edward O. 1975. *Sociobiology: The new synthesis.* Cambridge, MA: Belknap Press of Harvard University Press.

Winkelman, Michael 1986a. Magico-religious practitioner types and socioeconomic conditions. *Behavior Science Research* 20:17–46.

Winkelman, Michael. 1986b. Trance states: A theoretical model and cross-cultural analysis. *Ethos* 14:174–203.

Winkelman, Michael, and John R. Baker. 2010. *Supernatural as natural: A biocultural approach to religion.* Upper Saddle River, NJ: Pearson Prentice Hall.

Winkelman, Michael, and Philip M. Peck, eds. 2004. *Divination and healing: Potent vision.* Tucson: University of Arizona Press.

Winterhalder, Bruce. 1990. Open field, common pot: Harvest variability and risk avoidance in agricultural and foraging societies. In *Risk and uncertainty in tribal and peasant economies,* ed. E. Cashdan. Boulder, CO: Westview Press.

Witkowski, Stanley R. 1975. *Polygyny, age of marriage, and female status.* Paper presented at the annual meeting of the American Anthropological Association, San Francisco.

Witkowski, Stanley R., and Cecil H. Brown. 1978. Lexical universals. *Annual Review of Anthropology* 7:427–51.

Witkowski, Stanley R., and Harold W. Burris. 1981. Societal complexity and lexical growth. *Behavior Science Research* 16:143–59.

Wittfogel, Karl. 1957. *Oriental despotism: A comparative study of total power.* New Haven, CT: Yale University Press.

Wolf, Naomi. 1991. *The beauty myth: How images of beauty are used against women*. New York: Morrow.

Wolff, Ronald G. 1991. *Functional chordate anatomy*. Lexington, MA: D. C. Heath.

Wolpoff, Milford H. 1971. Competitive exclusion among lower Pleistocene hominids: The single species hypothesis. *Man* 6:601–13.

Wolpoff, Milford H. 1983. *Ramapithecus* and human origins: An anthropologist's perspective of changing interpretations. In *New interpretations of ape and human ancestry*, eds. R. Ciochon and R. Corruccini. New York: Plenum Press.

Wolpoff, Milford H. 1999. *Paleoanthropology*. 2nd ed. Boston: McGraw-Hill.

Wolpoff, Milford H., and Abel Nkini. 1985. Early and Early Middle Pleistocene hominids from Asia and Africa. In *Ancestors*, ed. E. Delson. New York: Alan R. Liss.

Wong, Kate. 2003. An ancestor to call our own. *Scientific American* (January):54–63.

Wong, Kate. 2005. The littlest human. *Scientific American* (February):56–65.

Wood, Bernard A. 1992. Evolution of australopithecines. In *The Cambridge encyclopedia of human evolution*, eds. S. Jones, R. Martin, and D. Pilbeam. New York: Cambridge University Press.

Wood, Gordon S. 1992. *The radicalism of the American Revolution*. New York: Knopf.

Wood, James W., George R. Milner, Henry C. Harpending, and Kenneth M. Weiss. 1992. The osteological paradox: Problems of inferring prehistoric health from skeletal samples. *Current Anthropology* 33:343–70.

Wood, Wendy, and Alice H. Eagly. 2002. A cross-cultural analysis of the behavior of women and men: Implications for the origins of sex differences. *Psychological Bulletin* 128:699–727.

World Bank. 2004. *World development indicators 2004*. Washington, DC: World Bank Publications.

Wright, Gary A. 1971. Origins of food production in Southwestern Asia: A survey of ideas. *Current Anthropology* 12:447–78.

Wright, George O. 1954. Projection and displacement: A cross-cultural study of folktale aggression. *Journal of Abnormal and Social Psychology* 49:523–28.

Wright, Henry T. 1986. The evolution of civilizations. In *American archaeology past and future*, ed. D. Meltzer, D. Fowler, and J. Sabloff. Washington, DC: Smithsonian Institution Press.

Wright, Henry T., and Gregory A. Johnson. 1975. Population, exchange, and early state formation in southwestern Iran. *American Anthropologist* 77:267–77.

Wulff, Robert, and Shirley Fiste. 1987. The domestication of wood in Haiti. In R. M. Wulff and S. J. Fiste, *Anthropological praxis*. Boulder, CO: Westview Press.

Yamei, Hou, R. Potts, Y. Baoyin, et al. 2000. Mid-Pleistocene Acheulean-like stone technology of the Bose Basin, South China. *Science* 287 (March 3):1622–26.

Yergin, Daniel. 2002. Giving aid to world trade. *New York Times*, June 27, p. A29.

Yinger, J. Milton. 1994. *Ethnicity: Source of strength? Source of conflict?* Albany: State University Press.

Young, Frank W. 1970. A fifth analysis of the Star Husband Tale. *Ethnology* 9:389–413.

Young, T. Cuyler, Jr. 1972. Population densities and early Mesopotamian urbanism. In *Man, settlement and urbanism*, eds. P. J. Ucko, R. Tringham, and G. W. Dimbley. Cambridge, MA: Scherkmn.

Younger, Stephen M. 2008. Conditions and mechanisms for peace in precontact Polynesia. *Current Anthropology* 49:927–34.

Zebrowitz, Leslie A., and Joann M. Montepare. 2005. Appearance *does* matter. *Science* 308 (June 10):1565–66.

Zeder, Melinda A. 1991. *Feeding cities: Specialized animal economy in the ancient Near East*. Washington, DC: Smithsonian Institution Press.

Zeder, Melinda, and Brian Hesse. 2000. The initial domestication of goats (*Capra hircus*) in the Zagros mountains 10,000 years ago. *Science* 287 (March 24):2254–2257.

Zihlman, Adrienne L. 1992. The emergence of human locomotion: The evolutionary background and environmental context. In *Topics in primatology*, vol. 1, eds. T. Nishida, et al. Tokyo: University of Tokyo Press.

Zimmer, Carl. 1999. Kenyan skeleton shakes ape family tree. *Science* 285 (August 27):1335–37.

Zimmer, Carl. 2004. Faster than a hyena? Running may make humans special. *Science* 306 (November 19):1283.

Zohary, Daniel. 1969. The progenitors of wheat and barley in relation to domestication and agriculture dispersal in the Old World. In *The domestication and exploitation of plants and animals*, eds. P. J. Ucko and G. W. Dimbleby. Chicago: Aldine.

Photo Credits

Text, Tables, and Figures

Chapter 1 Page 17, Table 1.1: Adapted from John W.M. Whiting. "Effects of climate on Certain Cultural Practices" in Ward H. Goodenough, ed. EXPLORATIONS IN CULTURAL ANTHROPOLOGY, p. 520 Copyright (c) 1964. New York: NY: McGraw-Hill Companies. Reprinted by permission of the author.

Chapter 2 Page 32, Figure 2.1: "Radiocarbon Dating" in R.E. Taylor et al CHRONOMETRIC DATING IN ARCHAEOLOGY, Figure 3.1, page 67 Copyright (c) 1997 Reprinted by permission.

Chapter 3 Page 48, Figure 3.4: From Noel T. Boaz and Alan J. Almquist, BIOLOGICAL ANTHROPOLOGY: A Synthetic Approach to Human Evolution, 2/e Copyright 9c) 2001 Reprinted by permission of Pearson Education, Inc., Upper Saddle River, NJ. Page 40: From Huxley, Thomas H., Man's place in nature (1863). In Evolution of man, ed. L. Young. New York: Oxford University Press, 1970. Page 46: From Beadle, George, and Muriel Beadle. 1966. The language of life. Garden City, NY: Doubleday, p. 216. Page 50: From Dobzhansky, Theodosius. 1962. Mankind evolving: The evolution of the human species. New Haven, CT: Yale University Press.

Chapter 4 Page 63, Figure 4.1: Figure 2 from "Body Weight, Race, and climate" by D.F. Roberts in American Journal of Physical anthropology, 11 (1953). Copyright (c) 1953. Reprinted by permission of John Wiley & Sons, Inc. Page 64, Figure 4.2: From Stephen Jones, Robert D. Martin, and David R. Pilbeam (eds) THE CAMBRIDGE ENCYCLOPEDIA OF HUMAN EVOLUTION. Copyright (c) 1992 Cambridge University Press. Reprinted with permission.

Chapter 5 Page 82, Figure 5.1(B-F): From Stephen Jones, Robert D. Martin, and David R. Pilbeam (eds) THE CAMBRIDGE ENCYCLOPEDIA OF HUMAN EVOLUTION. Copyright (c) 1992 Cambridge University Press. Reprinted with permission. Page 85, Figure 5.2: Based on Noel T. Boaz and Alan J. Almquist, BIOLOGICAL ANTHROPOLOGY: A Synthetic Approach to Human Evolution. Copyright (c) 1997 Reprinted by permission of Pearson Education, Inc., Upper Saddle River, NJ. Page 88, Figure 5.3: Adapted from Noel T. Boaz and Alan J. Almquist, ESSENTIALS OF BIOLOGICAL ANTHROPOLOGY, Copyright (c) 1999 Reprinted by permission of Pearson Education, Upper Saddle River, NJ. Page 96, Figure 5.4: From Robert D. Martin, Primate Origins and Evolution: A Phylogenetic Reconstruction (Princeton, NJ: Princeton University Press, 1990). The dates for the Paleocene, Eocene, Oligocene, and the beginning of the Miocene are from William A. Berggren, Dennis V. Kent, John D. Obradovich, and Carol C. Swisher, III, "Toward a Revised Paleogene Geochronology,"in Donald R. Prothero and William A. Berggren, eds., Eocene-Oligocene Climatic and Biotic Evolution (Princeton NJ: Princeton University Press, 1992), pp. 29–45. The dates for the end of the Miocene, Pliocene, and Pleistocene are from Steve Jones, Robert Martin, and David Pilbeam, eds., The Cambridge Encyclopedia of Human Evolution (New York: Cambridge University Press, 1992). Page 97, Figure 5.5: Noel T. Boaz and Alan J. Almquist, BIOLOGICAL ANTHROPOLOGY: A Synthetic Approach to Human Evolution. Copyright (c) 1997 Reprinted by permission of Pearson Education, Inc., Upper Saddle River, NJ.

Chapter 6 Page 118, Figure 6.1: Adapted from "The fossil Trail" by New York Times Graphics, The New York Times, September 5, 1995, p. C9. Copyright (c) 1995 by The New York Times Company. Reprinted by permission of New York Times Graphics. Page 120, Figure 6.2: From R. Freyman, "The First Technology," in Scientific American (April, 1987): 112, Reprinted by permission of the artist, Ed Hanson. Page 122: From Dobzhansky, Mankind evolving: The evolution of the human species. New Haven, CT: 1962. Yale University Press. Page 123, Figure 6.3: Tattersall et al ENCYCLOPEDIA OF HUMAN EVOLUTION AND PREHISTORY (New York: Garland, 2000) Copyright (c) 2000 Reprinted in the formats of Text and Other book via Copyright Clearance Center for Routledge, Inc. a part of the Taylor & Francis Group. Page 132, Figure 6.7: Copyright © 1969 by Eric Mose. Reprinted by permission of Eric Mose, Jr.

Chapter 7 Page 139, Figure 7.2: From Matthias Krings, et al "Neandertal DNA Sequences and the Origin of Modern Humans" Cell, Vol 90: 25 Copyright (c) 1997 Reprinted by permission of Elsevier. Page141, Figure 7.3: From Richard G. Klein,

"Ice-Age Hunters of the Ukraine" Scientific American (June 1974): 96–105. Copyright (c) 1974 Reprinted with permission. Page 155, Figure 7.6: David J. Meltzer, "Pleistocene peopling of the Americas" EVOLUTIONARY ANTHROPOLOGY, Vol 1(5) Copyright 1993 Reprinted by permission of John Wiley & Sons, Inc. Page 147: From Alan Templeton, "Gene lineages and human evolution." Science 272 (May 31 1996):1363. Page 157, Figure 7.7: From Christy G. Turner, II, "Telltale Teeth." Natural History (January 1987):8. Copyright 1987 Reprinted with permission.

Chapter 8 Page 164, Figure 8.1: From Stephen Jones, Robert D. Martin, and David R. Pilbeam (eds) THE CAMBRIDGE ENCYCLOPEDIA OF HUMAN EVOLUTION. Copyright (c) 1992 Cambridge University Press. Reprinted with permission. Page 165, Figure 8.2: From Stephen Jones, Robert D. Martin, and David R. Pilbeam (eds) THE CAMBRIDGE ENCYCLOPEDIA OF HUMAN EVOLUTION. Copyright (c) 1992 Cambridge University Press. Reprinted with permission.

Chapter 9 Page 196: From Linton, Ralph. THE CULTURAL BACKGROUND OF PERSONALITY. New York: Appleton-Century-Crofts, 1945. Page 199: From Miner, Horace, Body rituals among the Nacirema. American Anthropologist 58: 504–05.© 1956 Reprinted by permission of the American Anthropological Association from American Anthropologist 58:3, June 1956. Page 209: From Linton, Ralph. 1936. The Study of Man. New York: Appleton-Century-Crofts, 1936, pp.326–327.

Chapter 10 Page 223: Helen Keller, The Story of My Life. New York, NY: Random House, Inc., 1974. Page 233: Lewis Carroll, Through the Looking Glass and What Alice Found There. Philadelphia: Henry Altemus Company, 1897. Page 233: From Chaucer, Canterbury Tales. From Chaucer, Geoffrey. 1926. The prologue to the Canterbury Tales, the Knights Tale, the Nonnes Prestes Tale, ed. Mark H. Liddell. New York: Macmillan.

Chapter 11 Page 266, Figure 11.1: From James A. Levine et al "The Distribution of Work Tasks for male and Female Children and Adults Separated by Gender" in "Looking at Child labor" Science 296 (May, 2002) 1025 Copyright (c) 2002 Reprinted by permission of the author.

Chapter 12 Page 293: From Sahlins, Marshall D. 1958. Social stratification in Polynesia. Seattle: University of Washington Press.

Chapter 13 Page 299, Table 13.1: Mostly adapted from George P. Murdock and Caterina Provost, "Factors in the Division of Labor by Sex: A Cross-Cultural Analysis," Ethnology, 129(1973): 203–25. The information on political leadership and warfare comes from Martin K. Whyte, "Cross-Cultural Codes Dealing with the Relative Status of Women," Ethnology, 17(1978): 217. The information on child care comes from Thmas S. Weisner and Ronald Gallimore, "My Brother's Keeper: Child and Sibling Caretaker," Current Anthropology, 18(1977): 169–80.

Chapter 14 Page 328: Approx 50 words from Oliver, Douglas L. 1955. A Solomon Island Society. Cambridge, MA: Harvard University Press. Page 332: Approx 40 words from Mead, Margaret. 1961/1928. Coming of age in Samoa. 3rd ed. New York: Morrow.

Chapter 15 Page 350: From Mathiassen, Therkel. 1928. Material Culture of Iglulik Eskimos. Copenhagen: Glydendalske, p. 213. Page 353: From Sahlins, Marshall D. 1962. Moala: Culture and nature on a Fijian island. Ann Arbor: University of Michigan Press. Page 361: From Simpson, S. P., and Ruth Field. 1946. Law and the social sciences. Virginia Law Review 32:858. Page 362: From Boas, Franz. 1888. The Central Eskimo. Bureau of American Ethnology Annual Report. Washington, DC: Smithsonian Institution. Reprinted by University of Nebraska Press, 1964.

Chapter 16 Page 387: Raymond W. Firth, RANK AND RELIGION IN TIKOPIA: A Study in Polynesian Paganism and Conversion to Christianity. Copyright (c) 1970 Reprinted by permission of Allyn & Uwin.

Chapter 17 Page 396, Table 17.1: Artistic Differences in Egalitarian & Stratified Societies. Based on Fischer, John. 1961. Art styles as cultural cognitive maps. American Anthropologist 83:80–83. Page 401: From Thompson, Stith. 1965. Star Husband Tale. In The study of folklore, ed. A. Dundes. Upper Saddle River, NJ: Prentice Hall, p.449

Chapter 19 Page 437: E. Fuller Torrey, THE MIND GAME: Witchdoctors and Psychiatrists. Copyright (c) 1973 Bantam Books, a division of Random House, Inc. Reprinted with permission of the author.

Index

Note: Page numbers followed by *t* indicate tables, those followed by *f* indicate figures, and page numbers in bold indicate glossary terms.